RICHARD III's BOOKS

IDEALS AND REALITY IN THE LIFE AND LIBRARY OF A MEDIEVAL PRINCE

T0323271

ANNE F. SUTTON AND LIVIA VISSER-FUCHS

Front cover: Contrary to normal convention, the main body of this manuscript is foliated in Roman numerals, but preceded by a section in Arabic numerals. Illumination attributed to the Bruges Master of 1483. (© Bodleian Libraries, University of Oxford)

First published 1997
This paperback edition first published 2024

In association with the Yorkist History Trust

The History Press
97 St George's Place, Cheltenham,
Gloucestershire, GL50 3QB
www.thehistorypress.co.uk

© Livia Visser-Fuchs and the Yorkist History Society, 2005, 2024

British Library Cataloguing in Publication Data.
A catalogue record for this book is available from the British Library.

ISBN 978 1 80399 631 8

Typesetting and origination by The History Press
Printed and bound in Great Britain by TJ Books Limited, Padstow, Cornwall.

Trees for Life

Contents

List of Illustrations

Black and White

Colour Plates

Acknowledgements

We are very grateful to Julia Boffey and Paul Christianson for kindly reading our text and for their helpful suggestions, comments and additions; to Paul also for allowing us to read and use the typescript copy of his chapter in the forthcoming *A History of the Book in Britain*, vol. 3 (1400–1557); and to Mary Erler for her interest and support and for looking at the Wycliffe Bible. We also thank Jim Bolton and Elizabeth Watson for kindly reading parts of the text and their helpful suggestions and corrections, and Tony Pollard and Jeremy Potter for their support. We are indebted to Christopher de Hamel for telling us about the spurious 'hours of Richard III', and to Lotte Hellinga, Kate Harris, Meg Ford, Nicholas Rogers, Dorothy Clayton, Robert Yorke and Tony Edwards for their help. We would like to thank again all those people who have assisted us over the years in our pursuit of Richard III's books.

The Yorkist History Trust

The Yorkist History Trust is a charity founded in 1985 to advance and disseminate research and education related to the history of late medieval England (and in particular the reign and life of King Richard III). We fulfil these aims by offering research grants to scholars working on the period, by offering publication grants to titles of relevance, and by publishing critical primary source editions, volumes of collected essays, and academic monographs. Recent publications include Peter Fleming's *Late Medieval Bristol: Time, Space and Power*, an edition of *The Lordship of Middleham in 1465–66 and 1473–74*, edited by Livia Visser-Fuchs, Jonathan Mackman, and Anne F. Sutton, and the late Dr Sutton's magisterial *The King's Work: The Defence of the North under the Yorkist Kings*.

Future projects include editions of the executors' accounts of Sir Ralph Verney, the probate accounts and inventories of Sir Thomas Charlton, documents relating to the Smithfield Tournament, and London's Common Council Journal covering the reign of Richard III, as well as a monograph on the chronicler Robert Fabyan. We have recently funded projects on the gentry of the fifteenth century and the Brewers' Company of London. We welcome applications for editions and monographs to be published by the Trust and to support other publications and research on the fifteenth century. To submit an application, or for more information, please see our website: www.yorkisthistorytrust.org.

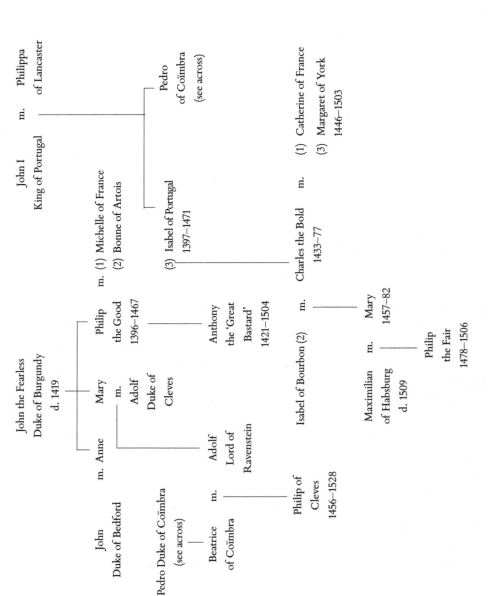

THE HOUSE OF BURGUNDY

John I   m.   Philippa
King of Portugal   of Lancaster

Pedro
of Coïmbra
(see across)

John the Fearless
Duke of Burgundy
d. 1419

John   Mary   Philip
Duke of Bedford   m.   the Good
                          Adolf   1396–1467
                          Duke of
                          Cleves

m. (1) Michelle of France
   (2) Bonne of Artois

(3) Isabel of Portugal
    1397–1471

Charles the Bold   m.
1433–77

(1) Catherine of France
(3) Margaret of York
    1446–1503

Pedro Duke of Coïmbra
(see across)

Anthony
the 'Great
Bastard'
1421–1504

Adolf
Lord of
Ravenstein

Beatrice   m.
of Coïmbra

Philip of
Cleves
1456–1528

Isabel of Bourbon (2)   m.

Mary
1457–82

Maximilian   m.
of Habsburg
d. 1509

Philip
the Fair
1478–1506

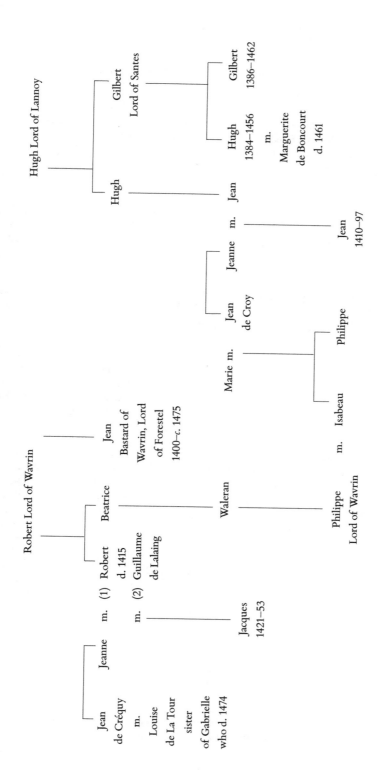

THE FAMILIES OF LANNOY, CROY AND WAVRIN

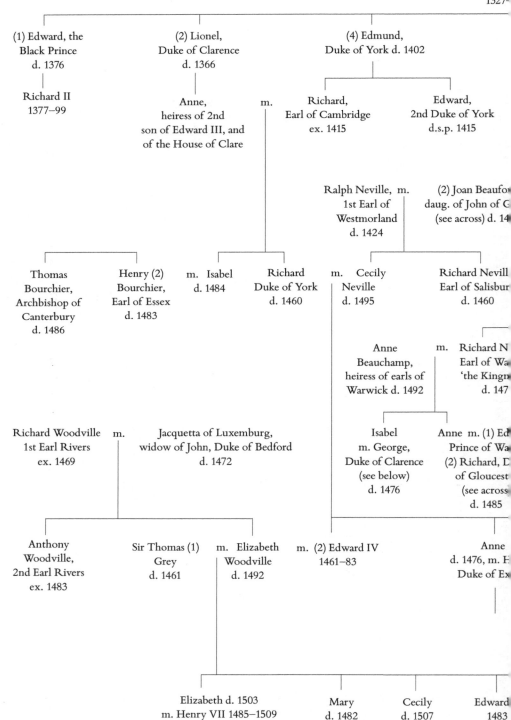

Edward I
1327-

(1) Edward, the
Black Prince
d. 1376

Richard II
1377–99

(2) Lionel,
Duke of Clarence
d. 1366

Anne,
heiress of 2nd
son of Edward III, and
of the House of Clare

m.

(4) Edmund,
Duke of York d. 1402

Richard,
Earl of Cambridge
ex. 1415

Edward,
2nd Duke of York
d.s.p. 1415

Ralph Neville, m.
1st Earl of
Westmorland
d. 1424

(2) Joan Beaufo
daug. of John of G
(see across) d. 14

Thomas
Bourchier,
Archbishop of
Canterbury
d. 1486

Henry (2)
Bourchier,
Earl of Essex
d. 1483

m. Isabel
d. 1484

Richard
Duke of York
d. 1460

m. Cecily
Neville
d. 1495

Richard Nevill
Earl of Salisbur
d. 1460

Anne
Beauchamp,
heiress of earls of
Warwick d. 1492

m. Richard N
Earl of Wa
'the Kingm
d. 147

Richard Woodville
1st Earl Rivers
ex. 1469

m.

Jacquetta of Luxemburg,
widow of John, Duke of Bedford
d. 1472

Isabel
m. George,
Duke of Clarence
(see below)
d. 1476

Anne m. (1) Ed
Prince of Wa
(2) Richard, D
of Gloucest
(see across
d. 1485

Anthony
Woodville,
2nd Earl Rivers
ex. 1483

Sir Thomas (1)
Grey
d. 1461

m. Elizabeth
Woodville
d. 1492

m. (2) Edward IV
1461–83

Anne
d. 1476, m. H
Duke of Ex

Elizabeth d. 1503
m. Henry VII 1485–1509

Mary
d. 1482

Cecily
d. 1507

Edward
1483

THE HOUSE OF YORK

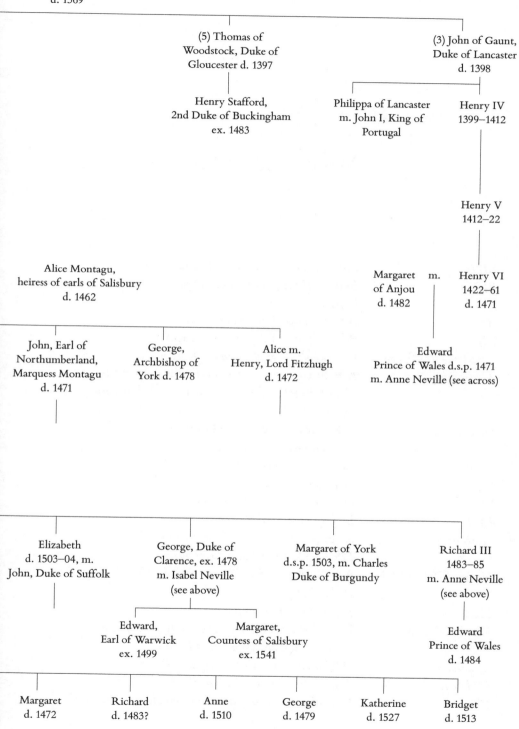

Philippa of Hainault
d. 1369

(5) Thomas of
Woodstock, Duke of
Gloucester d. 1397

(3) John of Gaunt,
Duke of Lancaster
d. 1398

Henry Stafford,
2nd Duke of Buckingham
ex. 1483

Philippa of Lancaster
m. John I, King of
Portugal

Henry IV
1399–1412

Henry V
1412–22

Alice Montagu,
heiress of earls of Salisbury
d. 1462

Margaret
of Anjou
d. 1482

m.

Henry VI
1422–61
d. 1471

John, Earl of
Northumberland,
Marquess Montagu
d. 1471

George,
Archbishop of
York d. 1478

Alice m.
Henry, Lord Fitzhugh
d. 1472

Edward
Prince of Wales d.s.p. 1471
m. Anne Neville (see across)

Elizabeth
d. 1503–04, m.
John, Duke of Suffolk

George, Duke of
Clarence, ex. 1478
m. Isabel Neville
(see above)

Margaret of York
d.s.p. 1503, m. Charles
Duke of Burgundy

Richard III
1483–85
m. Anne Neville
(see above)

Edward,
Earl of Warwick
ex. 1499

Margaret,
Countess of Salisbury
ex. 1541

Edward
Prince of Wales
d. 1484

Margaret
d. 1472

Richard
d. 1483?

Anne
d. 1510

George
d. 1479

Katherine
d. 1527

Bridget
d. 1513

Abbreviations

BIHR	*Bulletin of the Institute of Historical Research.*
BJRL	*Bulletin of the John Rylands Library.*
BL	British Library.
BN	Bibliothèque Nationale, Paris.
BR	Bibliothèque Royale Albert I, Brussels.
Charles le Téméraire	P. Cockshaw *et al.*, *Charles le Téméraire.*
'Choosing a book'	A.F. Sutton and L. Visser-Fuchs, 'Choosing a book in late fifteenth-century England and Burgundy'.
Coronation	A.F. Sutton and P.W. Hammond, eds, *The Coronation of Richard III.*
CPR	*Calendar of Patent Rolls.*
CS	Camden Society.
EETS	Early English Text Society.
EHR	*English Historical Review.*
Harl. 433	R. Horrox and P.W. Hammond, eds, *British Library Harleian Manuscript 433.*
Hours of Richard III	A.F. Sutton and L. Visser-Fuchs, *The Hours of Richard III.*
HRB	*Historia regum Britanniae.*
John Vale's Book	M.L. Kekewich *et al.*, *The Politics of Fifteenth-century England: John Vale's Book.*
Manual	*A Manual of Writings in Middle English.*
Middle English Prose	A.S.G. Edwards, ed., *Middle English Prose.*
PL	J.P. Migne, *Patrologiae cursus completus. Series latina.*

'R III books'	A.F. Sutton and L. Visser-Fuchs, 'Richard III's books: I–XIV' and Hammond, P.W., 'Richard III's books: III'.
Richard III	P. Tudor-Craig, *Richard III.*
RP	*Rotuli Parliamentorum.*
VCH	Victoria County History.

Why Richard III's Books?

As in all our dealings with the Middle Ages – or, for that matter, with any period remote from our own – we find that the most important question to ask is not, straightaway, 'What is this worth to me?' but 'What was this worth to them?'.1

In exploring in detail the surviving books which can be associated with Richard III – a man remarkable among his English peers for his habit of *signing* his books and thereby recording his ownership for us – we wished to discover not only the circumstances of his ownership but also the meaning of the texts themselves in his time, and to attempt to know their owner and understand his contemporaries, who also read these texts, a little better.

As Richard acquired his books gradually, at various stages of his life, and appears to have acquired them consciously, the events of his life must form part of our analysis. The changes in his signature when related to the evidence from datable documents allow us to make conjectures, or occasionally to be certain, about when he obtained various books. Similarly his use and awareness of some of the works can be illustrated by events in his life and his other known interests, and tell us why he had them – this is particularly true for his religious and chivalric texts. The books were *part of his life* and our knowledge both of his books and of his life benefit from an inter-related study. Too often little or nothing is known about an

---

1 Stevens, *Medieval Romance*, pp. 29–30. Professor Stevens continues that: 'systems of thought ... styles in literature ... are not invented for their own sake ... They come into being because they are needed ... primarily for explanation ... to impose meanings on life'.

owner of a surviving medieval text or the precise context in which it was used, but Richard is in this case a happy exception.

As his books are among the few personal possessions that survive for Richard they also demand to be briefly described as objects; some of them are intact and in their original bindings; some, though not many, are decorated, and the quality of their illumination and general workmanship may inform us about Richard's likes and dislikes and how his taste compared to that of other book owners. Some of the texts are still very well known and have been endlessly studied, such as the two *Canterbury Tales* which Richard had. There is no need to explore these in the same detail as the lesser known texts – such as the rare *Prophecy of the Eagle* or the *Life of St Katherine* – but in each instance an attempt at least must be made to find out what Richard and his contemporaries themselves thought of these texts in their time, and how the works that he chose to own relate to others in the same genre.

It is a curious coincidence that a king about whom so much has already been written for other reasons also turns out to be interesting for research into the social and cultural history of his time, but it is undeniable that there are some remarkable aspects of Richard's book ownership. For no medieval English prince do we have so many books which were signed by the owner's hand, or clearly marked as his, and which can also be assumed to have held their owner's personal interest. It is well known that Humphrey of Gloucester's 'library' earlier in the century was immense and incomparable, but it is difficult to find evidence that he was genuinely interested in the contents of the books. More importantly, it is impossible to use Humphrey's collection as an indication of what other people of his age and class liked to read, while comparison with the more fragmentary and scattered but, when taken together, ample remains of other 'libraries' of Richard's milieu shows that his was an 'average' one, in the sense that his taste was very similar to that of other noble men in the 1470s and '80s; there is much overlap between the single or few surviving items of lesser known collections and Richard's more numerous and better documented manuscripts. It is also fortunate that Richard's surviving titles offer a good, working cross-section of what was available and popular at the time in almost every genre except 'professional' books – medical, legal and theological texts – and allow the student and the reader an interesting overview of fifteenth-century attitudes to lay piety, chivalry, history, books of advice or 'mirrors' for princes, ancestry and noble lineage, prophetic material, and romances. Studying Richard's books is to take a crash-course in the literature of his time.

Comparison with the collections of continental princes reveals that there was great similarity between, for example, English and Burgundian courtiers in their areas of interest, though the scale and magnificence of their book ownership differed considerably. There is neither positive nor negative evidence that Richard ever collected any of the illuminated Flemish manuscripts which made the library of his brother, Edward IV, so famous, and it is likely that if he had any such volumes, decorated with his arms, they were coveted by his successors and their marks of ownership have obliterated his. Some splendid manuscripts of the period survive that contain the royal arms but no indication of which king of England commissioned or owned them.

It is a strange fact, no doubt due to the quirks of survival but nonetheless fascinating, that many of Richard's extant manuscripts represent the unique or one of the very few known copies of a number of texts. He owned one of the two surviving copies of the English translation of Mechtild of Hackeborn's *Liber Specialis Gratiae*, the only extant copy of the prose *Ipomedon*, the only manuscript of Geoffrey of Monmouth's *Historia regum Britanniae* known to have belonged to a medieval king of England, one of the two surviving texts of the verse paraphrase of the Old Testament, one of the two surviving texts of the *Prophecy of the Eagle* with this particular *Commentary*; and even his ownership of romances makes him disproportionately important in any analysis of owners of romances in English in the fifteenth century.

Finally, we know that Richard and the decision-making members of his only parliament were sufficiently enlightened, at a time when the printed book was beginning to gain a share of the market and when manuscript books were still produced in great numbers, not to allow insular and chauvinist mercantile measures against alien artisans and traders to interfere with the import into England of any kind of book or with the work of any book artisan. Many aspects, therefore, of Richard III's books deserve our curiosity and the man himself is merely one facet.

ONE

A Chronology of Richard III's Life and Library

Whoever ... claims to be zealous of truth, of happiness, of wisdom, or knowledge, aye, even of the faith, must needs become a lover of books.

Richard of Bury, Bishop of Durham 1281–1345, wrote this sentiment in his *Philobiblon* (*The Love of Books*) and believed it sincerely. His work was still well known among scholars in the fifteenth century, particularly in Germany and England, and printed for the first time in Cologne in 1473. It is possible that Richard III had heard of it: it was after all written by an Englishman and appreciated throughout the Latin-speaking world. In Richard's own time the text was owned by many religious houses in England; the Bridgettine house of Syon, for example, often visited by the royal family, had as many as three copies.[1]

Any book lover who reads Richard of Bury's views inevitably agrees with most of what he says, even if he lacks the bishop's collector's obsession; and in the fifteenth century his sentiments were accepted without question. The educated and cultivated aristocrat of Richard III's day knew that a collection of books was a necessity, an indication of his social status as well as an ever ready source of advice, entertainment, consolation and instruction.

---

1 For the quotation, see Richard of Bury, *The Love of Books*, p. 18. On the mss. and printed versions Altamura, *Riccardo da Bury, Philobiblon*, pp. 19–44.

Richard III was born into a family and social class that owned books. He himself had thirteen volumes which survive, containing eighteen separate texts; four other texts which he owned do not survive. This study seeks to bring together all we know about Richard's books and to put them into the context of the books owned by his immediate family – parents, siblings, their spouses and their children. It also takes into consideration the book trade that supplied them and the contemporary libraries of Richard's peers in England and abroad, in particular those of the dukes of Burgundy and some members of his court. By using this background, and by comparison and analogy a fairly complete and trustworthy picture emerges.

Richard's surviving books provide us with a self-selected sample whereby we can assess him, and more important, learn more about the opinions on many subjects available to a man of his background. His books hold the knowledge, the points of view and the accepted ways of thought; they were on his shelves and could be looked at by him at any time. Whether he accepted their stories and opinions, whether he even read them, can be debated, but in some cases it can be assumed that he did. With all possible *caveats* allowed, these books show some of the prejudices, misinformation, enthusiasms and hopes available to the curious reader of Richard III's day. Some of his books were ancient and revered texts, others as recent as William Worcester's exhortations to Edward IV to renew the war with France, others again were hot off Caxton's press.

Richard's surviving books included three texts that were straightforwardly religious: his book of hours, his New Testament translation and the *Book of Special Grace* by Mechtild of Hackeborn. With these should probably be included his verse paraphrase of several Old Testament stories, though this may have been regarded as narrative entertainment, teaching holy writ to a child. When he was king the Italian humanist Pietro Carmeliano presented to him a Latin verse *Life of St Katherine*, patron of scholars. He owned four romances, stories of entertainment in prose or verse: *Palamon and Arcite* (*The Knight's Tale*) and *Patient Griselda* (*The Clerk's Tale*) by Geoffrey Chaucer, a prose *Ipomedon* – the career and adventures of a perfect knight – and the beginning of the story of Tristan and Isolde. Lydgate's *Siege of Thebes* could also be classified as a romance, but Richard may well have considered it history. His straightforward history books were Guido delle Colonne's *Historia destructionis Troiae*, Geoffrey of Monmouth's *Historia regum Britanniae*, the *Grandes chroniques de France* and the Anonymous or Fitzhugh Chronicle of England; between them these covered large swathes of world history from the siege of Troy to nearly 1400. Advice on the conduct of princes, knights and soldiers, as well as practical military advice, was represented by Giles of Rome's *De regimine principum*, Caxton's translation of Ramon Lull's *Order of Chivalry*, Vegetius' *De re militari* in English, William Worcester's *Boke of Noblesse*, and the *Letters of Phalaris*. Further useful advice for a soldier was contained in his two rolls of arms, but these could also be seen as texts about ancestry and the descent of princes, comparable to the kingly histories of the *Historia regum Britanniae*. One short text was an oddity by twentieth-century standards, the *Prophecy of the Eagle* with a commentary, one of the texts that helped to prove the right to rule of the House of York. The subject coverage of Richard's books is varied and well balanced for such a small collection. The only subjects obviously lacking are theology, the law, astronomy and alchemy, all subjects that he could have left to professionals.

Richard's Education, His 'Tutors', and His Books before 1470

The future Richard III was the eleventh child of Richard, Duke of York, and Cecily, daughter of Ralph Neville, Earl of Westmorland; he was one of four sons who survived infancy. His father was killed at the battle of Wakefield, 30 December 1460, when Richard was eight years old, a moment of such crisis in the family's fortunes that Richard and his nearest elder brother, George, were sent into safety and exile at the court of the Duke of Burgundy, Philip the Good. Four months later they were recalled to take part in the coronation of their elder brother as Edward IV, and shortly after Richard was created duke of Gloucester.

A partial picture of Richard's childhood can be gleaned from his books and those of his son. Most people acquire their first book as a child: the first books of members of the best-documented family of book-owners in the fifteenth century, the dukes of Savoy, are known to have been acquired early, for the schoolroom or by gift. The noble child required educational texts like the *Donatus*, the fourth-century Latin grammar of which versions were still in use in the fifteenth century, or the basic religious text of a psalter; later came collections of moral stories.[2] Gifts and

---

2   Edmunds, 'Savoy', 24 (1970), pp. 320–21.

inheritance might expand a collection until the owner began to commission or buy on his or her own account.

There are no texts obviously and solely designed for a child among Richard's books, but if we turn to what we know about the education of his son, Edward of Middleham, we may learn a little about Richard's ideas on education. The evidence is slight, and there is really only one personal detail but it is of great interest: the presence of Anne Idley as mistress of the nursery of young Edward. She was the widow of Peter Idley, of Drayton, Oxfordshire, a government official and author of a book of moral guidance for his own son. It was a translation in rhyme royal of earlier Latin and English authorities and covered systematically all the moral issues of life, social behaviour, vices and virtues; it taught the child and young man to be restrained in speech and dress, to avoid women and taverns, and to take good advice; it also contained simple religious knowledge, such as the Ten Commandments, the Seven Deadly Sins and the Seven Sacraments.[3] Though there is no indication that Anne Idley ever introduced her husband's book into the Gloucester household, its impeccable contents and the fact that it was popular enough to survive in ten manuscripts, eight from the Yorkist period, make it possible that Edward of Middleham's early education was aided by Idley's 'Instructions to his Son'. Like so many simple fifteenth-century texts the book has been said to make tedious reading, but it is in fact full of small delights:

> The most vengeable thing that may be
> Of any man, worm, fowl, or beast,
> I remember it is the little, small bee
> That anon to battle is ready and prest;   [prepared]
> For though an armed man come to her nest,
> She is not afraid him to assail
> And with her little spear proffer him battail.[4]

Books were given to improve the mind of the growing aristocratic child and to teach him the things relevant to his status and background: the simple, attractive copy of the English translation of Vegetius' military manual may have been made for Edward of Middleham: the griffin of his

---

3   D'Evelyn, *Peter Idley's Instructions*, passim; *Manual*, vol. 7, XX [5].
4   D'Evelyn, *Peter Idley's Instructions*, pp. 96–97; spelling modernised.

Fig. 1 Richard's signature on a document nominating Charles, Duke of Burgundy, a knight of the Garter, 13 May 1469. Redrawn by Piet Design from Lille, Archives départementales, série B, 862/16.161.

earldom of Salisbury is included in the decoration of the first page (see fig. 35). He could have learned his family's history from the illustrated *Rous Roll* and *Beauchamp Pageant*, both made in his father's reign, as well as from the genealogical rolls that every noble family owned. Richard himself could have learned the ancestry of the House of York from similar texts or from the family tree in verse made by Osbern Bokenham of Clare, now called the Clare Roll.[5]

Among Richard's own books there are some that may have been suitable for a growing boy and adolescent, but it is difficult to establish whether he actually acquired any of these in his youth. Any conclusions about the date of acquisition of his books must be based on his signature, which varies and is sometimes accompanied by a motto. The books he acquired while king are a clearly defined group and present no problems. Of his other books the one that most readily falls into the category of educational texts is his collection of romances and Old Testament stories, possibly signed by him as an adolescent. The romances included Chaucer's *Knight's Tale* and the story of Ipomedon, the best knight in the world; the Bible selection included *Joshua, Job, Judith, Tobit* and *Maccabees*. All were chivalric and/or eminently moral tales, their educational message presented as agreeably as Gower or Caxton advised. Gower in his *Confessio Amantis* had attempted to strike such a happy mean between education and entertainment:

> ... men sein, and soth it is,
> That who that al of wisdom writ
> It dulleth ofte a mannes wit
> To him that schal it aldai rede,
> For thilke cause, if that ye rede,

---

5   For all these texts see below.

I wolde go the middel weie
And wryte a bok betwen the tweie,
Somwhat of lust, somewhat of lore,   [pleasure]
That of the lasse or of the more
Som man mai lyke of that I wryte ... [6]

The same idea was voiced by the author known as *Caton*, translated by
Caxton in 1483. He advised that no one read 'foule sciences' which are
'ful of errour as ben foles questyons and scyences seculers, ne also the fictions of poetrye', but he also knew very well that it was much easier to
learn if the lesson was made palatable and pleasant:

Thou oughest to rede and to receyve and to put in thy memorye that
that thou shalt rede, and to take to hit dylectacion and plesure, and that
thou forgete hit not lightly, as done many one that rede without takyng
of hyt ony plesure, for that that entryth in to one of theyr eerys yssueth
out ageyn by theyr other eere. [7]

The details of Richard's more serious education are largely unknown.
Before his exile in 1460 and before the deaths of his father and his second
eldest brother, Edmund, Earl of Rutland, at Wakefield, it is possible
that he was destined for the Church as the youngest son. Some of the
books he owned actually suggest that he had received the sound grammar education a future cleric needed: the highly abbreviated Latin text of
De regimine principum and the large, Latin Fitzhugh Chronicle demanded
good Latin of their readers, and Richard was obviously pleased to receive

---

6   Gower, *Complete Works*, vol. 2, *Confessio Amantis*, Prologue, lines 12–20. The translation by
    Tiller, p. 15, reads:

        ... men say – and truth it is –
        That works of wholly solemn kind
        Will often dull a reader's mind,
        Who studies in them every day;
        So I will walk the middle way,
        If you advise me so to do,
        And write a book between the two –
        Something to please, something to profit – ...

7   There is no modern edition of Caxton's translation of the French book of *Caton*: BL, B 5719,
    f. ix.

Latin copies of the *Historia Troiae* and the *Historia regum Britanniae*. These were books only a man with good Latin and a habit of industrious reading – even a scholarly bent – could appreciate. His ownership of one of the earlier English translations of the New Testament and an unusually extensive book of hours and prayers, originally put together for a clergyman, is equally important. The Italian Pietro Carmeliano did not think it odd to dedicate his Latin *Life of St Katherine*, the patron saint of scholars, to Richard III; he also presented the text to the learned John Russell, Bishop of Lincoln. Lastly, Richard's handwriting, when he chose, was conspicuously neater than the scrawls of the rest of his family, a fact that may betray a more scholarly education. If Richard did receive such an education it must have faltered after 1461, when he was sent to live in the household of Richard, Earl of Warwick, where he may have stayed for as long as seven years. Here schooling would have emphasised the knightly and social skills that were indispensable to a young nobleman, but a good grounding in grammar would also have been supplied. Among those who could have encouraged a natural inclination and ability to profit from an intellectual education was the earl of Warwick's brother, George Neville (died 1476), Archbishop of York, whose enthronement feast Richard attended as a boy in 1465. George Neville was a man 'of blood, virtue and cunning',[8] chancellor of Oxford University at a very early age, a genuine scholar as well as a valuable member of the Neville clan in their struggle for power and impressive enough to stimulate a young man's ambition. Some of the learned ecclesiastics Neville patronised continued in Richard III's service and he may have transmitted to Richard an appreciation of learning in others, for example, of a knowledge of Greek.[9]

It is possible that some of Richard's teenage education was spent at an inn of court; the inns were increasingly seen as providing a useful secular education for young men who had no intention of pursuing law as a career.[10] Certainly Richard as duke and king showed a good understanding of the law. This may, of course, have been a natural consequence of his daily duties as a prince, but it could have derived from some more direct experience. Wherever else he received instruction there is no doubt Richard completed his schooling at his brother's court. A sum-

8   *RP*, vol. 5, p. 450, quoted in Davies, 'The episcopate', p. 56.
9   Sutton, 'Curious searcher', pp. 68–69.
10 Ives, 'Common lawyers', pp. 198–99, 209. See also Ross, *Edward IV*, pp. 8–9.

mary picture of the education provided by the royal household is given by Sir John Fortescue in his *De laudibus legum Angliae* (c. 1468–70). He praises it as the 'supreme academy for the nobles of the realm, and a school of vigour, probity and manners'; its education concentrated on military training and produced men who would be able to protect the realm. Elsewhere he expands on the education of the prince himself: he should know the laws of his country and be thereby stimulated to justice, his knowledge to be 'in general terms' only. Similarly he should learn holy scripture, but not 'profoundly' like a cleric.[11] In other words, princes were for fighting and they were to leave religion and the law to professional men like Fortescue. A more varied and balanced picture of the education provided by 'the schools of urbanity and nurture of England' at the king's court is found in the so-called *Black Book*, the regulations for the royal household (1478). The 'henchmen' (the boys in this school) were presided over by the king's 'master of horse and henchmen' and a grammar master, who were

> to learn them to ride cleanly and surely, to draw them also to jousts, to learn them wear their harness; to have all courtesy in words, deeds, and degrees, diligently to keep them in rules of goings and sittings, after they be of honour. Moreover to teach them sundry languages and other learnings virtuous, to harping, to pipe, sing, dance, and other honest and temperate behaving and patience ... and each of them to be used to that things of virtue that he shall be most apt to learn, with remembrance daily of God's service accustomed.[12]

Something of this same variety and balance is reflected in Richard III's books: both the Old and the New Testament were part of his collection and he had his book of hours and a few other devotional texts; military matters are well represented by the standard texts of *De re militari* and the *Order of Chivalry*, by all the history books which were largely one battle or campaign after another, and by the romances of *Palamon and Arcite* (*Knight's Tale*), *Ipomedon* and the romance/history of the *Siege of Thebes*. All this is the stuff that virtuous knights were made of and Richard's collection as a whole matches the instructions given by the wise French

---

11 Fortescue, *De laudibus*, pp. 111, 137. Compare the view of Giles of Rome, ch. 5 below.
12 Myers, *Household*, pp. 126–27; spelling modernised.

Fig. 2 Richard's signature with the motto *tant le desieree* (I have longed for it so much) on a page of the story of *Ipomedon*, the 'best knight of the world'. Redrawn by Piet Design from Longleat, MS 257, f. 98v.

courtier Philippe de Mézières in 1386–89, on princely reading for the future Charles VI, in his *Songe du Vieil Pelerin*.

First the prince was to read the scriptures and the service books of the Church, carefully not taking too much pleasure in apocryphal works. He was doubtful concerning romances about such characters as Lancelot, which 'may excite the reader to knightly deeds, but they excite, too, to fleshly love' – these books were to be read once only. Of the Bible he recommended especially the historical books of Judges, Kings and Maccabees, and Solomon and Wisdom. He recommended Nicholas Oresme's renderings of Aristotle, *De regimine principum* of Giles of Rome, the works of Livy, Valerius Maximus, Seneca and Boethius, and certain histories of later kings such as Charlemagne; the fictions concerning Arthur he considered suspect. Augustine's *City of God* and his other works were also on the list. Above all, de Mézières concluded, coming back to where he started, the prince should read the Bible, like his father, Charles V, who read it through every year. It was preferable to read in Latin 'for one moral or historical book in Latin will give you more pleasure that half a dozen in French … If you read them [the Holy Scriptures] in French you will be drinking from a tributary and not from the main stream'.[13]

Very similar – perhaps even inspired by de Mézières – and very close to Richard's surviving collection is the 'booklist' for the virtuous knight given by the poet Hoccleve in his *Remonstrance against Oldcastle* (written 1415):

Rede the storie of Lancelot de Lake
Or Vegece, *Of the aart of chivalrie,*

---

13 Mézières, *Songe*, vol. 2, pp. 18–20, 221–24; his list also includes the works of Eustache Morel, an officer of the court. For later advice on the education of French princes, see Willard, *Christine de Pizan. Her Life and Works*, ch. 9, 'The education of the Dauphin', pp. 173–93.

Fig. 3 An author or librarian at work is visited by a nobleman and his dog. Grisaille illustration at
the beginning of the romance of *Jean d'Avesnes*. Flemish, *c.* 1470. Paris, Bibliothèque de l'Arsenal,
MS 5208, f. 1. By permission of the Bibliothèque Nationale.

The *Seege of Troie* or *Thebes*. The applie
To thyng that may to th'ordre of knyght longe ...
If thee list thyng rede of auctoritee   [like]
To thise stories sit it thee to goon,   [befits]
To *Iudicum*, *Regum* and *Iosue*,
To *Iudith*, and to *Paralipomenon*,
And *Machabe* ... [14]

---

14 *Paralipomenon* is the same as *Chronicles* which is 3–4 *Kings*. Richard's collection of Old
    Testament stories contained paraphrases of *Genesis*, *Exodus*, *Numbers*, *Deuteronomy*, *Joshua*,
    Judges, *Ruth*, 1–4 *Kings*, *Job*, *Tobit*, *Esther*, *Judith* and parts of 2 *Maccabees*.

More autentik shalt thow fynde noon
Ne more pertinent to chivalrie.[15]

Books Acquired 1471–85

Richard of Gloucester's years of formal education ended early. By 1469 he was probably embroiled in the politics that led first to the Earl of Warwick's desertion of Edward IV for the cause of Lancaster, and then to his invasion of England in September 1470 and Edward's escape to the lands of his brother-in-law, the Duke of Burgundy. Richard joined him and spent more than four months in Holland and Flanders. Any assessment of whether this second exile affected Richard's cultural outlook founders on lack of evidence. The commonly repeated assertion that Edward IV became a bibliophile only after he had seen the magnificent library of his host, Louis of Gruuthuse, has no basis in fact when it is critically examined; it would be hazardous to suggest Richard made any cultural discovery in this period that he could not have made outside the territories of the dukes of Burgundy. He did, however, visit his sister Margaret of York, Duchess of Burgundy since 1468, who had become a collector of beautiful manuscripts, and no doubt he also met some of the duke's influential courtiers, such as Philip of Cleves, Philip of Croy and Anthony of Burgundy, the *Grand Bâtard*, half-brother to the duke, all of whom patronised authors, illuminators and scribes.

Edward IV regained his throne after a campaign that included the two victories of Barnet and Tewkesbury, with Richard playing an increasingly conspicuous role. In the dozen years that remained of his brother's reign Richard was given the rule of most of the north of England: he led a series of short campaigns against the Scots in 1480–82, and in 1482–83 his service to his brother was rewarded by what amounted to a palatinate in the western marches of England and Scotland. During this time in the north he put his name in a massive chronicle covering the history of England from the conversion of the Anglo-Saxons to 1199, that became the possession of the Abbey of Jervaulx in Wensleydale not far from his

---

15 See e.g. Hoccleve, *Selections*, p. 66; Hoccleve's point was actually that a knight such as Sir John Oldcastle, the famous Lollard, should not spend too much time on theology and risk becoming involved with heretical views.

Fig. 4 Richard of Gloucester's signature in the Anonymous or Fitzhugh Chronicle. Redrawn by Piet Design from Cambridge, Corpus Christi College, MS 96.

Fig. 5 Richard's signature in his copy of the *Grandes chroniques de France*. Redrawn by Piet Design from BL, MS Royal 20 C vii, f. 134.

main castle of Middleham. Richard's participation in the invasion of France in 1475 may have prompted his acquisition of a magnificently (if idiosyncratically) illuminated volume of the *Grandes chroniques de France*, covering the years 1270–1380, either before the event, in search of advice, or during the campaign, out of curiosity. This he signed about halfway through on folio 134 in a convenient space in the text; his signature, *Richard Gloucestre*, is mature and is compatible with an acquisition in the 1470s (see also fig. 56). Between 1471 and early 1483 he also put his name, or had it inscribed by others, in three unpretentious reading texts: a New Testament translated into English by Lollard scholars at the end of the previous century; a copy in French of the first sections of what is now called the *Prose Tristan*, the standard compendium of Tristan stories in their Arthurian setting; and thirdly, Giles of Rome's *De regimine principum*, the most famous 'mirror' of princes. The New Testament was a plain, working text, made *c.* 1390, and has the serviceable binding of so many copies produced for early Lollards. The text was unglossed and so free of heresy. Richard may have received an episcopal assurance that the contents were orthodox.[16] On the Bible's first page he put the motto *a vous me ly* and *Gloucestre*. The Giles of Rome may have come into Richard's hands from a northern source, perhaps as a gift from a Percy, as it had probably been made for Henry Percy, 1st Earl of Northumberland, soon after Henry V had regranted him the earldom in 1416. Someone other than Richard seems to have inscribed its first page with the ownership of 'the prince the Duke of Gloucester'. It may also have been someone else

---

16 Deanesly, *Lollard Bible*, pp. 319–20.

who recorded the duke's ownership in the *Prose Tristan* — *Iste liber constat Ricardo duci Gloucestre* — but the writing is sufficiently like Richard's to be possibly an early effort by him at a formal *ex libris*; the phrase does not occur in any of his other manuscripts. The *Tristan* was acquired no doubt for its stories of chivalry and adventure which would help a young man to pass the time.

In 1472 Richard married Anne Neville, daughter of Richard Neville, the 'Kingmaker', killed at Barnet, and of Anne Beauchamp, heir of the Beauchamp Earls of Warwick, and Countess of Warwick in her own right. Richard must have known his wife from the time of his adolescent sojourn in her father's household. There is only one book that contains any evidence that it may have been Anne Neville's: the *Booke of Gostlye Grace* by Mechtild of Hackeborn. It bears the names of both *Richard Gloucestr'* and *Anne Warrewyk*. It is possible that she was also the *vous* of the *a vous me ly* motto in the New Testament. It remains arguable, however, that the Anne Warwick in the *Booke of Gostlye Grace* was Anne, Countess of Warwick, Richard's mother-in-law, in the role of donor rather than co-owner, and not Anne Neville, her daughter. The inscription in the *Booke of Gostlye Grace* is almost certainly by Richard himself,[17] that in the *Tristan* is probably also by him, and both, like the signature in the *Grandes chroniques*, tie in with a 1470s date. The *ex libris* in the New Testament is damaged almost to illegibility and that in *De regimine principum* is very rubbed, so these texts cannot be forced into a chronological sequence of acquisition.

The influence of Anne Beauchamp on Richard's education may have been important, but its details are irrecoverable. The same is true of the bookish and cultural interests of his wife, Anne Neville. She can only be allotted a share (at least) in the ownership of the *Booke of Gostlye Grace*[18] and a share in the parental choice of Anne Idley as the governess of the nursery of her son. As duchess of Gloucester she had every opportunity to 'collect' her own manuscripts from Flanders and elsewhere. Some of the mysterious books made in the 1460s–80s that survive in the English royal library suggest that a royal lady of

---

17 See for example the document granting the Order of the Garter to Charles the Bold of Burgundy, dated 13 May 1469 Lille, Archives du Nord, Archives Civiles, Série B, Chambre de Comptes de Lille, no. 862 (3), or the so-called 'Castle Rising letter' of 23 June 1469, BL, MS Cotton Vesp. F iii, item 19; see also ch. 3 below.

18 We return to this text and her ownership in ch. 3 below.

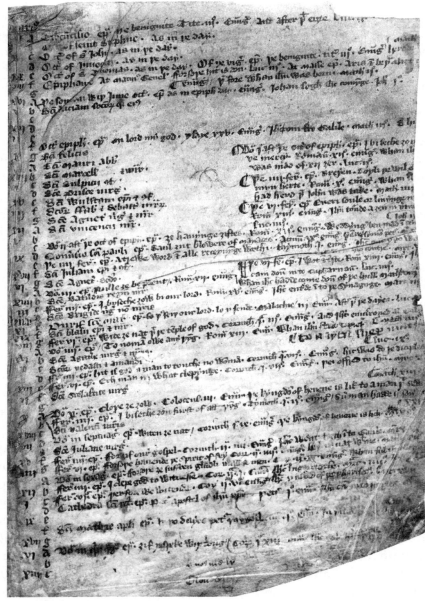

Fig. 6   The first page of Richard's copy of the Bible in English; it has the beginning of the calendar with saints' days and liturgical instructions. In the bottom margin is written, very small, *A vo[us] me ly Gloucestre*. New York Public Library, MS De Ricci 67. By permission of the New York Public Library.

Fig. 7 Richard's formal *ex libris*: *Iste liber constat Ricardo duci Gloucestre* (this book belongs to …) in the French prose version of the story of Tristan and Isolde. Redrawn by Piet Design from BL, MS Harl. 49, f. 155.

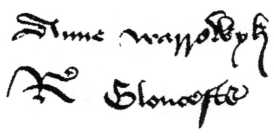

Fig. 8 The signatures *Anne warrewyk* and *R Gloucestr'* on the first flyleaf of a copy of the English translation of Mechtild of Hackeborn's *Liber Specialis Gratiae*, the *Booke of Gostlye Grace*. Redrawn by Piet Design from BL, MS Egerton 2006.

the House of York may have acquired them, obvious candidates being Elizabeth Woodville and her daughters, and Anne Neville.[19] It is likely that the duchess of Gloucester had her own selection of stories for entertainment and improvement of the mind, as well as her religious manuals and service books. Her library must have been similar – though not as impressive artistically – to that of her sister-in-law, the duchess of Burgundy and the *Booke of Gostlye Grace* may be the only survival. Margaret's surviving library has a heavy bias towards piety and it should be balanced with the inventory of another well-born female contemporary: the impressive collection of books of Gabrielle de la Tour, eldest daughter of the count of Auvergne and Boulogne, acquired apparently during her marriage and before her death in 1474. It ranged over history, religion, verse, romance, books of advice and information and beautiful books of hours, and included many of the titles owned by Richard of Gloucester; it offers persuasive evidence that such rich ladies could obtain books easily and had wide interests.[20]

---

19   See 'Choosing a book', pp. 82–83.
20   See ch. 2 below.

Fig. 9 Richard's subscription and signature on a letter to Louis XI of France, thanking the king for his gift of a 'great bombard', 16 June [1480]. Redrawn by Piet Design from BN, MS fr. 2908, f. 13.

Fig. 10 Richard's motto and signature on a document also signed by Edward V and Henry, Duke of Buckingham, April–June 1483. Redrawn by Piet Design from BL, MS Cotton Vesp. F xiii, f. 123.

The story of Richard's accession to the English throne, displacing his nephew, Edward V, and the rest of his brother's children as bastards, is too well known to need repetition here. Neither of Edward's sons were seen again after October 1483. Richard's 'active assumption of power' included the executions of William, Lord Hastings, Anthony, Earl Rivers, his nephew Richard Grey, and Thomas Vaughan. Richard and his queen were crowned on 6 July 1483, the first double coronation since 1308. Richard's reign lasted little more than two years. He survived a series of rebellions in 1483, and had several diplomatic successes, notably a peace with the Scots, but these were offset by the personal misfortune of losing his only son, Edward, Prince of Wales, in April 1484, and his queen in March 1485, and having to live with the rumours that he had murdered his nephews and even poisoned his wife. Opposition focused on the exiled Henry Tudor and on 22 August Richard was defeated and killed at the battle of Bosworth. His two years as king are hard to judge in cultural terms – he had barely time to stamp any aspect of government with his personality.[21] As regards his books, while king he acquired his book of hours in which he

---

21 For a brief overview, Sutton, 'Court and culture in the reign of Richard III', *passim*.

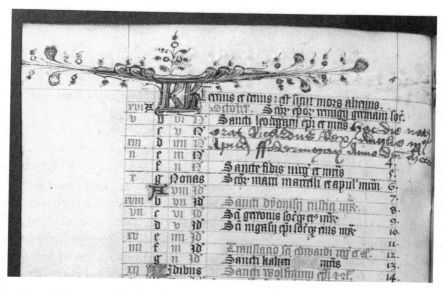

Fig. 11 Calendar page of Richard's book of hours with his autograph note recording his birthday on 2 October, written as king; it reads: *hac die natus erat Ricardus Rex Anglie iij[us] apud ffodringay anno domini M CCC[Clij]* (on this day was born Richard the Third, King of England, at Fotheringhay in the year of our Lord 1452). London, Lambeth Palace, MS 474, f. 7v. By permission of Lambeth Palace Library.

wrote his birth-date as *Ricardus Rex* and had a prayer inserted that includes his name and title. So clean is this book of all references to its original commissioner and previous owners that it was probably selected for the king for that reason. It was also designed to take over from the book of hours that Richard must have used until then: the earlier volume may have contained too many reminders of his early life as duke of Gloucester, of his brother Edward, and of his dead wife and son. Three other books were also acquired while he was king: his *Historia Troiae* and his *Historia regum Britanniae* (with its appendix, the *Prophecy of the Eagle*), both signed *Ricardus Rex* on their first pages (see figs 53, 54), and the *De re militari*, decorated with his crowned arms. The first two were second-hand, very ordinary looking books, both valuable for their texts alone. Richard was so glad to have them that he signed both companion volumes, each on its first page. The *De re militari*, by contrast, is a handsome, well-finished if unlavish book, made and decorated in London in the standard London style. Richard may have commissioned it himself for his son or he may have been given it as a present for himself or his son (see fig. 35).

Fig. 12 Richard's signature on a letter to the city of Danzig, 28 March 1484. Redrawn by Piet Design from Danzig, National Archives 300 D/16/135.

During his reign he also received the dedications of three books: the son of the antiquarian William Worcester presented him with his father's treatise on the need to reoccupy the lost territories in France and its accompanying collection of supporting texts; Pietro Carmeliano, the wandering scholar from Italy in search of a living, dedicated his verse *Life of St Katherine* to the king, at the same time presenting copies to two of Richard's councillors. Lastly Richard received the dedication of his translation of Ramon Lull's *Order of Chivalry* from William Caxton, the first English printer. All three dedications wanted something from the king: direct financial reward in the case of Worcester and Carmeliano and for Caxton the less direct recommendation of his book to other purchasers. Young Worcester and Caxton flattered the king's military pretensions and Carmeliano praised his learning and piety.

Caxton's press was at the height of its achievement at the end of Edward IV's reign and throughout Richard's.[22] That in itself was enough to secure Richard's reign a permanent place in the history of the English book trade, but in January 1484 his parliament made a significant gesture of favour towards books and education. It refused to allow chauvinist legislation to curtail the activities of immigrant alien workers in any section of the trade, or to impede the import of books, manuscript or printed, in any way. The extent to which Richard and his council were involved in this will be discussed in detail below. This famous proviso to chapter nine of his statutes ran until it was repealed at the request of the English stationers, binders and printers eager to limit foreign competition in the reign of Henry VIII. The proviso offers a focus for inquiry into the state of the book trade in the reign of Richard III at a time when manuscript production was still very important and when the advantages of print were being quickly grasped but not yet fully understood.

---

22 For figures see 'R III's books XI', pp. 117–18.

Standard Books in Late Medieval Noble Libraries

By Richard's time there were certain generally esteemed texts that anyone with the means to acquire them might be expected to own. Among these were Jean Mansel's *Fleur des Histoires*, a convenient summary of world history, of which large numbers of fine manuscript copies were produced in the Low Countries;[23] a version of the life of Alexander the Great or at least the so-called *Letter from Alexander to Aristotle*;[24] Valerius Maximus' *Dicta et facta memorabilia*, a collection of stories from Roman history arranged by subject and providing plenty of material for the moralist;[25] Vegetius' *De re militari*, the standard textbook on the art of war;[26] the *Roman de la Rose*, the long French poem on love by two poets, full of stories, the second half being notoriously misogynic; a 'mirror for princes', usually Giles of Rome's, but there were many other versions;[27] Boethius' *De consolatione philosophiae*, which gave comfort to all those under constraint or in distress;[28] a vernacular text of the *Golden Legend*, a compendium of saints' lives and other stories relevant to all religious feast-days;[29] and a national chronicle of one's own country, such as the *Brut* of England[30] or the *Grandes chroniques* of France.[31]

Of these titles some were and some may have been owned by Richard. About the *Fleur des histoires* we know, for example, that a man of similar tastes and status, the Burgundian Philip of Cleves (see below), as well as Richard's sister, Margaret of York, had one. As far as Valerius Maximus is concerned, there are two copies of the French translation among the

---

23 Saenger, 'Colard Mansion', pp. 405–18, esp. 408.

24 This text contained a description of the marvels of the East; it was also translated into English by John Multon, the London scribe, and could be bought in his bookshop, see *John Vale's Book*, p. 109; DiMarco and Perelman, *Letter of Alexander to Aristotle*.

25 The surviving mss of the French translation of Valerius Maximus are listed in Schullian, 'A revised list of manuscripts of Valerius Maximus'.

26 For the popularity of the text and the mss of the English translation see e.g. Lester, *Earliest English Translation*.

27 See ch. 5 below; also references given in 'R III's books V', pp. 61–73, esp. nn. 2, 3, 6 and 10.

28 See e.g. Patch, *Tradition of Boethius*.

29 See also ch. 3 below.

30 See also ch. 7 below; and e.g. Matheson, 'Historical prose', pp. 209–14; *Manual*, vol. 8, XII [2].

31 See ch. 5 below; and references in 'R III's books IX', pp. 494–514.

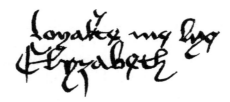

Fig. 13 Autograph motto, *loyalte me lye*, and signature of Elizabeth of York, later queen of Henry VII, in a French translation of Boethius' *De consolatione philosophiae*. Redrawn by Piet Design from BL, MS Royal 20 A xix, f. 195.

present Royal manuscripts; one has the arms of Edward IV's and his sons, the other bears the royal arms only. The latter manuscript could have been owned by any English king after *c.* 1470.[32] A *De re militari* was owned as a gift or a commission by Richard or his son, but even if this copy had not survived it could be taken for granted that the duke of Gloucester acquired this text at some stage of his life.

Ownership of the *Roman de la Rose* has to be hypothetical, but again, as many as three copies are found in the library of Philip of Cleves, who also possessed several 'mirrors' in contrast to the one *De regimine principum* that Richard owned. A copy of a French translation of Boethius, now in the Royal collection, is inscribed with the fascinating combination of Richard's best-known motto, *loyalte me lye*, and Elizabeth of York's first name, both in her handwriting.[33]

Though many copies or versions survive, no *Brut* chronicle is certain to have been owned by Richard or any member of his family.[34] He did have, however, the original of all *Bruts*, the *Historia regum Britanniae* of Geoffrey of Monmouth, his copy so plain and 'cheap' and so poor in its Latin that it was certainly acquired by him because he wanted the text. He signed it with his royal signature on the first page (see fig. 54). He was interested in the origins of his country and the British ancestors of the House of York – he signed the book as a descendant of Brutus, the

---

32 BL, MSS Royal 18 E iii, iv, and 17 F iv. The latter is not one of the very large mss made in Flanders in the 1470s or 1480s, but a French production of the 1450s or 1460s. The royal arms on the first page are very small and were clearly painted in as an afterthought.

33 BL, MS Royal 20 A xix; for a discussion of the ms. and the motto see Visser-Fuchs, 'Where did Elizabeth of York find consolation?', pp. 469–74.

34 See ch. 2 below, for a *Brut* that may have been owned by a member of the House of York. Caxton's *Chronicles of England* had no specific patron; his edition concludes with a prayer for the welfare of the newly crowned Edward IV.

founder of Britain. It is likely that the royal family, like 'everyone else' had a *Brut*, from Edward IV down. It was the most popular secular book in England and made even more available by Caxton's edition of 1480 as *The Chronicles of England* (see fig. 61).[35]

It must also be remembered that in addition to such secular works the duke of Gloucester, like all his social equals, certainly owned a collection of about forty service books, bibles, missals, graduals, antiphoners, as well as other – less personal but perhaps more magnificent – books of hours.[36] Patterns of ownership were also established by the particular background of the individual: a cleric had more theological works and religious manuals; women might have more devotional material, especially from the female mystics like Mechtild of Hackeborn, or copies of the *Cité des dames* by the famous champion of women, Christine de Pizan; men might be more inclined to read 'feats of arms', and if actively engaged in military affairs they needed Vegetius' *De re militari* or Bonet's *Tree of Battles*; heralds needed various rolls of arms; and 'everybody' might be expected to like stories, whether true or fictional, religious or secular, moral or bawdy, in prose or in verse.

Richard III's Collection

Without a complete inventory of Richard's entire collection little can be said with certainty about his tastes. We have eighteen texts in fourteen surviving volumes, most of them second-hand when he acquired them; and he is known to have received three dedications. Are we looking at the total of his books or only at the more modest volumes out of a large and magnificent library, long since dispersed and all signs of Richard's ownership obscured by the *ex libris* of later owners or the loss of flyleaves? It is salutary to remember that the recent discovery in Russia of three texts in two volumes belonging to him – Latin texts signed by him as king – has completely changed the balance of his known collection, and therefore

---

35 The text was also printed by the St Albans printer and Machlinia, Matheson, 'Middle English prose *Brut*: a location list', pp. 254–66.

36 See the estimate in 'Choosing a book', p. 63, 88; Edmunds, 'Savoy', 24 (1970), p. 324.

destroyed any conclusions about his likes and personality that might have been made in their absence.[37]

Apart from considering the number of Richard III's books and the subjects they cover we can also classify them by their illumination, or rather their overall lack of it. Only four are illuminated in any way, that is they have painted decoration which includes gold. His book of hours has one page of fine illumination, the rest of the decoration being of lesser quality, although few pages lack either colour or gold; his *Grandes chroniques* is substantially illustrated by five artists of high quality, but the illumination programme was never finished and the work of a sixth 'artist' – unfortunately near the beginning of the book – is abysmally bad; the *De re militari* and the *De regimine principum* are modestly decorated with standard London work of 1483–84 and of the 1420s respectively; the composite volume of romances and Bible stories has painted marginal decoration of a cheerful, probably provincial quality, composed mainly of foliage with a few fabulous animals, but it is also not finished and the series of shields of arms have not been filled in. Richard certainly did not acquire any of these books for the sole pleasure of looking at their pictures. As regards the *Grandes chroniques*, some of its illumination was sufficiently disastrous to put off anyone who was a mere collector of books. The pictures in Richard's hours made it a pleasant book to use every day, no more, and it had probably been chosen by Richard, or for him, with some care. It is possible that he only signed his second-hand books, while any splendid new work, commissioned from Flemish, French or English workshops, would have contained the arms or emblems of ownership most vulnerable to obliteration. The single commissioned volume that survives, the *De re militari*, which was possibly given to him or his son or commissioned by him for his son, is tantalising in its rarity (see fig. 35). It is attractive but uninspired in its workmanship and it provides no evidence to support an argument that Richard wanted to be surrounded by fine books; and it is always possible that it was a gift from someone who could afford nothing better. We have little means by which to discuss Richard's patronage of the decorative arts as applied to books,[38]

---

37 For judgments – such as they are – on Richard's library see e.g. Ross, *Richard III*, pp. 128–29; Lander, *Government and Community*, p. 328.

38 Compare Meale, 'Patrons, buyers, and owners', pp. 203–04, referring to the Vegetius: 'It is possible that Richard III, had he reigned longer, would have been more active in utilising native talents, though, as it is, only one of the several manuscripts which are known to have belonged to him was certainly made to his order'.

apart from noting that his book of hours contains some fine English illumination; his patronage of the book as a disseminator of knowledge, however, seems to be beyond doubt (see below ch. 10 and pl. VII).

Richard owned two French texts, ten English and seven Latin (excluding the rolls of arms, and William Worcester's volume of documents which is in all three languages), but this is slightly misleading as five of the English texts were comparatively short pieces for 'light' reading. As regards length he had more Latin, with English and French fairly equally in second place.[39] This emphasis fits in with our other findings on the Yorkist royal family: as far as can be concluded from their surviving books Richard of York and his sons owned a relatively large number texts by classical and medieval authors in the 'original' language. This apparent 'scholarliness' may have been due to a scarcity of English and French translations and the natural bias towards Latin in any medieval library, but that does not alter the fact that the owners could not have appreciated their Latin texts without a good passive knowledge of the Latin they had been taught in childhood.[40]

Most of the books that Richard had are on vellum of varying quality, only the *Boke of Noblesse*, and the composite volume of the *Historia Troiae*, *Historia regum Britanniae* and the *Prophecy of the Eagle* being on paper. the *Booke of Gostlye Grace* and the New Testament are the most crudely produced, and fairly typical for their date and subject matter: they were designed for serious use by devout people. The paper texts of the *Historia Troiae* and *Historia regum*, for all their faults, were written for use by a scholar; they have no pretensions to elegance except for the introductory initial of the former, but they are legible and competently laid out. Legibility, fine script and competent layout characterise all the other volumes. Several, such as the *Tristan* and the *De regimine principum*, have excellent pen-work initials and decorative flourishing as well as lists of contents.

All Richard's surviving books were second-hand, except for the modest Vegetius, but as second-hand books were the norm rather than the exception in his day, it is difficult to be certain that this characteristic is another piece of evidence that Richard was primarily interested in the contents

---

39 These proportions are comparable to those of the library of the dukes of Savoy, Edmunds, 'Savoy', 24 (1970) p. 327; 1498 inventory containing 298 volumes, of which roughly 150 were Latin, 91 French, 15 Italian and Spanish.
40 See 'Choosing a book', pp. 62, 74–77.

of his books. It does mean we are quite unable to assess him as a patron
or commissioner of books solely on the evidence of his surviving books.
All the manuscripts were made in England except the French *Grandes
chroniques* and the volume containing the *Historia Troiae, Historia regum
Britanniae* and the *Prophecy of the Eagle.*

For the modern scholar of books it is useful to realise that Richard's
collection was so ordinary. When examined in detail each book discloses
its unique qualities and its attractions for Richard, but it is also significant
that a man of his position who was neither an obsessive collector, nor an
ostentatious maecenas, needed and wished to possess this particular range
of books. This range was standard and unexceptional: Richard III was
more typical of English book owners of his day than was the frequently
cited Humphrey of Gloucester. Richard's books show us not only what
ideas, guidance and entertainment were on the king's shelves – which may
or may not be of interest – but also what was available to all his better
educated subjects.

Some aspects of Richard's book ownership can only be considered by
looking at analogous cases. Where, for instance, did he keep these books he
had acquired over the years? Few details are known about the location and
care of books under the Yorkist kings: from the records of their predecessors it is known that book-rooms or libraries existed at some of the major
palaces such as Eltham,[41] and the ordinances made for Edward's household show that a yeoman of the crown had special responsibility for the
royal books.[42] When Edward's books were transported they were carefully
packed in wooden crates ('cofyns of fyrre'); many were bound in sumptuous velvets and decorated with silk tassels and laces and metalwork.[43] Once
he was king, these details apply to Richard III, but there is no information
about the care of his books when he was still duke. The king had enough
books to warrant a special official to look after them, whether the duke had
we do not know. He may have had a book-room in each of his major residences, as carefully set up as those created by Jacques, Count of Armagnac
(died 1477),[44] or he may have had a single book-store from which a small

---

41   Stratford, 'Royal library in England', pp. 187–97.
42   Myers, *Household*, p. 116.
43   Nicolas, *Privy Purse Expenses of Elizabeth of York*, pp. 117, 125–26, 152. For other details of
storage see Edmunds, 'Savoy', 24 (1970), p. 321.
44   Pickford, 'Fiction and the reading public', pp. 428–29.

Fig. 14 The chronicler and poet, Jean Molinet (died 1507) presents his moralised version of the *Roman de la rose* to Philip of Cleves. Presentation scene from Philip's own copy. French, *c.* 1500. The Hague, Royal Library, MS 128 C 5, f. 1. By permission of the Royal Library.

travelling collection could be extracted to suit the occasion, like that taken by John Howard on the expedition to Scotland in 1482.[45]

A useful comparison for Richard's collection may be found in the short inventory of the books of the young heir to the dukedom of Savoy, who died in 1431: a book on the French wars, three romances, Bonet's *Tree of Battles*, a Life and a Passion of Christ, the *Book of Good Manners*, a book on chess (probably James de Cessolis' 'mirror'), *The Dicts of the Philosophers*, a book of songs, a Bible, and a book of hours.[46] The best inventory found to date which can be regarded as suggestive of what a book-list of Richard's could have been like is the one made of the collection of the Burgundian courtier Philip of Cleves. It was made after Philip's death in 1528 and

45 Crawford, *Household Books of John Howard*, II, p. 277. See below, p. 223, n. 41.

46 Edmunds, 'Savoy', 24 (1970), pp. 322–23, lists *Des nouvelles guerres de France*, a 'book on chess', '*Roman de la Rose*', '*Roman de Bertrand de Claquin*' [probably the verse life of Bertrand du Guesclin by Cuvelier, or its later prose version], 'Honnoré Bonnet's *Arbre des Batailles*', 'two copies of the *Narbonne*' [the *Narbonnais*, a *chanson de geste*?], a 'Bible', a '*petites matines*', '*La vie de nostre seigneur*', a '*Passion nostre-seigneur*', 'Jacques Le Grand's *Livre des bonnes moeurs*', '*Les dits des sages*', and a 'book of songs'.

covers the books in his 'house in Ghent'; it is an impressive list but he may have had other collections kept at other places.

Philip of Cleves, Lord of Ravenstein,[47] was a man sufficiently close to Richard in age, status and perhaps in interests, for his books to serve as an example of what Richard's library 'might have been'. Philip was born in 1456, four years after Richard, of royal and ducal blood, brought up at court, in the proximity of Mary of Burgundy, and in the service of Charles the Bold whose sudden death in 1477 brought about as traumatic a change in the lives of courtiers and relatives as did Edward IV's early death. Philip was a cultured man who became a soldier and who was forced into momentous choices and harsh action from an early age. It is still a matter for argument whether his choices were always right and honourable. Towards the end of his life he wrote a treatise on the art of war, both on sea and land. It allows us glimpses of what mattered to him and what aroused his emotions: the issue of the crusade – he was still willing to go on one when already an old man; the importance of practical military experience – he wrote that a war council should not comprise clergy and learned men who only knew war from books; the splendour of war – he took pleasure in chivalric ceremony, martial music and the magnificent beauty of a fleet of triumphant galleys.[48] The books he owned at his death reflected his interests as an educated man, a courtier and an active soldier. Most of them were in French, quite a number in Latin, a few in Italian. Practical, informative books, mainly on military matters and chivalric display (*c.* 20), were outnumbered by works on classical and contemporary history (*c.* 35);[49] classical literature and philosophy (*c.* 17) were balanced by Christian religion (*c.* 16). Didactic books, both narrative and 'plain', were present in the same number (*c.* 17); romances were few (*c.* 8). Liturgical texts were not mentioned in this inventory, except for a Bible in French and one book of hours; the fact that at least two of his books of hours survive again proves the unreliability of such lists, particularly as regards liturgical texts. The inventory also included paintings of cities of military importance, and a large number of documents concerning the ownership and revenue of

47 For Philip, his books and his own treatise see Finot, *Inventaire*, pp. 433–34; de Fouw, *Philips van Kleef*; Contamine, 'L'art de guerre selon Philippe de Clèves', pp. 363–76.
48 For Richard's interests in this field, see ch. 4 below.
49 He owned, for instance, one of the two surviving illustrated copies of the story of Edward IV's regaining of the crown in 1471.

land, a class of material that calls to mind the one surviving manuscript from Richard's ducal muniment room, a cartulary of the evidences of his lands and titles.[50] Like Richard, Philip of Cleves was also one of the few owners who signed their manuscripts neatly and systematically.

Philip had fifty years more than Richard in which to collect books so no comparison can be perfect, but the similarity of their backgrounds, interests and early lives makes him an interesting parallel. The books that do survive suggest that when Richard died his library had similar proportions and emphases, but no inventory has as yet been found and nothing is known about the immediate fate of most of his books. His book of hours was probably among the booty taken from his tent by the victors on the field of Bosworth; it passed to the new king's mother, Margaret Beaufort, and was given away. Of the other books, at least six must have been in royal residences and they remained in the Royal Library for several generations or until today;[51] some may have been in his ducal castles or had already been given away and they wandered through many collections throughout the world. They remain identifiable because Richard liked them enough to put his name in their text part, rather than on the more vulnerable flyleaves; he thereby ensured the survival of his signature – perhaps even saving some of the manuscripts themselves from destruction or neglect – and made the study of his 'library' possible.

---

50 BL, MS Cotton Julius B xii; the present authors hope to publish a detailed study of this ms.; see also Hicks, 'Cartulary of Richard III'.

51 The *Boke of Noblesse*, the *Grandes chroniques*, *De re militari*, *Historia Troiae*, *Historia regum* and the Longleat collection, see Catalogue, below.

TWO

The Books of the House of York

Richard was born into a family and social class that owned books. So much is certain, but whether the taste of his relatives influenced his own is something that can never be established beyond doubt. The surviving evidence of their book ownership and attitude to books is interesting in itself.

Richard's great-uncle, Edward, Duke of York, killed at Agincourt in 1415, was one of the few members of the English aristocracy of his time who actually wrote himself. He translated and expanded the popular French hunting treatise of Gaston Phébus, Count of Foix (died 1391)[1] and dedicated it to the future Henry V. The *Master of Game* discussed the nature of each beast and how it could best be hunted, but also elaborated on such joys of the hunter's life as the beauty of an early morning in the woods. Edward of York was the recipient of a poem by Thomas Hoccleve which claimed that the duke had expressed a wish to have as many of the poet's *ballades* as possible,[2] and he himself may have been the composer of a formal love poem, *A Lover's Farewell to His Mistress*. The date of the sole surviving copy of this poem also allows for the possibility that it was Richard III's father, Richard, Duke of York, who wrote it, but there

---

1 Tilander, *Gaston Phébus. Livre de Chasse*. York translated the text *c.* 1406 and added chapters on hunting in England. Twenty-six mss and fragments survive; Baillie-Grohman, *The Master of Game*; Braswell, 'Utilitarian and scientific prose', pp. 343, 367–68; Lewis, Blake and Edwards, *Index of Printed Middle English Prose*, 775.

2 Hoccleve, *Selections*, p. 55; Schulz, 'Thomas Hoccleve, scribe', pp. 71–81, discusses the possibility that Richard of York was the ballad's recipient but decides against it.

can be no certainty over its authorship. The verse contains no personal
thoughts or revealing images:

Farewell creature comely of kynde,
Farewell lanterne lussome of light,   [beautiful]
Farewell mynder most of my mynde,
Farewell souverain, semely in sight.[3]

Richard, Duke of York, and Cecily Neville

Richard III's father, Richard, Duke of York (1411–61), can be associated
with a small number of unusual books, which have never been discussed
in the context of his patronage. His book of hours is not unusual at first
sight (see pl. I).[4] It was one of many produced in the Low Countries for the
English market, but it has no less than twenty-three pages of extra devotions added for York himself in England.[5] These additions begin with two
prayers to the guardian angel, and apart from memorials[6] to such popular
saints as George, Christopher, Anthony and Barbara, there are less usual
ones to St Edward, king and confessor, who would have been important
to York as an ancestor, royal saint and law-giver,[7] to St Anne, and to the
Three Kings, whose cults were growing in the fifteenth century. St Anne
was particularly venerated by the ancestor-conscious nobility of western
Europe as the mother of the sacred dynasty and as the link between Christ

---

3   Robbins, *Secular Lyrics*, no. 205, lines 104–08, from Bodleian Library, MS Douce 95, ff. 1–3.
    The ms. has been dated to the second half of the 15th century.
4   Ushaw, St Cuthbert's College, MS 43.
5   York's coat of arms decorates the opening initial of the first prayer; the contents are described
    in Ker, *Medieval Manuscripts*, vol. 4, pp. 549–50.
6   Short prayers asking for a particular saint's intercession; also called suffrages. There is usually
    a standard series of such prayers included at the end of the office of Lauds in the text of
    the Hours of the Virgin, but the owner's special saints had their prayers separately at the
    beginning of a book of hours; see e.g. *Hours of Richard III*, pp. 44, 47, 94; Wieck, *Book of Hours
    in Medieval Art and Life*, pp. 111–23, 165–66; and ch. 3 below.
7   The memorials to male saints are to Sts Edward, George, Christopher, Anthony in that order;
    the one to St Anne is followed by Barbara only. St Edward had been particularly venerated by
    Henry III and Richard II for personal and propaganda reasons.

and his royal forebears.[8] The other additions to York's hours include well-known prayers to be said at the elevation of the host, a devotion to the Seven Words of Christ on the cross and pleas for general protection against temptation and spiritual enemies. It is interesting that both Richard and his father had books of hours to which they added numerous devotions.[9]

Richard of York's other surviving books are all dedications. The political situation *c.* 1440–*c.* 1460 and York's position as protector and heir to the throne, ensured that men increasingly sought his patronage. John Hardyng, soldier and antiquarian, re-dedicated his *Chronicle* (from the earliest times to 1437) to the duke and duchess of York shortly before, or in, 1460.[10] Hardyng's work had originally been composed for Henry VI; its main aim was to justify and facilitate the English conquest of Scotland, but he also sought reward for his long years of labour in gathering evidence.[11] In his *Proheme* Hardyng assumed that York took pleasure in reading chronicles and rehearsed in detail the duke's claim to the thrones of England, France and Spain, and even Jerusalem, as well as to the lordship of Ireland, Gascony and many other French territories. All the evidence, he maintained, was to be found in chronicles, for 'of olde bookes commeth our cunnyng newe'. He added that he wrote in English to allow the duchess, who did not have much Latin, and the duke's heirs to read the text and get 'a clere knowledge' of the history of Britain and their inheritance.[12] A few years later Hardyng re-dedicated his book again, this time to Edward IV; it is possible that Richard of Gloucester

---

8   Ryan and Ripperger, *Golden Legend*, pp. 520, 521. Brandenberg, *Heilige Anna, Grote Moeder*, pp. 12, 16–17. The name Anne was unusual in England before the marriage of Richard II to Anne of Bohemia in 1382. Richard of York claimed the crown of England through his mother, Anne Mortimer, and his other dynastic claims also derived from female ancestors; his eldest child was called Anne. The memorial to the Three Kings, patrons of travellers – and of the emperors of Germany – is also relatively rare; it begins *Ab oriente venerunt Magi*.

9   The prayers in York's hours have masculine forms and have the anonymous .N. common to such devotions if the owner's name was not filled in. For Richard's hours see *Hours of Richard III*, passim. Compare also the large, originally single volume owned by the dukes of Burgundy to which several generations added their favourite texts. Because of its size the book eventually had to be divided and is now Cambridge, Fitzwilliam Museum, MS 3-1954, and The Hague, Royal Library, MS 78 J 49.

10 See also ch. 7 below.

11 Hardyng, *Chronicle*. Gransden, *Historical Writing II*, pp. 274–87; Kingsford, 'The first version of Hardyng's chronicle', pp.462–82, 740–53; Edwards, 'The manuscripts and texts of the second version of John Hardyng's *Chronicle*', pp. 75–84. Riddy, 'John Hardyng's chronicle', pp. 91–108.

12 Hardyng, *Chronicle*, pp. 15–23.

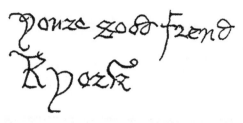

Fig. 15 Signature of Richard's father, Richard, Duke of York. Redrawn by Piet Design from [Owen and Blakeney]. *History of Shrewsbury*, vol. 1, p. 252.

also knew it and used some of its information about the geography of Scotland for his campaigns of 1480–82.

The other dedications to York are more individual and revealing. Their author, Osbern Bokenham (*c.* 1393–after 1464), was an Austin friar at the parent house of his order at Clare, Suffolk, built in the shadow of Clare Castle and closely associated with the lords of Clare since the time they brought the order to England.[13] In Bokenham's time York was Lord of Clare through his mother, Anne Mortimer,[14] and the friar/author must have known the duke well. Bokenham wrote for a circle of friends and patrons,[15] among them York's only sister, Isabel Bourchier, Countess of Eu, for whom he composed a life of St Mary Magdalene.[16] One work of Bokenham that may have been composed especially to please the duke of York himself is a 'chatty' genealogy of the lords of Clare, written in 1456, as a dialogue between a visitor to the priory and a friar who explains which lords and ladies are buried in the church (see pl. III and fig. 50). He lists the prominent members of the family from Joan of Acre, daughter of Edward I, at whose tomb the conversation takes place, concluding with the duke and duchess of York and their children, dead and alive. The poem is written on a roll; an English text down the left side and a

13 VCH *Suffolk*, vol. 2, London 1907, pp. 127–29; Roth, *Austin Friars*, vol. 2, pp. 302, 323, 334–35, 345, 347.

14 *CP* s.v. Clare, p. 246. The Honour of Clare was also important to York because his great-great-grandfather, Lionel of Antwerp, through whom he claimed the crown, was given the title of duke of Clarence (1362) deriving from the name Clare. On Edward IV's accession the title and the honour merged with the crown and were regranted to George, Edward IV's brother.

15 See e.g. Edwards, 'The transmission and audience of Osbern Bokenham', pp. 157–67.

16 When describing the evening on which the countess asked him to write her a life of Mary Magdalene, Bokenham explains at some length York's claim to the crown of Spain (see below).

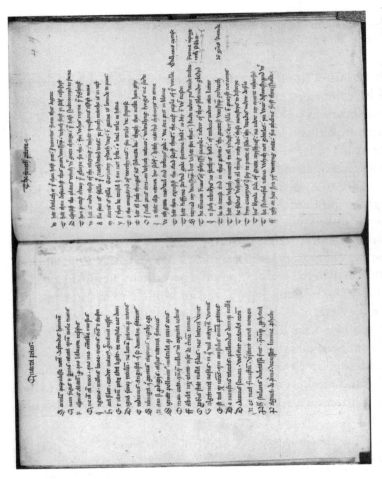

Fig. 16 An English translation, on the right, with parallel Latin text, on the left, of part of Claudian's *Consulship of Stilicho*, in which the poet praises the virtuous general Stilicho, voicing the wish of the Roman empire that he should become consul and save the country. The manuscript was made for Richard, Duke of York, in 1445 and has historiated initials with York's emblems: the closed fetterlock, the falcon, the white rose and the white hart. There are explanatory notes in the margin; the last one on the right-hand page reads *deo gracias Ricarde*, exhorting York to give thanks to God for his good name and success. BL, MS Add. 11814, ff. 18v–19. By permission of The British Library.

Latin version down the right, with the coats of arms of the lords of Clare, painted in full colour, running down the centre. At the top stand the visitor in a pink, fashionable gown and the friar in black, gesturing across a tomb on a green grassy knoll. One copy of this decorative roll, which is almost 3 feet long, may have hung in the priory for the entertainment of visitors; the lords of Clare may have been offered another.[17] The Latin text is very flattering to York (far more than the English version):

His sword shines forth, he is glorious in his titles and war triumphs. Nature gave him many talents, and fortune adorned him with great gifts. May he also have the blessing of a long life, happy and virtuous, and be redeemed at the end.[18]

Even more remarkable is an earlier manuscript which can probably also be ascribed to Osbern Bokenham: a small book containing part of the *Consulship of Stilicho*, a poem by the Roman poet Claudianus (*c.* 400 AD) celebrating the virtues and talents of the general Stilicho on whom, according to the poet, centred all the hopes of the empire and city of Rome.[19] The Latin text is given alongside the English translation — as in the Clare Roll — and was produced by someone whose scholarly intentions as well as devotion to York cannot be doubted. Notes in the margin give learned explanations of classical terms,[20] but also draw attention to the book's real protagonist, Richard, Duke of York; historiated initials contain York's badges of the fetterlock, falcon, white rose and white hart,

---

17 A gap and an error in the text suggest the surviving roll is a copy; it is now in the College of Arms, London; see also *Manual*, vol. 3, VII [38], and the present authors, 'Richard liveth yet'.

18 These phrases do not appear in the Latin text and one may wonder who was not supposed to read them.

19 BL, MS Add. 11814. For the ms. see Wright, *English Vernacular Hands*, no.19; Kirchner, *Scriptura gothica libraria*, no. 56b. For the text see Flügel, 'Eine mittelenglische Claudian-Uebersetzung (1445)', pp. 255–99, 421-38. On the translation see Fahrenbach, 'Vernacular translations', pp. 150–82. For discussion of the context see Watts, '*De consulatu Stiliconis*', pp. 251–66, which rejects the date given in the ms. and overlooks the emphasis on Spain; more relevantly Goodman and Morgan, 'The Yorkist claim to the throne of Castile', pp. 61–69, who explain the importance of this claim in 1444–45 and relate it to Bokenham's preface to the life of Mary Magdalene and to the translation of *De consulatu Stiliconis*, without naming the author of *De consulatu*.

20 Some draw attention to interesting lines, others explain words, such as *pallas tritonia minerva dea sapientie* or *mary was the name of Stillicoes ladi* (BL, MS Add. 11814, f. 21).

and one marginal note reads *deo gracias Ricarde*.[21] According to the colophon the manuscript was written and translated at Clare in 1445 and this date is confirmed by the contents and the author's emphasis on York's claim to the crown of Castile which, because of the political situation in Spain, took on a special significance in 1445.[22] The last lines seem irrelevant and owe little to the original Latin but they give an attractive, if exaggerated, picture of York's popularity with the estates who gather in his honour for the next meeting of parliament:

> ... tydyng with woordy wyngis
> Ovir the grete occian fleugh, commaundyng tappiere
> Swich high estatys as somownyd were; no man was lettid for age.
> Loong wey withstode not the western Iryssh, which ferthest duel of folke;
> For al alpees and mownteyns high, yit shippis sailed with wynde:
> The first love of thi gode life passid al hir labourys
> And gladly come to worship the, which venger of worship were.[23]

The author – who is likely to have been Bokenham – was an enthusiastic supporter of York, praising his patron's clemency, loyalty, prudence and 'vertuous dedys' in the person of Stilicho, and including the allegorical figures of Spain, France and England who entreat the hero to help and defend them. The author slightly altered the drift of the Latin text, raised the moral tone, but he did not change many actual words; there was, in fact, little need to do so and he must have been pleased to have found a text that suited York so well.[24] The work could be called a 'mirror of

---

21 BL, MS Add. 11814, f. 19.

22 *Ibid.*, section 15, ff. 15v–16, *Spayne compleyneth that stilico wil not rule* (Flügel, pp. 248–49). In the same year Bokenham went on pilgrimage to Compostella and may have become personally more conscious of York's claim and its possibilities Also in the same year he composed a life of Mary Magdalene for Isabel, York's sister (see above); in its introduction he dwells on the details of York's claim to the crown of Castile, ending enthusiastically: 'Wych god hym send, yf it be hys wyl'.

23 BL, MS Add. 11814, f. 25. The parliament of 1445–46 was summoned in Jan. 1445 and opened 23 Feb. York arrived from France before 21 Sept. in time to attend the session of 20 Oct. to 15 Dec., and the final one of 24 Jan. to 9 April 1446.

24 This is not the place to go into detail about the extent to which medieval scholars knew the works of Claudian, but a number of mss of his collected works survive, most of them from the 12th or 13th century; see Reynolds, *Texts and Transmission*, pp. 143–45; Platnauer, *Claudian*, vol. 1, pp. xix–xxiij. Bokenham had been to Italy as well as Spain. He mentions Claudian's *De raptu Proserpine* in his life of St Anne, but this was a very well-known text.

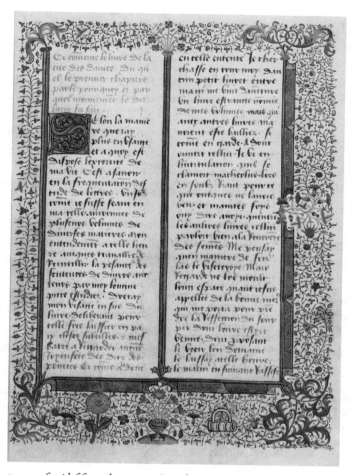

Fig. 17 First page of mid-fifteenth-century French copy of Christine de Pizan's *Cité des dames*, which probably belonged to Cecily Neville. In the centre of the lower margin is a 'Garden of Adonis' and the Yorkist emblems of the closed fetterlock and white rose were added in on either side. BL, MS Royal 19 A xix, f. 4. By permission of The British Library.

princes', but the author also set out to praise York for what he has already achieved, rather than present him with an example.

No other manuscripts have been found that can be definitely linked to Richard of York,[25] but two texts can be mentioned tentatively. He is likely to have owned at least one genealogical roll proving his descent and his claim to the crown of England (and France) of which a few examples survive,

25 York may also have owned some hunting tracts, see Sotheby catalogue, 12 March 1946, lot 2255, and Edwards, 'Transmission and audience of Bokenham', p. 165n.

although none can be specifically linked to York himself. They show York's descent from Brutus, the founder of Britain, via the Welsh princess Gwladys Ddu and the Mortimers.[26] There is also a *Brut* chronicle that could possibly have belonged to York, or someone close to him. The chronicle is the main item of a manuscript written and illuminated (first page only) in the 1440s. At the beginning of the book are inserted two short texts: schematic notes on some kings of England, Henry III to Edward III, and members of the Clare family of the same period, and another family tree proving Edward IV's claim to the crowns of England, France and Castile by right of his father.[27]

About the lifestyle and reading habits of York's wife, Cecily Neville, much is known from the period when she had retired from public life, after the defeat of her son, Richard III, in 1485.[28] She had a semi-monastic routine that must have differed greatly from her earlier worldly and peripatetic life when she was one of the first ladies of the land and a possible future queen.[29] There is no reason to doubt that her interests and therefore her book collection, whatever its size, were similar to those of such contemporaries as the duchesses of Burgundy and other aristocratic ladies at the English and continental courts. Unfortunately few inventories of female owners survive,[30] not even for Cecily's daughter, Margaret

---

26 Cambridge, Corpus Christi College, MS 98; the text of this roll also mentions Cecily, and Edward IV as king; BL, MS Add. 46354, ff. 59–61, is a 16th-century copy no longer in roll form, nor schematic, but written as continuous narrative. In all family trees of Edward IV his father's position and claims are crucial, see ch. 8 below.

27 New Haven, Yale Library, Beinecke, MS 323; Shailor, Catalogue, vol. 2, pp. 135–36; the insertions are slightly earlier or of the same date as the main text.

28 She may have 'retired' after Edward IV's death, or even when her husband died. She was born in 1415 and died in 1495.

29 Armstrong, 'Piety of Cecily Nevill', pp. 135–56; this article, mainly based on Cecily's will, is so well known that one tends to forget she had a previous career as a great lady.

30 Of particular interest are: **1.** the inventory of Gabrielle de la Tour, Countess of Montpensier (died 1474) printed in full: Boislisle, 'Inventaire', pp. 269–309; it contains more than 175 titles (a few doubles), all apparently her own or for her use as a number of her husband's books are listed separately. **2.** the will of Marguerite de Boncourt, Dame de Santes (died 1460), who left 22 books to male and female friends and servants among many jewels and *objects d'art*, see Lannoy, *Hugues de Lannoy*, pp. 281–95. The books vary in content and only one is strictly devotional (a psalter). See also *Histoire des bibliothèques*, vol. 1, p. 249, tableau 6, *Les bibliothèques des princesses*, a list of inventories and collections with the proportion of books on religion, literature and history; it shows that on average such ladies in the 15th century had 45 per cent moral and religious books, 45 per cent literature and 10 per cent history. See also Edmunds, 'Savoy', 24 (1970), pp. 324–25, for the library of Yolande, sister of Louis XI and wife of Amadeus II of Savoy (80 books).

of York, whose library appears to have been exceptional (see below). Arguing from analogous cases, it may be assumed that Cecily used her husband's books as well as having a number of her own. In the well-documented, later stage of her life she owned stories about the life of Christ, a *Golden Legend*, works by Sts Mechtild, Katherine of Siena and Bridget, and many liturgical books, most of which she bequeathed to her granddaughters and to the colleges at Stoke Clare and Fotheringhay, and the Bridgettine house at Syon, Isleworth.[31] It is likely, however, that in her youth she also had romances and perhaps some informative and history books. One manuscript, a copy of Christine de Pizan's *Cité des Dames*, a collection of stories of women famous for their learning, saintliness or courage, may be connected with Cecily as it is decorated with York's badges of the white rose and the fetterlock with a falcon; it is a typical 'ladies' book.[32]

It is unfortunate that Cecily appears to have left behind her little besides material for the study of the piety of her widowhood, and nothing to show whether she was in any way like Charles the Bold's mother, Isabel of Portugal, of any influence on the cultural and intellectual life of her sons, Edward IV and Richard III. Of almost equal social status – though not of equal political influence – both Isabel and Cecily lived the latter parts of their lives in semi-religious retirement. Both were religiously 'active' and shared, for instance, an interest in the revelations of St Bridget. There is evidence that Isabel of Burgundy also actively supported and stimulated the translating work of a humanist like Vasco de Lucena: though officially his translations of Curtius' *Alexander* and Xenophon's *Cyropaedia* were done for Charles, they may have been commissioned by his mother, who hoped that they might instruct him in temperance and statesmanship.[33] No evidence of any such activity on Cecily's part survives.

It is possible that Richard of York and Duchess Cecily during their moments of leisure were close to an East Anglian circle of neighbours

---

31 See Armstrong, 'Piety of Cecily Neville'.
32 BL, MS Royal 19 A xix; the illumination is French, c. 1430–50. Christine de Pizan was the most popular author in 15th-century women's libraries in France; *Histoire des bibliothèques*, vol. 1, p. 252.
33 Armstrong, 'Piety of Cecily Neville', pp. 135–36; Willard, 'Isabel of Portugal, patroness of humanism?', pp. 519–44; Lemaire *et al.*, *Isabella van Portugal*, which gives the latest research on Isabel's life and interests, with a bibliography; hardly any books that can be firmly ascribed to Isabel's personal ownership survive.

and relatives who shared an interest in religion, literature and art. Osbern
Bokenham may be seen as one of the providers of its needs, in the tradition of the poet John Lydgate, whom Bokenham admired and who may
also be loosely linked to the same circle.[34] Among Bokenham's patrons
were not only York's sister, but also Katherine Denston, neé Clopton,
whose brother, John, built part of the Clopton chapel in Long Melford
church, later decorated with verses by Lydgate.[35] John Clopton's step-
mother was Margery Drury, sister of the wife of John Baret,[36] a wealthy
clothier of Bury St Edmunds, close associate of John Lydgate and an amateur poet himself. The other dedicatee of Bokenham's *Life of St Katherine*
was another Katherine, first wife of John Howard, later Duke of Norfolk;
she is known to have been a sister of the lay confraternity of Clare Priory
(from 1445)[37] and it is likely that many of her acquaintances, including
Isabel Bourchier and her husband, and the duke and duchess of York,
were also *confratres* and *consorores*, thereby further cementing their association and shared interests.[38] It may be justifiable to create a picture of
a local network held together by social ties as well as religious and literary preoccupations[39] – in which the women may have had more leisure
to take part but which the men also shared. It flourished particularly in
the 1440s and early 1450s, before civil war temporarily split them, forc-
ing, for example, the abbey of Bury St Edmunds, John Baret and John
Clopton to choose Lancaster and the friars of Clare to stay loyal to their
patrons of the House of York.

The evidence for this social circle centred on Clare is slight, but it is
an intriguing addition to the suggestions of such literary communi-

---

34 See Edwards, 'Transmission and audience of Bokenham'; Moore, 'Patrons of letters in
    Norfolk and Suffolk'.
35 See Trapp, 'Verses by John Lydgate at Long Melford', pp. 1–11; the link of the Cloptons with
    Lydgate via the Drury family and John Baret was unknown to the author.
36 *Ex inf.* Margaret Statham. Baret left 3s. 4d. to *Maister Osberne Frere of Clare*. On Baret see his
    will, printed Tymms, *Wills and Inventories*, pp. 15–44; *John Vale's Book*, pp. 118–21.
37 Roth, *Austin Friars*, no. 804.
38 Membership of such fraternities was widespread and fashionable; brothers and sisters were
    included in all the spiritual benefits of the order, especially in their prayers for the soul. Many
    religious houses had such fraternities and people often joined several.
39 This is not the place to follow in detail all the possible family and other connections that
    can be made between Bokenham's patrons, other people named here and prominent Yorkists
    and Lancastrians, but see e.g. Moore, 'Patrons of letters in Norfolk and Suffolk', passim;
    Roth, *Austin Friars*, p. 327, no. 292, p. 334, no. 295; Edwards, 'Transmission and audience of
    Bokenham', passim; Johnson, *York*, p. 232 (Flegge), p. 229 (Bourgchier).

ties among the nobility in fifteenth-century England that stand up to any examination.[40] It seems to be quite impossible, in contrast, to suggest any literary community for the household of Richard Neville, Earl of Warwick, at his great northern castles of Middleham and Sheriff Hutton, where Richard of Gloucester lived for seven years. Warwick may have had a great influence on Richard's life, as may his countess, Anne Beauchamp, the heiress of the earls of Warwick. Although she employed artists at Warwick Castle while she was building a magnificent chantry for her father, Richard, Earl of Warwick, in the 1450s, nothing is known about Richard Neville's patronage and attitude to the arts. Both of them suffer from the complete loss of the Neville archives. The antiquarian John Rous, who praised so many of his Beauchamp and Neville patrons for their building and charitable actions, could merely mentioned Warwick's *intended* enlargement and improvement of the chantry at Guy's Cliff which was so dear to Rous.

Only one surviving manuscript can be associated with the earl of Warwick, but it is one that is an immediate reminder of Warwick's accomplishments and position as an experienced politician and diplomat in England and across the channel: the *Enseignement de la vraie noblesse*, a moral treatise criticising contemporary society in the shape of a dialogue between a young Flemish knight and an allegorical lady, *Imagination*, instigator of all human activity.[41] She teaches him what true nobility is and wishes him to go and give her message to one of the three classes of society, the clergy, the princes and knights, or the people of the towns. He offers to go to the knights 'among whom I have been brought up'. The author of the treatise is unknown but is likely to have been one of the brothers Hugh and Gilbert de Lannoy, noble courtiers and diplomats

40 Fleming, 'Hautes', pp. 85–102. The 'Woodville circle', created by Kipling in his *Triumph of Honour*, evaporates on closer examination: at best it consisted of two people, Antony, Lord Rivers, and John Tiptoft, Earl of Worcester, and only Rivers can still be considered to have been literarily *active* (if it was not his 'secretaire', mentioned by Caxton in the epilogue to the Moral Proverbs (Blake, *Caxton's Own Prose*, p. 119), who did most of the actual work!). For the strong possibility that Tiptoft did not write anything, see 'R III's books XII', pp. 160–61. Communities resembling the one around Bokenham are mostly middle class, for example the very active community living in St Bartholomew's Hospital, see Doyle, 'More light on John Shirley'; present authors, 'Cult of angels'.

41 Geneva, Bibliothèque Publique et Universitaire, MS fr. 166; Gagnebin, 'L'enluminure de Charlemagne à François Ier', pp. 155–56, no. 68; for the text see Hachez, 'Un manuscrit de l'*Enseignement de la vraie noblesse*', pp. 91–104.

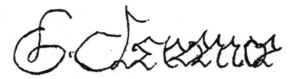

Fig. 18 Signature of Richard's brother, George, Duke of Clarence, on a document nominating Charles, Duke of Burgundy, a knight of the Garter. Redrawn by Piet Design from Lille, Archives départementales, série B, 862/16.161.

in the service of Philip the Good, both of whom wrote works of this type. Warwick's copy of the text has his full coat of arms, surrounded by the Garter, in the lower margin of the main, full-page miniature, which shows a broad landscape with trees and distant views; in the foreground the knight is kneeling beside his horse and listening to the Lady Imagination in front of a church (see pl. IV). In the right margin is a white bear, standing on its hind legs on a little island of green and chained to a bare tree trunk, clearly the Flemish illuminator's version of Warwick's emblem of the bear and ragged staff. The manuscript was written in 1464 at a time when Warwick was heavily involved in Anglo-French and Burgundian diplomacy and in frequent contact with Jean de Lannoy, a cousin of the author.[42] It could have been commissioned as a gift for Warwick.

For Warwick's elder brother, John, Earl of Northumberland and Marquess Montague (died 1471), again only one book survives: a de-luxe copy of English statutes.[43] The books of Warwick's younger brother, George, Archbishop of York, are those of an active scholar and patron of scholars and are not comparable to anything that Warwick or Montague may have owned. It is only possible to conclude that the libraries of the two secular Neville brothers would have probably held the usual selection of moral treatises and practical information, as well as the inevitable historical, devotional and liturgical texts.[44] It is unlikely that men in their

42 There is no evidence that the ms. was ever actually in Warwick's possession, or even that it reached England. The de Lannoys did give copies of their relatives' works as gifts: Hugh de Lannoy's widow in her will left two copies of her husband's work to friends; see de Lannoy, *Hugues de Lannoy*, pp. 281–95. Jean, too, was an author; he wrote a 'letter' of moral instruction to his new-born son whom he thought he would not live to teach personally, see ch. 5 below.

43 Now London, Lincoln's Inn, MS Hale 194, Ker, *Medieval Manuscripts*, vol. 1, p. 140.

44 See for example, *Histoire des bibliothèques*, vol. 1, p. 249, tableau 5, *Les bibliothèques des princes*

position – and in particular Warwick – did not possess a considerable number of sumptuous books acquired by purchase and gift.

Edward IV and Queen Elizabeth Woodville

Among Richard's brothers and sisters, both George of Clarence (died 1478) and Elizabeth of Suffolk present similar problems: no book of theirs is known to be extant. Caxton dedicated the first edition of his *Game of Chess* to Clarence (1474), bestowing on him standard praise in a standard prologue which reveals nothing except that the printer hoped that 'other, of what estate or degre he or they stande in, may see in this sayd lityll book yf they governed themself as they ought to doo'.[45] This scarcity of information cannot be said to prove that neither George or Elizabeth possessed books – it only indicates how many books do not survive. The eldest York sister, Anne (died 12 January 1476), inherited through her husband, Henry Holland, Duke of Exeter, the psalter of the famous 'Beaufort Hours and Psalter',[46] and there is a book of hours which shows her kneeling before the Virgin and dressed in a mantle showing her coat of arms.[47]

Edward IV himself had a more varied collection than has often been suggested, and as many as forty-five titles either survive or can be identified.[48] If all the books associated with him are considered in the same prosaic way that other fifteenth-century libraries and their owners are studied, and his library reconstructed by *including* dedications to him and texts owned by him in his youth and *excluding* purely speculative links, it turns out to be as miscellaneous in quality and contents as Richard of Gloucester's. His collection ranges from a small Latin formulary to English translations of Cicero printed by Caxton[49] and Guillaume Caoursin's *Siege of Rhodes*,[50]

---

45 Blake, *Caxton's Own Prose, Game of Chess*, p. 85, lines 29–31.
46 Now Rennes, Bibliothèque Municipale, MS 22; the hours are now BL, MS Royal 2 A xviii; see Rickert, 'The so-called Beaufort Hours and Psalter', pp. 238–46, corrected by Rogers, 'Books of Hours produced in the Low Countries', pp. 85–91.
47 Cambridge, Sidney Sussex College, MS 37; the picture is on f. 115v; see e.g. *Hours of Richard III*, p. 109 n. 267.
48 List of Edward's books in 'Choosing a book'.
49 *De amicitia* and *De senectute*, translated by William Worcester in the 1450s and printed and dedicated to Edward IV by Caxton in 1481.
50 See ch. 3 below.

Fig. 19 A book of hours belonging to Richard's sister, Anne, Duchess of Exeter. The duchess, in a mantle of her arms, kneels before the Virgin and Child, at the beginning of a prayer to the Virgin and St John the Evangelist. Cambridge, Sidney Sussex College, MS 37, ff. 116v–117. By permission of the Master and Fellows of Sidney Sussex College, Cambridge.

Fig. 20 *Ex libris* of the future Edward IV while he was duke of York (1461) in a small book of legal formulas compiled after 1445. The capital *I* of *Iste* contains a falcon on a closed fetterlock. BL, MS Harl. 3352, f. 1v. By permission of The British Library.

and from St Augustine's *City of God* to tracts on alchemy[51] and Lorenzo Traversagni's *Triumphus justitiae*.[52] Long before Edward acquired the well-known large Flemish manuscripts he owned some simple books which date from his youth: a book of legal formulas, a collection of medical treatises and a mirror for princes, all in Latin.[53] During his early years as king he received a number of dedications: the *Chronicle* of John Hardyng (1463?) and John Capgrave (1462-63),[54] and the *Compound of Alchemy* by George Ripley (1471).[55] In 1472 he was given what was probably his first printed book: the so-called *Orationes* of Cardinal Bessarion, the Greek book-collector, humanist, theologian and papal legate. It contained a vigorous and learned plea to the leaders of western Europe to settle their differences and join forces against the Turks. Printed in Paris in 1471, copies were presented, each with a letter of dedication, to the emperor, the kings of France and England, the dukes of Burgundy and Savoy, as well as to prelates and abbots, and others whose copies do not survive. Edward's copy was printed on vellum, has a hand-painted presentation page and survives in the Vatican (see fig. 21).[56]

In the late 1470s and early 1480s Edward acquired a number of bulky illuminated manuscripts from Flemish workshops, all written in a large script that made them suitable for reading aloud from a lectern. They were standard titles in French or translated into French: Valerius Maximus' *Memorabilia* and other collections of ancient history such as Josephus' *Jewish Wars* and versions of the work of Julius Caesar; the chronicles of the crusades by William of Tyre and the well-known, (near) contemporary histories of Jean Froissart and Jean de Wavrin; religious/didactic texts such as St Augustine's *City of God* and Pierre Richart's *Fortress of*

---

51 Edward IV may have been particularly interested in alchemy: Thomas Norton dedicated his *Ordinal of Alchemy* to him (see *Thomas Norton's Ordinal of Alchemy*, ed. John Reidy, EETS OS 272 (1975), introduction), and George Ripley his *Compound of Alchemy* (see *DNB*, vol. 48, and the facsimile, Amsterdam 1977, of the edition of 1591). Norton is said to have accompanied Edward into exile; Ripley maintained in the dedicatory epistle that Edward had *asked* for the text and that he (the author) was willing to share his knowledge only with the king, who was sworn to secrecy!

52 See 'Choosing a book', p. 76. The text of the *Triumph of Justice* survives in an autograph copy, Vatican Apostolic Library, MS Vat. lat. 11608, ff. 90–157v.

53 BL, MSS Harl. 3352 (formulas) and Royal 12 E xv (treatises and mirror).

54 See ch. 7 below.

55 See n. 51 above.

56 Rome, Vatican Apostolic Library, MS [sic] lat. 3586; 'Choosing a book', pp. 76, and ch. 11 below, for the presentation of the book to Louis XI.

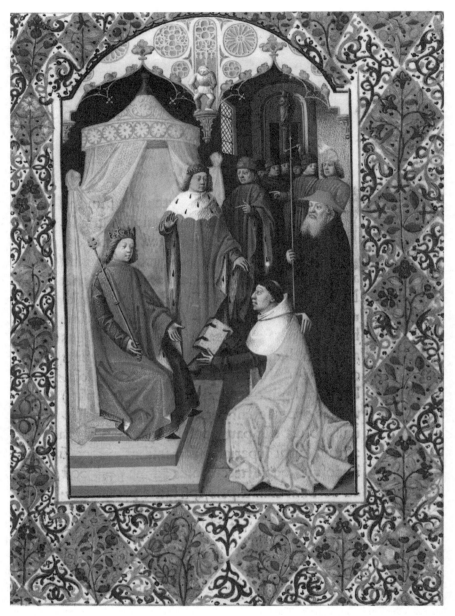

Fig. 21 The printer Guillaume Fichet presents Cardinal Bessarion's *Orationes* to Edward IV; the cardinal stands behind the printer in this probably fictional scene. Miniature and marginal decoration were added to the book, which was printed at Paris in 1472. This particular copy bears a dedication to Edward. Rome, Vatican Apostolic Library, MS [sic] 3586, f. 1. By permission of the Biblioteca Apostolica.

Fig. 22 Signature of Edward IV on a document nominating Charles, Duke of Burgundy, a knight of the Garter. Redrawn by Piet Design from Lille, Archives départementales, série B, 862/16.161.

Faith, as well as short chivalric/didactic treatises including Christine de Pizan's *Letter of Othea* and Alain Chartier's verse *Breviary of Noblemen*; and informative books, including the agricultural and general encyclopaedias of Pierre de Crescens and Bartholomew the Englishman. The format and didactic and historical contents of all these manuscripts made in Flanders suggest that they could have been used in the education of his sons, whose coats of arms are often included in the decoration of the margins.[57] The same titles were to be found in the – much larger – collections of Edward's contemporaries at the Burgundian court, but his copies have a different format, they show signs of 'mass-production' and their execution and illumination is not as lavish as one would expect in the library of a man of unlimited means. A few of this particular group of manuscripts have the royal arms only and could have belonged to either Edward or Richard or Henry VII. It is in fact likely that Richard also acquired some Flemish manuscripts, though all marks of his ownership have disappeared and no surviving copy can be said to have been his with certainty. The available evidence concerning Flemish artists, their workshops and patrons suggests a complicated pattern of commission and purchase by members of the Burgundian court, and by a few Englishmen. Clearly some ateliers were popular with certain patrons; Edward IV, Lord Hastings, Sir John Donne and Sir Thomas Thwaytes bought work from the same sources as Anthony of Burgundy, Louis of Gruuthuse, Philip of Cleves and members of the Nassau family. Richard of Gloucester no doubt shared the same fashionable taste in some way.

The books of Edward IV's queen, Elizabeth Woodville, form a problematic collection.[58] Superficially, the most important item is the large, early fourteenth-century volume which in Elizabeth's day contained

---

57 'Choosing a book', pp. 79–82.
58 For all her books see the present authors, 'Elizabeth Woodville', pp. 227–32. Meale, 'Manuscripts, readers and patrons', pp. 103, 120–22, also deals briefly with her books.

two of the three parts of the French prose *Lancelot*, the *Queste del Graal* and the *Morte Artu*, with the prologue, the *Estoire del Saint Graal*, all on vellum, and a stray story from the Tristan cycle on paper. It is just possible Elizabeth may have owned and signed the book while still plain *E Wydevyll'* and still been its owner when the names of her daughters, Elizabeth and Cecily, each described as the king's daughter, were added, but it is in fact more likely that the signature was that of her brother, Edward (died 1488); as queen Elizabeth signed as *Elyzabeth*.[59] The only other secular text associated with her is a copy of Caxton's *Recuyell of the Histories of Troy*, inscribed 'This boke is mine quene elizabet' after her death by Thomas Shukburghe junior.[60] She received at least three dedications and gifts. In 1471 a Londoner dedicated to her his poem celebrating the return of Edward IV from exile and the victories against Warwick and Fauconberg at Barnet and at the gates of London, and in 1465, during her crossing of London Bridge into the city before her coronation, the city of London presented her with six ballads written out and decorated by John Genycote.[61] Another likely gift is an hours of the Guardian Angel

---

59 BL, MS Royal 14 E iii; the *Queste* is extensively illustrated, the *Morte* less so. For a reproduction of this problematic *E Wydevyll'* signature and two of her regnal signatures of [1482] and 1491, see MacGibbon, *Elizabeth Woodville*, frontispiece and opp. p. 196. The inscriptions for Elizabeth's daughters could be by either of the princesses or by another hand. The book was the property of Sir Richard Roos (d. 1482), who wrote 'cest livre est a moy' (f. 2v) and described the contents as they were then and probably annotated the text (e.g. ff. 84v, 87, 88); he bequeathed it to his niece 'Alianore Hawte' who also claimed 'thys boke ys myne' (f. 162). 'Jane Grey' who is to be identified as Elizabeth's sister, Jane or Joan, who married Sir Anthony Grey of Ruthin, added her name (ff. 1, 162). All the signatures could date from *after* the bequest from Roos in 1482, including *E Wydevyll'* as Edward. This simplifies the scenario very helpfully. For a full analysis, the present authors, 'Elizabeth Woodville', pp. 228–30. Compare Meale, 'Manuscripts, readers and patrons', p. 103.

60 San Marino, Huntington Library R.B. 62222, the copy with the unique engraving of Caxton presenting his translation to Margaret of York. The inscription runs:
This boke is mine quene elizabet late wiffe unto the moste noble king edwarde the forthe off whose bothe soolis y be seche almyghty Gode Take to his onfinyght mercy above Amen. Per me Thomam Shukburghe iuniorem.
See the present authors, 'Elizabeth Woodville', p. 230. The association of Elizabeth with the anonymous dedicatee of Caxton's translation of the *Book of the Knight of the Tower*, by Blake, *Caxton and His World*, pp. 92–93, and later in his 'The "Noble Lady" in Caxton's "The Book of the Knight of the Tower"', pp. 92–93, cannot be sustained, see 'R III's books XI', pp. 115–16.

61 Sole copy BL, MS Royal 17 D xv, f. 327 ff., possibly sold in John Multon's shop; printed Wright, *Political Songs*, vol. 2, pp. 271–82, esp. 281–82; *John Vale's Book*, pp. 109–10. For the ballads CLRO, Bridge House Accounts, p. 95. For both the present authors, 'Elizabeth Woodville', pp. 224–27.

presented to her 'sovereyn princes' by an unknown woman who made an acrostic of the name 'Elisabeth' in her dedicatory poem and described how the text had been specifically requested (see pl. V).[62] Similarly she may be the unnamed late fifteenth-century queen who was given Lydgate's *Life of Our Lady* 'ffor to comffort and to passe tyme in redyng'.[63] That Queen Elizabeth Woodville owned and bought expensive books is undoubted,[64] but her collection is irrecoverable.

One particular group of books still in the royal collection is a reminder of how unknown is the role of the queen in Yorkist book collecting. This group can be tentatively linked to Edward himself but seems to be separate from the texts concerned with antiquity, the big manuscripts acquired from the Low Countries, and the dedications mentioned above. Using the early inventory numbers in royal library manuscripts[65] some suggestions can be made. A group of three surviving books all bear the same type of distinguishing inventory number, the highest number of the three being ninety-three.[66] All three texts are fine manuscripts; two were made in the late 1470s or early 1480s before 1485; the third dates from the 1430s–50s and bears Yorkist emblems. The three books contain four texts, mostly didactic literature, and one volume of lives of saints. All are comparatively small, slim volumes and one has exceptionally fine illumination: they were books for private study, not for reading aloud. It

62 Liverpool Cathedral, MS Radcliffe 6. See the present authors, 'Elizabeth Woodville', pp. 230–31, and 'Cult of angels'.

63 New Haven, Yale University Library, Beinecke MS 281, verso of front flyleaf; the present authors, 'Elizabeth Woodville', p. 232.

64 In 1466–67 she spent £10 on an unspecified book from Master Wulflete of the University of Cambridge, Myers, 'The household of Queen Elizabeth Woodville', p. 318. The one other ms. that has been linked to her is ex-Bradfer-Lawrence MS 15, sold at Sotheby's 6 Dec. 1983, lot 65, and now Toronto, Bergendal Collection, MS 60, fragments of a 14th-century missal. It bears – among others – the inscriptions 'Elizabeth dei gratia' and 'To my good friend [Mortimer]' which have been interpreted as Elizabeth of York's; it has also been suggested that it was her mother's, because of references to Westminster Abbey and the 'victorious king Henry', *Richard III*, item 156, p. 64. These suggestions do not stand up to scrutiny. See the present authors, 'Elizabeth Woodville', pp. 228, 231–32 and esp. nn. 100–02.

65 A provisional list of these numbers was kindly supplied by Professor James Carley; 'Choosing a book', pp. 82–83.

66 BL, MS Royal 19 A vi, numbered 60: *Ung tractie de conseil extraict du second livre de la thoison d'or*, by Guillaume Fillastre, and *Tulle de veillesse*, before 1477; MS Royal 20 B ii, numbered 62: lives of saints in French, with good quality illumination, 1480s, arms of John Donne; MS Royal 19 A xix, numbered 93: *Cité des Dames*, French, c. 1430–50, tentatively ascribed to the ownership of Cecily of York, see above.

is therefore likely that a different type of book was being acquired while Edward bought his lectern books in the Low Countries: these could have been the purchases and acquisitions of women of the House of York. The little evidence that survives suggests that the queens and princesses of the House of York owned varied collections, and if this was indeed the case, then their cultural and literary interests should be seen as comparable to those of their noble female contemporaries abroad, including the collection of Margaret of York, Duchess of Burgundy.

Margaret of York, Duchess of Burgundy

Much has been written about Margaret's ownership of books and patronage of authors, but some aspects remain mysterious. Why, for example, does she appear to have had no English books at all? And did her collection really contain such an overwhelming proportion of devotional works as the surviving manuscripts suggest? Again, all conclusions have to be drawn from the surviving manuscripts and from indirect references to her gifts or ownership, as no inventory has come to light.[67] To date about thirty volumes have been associated with Margaret, either because they were commissioned by her, contain her arms or signature, or because they were given to her or by her. Some are mere fragments, others are composite volumes containing several separate works; in all there are seventy-three titles, including a few doubles. Apart from the usual books of hours, breviaries and a gradual, there are four saints' lives – Colette, Gommaire, Edmund and Katherine – and many works of devotional instruction, ranging from a couple of pages to full-length books.[68] Not all of these devotional texts can have been of equal importance to, or even consciously chosen by, their owner. Some of the very short texts are mere 'fillers' of the manuscripts in which they are found; workshops often included short works in this way and this practice partly explains the presence of a number of doubles among Margaret's surviving books. Many of her devotional texts explained the basic truth of Christian teaching, each in their own way, and again and again rehearsed the tenets of the Church and other simple moral maxims: the Ten Commandments, the Seven

---

67 The latest study of Margaret's books is the collection of essays in Kren, *Margaret of York*.
68 Morgan, 'Texts of devotion and religious instruction', pp. 63–76.

Deadly Sins, the Four Cardinal Virtues; putting them in ever-changing but nonetheless very similar, schematic patterns; presenting them as dialogues, admonitions addressed to the reader or plain narrative. It is clear, however, that Margaret of York also owned some important works, not to be found in every library and probably unknown to her before she came to Burgundy, such as Thomas à Kempis's *Imitation of Christ*, meditations by St Bernard, treatises by Jean Gerson and the religious advice of St Peter of Luxemburg. Particularly splendid is her copy of the *Visions of Tondal*, which describes and illustrates a journey to the next world. She also had Boethius' *Consolation of Philosophy* (see pl. II), an *Apocalypse* with commentary and part of a *bible moralisé*.

Five surviving manuscripts associated with her were informative or historical: one volume of Brunetto Latini's *Livre de Tresor*, a thirteenth-century encyclopaedia; a chronicle of Flanders; Curtius' *Life of Alexander the Great*; Justinus' epitome of ancient history, in Latin; and at least one volume of the *Fleur des histoires*, a very popular history of the world. Of these five books two have been only recently been 'discovered' and have redressed the balance of her library which was so heavily weighed in favour of devotional texts. Her lack of English books may be explained by the disastrous fire in the castle of Male, near Bruges, in the summer of 1472, which was said at the time to have caused the loss of many of her most personal belongings. The survival of her English books would have been also at risk after her death, when there were few people in her immediate circle who could read the language.[69] Margaret's facility in French and Flemish may have meant that she never attempted to acquire any of the English devotional or other texts that were popular with her noble countrywomen during her lifetime after the books of her youth had been burnt.

Many of the books connected with Margaret were actually given away by her to others. These gifts show how she cared for the instruction and entertainment of her family and friends, and present an interesting picture of the way in which books were passed from one owner to another

---

69　It is known that after the death of Jacqueline of Bavaria, Countess of Holland, who had been married to Humphrey of Gloucester, her English books were sold to an English merchant for the very reason that no one could read them. Similarly, it is still a mystery why there are no Flemish books among the many manuscripts of Louis of Gruuthuse, whose collection ended up in the French royal library; Flemish was his mother tongue, but any books in that language may have been sold off by their French owners.

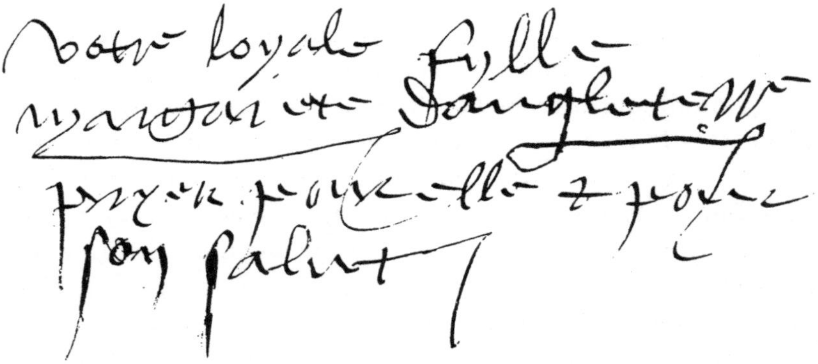

Fig. 23 Autograph note of Richard's sister, Margaret of York, Duchess of Burgundy. It reads: *votre loyale fylle margarete dangleterre pryez pour elle et pour son salut*, your loving daughter, Margaret of England, pray for her and for her well-being. Redrawn by Piet Design from Ghent, Poor Clares, MS 8, f. 163.

and were used as a means of ensuring a place in the recipient's memory and prayers. She gave her *Dialogue between the Duchess of Burgundy and Jesus Christ*, which had been composed at her request to instruct her how she might reconcile her exalted position in society to a true Christian way of life, to her friend and lady-in-waiting Jeanne de Haluin, Lady of Wassenaar, in 1500. To her stepson-in-law, Maximilian, or to her stepdaughter, Mary, she presented a beautiful Italian manuscript in Latin of Justinus' epitome of Trogus Pompeius' books of ancient history. Together with Mary she may have given a copy of Curtius' *Life of Alexander* to her brother Edward IV's servant and courtier, Sir John Donne,[70] and Mary herself in her turn gave Margaret a chronicle of Flanders, written when Mary became duchess of Burgundy and countess of Flanders on her father's death in 1477. Like most female members of her own and her husband's family Margaret was a patroness of many religious houses and also presented books to them: a beautifully illuminated life of the Franciscan saint Colette to the convent of the Poor Clares at Ghent, choirbooks to the church of St Ursmer at Binche, a gradual to the Observant Grey Friars at Greenwich, and perhaps a book of hours to the Bridgettines at Dendermonde.[71] In 1473–74, she is said to have laid with her own hands the first stone for the new library wing

70 BL, MS Royal 15 D iv, Backhouse, 'Sir John Donne's Flemish manuscripts', p. 49. The *Dialogue* is now BL, MS Add. 7970.

71 For the first three see Kren, *Margaret of York*, Appendix; for the Bridgettines see Reynaert, 'Het middelnederlandse gebedenboek van de Brigitinessen van Dendermonde', pp. 29–48.

of the Dominican house at Ghent. Visible reminders of this public act of patronage survive in the stone's inscription, describing the ceremony and her gifts to the house on the occasion, and in the decoration of the ceiling of the library which includes her *M* and the pomegranate, said to have been one of her devices.[72]

The members of the House of York may not be well served by the survival of either their books or inventories of their libraries, but once every reference has been collected and the essential service books allotted, the accumulated evidence reveals that they were comparable to any other noble house of the time. Their interests and purchases, the dedications and gifts they received, their use of books as presents for others, the means by which they claimed their books as their own by signature, *ex libris* and personalised decoration, are all very similar to the better documented practices of the dukes of Savoy, for example, or the dukes of Burgundy and their families. Edward IV, Margaret of York and Richard III stand out – they are best served by survival and reference – but the information about their parents is not negligible. Both children and parents clearly show they belonged to a family in which books were an expected part of daily life.

---

72 De Jonghe, *Belgium Dominicanum* ..., p. 29; Simons, *Het Pand*, pp. 60–95.

THREE

Devotional Books, Saints and Piety

There is no doubt that Richard, both as duke and king, owned many religious books. It has been calculated that a nobleman's household in the later Middle Ages needed thirty to forty liturgical books for the use of its chapel,[1] apart from the devotional treatises and saints' lives which were to be found in many collections, and the duke of Gloucester's household would not have been an exception. Only five such books survive for Richard, but they present a good cross-section of the devotional texts that were available and popular at the time, and allow some insight into the nature of the piety of their owner.

Books of Scripture

Taking the books in the order we can assume he acquired them, the first to be mentioned is the English verse translation of a large section of the Old Testament which Richard owned as an adolescent. It was part of the anthology that included stories by Chaucer and Lydgate and the romance of *Ipomedon*.[2] The New Testament in Richard's collection was represented by a copy of the Wycliffite or 'Lollard' translation, made about 1390 and owned

---

1 'Choosing a book', pp. 62–63 n. 25.
2 See ch. 9 below, and Cat. II; 'R III's books II'.

Fig. 24 Capital *I* in the shape of a wyvern at the beginning of the fourth Book of Kings in Richard's verse paraphrase of stories from the Old Testament. Redrawn by Piet Design from Longleat, MS 257, f. 176.

by Richard before he became king (see fig. 6).[3] Together with his wife he owned a manuscript of the English translation of Mechtild of Hackeborn's *Book of Special Grace*, which is both a saint's life and a collection of mystical revelations (see fig. 8).[4] Richard's book of hours for daily use, acquired when he was king, also survives; it is likely he had other and more elaborate *horae* as well.[5] Finally, we know that the Italian humanist scholar and poet Pietro Carmeliano, who had settled in England in 1481, composed a *Life of St Katherine of Alexandria* in Latin verse for the king as a New Year's gift in

3　'R III's books III'; Cat. III, below.
4　'R III's books I'; Cat. I, below. See also Bromberg, *Het Boek*; Bynum, *Jesus as Mother*, ch. 5, 'Women mystics in the thirteenth century: the case of the nuns of Helfta'; and Finnegan, *Women of Helfta*, esp. ch. 4, the '*Book of Special Grace*', which all discuss the devotional aspects of the original in detail.
5　*Hours of Richard III*, p. 2.

1484 or '85 (see pl. VI).[6] Further evidence of Richard's piety and interest in religious matters must be sought in the book ownership of his closest relatives and intimates, his own public acts and official publications, and his religious foundations. His attitude to the need for a new crusade against the continued threat from the infidel armies can also be traced.

The Old Testament text that Richard owned is part of a manuscript made and illuminated in his own lifetime. The first part of the book contains romances, the second, written in a slightly different hand but in the same workshop, has the Old Testament text. The illumination of the whole manuscript is unpretentious and pleasant, but the decoration of the romance section is more elaborate. The Old Testament text is an alliterative verse paraphrase in twelve-lined stanzas of the most dramatic, narrative parts: Exodus, Numbers, Deuteronomy, Joshua, Judges, Ruth, 1–4 Kings, Job, Tobit, Esther, Judith and parts of 2 Maccabees.[7] The text originally started with Genesis and the creation of the world, but these pages are now lacking in Richard's copy. These Bible stories, no less than the romance *Ipomedon*, were meant to hold the reader's attention as well as edify him. The Flemish author Jacob van Maerlant, who composed a 'Rhyming Bible' in the vernacular in 1271, had already complained that people would rather listen to the stories of Tristan and Lancelot, Percival and Galahad, and that 'all over the wide world, people read trifles of love and war, but the Gospel is too much for them ...'. Both van Maerlant's work and the English paraphrase were written to ease the way to devotion and salvation for the lazy and illiterate layman.[8]

Van Maerlant, as well as the unknown author of the paraphrase, relied heavily on a twelfth-century Latin prose *adaptation* of the Bible (see below), which was accepted by the Church as less dangerous, that is, less likely to tempt the reader to a personal interpretation of God's Word – and thus to heresy – than reading the Bible itself. Even so van Maerlant's translation was not welcomed in his day.[9] How the author of the English poem fared

---

6 'R III's books XIV', and Cat. XIV, below.
7 For a detailed description of the ms. and its illumination see 'R III's books II', pp. 426–30. The chapters from 2 Maccabees are 6: 10 and 18–31; 7: 1–42; 9: 4–29; they are called *De matre cum septem pueris* and *De Antioco*.
8 Van Maerlant is mentioned and quoted by Deanesly, *Lollard Bible*, pp. 71–75, 294, 441. The quotation is from van Maerlant's *Leven van St Franciscus*, lines 37–40. The author had translated several romances himself before a complete change of mind led him to concentrate on religious and didactic work.
9 For van Maerlant and Comestor see also Hindman, 'Fifteenth-century Dutch Bible illustration and the *Historia Scholastica*', pp. 131-44, and references given there.

in this respect is not known; the fact that the young Richard of Gloucester possessed a copy suggests that by the 1460s the work was considered 'safe'.

The author of the text has been called a late exponent of the four-teenth-century religious didactic movement in the north of England; the work has been related to the Old Testament stories of the *Cursor Mundi*, the homily cycle known as the *Northern Cycle* and to the *York Plays*, but it is not clear, for example, whether the paraphrase was inspired by the plays or the plays by the paraphrase.[10] His knowledge of religious litera-ture is evident, and the author may have been a cleric himself, writing for fellow religious who had no Latin,[11] or an educated layman like van Maerlant. He leaves no doubt as to his purpose: to select the most valu-able parts of the Bible, to be brief and comprehensible to all. He is true to his word, including such stories which might be thought suitable to an audience used to popular romances, adding legends and description and leaving out the duller parts. Like many medieval religious texts the paraphrase derives much of its method and material from the *Historia Scholastica* of Peter Comestor, chancellor of the university of Paris until his death in 1178. The *Historia* was composed between 1169 and 1175 and became the favourite handbook of sacred history. It included most of the Bible books, from Genesis to the Acts of the Apostles, interspersed with quotations and excursions containing much of the current learning of the day. In its many redactions and translations it became a standard part of monastic and private libraries.[12]

A modern reader would not care to wade through all 18,372 lines of Richard's Old Testament paraphrase, but a number of them make quite enjoyable reading. Take, for example, the story of Tobit. Where the Bible text merely has *canis secutus est eum* (his dog followed him, Tobit 6: 1) and the *Historia Scholastica* is equally brief, the paraphrase reads:[13]

> A litle hound at home they had
>   that went aboute noght bonne in band.   [not tied up]
> What yong Thoby unto him bad
>   he wold take hede unto his hand;

---

10   For the edition see Cat. II, below; also Morey, 'Peter Comestor', p. 30.
11   Morey, 'Peter Comestor', p. 31.
12   E.g. Morey, 'Peter Comestor', passim.
13   Stanza 1306; *Historia*, printed in *PL*, vol. 198, col. 1434.

and to wende with him he was glad
    becaus that he him frendly fand.
In ich stede where they were stad
    the hound would stabley with him stand.

Or 2 Maccabees 7: 8, where the last of the seven sons of a Jewish family that has refused to eat 'swynes flesh' (and thus break Moses' law) is about to be killed at the command of the heathen King Antiochus; the son is reminded by his mother of God's love for His Creation, that He made out of nothing:[14]

Behald, sonne, to heven on hyght
    and to this werld that is full wyde,
to bestees and fishes and fowles in flyght,
    how erth and ayre ere occupyed,
and how God made all with his myght
    with out substance o many syde.
And men he made of reson ryght
    ay in his blyse to beld and byd.   [beld – find refuge]
He askes noght elles therfor,
    nawder in dede ne in saw,   [saw – word]
bot that men shal ever more
    luf hym and luf his law.

The stories from the Old Testament go very well with the other items in Richard of Gloucester's collection preserved in Longleat, MS 257.[15] All emphasise the need for order and law in society, and the value of stabilising virtues like loyalty and perseverance. The *Siege of Thebes* teaches many lessons: truth, kindness and generosity should be a ruler's virtues; vice and falsehood come to no good end. In the *Knight's Tale* all crimes are duly punished and order is restored from above. The *Clerk's Tale* (*Patient Griselda*) is almost a saint's life, stressing that everybody should live according to his degree and that God's law must be kept in this world (and in marriage). The importance of loyalty to God's law is a very evident

---

14 Stanza 1517.
15 See also ch. 9 below. The story of Judith is printed with an introduction and a commentary in Peck, *Heroic Women*, pp. 109–53.

and recurring element in the Old Testament paraphrase. An anthology of this nature could in its entirety have been made for the young Richard of Gloucester; it is a well balanced collection of secular and religious texts, probably put together at the request of somebody who had one specific person's instruction and entertainment in mind.

Far less readable and perhaps more controversial was Richard's copy of the New Testament in the English translation made by Wycliffite scholars in the last decades of the fourteenth century. The manuscript belongs to a relatively early stage in the long process of development and revision by which these dedicated translators, inspired by the reformist views of John Wycliffe, attempted to create an accurate and comprehensible vernacular Bible text, and it is still too self-consciously literal and close to the Latin to allow easy reading.[16] The manuscript appears to be in its original rough sheepskin binding; the text is written in two columns; its decoration is limited to some penwork for the initial of each chapter; and there are various annotations in seventeenth-century hands. Like the serviceable manuscript of Mechtild of Hackeborn's *Book of Special Grace* (see below), this was a book originally designed for the devotion of people who lived relatively simple lives. The text itself demands to be carefully studied to be understood at all:

In the begynnyng was the word, that is Godis sone, and the word was at God and God was the word. This was in the bigynnyng at God. Alle thingis ben mad by Hym and withouten Hym is maad noght that thing is mad; was lif in Hym and the lif was light of men; and the light shyneth in derknesses and derknesses conprehendiden, or token, not it. A man was sent fro God to whom the name was Jon. Thys man cam in to witnessing that he shulde bern witnessing of the light that alle men shulden bileeven by hym. He was not that light, but that he shuld bern witnessing of the light. It was a verre light, the wiche lightneth eche man comende in to this world, he was in the world and the world was maad bi hym, and the world knegh hym not.[17]

---

16 See e.g. one of the more recent studies on the subject: Hudson, *Premature Reformation*, ch. 5, 'Lollard biblical scholarship', pp. 228–77.

17 John 1, 1–10, p. 98 of the ms.; thorn, yogh, punctuation and capitals modernised.

Richard's copy includes all the books of the New Testament with introductions to some individual sections, but not the General Prologue,[18]
which contains the most 'dangerous' and heretical parts of the Wycliffite
redaction and is therefore lacking in most surviving copies. Nor does the
text contain any of the famous glosses on the Gospels that Chaucer in the
early days of Lollardy regarded as representative of Lollard 'puritanism'.[19]
Among the heretical views held by Wycliffe and various followers at
various times were reservations about the authority of the Church and
the legitimacy of the papacy, contempt for post-biblical saints and their
worship, the rejection of good works as a means to salvation and, most
dangerous of all, the denial of the host being the body of Christ.

It is of particular interest to explore what owning an English Bible by
Richard of Gloucester, or by any man of his background and his period,
actually meant in terms of religious interest, independence of mind,
and 'bookishness' or literacy. It is too easy to dismiss his ownership as
meaningless and ordinary, simply because royalty and noble persons were
allowed to possess such texts. It is indeed tempting to suppose that he
'was something of a Puritan' and that his religious experience was 'more
powerful and more private than conventional piety'.[20]

Always provided that Richard is the 'Gloucester' who wrote his title and
motto in the manuscript (see fig. 6) – and always provided that he did study
its contents at all – there is no doubt that it is remarkable that he owned
this book. Known (or avowed) ownership of a vernacular prose Bible in
the second half of the fifteenth century was very rare, even among those
who could have owned one legitimately. All that survives, for example, for
Edward IV is a copy, written and illuminated in Flanders, of an extended
version of the French redaction by Guiard des Moulins, composed in 1295.[21]
Des Moulins, like his main source, Peter Comestor's *Historia Scholastica* (see
above), treated the Bible as history and thus avoided all doctrinal controversy. No Bible of any kind occurs in the well-known list of devotional

---

18 The General Prologue is the introduction to the Old Testament, summarising its contents;
    it not only contains an exhortation to study the Bible in one's own language, whatever the
    consequences to oneself, but also general, scholarly remarks on the problems and purpose of
    translation.

19 The *Shipman's Prologue*, line 1180 quoted by Thomson, 'Orthodox religion and the origins of
    Lollardy', p. 42.

20 Kendall, *Richard III*, p. 320.

21 Warner and Gilson, Royal 15 D i, 18 D ix, x; see e.g. *Dictionnaire des lettres françaises*, pp. 187–89.

books in the will of Edward's and Richard's mother, Cecily Neville, which does include several books of hours and liturgical books.[22] Among the many religious treatises and other texts associated with Richard's sister, Margaret of York, there are only an Apocalypse with commentary and an extract of a moralised book of Exodus, both in French.[23] The members of the royal family known to have had an English Bible are Henry VI and Henry VII. Henry VI's copy[24] was made before 1420; it contained the Old and the New Testament in a later version and only the first chapter of the General Prologue, not the parts that were considered heretical. It was given by the king to the Charterhouse at Sheen. Henry VII also had both testaments in a later version; the manuscript had been made *c.* 1440, but had a leaf inserted at the beginning, decorated with red and white roses and the royal arms, in Henry VII's time. It is a good text, corrected throughout in a contemporary hand and has none of the heretical additions.[25]

Bibles, Latin or English, were always of great value: in 1488 John Olston alias Colt, parson of St Michael Bassishaw, London, left George Wilkinson 'my bible for the terme of his lief under the condicioun that he at the tyme of his dethe take and deliver hit to a nother devoute disposed to preche the word of god ... and so from oon to a nother as long as the saide bible shall endure'.[26] Bibles, or parts of them, specifically described as English are rarely found in wills and inventories.[27] One of the exceptions is the will of John Clopton, great benefactor of the church of

22 Nichols and Bruce, *Wills*, 1863.

23 BR, MS 9030–37 and New York, Pierpont Morgan Library M. 484; see Kren, *Margaret of York*, p. 261.

24 Oxford, Bodleian Library, MS Bodl. 277; see Forshall and Madden, *Holy Bible*, vol. 1, p. xlvij; Catto et al., *Wyclif and his Followers*, pp. 47–48 and pl.; Deanesly, *Lollard Bible*, pp. 7n., 261, 331n., 335.

25 BL, MS Royal 1 C viij; Forshall and Madden, *Holy Bible*, p. xxxix. The inserted leaf with Henry's emblems emphasises the second-hand nature of the ms.; it would be of great interest to know the previous owner(s).

26 PRO, PCC 32 Milles, PROB. 11/8, f. 257v.

27 Deanesly, *Lollard Bible*, pp. 391–98. It is often impossible to ascertain whether the Bible mentioned was in Latin or English, e.g.: Thomas Walsingham, 1457 (PRO, PCC 8 Stokton, PROB. 11/4, f. 61) 'the Grete Bibille that my lord Cardinalle gave wretyn of boleyn hand'; Baldwyn Hyde, 1472 (PRO, PCC 6 Wattys, PROB. 11/6, f. 46v) 'my bible ... be sold ... and the money ... disposed ... for my soule'; Stephen Preston, 1473/74 (PRO, PCC 14 Wattys, PROB. 11/6, f. 100v) 'my byble'; Anne Bonyfant and Joan Baret recorded a debt between them in a Bible, 1497, both note and Bible probably being in Latin (see the will of the former, PRO, PCC 16 Horne, PROB. 11/11, f. 134); the will of Eleanor Hull (1460/61) is specific: 'my blue byble of Latyn' (Barratt, *Seven Psalms*, p. 204). See also the Bibles in York wills mentioned in Moran, *Education and Learning*, p. 35; Vale, *Piety, Charity and Literacy*, pp. 29–30.

the Holy Trinity at Long Melford, who died in 1494. He left a 'Bible in English' to one of the supervisors of his will and, though this must have been a Wycliffite text, the rest of his will proves the orthodoxy of his faith beyond doubt, actually stressing the tenets of the Church that were rejected by the Lollards:

> I knowe well that prayers is a singuler remedie for the deliveraunce of soules in purgatory, and especially the offering of the Blessed Sacrament of our Lorde's body … .[28]

More usually when Bibles or Bible texts in English were mentioned in any context in the fifteenth century, it is against a background of religious dissent and potential heresy, secret readings to small gatherings of craftsmen and farmers, at night, or in fields and behind hedges.[29] Such scenes are far removed from the aristocratic, orthodox circles to which Richard of Gloucester belonged, but if he had obtained a licence from his bishop and if he knew that people of a different class who were 'caught' reading the Bible in English were automatically suspected of heretical ideas, he was to some extent aware of the origins and implications of the text he owned. If, as we have suggested, he was destined for the Church in childhood,[30] he may have had a good appreciation of the value and reputation of the Wycliffite Bible; his copy might even have been a relic of that period of his life. There was nothing inherently heretical in the translation itself, only in the commentaries, and there is nothing in Richard's other books and in his actions throughout his life to show that he held any unorthodox opinion, but the English Bible did allow him and any owner of such a Bible to see and hear and think for themselves. His owning it is unlikely to have been accidental: the manuscript was old and the book was a conscious acquisition by the duke of Gloucester, who marked it as his own. The simplicity and age of the manuscript matches the rela-

---

28 For Clopton see also ch. 2, above. He gave the Bible to William Pykenham, Archdeacon of Suffolk, one of the supervisors of his will; PRO, PCC 17 Horne, printed in Howard, *Visitation of Suffolke*, vol. 1, pp. 34–40. The Bible may have belonged to his grandmother, Katherine de Tendryngge; her will of 1404 (BL, MS Harl. 10, f. 158), ibid. pp. 30–33, mentions *unum librum vocatum Byble*.

29 E.g. Thomson, *Later Lollards*, pp. 38, 41–42, 68, 130–31, 177, 217–18, 229; Aston, 'Lollardy and Literacy', pp. 198–99.

30 See ch. 1 above.

tive cheapness of Richard's other, mostly second-hand books. It again suggests a genuine interest in the *contents* of books and perhaps even in literacy generally, not merely as a useful accomplishment but as an aid to greater understanding and knowledge.

A Book of Revelations: The *Booke of Gostlye Grace*

The names of *Anne Warrewyk* and *R Gloucestr'* occur together on the first flyleaf of the manuscript of the *Booke of Gostlye Grace* (see fig. 8). There is no doubt that Richard's name was written by his own hand: the signature is identical to several others known to be autograph.[31] For Anne Neville's signature no comparative material exists,[32] but the names are written in a way that suggests they were inscribed at the same time and that indicates a joint and equal interest in the book. The manuscript Richard and Anne owned is written in a large mid-fifteenth-century hand; the decoration is very simple, consisting of alternate red and blue initial letters marking the descriptive titles of each chapter, and larger blue capitals at the beginning of each chapter. It is an attractive, plain book (10 × 7 inches) in its original leather binding, rough without any signs of tooling; the fragments of three clasps remain. Scattered throughout in the margin are roughly written comments of no particular importance, such as 'Nota bene' and 'Nota the praysynges of the sayntes'.[33]

Only two copies of the English translation of Mechtild of Hackeborn's *Liber Specialis Gratiae* and very few copies of the Latin text once owned by English readers survive. There is evidence that the majority of them, like the manuscripts of similar works, such as the revelations of St Bridget and St Catherine of Siena, can be linked to an elite of Carthusian monks, Bridgettine nuns and devout laywomen.[34] It may have been the

---

31 See ch. 1 above.

32 The way women signed their names has not been specifically explored. What seems certain is that ladies with titles in their own family or their husband's did not sign themselves by their husband's surname. Anne Beauchamp, Countess of Warwick in her own right, wife of Richard Neville, would not have signed herself merely as Anne Neville. Would her daughter have called herself Anne Warwick, as daughter of that title, or Anne Gloucester rather than Anne Neville? Once queen she would have written 'Anne' or 'Anne the queen'.

33 These notes are in a late 15th- or early 16th-century hand which has not been identified.

34 See e.g. Lovat, 'Library of John Blacman', pp. 195–230, esp. 207; Hutchison, 'Devotional reading', pp. 215–27, passim; see also the present authors, 'Cult of angels'.

Carthusians who brought a version of the *Liber* to England and translated it, addressing it to their 'sustrene' and 'brethere' in orders who were
unable to read Latin, and presumably also laymen and women; the translation emphasises the didactic element of the book.[35] Though there are few
surviving copies of the complete text, the work's influence and popularity can be deduced from the number of extracts that survive separately.[36]

Mechtild was the daughter of the Baron von Hackeborn and younger
sister of Gertrude, abbess of a Cistercian community of women, established originally at Mansfeld in Saxony but moved by Gertrude to Helfta.
The community was known for both its piety and its learning, and in
1261 became the home of St Gertrude the Great, editor and translator of
religious manuscripts, and a decade later of Mechtild of Magdeburg, a
beguine and author of mystical lyrics and *The Flowing Light of the Godhead*,
a book of her mystical experiences. According to the *Book of Special Grace*
Mechtild of Hackeborn entered the convent at the age of seven at her
own request. It is possible, however, that she stayed at home longer as her
experience of worldly feelings and her knowledge of aristocratic society
are perhaps too great for someone who retired into an all-female, devout
and scholarly community at a very early age.[37] She became the assistant
of her sister, the abbess, training the choir and the novices and teaching
in the convent school. She acquired a reputation for learning, devotion,
amiability and compassion, besides fame as an accomplished singer, the
'Nightingale of the Lord'. Her life was spent, and her reputation after
death remained, in the shadow of her greater contemporaries, her pupil
and friend St Gertrude, and Mechtild of Magdeburg. Mechtild herself
died in her late fifties, 1298–99, after a long, painful illness during which
she began to recount her visions in confidence. She was dismayed to discover that her words were being written down, but in another vision
Christ assured her that the recording of her experiences was part of the
divine plan and He gave her the title for her book.

---

35 Halligan, *Booke*, pp. 52–53; Blake, 'Revelations of St Matilda', pp. 322–24.

36 Joliffe, *Checklist of Middle English Prose Writings of Spiritual Guidance*, I, 32; Sargent, 'Minor
    devotional writings', pp. 130–31.

37 Bromberg, *Het Boek*, p. 12–13; compare Bynum, *Jesus as Mother*, who appears convinced
    that Mechtild entered the convent early because she shows no strong awareness of female
    inferiority or weakness, which society outside the convent would have instilled into her, and
    little sense of stereotypical male and female behaviour, unlike Mechtild of Magdeburg, who
    lived in the world much longer, albeit as a beguine, pp. 252–53 and note.

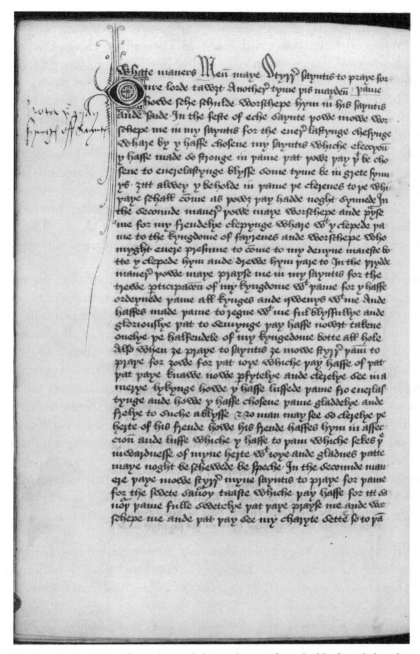

Fig. 25 An annotated page from the English translation of Mechtild of Hackeborn's *Booke of Gostlye Grace*, from the copy owned by Richard of Gloucester and 'Anne Warwick'. English, *c.* 1450. BL, MS Egerton 2006, f. 94v. By permission of The British Library.

Mechtild's 'special grace'[38] was her God-given ability of experiencing her intense faith through vivid images and describing them. They were visualisations of all the aspects of her faith: her devotion, above all, to the Sacred Heart, but also to the Humanity of Christ, Christ as Bridegroom, the Eucharist, the Virgin Mary, and all the saints. Very frequent, too, are her detailed references to the Nine Orders of Angels. Her images are colourful, lively and have great appeal; she had 'the eye of a painter and the fresh mind of a child'.[39] One modern editor suggested that she may have been particularly inspired by the miniatures made in the conventual scriptorium of which she was in charge.[40] Her visions also have an immediacy and a 'physicalness' which is amazing to the modern reader, but most of all they are full of joy, praise of Christ and awareness of glory.[41] They also possess a practical piety, closely linked to the daily liturgy, without any hint of unorthodoxy or doubt.

Mechtild's love of colour and pageantry may have appealed to the young duke and duchess of Gloucester. There are many descriptions of rich garments, often in the liturgical colours of red, green and white; in one instance the Virgin's golden mantle is embroidered with red doves, in another she has a sky-blue tunic covered with flowers; St Katherine wears a white robe with golden wheels; Mechtild's sister, the abbess, appears in a green robe with innumerable stars. There are feasts and processions, banners and coats of arms; Christ appears as a knight. Flowers are used to illustrate the virtues: the lily for innocence, the violet for humility and the rose for patience. The tree appears in many shapes. Mechtild's love of nature was so great that one day on her way to meet a funeral procession she felt such joy at the sight of the beauty of the fields, that she was later ashamed of her frivolity.

Many of her visions were inspired directly by the daily liturgy; during Advent she once had splendid vision of the Annunciation:

> In the tyme that the gospelle: *Missus est*,[42] was redde, sche sawe in spyrite howe the Archaungele Gabrielle … come into Nazareth and bare a kynges banere wryttene fulle of letters of golde. And hym folowede a

---

38 Latin *specialis* and *spiritualis* when abbreviated look very similar and the change to *Liber Spiritualis Gratiae* ('Booke of Gostlye Grace') is easily made.

39 Finnegan, *Women of Helfta*, p. 46.

40 Bromberg, *Het Boek*, pp. 13–14, 26.

41 Bynum, *Jesus as Mother*, p. 254.

42 *Missus est angelus*, read on the Wednesday after St Lucia (13 Dec.) in Advent.

grete multitude of aungellys, whiche sche cowthe nought nowmbere, ande allè thay were ordeyned to be alle abowte the howse whare that glorious ladye was.... thaye were als hitt hadde bene a walle in heyght fro the erthe to hevene. Ande within the ordere of aungellys were archaungelys, ande within the archaungelys were the ordere of vertues, and soo eche ordere withyn othere in such a manere that eche ordere was ... a wall rownde abowte the howse.... That specious [beautiful] spowse come than with the brennynge ordere of seraphyne ... [and] stode stylle besyde the banere ... als a yonge delectabylle spowse ... anone than the Holye Goste in lyknes of a culuere [dove] spredde abrod the wenges of Goddys swetnes, ande entrede into the sawle of that glo-rious vyrgyne, fullfyllynge here with Goddys sonne.[43]

Often the setting of Mechtild's vision is the convent itself: Christ appears on the altar, the angels in the choir, John the Evangelist stands at the bed-side of a fellow nun. Central to many visions is the unity of Mechtild's soul with God or Christ; it is described in purely physical terms, unlike the more 'academic' descriptions of other mystical authors. She is fre-quently embraced by Christ; he gives His heart to her and asks for it to be returned when she dies; she puts hers against His, to feel His heartbeats. Sometimes she explains the meaning of these scenes:

Ande att laste our lorde so ioynede and in a manere oonyde his herte, whiche passede honye in swetnesse, to that maydens herte and gaffe here alle his holye excercyse of his medytacion, devocion, ande of his blessede love, ande made here ryche habundauntlye with alle Goddys Graace. Ande so this chosene sawle was fullye to here semynge incor-porate to Cryste ande in the love of God softenede ande liquifiede. As softe waxe enpressede to a seele scheweth the lyknes of the seele, ryght so in suche a symylitude that blessede sawle of the maydene was made alle oone ande onede with here dere love.[44]

Mechtild was one of those thirteenth-century women mystics who paved the way for 'some of the most distinctive aspects of late medi-eval piety: devotion to the human, especially infant, Christ and devotion

---

43 Halligan, *Booke*, pp. 80–81 (on microfiche).
44 Halligan, *Booke*, p. 79 (on microfiche).

to the eucharist (frequently focused in devotion to the wounds, blood, body, and heart of Jesus)'.[45] In her own time she was a counsellor and advisor not only to her fellow nuns, but to clergy and laity from the outside world. She was a powerful mediator between Christ and the members of her community, telling people that they should act according to Christ's wishes, which meant above all saying prayers to help the souls of the dead through purgatory.[46] Though she was conscious that as a woman she could not participate fully in the life of the Church, she never dwelled on this but concentrated on her own important personal role, combining this with supreme serenity, confidence and complete trust in Christ as a just judge and caring parent and consoler. 'The visions of the nuns of Helfta projected them into the priestly role from which they were clearly by canon law excluded.' They derived their authority 'from their mystical union with Christ and the accompanying visions'.[47] A book like Mechtild's was bound to attract fifteenth-century female readers even if they were not as aware of these aspects of the text as are modern commentators.

The orthodoxy and piety of Mechtild's *Booke* are 'positive' and impeccable: religious life is praised, disrespect to the clerical authorities disapproved of, the official liturgy, in Latin, particularly the canonical hours, is to be faithfully and fervently observed. Her work is long but lively and could have been appreciated by any layman and, perhaps particularly, laywoman.

Book of Hours and Prayers

The book of hours that survives for Richard III was acquired possibly as late as the spring or summer of 1485 (see pl. VII). It had been made in the 1420s for an unknown person, probably a cleric as the book is remarkable for its number of additional prayers. It is a modest book in every way except for its textual contents. Its illumination includes three pages with one historiated initial each, of which only two survive. The page for Matins, the opening of the Hours of the Virgin, contains some

---

45 Bynum, *Jesus as Mother*, p. 172.
46 *Ibid.*, p. 181.
47 *Ibid.*, pp. 227, 249.

first class English illuminating work, and it is the illumination which dates the book. It was rebound for Richard III and a quantity of new pages with his special prayers was added. There are no ownership marks earlier than the date and place of birth of *Ricardus Rex Anglie* inserted in the calendar by Richard himself (see fig. 11), and his name, partly erased, in one of the prayers he had added to the book. The complete absence of any sign that he used it as duke suggests that this book of hours represented a break with the past, possibly after the deaths of his son and his wife – though it may be that his previous copy had simply worn out.[48]

A fifteenth-century book of hours[49] in England usually had the same, standard contents. It began with a twelve-page calendar, listing the feast days and saints' days of each month and incidentally allowing the owner some space to insert his or her own important dates, such as birthdays, deaths and national events that had affected the family. Before or after the calendar the owner sometimes included special prayers, called memorials, to his favourite saints; St George, patron of England, and St Christopher, who protected against many disasters, were very common in this position. The main text, the Little Office of the Blessed Virgin Mary, followed, divided into seven parts: Matins with Lauds, Prime, Terce, Sext, None, Vespers and Compline. Each section contained the prayers, lessons and psalms that were to be read or sung in honour of St Mary at set 'hours' of the day. Sometimes the book also included other daily offices, for example in honour of the Cross or the Holy Ghost. These offices were not the official ones said daily by the clergy from their breviary, but were shorter and did not vary, and were therefore easier for the laity to use and understand.

The 'hours' of the Virgin were usually followed by the Penitential and Gradual Psalms and the Litany. These first psalms were a group of seven selected because they expressed the grief of the faithful for their sins and engendered a spirit of penitence. The Gradual or Fifteen Psalms were traditionally thought to have been sung by Mary as a very young girl going up the steps (*gradus*) of the temple to dedicate herself to God's service. The Litany's main feature is its repetitive request for the intercession of all apostles and saints, led by the priest and the responses given by the people.

---

48   See *Hours of Richard III*, passim, esp. p. 39, and Cat. XV, below.
49   For all details of what follows see *Hours of Richard III*.

Fig. 26 St Julian and his wife ferrying Christ, dressed as a pilgrim, across the river. The saint accidentally killed his parents and spent the rest of his life doing penance by ferrying travellers across a river, until he was he released by Christ and died. Julian was the patron saint of travellers and a short prayer to him, meant to be said before setting out on a journey, was included in Richard III's book of hours (see ch. 3, n. 51). Grisaille miniature in a book of hours of Philip the Good. Flemish, *c.* 1454. The Hague, Royal Library, MS 76 F 2, f. 273v. By permission of the Royal Library.

A series of prayers, or collects, for various purposes was often attached to the Litany (as was the case in Richard's hours): 'for devoted friends', 'for peace', 'against evil thoughts'. Towards the end of most *horae* are to be found first the Office or Vigil of the Dead, to be said over the recently deceased before and during the funeral, or privately in memory of the dead; secondly the Commendation of Souls, meant to help the dying in their passage to the next world; and thirdly the Psalms of the Passion, traditionally said to be the psalms that Christ recited on the cross before he died but was unable to finish.

Many books of hours end at this point, but Richard III's book has a large number of extra devotions, so many in fact that it can justifiably be called a 'book of prayers' as well as an 'hours'. Few of these additional texts are unusual in themselves, but the presence of so many in the same manuscript indicates the deep piety of the person who originally ordered the book in the 1420s and also suggests that Richard had a similar interest in them. The theory that these additional prayers were the reason why he acquired *this* book of hours is supported by the fact that he had yet more devotions added to the book. Together all these extra prayers fill as much as sixty pages; there are long devotions to God and Christ and the Virgin, shorter ones to the angels, the guardian angel, St John and St Anne, and brief 'useful' texts to be said when going to bed, or to St Julian when departing on a journey.

The most interesting parts of the book are the devotions added for Richard III. At the very beginning, written in a later hand than the main text, is a collect of St Ninian:

O God who has converted the peoples of the Britons and the Picts by the teaching of St Ninian, your confessor, to knowledge of your faith, grant of your grace that by the intercession of him by whose learning we are steeped in the light of your truth, we may gain the joys of heavenly life. Through Christ our lord, Amen.

St Ninian, according to the anonymous chronicle that Richard may have owned,[50] was a Briton educated in Rome who returned to his native country to convert the Southern Picts to Christianity. He became the patron saint of the western march towards Scotland, of which Richard was warden as duke of Gloucester. Richard deliberately took up his cult and included his worship at each of his religious foundations at York, Middleham and Barnard Castle, and also at Queens' College, Cambridge (see below).

At the end of the book, on some pages originally left blank and some specially bound in for the purpose, two more significant and longer texts were added for Richard III. The first is a six-page prayer for deliverance from evil and affliction, which has been called the 'prayer of Richard III', because he is one of the best known owners of this

---

50 The so-called Fitzhugh Chronicle, see ch. 7 below.

Fig. 27 St Ninian shown with a supplicant and an angel. The saint is depicted as a bishop and holds fetters and a Bible, symbols of his releasing prisoners and his evangelism. Edinburgh, University Library, MS 42, f. 72v. By permission of the University Library.

devotion.[51] It is a very moving text with long, repetitive sections that read like powerful incantations:

> O most sweet lord Jesus Christ ... who was sent ... to forgive sins, to comfort afflicted sinners, ransom captives, set free those in prison, bring together those who are scattered, lead travellers back to their native land ... deign to release me from the affliction, temptation, grief, sickness, need and danger in which I stand ...

and:

> [deliver me] even as you delivered Abraham from the hand of the Chaldeans, Isaac from sacrifice by means of the ram, Jacob from the hands of his brother Esau, Joseph from the hands of his brothers, Noah from the waters of the flood by means of the ark, Lot from the city of the Sodomites, ... Susanna from false accusation and testimony and Judith from the hand of Holofernes, Daniel from the den of lions, ...

and:

> ... deliver me by your holy goodness, your incarnation, your nativity, your baptism, and your fasting, by the hunger and the thirst, the cold and the heat, by the labour and the suffering, by the spit and the buffets, by the blows and the nails ... by the words which you spoke on the cross.

---

51 And also because its composition and even its contents have been used as evidence of his supposed crimes. This 'evidence' of Richard's guilt was created by a failure to consult either the ms. itself or M.R. James's catalogue of the Lambeth Palace mss which describes the ms. precisely. Two folios are missing from the ms. which means that the beginning of Richard III's prayer and its explanatory rubric are lost, as well as the text of the preceding prayer to St Julian the Hospitaller, which was part of the original book and not one of Richard's additions. Some of the rubric of the prayer to St Julian survives. St Julian is famous as a saint who accidentally killed his parents and spent his subsequent life atoning for his mistake by ferrying travellers across a river and giving them hospitality; prayers to him asked for a safe journey and a good host at night. Failure to consult the ms. or the catalogue led certain scholars to conflate the rubric of the prayer to St Julian with Richard III's prayer and assume that Richard was praying to St Julian to obtain pardon for murder. See esp. present authors, 'Richard III and St Julian' and *Hours of Richard III*.

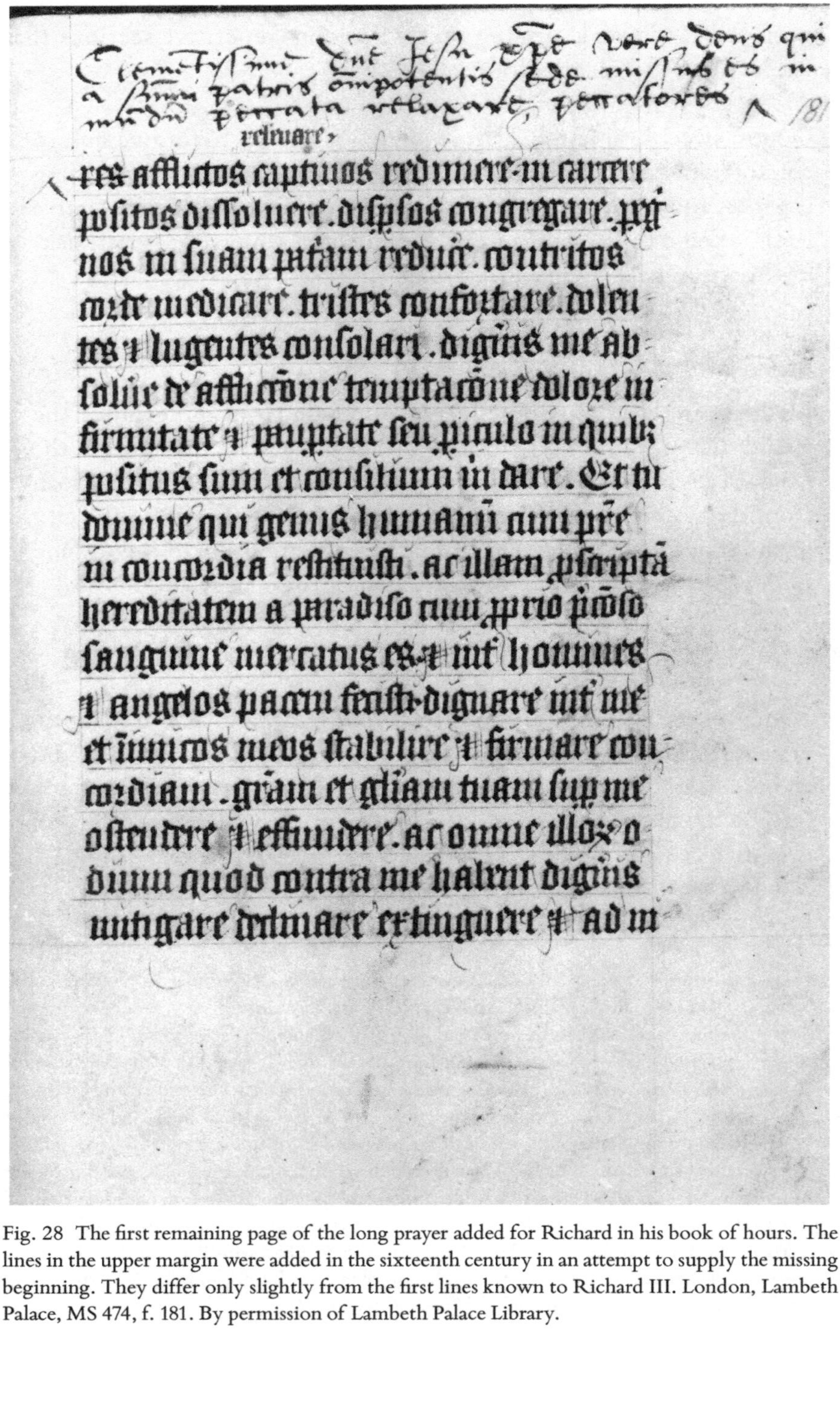
res afflictos captiuos redimere in carcere
positos dissoluere. dispersos congregare. pere-
nos in suam patriam reducere. contritos
corde medicare. tristes confortare. dolen-
tes et lugentes consolari. digneris me ab-
soluere de afflictione temptacione dolore in-
firmitate et paupertate seu periculo in quibus
positus sum et consilium in dare. Et tu
domine qui genus humanum cum patre
in concordia restituisti. ac illam perscriptam
hereditatem a paradiso cum proprio precioso
sanguine mercatus es et inter homines
et angelos pacem fecisti. digneris inter me
et inimicos meos stabilire et firmare con-
cordiam. graciam et gloriam tuam super me
ostendere et effundere. ac omne illorum o-
dium quod contra me habent digneris
mitigare declinare extinguere et ad ni-

Fig. 28 The first remaining page of the long prayer added for Richard in his book of hours. The lines in the upper margin were added in the sixteenth century in an attempt to supply the missing beginning. They differ only slightly from the first lines known to Richard III. London, Lambeth Palace, MS 474, f. 181. By permission of Lambeth Palace Library.

In a few pages the prayer manages to remind the supplicant of a great many examples of God's goodness, of His frequent intervention to deliver sufferers from their affliction, and of Christ's sacrifice for man. It is not surprising that this devotion became increasingly popular from the time it was composed, probably in Italy at the end of the fourteenth century, perhaps by members of the Franciscan order. All over western Europe owners of books of hours highly valued the text and knew it in Latin or in their own vernacular; it was frequently added specially to an existing collection and often the owner had his or her own name inserted, as did Richard III himself: ... *liberare digneris me, famulum tuum regem Ricardum* ...; ... *custodias me, famulum tuum regem Ricardum* ... (deign to deliver me, your servant King Richard; keep me, your servant King Richard).

The deeply penitent and humble tone of the prayer and its mention of, for example, the deliverance of Susanna from false witness have been used by modern scholars as indications of Richard's disturbed emotional state and a sense of guilt. When compared to other texts, however, this devotion, though impressive and obviously considered very effective by Richard's contemporaries, contains nothing that was unusual at the time and many anonymous, innocent and ordinary people knew and used it and hoped it would alleviate their misery. Because of the damage to the manuscript the rubric[52] to Richard's prayer is now lost, but we know from other copies that it was often ascribed to the authorship of St Augustine and claimed to be of great help to people, provided they were truly penitent, free from mortal sin and repeated the prayer on bended knees for thirty consecutive days. It would not only wash away one's own sins but could also be said for the sake of others. A later owner of Richard's book of hours, after the reformation, may have found these promises offensive and removed the pages that held the rubric, thus leaving us without the key to Richard's hopes and expectations.

After the 'prayer of Richard III', in the same hand as the collect of St Ninian and the long prayer itself, is another remarkable and unique text that was almost certainly added for the king during his reign. Three leaves were cut out of the manuscript by later owners and this

---

52 Introductory heading written in red ink; the rubric to Richard III's prayer may have been quite long and detailed.

last devotion, too, was made incomplete by the unfortunate attempts to 'clean up' the book, but enough of it is left to show that this was probably a 'private litany', similar to those that were composed in great numbers in the fifteenth and sixteenth centuries. Part of it must be quoted to give an impression of its form and purpose. The fragmentary text now begins:

> ... keep us from weakness (*languor*), Jesus, for the sake of your sublime name, cleanse us of all offence and crime.

After a series of verses and responses asking for God's mercy on the king and his people, the text continues:

> Almighty, ever-living God, in whose hand are all the powers and all the rights of kingdoms, come to the help of the Christians and let the peoples of the heathen who trust in their fierceness be destroyed by the power of your right hand. Amen. *Kyrie eleison. Kyrie eleison. Kyrie eleison...* . Look down, Lord, upon your people for whom our lord Jesus Christ did not hesitate to deliver himself to those that would harm him and to suffer the agony of the cross. Remember, Lord, your covenant and say to the destroying angel: Now stay your hand! And let not the earth be made desolate and do not destroy every living soul. May your anger, Lord, now be lifted from your people. And from your holy city, let it not be made desolate.

These are the remnants of a highly personal devotion, though compiled from existing formulas. If the text was complete its rubric would tell us what the exact purpose of the supplication really was, but the surviving section quoted here suggests that it was the threat from the East, the repeated incursions of the Turkish armies and events like the siege of Rhodes in 1480 that inspired this prayer, and made it focus on the slackness ('weakness', *languor*) of the Christian princes to deal with the problem. During the few years of Richard's reign he is known to have been aware of the dangers on at least two specific occasions. In May 1484 the Silesian nobleman Nicholas of Poppelau told Richard about the great victory the king of Hungary and the armies of the emperor had gained over the Turks not long before.[53] Richard was overjoyed and was heard to exclaim: 'I wish my kingdom lay on the Turkish border. With my own people alone and without the help of others, I would certainly drive away with ease not only the Turks but all my enemies!'. His remark not only proves his self-confidence in military matters, but also perhaps shows that he realised the difficulties of making the Christian princes cooperate.

Later in the same year the king's attention was again drawn to the seriousness of the situation: on 21 November Pope Innocent VIII sent an encyclical to the kings and princes of Europe, warning them of the increased Turkish threat to the western Church and culture. He asked for speedy assistance: ambassadors with sufficient powers should be sent and delay was no longer possible. This was, of course, not the first attempt of its kind by fifteenth-century popes, and like the others it proved entirely unsuccessful. Princes always found an excuse for not tackling the problem in the untrustworthiness of their neighbours.[54] Richard III, in spite of his enthusiasm, also took no decisive action, but he may have been sufficiently moved to have this special 'crusading litany' made and he included mention of the un-Christian and sinful *languor* that affected him and his fellow rulers.

Saints and the *Life of St Katherine*

Saints' lives were widely read in the fifteenth century, both for instruction and entertainment, and they survive in French, Latin and English, in prose and verse, in print and manuscript, in collections and separately. It

---

53 The surviving versions of von Poppelau's account imply this battle was fought on St Martin's day 1483, which could be either 4 July or 11 November. The only really memorable victory over the Turks had been the battle of Brodfeld, 13 Oct. 1479, at which Matthias Corvinus, King of Hungary, was not present but members of his court were, as well as Saxons, Serbs, Wallachians, etc. Corvinus was actually fighting the Emperor Frederick III during these years, and in 1483 made a truce with the Turks, but there was an occasion in the autumn of 1483 when soldiers of Matthias defeated a retreating Turkish army and liberated their captives; this was made much of by Matthias in a letter to Pope Sixtus IV of 6 November, see e.g. Kupelwieser, *Kämpfe Ungarns*, pp. 166–75. It is likely von Poppelau was confused, or lied, or the many copyists, translators and editors of his journal confused the facts. If Richard had known the real political situation in eastern Europe he would have seen no reason for rejoicing.

54 See e.g. Walsh, 'Charles the Bold and the crusade', pp. 53–86.

has been said convincingly that late medieval hagiography had lost some
of the simplicity and direct emotional involvement of both author and
reader that it had, for example, in Anglo-Saxon works. Saints' lives had
become objects of aesthetic appreciation, celebrations of the visible glory
and perfection of the saints and teaching moral lessons rather than religious awareness. They were written by clever craftsmen, who were often
equally good at writing secular texts, and the distinction between hagiography and romance writing was, and is, often not clear.[55] The change in
character of such works was also due to increasing sophistication: saints'
lives had a long history as a genre and in the fifteenth century reached
almost the end of their development; they had begun to change into mere
biographies without much devotional content.[56] Comparison may be
made to the visualisation of the cult of saints in votive jewellery, such
as reliquaries or statues, or in panel paintings, where splendid portraits
of rich donors were placed beside equally magnificent depictions of their
saintly patrons supporting them.[57] The saint's written life, the goldsmiths'
work and the paintings were tangible acts of devotion and expressed the
hope of practical reward for the maker and the user through the intercession of the saint they celebrated.

There is evidence for devotion to saints among Richard III's family
and circle in the books they owned and their public display of piety and
charity. Richard's father, Richard of York, had memorials (prayers) in his
private book of hours to the Guardian Angel (see pl. I), Sts Edward the
Confessor, George, Christopher, Anthony, Anne, Barbara and the Three
Kings.[58] At his reburial the religious banners borne alongside his body on
its journey from Pontefract to Fotheringhay showed St George and the
royal saints, Edward and Edmund, his official patron saints as the King of
England who never was. No other indications of his personal preference

---

55 Wolpers, *Heiligenlegende*, pp. 259–62, 348; Nevanlinna and Taavitsainen, *St Katherine*,
    p. 16. The discussion about the relation between romances and saints' lives is ongoing, see
    e.g. Childress, 'Between romance and legend', pp. 311–22; Reiss, 'Romance', pp. 108–30, esp.
    114–17; Barron, *English Medieval Romance*, pp. 57–58, 76–77, 245–47; Williams, 'Hunting the
    deer', pp. 187–206, esp. 187–88.
56 Nevanlinna and Taavitsainen, *St Katherine*, p. 14; according to Wolpers, *Heiligenlegende*,
    p. 402, by the time Caxton compiled his *Golden Legend* the medieval saint's life – in lay hands
    at least – had outlived itself and was incapable of renewal.
57 Wolpers, *Heiligenlegende*, p. 348.
58 See ch. 2 above.

survive.[59] Cecily of York's piety late in life is well documented in her will and the household ordinances that record her daily life.[60] Among the books that were thought suitable for reading to the duchess and her household during the main meal of the day was a *Legenda aurea*, the most famous collection of saints' lives, presumably used in an English translation. Cecily's preferred saints must be sought among the many patrons and protectors of the houses of Neville and York depicted in the stained glass of the church at Fotheringhay – for a while the intended mausoleum of the House of York[61] – and there is supporting evidence for a few of them. St Bridget of Sweden was worshipped by many members of Cecily's family and she herself owned her *Revelations*. St Erasmus, and St Barbara (who does not survive in the Fotheringhay glass), were each represented on a golden *Agnus Dei* (reliquary) that Cecily bequeathed in her will. St Erasmus, according to some legends, was subjected to every conceivable form of torture,[62] and helped sufferers of disease and all bodily pains, especially women in childbirth. Barbara (see below) protected against sudden death. Cecily also owned a relic of St Christopher. Most special to her must have been St John the Baptist: she twice expressed particular trust in his intercession at the beginning of her will.[63] On a practical plane St John was invoked against headaches and sore throats, but he was also the greatest prophet who foretold the coming of the rightful king.

Edward IV is not known to have owned any saints' lives and very little is known about his preferences, but it can be assumed that he venerated

---

59 See e.g. Rosenthal, 'Richard, Duke of York: a fifteenth-century layman and the church', pp. 171–87; present authors, *Reburial of Richard, Duke of York*.

60 See ch. 2 above.

61 See Marks, 'The glazing of Fotheringhay church', pp. 79–109. The saints that occurred in the glass – as far as they have been identified from surviving fragments and antiquaries' reports – include Denis, Blaise, George, John the Baptist, Alban, Armel, Vincent, Guthlac, Erasmus, Clement, Richard Scrope, Avitus (?), Ambrose, Jerome, Augustine, Gregory, Edmund, Scholastica, Ursula, Frideswide, Ethelreda, Agatha, Sitha, Margaret, Bridget.

62 Fifty-two 'passions' are listed in BL, MS Add. 36983, f. 280, a ms. of *c*. 1442, printed in Horstmann, *Sammlung Altenglischer Legenden*, pp. 202–03.

63 The mention of a saint in this position may be important. Compare the will of Isabel, Dowager Duchess of Burgundy, who recommended herself to the Virgin and all the saints – as Cecily and most testators did – and then to St Anthony of Padua, who was Portuguese like the duchess herself, and whom she also venerated because of his link with the Franciscan order, Sommé, 'Le testament d'Isabelle de Portugal', pp. 27–45, esp. 29, 38. Cecily of York also owned an arras with the story of John the Baptist (and one of Mary Magdalene), Nichols and Bruce, *Wills*, pp. 1–8.

St George, as patron of England and the order of the Garter, St Bridget, who wrote the politically useful prophecy about the need of the rightful royal heir coming into his own for the good of the kingdom, and perhaps St Anne, mother of the sacred dynasty, who may have been important to his father and who granted Edward himself a good omen on his return from exile.[64] He probably worshipped officially others of the 'Fotheringhay' family saints, such as St Richard Scrope, a martyr of the opposition to the Lancastrian kings and defender of the 'true' line, and one of the prophets who foretold Edward's accession.[65] The arms of St Edmund, king and martyr, St Edward, king and confessor, and St Louis IX of France appear alongside the magnificent family tree in the so-called Philadelphia Roll, an elaborate, visual proof of Edward's right to the throne.[66] His queen, Elizabeth Woodville, appears to have been particularly devoted to her namesake St Elizabeth, the mother of St John the Baptist, and like her mother-in-law (another frequently pregnant woman), to St Erasmus.[67]

Margaret of York's patron saints are not known but she probably shared her husband's, Charles, Duke of Burgundy, veneration of St George, patron of the order of the Garter of which he was pleased to be a member, and of St Anne who married three times like Charles himself. Like her mother Margaret worshipped St Bridget, whose order she supported with money and patronage,[68] and she may have displayed an official devotion to such local saints as St Gommaire (Gummarus) of Lier, whose *Life* was given to her by the monks of the abbey of Lier when she visited them.[69] It is likely she had a genuine personal devotion to the ascetic recluse and spiritual counsellor, St Colette of Corbie, of whom she and Charles owned a beautifully illuminated manuscript *Vita*.[70] Margaret also had Jean Mielot's long and detailed redaction of the *Life of St Katherine*,

---

64 For St Bridget's prophecy see ch. 8 below. For St Anne's omen see Bruce, *Historie of the Arrivall*, p. 14.
65 See McKenna, 'Popular canonization', pp. 608–23; Hughes, *Pastors and Visionaries*, pp. 305–12.
66 Philadelphia Free Library, MS E 201; see also ch. 8 below.
67 Present authors, 'Elizabeth Woodville', pp. 233–34.
68 See ch. 2 above.
69 The implication, suggested by Blockmans, that Margaret worshipped St Gommaire because he helped people who were unhappily married was, one hopes, made in jest, see Blockmans, 'Devotion of a lonely duchess', p. 43.
70 Ghent, Poor Clares, MS 8; see Corstanje, *Vita Sanctae Coletae*.

Fig. 29 St Anne and the Holy Kinship appear to St Coleta and St Francis. St Anne had married three times, like Charles the Bold, Duke of Burgundy, who is shown kneeling with his third wife, Richard's sister, Margaret of York. Miniature from Margaret of York's copy of the *Life of St Coleta*. Flemish, 1468–77. Ghent, Poor Clares, MS 8, f. 40v. By kind permission of the Abbess and Convent of the Poor Clares, Ghent.

which had been put into French at the command of Philip the Good,[71] and two chapters on the life of St Edmund, king and martyr, based on the *Golden Legend*, her only text that represents a link with England, though her copy was in French.[72]

Richard of Gloucester himself listed 'suche saints as that I have devocion unto' in the statutes for the foundation of his college of priests at Middleham in 1478: John the Baptist, John the Evangelist, Peter and

---

71 Modernised French version in Mielot, *Vie de Ste Catherine d'Alexandrie*. Only one folio of Margaret's copy survives and the present whereabouts of this fragment is not known, see Christie's sale catalogue, 26–27 May 1963, lot 195; De Schryver, 'The Louthe Master and the Marmion case', p. 171, fig. 129.
72 New York, Pierpont Morgan Library M. 484, see Kren, *Margaret of York*, p. 261.

Paul, Simon and Jude, Michael, Anne, Elizabeth, Fabian and Sebastian, Anthony, Christopher, Denis, Blaise, Thomas, Alban, Giles, Eustace and Erasmus, Eloy, Leonard, Martin, William of York, Wilfred of Ripon, Katherine, Margaret, Barbara, Martha, Winifred,[73] Ursula, Dorothy, Radegund, Agnes, Agatha, Apollonia, Sitha, Clare, and Mary Magdalene. Any attempt to link this great number and variety of protectors to specific interests or preoccupations of Richard is of doubtful benefit,[74] and his real preferences have to be discovered elsewhere. This is facilitated by other sections of his Middleham statutes: 'I wol that Seint George and Seint Nynyane be served as principal fests, ..., and also Seint Cuthbert day in Lent, and Seint Antony day that falls in Janiver'.[75] The stalls of the dean and six priests of the college were to be called after Our Lady, St George, St Katherine, St Ninian, St Cuthbert, St Anthony, and St Barbara,[76] strictly in that order of precedence. Richard's endowment of four fellowships at Queens' College, Cambridge, in 1477, was to the worship of the Virgin, and Sts George, Anthony and Ninian; prayers were to be said to them and masses celebrated.[77] In 1478 Richard was granted permission to found a college of a dean and twelve chaplains within the castle

---

73 Richard's mention of St Winifred in 1478 is intriguing given the growth of her cult at this time, culminating in the establishment of her fraternity at Shrewsbury in the first years of Henry VII; the circumstances of the foundation and the 1484 publication of the *Life of St Winifred* suggest that the fraternity might have been established earlier but for the political changes of 1485. Caxton's *Life of St Winifred* can be dated to 1484 on the evidence of the paper used; it was also a text that emphasised the saint's connection with Shrewsbury. For a group of influential and pious people with Shrewsbury origins and connections with the fraternity, who were living in London and court circles in 1483–85, see the present authors, 'Cult of angels'. For the date of Caxton's text, Lowry, 'Caxton, St Winifred and the Lady Margaret Beaufort', p. 116 and n. 33; and [Owen and Blakeway], *History of Shrewsbury*, vol. 2, pp. 124–28.

74 Raine, 'Statutes', p. 169. This great number also shows by implication that linking the specific properties of any saint to an historical person without supporting evidence is fraught with danger and may easily lead to gratuitous conclusions, compare e.g. the notes on St Julian and St Gommaire, above.

   The special prayers in Richard's book of hours are to Ninian, George, Christopher, Joseph the Patriarch, and Julian; of these only Ninian was added for him personally. The *memoriae* in lauds, which were part of the original book, are to the Holy Spirit, the Trinity, the Cross, All Angels, John the Baptist, Peter, Laurence, Nicholas, Mary Magdalen, Margaret, Sitha, the Relics of the Saints, All Saints and Peace. The list of saints invoked in the Litany is very long and no conclusions can be drawn from it.

75 Raine, 'Statutes', *ibid.*

76 *Ibid.*, p. 161.

77 Searle, *History of Queens' College*, vol. 1, pp. 89–90.

Fig. 30 St Margaret emerging from the dragon (the devil) that devoured her; part of her dress is still hanging from its mouth. Margaret was one of the great virgin saints and the patroness of women in childbirth. Grisaille miniature in a book of hours of Philip the Good. Flemish, *c.* 1454. The Hague, Royal Library, MS 76 F 2, f. 276v. By permission of the Royal Library.

of Barnard Castle; it was dedicated to Christ, the Virgin, St Margaret, the saint of the church's original dedication, and St Ninian.[78] Little is known with certainty about Richard's proposed grandiose college of a hundred priests at York Minster, except that they were to 'sing there in the worship of God, Oure Lady, Seint George and Seint Nynyan'.[79]

Among Richard's six favourite saints the Virgin Mary and St George are obvious choices, though Richard's devotion to them may have been none the less genuine; they need no further explanation. St Ninian's importance to Richard has been mentioned above in the description of his book of hours. He had been the apostle of the north; his cult focused on Whithorn in Galloway and devotion to him emphasised Richard's association with

---

78 VCH Durham, vol. 2, pp. 129–30; *CPR 1476–85*, p. 67.
79 BL, MS *Harl. 433*, f. 72, punctuation and capitals modernised. See Dobson, 'Richard III and the church of York', pp. 145–46.

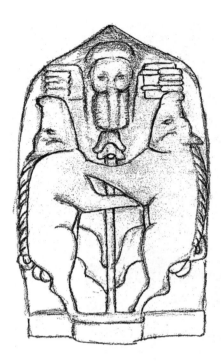

Fig. 31 Sketch of a very worn stone relief of St Anthony with boars resembling the supporters of Richard's arms. The saint has a forked beard of three points; in his left hand he holds a book; the boars support his staff with its T-shaped top and a bell immediately below (see also ch. 3, n. 58). Barnard Castle, St Mary's church.

the north, especially the western march, and by implication with any claims the English might have to regions of Scotland that Ninian Christianised and civilised. The see of York, moreover, claimed many Scottish bishoprics, but especially Whithorn, as subject to its spiritual rule.[80] Ninian was primarily a Scottish saint and prayers to him are usually found in the books of hours of Scottish owners; his symbols are a bishop's crook, a book, representing his evangelism, and a chain, because he released prisoners, in other words the pagans whom he converted and delivered from the bondage of the devil (see fig. 27). Ninian's real popularity dates from the late fifteenth century,[81] but St Cuthbert's cult, associated with Durham and the western march, was long established. Cuthbert rivalled Thomas Becket in popularity throughout England but was the particular patron of the north and invoked during campaigns against the Scots, when banners with his image were carried along.[82] In 1474 Richard and his wife were admitted

---

80 Dobson, 'Richard III and the church of York', p. 153 n. 84.
81 *Hours of Richard III*, p. 41–44, 84, 94n.; and e.g. Anderson, *St Ninian*.
82 Dobson, *Durham Priory*, pp. 25–32.

to the Fraternity of St Cuthbert at Durham.[83] At the creation of Richard's son, Edward of Middleham, as Prince of Wales in 1483 banners showed Sts George, Edward and Cuthbert.[84]

St Anthony, who had a memorial in the hours of Richard's father, was closely associated with the pig or boar, the animal that supported Richard's arms and, when white, was a symbol of resistance to temptation and the rejection of evil. St Anthony had been the first monk, a healer of men and animals, patron of hospitals for the poor and the sick and of a spiritual order of knighthood.[85]

St Katherine and St Barbara are the female patronesses clearly preferred by Richard at his Middleham foundation. The stories of these two virgin martyrs are similar; both rejected marriage and refused to offer to the pagan gods, and both before they died asked Christ to help people who prayed for their intercession. St Barbara was forced to live in seclusion in a tower where she was secretly converted; after much suffering she was finally beheaded by her own father, who was struck by lightning and burned to ashes for his cruelty. Her symbol became a tower and her special function to protect against sudden death, particularly by fire and explosions; armourers, gunners and miners as well as soldiers of all kinds worshipped her.[86] Richard, with his avowed interest in artillery (see

---

83 Pollard, 'St Cuthbert and the hog', pp. 109–29, esp. 111.

84 *Harl. 433*, vol. 2, p. 42.

85 For Richard's boar see ch. 11 below. An intriguing link between Richard, St Anthony and the boar is to be found in St Mary's church, Barnard Castle. There are several stone reliefs of boars in the town, e.g. in the outside wall of St Mary's, in the castle and on houses (Pollard, 'St Cuthbert', p. 113 and n.) but inside St Mary's there is a large, rectangular stone slab, set into the wall but obviously not now in its original position. It is very weathered and looks as if it has been in the open air for many years. It depicts an old man with a forked beard of three points; in his left hand, raised to the level of his face he appears to hold a book, in his right hand, similarly raised, is another object. In front of his body, down the middle, is a staff with a tau-shaped top and a bell immediately below. The man is dwarfed and almost embraced by two very large boars, standing on their hind legs, snouts high in the air and reaching to the man's chin, their front feet stretched across his body and the staff; they have obvious bristles down their backs and very prominent members. The man is certainly St Anthony and the boars look like heraldic supporters. Nothing appears to be known about the relief; by its shape and condition, it could have been set over an entrance door of, for example, a hospital or another building dedicated to St Antony; association with Richard of Gloucester seems inevitable, but at the moment we can only speculate.

86 St Barbara was one of the two female saints specially honoured in the book of hours of Richard's father, see ch. 2 above. The most complete study, with a continental focus, is Nemitz and Thierse, *St. Barbara*.

below and fig. 40), undoubtedly was aware of his need of her protection.[87]
St Katherine, a learned princess who vanquished fifty pagan philosophers in theological debate, was threatened with death between spiked
wheels and finally beheaded; her story will be discussed in more detail
below. She became the protector of wheelwrights and millers, but also
of learned men and scholars; her main emblem was a wheel. Katherine
and Barbara often appear together, for example in some of the most
famous paintings by Memling. In such pictures they are usually taken to
represent the two ways of life open to medieval men and women: the
active and the contemplative.[88] It is possible Richard was aware of this
and consciously chose these two symbols of the dilemma that confronted
any devout layperson conscious of his or her spiritual obligations, and
particularly people in high positions who were even less able than others
to compromise and lead the 'medled lyf that is to saye somtyme actyfe
and sometyme contemplatyf'.[89] We have no other evidence of Richard's
devotion to St Barbara, but in 1483 or '84 a *Life of St Katherine* was dedicated to him (see below).

Literate people owned saints' lives in various forms, either in a complete
set, such as James de Voragine's *Legenda aurea*, or more often separate lives
in miscellaneous collections or commonplace books, among items of a
very different nature. The Beaufort family, for example, had a French
text of the *Golden Legend* in the translation by Jean de Vignai, which was
very rare in England.[90] Latin copies of the collection were mostly owned
by religious houses, parish churches and cathedral libraries,[91] and such
texts could serve as the basis for a translation by one of the inmates. Parish
churches preferred an English copy of the *Golden Legend*. In 1485 Sir John
Scott, controller of the household of Edward IV 1461–70 and later marshal of Calais, in his will bequeathed 'a legend complete', 'another legende
complete' and 'my old legend ... hit tabe complete' to three neighbouring
churches; they were to be made or completed by his chaplain at Sir John's

87 See ch. 4 below.
88 Jameson, *Sacred and Legendary Art*, vol. 2, p. 496; the same, *Legends of the Madonna*, p. 90; de
    Vos, *Memling*, pp. 152–53, 166–67, 180–81, 234.
89 See e.g. Carey, 'Devout literate laypeople and the pursuit of the mixed life', pp. 360–81; the
    quotation (p. 373) is from Walter Hilton's *Epistle on the Mixed Life*. See also ch. 5 below.
90 BL, MS Royal 19 B xvij, made in France, 1382, see Warner and Gilson.
91 See e.g. Ker, *Medieval Libraries*, pp. 13, 23, 30, 61, 74, 76, 90, 121, 132, 173, 197, 199, 210, 212,
    220, 223.

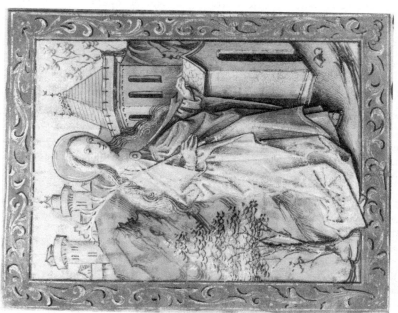

Fig. 32 a and b St Barbara, on the left, with her tower, and St Katherine, on the right, with her broken wheel; together they represented the active and contemplative life. Grisaille miniatures in a book of hours of Philip the Good. Flemish, c. 1454. The Hague, Royal Library, MS 76 F 2, ff. 280 and 276. By permission of the Royal Library.

expense.[92] Thomas Berby, mercer, in his will of 1464 freely returned to the parishioners of St Stephen Coleman Street, London, a *legenda* that he had received from them as surety; all he asked in return was their special prayers for his soul.[93] Various older English translations existed but relevant in the present context are the so-called *Gilte Legende* of 1438, which are probably the work of the Austin friar Osbern Bokenham who has already been mentioned,[94] and Caxton's compendious redaction of the *Golden Legend* that came out in November 1483.[95]

The translator of the *Gilte Legende* had 'Englished' the *Legenda aurea* in more ways that one: he omitted passages that English readers might find objectionable, such as the story of the cowherd from whom all English kings were descended in the life of St Germain, and he added lives of insular saints, such as St Chad and St Erkenwald. His style and language have been generally praised by commentators, but the text did not survive on its own after it had been absorbed into Caxton's edition: all the surviving manuscripts date from the middle or the second half of the fifteenth century. One manuscript is known to have been given by the London mercer, John Burton, to Halliwell Priory near London, where his daughter was a nun;[96] another was written by a scribe, probably from London, known as Ricardus Franciscus, who produced literary as well as legal texts *c.* 1450.[97]

William Caxton was the first layman in England to edit a large hagiographical collection. He had been encouraged in his publication by William, Earl of Arundel, who had promised 'to take a reasonable quantyte of them when they were achyeved'.[98] Caxton regarded the lives in his vast *Golden Legend* as very close to his historical publication the *Polychronicon*: both were 'historye' and therefore 'precious and profytable',[99] providing

92 Fleming, 'Hautes', p. 95 and n.; PRO, PCC 15 Logge, PROB. 11/7, f. 115r–v. A *legend* in the singular *may* mean a legendary or lectionary, a book containing the lessons or other readings of mass or divine office.

93 PRO, PCC 4 Godyn, PROB. 11/5, f. 29v. And see previous note.

94 Called the '1438 Golden Legend' in *Manual*, vol. 2, pp. 423–25, 432–36, 559–60; Wolpers, *Heiligenlegende*, pp. 373–83; Jeremy, 'English prose translation of the *Legenda aurea*', pp. 181–83.

95 *Manual*, vol. 2, pp. 436–39, 560–61.

96 Oxford, Bodleian Library, MS Douce 372. Sutton, 'Alice Claver', p. 140.

97 BL, MS Harl. 4775; for Franciscus see Christianson, *Directory*, p. 107.

98 Caxton's prologue and additions, Blake, *Caxton's Own Prose*, pp. 88–96, esp. 90.

99 Blake, *Caxton's Own Prose*, p. 131, lines 116–23; see also ch. 7 below. A layman who had both of these works by Caxton was John Skirwith, leatherseller of London (d. 1486), PRO, PROB 2/15; an edition of this inventory is forthcoming in *The Ricardian*.

Fig. 33 God, the Virgin Mary and the company of saints, many of them identifiable by their emblems. Grisaille miniature in a book of hours of Philip the Good. Flemish, *c*. 1454. The Hague, Royal Library, MS 76 F 2, f. 283. By permission of the Royal Library.

examples for his readers to follow. While earlier fifteenth-century redactions of saints' lives have been compared to the delicate and splendid panel paintings and miniatures in books, Caxton's version, with its simplification of his sources' language, its bourgeois celebration of ceremony and its lack of spiritual involvement, has been associated with the English woodcuts of the time, simple, crude and heavily outlined.[100]

Individual saints' lives were owned in various forms and for various reasons. Sir John Donne, a Calais administrator serving Edward IV, Richard III and Henry VII, acquired a Flemish manuscript with an account of the Assumption of the Virgin, a life of St John the Evangelist, a miracle of the same St John taken from the life of Edward the Confessor, and a life of St Mary Magdalene, all in French. It may be assumed that he chose the book primarily because part of it concerned his name saint.[101] Sir John Paston had a *Lyffe of Seynt Cry* ... , either Christopher or Christiana, or a more obscure saint, in a separate booklet.[102] Sir Roger Townshend, a lawyer who served the Woodville family, at the end of his life possessed separate manuscripts of the lives of St Thomas, either the archbishop or the apostle, and St Blaise, who was invoked on behalf of sick animals as well as humans, and was the patron of woolcombers.[103] William Bodley, grocer of London, and his two wives had a *Life of St Katherine*, which had probably belonged to his father and had been made in London *c.* 1480. None of the ladies in the family appear to have been called Katherine.[104] Anne Harling, of East Harling in Norfolk, a wealthy heiress and widow of the fifth Lord Scrope of Bolton, mentioned St Anne, together with Sts Peter, Paul and John the Evangelist, in her will and was buried in St Anne's chapel at Harling; she owned a stanzaic life of St Anne, as well as lives of Sts Katherine, Margaret and Patrick.[105] The same life of St Anne occurs in the collection of Robert Reynes, of Acle near Norwich, put

---

100 Wolpers, *Heiligenlegende*, pp. 386, 400; to illustrate his image Wolpers compares Caxton's woodcut of the assembly of saints in the first edition of the *Golden Legend* to the Wilton Diptych and the Eton wall paintings.

101 BL, MS Royal 20 B ii, see Backhouse, 'Sir John Donne's Flemish manuscripts', in Monks and Owen, pp. 48–53, esp. 51–52. In the Memling triptych commissioned by Donne both the Sts John are very conspicuous, but it has been said that this painting was inspired by the similar one made for St John's Hospital, Bruges, see Vos, *Memling*, pp. 180–83.

102 See Lester, 'The books of ... Sir John Paston', pp. 200–15, esp. 204.

103 Moreton, '"Library" ... of a lawyer', pp. 338–46, esp. 342, 345–46.

104 Cambridge, Corpus Christi College, MS 142, see Sutton, 'Lady Joan Bradbury', p. 212n.

105 BL, MS Harl. 4012; *Testamenta Eboracensia*, vol. 4, pp. 149–54.

together between 1470 and 1500. Reynes was a member of the local guild of St Edmund and probably also of the guild of St Anne. The first two lines of the last but one stanza in Reynes's copy reads:

And Mary and her moder maynteth this gylde,
To the worchep of God, and of His plesaunce, ... [106]

Personal dedications and commissioned saints' lives confirm this picture of the reasons why people owned the story of a particular saint in writing. Usually the recipient had a special devotion to the saint, because he or she was his or her name saint, or the patron of guild, craft, religious house or order. In the 1440s, for example, Osbern Bokenham wrote his English verse passion of St Katherine for two female patrons, Katherine Howard, first wife of John Howard, later duke of Norfolk, and Katherine Denston, *née* Clopton.[107] John Lydgate and John Capgrave composed most of their saints' lives for specific individuals or institutions. Lydgate's *Legend of St George* was written in honour of the armourers of London, and his *Life of St Alban and St Amphibal* for John Whethamstede, Abbot of St Albans.[108] Capgrave's *Life of St Gilbert of Sempringham* was composed at the request of the master of the Gilbertine Order to provide his nuns with an English text.[109]

At Christmas 1484[110] the Italian humanist scholar Pietro Carmeliano, who had arrived in England in 1481, dedicated a verse life of St Katherine of Alexandria in Latin to Richard III.[111] Carmeliano made at least three copies of his text for different dedicatees. The manuscript he presented to Richard III does not survive, but his dedicatory letters in the two extant copies provide evidence of the royal dedication. The two other recipi-

106 See Louis, *Commonplace Book of Robert Reynes*, p. 228.

107 Bokenham, *Legendys*; and see ch. 2, above.

108 E.g. Schirmer, *John Lydgate*, ch. 18.

109 E.g. Meijer, 'John Capgrave', pp. 400–40, esp. 424. John Capgrave's *Life of St Katherine* appears to have no specific dedicatee, but one of the owners of a copy of the text – who presented it perhaps to a community of nuns – was called Katherine (Babyngton), BL, MS Arundel 396, f. 130v (*c.* 1440).

110 Christmas 1484 is the most likely date but Christmas 1483 is possible.

111 See 'R III's books XIV', where both mss of this text are illustrated, and Cat. XIV, below. See also Carlson, *English Humanist Books*, pp. 42–48. The text was printed and edited with an introduction, full critical apparatus and both dedications by Orbán, *Vitae Sanctae Katharinae*, vol. 119, pp. 263–97.

ents were Sir Robert Brackenbury, Constable of the Tower, and John Russell, Bishop of Lincoln and Chancellor of England. To Brackenbury Carmeliano wrote that he had shortly before dedicated and presented the work to the king; to Russell he mentioned the fact that he had dedicated the 'main copy' to Richard. It may be assumed that he gave the text to the king first and that all three copies were New Year gifts, though the occasion is only mentioned in the Brackenbury dedication.

The two surviving 'dedicatory letters' are cleverly composed. The one to Brackenbury consists mainly of praise of the king, explaining that Carmeliano had dedicated his work to the king in imitation of other authors who wished to honour princely patrons of learning. He could not find a prince more worthy than Richard:

> If we look for religious devotion, which prince is more devout? If we look for justice, who is greater? If we look for prudence in preserving peace and waging war, where shall we find his equal? Who is more wise, temperate, liberal, more intolerant of crime and heresy?

No one, as Brackenbury could testify. Carmeliano asks Brackenbury to recommend him to the king. It is clear that Carmeliano expected to touch the right chord by this praise of Richard. In his dedication of the third copy of the *Life of St Katherine*, to Chancellor Russell, the poet struck an altogether different note; here it was the scholar and cleric who was being flattered (see pl. VI). By accident, he says, he had opened a book of saints' lives at the life of St Katherine,[112] and when he read it his tears flowed freely and his hair stood on end. He chose her as his protectress and dedicated all his energy to put her life into verse, presenting his main copy to the king, but also thinking it right to produce one for the chancellor, who is expert in Latin and all the liberal arts and a kind benefactor of learned men. Considering Carmeliano's general astuteness, the cleverness of his two surviving dedicatory letters and the fact that he intended the book first and foremost for the king's use, it must be assumed that he knew that this particular text would please Richard III; circumstantial evidence for Richard's devotion to St Katherine may be sought partly in

---

112 The number of surviving ms. copies of the so-called 'vulgate' text is considerable, probably almost 200, and it was printed from the late 15th century on. See the edition of the text included in d'Ardenne and Dobson, *Seinte Katerine*, pp. xvi–xvii, 132–43.

this very dedication. The introduction in the royal manuscript is likely to have been similar to Brackenbury's: glowing praise of the king and his beneficent rule, and a clear reference to his patronage of learned men, of whom the saint was special protectress. Though Richard's copy does not survive, it can be described as there is little doubt that it was very similar to the manuscripts of Russell and Brackenbury: a small (8 × 5 inches) vellum book of eighteen folios, containing a few pages with praise of the king and a half-page miniature depicting St Katherine with her sword and wheel; the text was written in Carmeliano's neat humanist hand; the first page had some minor decoration.[113]

Though there is no historical evidence that anyone like her ever existed, St Katherine was one of the most venerated saints from the tenth century on. She was not only a virgin and a martyr, but also a doctor of the Church; she was the bride of Christ, joined to him in a mystical marriage which became the subject of many medieval and later works of art.[114] The story of the earlier part of her life, her *vita* or *conversio*, which also circulated separately from that of her martyrdom, or *passio*, claimed that she was a heathen princess, learned in all the arts and sciences, who succeeded to her father's throne. Urged by her mother and her councillors to marry, she described the perfect husband and it was clear only Christ fitted her description. In a vision she was allowed to see Him and she professed herself willing to be His servant. After conversion and baptism she was affianced to Him by the Virgin Mary herself.

The oldest version of the legend contained only the saint's martyrdom,[115] starting with her first confrontation with the Emperor Maxentius, who has ordered all his subjects to sacrifice to the gods. Katherine tells him he should acknowledge God and offer love and devotion rather than the blood of animals. The emperor ridicules the Christian faith but Katherine's eloquence amazes him and he summons fifty doctors and philosophers to convince her of her errors. The learned men arrive, indignant at being asked to argue with a single young woman. The details of the saint's arguments in the ensuing disputation are variously given;

113 See the descriptions and illustrations in 'R III's books XIV'.

114 Her feast day is (usually) 25 November, Butler *et al.*, *Lives of the Saints*, vol. 11, pp. 296–97; Jameson, *Sacred and Legendary Art*, vol. 2, pp. 467–91; the introductions of Ardenne and Dobson, *Seinte Katerine*, and of Nevanlinna and Taavitsainen, *St Katherine*, and references given there.

115 See e.g. *Bibliotheca Sanctorum*, vol. 3, cols 955–57.

in the early versions they are very brief; in some later texts, such as John Capgrave's *Life of St Katherine*, they include long doctrinal points.[116] Eventually all fifty doctors are convinced and converted; supported by St Katherine they suffer a martyr's death by fire and she herself is tortured and imprisoned. In the emperor's absence his wife and the commander of his army visit Katherine; they find her cell filled with celestial light and are immediately converted. Katherine explains Christ's goodness and the blessings of heaven to them and predicts their death by martyrdom. On his return Maxentius tries to force the saint into submission by showing her four spiked wheels built to lacerate whoever is put between them. At her prayer the engine is shattered by angels, the flying fragments killing 4,000 pagans, but no Christians. The empress intercedes for Katherine, confesses to her conversion and both she and the commander of the army are put to death. Before St Katherine, too, is beheaded she prays that in future anyone in distress calling on her shall be heard and comforted. Christ promises that it shall be so.

Carmeliano's *Beatae Katerinae Egyptiae Christi Sponsae Vita* ('The Life of Saint Katherine of Egypt, Spouse of Christ') is not actually a 'life' but only the 'passion' of the saint, based on the Latin so-called 'vulgate' version of her martyrdom. Carmeliano followed closely the order and events of his original and hardly added any material of his own. His approach was entirely classical; there are no biblical quotations, many mythological allusions and the metre is faultless, imitating classical usage in every way. Though it omits the contents of her speeches, the text focuses on St Katherine's defence of the Christian faith, her learned refutation of the philosophers, her conversion of them and others and her final martyrdom. It is likely that Carmeliano knew Caxton's 1483 edition of the complete *Golden Legend*, which contained the much longer life of St Katherine, including her English connection, childhood, conversion and her mystic marriage to Christ, all the elements that made the story universally popular and attractive. Carmeliano clearly expected his work to be appreciated mostly for its elegant form.

In spite of its un-English form Carmeliano's reasons behind his decision to compose the life of a saint and of this saint in particular must be sought in the existing English literary tradition, which he had no doubt learned about. St Katherine may have been Carmeliano's own favour-

---

116 Ed. Horstmann, *Life of St. Katherine of Alexandria*, pp. 294–335.

ite saint, as he claimed in his dedication to Chancellor Russell: she was the patroness of the city of Venice — which ruled Brescia, Carmeliano's native city — and the special protectress of the university of Padua[117] where Carmeliano may have been a student. She was also an example of someone who is victorious through learning and eloquence as he himself hoped to be. It is equally possible that Carmeliano was well aware of Richard III's personal preference for St Katherine.[118] Carmeliano's choice was impeccable; he can only be blamed for not making the most of the story. Because he was determined to use the short and convenient Latin text instead of one of the longer and more detailed English legends, he omitted to mention St Katherine's English connection and the fact that she was related to St Helena, daughter of King Coel of Colchester, and her son, Constantine, the first Christian emperor. Caxton, in contrast, knew what people in general liked and included all these interesting facts in his publication.

'His most simple creature, nakidly borne into this wretched world'

Piety in the individual was a required characteristic in the fifteenth century — devotion to God and His saints was expected. The purpose of piety was to ensure the salvation of the soul, but the greater the social consequence of the individual the more difficulty he or she might experience in achieving that aim, and the more the responsibility he or she bore for those less able to care for themselves. Public piety and charity went hand in hand and were rarely distinguished as separate activities: they both benefited the soul.

When tested on his public piety and charity Richard III seems to have passed with flying colours in the opinion of most of his judges. His foundations at Middleham, Barnard Castle and York, and his endowment of four fellows at Queens' College, Cambridge, not only provided prayers for the living and the dead, they were also conscious contributions to the better education of the clergy and the improvement of the service they could provide for the people entrusted to their

---

117 See Jameson, *Sacred and Legendary Art*, vol. 1, p. 476 n. 1.
118 It may be also remembered that Richard's illegitimate daughter was called Katherine.

spiritual care. Gifts, large and small, went to religious establishments throughout Richard's adult life, ranging from a bell to the shipmen's fraternity in Hull, to contributions to windows at Great Malvern and Carlisle Cathedral Priory.

Richard's patronage and employment of learned and able men has also been praised; Pietro Carmeliano had good reason to hope for appreciation and reward. Accepting the manuscript of the *Life of St Katherine* as a formal gift must be seen as part of a prince's public obligations, though Richard's interest in the particular contents of the book were a matter of his private devotion to the saint. His patronage of learning was closely related to the religious establishments he founded and was another aspect of his support of the Church and his awareness of the need to improve the condition of his subjects as well as provide himself with good counsellors and administrators. Only two bishops were appointed during Richard's reign, Thomas Langton of Salisbury and John Shirwood of Durham, but both were noted for their learning and Langton was an enthusiastic educator himself.

Richard's private piety should also be discussed. Everyone in the late Middle Ages who had attained a certain level of education knew what God and His Church expected of the faithful – by the late fifteenth century the laity were extremely well provided with information about these expectations and how to satisfy them and save themselves from too long a term in purgatory. Ideally everyone should lead a life wholly devoted to God and spend their days in prayer and meditation. Even busy men and women of the world could go about their duties in an awareness and love of Christ and devote time to religious matters as often as possible, leading the so-called 'mixed' or 'meddled life'. Richard's particular veneration of St Katherine and St Barbara, who represented the contemplative and the active life, appears to symbolise his recognition of the dilemma. It has been suggested with some credibility that late fifteenth-century princes tried to reconcile their ostentatious life-style with their religious consciences by increasing their charitable activities and by reforming their households morally as well as financially. The observant or sensitive prince could have been painfully aware of how far his way of life fell short of the ideal and how dangerously near everlasting punishment he stood. One way of salving his conscience could be a meticulous correctness in his minor charities; another could be princely generosity to the Church and the grand scale of his foundations, such as

Richard's proposed college of the unprecedented number of a hundred priests at York.

His religion should make a prince aware of his own exalted position, of God's goodness to him, and the fickleness of fortune. The last would not have needed expounding to Richard: in his preamble to the statutes of the foundation at Middleham he expressed his deep gratitude to God:

> Know ye that where it haith pleasid Almighty God, Creatour and Redemer of all mankynd, of His most bounteuouse and manyfold graces to enhab-ile, enhaunce and exalte me His most simple creature, nakidly borne into this wretched world, destitute of possessions, goods and enheretaments, to the grete astate, honor and dignite that He haith called me now unto, to be named, knowed, reputed and called Richard Duc of Gloucestre, and of His infynyte goodnesse not oonly to endewe me with grete possessions and of giftys of His divyne grace, bot also to preserve, kep and deliver me of many grete jeoperdes, parells and hurts, for the which and other many-fold benyfits of His bounteuouse grace and godnesse to me, without any my desert or cause in sundry behalves shewed and geven, I, daily and ourly according to my deuty remembring the premisses, and in recognicion that all such goodness cometh of Hyme ...[119]

These were not idle words for a man who now ruled most of the north of England, but a few years earlier had been in exile for the second time in his life and had to borrow a few shillings to be able to continue his jour-ney through a foreign country.[120]

The most personal document that survives to throw light on Richard's personal piety is his book of hours. The book is beautiful, but simple and unostentatious and cannot have been chosen for its outward appearance. Here as with all his surviving books, including the enigmatic English Bible, it is an inevitable conclusion that Richard actually owned books because of what was in them. To the many prayers in the original text of his *horae* the king had yet another ten pages of devotions added; these prove that he was genuinely devoted to St Ninian, deeply concerned about the crusading movement, and particularly in need of a prayer that

---

119 Raine, 'Statutes', p. 160.
120 For Richard's exiles see Visser-Fuchs, 'Richard in Holland, 1461 and 1470–71'; for the loan *ibid.*, p. 227 n. 20.

could give him comfort in his sorrow and grief. The so-called 'prayer of Richard III' is an entreaty for comfort and help against an inimical world, but it is also full of hope. In conventional words and phrases well known from the daily liturgy there is trust and hope and a desire to trust and hope; the many examples rehearsed in the prayer of people who were saved by God's goodness justify such hope. The revelations of St Mechtild, too, bear witness vividly and almost tangibly to God's justice and mildness and love of man. The repetitive incantations of the prayer and the colourful scenes of the visions are still very moving and no doubt could bring a mind brought up in the Christian beliefs of the late medieval world, steeped in its conventions, fed on its images, and daily absorbing its liturgy and language, to the intense devotional concentration that was thought so desirable, leading the reader and supplicant from sorrow to joy.

The evidence of the religious books that Richard owned as duke and king is not unequivocal, but it is positive rather than negative. The contents of his hours, his worship of particular saints and the mere ownership of Mechtild's *Booke of Gostlye Grace* and the English Bible show us a man whose piety may have been conventional but certainly not lukewarm.

FOUR

Chivalric Ideals and Reality

A young man of noble family, such as Richard himself, was surrounded from the day he was born with the panoply of chivalry: halls would be hung with weapons and armour and hunting trophies; almost every story he was told concerned feats of arms, and the books he knew might be illustrated with dramatic battle-scenes and colourful heraldry. Larger-than-life heroes killing their enemies with one stroke, surrounded by the rewards of success, fine tents and richly caparisoned horses, were commonplace in the historiated sequences of tapestries in great palaces. Subjects included the stories of Jason, Hector, Arthur, Charlemagne, Guy of Warwick, as well as the military heroes of the Old Testament.

A nobly-born youth was considered to have an innate inclination towards 'chivalry' from which nothing could deflect him. Even if he were brought up among peasants he would show his true nature in the end. The stories and ceremonies of chivalry were supposed to act upon him as the scent of game on a hound. The hero of *Blanchardyn and Eglantine* was just such a young man. He was brought up by his father, the king, in ignorance of war, military heroes, heraldry or jousting, and instead taught 'lytterature', 'good manners', grammar, logic and philosophy, with 'tables', chess, and hunting and hawking as his 'passetymes'. He excelled at all these, but nevertheless longed for something that was missing. The inevitable happened:

... walkyng wythin the paleys. And by adventure entred in to a chambre, hanged wyth right fayre and [p. 15] riche tapysserye of the destruction of Troye, well and alonge fygured. Blanchardyn, that nevere had taken theratte noo hede, ryght instantly dyde advyse and sette his syght toward the sayde tappysserie. And coude not merveylle hym self to moche, in beholdynge upon the same ... of thystorye and of the personnages. And first recounted unto hym his mayster the puyssaunce, the right great cyrcuyte and the noblesse of the cyte of Troyes ... merveyllous batayles ... grete valyaunce of Hector, of Troylus, Parys ... of whom he sawe the representacyon in the sayde tappysserye, that sore movyd and styryd his noble and hyghe corage and gaffe hym awylle for to be lyke unto those noble and worthy knyghtes ... he demaunded ... the names and blasure of the armes ... to fore they departed fro the chambre ... he was ... endoctryned of the names and usages for the moost parte of thabylymentes necessary, and servynge [p. 16] to the werre ... Blanchardyn concluded in his corage, that he shold fynde hym self, yf god graunted hym helthe, in som place where by experyence he shuld lerne to bere armes, and shuld exercyce and take payne and dyligence upon hym selfe to knowe the wayes of the same, for the grete plesure that he toke in herynge therof speke, thynkyng in hym self that the use therof shulde be to hym ryght moche agreable and plaisaunt ... [1]

The charming trappings of this story mask the crude facts of what is really happening: the boy's natural aggressive energy is stimulated by the military display and is ready for release in action and adventure. Such aggression was much admired in the Middle Ages but needed to be organised, and it was chivalry which channelled all this surplus energy of the upper or knightly class. By Richard's day generations of clergy and other theorists of chivalry had imposed certain controls over secular rulers and their fighting men which were occasionally successful and of which the *Order of Chivalry* by Lull was one of the most important texts: war was to be in a just cause; the knight was to be a protector of the weak; and the highest glory was to fight the infidel. The knight was expected to fight for his lord, or his employer, and the Church; only in romances was he allowed to fight for love and his lady; and always and everywhere he was fighting for reputation, honour and fame.[2]

---

1 Caxton's *Blanchardyn and Eglantine*, pp. 13–16; *u* and *v*, some punctuation and capitals have been modernised by the present authors.

2 The main books on chivalry which have been used are: Barnie, *War in Medieval Society*; Benson and Leyerle, *Chivalric Literature*; Vale, *War and Chivalry*; Keen, *Chivalry* (for a general definition of chivalry see his ch. 1); Contamine *et al.*, *Guerre et Société*.

Fig. 34 The arming of the young Pyrrhus, Achilles' son, in the famous armour of his father, by Ajax and Agamemnon. Engraving of one of a set of tapestries, each *c.* 15 feet high and *c.* 30 feet long, telling the story of the Trojan War, made at Tournai 1475–90. Engraving by Henry Shaw. This tapestry is now at the Victoria and Albert Museum, London.

The fact that all soldiers, including knights, were brutalised by war, often encouraged war for their own gain, looted, ruined the country they fought over, and ill-treated and slaughtered the poor was rarely discussed and certainly led to no pacifist conclusions. Nevertheless some questioning of the accepted point of view went on. Even that admiring chronicler of chivalry, Froissart (died *c.* 1404–10), was shocked at the needless slaughter of citizens of Limoges by the Black Prince he so revered.[3] The poet John Gower (died 1400) realised the divergence between the pretensions of knights and their actual motives; he recognised the vanity of fighting

---

3 It seems cynical to ascribe Froissart's disapproval to French 'partisanship' only, Barnie, *War in Medieval Society*, p. 77. For the increasing expense of war and the dependence on rewards and looting, Vale, 'Warfare and the life of the French and Burgundian nobility', pp. 169–93. And see Keen, *Chivalry*, ch. 12, for a comparison of chivalry to real war.

for a woman's love or one's own fame, and condemned the greed that
motivated the English war in France and the misery it caused.[4] A nobleman like Gilbert de Lannoy (died 1462), soldier and traveller, diplomat
and counsellor of Philip the Good, who had been fighting battles all his
life, insisted that war was to be avoided as much as possible, and advised
his prince that when the wish to win battles and glory became too strong
he should go and fight the heathen.[5] In Chaucer's *Knight's Tale* – of which
Richard owned a copy from his youth – the victorious Theseus is at first
irritated by the ill-timed interruption of his triumphal progress by the
entreaties of the widowed queens, but the next moment he is gentle and
full of pity for them and immediately sets off on a campaign on their
behalf.[6] Chaucer shows Theseus caring for the queens and their dead husbands, but at the same time allowing his dead enemies to be plundered
and arbitrarily imprisoning the two heroes of the story. One moment he
decides that two hundred well-armed knights shall fight over the trivial
matter of who is to marry the heroine and the next he imposes extra rules
to prevent the shedding of 'gentle blood'.[7] Chaucer makes this paragon
of chivalry a violent, unpredictable prince who sometimes obeys the
strict rules of chivalry. In short, Theseus was not unlike the heroes of the
Hundred Years War.

A variety of such contradictory images would be imprinted on a young
man's mind from the books he read: balancing the continual diet of war
and battle in most chronicles and romances, there would be chapters of
sage advice, counselling pity, restraint and justice. William Worcester's
Boke of Noblesse (see fig. 37), encouraging Edward IV and then Richard
III to make war on France and advising on how to do so successfully, is a
case in point. On one page there is the exhortation to follow 'the example
of the boar': 'avaunsing your corageous hertis to werre ... furious, egre
... ayenst all tho nacions that ... wolde put you frome youre ... rightfull enheritance', as there is no 'more holier, parfiter, or a juster thing'
than to fight such enemies; while a few pages on Worcester is moved
by the 'oppressions and tirannyes, ravynes, and crueltees' that the king's

4   Barnie, *War in Medieval Society*, p. 123.
5   Van Leeuwen, *Denkbeelden van een Vliesridder*, pp. 30–34. See also ch. 5 below for the advice
     on war in 'mirrors'.
6   The Black Prince, according to Chandos Herald, undertook his Spanish campaign *pur pitie*,
     quoted Mathew, 'Ideals', p. 359.
7   *The Knight's Tale*, lines 893–1032, 2537–64.

officers have done against 'the pore comons, laborers, paissauntes of ...
Normandie', these being, of course, the king's rightful subjects.[8]

Richard III's books illustrate all the diverse aspects of chivalry. The
romances of *Palamon and Arcite*, the *Siege of Thebes*, *Ipomedon* and *Tristan* entertained with 'many joyous and playsaunt hystoryes ... of ... chyvalryes',[9] and
his more solid history books gave him similar stories. The reputations of the
heroes of *Tristan* and *Ipomedon* inspired an interest in hunting which developed the skills of horsemanship essential to the knight. Practical instruction
was to be found particularly in Vegetius, and to a lesser extent in the *Boke of
Noblesse* and its supporting Collection of documents. The classic rehearsal of
the ideals of knighthood was contained in the *Order of Chivalry*, reinforced
by episodes in the works of history and fiction. Can these texts and their
advice be related to the realities of Richard of Gloucester's life and career,
particularly as two of them were dedications and given to him? Did Richard
share his contemporaries' attitude to chivalry? Did he enjoy the wars and
battles in which he took part and long for a military reputation equal to
those of Arthur, Edward III or Henry V? Did he wish to conquer France
and go on a crusade? Could he distinguish between the rhetoric of war and
the lure of fame and success on the one hand and the ideals of justice and
restraint on the other? Did he set store by the chivalric code of honour and
his reputation as a knight *sans peur et sans reproche*? Precise answers cannot
be given, but his surviving collection of chivalric texts – like his religious
books – provide both substantial material for a comparison of ideals and
reality and an excellent cross section of the kind of texts about these subjects to be found in an average noble library of his time.

Chivalric Treatises

All Richard's books of chivalric theory came to him during his reign,
although he would certainly have been brought up on two of the texts as a
young man. Flavius Vegetius Renatus, the author of what was to become
the standard military treatise used by soldiers from the end of the fourth
century to the nineteenth century was not a professional soldier himself,

8 Worcester, *Boke of Noblesse*, pp. 22, 73.
9 Caxton's prologue to his edition of Malory's *Morte DArthur* (1485), see Crotch, *Prologues and
   Epilogues of William Caxton*, p. 94.

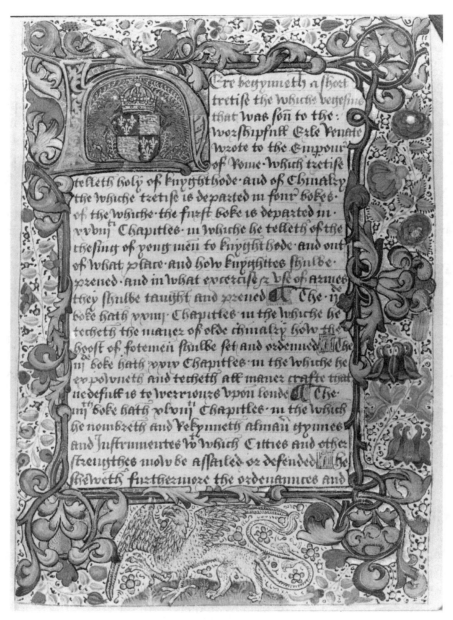

Fig. 35 The beginning of the English translation of Vegetius' *De re militari*, showing the royal arms supported by boars in the initial *H*; the griffin of Salisbury in the lower margin suggests that the manuscript was made for Richard III's son, Edward, Prince of Wales and Earl of Salisbury, before his death in April 1484. BL, MS Royal 18 A xii, f. 1. By permission of The British Library.

but a minister of finance at the Roman imperial court. He admitted that his work relied on earlier books as readily as many of his innumerable copyists, redactors and pilferers admitted that he was their source; they ranged from John of Salisbury, Vincent of Beauvais and Giles of Rome to Christine de Pizan, all as innocent of actual military experience as himself.[10]

The text owned by Richard III is divided into the four books usual to it in the Middle Ages. According to the original preface, the first teaches what kind of men make suitable recruits and the exercise needed for their training: running, marching, leaping and swimming; the use of shield and sword, the handling of other weapons, and feats such as the leaping on and off horseback sword in hand. They are taught how to set up and fortify camps both when the enemy is far way and when he is dangerously near. The second book was of less interest to medieval users and is concerned with the composition of the Roman legion and the titles and duties of its officers; it ends with a list of the engines of war which was adapted to their own times by medieval translators. Book Three was the most popular and frequently used part of the manual; here is the famous maxim, *qui desiderat pacem praeparet bellum* ('who desireth pees array him to werre'),[11] and here are the general rules of war, the earliest and most influential attempt to summarise military theory. The following quotations will give an idea of the tenor of these maxims and of their wording in Richard III's copy:

There beth no counselles better ten tho of which thyn ennemy hath no knowing till they ben doon in dede.

---

10 Vegetius' book became known as *Epitoma rei militaris* or *De re militari*. Most of the following is based on: *Geschichte der Wissenschaften in Deutschland*, vol. 21; Jähns, *Geschichte der Kriegswissenschaften*, pt 1, pp. 109–205; Springer, 'Vegetius in Mittelalter', pp. 85–90; Bornstein, 'Military manuals', pp. 469–77; Wiseman, '*L'Epitoma rei militaris*', pp. 12–31; Shrader, 'A handlist of extant manuscripts containing *De re militari*', pp. 280–305, 243 mss in Latin, 46 in French, 17 in English and 18 in other vernaculars. The summary was made with the help of the Teubner edition of the Latin text, Lang, *Flavi Vegeti Renati Epitoma Rei Militaris*, which should be used in conjunction with Anderson, *Studia Vegetiana*. For the 1408 trans., see Lester, *The Earliest English Translation of Vegetius*, and also his *John Paston's 'Grete Boke'*, pp. 50, 159–63. For a modern trans. of the original text, Milner, *Vegetius: Epitome of Military Science*.

11 BL, MS Royal 18 A xii, f. 50. All quotations are taken from Richard III's copy of the 1408 translation. No attempt has been made to correct its errors; ampersands have been extended and punctuation and the use of capitals modernised.

Every hooste with travaill and labour profitteth and sutteleth, but with
ydilnes he dulleth.

Good dukes ne fighteth never openly in felde, but they be dryven therto
by sodeyn happe or grete nede.[12]

The main part of the third book deals with strategy and tactics: the various kinds of warfare and how the health of an army may be preserved;
it claims that 'oure olde wise werriors tolden that usage, exercise and
besy occupacion in dedes of armes profiteth more to the keping of bodily
helthe of her knyghtes then leches or medycynes';[13] and it explains how
to prevent a mutiny, what to do when in command of an inexperienced
army, how to dispose one's troops for battle and where to place the commanders. The fourth book discusses the use of fortifications and their
component parts; it contains a description of various siege engines and
the use of mines. The last chapters are devoted to naval warfare, ships and
their building, the winds and the signs of storms.

It was not only Vegetius' detailed practical advice that attracted readers
through the centuries, but his patriotism, his emphasis on exercise, and
his moralising. His precepts were endlessly repeated in edifying books.
The *Livre des faits d'armes et de chevalerie* by Christine de Pizan (1408–9),
translated and printed by Caxton 1489, was one of the most important
adaptions available to Richard III's generation.[14] Between *c.* 1250 and
the end of the sixteenth century the *De re militari* was translated into the
vernaculars of Europe including English. The text owned by Richard III
is one of the eleven extant copies of the first English translation, made
in 1408 for Thomas, Lord Berkeley.[15] The text produced was readable,
if slightly long-winded, and the general spirit of the original manual
was preserved.

De re militari was considered an ideal teaching aid for the young, and it
would automatically have been part of the education of a young noble-

---

12 BL, MS Royal 18 A xii, ff. 95–96v.

13 *Ibid.*, f. 53.

14 Pizan, *Book of Faytes of Armes and Chevalrye*, trans. W. Caxton.

15 Lester, *Earliest English Translation of Vegetius*. A verse paraphrase was made 1457–60, Dyboski
    and Arend, *Knyghthode and Bataile*. For comments on this and other versions, MacCracken,
    'Vegetius in English', pp. 389–403. For the identity of the translator, Science, *Boethius: De
    Consolatione Philosophiae* translated by John Walton, introd., and MacCracken.

man like the duke of Gloucester.[16] Giles of Rome had included its military advice in the last section of his *De regimine principum* for the heir of the king of France. It is possible that Richard III's copy was in fact intended for his son as the gold griffin of Salisbury, Edward's principal badge from 1478, is prominent in the lower border of the first folio. The copy is comparatively small, written in a clear hand with important words given in red;[17] each of the four books has a full decorated border of formalised foliage, the arms of England beneath an imperial crown and supported by the white boars of the king appearing in the opening initial of Book One (f. 1), and the arms of Queen Anne Neville in the opening initial of Book Three (f. 49). Who commissioned the book and for whom is not certain. What is certain is that it was made 1483–84, before the death of the prince of Wales in April 1484. It was a modest but attractive commission from a London workshop producing a type of standard text with standard illumination which is well known for the 1480s.[18]

The *Order of Chivalry* is perhaps the most important of the chivalric works associated with Richard III. Its author, Ramon Lull (c. 1235–1315), the son of a wealthy Majorcan knight, devoted his life to the conversion of the Saracens of North Africa.[19] The *Order* represents his hopes of training knights in the highest ideals of Christianity as part of this crusading endeavour. He wrote the text in Catalan but it was soon circulating in several languages, including Latin.[20] By the mid-fifteenth century there were a number of French versions and Caxton used one for his translation; another version was bought by Edward IV among the many texts he acquired from Bruges in the 1470s and 1480s (see fig. 36).[21] Five copies of

---

16 Orme, *From Childhood to Chivalry*, pp. 185–88.

17 The scribe of Richard's copy is unlikely to have known Latin well for he did not correct the simple errors in some of the chapter headings still in Latin.

18 A full discussion of the illumination is in 'R III's Books IV', pp. 543–49. Reference should also be made to Scott, *Mirroure*, pp. 45–50, 66–68, and her '*Nova Statuta* manuscripts', pp. 103–05.

19 Byles, *Ordre of Chyvalry*, pp. xi–xiii. See also Minervini, *Ramon Lull, Livre de l'Ordre de Chevalerie*, for mss and eds; and Keen, *Chivalry*, pp. 8–11.

20 Byles, *Ordre of Chyvalry*, pp. xiii–xvi. There is no extant Latin text. Lull's command of Latin was slight but most of his work exists in Latin translations.

21 The textual differences between the version owned by Edward and the one dedicated to Richard III are slight and consist mostly of different words or phrases. 'The cumulative effect is impressive', however, Byles, *Ordre of Chyvalry*, pp. xxxiii–xxxvi. Edward's copy occupies a mere sixteen folios of BL, MS Royal 14 E ii, Byles, p. xviii; Ward, *Catalogue of Romances*, vol. 1, pp. 922–23; and Warner and Gilson, vol. 2, pp. 139–40.

Caxton's *Book of the Order of Chivalry or Knighthood* survive, an elegant and mature typographical product of his workshop.[22] He chose to make it a quarto book, the only one of his chivalric texts not to be a folio volume,[23] but the smaller size was appropriate, perhaps essential, to such a short text, and consistent with its purpose as a 'manual' of chivalry. As a small book and a very famous one the *Order of Chivalry* had recommended itself to Caxton as both translator and publisher: it was short to translate and correspondingly inexpensive to print. An examination of its text[24] shows clearly how Caxton's epilogue and dedication to Richard III grew naturally out of what he had just read and translated.

Lull's treatise of instruction for young men in the virtues of knighthood starts in the form of a dialogue between a potential knight – a squire or examinee – and a knight of long experience.[25] Their meeting is contrived as though it was a charming, minor adventure in a romance. A wise and virtuous knight has retired to be a hermit, not wishing to dishonour chivalry by his old age; each day he prays in a meadow beneath a fruit tree close by a fountain. Meanwhile a king 'moche noble, wyse and ful of good custommes sente for many nobles by cause he wold hold a grete courte', and a young squire sets out to attend and be dubbed a knight there.

> Thus as he wente all allone rydynge upon his palfroy, it happed that for the travaylle that he hadde susteyned of rydynge he slepte upon his horse ... his palfroye yssued oute of the ryght way and entryd in to the forest where as was the knyghte heremyte. And soo longe he wente that he came to the fontayne at the same tyme that the knyght ... was there comen for to praye unto God and for to despyse the vanytees of this worlde ... Whan he sawe the squyer come he lefte his oroyson and satte in the medowe in the shadow of a tree and beganne to rede in a lytyl book that he had in his lappe. And whan the palfroy was come to the fontayne he beganne to drynke, and the squyer that slept anone felte

---

22 None of the copies are perfect. De Ricci, *A Census of Caxtons*, p. 84, item 81; Duff, *Fifteenth-century English Books*, p. 16, item 58; Byles, *Ordre of Chyvalry*, pp. xxii–xxv.

23 Blake, *England's First Publisher*, p. 63, finds the size inexplicable.

24 Reading the texts has often been lacking in Caxton studies, as pointed out by Blake, 'William Caxton: the man and his work', pp. 67–68. For an unfanciful biography of the printer, see 'Richard III's Books XI', pp. 110–12.

25 Byles, *Ordre of Chyvalry*; punctuation, capitalisation, the usage of *u* and *v* and the Anglo-Saxon letters have been modified for the quotations used here.

that his hors meved not and lyghtly awoke. And thenne to hym came
the knyght whiche was moche old and had a grete berde, longe heer
and a feble gowne worne and broken for over longe werynge, and by
the penaunce that he dayly made was moche discolourd and lene, and
by the teres that he had wepte were his eyen moche wasted ... Eche of
them merveylled of other, for the knyght ... had sene no man sythe
that he had lefte the world, and the squyer merveylled hyn strongly
how he was comen in to that place. Thenne descended the squyer fro
his palfroy and salewed the knyght ... and after sette them upon the
grasse that one by that other, and er ony of them spak eche of them
byheld eche others chere.[26]

The knight learns the purpose of the squire's journey and has all his
memories of his former life awakened: 'he caste oute a grete syghe'. He is
horrified to learn that the young man knows nothing of the duties of the
order to which he is seeking admittance:

'I mervaylle how thow darest demaunde chyvalrye or knyghthode ...
noo knyght maye not love the ordre ne that whiche apperteyneth to his
ordre but yf he can knowe the deffautes that he dothe ageynst the ordre
of chyvalrye. Ne no knyght ought to make ony knyghtes but yf he hyn
self know thordre ...'[27]

The squire begs the knight to teach him.

'Frend', sayd the knyght, 'the rule and ordre of chyvalrye is wreton in
this lytyl booke that I hold here in myn handes, in which I rede and
am besy ...'[28]

The knight-hermit finally tells the squire to take the book
...

to the courte ... to shewe to alle them that will be made knyghtes ...
And whan he was comen, he presented the booke ... to the noble kyng,
and furthermore he offryd that every noble man that wold be in thordre

---

26 *Ibid.*, pp. 5–8. Palfreys could be expensive but they were not war horses, Vale, 'Warfare and
the life', p. 172.
27 Byles, *Ordre of Chyvalry*, p. 10.
28 *Ibid.*, p. 11.

Fig. 36 The hermit-knight instructing the squire in the duties of knighthood, from Edward IV's copy of the French translation of Ramon Lull's *Ordre de Chevalerie*. BL, MS Royal 14 E ii, f. 338. By permission of The British Library.

of chyvalry myght have a copye of the sayd book, to thende that he myght see and lerne thordre of knyghthode ...[29]

The rest of the text (Chapters Two to Eight) is presented as the text of the 'little book'. The second chapter sets out the mythical origins of knighthood and advises how a knight should be trained. Lull begged princes to set up special schools for knights just as there were for clerks, rather than rely upon the haphazard results of parental training.[30] The third chapter describes the duties of a knight: to defend the Christian faith and protect the Church; to defend his lord; and maintain justice. A knight should uphold his lord's authority and see that the peasants till the land; he should defend the weak and be merciful; he should punish

29 Byles, *Ordre of Chyvalry*, p. 14.
30 *Ibid.*, pp. 14–23.

wrong-doers. In order to keep his body in training he should joust, tourney and hunt, while his soul should be exercised in justice, wisdom, charity, loyalty, truthfulness, humility, strength, hope, swiftness and 'al other vertues'.[31] Much of this reads as an idealised and Christianised version of Vegetius.

The fourth chapter sets out how the squire should be examined and by whom. A wicked knight is not a fit examiner and here the author expands on the duty of good knights to execute the bad. The candidate's character, past life and the real reasons for his candidature have to be established; he must not be too young; good looks are not enough, but he must not be disabled 'or over fat'; and he should be well born.[32] Chapter Five goes through the ceremonies that turn the squire into a knight, setting out the twelve articles of belief to which he has to subscribe – very much those of any member of the Christian Church.[33] Chapter Six gives the significance of each of the new knight's arms. The sword is in the shape of the cross to defeat the enemies of Christ, its two edges are chivalry and justice, the helmet signifies dread of shame, and so on.[34] Chapter Seven sets out the 'custommes' of a knight. He must know each of the seven virtues and their relevance to him is explained. The seven deadly sins are rehearsed in comparable detail, the last one being temperance, an example to a knight to seek moderation in all things. He should hear mass and pray; he must not credit divination or superstition for that is to take leave of reason 'lyke to a foole that useth no wytte ne reason'. He must love 'the comyn wele, for by the comynalte of the people was the chyvalrye ... establysshed. And the comyn wele is gretter and more necessary than propre [personal] good and specyall'. He must be well spoken and hospitable. Virtue comes from within.[35] The last chapter describes the honours rightfully due to the order of knighthood which is so essential to the maintenance of government in this world.[36]

It is a book of ideals.[37] Despite the author's tendency to repeat himself and ramble, it is stirring stuff. It is impossible to read it without

31 *Ibid.*, pp. 24–46. Quotations, pp. 32, 31.
32 Byles, *Ordre of Chyvalry*, pp. 47–65. Quotation, p. 63.
33 *Ibid.*, pp. 66–76.
34 *Ibid.*, pp. 76–89.
35 *Ibid.*, pp. 89–115. Quotations, pp. 92–93, 108–09, 109–10, 113.
36 *Ibid.*, pp. 115–20.
37 For some 15th-century books rehearsing chivalric ideals see Vale, *War and Chivalry*, ch. 1, and below, ch. 5.

being moved to enthusiasm, while at the same time being aware that
its ideals have been mostly ignored. Caxton was certainly so carried
away by it that he wrote an equally stirring epilogue which is one of
his most admired pieces of writing.[38] He tells us first that he translated
the book at the request of the 'gentyl and noble esquyer' who gave it
to him,[39] and in this way he neatly uses the inspiration of the opening
adventure when the squire acquires the treatise, takes it to court and
presents it to his king who orders it to be circulated to all knights and
squires. At the end of his epilogue the optimistic printer picks up this
theme again and says:

> thys lytyl book I presente to my redoubted … lord, Kyng Rychard
> … to thende that he commaunde this book to be had and redde unto
> other yong lordes, knyghtes and gentylmen within this royame that
> the noble ordre of chyvalrye be herafter beter used and honoured than
> hit hath ben in late dayes passed. And herin he shalle do a noble and
> vertuouse dede.[40]

No doubt Caxton was well pleased with his conceit of reusing Lull's
adventure so appositely. The rest of his epilogue continues on the main
theme of the *Order* itself, namely the decay of chivalry and the need for
its revival – an ever-present problem not unique to any period.[41] Caxton
suggests that King Richard should order jousts to be held regularly to
encourage men to maintain their fighting skills, exactly as Lull had done.
It is Caxton himself who then laments that now there are no heroes in
England to compare to those of King Arthur's day; he wants knights to
give up going to bath-houses and playing at dice.

---

38 Byles, 'William Caxton as a man of letters', p. 22. Caxton's translation of *Aesop*, also done in
    1484, is similarly admired. See also Blake, 'Caxton's Language', pp. 123–27.
39 Byles, *Ordre of Chyvalry*, Crotch, *Prologues and Epilogues of William Caxton*, and Blake, *Caxton's
    Own Prose*, pp. 126–27, for the epilogue. There is no means by which the anonymous squire
    can be identified: for a summary of past efforts to do so, 'R III's books XI', p. 129 n. 94.
40 Richard's Prince of Wales was not involved in this dedication, as Painter, *William Caxton*,
    p. 192, suggests. He appears to have misread 'the Prynce' whom Caxton imagines presiding
    over the tournament, see Blake, *Caxton's Own Prose*, p. 127.
41 Vale, *War and Chivalry*, p. 163. Compare Painter, *William Caxton*, p. 142, who sees Caxton
    courageously lecturing Richard on the state of the country under his rule! See 'R III's books
    XI', p. 126 n. 37, for the current myths about Richard III, Caxton and Rivers.

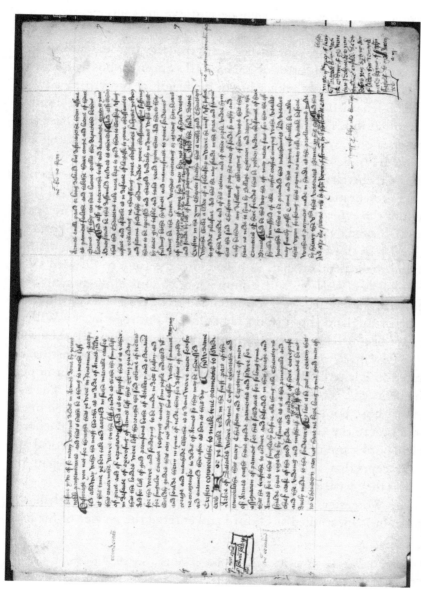

Fig. 37 Two pages from William Worcester's *Boke of Noblesse*. The insertions are in Worcester's hand; one of them refers to documents which had been in the keeping of Sir John Fastolf and given by Worcester to Edward IV. BL, MS Royal 18 B xxii, ff. 14v–15. By permission of The British Library.

Leve this. Leve it and rede the noble volumes of Saynt Graal, of Lancelot,
of Galaad, of Trystram, of Perce Forest,[42] of Percyval, of Gawayn and
many mo. Ther shalle ye see manhode, curtosye and gentylnesse.

He then goes on to list some more recent military heroes, ending with
the earl of Salisbury, ancestor of Richard III's queen, 'whos names shyne
gloryously'. Caxton wrote this when at the height of his writing powers.
Whether Richard III appreciated it we cannot know, but the compliment implicit in his being put in the role of the king in the *Order* who
was 'moche noble, wyse and ful of good custommes' was not an ungrace-
ful one. We can be certain, however, that Richard did read this classic
and essential chivalric text at some time in his life, even if he never read
Caxton's presentation copy. The relevance of the text to Richard III in
the light of the evidence of his interest in a crusade is obvious – no reader
can be unaffected by Lull's preoccupation with the Christian knight.

Richard III's third 'chivalric' text was another dedication, and a second-hand dedication at that, as it had already gone to Edward IV in
1475. The *Boke of Noblesse*, with a supporting volume of documents concerned with the French war, was intended to be read and consulted by
any king of England about to invade France.[43] Put together by William
Worcester originally in the hope of presentation to Henry VI, they were
given to Edward IV on the eve of his French enterprise, and were then re-
dedicated to Richard III, presumably because it was thought, or hoped,
that he believed a reconquest of the lost territories still feasible. The evidence that both books were presented to Richard III is contained in the
introduction to the Collection. The *Boke* is the least known of Richard's
chivalric books and deserves to be better known. It gives practical and
moral precepts that, if followed, would enable the English to regain the
territories they have lost.

William Worcester, alias Botoner, 'of Bristol and Norfolk, gentleman',[44]
was born in 1415, studied at Oxford and entered the service of Sir John

---

42 Perceforest linked the Alexander cycle to that of Arthur, see ch. 9 below, n. 114. It is
    interesting that Caxton relies so heavily on Arthurian and romance examples at a time when
    Burgundian writers were increasingly emphasing the virtues of the more respectable heroes
    of antiquity, Vale, *War and Chivalry*, p. 163, and ch. 9 below.
43 'R III's books XII' and Cat. XIIA and B below.
44 He is thus described in what is still the main study of his life and work: McFarlane, 'Willam
    Worcester', pp. 196–221, repr. McFarlane, *England in the Fifteenth Century*, pp. 199–224.

Fastolf. He acted as his secretary, agent and personal attendant until Fastolf's death in 1459.[45] Worcester served his master long and intimately, writing for his entertainment and ministering to him during his long illness. His duties also took him on extensive journeys through England and into Normandy, collecting evidence for lawsuits, looking after the Fastolf estates, even sorting out the confused affairs of the late duke of Bedford, regent of France. Worcester's own interests were wide ranging:[46] he liked 'a good boke of Frenshe or of poetre';[47] and he made several translations; he is known to have sampled the 'new learning'; medicine, astrology and biology also intrigued him. Worcester was an antiquarian first, however, and enjoyed collecting historical, architectural and topographical facts, stimulated by his travels in Fastolf's service and by Fastolf's needs and wishes.

Sir John Fastolf personally encouraged the creation of a remarkable amount of literary work and Worcester appears to have been involved in many instances; for example he assisted three of Sir John's old companions-in-arms to write an account of military events in Normandy, 1415 to 1429, not finished before Fastolf's death.[48] Among several translations produced for Sir John's entertainment in his old age Worcester himself made a compilation called *Acta Domini Johannis Fastolf* ('The Deeds of ...'), now lost, a translation of Cicero's *De senectute* and *De amicitia* and Buonaccorso da Montemagno's *Controversia de nobilitate* (*The Declamation of Noblesse*). Not long after 1451 he also wrote the *Boke of Noblesse*, the title and argument based on a quotation from Montemagno's text.[49] Reference to the misery of the common people of Normandy and to Charles VII as 'youre grete adversarie'[50] suggest that it was made not long after the expulsion of the English and before 1461. Worcester later made

---

45 See also *Paston Letters*, ed. Gairdner, vol. 1, pp. 152–53 and passim; Kendrick, *British Antiquity*, pp. 29–33; Mitchell, *John Free*, passim; Emden, *Oxford*, pp. 2086–87, incl. a list of the books Worcester owned; Davis, 'The epistolary usages of William Worcester', pp. 249–53; *Paston Letters*, ed. Davis, passim; Gransden, *Historical Writing in England II*, pp. 327–32.

46 McFarlane, 'William Worcester', p. 219, offers mild criticism.

47 *Paston Letters*, ed. Gairdner, no. 370.

48 Peter Basset, Englishman, Christopher Hanson, of 'Almayn', and Luke Nantron, born in Paris. See Rowe, 'A Contemporary Account of the Hundred Years' War', pp. 504–13; McFarlane, 'William Worcester', pp. 207–08. The text is now London, College of Arms, MS M 9, ff. 31–66, see Campbell, *Catalogue*, vol. 1, p. 129.

49 For all above, 'R III's books XII'.

50 Worcester, *Boke of Noblesse*, p. 3.

a complete adaptation of the text for presentation to Edward IV,[51] and a fair copy with long marginal notes by Worcester was, it seems, written shortly before Edward's departure to France in 1475. Worcester wrote that the evil of the English defeat could still be remedied 'as youre hygnesse now entendyth'.[52] It also appears that some important documents had already been handed over by the author to the king:

> ... the statutes made by Johan regent of Fraunce, duc of Bedford, ... uppon the conduyt of the werre, that I delyvered to your hyghenes enseled, the day before your departyng out of London, that remayned yn the kepyng of ser Johan Fastolfe for grate autoritee.[53]

The Collection of supporting documents[54] is smaller than the *Boke*[55] and though neatly written it is a not very 'presentable' jumble of notes and copies. The first six pages contain the introduction which begins:

> Most hyghe myghtye and excelente Cristen prince Edwarde by the dyvyne prudence of God the thred kyng of Englande and of Fraunce
> ...

The first three letters of *Edwarde* are written on an erasure, *thred* is underlined (i.e. erased) in different ink and *fourth* added in substitution in the margin in the same ink as the underlining; the dedication to Richard III is thereby preserved. The dedication was written by Worcester's son, as he himself says, and the way the relatives of the king are described proves that it was meant originally for Edward IV ('the queneys moder, dame Jacques, ducese of Bedforde'), and altered for Richard III ('your most nobill brodyr and predecessoure'). The documents themselves include lists of Frenchmen who served under Bedford, some summary biographies, estimated revenues from English possessions in France, vari-

---

51 Phrases such as 'the erle of Marche your moste noble antecessour' (p. 15) and 'that highe and mighty prince Richarde duke of Yorke youre father' (p. 41), leave no doubt that the book was rewritten after 1461.
52 Worcester, *Boke of Noblesse*, p. 9.
53 *Ibid.*, p. 31.
54 Lambeth Palace Library, MS 506; described James, *Lambeth Palace*, pp. 710–14. Most of the documents were printed by Stevenson, *Letters and Papers*.
55 See Cat. XIIA and B below for sizes.

ous wages, receipts and expenses; ordinances, inventories, and several reports by Fastolf. In all, this is a collection that might be of use to a new English conqueror.

The title of the *Boke of Noblesse*[56] is explained by the Latin quotation which Worcester chose as his beginning and as his 'argument'. This is emphasised by red underlining and other attention-marks which do not appear elsewhere in the manuscript. It is the description of hereditary nobility glorified by one of the contestants in Buonaccorso da Montemagno's *Controversia de vera nobilitate*,[57] which maintains that the highest kind of nobility derives from the great deeds of one's ancestors, the status and privileges inherited from them and one's mental and physical resemblance to them (translation from the Latin, p. 1):

> This is the highest kind of nobility: to be able to relate the great deeds of one's ancestors; to be able to strive for public office because they did well; to be able to protect the common good by hereditary right and above all to be able to call oneself part of them and show that one is made in their image. Only those born from noble parents are called noble by the people.

Worcester chose to ignore the actual problem discussed in the *Controversia* – whether nobility of virtue or nobility of blood is to be preferred and whether virtue can ennoble a man (see ch. 6 below) – the quotation was enough for the purposes in hand. The *Boke* argues that by remembering the feats of arms of his predecessors the king will find the courage to reconquer France, and that it is the 'comyn profit' and 'wele' that will benefit. There is not only great emphasis on the rightful, inherited title of the king to each of his French dominions, but the author is also careful to describe the people of Normandy and elsewhere as the king of England's true subjects to be protected and treated justly. The subsequent introduction by the younger Worcester picked up the theme of duty to one's ancestors and the need to 'governe the comyn publique'.

The argument of the *Boke* itself (such as it is) rambles from one topic to another and is difficult to follow. Much of its material is taken from

---

56 The contents are not very adequately described in the introduction to the Nichols edition, pp. i–xvii; briefly in Bornstein, 'Military manuals', pp. 474–75. For an evaluation, Allmand, 'Boke of Noblesse', pp. 103–11.

57 For the disputed authorship of this text see 'R III's books XII', pp. 160–61.

recent history – Worcester no doubt used Fastolf's memory and knowledge – describing the valorous deeds of the English and the treachery of the French in an attempt to prove that all is not lost and defeat can be reversed. There is a discussion of the problem of war between Christians (taken from Christine de Pizan), excursions into mythology (taken from Cicero) and many examples of civic and military virtue from Roman history. Disproportionately long passages are quoted from Cicero's *De senectute* which Worcester had translated, and his other literary source responsible for a few long sections was Christine de Pizan's *Livre des faits d'armes et de chevalerie.*

Among the more interesting sections of the book are those urging the regular payment of soldiers so that the country may be saved from plunder and oppression, and exhorting the English not to seek riches before victory is assured. They should gain 'worship' first, the rewards will follow. Behind the exclamations and exhortations – 'by lak of simple payment' the dukedom of Normandy was lost, 'wolde Jhesus of his highe grace' that all commanders rewarded their men – behind these, one can hear the excitement and the regrets of old Sir John Fastolf whose efforts over several decades had all been brought to nothing. Moral precepts are also given: 'noble men' are to eschew 'sensualite' and 'pomp in clothing', and above all sloth, exercising themselves continually in arms. The last chapter elaborates on the willingness of the nobility of Rome to sacrifice its wealth to the state when 'a gret armee' and 'men for to defende and kepe the see as the lond' were needed. The 'comons of Rome' followed the example of the nobility and the country was bought 'to worship, prosperite and wellfare'.[58]

It is difficult to gauge what Worcester's motives were in writing the original version of the *Boke of Noblesse* and its *pièces justificatives*. The prospect of presenting the *Boke* to Henry VI, whether it ever actually happened or not, may have kept the ageing Fastolf happy. Worcester's own travels in France could have made him aware of the magnitude of the loss of Normandy, and daily contact with his master and frequent conversations with old soldiers like Basset and Hanson may have convinced him, too, that the English presence in France could not be allowed to become merely a thing of the past. Nationalist sentiment and an interest in history, as well as a desire to display his literary knowledge, also played

---

58 Worcester, *Boke of Noblesse*, pp. 30–33, 71–74, 83–85.

a part. On the eve of Edward IV's invasion of France, fifteen or more years after Fastolf's death, the work was actually presented to a king of England about to invade France but the precise circumstances are not clear. It may be that Worcester had already adapted the text for Edward, and that his additions concerning Sir John – stories on the old man's authority or references to his successful activities which all seem to be last-minute insertions – were only done when he realised how much of an asset Fastolf's name was. It could have been Edward himself or some-one close to him who expressed an interest in the old soldier; Edward may also have been well pleased with a piece of propaganda that ended so conveniently with an injunction to nobles and commons to help finance the war and provided a historical precedent for his benevolences![59] The circumstances of the gift to Richard III of these two texts is as difficult to assess as Richard's attitude to France and its conquest, to which we will return.

Knightly Training: Theory and Exercise

Even a comparatively pedestrian English romance like the *Siege of Melayne* (Charlemagne's rescue of Milan from the Saracens), written *c.* 1400, could rise to oratory when describing the main themes of chivalry. The duke of Normandy has been fatally wounded by the pagans and makes his dying speech to Roland asking him to commend him 'to all chevalrye', to knight his son and to see him made duke in his father's place:

> Bid hym hawkes and houndes forgoo
> And to dedis of armes hym doo,
>   Thase craftes forto konn;
> Appon the cursede Sarazens forto werre,
> Venge me with dynte of spere,
>   ...
> A, Rowlande! Byhaulde nowe whatt I see'...
> Loo! I see our vawarde ledde to heven

---

59 Like most authors of his time Worcester had to peddle his wares and profit was probably uppermost in his mind in 1475. E.g. in 1473 he offered the translation of *De senectute* to William Waynflete, Bishop of Winchester, but was not rewarded, see Harvey, *William Worcestre, Itineraries*, p. 252.

With angells songe and merye steven   [voice]
Reghte as thay faughte in the felde![60]

In a speech of thirty short lines some of the main tenets of chivalry are summarised: loyalty to one's country, king and family, the training field of hunting, which must be given up at last in favour of real war, the ultimate goal of fighting the pagans and, at the end, the assured and glorious reward of marching into heaven as Christian soldiers in full military formation. It is a simple viewpoint and has never gone out of fashion.

The road to this heaven was a long one, however, and the young man had to start early to master all the accomplishments that would make him a knight in the eyes of the world and help him reach his final goal. In *Ipomedon* the young hero, who is to become the best knight in the world, is taught in childhood 'to read, sing, carol, dance, hunt, hawk, joust and tourney'. These accomplishments appear to be given in a more or less rising scale of importance.[61] Continual physical training in the shape of hunting and exercise in arms was given first priority by all writers on the subject of chivalry, but many mention the need of theoretical grounding as well. The *Order of Chivalry*[62] advises going to jousts and tournaments, and hunting the hart and the boar for 'in doyinge these thynges the knyghtes excercyse them to armes for 'to mayntene thordre of knighthode'. The author is equally clear, however, that a knight needs a 'textbook' on chivalry, hence the composition of the book itself. Vegetius' *De re militari*'s main, endlessly quoted lesson is again a need for continuous exercise, but balanced by the use of books. Vegetius praises the Athenians for having made such 'bookys and reweles, and commaunded the maystres of her yonge chivalrie to teche and rede thilke bookys to the yonge werriours'[63]. Worcester's *Boke of Noblesse* was another book for soldiers and commanders, though it cannot be called a manual and was not meant for the beginner. It stresses what a 'riche tresour' is a well-trained army and gives examples of battles lost by men no longer 'accustomed' to war, or won by a small company of thoroughly trained ones.[64]

---

60 'Sege of Melayne', in Mills, *Six Middle English Romances*, p. 9, lines 295–324.
61 Kölbing, *Ipomedon*, p. 324. Meale, 'The Middle English romance of Ipomedon', pp. 153–54, stresses the story's importance as a didactic tale of courtesy. In the version discussed by Meale the emphasis on the hero's education is greater than in the text owned by Richard.
62 Byles, *Ordre of Chyvalry*, p. 31; the italics are ours.
63 BL, MS Royal 18 A xii, f. 49. Lester, *The Earliest English Translation of Vegetius*, pp. 103–04.
64 Worcester, *Boke of Noblesse*, pp. 26–29.

How seriously did Richard as duke or king take these and similar injunctions to hunt, joust and read? We do not have any book of hunting that he owned, but his interest in *Tristan* and *Ipomedon* when a young man may have been partly inspired by their both being hunters *par excellence*.[65] There is plenty of evidence of hunting at the royal court in Edward IV's time and in Richard's. The king and his court needed their 'disport' and there was an elaborate hierarchy of officials, animals, parks, forests and chases to provide the most royal hunting and hawking. The English court could lay on an elegant party for Louis de Bruges, Lord of Gruuthuse, at Windsor in 1472,[66] and a more jolly and relaxed outing was organised by Edward IV for the mayor and aldermen of London in 1478.[67] During the last months of his reign in anticipation of a military campaign Richard made extensive use of the hunting around Nottingham, where there was a park and a lodge appropriately called the 'ermitage'.[68] As king, Richard was as energetic as any other in preserving his game, guarding against over-hunting and poaching.[69]

Hunting, however enjoyable and useful, was not the real thing. Ipomedon is supremely skilful as a hunter, his expertise may prove his social status and make his lady fall in love with him, but he is still suspected of a lack of 'manhood', and he can only genuinely establish his reputation by performing deeds of arms and participating in tournaments. There is no evidence of Richard's participation in a joust or tournament, but it is unlikely he could have avoided them as an adolescent because they were an essential part of the training for war once basic skills had been learnt. We can also safely assume that he was at least a spectator on several of the more splendid 'staged' occasions. The reports of the great tournament at Smithfield in June 1467, when the Bastard of Burgundy, half-brother to the future Duke Charles, came to answer the challenge of Anthony Woodville, Lord Scales, do not mention Richard's presence: he was only fourteen years old at the time and may have been in Warwick's household

---

65 For the hunting in these texts, see 'R III's books II' pp. 328–29; and 'R III's books X', pp. 30–31. For the physical and moral benefits of hunting as portrayed in the prologue of Gaston Phébus's classic on the sport (trans. by Richard's great-uncle), see Strubel, 'Ecrire la chasse', pp. 491–502.

66 Kingsford, *English Historical Literature*, pp. 382–88.

67 *The Great Chronicle*, pp. 228–29.

68 Kendall, *Richard III*, pp. 436–37; *Harl. 433*, vol. 1, p. 208; vol. 2, p. 216.

69 *Harl. 433*, vol. 1, p. 158; vol. 2, pp. 117, 142, 216, 219.

in the north or overlooked by the chroniclers of the event. Olivier de
La Marche, the Burgundian courtier and expert on court ceremony, who
was present, makes mention of *l'admiral* as one of the officials who formally allows the participants to enter the lists. Richard had been 'admiral
of the sea' since at least August 1462 and it is just possible that he is the
person referred to.[70]

In 1478 during the festivities of the wedding of young Richard, Duke
of York, and Anne Mowbray, Richard fulfilled a ceremonial role suitable
to his rank as duke and constable. He did not take part in the tournament
that followed.[71] It is likely that in the week after Richard's coronation
another tournament was held. The relevant sources have disappeared, but
since such festivities were part of the coronations of Elizabeth Woodville,
Henry VII and Elizabeth of York there is no reason to assume that
Richard made an exception during the splendid celebrations of his own
accession.[72] Finally there is Caxton's well-known exhortation to Richard
III in his epilogue to the *Order of Chivalry*, that 'twyes of thryes in a yere
or at lest ones he wold do crye Iustes of pees to thende that every knight
shold ... tornoye one ageynste one or ii ageynst ii. And the best to have a
prys, a dyamond or Iewel suche as shold please the prynce'.[73] Is this a mere
repetition of Lull's own request or did Caxton really feel that the number
of tournaments held in recent years had fallen off?

As regards Richard's use of textbooks on war and the preparation for
war, Vegetius' *De re militari* is the main text to consider: it was a purely
practical book, of which a copy was actually made for Richard. That soldiers have to be well trained and commanders well prepared is what the
book's 'philosophy' amounts to, but the fact that such as John of Salisbury
and Giles of Rome quoted Vegetius extensively gave an additional, spurious theoretical aura to the manual. Vegetius' practical examples were
borrowed by others to *illustrate* in truly Aristotelian fashion their own
arguments and prove their point. These medieval commentators were
greatly attracted by his emphasis on constant training: 'Thorugh exercise

---

70 For this event see mainly Anglo, 'Anglo-Burgundian feats of arms', pp. 271–83. For La
    Marche's memoirs see edition by Beaune and d'Arbaumont, vol. 3, pp. 48–56; *l'admiral* could
    be a mistake or copying error for *marechal* or *connetable*.

71 Black, *Illustrations of Ancient State and Chivalry*, pp. 27–40.

72 Sutton and Hammond, *Coronation*, p. 46.

73 Byles, *Ordre of Chyvalry*, p. 124.

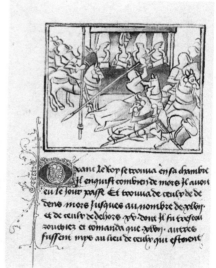

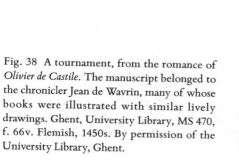

Fig. 38 A tournament, from the romance of *Olivier de Castile*. The manuscript belonged to the chronicler Jean de Wavrin, many of whose books were illustrated with similar lively drawings. Ghent, University Library, MS 470, f. 66v. Flemish, 1450s. By permission of the University Library, Ghent.

texclude slouth'. Inspired by this, Lydgate the monk, for instance, in the prologue to his *Troy Book* assumes that Prince Henry (later Henry V),

> He besyeth evere, and ther-to is so fayn
> To hawnte [practise] his body in pleies marcyal,
> Thorough exercise texclude slouth at al,
> After the doctrine of Vygecius.[74]

Soldiers among the book's readers were equally impressed: as late as 1805 the prince de Ligne thought it should be in every general's pocket. For a soldier and commander like Richard, and many of his contemporaries, the book had much to offer: it gave sound advice and they had only to follow it.

The advice set out in Willam Worcester's *Boke of Noblesse* was not of such practical use. It was focused on the war in France and was old-fashioned by Richard's time, but it may have offered material to the king and his commanders for a discussion of the possibilities and problems of invasion and occupation. The knowledgeable comments of Sir John Fastolf preserved in the Collection of documents that accompanied the *Boke* may have been especially appreciated for their practical usefulness.

---

74 *Lydgate's Troy Book*, vol. 1, lines 86–89; *u, v* and *yogh* modernised.

Ey commence le premier chapitre du liure de frontin

our la decla
ration de la
premiere
soubtilite

contenant que on doit
es fais de guerre et de
bataille tresbien celer
ce que on veult faire.

Fig. 39 Frontinus teaching young knights. Grisaille miniature from a manuscript containing Vegetius' *De re militari* and Frontinus' *Strategemata*, both in French translation. The initial has the coat of arms of the Wavrin family. Flemish, 1450–75. The Hague, Royal Library, MS 73 J 22, f. 93. By permission of the Royal Library.

Richard's Reputation as a Soldier

Few people have denied Richard some personal merit as a soldier and commander.[75] For Pietro Carmeliano, an Italian scholar in need of patronage, he
was unequalled in the prudent keeping of peace and waging of war, a veri-
table *christianus imperator*;[76] at the other end of the scale there is the statement
that 'Even his hostile critics did not stoop to deny his martial prowess on that
day [of Bosworth]'.[77] Apart from a 'reputation for military valour' Richard
has also been given a 'professed taste for war', a statement apparently founded
on his rejection of the treaty with Louis XI and his campaigns in Scotland.[78]
Any deprecation of a taste for war is, however, entirely anachronistic. As
mentioned above 'noble' men were expected to have such a 'taste', even an
aptitude, for war: men admired their own energy and aggression and the
panoply of chivalry was devoted to showing them off. Kings who did not
take an active part in these wargames, like Henry VI, failed to command the
respect of the 'naturally' warlike among their subjects.

Whatever his personal inclination – and our present-day judgment
– Richard did conform and behave as expected: at eighteen he took an
active part in his brother's campaign to regain the throne. He fought
at Barnet and was sufficiently in the thick of battle to get wounded. At
Tewkesbury he successfully led the left wing.[79] Richard's role at Barnet
gained him a literary comparison to one of the Nine Worthies, the great
heroes of chivalry, Hector of Troy:

> The duke of Glocetter, that nobill prynce,
>   Yonge of age and victorius in batayle,
> To the honoure of Ectour that he myghte comens,
>   Grace hym folowith, fortune, and good spede.
>   I suppose hes the same that clerkis of rede,
> Fortune hathe hym chosyn, and forthe wyth hym wall goo,
> Her husbonde to be, the will of God is soo.[80]

---

75 E.g. Ferguson, *Indian Summer*, p. 168: '... the militarily impeccable but otherwise
reprehensible Richard III'.
76 For Carmeliano see ch. 3 above.
77 Ross, *Richard III*, p. 225.
78 *Ibid.*, p. 191.
79 E.g. Hammond, *Barnet and Tewkesbury*, pp. 76, 95.
80 BL, MS Royal 17 D xv, f. 327; printed in Wright, *Political Songs*, vol. 2, pp. 271–82.

In his own book of the story of Troy Richard could read about Hector's virtues: '... a knight of unheard valour ... Of the sons of King Priam, there was none who was distinguished by as great a spirit as Hector ... No offensive or improper word ever left his mouth'.[81] The London author also singled out Hastings and Clarence, and Earl Rivers was especially praised for his defence of London from the Bastard of Fauconberg. Although the likening to Hector was standard panegyric, it was no mean compliment and Richard is the only character compared to a named hero.

To Edward's French enterprise in 1475 Richard contributed apparently more men than any other English noble[82] and was therefore arguably enthusiastic for the campaign. During the conference at Picquigny at which peace was made with Louis XI in return for a pension, Richard was absent *comme mal content* at this treaty, but later, it is said, he had second thoughts and visited the French king at Amiens, apparently accepting a gift of *vaiselle et ... chevaux bien accoutres*.[83] The French historian Philippe de Commines, an expert at subtle calumny, implied – and modern historians have accepted – that Richard became reconciled to the purchased peace when he accepted Louis's presents. It is equally possible, however, that Richard viewed the visit to the French king as an opportunity to meet him personally and size him up, the acceptance of the presents being a matter of courtesy to both Edward IV and Louis XI. We catch a similar glimpse of Richard on the day of Picquigny itself, having a look at the French army: *monsieur l'admiral de France montra au duc de Clochetre et aultres seigneurs l'armee du roy de France, qui estoit en plain champ* ('the admiral of France showed the duke of Gloucester and other lords the army of the King of France which was drawn up in the field').[84] It has a ring of truth: what commander would forgo the opportunity of having a good look at the opposing army, as well as at its commander. It also indicates

---

81 Meek, trans., *Guido delle Colonne. Historia destructionis Troiae*, pp. 43, 84, and see also ch. 7 below.

82 Scofield, *Edward IV*, vol. 2, p. 117.

83 Commines' memoirs, bk. 4, ch. 10 (Jones, trans. p. 259): 'plate and well equipped horses'. Richard's disapproval became widely known; Molinet, *Chronique*, vol. 1, p. 109, mentions no other objectors and does not suggest that Richard later accepted the peace.

84 Commines, *Mémoires*, ed. Dupont, vol. 3., pp. 307–08, preuve 27. The admiral also visited the French army. The same report from Amiens goes on to say: 'And while the King of France was at Amiens, the said English each came in peace and the King had them made very welcome'. Amiens is only 10 miles from Picquigny.

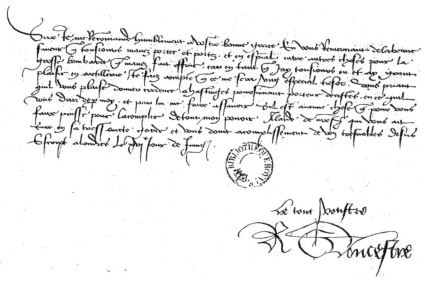

Fig. 40 Letter from Richard of Gloucester to Louis XI, 16 June [1480], thanking the king for his gift of a 'great bombard'. The heading: *Au roy, mon treshonnoure seigneur et cousin* is on the other side of the paper. The whole of the subscription appears to be in Richard's own hand. Paris, BN, MS fr. 2908, f. 13, item 1. By permission of the Bibliothèque Nationale.

Gloucester did not distance himself from the scene of the treaty, only from the actual interview on the bridge.

One small incident five years later continues this 'story'. On 16 June 1480 Richard wrote to Louis XI to thank him for

> the good favour you have always shown me and still show me, and among other things especially for the great bombard which you caused to be presented to me, for I have always taken and still take great pleasure in artillery and I assure you it will be a special treasure to me. I pray you … let me know if there is anything I could do for you …

This conventional letter is in the same mode as Richard's letters to Louis when he was king.[85] In 1480 Edward IV was still hesitating between a French and a Burgundian alliance and Louis was seeking the support of Edward's counsellors for the cause of France; his ambassadors had been in England since February and had probably conveyed the bombard

---

85 For a full text and discussion, present authors, 'Richard of Gloucester and *la grosse bombarde*'.

to the duke. As England declared war on the Scots in May the bombard may have been immediately useful against Louis's allies, the Scots. The interesting facts are that Louis XI gave Richard a bombard – the equivalent of giving a young man his own aeroplane nowadays – rather than anything else,[86] and that Richard confessed in an otherwise short and formal letter to a liking for guns, a liking of which Louis may have known and which there is no reason to doubt as genuine. Richard's known devotion to St Barbara, the patron saint of gunners and gunmakers and especially invoked against sudden death, may be relevant. Nor would Richard have been unusual among his contemporaries in liking guns: Louis XI actively promoted their development; Edward IV built up an impressive artillery train; and Louis of Gruuthuse had a gun (mortar) as his personal crest. By Richard's day they were an accepted and very important part of the equipment of any general in pursuit of victory.[87]

Richard's foreign policy provides meagre evidence about his attitude to large-scale foreign war and the particular attractions of an invasion of France. Nevertheless it seems to have been the fear he inspired in France as a potential aggressor which was to be a major cause of his defeat at Bosworth.[88] He succeeded to a difficult legacy: on 23 December 1482 Louis XI and Maximilian of Austria, the widower of the duchess of Burgundy, had reached an agreement in the treaty of Arras that excluded England. Louis had ceased some time before to pay Edward IV the 'pension' agreed at the treaty of Picquigny in 1475, and now he repudiated the proposed alliance between Edward's eldest daughter and the dauphin who was instead promised to Maximilian's daughter. Within the month Edward's parliament was discussing war and voting supplies for defence. To inflame English public opinion sections of the violated treaty of 1475 and the clause of the 1482 treaty repudiating Princess Elizabeth

86 We are grateful to Ian Eaves for discussing this gift with us.
87 See Vale, *War and Chivalry*, pp. 129–46, for a summary of evidence and arguments about the use of firearms in the 15th century. Large guns were usually given names; unfortunately the name Richard gave to his bombard is not known.
88 The best analysis of Richard's foreign policy in this respect is Davies, 'Richard III, Brittany and Henry Tudor', pp. 110–26. For important details, Hanham, *The Celys*, ch. 11; and Davies, 'The alleged "sack of Bristol", pp. 230–39. See also Ross, *Richard III*, pp. 191–92, 194–203 (*The Promise of Matrimony* is not mentioned); and Grant, 'Foreign affairs under Richard III', pp. 113–32.

were printed and circulated, underlining the treachery of the French and making them the special focus of hostility.[89]

When Richard became king he was faced with a nation already inclined to war with the treacherous French. What expectations were as to the form which the war might take and its extent is difficult to gauge. As he enjoyed a reputation for disagreeing with the treaty of Picquigny, both Richard's subjects and the French might expect an aggressive policy from him. Richard was offered help against France by Castile as early as the summer of 1483, and was continually being urged to action by Maximilian who was grateful for anything that might distract the attention of the King of France from the Low Countries, the safety and peace of which were also of prime importance to England's leading merchants. Until the death of Louis XI on 30 August 1483, Brittany also hoped for English aid against France. From Louis's death to the end of Richard's reign, relations between France, Maximilian, England, Brittany and Scotland consisted of a series of minor diplomatic exchanges, truces, and small military or piratical campaigns mostly at sea; it was a time when any policy or alliance was only retained as long at it accorded with the self-interest of the five rulers, each of whom were plagued by their own internal rebels.

It seems to be certain, however, that for a considerable portion of Richard's reign after Louis's death and particularly after January 1484, the regency government of France feared that the English king might attack France in strength.[90] From 8 June 1484 England and Brittany enjoyed a precarious truce; London merchants were expecting war with France in the summer and in June and July Richard III was conducting naval operations at Scarborough against the French and Scots. In August Richard ordered his subjects to cease piratical attacks on all foreign shipping except that of France, and a French attack on Calais was feared. In September

---

89 This pamphlet, *The Promise of Matrimony*, survives in one copy, once bound in BL, MS Royal 17 D xv, now BL, IB 55451; it is not certain whether Caxton or Machlinia printed it. Published Ellis, *Archaeologia*, 32 (1847), pp. 325–31, and in facsimile, Picot and Stein, *Recueil de pièces*, pp. 233–38, 301–03; and see *John Vale's Book*, pp. 253–56, for the text of a contemporary ms. copy and other relevant documents.

90 Davies, 'Richard III, Brittany and Henry Tudor', esp. p. 121. By January 1484 the French people, especially in Picardy and Normandy, were asking for protection, Bernier, ed., *Journal des États généraux*, pp. 314–15, 592–93.

Richard concluded a truce with Scotland,[91] and about the same date
France heard alarmingly exaggerated rumours of promised English aid to
Brittany in the shape of a contingent of archers. In October Henry Tudor
fled to France and the French regent's support for his invasion of England
was the most concrete result of the French conviction that Richard III
needed to be kept busy at home. At any point, therefore, from about
January 1484 especially, hopes of a French campaign may have been sufficiently vocal to have prompted the young William Worcester to adapt
his father's *Boke* and Collection for the king.

The wider issues of whether Richard and his subjects viewed a large-
scale invasion to *reconquer* France as worthy of serious consideration
is another matter: alliances were uncertain, the logistical problems of
invading and then keeping the territories were great, and the experiences
of the 1450s and 1475 were not encouraging. The supposed attractions of
profit to English soldiers of all ranks, if the war were successful and the
advantages to the king of keeping the unruly elements of English society
occupied, carried increasingly less weight as regards a French war of conquest: the conclusion of the invasions by Edward IV and Henry VII in
French pensions were perhaps surer signs of the times.[92] Ultimately any
discussion of an invasion of conquest by Richard is entirely speculative:
he would have to have been as motivated to seek glory as a Henry V or
as responsive to demand as Edward IV had been, and we cannot know if
he was either of those things. On the other hand, it is just possible that
Richard, as the brother of a sister who was fostering the heir of the last
duchess of Burgundy, may have regarded war with France as one of the
responsibilities of the English crown, in the same way as did Jean Molinet,

---

91 Ross, *Richard III*, p. 193, blames Richard for lack of warmth towards James III, but Pollard,
    North-Eastern England, is more positive and thinks Richard abandoned his ducal plans to
    invade Scotland because of lack of money, pp. 242–44. And see Grant, 'Foreign affairs
    under Richard III', pp. 113–32, and his 'Richard III and Scotland', pp. 127–45, and app. of
    Whitelaw's speech.

92 Discussion of this question as regards Richard is usually confused. Modern commentators not
    only regard an invasion of France as unrealistic by Richard's reign but are also unwilling to
    allow Richard to get anything right. Evidence that he did plan a foreign war is said to suggest
    an attempt to assuage trouble at home, and evidence that he decided against reconquest of the
    French territories is said to prove he faced too much rebellion in England to risk leaving the
    country. For indications that contemporary reactions may have been much more subtle, see
    the changes in many Englishmen's attitudes to the French war at earlier dates, Keen, 'The case
    of Grey v. Hastings', pp. 123–36, esp. 135–36. Compare the traditional view of Richmond,
    '1485 and all that', pp. 186–91, and Grant, 'Foreign affairs under Richard III', pp. 113–32.

the Burgundian poet and chronicler who had seen many battles, alliances and political changes in his lifetime. In July 1485, only a month before Richard's death, Molinet still looked to the island kingdom of England and its king [Neptune] for help against the dreaded French:

> ... if only Neptune, god of the seas, would rid the world of this unclean mist of trouble and discord, and not keep himself in isolation ... [93]

To turn to Richard's reputation as a commander, this seems currently to hinge on judgments of his Scots campaign of 1482; and it is unlikely there will ever be agreement on whether this was a success or not.[94] The *Crowland Chronicle* continuator, who liked neither Richard nor anything northern, testifies to Edward's dismay at Richard's wasteful expenditure and righteously regrets that such a wealthy town as Edinburgh was not sacked. In contrast to this cleric's opinion there is Edward's letter to the Pope exulting over his brother's expedition and the restoration of Berwick to England. The truth must lie in the middle. In some ways it was a model campaign, as Richard started and finished it with a given number of troops within a set period and gained what was probably the main objective by the capture of Berwick. Putting the rebel prince, the duke of Albany, on the Scots throne – if that was an objective – proved impossible since Albany received no support in his own country. Deciding the issue by a pitched battle was also impossible as no Scot turned up to fight. Despite the Crowland chronicler it is difficult to blame the English commanders for not sacking Edinburgh – there was no lack of burning and plundering on the way – or for not seeking to establish English rule in Scotland. This particular campaign, and all military and diplomatic activities in the years immediately before and after, remain debatable for lack of sources, but a recent reaction to it has been among the most positive and realistic: 'from the point of view of northern England, Gloucester's achievement in the field was anything but trivial'. He 'brought back a sense of pride to northern English society by his exploits against the old enemy'.[95]

---

93 Molinet, *Faictz et dictz*, vol. 1, p. 218.
94 *Crowland Chronicle*, pp. 146–49; Ross, *Richard III*, pp. 288–90; Scofield, *Edward IV*, vol.2, pp. 344–49; Macdougall, *James III*, pp. 168–70; the same, 'Richard III and James III', pp. 148–71; Pollard, *North-Eastern England*, pp. 235–44.
95 Pollard, *North-Eastern England*, p. 244.

In Richard III's copy of Guido delle Colonne's *Historia Troiae* there is a passage marked by two marginal comments. It concerns the great advantages of fighting to protect one's own home with relatives and friends – 'note well the fair words' a fifteenth-century hand wrote in Latin in the margin – a dictum illustrated by the image of the crow courageously defending its nest against the stronger falcon.[96] It is impossible to say if Richard wrote the marginalia, but that he would have agreed with the underlying sentiment is supported by his expressed desire to fight the Turks with 'his own people alone' (see below). Whatever may be said about the lack of support he received at Bosworth, that is also how he may have regarded the battle and his fatal effort to decide its outcome. According to Lydgate's *Siege of Thebes*, which he read in his youth:

> ... better it wer to every werryour
> Manly to deye with worship and honour,
> Than lik a coward with the lyf endure.[97]

A follower of the Stanleys put into Richard's own mouth a dramatic version of this commonplace of the chivalrous:

> He said, 'Give me my battle axe in my hand,
> Set the crown of England on my head so high,
> For by him that shope both sea and land,
> King of England this day I will die!
> One foot will I never flee
> Whilst the breath is my breast within!'[98]

Richard's Reputation as a Christian and Courtly Knight

Thoffyce of a knyght is to mayntene and deffende wymmen, wydowes and orphanes ... To doo wrong and force to wymmen, wydowes that have nede of ayde, and orphelyns that have nede of governance ... and

---

96 St Petersburg, Saltykov-Shchedrin State Public Library, MS Lat. F IV 74, f. 43: *nota bene pulcra verba*, and *nota de cornice et eius strenuitate* ('note the crow and its vigour'). See Cat. VII below.
97 *Lydgate's Siege of Thebes*, lines 4122–24.
98 'The Ballad of Bosworth Field', in Hales and Furnivall, *Bishop Percy's Folio Manuscript*, vol. 3, p. 257 (punctuation and spelling modernised).

to take awey fro them that is gyven to them, these thynges may not accorde to thordre of chyvalrye ...

So wrote Lull in the *Order of Chivalry*,[99] but we will never know to what degree Richard appreciated this idealistic, semi-religious treatise.[100] Their chivalric principles failed most knights and princes in their conduct towards women, the poor and those weaker than themselves whenever they stood in the way of their political or material advantage. One of the famous examples of 'realistic' behaviour of contemporary princely knights is the case of Jacqueline of Bavaria, in her own right Countess of Holland, Zeeland and Hainault, who was exploited and abandoned by that paragon of English aristocratic learning, Humphrey, Duke of Gloucester, and disinherited by Philip the 'Good', 'Grand Duke of the West'.[101]

Richard of Gloucester cannot be exonerated from similar treatment of his mother-in-law, Anne Beauchamp, Countess of Warwick in her own right, and Elizabeth Howard, Countess of Oxford.[102] We need not believe all the gruesome details of eye-witness reports recorded long after Richard's death, and Edward IV may have been eager to keep wealth and land out of the hands of political opponents, but the way in which both countesses were deprived of the greater part of their lands can hardly be called chivalrous. Probably this did not damage Richard's reputation at the time – Philip the Good's certainly survived – as most people did not expect anything else and once greed had been satisfied such behaviour could be covered up by the formal courtesies of chivalry and gifts and annuities to the victim. The reality of princes' behaviour did not mirror

---

99 Byles, *Ordre of Chyvalry*, pp. 38–39.

100 It is difficult to establish what ownership of Lull's *Order* meant by the end of the 15th century. Vanderjagt, *Qui sa vertu anoblist*, pp. 68–70, suggests that in the Burgundian court circle it was a mark of 'conservatism'. He maintains that Philip the Good and Charles the Bold ignored the work and only the 'conservative' Croy family owned a copy (Brussels, Bibliothèque Royale, MS 10493–7). The dukes, however, had copies 'in the family', and the experienced and literate soldier and historian of England, Jean de Wavrin, also owned the *Order* (Paris, BN, MS fr. 1973); his taste in books was not 'conservative'. In BL, MS Royal 14 E ii, made in Flanders for Edward IV or his sons, the *Order* was used to fill out a volume of didactic chivalric texts, which suggests it was still reasonably popular, as does the choice of the text by the bookseller, Caxton.

101 E.g. Vaughan, *Philip the Good*, pp. 31–53. See also ch. 9 below.

102 Hicks, 'Descent, partition and extinction: the Warwick inheritance', pp. 116–28; and his 'Last days of Elizabeth, Countess of Oxford', pp. 76–95; Crawford, 'Victims of attainder: the Howard and de Vere women', pp. 59–74.

the wishes of Lull or the authors of romances, and yet the main interest of romances such as the *Prose Tristan*, and the section owned by Richard in particular, is likely to have been its chivalric adventures, the knight errantry, which Sir Thomas Malory loved so much. Malory's readers liked it, too – his publisher Caxton was sure of that – and Richard may have shared that liking. Knight errantry was a noble activity for an honourable man as defined by Tristan himself in another part of the *Prose Tristan*:

> I am a knight errant, and knights errant always wander through the kingdom of Logres and other countries in search of adventures, because, as far as they are able and have the opportunity, they must defend the weak against the strong and uphold loyalty wherever they are. And if they come across any wrong done to a knight, a lady or a maiden and they can put it right, they must do so immediately; and if they do not, they can no longer be considered knights or men of honour, for they will have failed to keep their oath to God, to all chivalry and the world as well.[103]

Philip the 'Good', Edward IV and Richard III were never knights errant, but they knew from their books the ideals that *should* govern their conduct.

Another instance of Richard's failure to be an ideal knight was the protection of his nephews. If he did not kill them he certainly deprived them of their inheritance, however needful, justifiable and even inevitable his action may have seemed to him. His own defence would probably have been that he wished to serve the 'common good' of the realm which could never benefit from the rule of an illegitimate minor. How Richard wanted to be seen in his earlier role as protector can only be gleaned from Chancellor Russell's draft speech for the opening of Edward V's first parliament, which Richard may have read and approved of, if not inspired:[104] the Protector is the 'stable land' in which is to be found the 'suerte or fermenesse' of the world. He will protect the kingdom against external and internal enemies and emulate the Roman Lepidus who fulfilled the office of protector of the young king of Egypt to such perfection that it was not certain whether his charge eventually owed more to his father or to

---

103 Tristan 'on chivalry', quoted by Baumgartner, *Le Tristan en prose*, p. 181. This passage from the *Prose Tristan* does not occur in Richard's ms.
104 Nichols, *Grants*, pp. xxxvii–xlix; Chrimes, *English Constitutional Ideas*, pp. 168–78.

his guardian. The source of the story, Valerius Maximus,[105] saw Lepidus' conduct as an example of *fides publica*, loyalty to the state, and Richard no doubt would have wished to have his subsequent progress to the throne regarded in the same light. The 'loyalty' that 'bound' him need not always have been to an individual when a wider application was more relevant, or more opportune.[106]

Faithfulness to and the care of one's companions was major feature of knightly conduct: Richard's chantry at Queens' College Cambridge established in 1477 included prayers for

> the soules of Thomas Par, John Milewater, Christofre Wursley, Thomas Huddleston, John Harper and all other gentilmen and yoman servanders and lovers of the saide duke of Gloucetr', the wiche were slayn in his service at the batelles of Bernett, Tukysbery or at any other feldes or jorneys ...

The specific names and battles mentioned record the effect on Richard of his first military campaign; he did his duty to the dead.[107]

The crusade played an important part in chivalric ideals in Richard's lifetime – among his books it fitted best with the preoccupations of the *Order of Chivalry*. Fighting the infidel was still the best justification for war and aggression. Though western Europe was at a safe distance from the actual theatre of war, people were conscious of the Turkish threat; princes all had the defence of Christendom as the *next* item on their agenda, to be tackled just as soon as their own dynastic and regional problems had been solved. In 1480 people in England and everywhere in western Europe had the danger brought home to them when the long-expected attack of the Turkish fleet on the Hospitaller stronghold of Rhodes finally took place. The island was besieged from early June to the end of July; news was avidly sought in England, large sums of money

---

105 Valerius Maximus, *Acta et Facta Memorabilia*, bk. 6, ch. 1, 'De fide publica'.
106 Two other less well-known examples of a lack of chivalry in Richard are the account in Wavrin of the plan to kill Martin del See in 1471, and the circumstances surrounding the execution of the Bastard of Fauconberg. The first is a curious story unlikely to be confirmed or explained; the latter does not appear to redound particularly to Richard's discredit. Discussed in 'R III's books XIII', pp. 198–99, and Britnell, 'Richard Duke of Gloucester and the death of Thomas Fauconberg', pp. 174–84. For Richard's motto, see chs 5 and 11.
107 Ross, 'Some "servants and lovers" of Richard in his youth', pp. 2–4. And see Keen, 'Brotherhood in arms', pp. 1–17, and Allmand, 'Changing views of the soldier', p. 182.

were collected in England and Ireland to support the Hospitallers, and Sir John Weston, the prior of the Order of St John in England departed to assist the grand master in Rhodes. Despite Edward IV's objections to so much bullion, and the prior leaving the country, he was later to own an English translation of the best-known contemporary account of the siege and its successful conclusion for the knights; and it is likely that Richard, too, knew of this text.[108]

Richard does appear to have had a genuine interest in the crusading movement. The evidence is not extensive but it is strongly personal. First there is the king's well-known, self-assured remark to the admiring German visitor, Nicholas von Poppelau, telling him that given the opportunity he would defeat the Turks with only his own people to help him. Secondly, there is the surviving fragment of what may have been a 'crusading litany' among the additions to Richard's book of hours. This text appears to be unique and may at least point to an awareness of the *languor* (inactivity) that affected western leaders as soon as they were actually asked to unite, organise themselves and rise above chivalric display. The litany beseeches God to destroy 'the peoples of the heathen' and preserve the earth from desolation. 'May your anger, Lord, now be lifted from your people'; its words are conventional but none the less forceful.[109]

Equally important in this context is the evidence of Richard's veneration for the oil given by the Virgin Mary to St Thomas Becket to anoint the English kings at their coronation. Divine assistance against all enemies, both Christian and pagan, was expected from the holy oil: the first king to be anointed with it would recover Normandy and Aquitaine, 'build churches in the holy land and chase all the heathen from Babylon', and all kings who used it would be vigorous champions of the Church. When 'carried in the breast' the oil would bestow victory over all enemies. Richard III was the king who decided that the holy relic of the oil should be kept with the other regalia in Westminster Abbey, making the particular reservation that it should be returned to him 'whensoever it shall

---

108 Hanham, *Cely Letters*, pp. 103, 107, 108 (nos 114, 117, 118). Tyerman, *England and the Crusades*, p. 356. Kaye/ Caoursin, *Siege of Rhodes. Manual*, vol. 8, [86].
109 See ch. 3 above.

please hym to ask it'![110] The overall message seems to be clear: Richard was both aware and moved by the contemporary demand for a crusade.

The Display of Chivalry

There is evidence that Richard appreciated the outward display of knighthood as well as kingship. As a boy he may have been impressed by it, as a man his own contribution to the 'public face' of chivalry could inspire the next generation. When he went to inspect the French army on the day of Picquigny it may have given him the kind of pleasure that a similar visit gave to Sir John Chandos over a hundred years earlier shortly before the battle of Poitiers 'to see such a great number of noble knights newly armed and equipped'; to be defeated by such a fine company would be no disgrace, to defeat them would bring great glory.[111] Richard's *Grandes chroniques* would have provided him with many other similarly splendid scenes.

He took seriously the ceremonial side of the office of constable, a post he held from 1469,[112] especially the supervision of the heralds, which he shared with the marshal. He issued a set of ordinances for the reformation of the office,[113] in which the heralds were above all instructed to record the ceremonies and the deeds of chivalry. By letters patent of 2 March 1484 Richard made the heralds and pursuivants a body corporate and conveyed to them the house 'Coldharbour' for the use of the twelve principal heralds, 'a high mark of royal favour'.[114] Richard himself owned several heraldic manuscripts, privately and professionally: a 'general' roll and an ordinary, neither of which survive, and he may have had a copy made of the 'Salisbury Roll', the splendid pictorial roll of the earls of Salisbury

---

110 Sutton and Hammond, *Coronation*, pp. 7–10. A French prophecy developed in Charles V's time and later by Charles VII said a king of France would drive out the English and go on a crusade, Chaume, 'Une prophetie'.

111 Froissart, *Chroniques*, quoted Barnie, *War in Medieval Society*, p. 73.

112 In this capacity Richard also sat in judgment, together with the marshal, John Mowbray, Duke of Norfolk, on a number of defeated opponents after the battle of Tewkesbury; see Squibb, *High Court of Chivalry*, ch. 1; Keen, 'Treason trials under the law of arms', pp. 85–103, on such a court and its authority. It is possible that Richard also presided as constable at a summary trial of the Bastard of Fauconberg. See also chs 6, 7 below.

113 Wagner, *Heralds of England*, p. 68.

114 *Ibid.*, pp. 123 ff., 131. Marks and Payne, *British Heraldry*, item 78.

and their ancestors. Richard must have also been acquainted with a roll-chronicle made by John Rous to celebrate the Beauchamp and Neville earls of Warwick, as well as with the Beauchamp Pageant, the pictorial life of Richard Beauchamp, both ending with himself and his son in right of his wife, and both full of heraldic and chivalric display.[115] The ceremonial of the coronation vigil procession and the investiture of the prince of Wales show Richard exploiting and enjoying chivalric display exactly as other contemporary princes did. He also was no exception in his political and ceremonial use of the English orders of chivalry and the lower orders of knighthood.

One of the privileges of a knight was to create others. During the Scottish campaigns, 1481–82, Richard as Duke of Gloucester dubbed seventy-five knights and knights-banneret.[116] After a military expedition of undoubted success knighthood in the field was one of the expected rewards. Few of those taking part in such extempore ceremonies would have remembered the idealistic strictures of Lull's *Order* that the prospective knight be virtuous and prepared to receive the honour, and that the donor be himself a knight of undoubted honour and virtue. No details of the feast and ceremonies – if there were any – accompanying these dubbings by Richard are known: it is unlikely the knights received any of the instruction hoped for by Lull; they may have been expected to confess and hear mass. Such knighting in the field was essentially a secular ceremony, a reward for fighting, and only the great orders of chivalry had refined their ceremonies in line with the vision of such as Lull. Knighthood received in the field was one of the most ancient rewards for prowess and in theory mere martial merit was sufficient to raise a man to such status, but in practice it was conferred, by Richard's lifetime, on those who had the family and means to support the rank. These considerations would have guided Richard of Gloucester's choice of knights in 1481–82 just as it guided his choice of young men of good family, county standing and sufficient wealth summoned to become knights of the Bath at his coronation – and rank and wealth were also among Lull's qualifications for knighthood.

Knights created by Richard as king included the Spanish ambassador at the investiture of the Prince of Wales in York (1483) and two of his three

---

115 For all these mss see ch. 6 below.
116 Metcalf, *A Book of Knights*, pp. 5–7.

mayors of London, Edmund Shaa (1482–83) and Thomas Hill (1484–85). The choice of these recipients was guided by his desire to reward supporters and friends and encourage diplomatic friendship. Following the same considerations he gave the Order of the Garter to Sir John Conyers, the Earl of Surrey, Lord Lovell, Richard Ratcliffe, Thomas Burgh, Lord Stanley and Richard Tunstall. No foreign princes were admitted in his short reign, nor did Richard receive the Golden Fleece.[117] He never presided at the April feast of the fraternity of St George at Windsor: he ordered the accustomed livery to be issued in 1484,[118] but his son had recently died and he did not attend; in 1485 the day before the feast Richard ordered Lord Maltravers to observe the full ceremony in his absence and it was probably the queen's death in March that prevented his attendance.[119]

Conclusion: Richard III and Chivalry

Richard appears to have been a knight *sans peur*, but it would seem hard to maintain that he was *sans reproche*, and to attribute to him an 'unsophisticated and chivalrous heart' is to oversimplify his character.[120] To be a prince and at the same time a paragon of chivalry was impossible.

Did Richard fail as a knight in his own eyes and did he use his books to set himself a standard? He probably regarded himself as a reasonably successful soldier, who had had the right training and read the right books. His activities as a young man under his brother's command, and his own campaigns in Scotland and against the 1483 rebels were well organised and successful. He can hardly have doubted that he would crush the Tudor rebellion as well. His wish to go on crusade may have been genuine – though the problem of France would have to be solved first[121] – and he may have considered himself a failure as a Christian soldier and champion of the Church so long as he took no action. Intoning his crusading litany every day, alone or with

---

117 Ashmole, *Institutions ... of the Garter*, p. 712.
118 *Harl. 433*, vol. 2, p. 129.
119 *Ibid.*, pp. 215–16.
120 Ferguson, *Indian Summer*, p. 139, a view based on the work of P.M. Kendall.
121 N. Pons, 'Guerre de Cent Ans et polémistes du xve siècle', esp. pp. 148–49, for the contemporary view, held in France at least, that the Anglo-French war had been started by the devil to prevent a crusade.

his chaplain, may have been a genuine and necessary outlet at a time when people had no doubts about the power and effect of prayer.

Harsh political actions such as the extinction of Henry VI and the confiscation of the lands of the countesses of Oxford and Warwick probably did not cause the duke of Gloucester and brother of Edward IV any loss of sleep. Deposing and disinheriting his own nephews was another matter, but he would not have seen that as failing in his 'knighthood', rather it was his duty as a prince and ruler. If he disposed of them as well, he, too, like his contemporaries, knew that the death of his son was divine retribution, played out finally at the battle of Bosworth.[122] He, too, knew the stories, not only of Herod, but of the wicked uncles and tyrants of history and romance, such as the wicked uncle-protector of the hero of *Jason* translated and printed by Caxton, probably in 1477, for the future Edward V, by the licence of Edward IV. At times Richard may have linked these stories to himself.

Nevertheless, it is likely that Richard was untroubled by the ambiguity of some of the precepts of chivalry or by the clash between courtly display and crude reality: he had been born to it. Ostentation and magnificence was as natural to him as to his brother, Edward IV, the Valois Dukes of Burgundy, or any of his social equals. To do less than others would have been foolish in the extreme, and there was great similarity, and continuity, between the ceremonial display of the courts of Henry VI, Edward IV, Richard III and Henry VII, as well as between the Burgundian ducal court and those of the kings of France and England. Indications of individuality are few and faint. The 'real' Richard III must be sought in such small personal things as we know about him and the books he owned should be prime witnesses, but even their evidence remains difficult to interpret and subject to our prejudice. He owned the usual chivalric texts, and as regards his 'chivalry' it can be tentatively concluded that he was an active, practical and ambitious man, both in politics and straightforward military matters. He was conscientious in his fulfilment of his offices and not averse to the display they, and his status, demanded; and he was as pious about the ideals of chivalry as were his princely contemporaries.

---

122 Keen, 'Introduction', to Contamine *et al.*, *Guerre et société*, pp. 12–13: '... the enormous difficulty of shaking free from the shackles of a providentialist conception of the causes of defeat and victory ...'; the part played by chance in the outcome of war was so great in the Middle Ages that 'it was hardly irrational to think more in terms of Providence, and less in terms of God's natural predeliction for the side with the bigger battalions'.

FIVE

Mirrors for Princes:
Books with a 'Handsome Title'

The book has been given a handsome title: it is called *Speculum Regale*, not because of pride in him who wrote it, but because the title ought to make those who hear it more eager to know the work itself; and for this reason, too, that if anyone wishes to be informed as to proper conduct, courtesy, or comely and precise forms of speech, he will find and see these therein along with many illustrations and all manner of patterns, as in a bright mirror. And it is called *King's Mirror*, because in it one may read of the manners of kings as well as of other men.[1]

In this way an unknown cleric introduced his *King's Mirror* to the court of Haakon IV of Norway (1217–63).[2] He also provided a neat description of the type of book he was writing. Mirrors for princes were one of the most popular forms of didactic and educational literature throughout the Middle Ages – Richard of Gloucester owned a copy of the most influential of these texts, the *De regimine principum* by Giles of Rome. The analogy of the mirror (*speculum*) in their title was applied generally to any book that provided advice and examples for all aspects of life and behaviour, not only the spiritual and not only to princes; the ultimate mirror for mankind was always the Bible:

---

1   Larson, *The King's Mirror*, p. 74.
2   Finished in 1240s, Larson, pp. 64–65. And see Bagge, *Political Thought of the 'King's Mirror'*, pp. 218–24.

Fig. 41   A typical presentation scene; it shows the author, Vasco de Lucena, presenting his translation of Xenophon's *Education of Cyrus* to Charles, Duke of Burgundy, whose arms appear on the cloth of estate. The English royal arms in the marginal decoration indicate that the manuscript was made for Edward IV. Flemish, *c.* 1470. BL, MS Royal 16 G ix, f. 7. By permission of The British Library.

Holy Scripture offers our spiritual eyes in some ways a mirror ...
There we recognise what is deformed and what is beautiful in our-
selves ... we may see in the victory of the great what we have to
imitate, and in their falls what we have to fear.
(St Gregory the Great, *Moralia*, book 8, chapter 1).[3]

Books discussing the government of states and the rule and education of
princes had flourished in classical times and formed a strong Christian
tradition from St Augustine's *De civitate dei* onwards. Closely related
and equally useful were the biographies of famous men; history was
seen as the supreme example for the present and, in particular, lives of
princes that concentrated on their education, military success or good
government could also serve as mirrors. Very popular in this genre were
Xenophon's *Education of Cyrus* and Curtius' *Life of Alexander*.[4] Recently
there has been a plea for a more precise definition of the many categories of books of this type, focusing on a distinct group of works, known
as 'mirrors of princes', which began to proliferate in the thirteenth century, promoted by the kings of France. These were inspired by St Louis's
vision of himself as an ideal king and by the new political literature
publicised by the mendicant orders. These particular, 'serene, didactic'
works set out to teach Christian ethics and morals to the laity; they
were highly authoritarian and contained a new blend of Augustinian
and Aristotelian teaching.[5] Of several texts produced at the end of the
thirteenth century that by Giles of Rome was the most important. The
promotion of the 'ideal king' was entirely appropriate to the period and

3   Bradley, 'Background of the title *Speculum*', pp. 100–15, for a full discussion of the use of
     the word 'mirror' from St Augustine (and before) to the later Middle Ages; quotation from
     St Gregory, pp. 109–10 and n. 53.
4   German scholars have attempted to list the kind of texts that can be described as 'mirrors of
     princes' (*Fürstenspiegel*). The main categories are: 1. biographies of famous men emphasising
     their government and deeds; 2. idealised, literary biographies of historical figures; 3. works
     that discuss the theoretical rules and norms by which a prince should live, illustrated by
     historical examples. Closely related are treatises that discuss the obligations of all classes and
     include rulers, instructions written by princes for their sons, and also funeral or welcoming
     speeches and poems praising a living or dead ruler and his life and deeds. See Singer,
     Fürstenspiegel, introd., esp. pp. 15–18.
5   Guenée, *States and Rulers*, pp. 69–74, for overview. Genet, *Four English Political Tracts*, pp. ix–
     xiv; quotation, p. xi. And his 'Political theory', pp. 23–24. Gilbert, *Machiavelli's 'Prince'*, esp.
     introd. and conclusion.

'a system in which everything depends on the just and good (or unjust and bad) will of the ruler'.[6]

The Model Mirror and the Perfect Prince

The 'mirror' of which Richard of Gloucester owned a copy was composed probably in 1277–79 by Giles of Rome also known as Aegidius Romanus, tutor of the future Philip IV of France (1285–1314), supposedly at the prince's request.[7] The title *De regimine principum* may be best translated as *The Guidance of Princes*.[8] Giles himself had been a pupil of St Thomas Aquinas and at an early age had joined the newly formed mendicant order of Augustinian Friars. In 1285 he became the order's first master at the university of Paris and in 1292 its prior general. During his period at the university his teaching was adopted as the official doctrine of the order and by 1304 about twenty-five of his philosophical and theological works were in use; he was regarded as one of the greatest theologians of his day. Created archbishop of Bourges in 1295, he died in 1316 at the papal court of Avignon.[9] It was Giles, following in the footsteps of his master St Thomas Aquinas, who most successfully recreated the mirror of princes in an Aristotelian tradition, blending pagan and Christian thought in a way that made any other, earlier, approach outmoded.[10] Giles followed Aristotle (and Aquinas) in considering ethics and politics to be parts of a single discipline devoted to the promotion and maintenance of human happiness. Every individual must learn to rule himself, and the moral health of each citizen, and especially of the ruler, will lead to the political health of the state and the happiness of all its members. This adoption of the notion of self-governance was not unique to Giles but his was an exceptionally elaborate treatment of the theme.

No detailed analysis of Giles's text has ever been made and it has never been made readily accessible to modern readers despite its immense

---

6   Genet, 'Political theory and local communities', p. 24.
7   Philip became king at the age of 17. For the history of Giles's work, Berges, *Fürstenspiegel*, pp. 320–28.
8   Alternatives are: 'On the Governance of Princes'; 'Government' or 'Education of Princes'.
9   Hewson, *Giles of Rome*, pp. 3–37; Scholz, *Publizistik zur Zeit Philipps des Schönen*, pp. 32–42.
10 E.g. Genet, *Four English Political Tracts*, p. xiv. Born, 'Perfect prince', pp. 502–04, on the differences between 'pre-' and 'post-Aristotelian' mirrors.

popularity in the Middle Ages: hundreds of manuscripts, twenty-seven recensions and many translations and abridgements.[11] There has been no English translation of *De regimine* since that of John Trevisa (died 1402), made for Lord Berkeley, which survives in one copy.[12] Summaries of the book's contents have been published,[13] but the full flavour of Giles's style still needs to be obtained from the Latin text.[14] 'In ethics,' he said, 'in which we search for righteousness and [learn how] to do good, we have to proceed by way of persuasion and illustration'.[15] He supported his arguments by an authoritative style that leaves no room for doubt on the part of his audience, a very orderly approach and detailed practical advice. He gives references to the works of 'the Philosopher' (Aristotle) and the other authorities in his text and he regularly recapitulates his arguments. His three books cover three main subjects: how a king should rule himself, how he should rule his household, and how he should rule his kingdom.[16] Within these books the treatise is extremely systematic, its contents divided and subdivided almost to excess. Giles's method tells of his experience in the university school-room and was ideally suited for the teaching and learning process.

Book One deals with the self-rule of the prince himself, or of any individual: the good man is in control of himself (*seipsum habet*), the bad man is not (*seipso caret*). Just as a king is not in control of his kingdom if there are some people who do not obey him, so an individual is not in control of himself if his desires (*appetitus*) do not agree with his reason (*ratio*).[17] 'Who rules himself is worthy to be made ruler or lord of others'.[18]

To be able to rule himself a prince must know everything about himself: how to live, what good things to pursue, what virtues there are

---

11 Genet, *Four English Political Tracts*, p. x.
12 Oxford, Bodleian Library, Digby MS 233, ff. 1–182, a copy that descended to Lord Berkeley's great-great-great-grand-daughter, Mary Hungerford, heiress of many titles (d. 1534), see the present authors, '*Loyaulte me lie*: another user of this motto', pp. 120–21. Childs, 'Study', pp. 79–107, in favour of Trevisa's authorship.
13 The most detailed is Berges, *Fürstenspiegel*; see also Born, 'Perfect prince', and for a short English summary, Jones, *Royal Policy of Richard II*, pp. 155–57.
14 Aegidius Romanus, *De regimine principum* ..., Rome 1556, repr. Frankfurt 1968. Our own translations are used here.
15 *Ibid.*, bk 1, pt 1, ch. 1, f. 2v.
16 *Ibid.*, bk 1, pt 1, ch. 2, passim.
17 *Ibid.*, bk 1, pt 1, ch. 3, f. 6.
18 *Ibid.*, bk 1, pt 1, ch. 3, f. 6v.

and what passions. He must be aware that there are three ways in which one can live: the pleasure-loving (*voluptuosa*), like an animal; the socially active (*politica*), like a human being; and the contemplative (*contemplativa*), like an angel. A prince should, of course, avoid the 'bestial' life and he should combine in himself the active and the contemplative, for the active life will allow him to have time for others, do great things and rule his subjects, and the contemplative will allow him to consider himself, through inward devotion and love of God, and progress (*proficiendo*) in the love of God.[19]

The prince should have all the twelve virtues: prudence, justice, strength of mind, moderation, love of honour, greatness of soul, liberality, nobility of mind, clemency, truthfulness, courtesy and a pleasant and ready wit. Giles explains that the first four are the cardinal virtues and are essential to princes, and proceeds to discuss all twelve separately, each with its opposing vice, and to what degree the ruler should possess them. Justice, according to Giles, is different from the other virtues. It is divided into two: justice according to the law (*justitia legalis*) and the justice which gives everyone his due (*justitia aequalis*) and it is the justice according to the law that he puts above all other virtues. Following Aristotle and St Thomas Aquinas, Giles states that it is, as it were, all virtues in one. This justice only exists in relation to others; just as the parts of the human body support each other when they function healthily, so the members of a state are well and virtuous if they live together according to the law. Without the law a state cannot survive and a ruler cannot rule; the prince is the living law (*lex animata*); and as each virtue is at its most perfect when it can bestow its own quality on others, so a just prince is genuinely great and virtuous if he can make others just.[20] Giles concludes that all the virtues are interconnected and if a prince lacks one he lacks them all![21]

The Second Book, on the management of the household, discusses the treatment of wives, children and servants. All men should marry; if they do not they live like beasts or gods. They should be faithful to their wives and live in friendship with them. Men should have only one wife and women only one husband. Giles is of the opinion that no one, and least of

---

19 *Ibid.*, bk 1, pt 1, ch. 3, f. 8r–v.
20 *De regimine*, bk 1, pt 2, chs 10–12.
21 *Ibid.*, bk 1, pt 2, ch. 31.

all princes, should marry a close relative, and as usual he has a three-fold argument. First, the way a man and wife live together is incompatible with the respect that relatives should feel for each other; secondly, relatives already live in amity because of their relationship and the extra bond that marriage to a stranger would forge is wasted when a prince marries a relative – and princes need every safeguard available to them. Lastly, says the friar, if conjugal love is added to the natural affection of relatives, the resulting love would be too strong and 'it is better for those who wish to be healthy in reason and understanding not to exert themselves too much in sexual love'.[22]

A large part of Book Two is devoted to the education of boys and to a lesser degree that of girls. 'Habit is like a second nature',[23] and the need to start a child's education early is emphasised. Practical details about the proper behaviour of young people, their exercise, dress and the way they should move are given. The sons of princes in particular should receive a good education because of their eventual influence over others. They should be taught the main maxims of the Christian faith, but there is no need for them to understand as much as clerics do. Good habits should be instilled into them, and they should be taught to read (*studio litterarum*). The sons of noblemen, and especially the sons of kings, must study the liberal arts: grammar, that is Latin grammar, to be able to speak correctly; dialectic, to argue subtly; rhetoric, to argue in such a way that simple people can understand. Also music, to have an innocent pastime that protects young people who have no need to work against the dangers of idleness; arithmetic, to help with the music; and geometry, the sixth science, which is needed for the seventh, astronomy. Giles, in one of his rare divergences from Aristotle, adds that astronomy used to be important but that natural philosophy and metaphysics were now far more necessary. Theology is the greatest of all, and economics, medicine and politics are also worthy of consideration. All knowledge is useful to a prince if it gives him the moral awareness which enables him to rule well.[24]

The first part of Book Three treats of the state as a whole, its origins and reason for existence. The opinions of some ancient philosophers are refuted; for instance, Giles is against the notion that holding all goods

---

22 *Ibid.*, bk 2, pt 1, ch. 11.
23 *Ibid.*, bk 2, pt 2, ch. 7, f. 181.
24 *De regimine*, bk 2, pt 2, chs 2, 6–8.

and even wives and children in common will solve all the problems of society: 'we have experienced that when people own something together they have more quarrels among themselves than when each possesses his own'.[25] The last two parts discuss the governing of the state in peace and war. Giles advises on how to encourage and maintain peace and learning and education in the kingdom. Those princes who need to maintain themselves by keeping their subjects continually at odds with each other and by promoting foreign wars to ensure they are occupied abroad, are merely tyrants. Only tyrants leave their people in ignorance. 'A real king is virtuous, a tyrant is not, but he pretends to be'.[26]

In his final chapter, before he turns to military matters and how a prince should be a good general (a section heavily indebted to Vegetius' *De re militari*[27]), Giles analyses how a prince should act if he wishes to be loved by his people.[28] He should be beneficent and liberal for people are susceptible to tangible rewards and gifts; he should be strong and magnanimous for then his subjects will feel safe and protected; but most of all he should be fair and just, for the just are loved above all others. In this he harks back to his earlier description of love as a power for unity. This power of love in relation to princes is analysed as follows: it is in the love of God that human beings find happiness; a prince is sure to be happy when he loves God; since the proof that one person loves another is doing what the other person wishes him to do, a prince will be happiest when he is obeying God, and God's greatest wish is that the prince rules the people entrusted to him justly and piously.[29]

Following Aristotle and St Thomas Aquinas, Giles of Rome's work concentrates on the need for a perfect and just ruler, who is personally good. Always present behind Giles's teaching was the basic, intellectual ideal of the philosopher-king first described by Plato. On this subject Giles could not be bettered: his was the standard work which everyone copied or claimed as one of their authorities.[30] Giles's prince had to be

25 *Ibid.*, bk 3, pt 1, ch. 11, f. 253.
26 *Ibid.*, bk 3, pt 2, ch. 9, f. 282. His section on how a tyranny is maintained was taken from the fifth book of Aristotle's *Politics*; much of it was to be repeated by Machiavelli in *The Prince* (1513) from a different point of view.
27 *De regimine*, bk 3, pt 3, chs 1–22, summarises Vegetius.
28 *Ibid.*, bk 3, pt 2, ch. 36, passim.
29 *Ibid.*, bk 1, pt 1, ch. 12, f. 24r–v.
30 E.g. Fortescue says Giles is one of his authorities to a degree which his editor finds hard to justify, Fortescue, *Governance*, pp. 176–77. Hoccleve claims Giles as a source, but the debt is in fact small, Childs, 'Study', p. 18.

prudent, dignified but sympathetic, and above all, truthful. He must be energetic and just, his justice always tempered with mercy; courageous but not rash; moderate in all things; great hearted (magnanimous) and magnificent in all his undertakings, and a liberal but careful rewarder of the deserving. He must love honour, be humble and friendly while commanding respect, and he should have an equal such as his wife with whom he can share secrets. Above all he must love the common good and welfare of his kingdom and not merely his own advancement. He should actively promote the virtue, education and wealth of his subjects of all ranks, with a special emphasis on townspeople. He should encourage wise men and priests and choose the best councillors from among them for their practical qualities and truthfulness. The king's laws were of paramount importance – Giles spends much time on the law; they were to be made known and to be observed and not changed lightly.[31] *De regimine principum* (and the other major mirrors for princes) set out what a prince should try to be – contrariwise, it set out those criteria by which a prince could be judged; it itemised points for public opinion to check and consider, and public opinion could be particularly important in fifteenth-century England, a country used to changing unsatisfactory princes.[32] Giles himself provided for criticism by emphasising the duties of the prince and the duty of subjects to obey for the sake of the good of the state. Though his emphasis was on the need for a prince to be personally good his text was to become one of the cornerstones of the theory of royal absolutism.[33] Few princes could hope to achieve full success in following Giles's

---

31 Born, 'Perfect prince', pp. 488–91.

32 See Genet, 'Political theory', p. 19. The Scots ambassador William Whitelaw, in his speech in Richard III's presence during the peace negotiations in September 1484, ascribed many of these virtues to Richard himself: mildness, clemency, liberality, loyalty, justice, greatness of heart, wisdom, affability to everyone, and prudence, as well as all the virtues that a commander should have. See BL, MS Cotton Vesp. C xvi, f. 75v, and also the translation of the speech in Grant, 'Richard III and Scotland', appendix 4, p. 194.

33 *De regimine*, bk 3, pt 2, ch. 34. In fact, though Giles without doubt or hesitation supports monarchy as the best form of government, his discussion of the obedience of subjects is *very* brief – limited to one chapter – stating that they should 'obey kings and princes and the royal laws'. First, because obeying the law and the lawmaker results in virtue, and secondly, because it is a mark of freedom rather than servitude – beasts obey no law and they are slaves – and as the mind rules the body so the king governs the land. Thirdly, obedience to the king and the law leads to peace and abundance. For Giles's place in the history of political thought, e.g. Carlyle, *History of Medieval Political Theory*, vol. 5, pp. 70–77, and Gilbert, *Machiavelli's 'Prince'*, introd. and passim.

advice to be a perfect prince and above criticism – save perhaps Louis IX, so speedily sanctified after his death (1270; 1297) – but at the least later medieval princes had to ensure their propaganda conformed to these criteria of perfection.[34]

Fifteenth-century Readers of Mirrors of Princes: Richard of Gloucester and Others

If Richard III appreciated the original authorities on the fall of Troy and the history of Britain, as we contend he did, he may also have appreciated the 'masterpiece' among the mirrors of princes. Our purpose is to assess the relevance of the book to Richard of Gloucester and his contemporaries; at the crudest level, would Richard have read some, all or any of the text? Was Giles a bore, too theoretical for the taste of a late fifteenth-century prince, or was he out of date? Was Giles's taste for the philosopher-king too foreign for the English? Other mirrors had been written since the time of Giles, several had been adapted to suit particular recipients and both princes and the political scene had changed since the 1270s. Machiavelli completed his version of advice to a prince in 1513[35] and Erasmus was working on his *Institutio principis christiani* in 1515–16.[36] Machiavelli's *Realpolitik* may have been more in tune with what princes thought, even though his work was condemned and princes continued to endorse Giles's views in their propaganda. Was Erasmus's milder and intellectual, but equally modern, version more suited to the princes of

---

34 Sutton, 'Curious searcher', passim, for an assessment of how Richard III might have had to judge himself by the criteria of the 'perfect prince'. Harriss, *Henry V*, introd., summarises the ideals of kingship shared by Henry V and his subjects. Compare Machiavelli to whom reputation is less important than the safety of the prince and his power, *The Prince*, ch. 15.

35 See e.g. Gilbert, *Machiavelli's 'Prince'*, where it is shown that Machiavelli was indebted to many predecessors. *The Prince* was first published in 1532, six years after Machiavelli's death; Thomas More's *Utopia* came out in 1516.

36 See e.g. Born, 'Erasmus on political ethics', pp. 520–54, for a summary of Erasmus's work and a list – with several errors – of similar works from the 12th to the 17th century; Born indicates that Erasmus was also deeply indebted to a great number of predecessors. *Institutio principis christiani*, ed. Herding, translation in *Collected Works of Erasmus*, vol. 27, ed. A.H.T. Levi, Toronto 1986.

his time?[37] At a more domestic level, less pretentious and non-clerical advice on marriage – for example – written by an 'ordinary' author of the mid-fifteenth century might be very much more acceptable and under-standable to a fifteenth-century reader than that of a learned, celibate, long-dead theologian (see below).

It can be stated categorically that all princes sooner or later owned a mirror of princes.[38] Many of them were specifically adapted to the pre-tensions of a particular king in exactly the same way as Giles of Rome's text had been made for the heir to the crown of France, the future Philip IV. A list concentrating on fifteenth-century royalty and nobility pro-duces an impressive number.[39] Henry of Monmouth, who seems to have had almost as definite an image of himself as king as that expressed by Louis IX,[40] commissioned Thomas Hoccleve, a clerk of the privy seal, in about 1409 to produce *The Regement of Princes*. According to its author the text was based on Giles, the *Secreta secretorum*, and James de Cessolis' *Game of Chess*. Later, as king, Henry commissioned Lydgate's *Troy Book* (1412), another utilitarian work that has much of the mirror in it and was calculated to foster good public relations.[41] Several 'mirrors' were pre-sented to Henry VI, the *Tractatus de regimine principum* being tailored to the king's interest in educational and religious foundations.[42] Margaret of Anjou was presented with a copy of the standard French translation of Giles of Rome's work,[43] and her son Edward, Prince of Wales (1453–71) was the intended recipient of the *Active Policy of a Prince* by the aged George Ashby, past clerk of his mother's signet. Ashby mentioned sev-eral of the immediate problems that the prince had to face – rebellious subjects, maintenance, the carrying of weapons by the lower classes. His

---

37 Princes like Charles the Bold and Richard himself would have been surprised to read Erasmus's warning that boys should take an 'antidote' before they read about such 'tyrants' (*tyranni* may even mean 'criminals') as Achilles and Alexander, *Institutio*, Herding, p. 179.

38 See e.g. Green, *Poets and Princepleasers*, ch. 5, on books of advice for princes. Orme, *From Childhood to Chivalry*, pp. 88–103, on their general inclusion in the education of princes.

39 Orme, *From Childhood to Chivalry*, pp. 95–98. Green, *Poets and Princepleasers*, ch. 5.

40 Harriss, *Henry V*, introd., esp. pp. 26–29.

41 Hoccleve, *Regement*, lines 2134–35. Childs, 'Study', p. 18, points out that Hoccleve in fact used little of Giles. See Harriss, *Henry V*, introd., pp. 8–9, and Pearsall, 'Lydgate and literary patronage at the Lancastrian courts' (forthcoming).

42 Genet, *Four English Political Tracts*, pp. 40–168.

43 By Henri de Gauchy, *c.* 1282; this was one of the several texts in BL, MS Royal 15 E vi presented to her by Sir John Talbot.

text was uninspired and is mainly interesting for his ready reference to the value of chronicles not merely as sources of example but as the recorders of the prince's future actions which he must therefore design to be wise and good.[44] While in exile at Bar, in France, Edward of Lancaster also received Fortescue's *De laudibus legum Anglie* in which the former chief justice set out to persuade the prince that a knowledge of the laws of his future kingdom was as essential to him as fighting skills.[45] Richard, Duke of York, received an English translation in a unique format of part of the *Consulship of Stilicho* by the Roman poet Claudian, which the translator intended to be a mirror for York (see fig. 16). It contained praise of what the duke had already accomplished and set out the virtues and good acts of the general Stilicho as examples to be followed.[46]

Edward IV can claim no dedication of a mirror text but he had a *Secreta secretorum* as a young man – in a version that contained little on the theory of government – and a *Gouvernal of Kinges and Princes* in his library as king.[47] He was also the owner of what is now the *Chemin de Vaillance* or *Songe Doré*, written in the 1420s by an aged Norman nobleman.[48] It consists of a dream (*c.* 42,000 lines) in which the author is guided by Nature, the World and Charity to the dwelling of *Dame Vaillance* (Lady Courage), while tempted by Vices and saved by Virtues on the way. Part of the journey is accomplished in the Ship of Law along the River of Contemplation and the final meeting with Lady Courage is preceded by a vision of Paradise. There is much lively detail on aspects of courtly life and war. The *Chemin* was essentially a manual for knights, not merely princes. The *Game of Chess* by James de Cessolis, a popular mirror which compared human society to the

---

44 *Ashby's Poems*, pp. v–vii, 12–41.

45 Fortescue, *De laudibus*, first printed *c.* 1546 and popular since then, Chrimes, ed., p. xcix; its earlier popularity in manuscript is impossible to gauge, but it is worth noting that the more accessible *English* text of the *Governance* was in the shop of the well-established London scrivener John Multon, by 1475, see n. 50 below.

46 See ch. 2 above.

47 *Secreta*, BL, MS Royal 12 E xv. The 1480 *Wardrobe Accounts*, ed. Nicolas, p. 152, refer to the 'Gouvernement of Kinges and Princes' among Edward's books; its text cannot be identified with certainty.

48 Jean de Courcy, Lord of Bourg-Achard, see e.g. Piaget, '*Le Chemin de Vaillance* de Jean de Courcy', pp. 582–91, for a summary of the story, and Dubuc, '"Le Chemin de Vaillance"', pp. 276–83. The text only survives in BL, MS Royal 14 E ii, where it is followed by three very short didactic texts, the *Epistre Othea* of Christine de Pizan, the *Bréviaire des Nobles* of Alain Chartier, the *Des ix malheureux et ix malheureuses*, and Ramon Lull's *Ordre de Chevalerie* (see ch. 4 above).

This chappytre of the first tractate shewyth who fond first the playe of the chesse   Capitulo   ij

This playe fonde a phylosopher of thorpent whych
ｆ was named in caldee Eperses or in greke philemes
tor which is as moche to say in englissh as he that louyth
Justyce and mesure / And this philosopher was renomed
gretly among the grekes and them of Athenes whyche
were good clerkys and phylosophers also renomed of their
connyng/This philosopher was so Just and trewe that he
had leuer dye / than to lyue longe and be a fals flaterer
with the sayd kyng / For whan he behelde the foul & syn-
ful lyf of the kyng ·And that no man durst blame hym

Fig. 42 Woodcut from Caxton's second edition of James de Cessolis' *Game of Chess*, c. 1483. The philosopher begins to explain, through the medium of the game of chess, the governance of the world.

game, using many *exempla* to illustrate its arguments, was translated and printed by Caxton in English for the first time on 31 March 1474 with a recommendation of its text to Edward IV's brother, George of Clarence; it was reissued by Caxton in about 1483 presumably in response to demand.[49] Either Edward of Lancaster or Edward IV may have been the original dedicatee intended for Fortescue's *Governance of England*, and the latter may have been the actual recipient – this was a book of advice that was tailored to the English situation and probably had greater immediate circulation through the London bookshops than his Latin *De laudibus*.[50] Edward V is not known to have owned or been presented with any 'mirror' text.[51] Richard III had Giles of Rome's classic of the genre, and possibly received the dedication of another in the shape of the *Phalaris Letters*. Henry VII apparently only had the Burgundian manual for knights, the *Enseignement de la vraie noblesse*, one of the many 'mirrors' composed for the Valois dukes of Burgundy and their court (see below).[52] The French kings were equally assiduous owners of mirrors: the French royal library in Charles V and VI's time contained eight copies of Giles of Rome and over twenty related works;[53] Charlotte of Savoy, queen of Louis XI, for example, owned a *Livre de Gouvernement des roys et princes*.[54]

Before turning to Richard's own copy of Giles's *De regimine principum*, it is worth considering the other text that can be described as a 'mirror for princes' and which may have been presented to him at the beginning of his reign. *The Letters of Phalaris* was a collection attributed to the Greek tyrant and edited by Pietro Carmeliano, an Italian scholar seeking preferment in England since 1481. Carmeliano had already dedicated Cicero's *De oratore* to Edward IV and his own poem *Spring* to Edward, Prince of Wales.[55] His one certain presentation to Richard III was a *Life of St Katherine* described

---

49 *Liber de moribus hominum et officiis nobilium ac popularium super ludo scaccorum*, see Born, 'Perfect prince', pp. 491–93. Cessolis, *The Game of Chess. Translated and Printed by William Caxton c. 1483*.

50 BL, MS Cotton Claudius A viii, ff. 175–97, which is in the hand of the scribe, John Multon, who died 1475, see *John Vale's Book*, fig. 1, pp. 53–54, 110; for the dating of the *Governance*, pp. 53–66.

51 His uncle Rivers thought that 'the understanding' of his translation of the *Dicts and Sayings of the Philosphers* would be 'full necessary' to the Prince, cited Orme, *From Childhood to Chivalry*, p. 103.

52 BL, MS Royal 19 G viii.

53 Green, *Poets and Princepleasers*, p. 140.

54 Fortescue, *Governance*, p. 176.

55 For a full discussion of all Carmeliano's dedications to the Yorkist kings and his patrons 1481–85, see the present authors, 'R III's books XIV'.

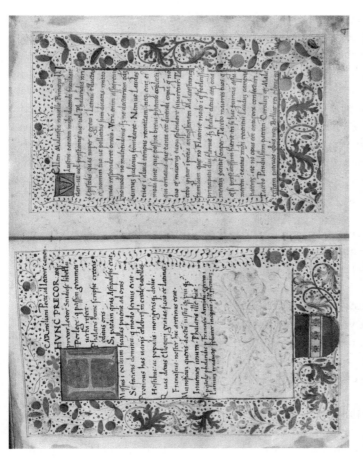

Fig. 43 The first two pages of the only surviving one of Pietro Carmeliano's autograph copies of the Latin translation of the *Letters of Phalaris*. On the left, f. 3v, is Carmeliano's poem addressing the reader; below it space was left for a miniature, probably intended for a picture of the tyrant Phalaris, but only filled with a drawing of crossed branches and foliage; in the lower border is the coat of arms of the Lee family. On the right, f. 4, is the beginning of the introduction of the translator, Francesco Griffolini, dedicating his work to Domenico Malatesta. Folio 3, on the left, was made separately, decorated with the arms of the future owner when the author had decided to whom he was going to give this particular copy, and then added to the book before it was bound. Dublin, Trinity College, MS 429, ff. 3v–4. By permission of the Board of Trinity College Dublin.

above,[56] but there is some evidence this may have been preceded by the *Letters*. Phalaris was a sixth-century ruler of Agrigento, Sicily, whose name became synonymous with tyranny and cruelty in the ancient and medieval world and the letters were accepted as his own defence against these charges until proved to be forgeries in the seventeenth century. They were widely used and praised as models of elegant Latin and persuasive argument; as they concerned political acts they were also used as a 'mirror of princes'. The opinion of the diplomat Sir William Temple, probably also reflects that of late fifteenth-century scholars:

> ... the Epistles of *Phalaris* ... have more Race, more Spirit, more Force of Wit and Genius, than any others I have ever seen ...; ... such Freedom of Thought, such Boldness of Expression, such Bounty to his Friends, such Scorn of his Enemies, such Honour of Learned men, such Esteem of Good, such Knowledge of Life, such Contempt of Death, with such Fierceness of Nature and Cruelty of Revenge, could never be represented but by him that possessed them.[57]

Some samples may be given of the rather simple rhetoric that was to make these letters so amazingly popular for many years:
Phalaris to Theusippus

> We have spared your son because of his youth and you because of your age, though you deserved no mercy. If you do not restrain yourself from further rashness his youth will not save him, nor your age you; on the contrary, we will inflict on you punishment in the same measure as we granted you mercy.[58]

Phalaris to Hiero
I could say much about you and your foolish speech against me, but I do not want to waste words; only this: an Indian elephant takes no notice of a mosquito.[59]

---

56 Ch. 3 above.
57 Temple, *Essays On Ancient and Modern Learning*, pp. 34–35.
58 Dublin, Trinity College Library, MS 429, f. 10–10v.
59 *Ibid.*, f. 28.

For his autograph 'edition' of the *Letters of Phalaris* Carmeliano wrote a page of verse recommending the book to his (nameless) reader, explaining who Phalaris had been and how famous and eloquent his letters were (f. 3v). At the end of the text itself he wrote: 'I, Carmeliano, moved by the request of a friend, wrote this text with my own hand in haste'.[60] Carmeliano's manuscript edition of the *Letters* exists in one autograph copy with the arms of the Lee family, probably representing John Lee, master of Maidstone College and a past student of some distinction of Padua University. The book is in the standard format Carmeliano used for presentation copies, readily duplicated by himself for any new patron/ maecenas. One inscription in this manuscript suggests a royal patron, and is written in Carmeliano's hand on the last flyleaf (f. 63):

> *Carmen pro homagio legeo reddendo.*
> Pro vita et membris necnon et honoribus ipsis
>   Incipio, o princeps, subditus esse tuus.
> Nam tibi fidus ero, vivam moriar quoque tecum
>   Contra omnes populos et genus omne virum.
> Denique prestabo tibi quicquid iure tenebor.
>   Sic Deus aspiret sanctaque turba mihi.

The most appropriate translation of this *Verse for the swearing of the oath of homage* can be found in the coronation *ordo* of Richard III – the copying out of the manuscript may have coincided with the planning of the solemnities for either Edward V's or Richard III's coronation – and Carmeliano may have been inspired by some of the ceremonial texts that he found new and interesting:

> [Prince], I become your liegeman of life and limb and of earthly worship, and faith and truth I shall bear unto you for to live and die against all manner of folk. [And I shall do you service for the lands I shall hold of you by right.] So God me help and his hallows.[61]

---

60 *repente*, 'in haste', 'recently', 'unexpectedly'? Compare Caxton's frequent claim that he produced a book at the request of 'a friend'.

61 Spelling modernised; words in square brackets added to make a complete translation of Carmeliano's text. The sentence beginning 'And I shall you do service ... (Latin *Denique prestabo* ...)* appears to be taken from the oath of spiritual lords, but the phrase 'of life and limb' (Latin *pro vita et membris*) definitely belongs to the oath of temporal lords. For the text of both oaths see Legg, *English Coronation Records*, p. lvj, and Sutton and Hammond, *Coronation*, p. 224.

The Latin text Carmeliano composed is actually a mixed text, containing elements from the oath of homage taken by temporal lords and the oath of fealty taken by spiritual lords. The mixture may be due to Carmeliano's ignorance.

If these verses were added and were a token of gratitude to a generous patron, like the poem added in later at the end of the prince of Wales's *Spring*, they suggest a patron who could be appropriately addressed by an oath of homage and, in 1483 or 1484, this could only be Edward V or Richard III. Such royal patronage would throw out the simpler theory of the dedication of these elegant letters to a member of the rich and cultivated gentry of England, the 'friend' of the colophon at the end of the text and the owner of the Lee arms. Should the manuscript also be connected to the court? Was it passed on to the king? Was its original dedicatee a king? If this text was indeed seen by Carmeliano and his English readers primarily as a 'mirror for princes' then a translation of the oath was an entirely appropriate expression of loyalty to the new king, Edward V or Richard III, who may also have been the dedicatee.[62]

Richard's own copy of Giles's *De regimine principum* was probably a gift, or purchase, from a member of the Percy family. It is a large, slim volume written in two columns in the second quarter of the fifteenth century, with an alphabetical list of contents at the end to assist the reader. Its clean, attractive text was easily readable by someone whose Latin was good enough not to be deterred by a text presented in an highly abbreviated form. Giles's style demanded concentration and intellectual stamina; it was only accessible to a young man with several years of grammar education behind him. Giles was a scholar who usually wrote for other scholars and a teacher who produced a highly organised text that was intended for instruction and learning by rote.

The scheme of heraldry used to decorate the opening of each section of Richard's copy (the arms of Richard II; of the House of Lancaster; St John of Beverley; St Cuthbert of Durham; St William of York; St George; the arms of probably Richard, Duke of York, 1415–60; Henry Percy,

---

62 Modigliani, 'Un nuovo manoscritto', pp. 86–102, is prepared to regard the oath as a straight-forward request for protection from a king, shortly after his coronation – though she does not seem to have recognised the text for what it is – and includes even Henry VIII among possible candidates. In view of the fact that the manuscript copy preceded the printed edition (Oxford, Hunt and Rood, 1485), an earlier date, close to the production of the very similar ms. of *Spring*, is almost certain; for details see 'R III's books XIV'.

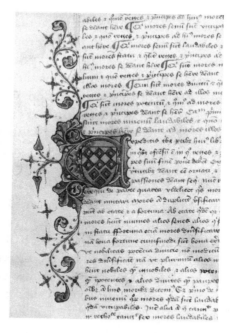

Fig. 44 Part of a page from Richard's copy of Giles of Rome's *De regimine principum*, showing the arms of St William FitzHerbert, Archbishop of York (died 1154). English, 1440s. Sion College, MS Arc. L 40.2/ L 26, f. 27v (now transferred to Lambeth Palace Library). Photograph by P.W. Hammond.

Earl of Northumberland with his wife, Eleanor Neville, daughter of Ralph, 1st Earl of Westmorland, married 1414; London; York; Beverley; and St Edmund)[63] suggests this book was made for Henry Percy, Earl of Northumberland (1416–55), perhaps to commemorate the year 1416 when he was given a new grant of his grandfather's earldom by Henry V and perhaps after the marriage of Richard, Duke of York to Cecily Neville, younger sister of Henry Percy's wife, which took place sometime before 1424; Henry Percy and Richard of York were both descendants of Lionel, Duke of Clarence. Henry Percy is known to have given another, older copy of *De regimine principum* in 1419 to William de Norham, his confessor.[64] Original Percy ownership and commission seem to be indisputable, but how it came to Richard of Gloucester is not known: after 1471 he had ample opportunity, while lord of the North, to receive the book from a Percy. The (now illegible) inscription in the top right-hand corner of the first page: *Egidius de Regimine Liber illustrissimus Principis Ducis Gloucestr'*, 'the most illustrious book of the prince, the duke of Gloucester', does

---

63 For more details on the heraldry see 'R III's books V' and Cat. V below.

64 Oxford, Bodleian Library, MS Laud Misc. 702, flyleaf: 'hunc librum contulit dominus Henricus Percy inclitus comes Northumbr' fratri Willelmo de Norham confessori eiusdem domini et sac' theo' doctori, xiij die Aprilis 1419'; an early 14th-century copy.

not help. It might be expected that the 'illustrious' *should* agree with the
duke not the book, but it may represent a compliment to the quality of
the book; and the addition of 'prince', although appropriate to Richard's
royal rank, may also underline the suitability of the mirror of princes for
him, especially if the inscription was the work of the donor.[65]

The two Percy copies of Giles's text alone indicate that certain English
nobles were well aware of its status and value;[66] Thomas, Lord Berkeley,
had it translated in the last years of the fourteenth century. Nevertheless,
it seems to be generally accepted that the particular mirrors of princes, of
which *De regimine principum* was the prime example, so assiduously promoted by the thirteenth-century kings of France and their descendants
including the dukes of Burgundy, were not as popular in England as other
similar texts. The Aristotelian basis of such works as Giles's *De regimine
principum* had had a mixed reception in England whereas it was nurtured
in France.[67] The English certainly owned French mirrors but they failed
to translate them, except for the Berkeley translation of Giles which was
apparently never circulated, and the *Three Considerations*, a translation of
a mid-fourteenth-century French tract in the mould of a classic mirror.[68]
The absence of translations may, however, be misleading: those English
who might expect to read such texts would happily read them in French;
De regimine principum, for example, had been available in French since
soon after its appearance,[69] and in 1450 Jean Wauquelin translated Giles's
work into French again at the request of Duke Philip (who already owned
three copies of the Latin text). Although only one copy of this particular
translation survives it may have been circulated on a wider basis.[70] The
English may have preferred the lessons of mirrors put into a more palatable form by a poet: Gower's *Confessio Amantis* or Hoccleve's *Regement
of Princes*, both of which gilded the pill with extensive stories to illustrate each point. There is some evidence that the English preferred the

---

65   For a full discussion of which duke of Gloucester owned this book, see 'R III's books V'.
66   For other noble English owners of the 15th century, see Orme, *From Childhood to Chivalry*,
     pp. 95–98, and Firth-Green, ch. 5.
67   Genet, *Four English Political Tracts*, p. xv; Jones, *Royal Policy of Richard II*, pp. 158–60.
68   Genet, *Four English Political Tracts*, p. xvi, 174–79.
69   Giles of Rome, *Li Livres du Gouvernement des Rois*. For other French translations of similar
     works, Genet, *Four English Political Tracts*, p. xiv n. 36.
70   Brussels, Bibliothèque Royale, MS 9043; see e.g. *Charles le Téméraire*, item 76; the ms. was
     made for Philip in 1452, after Wauquelin's death.

Secreta secretorum,[71] a text that derived its status from being erroneously understood to be a secret letter from Aristotle to Alexander the Great telling him how to rule in the philosopher's absence. The title suggested that the theory of government was a secret knowledge, revealed only to rulers. Versions of the manual on government circulating in the fifteenth century frequently included sections on physiognomy and the maintenance of health, also addressed to the prince, or astronomical or medical treatises – as did Edward IV's copy. These 'scientific' additions may partially account for the wide popularity of the work in England: there were about eight different versions of the *Secreta secretorum* in English prose alone, circulating in the fifteenth century, which included the section on the government of princes.[72]

There were more fundamental differences of tradition that might affect the reception of the French-inspired mirrors of princes. The English were used to commenting more directly on political events and specific problems: Edward III had received a mirror specifically directed at the evils of royal purveyance;[73] and from the time of Richard II many anonymous texts survive on political, social and economic evils, including some with a Lollard background. Many partisan broadsides, some containing material on the theory of government, were exchanged between the Yorkists and Lancastrians.[74] There was also a considerable contrast between the ways in which the English and French viewed their kings. The French kings had long fostered a sacred image to help them control their many over-mighty subjects and to answer the English threats to their legitimacy. Most important for its effect on the fifteenth century was the propaganda of Charles V (1364–80), who was determined to offset the disasters of his father's reign at the hands of the English. This propaganda was both historiographical, as in his careful new recension of the *Grandes chroniques de France*, produced at Saint-Denis and probably carried out by his chancellor, and it was also

71 Genet, *Four English Political Tracts*, p. xvi.
72 Manzalaoui, *Secreta Secretorum. Nine English Versions*, pp. xxv–xl, on the 15th-century English versions; only 7 of his 9 edited versions are 15th-century and only 5 of them include the section on government (nos 3, 4, 5, 6 and 7). See also Steele, *Three Prose Versions of the Secreta Secretorum*, and his edition of *Lydgate and Burgh's Secrees of Old Philosoffres*.
73 Moisant, *De speculo regis Edwardi III*; and see Jones, *Royal Policy of Richard II*, pp. 162–63 and n. 47; Genet, 'Political theory', p. 28.
74 Genet, *Four English Political Tracts*, pp. xviii–xix (list). *John Vale's Book*, passim.

Fig. 45 Aristotle instructing King Alexander, from a manuscript of an English version of the *Secreta secretorum*. The illumination is typical London work of the later fifteenth century, also to be found in Richard III's Vegetius (see fig. 35) and many copies of the statutes. The motto, *Oublier ne doy*, and the crest may be those of the Whetehill family of Calais. English, London, 1438–60. Oxford, University College, MS 85, p. 70. By permission of The Master and Fellows of University College, Oxford.

religious.[75] The French kings were sacred figures, anointed with the oil of Clovis; they had the power of healing and they were protected by particular saints, St Denis and St Louis; they were buried in their own necropolis of the abbey of Saint-Denis. Their view of their position and history was put into pictorial form in Charles VII's reign by an unknown artist: its central scene is the Crucifixion; to the right of Christ on the cross are St John the Baptist and Charles VII depicted as his ancestor, St Louis, in the full royal regalia of blue mantle powdered with fleurs-de-lis, crown and sceptre; on the left of Christ stand St Denis in episcopal robes and the emperor and Christian warrior, Charlemagne, another ancestor of Charles VII. The painting sums up the *religion royale* that hedged the French monarchy in the lifetime of Richard of Gloucester.[76] No such cult of their persons was consistently promoted by the medieval English kings. Neither Edward the Confessor nor St Edmund, the two English king-saints, nor the later adopted St George, ever held a position analogous to that of Sts Denis and Louis. The English kings never consistently maintained a royal abbey and necropolis, although Henry III, who had been shown the glories of Saint-Denis by his brother-in-law, St Louis, set out to make Westminster Abbey the burial place of himself and succeeding kings. He rebuilt it extensively and promoted the cult of Edward the Confessor, giving him a gold shrine. Richard II and Henry V and VII contributed to this programme, but all other fifteenth-century English kings were buried elsewhere. We cannot know if kings like Edward IV and Richard III would have liked to have had the status and sanctity of their French cousins, or whether they preferred the more limited and practical English pretensions to sanctity: touching for the king's evil and blessing the cramp rings at Easter.[77] They must have known instinctively that, as island kings, they could manage without the buttress of a *religion royale*. Each point of view had its own advantages. The French became adept at revering their 'most Christian' kings and developed a matching contempt for the 'habits' of disrespect and regicide of their English enemies. The French chancellor Guillaume de Rochefort's public criticism of Richard III's accession and displacement of Edward V

---

75 For a brief summary of the place of the *Grandes chroniques* in this propaganda and the differences between French and English historiography, see 'R III's books IX'.

76 Illustrated in Beaune, *Naissance*; it is now in the Louvre. The St Denis-Charlemagne panel is clearly by a different artist and replaces (and presumably copies) the lost original. And see Bloch, *Royal Touch*, passim; Beaune, *Naissance*, passim; Hinkle, *Fleur de Lis*, passim.

77 Sutton and Hammond, *Coronation*, pp. 6–7.

in the 1484 Estates General included a disparaging reference to the twenty-six changes of dynasty England had endured. De Rochefort was repeating the well-worn theme that the English had vicious characters and customs as proved by their regular killing of their kings. French propagandists asserted that their own kings enjoyed complete legitimacy of descent and the respect of their subjects, and they assiduously explained away the three breaks in the royal dynastic thread since the mid-fifth century.[78] A robust English response can be found in the work of Sir John Fortescue who pointed out the evils of unlimited royal government in France and how it impoverished and crushed the people. In contrast, the English were well fed and had lively, free spirits, as witnessed by the high level of violent crime in England. Fortescue would not have endorsed king-killing but he certainly thought the English method of controlling their kings by a mixed form of government – in which judges like himself played an important part – was preferable to the untrammelled power of the French kings which he had observed at first hand while in exile with Margaret of Anjou and her son.[79] This French–English difference of opinion over the government and treatment of kings adds an intriguingly ambiguous quality to any assessment of the reception of such an extremely theoretical and philosophical mirror as that of Giles.

At a more mundane level, how dated was *De regimine principum*? There is some evidence that by the middle of the fifteenth century at least some of its vocabulary was considered to be out of date although an intelligent reader might be able to supply the deficiency: the author of the *Tractatus* presented to Henry VI, 1437–43, altered certain words in his extensive quotations from Giles.[80] The lack of commentary in such texts as Giles's on the real problems of the day was not surprising, but in England the

---

78 Lewis, 'Two pieces of fifteenth-century political iconography', pp. 319–20, citing the examples used by Jean Juvenal des Ursins, Guillaume de Rochefort himself and Noël de Fribois – all the examples are Anglo-Saxon, but the French found ample support for their theory in the deaths of William II, Edward II, Richard II and the Wars of the Roses. For Fribois see Daly, 'Mixing business with leisure', p. 100. For other anti-English arguments on similar lines, Lewis, 'War propaganda and historiography', p. 12. For French explanations of their own dynastic embarrassments – the Carolingian displacement of the Merovingians, the Capetian seizure of power and the Valois succession – see Daly, pp. 100, 108.

79 Fortescue, *De laudibus*, pp. 80–89, his *Governance*, pp. 113–16, 137–40, 141–42. And see Lewis, 'France in the fifteenth century', pp. 3–27, 169–87.

80 Genet,' Political theory', pp. 19–28, esp. 20, 22; he examines the failure of such texts as that of Giles to discuss local communities.

lack might be more quickly noticed: Fortescue's *Governance of England*, which was circulating in London by 1475,[81] had a direct relevance to the English scene; certain texts like the *Tractatus* for Henry VI and the *De Consulatu Stiliconis* for Richard, Duke of York, in 1445 had been more or less tailored to their recipients. These alterations to texts for new princes show that new attitudes were being taken into account, and new works like those of Fortescue heralded the larger changes which overtook this type of political literature in the 1500s.[82]

More interesting to Richard and his contemporaries than Giles's standard work may have been the almost embarrassingly large number of new 'mirrors' written for the dukes of Burgundy by members of their entourage, as well as the several translations made for them of ancient authorities. These new Burgundian texts may be considered among the most likely to have found their way to England as the two countries were so often allies against France. Their tone is usually personal and direct, possibly derived from the duty of the knights of the order of the Golden Fleece to criticise each other's conduct, including their sovereign's, during the chapters of the order. Certain members of the Lannoy family, which included three founding knights of the order, were tireless writers of practical memoranda and moral advice.

In 1430 Hugh de Lannoy wrote a detailed plan of action for Philip the Good on the matter of Anglo-Burgundian cooperation; it had no theoretical content. In 1432–33 he even 'advised' Henry VI, and in 1436, a year after the Franco-Burgundian peace of Arras, he composed another memorandum for Duke Philip, explaining the difficult situation in the duke's lands and the urgent need to make peace with England, while at the same time assuring him that this could be done without loss of honour. A year later again he advised war, because the chances to preserve the peace had deteriorated. He also advised the duke on financial matters, though not always from altruistic motives.[83] Hugh's younger brother, Gilbert, another founding-knight of the Golden Fleece, travelled extensively round Europe and the East, writing practical reports for diplomatic purposes. He wrote a letter of fatherly advice to his son which became

---

81 *John Vale's Book*, pp. 53–54, 110.
82 Genet, 'Les idées sociales de Sir John Fortescue', pp. 446–61, and his 'Political theory', p. 28.
83 For Hugh see Lannoy, *Hugues de Lannoy*, and e.g. Vaughan, *Philip the Good*, passim.

well known outside the family circle,[84] and (probably) a book which can be considered a true mirror for princes and which became known as the *Instruction d'un jeune prince*.[85] The *Instruction* claims to be an ancient treatise on good government written by an aged courtier for a fictional prince at the request of his dying father, who did not want his son to make the same mistakes as he had done. The work stresses above all the need to fear God, next discusses the four virtues of prudence, justice, restraint and strength of mind, but also humility, the daughter of prudence, and honesty. A prince should avoid drunkenness, lust, ingratitude and laziness and be generous and high-minded. He should rule with reason and justice; his counsellors should be of high birth, sensible, pious, and not younger than thirty-six years of age. A prince should travel round his lands and see things for himself, thus keeping control of his officers. No unnecessary wars should be fought, and any youthful excess of energy should be vented on pagans not on Christians, and even that should only be undertaken after long consideration and with the greatest care. The good running of his own estates is also crucial, and a prince should gather round him perfect knights, whose duties and virtues Gilbert illustrates with the story of Hue de Tabarie, a famous crusader, who was said to have explained the duties of a Christian knight to Saladin. The book should probably be dated 1439–42; the author speaks to his masters so plainly that it almost comes as a surprise that both Philip and Charles of Burgundy owned copies. A cousin of Hugh and Gilbert, Jean, knight of the Fleece from 1451, also wrote a literary letter of paternal advice to his young son; its intentions are very similar to those of the texts discussed above and the book was known outside the family circle, but it was genuinely written for his son, who was so young that he feared he would not live to instruct him.[86]

The accession of Charles the Bold in 1467 provoked a flood of manuals on princely conduct. It was the character of Charles and the resulting fears of his courtiers and counsellors that gave rise to this sudden stream of 'mirrors'. Many of them survive from various courtiers' libraries; whether they had any effect on the main recipient is doubtful in the extreme. The court chronicler, George Chastellain, wrote his *Advertissement au duc*

---

84 The *Enseignements paternels* survive among others in mss that belonged to Charles the Bold and Margaret of York, and Louis of Gruuthuse.

85 Van Leeuwen, *Denkbeelden van een Vliesridder*, and Potvin, *Oeuvres de Ghillebert de Lannoy*.

86 Lannoy and Dansaert, *Jean de Lannoy*.

Fig. 46 A Burgundian 'mirror for princes', the *Instruction d'un jeune prince*, written under a pseudonym by a member of the influential Lannoy family for the duke of Burgundy. The scene shows the fictional author presenting his book to the equally fictional king of Norway. The manuscript was owned by a member of the Luxemburg family, relatives of Jacquetta, Duchess of Bedford, mother of Queen Elizabeth Woodville. Northern France, 1460s. Cambridge, Fitzwilliam Museum, MS 1816/165, f. 10v. By permission of the Fitzwilliam Museum.

Charles, soubs fiction de son propre entendement parlant a luy-mesme ('Advice to duke Charles, in the guise of his own mind talking to himself'), a dream in which the author saw Charles surrounded by many personages: Clear Understanding and Knowledge of Oneself speaking to him at length, and introducing such characters as Strong Desire, Proper Shame, Nobility of Mind, High Intentions, Profound Thought, Public Necessity and even Various Conditions of Your People, and Enmity of the Kings and Princes that Hate You. Some of them were Charles's personal virtues and shortcomings, others were part of the political situation in which he found himself. The main purpose of the text was to reconcile the young duke with his discontented subjects in the major towns, who, according to Chastellain, had to be won over by justice. The harsh message of the author in the 'dream' is obscured by its complicated language and images.[87] Another dream written at the time is *Le Lyon Coronné* in which the control over a young, princely lion is contested by Envy and various virtues such as Loyal Undertaking and Perseverance; Envy eventually drowns herself.[88] Charles Soillot, Charles's secretary, dedicated another, similar booklet to his master when he was still count of Charolais: in *Le débat de félicité*, Church, Nobility and Labour each claim that they are the happiest estate, but the judges – Theology, Logic, Arithmetic, Geometry and Music – decide that true happiness is only to be found in devotion to God and the Virgin Mary.[89]

Charles also received a selection of the 'mirrors' of antiquity. In 1468 the same Charles Soillot translated into French Xenophon's *Hiero*, a manual on good government consisting of a dialogue between the philosopher Simonides and the tyrant Hiero on the nature of tyranny and whether it is possible for a tyrant to be happy, of which the realist, Xenophon, did not exclude the possibility. The Burgundian editor claimed that the book contained *aucunes moult singulières doctrines ... bien convenables à tout prince.*[90] In the same year Jean Mielot, scribe, artist and author, translated Cicero's letter to his brother Quintus in which he pompously advised him on the proper rule of the province of Asia.[91] Quintus is said to have been an irri-

---

87 Doutrepont, *Littérature*, pp. 323–24; *Charles le Téméraire*, item 12.
88 Ed. Urwin; *Charles le Téméraire*, item 13. The text is short and its only two surviving copies occur in miscellanies
89 *Charles le Téméraire*, item 2; Doutrepont, *Littérature*, p. 325.
90 Quoted in Gallet-Guerne, *Vasque de Lucene*, p. 24.
91 *Epistulae ad Quintum fratrem*, I, i.

table young man – like Charles – and the letter is full of exhortations to be moderate, advice that Mielot clearly thought the young duke needed. Many details of the letter could be fitted to Charles, but the translator also assumed a more general interest:

> the letter contains many fine and helpful statements … addressed to kings and princes … how to acquire honour, good renown, and eternal glory at last.[92]

In 1470 Vasco de Lucena, humanist and servant of Charles's mother, Isabel of Portugal, made a French version of Xenophon's *Cyropaedia*, mentioned by Cicero in the letter to his brother already translated by Mielot. Cicero said that Xenophon had written a book about the education of 'great Cyrus', King of Persia, 'not in accord with the historical truth, but as a model of just government' in which no aspect of good government was left undiscussed. Vasco de Lucena, echoing Mielot, recommended the text for the many similarities between its hero and Duke Charles.[93]

No English prince of the fifteenth century received as much formally composed advice as the Burgundian princes; the English king had to accept more specific criticism and advice verbally in the English parliament.

Social Behaviour: The 'Well of Gentleness'

Giles's *De regimine principum* and most mirrors for princes also included advice of more general application, as the author of the Norwegian mirror, with whom we opened, carefully said: 'proper conduct, courtesy, or comely and precise forms of speech'. This included the conduct of a man's personal relationships with wife, family and servants. The need for princes to learn the skills of social interaction was as essential as it was for other young men. These themes offer another means of assessing how a fifteenth-century reader might have reacted to Giles's 200-year-old text.

---

92 Bossuat, 'Jean Miélot, traducteur de Cicéron', pp. 82–124, esp. 97.
93 Gallet-Guerne, *Vasque de Lucene*; her introd. is interesting on the books of advice written for Charles.

Giles of Rome, for instance, in *De regimine principum* is eloquent on correct social behaviour on several levels:

> If man is a social animal, as the first book of the *Politics* essentially proves,
> he should possess a kind of virtue which makes him behave correctly in
> the words and deeds by which he communicates with others. Reason
> expects that different people behave in different ways; although all men
> who want to live in a civilised manner must be amiable and kind, not all
> men need be amiable in the same way. Since too great familiarity breeds
> contempt, kings and princes, in order to be respected and to prevent the
> royal dignity from being held cheap, should behave in a more dignified
> manner than others ... so in his way of treating others, a certain famili-
> arity may be accounted a virtue in a king and he may be called amiable
> because of it. If a common person is too familiar this is accounted a
> vice, not a virtue, and he is not called courteous but rustic.[94]

Elsewhere Giles describes 'courtesy', the virtue that a 'courtier' should possess:

> ... courtesy (*curialitas*) combines every virtue because noble behaviour
> insists on sharing in every virtue.... . Men who give suitable gifts at
> the right time are called courteous, and that is liberality.... . Men who
> eat decorously are called courteous, and that is temperance. Men who
> honour their fellow citizens and respect their wives and daughters are
> called courteous, and that is chastity. A man is called courteous if he
> receives others kindly and pleasantly, and that is amiability. In brief:
> courtesy combines all virtues.[95]

There were many other sources of social instruction specifically geared
to the life of a courtier living in the houses of princes and available to
young men such as Richard of Gloucester; some were in the superficially
more attractive format of romances and gilded the pill with adventures
and a story-line. In *Partonope of Blois*, Queen Melior, although scarcely
older than her lover, the hero, instructs him regularly in courtly behaviour, which she calls 'chivalry'. As he is descended from a Trojan prince

---

94 *De regimine*, bk 1, pt 2, ch. 28, ff. 79v–80.
95 *Ibid.*, bk 2, pt 3, ch. 18, ff. 231v–33v.

(in common with all the princely houses of Europe in Richard's day), Partonope must be naturally inclined to courtly behaviour; she advises:

> ... fayle no curtesy
> And be lowly to smale as welle as to grete,
> That men mowe say that passe by the strete
> 'Loo, yender gothe the well of gentylnes'.[96]

A similar tutorial role is played by the older lady of *Le petit Jehan de Saintré*, who takes another adolescent hero through a course of education in the ways of the court. Love was recognised as a potential catalyst which encouraged young men towards social graces: it made a young noble suddenly aware of the value of courtesy and desirous of growing up fast in Christine de Pizan's *The Duke of True Lovers*, and in the Burgundian romances of *Gilles de Chin* and *Jean d'Avesnes* an uncouth youth tidies himself up after he has left home and is further polished and civilised when he meets the lady of his dreams. In the real-life romance of *Jacques de Lalaing* the hero's father says to his son: 'few noble men have reached true virtuous prowess and great fame without having a lady with whom they were in love'.[97] Although *la Fière* never schools him directly, his love of her makes Ipomedon strive to do great deeds and achieve renown. *Tant le desieree*, 'I have longed for it so much', in this context of aspiration, was not an inappropriate motto for Richard of Gloucester to write in the margin of his *Ipomedon* – Richard apparently grasped the point it was teaching (see fig. 2).[98]

Some of the romances circulating in Richard of Gloucester's day may give a better understanding of the social behaviour expected – or hoped for – from the well-educated 'courtier' fashioned in the school for the king's henchmen described in the *Black Book* of Edward IV's household, than the older books of advice written by clerics. *King Ponthus and the Fair Sidoine*, a prose romance put into English near the middle of the fifteenth century, is a prime example of a 'courtly' romance with an exemplary hero to excite the audience's admiration and imitation and with a strong undercurrent

---

96 Bödtker, *Partonope of Blois*, lines 1845–57. She gives almost identical advice, lines 2415–22.
97 La Sale, *Jehan de Saintré*. Christine de Pizan, *The Book of the Duke of True Lovers*. Chalon, ed., *Gilles de Chin*. Finoli, ed., *Jean d'Avesnes*. *Jacques de Lalaing*, printed Chastellain, *Oeuvres*, ed. Lettenhove, vol. 8, p. 15; quoted in Black, '*Jehan de Saintré* and *Le Livre des Faits*'.
98 See ch. 11 below.

of wholesome advice suitable for everyone, not merely princes. In *King Ponthus* the lessons are taught via the story of the education and career of Ponthus, another perfect knight and king.[99] He achieves perfection early on during his education, before he regains his inheritance:

> And above all thing he loved God and the chirche, and his first ocupacion in the morowe was to wesch his hondes, to say his prayers, and to here his messe full devoutely, and wold never ete ne drynke unto the tyme that he had his prayers all said. And of suche as he hade, he wold gyf to the poer men prively parte. And he wold never swere grete othe bot 'Truly' and 'As God me helpe'. And he wold be as glade when he loste and when he wan; if any man dide hym wrong, he wold sey att few wordes in faire maner that he had wrong, and he wold yeve upp his gamme in faire maner rather or he wold strive; and no man couth make hym wroth in his playng. And he lovyd never mokkyng ne scornyng ... for he was the best taght that any man sen in any place, and the best and fairest schapen in his live dayes.[100]

This is teaching the courtesy and civilised manners advised by Giles by example. At the end of *King Ponthus* there is also a long speech of direct advice given by Ponthus himself to his cousin on the occasion of the latter's marriage.[101] Ponthus turns to the bride, Genever, 'I wolle that my cosyn here love you and obey you, and that he have noo plesaunce to noon so myche as to you ...', and she replies, 'Ser ... he shall doo as a goode man owe to doo'. This is unlike the official tone of the celibate, clerical authors of mirrors such as Giles of Rome, learnedly advising princes on the conduct of their private lives; the romance is closer to the real life of the men and women who make up the bulk of its readership. Ponthus's more detailed advice to Pollides when they are alone, mirrors the perfections he himself achieved so early on. It is on a homely and intimate level: out of a total of sixty-seven lines he spends seven on the worship of God, a couple on love for his father, eight on his relationship with his social inferiors and servants (knights and esquires), nine on how to beware of flattery and malice and recognise honesty in men's conversation, but then he takes off

---

99 Specifically characterised as a *miroire* in *Dictionnaire des lettres françaises*, pp. 1202–03. For the background of this popular romance made for the family of La Tour Landry and printed seven times 1478–1550, see *ibid.*, and Mather, 'King Ponthus', esp. pp. iv–xxvii.

100 Mather, 'King Ponthus', pp. 11–12; *u* has been rendered as *v*, and an *e* added occasionally.

101 Mather criticises this as out of place, 'King Ponthus', p. xlviii.

with twenty lines on how to cherish his wife and another twenty on suc-
couring the poor. Much is standard advice but the balance is interestingly
weighted towards the priorities of 'real life': love and charity. 'Ye shuld
be curtes and gentle unto your wyf' for rudeness may cause her to stop
loving you 'wherof ye myght be right sorye ...'. He emphasises 'there
be gret perell and grete maistre to kepe the love of mariage'. He advises
Pollides to be faithful and never allow a quarrel between him and his wife
to last. This is a far cry from Giles of Rome's chilly, academic advice to a
man to seek friendship with his wife (see above).[102]

Equally striking is the last section of Ponthus's speech on the poor:

> ye come into the worlde as pouere as they did, and as pouere shall ye be
> at the day of your dethe; and ye shall have noo more of the erthe, save
> oonly your lengthe, as the pouere shall have, and ye shall be left in the
> erthe alone, as the pouere shall be.

These are the same sentiments expressed in Richard of Gloucester's
Middleham statutes, standard stuff but effective. The statutes stated that
God had exalted Richard 'the most simple creature, nakidly borne into
this wrethed world destitute of possessions, goods and enheretaments'
and 'in recognicion' of all the honours given him by God he determined
to use some of those goods to found, in this case, a college which would
bring benefit to a community.[103] Ponthus continues on a practical level,
speaking to 'all' men of property:

> Every friday in esspeciall here the clamour of the pouer people, of
> wommen and wydoys. Putt not their right in resspete ne in dilacion, ne
> beleve not allway your officers of every thyng that they shall tell you;
> enquer befor the truthe, for sum of theym wolle doo it to purchese damege
> to the pouere, for hate, and sume for covetyse, to have their goodes, when
> they see that they may not doo so with theym as they wold ...[104]

This text is worth quoting for its rendering of the rules of charity – the
social responsibility that the rich were supposed to shoulder – that a pros-

---

102 *De regimine*, bk 2, pt 1, ch. 11.
103 See ch. 3, above.
104 Mather, 'King Ponthus', pp. 145–47. Apparently this homily is faithfully translated from the
French, *ibid.*, pp. vi, xvi.

perous household was ideally expected to obey, according to its means. Active, day-to-day charity is a subject that Giles, for example, never dealt with specifically in the *De regimine principum*.

The most important of the surviving texts of the English translation of *Ponthus* belonged to the family of Sir William Hopton, briefly treasurer of Richard III's household before his death in early 1484,[105] the greatest secular household dispensing regular charity in England.[106] The Hopton family had it bound in a volume along with Hoccleve's mirror *Regement of Princes*, a *Brut* and two other stories. The Hopton collection contained a substantial proportion of educative and edifying matter which promoted the civilised and courteous society described in a more laboured way by Giles: 'it wasn't a bad sort of book to have about a house'.[107]

The Use of the Imagery of Mirrors of Princes in Richard's Reign

Is there any sign that Richard III and his clerks used the thoughts, images or words of 'mirrors' or other treatises on kingship or related matters in their pronouncements? Richard was capable of a grand gesture – a courtesy – to secure the favour of his subjects or to thank them in a manner that lives out the bare theory of Giles' *curialitas*, in particular its component 'liberality': he presented the city of London with a great cup decorated with pearls and gems at Epiphany 1484.[108] His visit to Canterbury later in January 1484 was the scene of another gesture over a gift: the leading citizens of Canterbury

---

105 Bodleian Library, MS Digby 185, dated to *c.* 1450, Mather, 'King Ponthus', pp. xxiii–xxvii. And see Richmond, *John Hopton*, pp. 136–39; Meale, 'The Morgan Library copy of *Generides*', pp. 89–104, esp. 102–03. The Hoptons also owned another courtly romance of the mid-15th century, *Generides*.

106 Little evidence survives of the day to day charity of the household of the Yorkist kings; better documented is that of Charles the Bold, whose almoner presented him with a list of deserving persons whenever he left a town: old people, prisoners, widows, merchants who had lost their goods. All were checked out and the deserving received amounts authorised by the duke, La Marche, 'L'Estat de la Maison du Duc Charles de Bourgoigne', in his *Mémoires*, vol. 4, pp. 2–3.

107 Quotation Mather, 'King Ponthus', p. xxvi. The other stories are that of Gerelaus and his wife, and Jonathan and his paramour, ibid., p. xxiii. Compare ch. 9, below, on the edifying character of romances in the 15th century generally.

108 Corporation of London Records Office, Journal of the Common Council 9, f. 43; for the background see Sutton, 'Richard III, the city of London and Southwark', pp. 289–95.

presented the king with an expensive purse and £33 6s 8d in gold, 'which the lord King with gracious actions ordered to be redelivered'.[109] Such gifts and their return were a feature of Richard III's progress through his realm after his coronation in 1483, continued in early 1484.

Richard III was also well aware of the value of due observance of the process of law – Giles' 'justice according to the law' – when he 'called all the justices before him in the inner Star Chamber and asked of them three questions', two of which concerned official malpractice or misprision.

> And afterwards all the justices ... consulted together how those who had been convicted of misprision should pay the fine. And they were all agreed that in every case where anyone had been convicted of misprision, trespass or otherwise, when a fine or ransom shall be paid, the justices before whom he had been convicted shall take security and pledges for the fine etc. and afterwards, at their discretion, they (and not the lord the King either by himself in his chamber or otherwise before him, unless by his justices) shall assess the fine.
>
> And this is the King's will to wit, to say 'by his justices' and 'by his law' is to say one and the same thing.[110]

The king's reply is a precise reflection of Giles of Rome's perception of the interaction between a king, the law and his subjects (see above).

Richard's reply to his justices is not only of great interest at a purely legal level, showing his proper concern for justice, it is also important for the dramatic weight and value attached to it by the clerk who recorded the king's answer and the justices' debate that preceded it. Richard's words have a dramatic value similar to the actions accompanying the gifts to London and Canterbury: they are image-making stuff and a potent part of kingship not to be lightly dismissed or disparaged especially if they have a beneficial, social effect as in these cases.

There is one significant image of a prince's power and duties that Richard III is known to have approved of: the sun-king. In 1480 William Caxton translated from the French and printed, at the request of Hugh Brice, alderman and goldsmith of London, the *Mirror of the World*. Originally called the *Image du monde*, this encyclopaedia was written by

---

109 See Sutton and Hairsine, ' Richard III at Canterbury', pp. 343–48.
110 Hemmant, *Select Cases in the Exchequer Chamber*, vol. 2, pp. 86–90, esp. 86, 90.

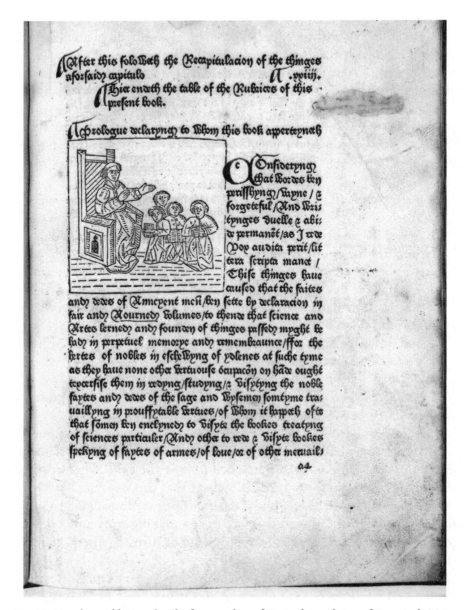

Fig. 47 A teacher and his pupils. The first woodcut of Caxton's translation of Gossuin de Metz, *Mirror of the World*, a popular encyclopedic work on science, geography and the natural world. John Rylands University Library of Manchester, 3469, f. 3. Reproduced by courtesy of the Director and University Librarian, the John Rylands University Library of Manchester.

Gossuin of Metz in 1246, and covered natural science, geography, meteorology and astronomy.[111] Brice wished to present the book to William, Lord Hastings, his superior at the royal mint and the king's friend.[112] It is possible that the text became generally known at the court of Edward IV, enabling Richard when he had become king, or his counsellors, to borrow a useful simile from it. In the eighth chapter of the third part, 'Of the vertue of heven and of the sterres', the position of the sun is described:

> Thus is he the right veyle[113] and patrone of all the other sterres, ffor it is the most fyn of all the other by the grete clerenesse that is in hym, and in all thynges by hym;[114] ... yet some tyme they [the stars] restrayne his heetes and after they enlarge them, ..., as he otherwhile hath nede; lyke unto a kynge which is the gretter lorde and the more myghty in hym self for his hyghnesse than any other of his people, neverthelesse he hath sometyme nede of them for to holpen and servyd of them; ffor how moche the nerrer he is to his peple, so moche more is he strong and puissant, and the ferther he wyth draweth fro his folke, so moche the lasse he exployteth of his werke.... But the other [stars] have their power everich in his degree.[115]

In August 1484, in the preamble to the instrument creating his son prince of Wales and earl of Chester, a document in which the king himself might have taken a close personal interest, Richard described his own position in a very similar way. He repeated the unique magnificence and beneficence

---

111 Gossuin de Metz, *L'Image du monde*, p. 176; Gossuin's work was based on the *Imago mundi* of Honorius of Autun (d. *c*. 1155), *PL*, vol. 172, col. 139, which is very brief on the sun, explaining that it does supply the light of the stars and is always shining even when it cannot be seen. Gossuin himself created the image of the sun as king. Another possible source which may have inspired the more learned among Richard's counsellors is Cicero's *De natura deorum* ('The Nature of the Gods', 2, 19, 49), a dialogue setting out the theological tenets of the main schools of Greek philosophy. The defender of the Stoics uses the phrase: 'the sun which holds the lordship of the stars' *(sol qui astrorum tenet principatum)* explaining how it rules nature like a god. See M. van den Bruwaene, ed., 3 vols, Brussels 1970–81, pp. 72–75. Cicero's philosophical works were known to men like John Gunthorpe who had attended the lectures of Guarino da Verona in Ferrara, Weiss, *Humanism*, e.g. p. 122.

112 Blake, *Caxton's Own Prose*, pp. 114–19; Caxton adds that the book has been produced under the shadow of Edward IV's noble protection. For a fine, illustrated copy made for the draper of London, Thomas Kipping, Scott, *Mirroure*, esp. pp. 2–10.

113 Watcher, supervisor, Fr. *veille*.

114 The French has *et toutes choses naissent par lui*, all things come to life through him.

115 Caxton's *Mirrour of the World*, pp. 147–48; *u* and *v* modernised.

of the sun as king; he, too, depicted his courtiers and officers as stars who derived their light from the sun-king, each according to his own degree 'transmitting' his light and ruling as his representative; he mentioned his need of these men, as he needed his son to be his deputy in Wales and Chester. Richard had two things added to the image of the orderly celestial court as depicted in the *Mirror of the World*: the first was the certainty that the sun's power, and the king's, is not lessened by any act of sharing, his greatness remains undiminished.[116] The second addition was his awareness of his duty to be king and the heaviness of his responsibilities, a theme stressed by many mirrors for princes:[117]

Such is the clarity and charity of the great solar light that, when it pours out whatever it has of light and splendour on the other heavenly bodies, the sun does not therefore shine the less, nor does it suffer any diminution of its strength and beauty. It is pleasant to see how the great sun, like a king seated in the midst of his nobles, together with the major and minor stars, each with their ordained light adorn the whole celestial court. Moved by this example and seeing the vocation to which we are called by God's favour, namely that we have to govern and be at the head of all the mortals of this kingdom, we turned the gaze of our inner eye to the immensity of this most noble state and its members, and took care above all that in these great responsibilities that press upon us those whom we need to bear part of them will not in any way be found to be lacking ...[118]

This is grandiloquent stuff, suitable for the document for which it was composed: it makes clear that Richard III was well aware of the contents of mirrors of princes and that he was equally aware of the positive and the negative sides of the task he had taken upon himself, the splendour as well as the burden of kingship.

---

116 We have not been able to find an exact equivalent of this image. There is a classical image of the sun not getting polluted even when it shines into cesspools, apparently going back to the ascetic philosopher Diogenes, see Diogenes Laertius, *Lives of Eminent Philosophers*, bk 6, ch. 63. Another fact known to the medieval scientist is that the sun's light never fails, even when we cannot see it, see e.g. Bartholomew the Englishman, *On the properties of things*, bk 8, ch. 18, quoted in Salvat, 'Barthélemi l'Anglais, traités du soleil et de la lune', pp. 339–57, esp. 347.

117 E.g. Singer, *Fürstenspiegel*, p. 30.

118 BL, MS Harl. 433, f. 27v; Visser-Fuchs, 'The splendour of the sun', pp. 229–30.

SIX

Ancestry and 'True Nobility'

To most of Richard's contemporaries, and especially his social equals, the past, in the shape of national and family history, was important and relevant to the present. There was a prevailing preoccupation with family: the lines of family descent proved the inheritance of lands and wealth, including the crown of England. These lines were subject to the rules of genealogy and chronology and to the common law on the descent of land, and they could be made visible and illustrated by the colourful displays of heraldry. For Richard Plantagenet, family history was national history, and as Duke of Gloucester, Lord of the North and King of England, he could put personal genealogy and heraldry to propagandist or educational use, especially when it had been made accessible in a visually attractive form. There was also, perhaps most important of all, the element of sheer pleasure given by fascinating facts about one's ancestors – however useful they were to prove a title, impress a supporter or educate a child in history – that once made the nineteenth-century antiquarian, Thomas Wright, describe members of a medieval family poring over their rolls of pedigrees to pass an evening in pleasant conversation and controversy about their ancestors, distant relatives, old victories and well-planned marriages to heiresses;[1] a pleasure not unknown in Wright's own time or even in the twentieth century. Reminding oneself of such links with the past has always contributed to an individual's sense of identity.

To pursue Wright's useful image, another possible topic of conversation which cannot have escaped the knowledge of Richard III and some of his

---

1   Wright, *Feudal Manuals*, pp. ix–x.

English contemporaries was the debate about the nature of true nobility as exemplified in Buonaccorso da Montemagno's *Controversia de vera
nobilitate* printed in English for the first time by Caxton in 1480: did a
man have his virtue from his blood and the inherited achievements of his
ancestors, or did his own personal merit bestow nobility on him, irre-
spective of his origins? It is unlikely that this debate troubled any but the
more literary members of the English 'nobility', but in theory it could
cast doubt upon the value of making any pedigree or book celebrating
any ancestor or family, and render pointless the use of an inherited coat of
arms. To an English gentleman or aristocrat, secure in a hierarchy of titles
beneath a king, this logic was esoteric, nobility by blood and the continuity of one's family, the longer the better, were all-important.

The inherent interest in the descent of kings – whether for propaganda,
mere historical knowledge, or for education – and the contemporary
debate about the nature of true nobility that was referred to, for example,
in Bishop John Russell's draft speech to the parliament of 1483 supporting Richard of Gloucester as protector,[2] are the background of a number
of manuscripts associated with Richard III. The Yorkist period has been
portrayed as one that saw a particular burst of production of royal pedigrees justifying the accession of Edward IV and the replacement of the
House of Lancaster with that of York. Richard has not been linked personally with any of these pedigrees and the shortness of his reign has
meant few survive with his name as king added during his lifetime. He
can be personally associated, however, with four manuscripts all containing pedigrees of various types in which he himself appears, one of the
lords of Clare,[3] a title of his father, one of the earls of Salisbury[4] and two
of the Beauchamp family;[5] the last two representing lesser families than
the Plantagenets but undoubtedly of great, perhaps greater, immediate
and personal interest to Richard, his queen and his son, the prince of
Wales. Richard also possessed two purely heraldic manuscripts for official
purposes, which he could also have used for reference or for the education
of his son.[6]

---

2   See below.
3   London, College of Arms, Clare Roll, see ch. 2 above.
4   BL, MS Add. 45122, Salisbury Roll; Cat. XX, below.
5   BL, MS Add. 48976, Rous Roll; Cat. XVIII, below. BL, MS Cotton Julius E iv, Beauchamp
     Pageant; Cat. XIX, below.
6   Cat. XIII A and B, below.

Pedigrees and Genealogical Chronicles

Medieval and later pedigrees and genealogical chronicles survive in great numbers throughout Europe. Scholars and patrons were not put off by St Paul's strictures on 'stories and interminable genealogies that only lead to controversy and do not teach us God's plan with us, which can only be learned through faith'.[7] Genealogy had become a convenient tool for the teaching of history by the end of the twelfth century, the main populariser being Peter of Poitiers, chancellor of the university of Paris (*c.* 1130–1205), in his *Compendium historiae in genealogia Christi.* This abbreviated biblical history, illustrated by a diagrammatic chart of descent from Adam and Eve to Christ, aimed to help his clerical students with their studies. The 'portraits' or names of the historical persons in the chart appeared in roundels linked by lines of descent. The nature of the work demanded that it be written as a roll which unrolled from top to bottom and this format remained the most popular for pedigrees for centuries. From France the biblical pedigree of Peter of Poitiers spread rapidly to other countries including England.[8]

It was inevitable that such a device was swiftly adapted for the descents of kings, and just as the ancestors of Christ gave a framework for teaching and remembering biblical history, so did the blood relationship and line of kings give a diagrammatic backbone to the history of a country. It was also inevitable that the genealogy of contemporary kings should be linked to those of long-dead dynasties and even to Christ's, and so take the ancestors of the present king back to the beginning of the human race in the Garden of Eden. The kings of England took their descent from Japhet, son of Noah, through the kings of Troy, the founders of Rome and Brutus, the first king of Britain, and down through the Welsh princes, the Anglo-Saxon kings and the Normans to the contemporary king, such

---

7 1 Tim. 1: 4: '… neque intendent fabulis et genealogiis interminatis, quae quaestiones praestant, magis quam aedificationem Dei, quae est in Fide'. Compare the use of St Paul's text on stories generally, ch. 9, below.

8 *Manual*, vol. 8, XII; Hilpert, 'Geistliche Bildung und Laienbildung', pp. 315–31; Morgan, *Early Gothic Manuscripts I*, pp. 91–92, points out that most early copies are English and surveys three, *c.* 1208–*c.* 1220. His vol. 2 *Early Gothic Manuscripts II*, pp. 180–81 surveys one ms. in the same tradition, BL, MS Royal 14 B ix, *c.* 1270–90. See also De La Mare, *Lyell*, MS Lyell 33, pp. 80–85, pl. vi. On rolls containing world histories and genealogies generally see also the rather confused article by Fossier, 'Chroniques universelles en forme de rouleau', pp. 163–83.

Fig. 48   The beginning of the family tree showing the descent of Edward IV: Adam and Eve, with
their sons Abel, Cain and Seth, and the names of Seth's descendants below. The text in the rim of
the roundel is from Genesis 4: 14–15, God's words to the serpent. Philadelphia, Free Library, MS
Lewis E 201. By kind permission of the Free Library of Philadelphia.

as Edward I for whom a number of rolls survive, created to support his
claims to the crown of Scotland.[9]

Latin and English versions of Peter de Poitiers's biblical genealogy continued to the current English king were common by the mid-fifteenth
century[10] and so were other purely secular royal pedigrees. The latter had
proliferated since at least the reign of Henry II, another king who needed
to emphasise his right to the crown. For their brief texts and explanatory notes some of these secular manuscripts relied on the *Little Brut*, a
short and often very independent version of the *Brut*, the national English
chronicle from the days of Brutus, the founder of Britain, via the stories
of Geoffrey of Monmouth, through several continuations to the reigning king. The *Little Brut* could be in Latin, French or English and usually

---

9   Sandler, *Gothic Manuscripts*, vol. 2, item 9, p. 26, a particularly magnificent example from
    Adam to Edward I, with a section showing Scotland and England running parallel. See also
    Heralds Catalogue, no. 113, pl. 39, for an example made 1296.
10 De La Mare, *Lyell*, pp. 81–85; *Manual*, vol. 8, pp. 2674–75.

started with the Heptarchy of Anglo-Saxon kings, represented by a complicated diagrammatic roundel.[11]

If kings of England felt no compunction about linking their descent to that of Christ, noble and gentle families of England had as little shame about attaching theirs to that of the kings of England (and so back to Adam). The Percys were one example (see fig. 49)[12] and the Botiller family had another such genealogy, compiled to celebrate the marriage of Thomas Botiller to Eleanor Talbot in 1448–49.[13] On the continent similar texts were produced in the same period. One example, made for the dukes of Burgundy in 1466–68, is particularly interesting because its prologue reveals something of the activities of the makers rather than the patron. It directly addressed Duke Philip the Good:

> Your humble servants, who love truth and do not wish to exalt you beyond reason but also do not want your glory, dignity and high descent to be diminished, hidden or belittled by people out of ignorance or envy, desiring to know your rights, have searched for old chronicles and studied them; they have worked very hard, travelled far, requested information from many people, at great expense and completely at their own initiative and without your command ... [14]

This particular genealogy was made to help prove Philip's 'natural' right to the various lordships he amassed, all of which he claimed in one way or another by right of inheritance; the makers knew that the result of their labours would be very welcome.

Genealogical chronicles of English history in English verse or prose with some literary pretensions were common by the early fifteenth century, constantly brought up to date by each succeeding generation.[15] The verse chronicles all derived from two poems called *The Kings of England since William I*, one by John Lydgate in the 1420s, and the other by an unknown

---

11 E.g. The Hague, Koninklijke Bibliotheek, MS 75 A 2/2, a roll, to Edward I; *Heralds Catalogue*, no. 65, pl. 39.

12 *Manual*, vol. 8, pp. 2677–78 [49]; it can be remembered that the Percys also added their name to the list of the 'Companions of the Conqueror'. See also Bodley Roll 5, discussed below.

13 New York, Public Library, Spencer MS 193, see Mooney, 'Lydgate's "Kings of England"', pp. 255–89, esp. 269.

14 This is a free translation of the text quoted in *Charles le Téméraire*, item 8; see also Doutrepont, *Littérature*, p. 453.

15 *Manual*, vol. 8, pp. 2675–76.

author written probably in 1445 to celebrate Henry VI's marriage. To date over fifty manuscripts are known of these verse chronicles, a clear indication of their popularity, although they are by no means the most commonly surviving genre of English royal pedigrees.[16] They were owned by monastic houses, aristocrats and heralds such as Sir Thomas Holme, Clarenceux 1476–83, and they were often expensive productions; like Peter of Poitiers's biblical genealogy they could also be used by schoolmasters.[17]

The change of kings in 1461 encouraged the production of new pedigrees ending with Edward and displacing the Lancastrian line. The Lancastrians had 'lopped off' the branch of York, but now events had shown the latter was the true line, still alive and flourishing once more. Edward's biblical descent was naturally much the same as that of any other king in Europe, but by using his Mortimer descent he could include Cadwalader and his angelic prophecy of the eventual return of the British race, described by Geoffrey of Monmouth to add dramatic panache to the rows of Celtic kings.[18] Edward could also self-righteously restore accuracy to those areas deliberately made hazy by his predecessors: the true positions of Edmund 'Crouchback' and John of Gaunt among the sons of Henry III and Edward III.[19] The change of kings necessitated active dissemination of the details of Edward's recent ancestry, proving his rights to the crown of England, as well as the crowns of France, Leon and Castile. Long, short and interpolated versions in English and Latin were produced of Peter of Poitiers's biblical genealogy and of other chroniclers, extending down to Edward, some of them expressing active Yorkist partisanship, others merely setting out the facts of descent.[20]

---

16 Mooney, 'Lydgate's "Kings of England"', passim.

17 *Ibid.*, pp. 271–72.

18 See ch. 8 below.

19 There was a contemporary tradition that Edmund, 1st Earl of Lancaster, had been older than his brother, Edward I, and that as a consequence Henry IV inherited the throne by right of his mother, Blanche of Lancaster, Edmund's great-granddaughter, *Complete Peerage*, vol. VII, p. 378n. Edward IV claimed the crown by right of his great-great-grandmother, Philippa, only child of Edward III's third son, Lionel of Clarence; John of Gaunt was Edward III's fourth son.

20 See Anglo, 'British History in early Tudor propaganda', pp. 41–45, for one list of such genealogies; Allan, 'Yorkist propaganda', pp. 171–92; and her 'Political propaganda', pp. 278–87; Ross, 'Rumour, propaganda and popular opinion', pp. 15–32; *Manual*, vol. 8, pp. 2675–78; De la Mare, *Lyell*, pp. 81–85; Scott, *Later Gothic Manuscripts*, on Oxford, Corpus Christi College, MS 207. We are most grateful to Dr Scott for allowing us to see her draft description of this ms., and to her and Jeremy Griffiths for discussing such mss with us.

A good example of a 'standard' roll of Edward IV is Oxford, Bodleian Library, MS Lyell 33, which used the beginning of the *Compendium* of Peter of Poitiers in translation and extracts from English chronicles. It substituted the Mortimer descent, on the left, for the list of popes in the 'Lancastrian' rolls. It was Yorkist in tone but without any great partisan emphasis; there was, for instance, mild praise of Henry V. Decoration was limited to the top margin, a few inches of the left margin from the top down and one roundel showing Adam and Eve and the serpent (see also fig. 48).[21]

Some of these English royal genealogies were visually striking and could have been decorative and loyalist displays in a public place such as a church or hall. The most famous pedigree known to have been actually put on display was that proving Henry VI's claim to the throne of France, which was hung in Notre-Dame, Paris, at the order of John, Duke of Bedford, in 1423, and consisted of a poem with a picture.[22] There is no surviving Yorkist propaganda pedigree that can *certainly* be said to have been displayed in this way,[23] but a candidate is the roll containing a delightful pedigree of Edward IV from Henry III (to include Edmund Crouchback), BL, Harley Roll 7353. It is done in the manner of a tree of Jesse, with Henry III reclining at the bottom and Edward IV and Henry VI emerging as opponents at the top. Each descendant sits in a cup rimmed with flower petals, apparently in animated conversation (or conflict) with each other.[24] Above the tree are five pairs of paintings, each pair illustrating an event of Edward's career on the right and its biblical 'type' or precedent on the left. The last pair are allegorical representations of Edward's success and the fulfilment of all prophecies that predicted his 'coming' (see figs 64, 66). It is possible that this roll once hung in a Dominican house at Gloucester, its religious typology being presumably second nature to its clerics.[25]

---

21 The ms. is described and compared to related mss in De La Mare, *Lyell*, pp. 80–85; see also *Manual*, vol. 8, p. 2676. Compare Allan, thesis, p. 279, who describes Lyell 33 as 'prejudiced'.

22 Rowe, 'King Henry VI's claim to France'.

23 Allan, thesis, pp. 307–08, on display; Mooney, 'Lydgate's "Kings of England"', p. 27. Most if not all surviving copies have holes at their top end, but it obviously cannot be established when these were made.

24 BL, MS Harl. 7353, see also ch. 8 below. Illustrated in A. Cheetham, *Richard III*, London 1972, p. 13; Pollard, *Richard III and the Princes*, p. 40.

25 Illustrated e.g. in Pollard, *Richard III and the Princes*, pp. 41, 53; Ross, *Edward IV*, pls 2, 3, 4. For more details of these rolls and other Yorkist rolls using genealogy and prophecy, see Allan, thesis, pp. 297–307, and ch. 8 below.

Equally striking is another Latin pedigree emphasising Edward's claims
to England, France, Leon and Castile, now in the Philadelphia Free
Library. It has pictorial roundels of God in splendour, Adam and Eve and
the Ark (see fig. 48), and includes a row of 'portraits' of kings, and a glorious display of heraldry and emblems of the house of York, with copious
use of Edward's motto *comfort et liesse* (comfort and joy). At the head of
the roll putting everything else in the shade is an equestrian 'portrait' of
Edward IV in full heraldic trappings (see pls VIIIa and b).[26]

Both the Harley Roll and the Philadelphia Roll were made in the 1460s
and the exuberance of both express the palpable relief that Yorkist supporters felt at Edward's succession and the end of civil war. The Harley
Roll rams its point home by the spectacular and apparently unique image
of Reason driving a spoke into Fortune's Wheel and so actually stopping it, for all time, with Edward IV sitting securely and triumphantly
on top as King of England for ever. The Philadelphia Roll's celebration is
conveyed by its immaculate presentation and artistic competence as well
as its religious persuasiveness: there is no escaping the evidence that the
Yorkist accession was God's will. God's right hand points to Edward, who
is surrounded by quotations like *A domino factum est istud* (This was done
by the Lord) and *Si deus nobiscum quis contra nos* (If God is for us who will
be against us?).[27]

The clerics who wanted the Harley Roll and the unknown aristocrat
who wanted the Philadelphia Roll were not alone in their support of
York and their desire to show it in such a work. Another genealogical
effusion was created, or copied, for the city of Coventry: a verse pedigree reciting Edward's position as the heir of Brutus, the Saxon kings, the
Norman kings, St Louis, Edward III, Isabella of Castile and Richard II.
It ended by celebrating at length the 'rose of grete plesaunce, ... wheche
ros alle the worlde schalle loye [praise? or love?]' now the lion [of March]
has torn up the thorns and briars stunting its growth, and the fox [Henry

---

26 Philadelphia Free Library, MS E 201, see also ch. 8 below. A discussion of this ms is to
   appear in Scott, *Later Gothic Manuscripts*. Edward is shown with neither queen (but spouses
   are not included in this roll generally) nor children; everything is focused on his rights by
   inheritance. See also the present authors, *Reburial of Richard, Duke of York*.

27 An equally pious note is struck by the final scene of a genealogy made shortly after Edward
   IV's marriage: Edward and his queen kneel before God's throne supported by Sts George and
   Margaret; Oxford, Jesus College, MS 114, described in Allan, thesis, pp. 285–87.

VI] has fled.[28] It is possible this pedigree, too, was for public display in the town hall for the leading citizens.

These English royal genealogies went everywhere, throughout England and examples were to be found in France, Flanders, Germany and Rome. A 'Lancastrian' roll originally ending with Henry VI and the birth of Edward of Lancaster, must have travelled to France between 1453 and 1460; this is clear from the additions made to it in French and Latin, which also indicate that the author was moderately knowledgeable about English events. It was brought up to date, eventually, to the reign of Henry VIII (*rex modernus*).[29] Early in the reign of Edward IV an old servant of his father, Thomas Derwent, had been arrested in the north and threatened with death because in his 'kasket' had been found 'a pedegre of the true and verray lynyall descent from noble progeniteurs to your highnesse as rightfull and verrey enheritour to the crownes of Englond and Fraunce'.[30] When the pope was informed of Edward's accession, a note with the Yorkist line of descent was included to convince him of the righteousness of the new king's claim.[31] Evidence of the general spread of this propagandist material is the letter of a Hanse merchant to his principal in Lübeck, 5 November 1468. He enclosed several records of recent events and among them 'a tree (*trunck*) of King Edward, King of England, who is heir to the crown and nearer to it than King Henry ... ; have it explained to you by doctors and clerks'.[32] As is clear from this merchant's comments the precise message of these rolls would not be immediately clear to anyone who could not study the text closely: they were clever and complicated, packed with symbols, heraldry and esoteric information, as well as being in Latin.

To concentrate on the propaganda element in these pedigrees and chronicles is to miss the main point for an incidental one. The very different

---

28 Louis, 'Yorkist genealogical chronicle', pp. 1–20. 'Fox' (*vulpes*) is one of the prophetic 'code names' describing Henry VI as opponent of the rightful heir, Edward IV, see ch. 8 below.

29 The roll is now The Hague, Koninklijke Bibliotheek, MS 78 B 24.

30 PRO, Special Collections, Ancient Petitions, SC8/107/5322, Derwent's complaint to the king. We are grateful to Dr Henry Summerson for this reference.

31 T. Rymer, *Foedera, Conventiones,* ... , 20 vols, XI, vol. 5, pt 2, p. 110, 22 March 1462; Pius II wrote back: 'We have been informed that Your Highness has assumed the government of the kingdom of England; you write that you have succeeded to the kingdom by direct line, as is contained in the note with your family tree which you have sent us'.

32 The text was probably part of a codex, not a roll; it is not known yet whether it survives; *Hanserecesse*, vol. 6, item 117, p. 87.

but closely related manuscripts and the working pedigrees and armorials of the heralds help to preserve a true perspective from which to view all these effusions. More than anything else they were a product of a passion for family, territorial pride and acquisition, fostering inheritance and judicious, profitable marriage and procreation. By the fifteenth century family and the descent of property was firmly guided by stringent rules in the care of heralds and lawyers. Each new heir required a new line for himself and his heir on the family pedigree and he might choose to edit out 'superfluous' uncles, brothers and sisters, change a few rich widows into heiresses, demote a childless elder son to the place of deceased younger son, all in the cause of tidying up and flattering the picture.

Richard III as the 'natural' successor to a reigning king hardly needed a new version of the Yorkist pedigree, but a few amendments, such as the omission of his various nephews and an emphasis on his father's descent and rights would have been essential. No 'roll' containing these elements seems to survive, nor is there any evidence of a sudden new spate of propaganda pedigrees being made during Richard's reign. He almost certainly owned one or more of these Yorkist pedigrees, but his own rule and that of his heir required different methods of legitimation: the arguments of canon law to make his nephews and nieces illegitimate, the arguments of practical politics against the rule of a minor and the obvious benefits of being ruled by such a good prince as himself.[33]

Royal pedigrees, however, were produced that included Richard III, his queen and son, one surviving example being prepared for the Percy family. Bodley Roll 5 is a careful and handsome product illustrated by pen portraits of kings, queens and some towns. It has no political point to make and the author's introduction is only concerned with the moral message that although the body dies as a consequence of the Fall, the soul does not.[34] His recent information is accurate: he shows all the duke of York's children and knows their fate; he truncates Edward IV's descent, but puts in roundels for all his children; and he similarly truncates Richard's descent but puts in his queen and son. In contrast the parallel line of the Percys continues and clearly is expected to continue. No

---

33 See e.g. Sutton, 'Richard III's "tytylle & right"', pp. 57–63; Helmholz, 'The sons of Edward IV', pp. 91–103.

34 The author tied himself into knots over his composition and ends desperately with 'etc.'! For the text of this roll see the description *Manual*, vol. 8, pp. 2677–78.

Tudor king has been added, dating the finishing of the roll to very soon after Bosworth.[35]

Richard III's Roll and Book of Arms

Less personal and more professional, but still concerned with family, descent and legitimacy, were the books and rolls that preserved purely heraldic information. Richard III is known to have owned two rolls of arms (rolls being inclusive of books in this terminology).[36] Few medieval rolls of arms survive in their original form, most existing in copies, and those owned by Richard are no exception. Some are now classified as 'occasional rolls', that is they recorded the arms borne by the persons present at a particular event, such as a tournament or funeral and usually bear the name of the 'occasion'. Others record the arms borne by the families or persons living in one region; some cover an entire country, or the 'whole world', starting with the king of England, the emperor, or the king of Jerusalem, as appropriate. One of Richard's rolls falls into this 'general' category. There were also 'ordinaries', that is rolls which group coats together by their use of a particular device such as the lion or the cross. Into this category falls Richard's other roll, now called 'Thomas Jenyns' Book'. Ordinaries were particularly useful to heralds in their professional capacity but rarely survive.

Rolls of all kinds were made by and for heralds from the earliest period of heraldry (twelfth century) and the language of the blazon (the precise description of a coat in a standard heraldic 'language') was fully formed by *c.* 1250. From the beginning heralds needed to make copies of the rolls and the information of their fellow-professionals for their own use, just as they needed to copy any roll that was wearing out with constant use. Their copies were usually very accurate.[37] It is their accurate copying that

---

35 The roll seems to date from very soon after Richard's death as his descent is firmly cut off, as was done in the case of other heirless kings, but the author did not choose to add in Henry VII. Some of the most recent Percy details may have been added shortly after 1489. Allan, thesis, ch. 11, has other examples of Yorkist genealogies being used by the king's subjects.

36 Wagner, *Aspilogia*, vol. 1, p. xi; *Aspilogia*, vol. 2 contains corrections and additions but these do not affect Richard's two rolls.

37 Wagner, *Aspilogia*, vol. 1, pp. xiv–xv; for Wagner's categorisation of the rolls, pp. xv, xvi, xix–xx

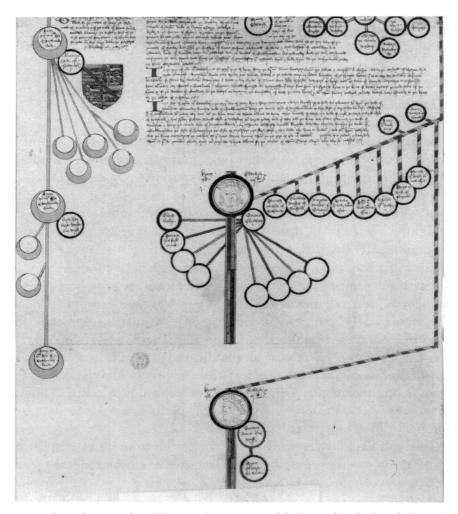

Fig. 49 The end section of a roll showing the succession of the kings of England, probably made for the Percy family, whose descent runs parallel and continues, unlike those of Edward IV and Richard III. The lines of both kings are clearly truncated although roundels have been drawn for their children. The failure to insert all the most recent names in the otherwise complete roll and the inclusion of the fifth earl of Northumberland suggests it was left unfinished shortly after the battle of Bosworth and the death of the fourth earl in 1489. Henry VII was not added and the roll was therefore probably made shortly after the battle of Bosworth. Oxford, Bodleian Library Bodley Roll 5. By permission of the Bodleian Library.

has preserved the record of Richard's possession of two such rolls. (Over the years it became usual to attach the name of an owner to a roll for identification,[38] and these names will be used here.)

Richard's rolls do not survive. The industrious Sir Thomas Wriothesley, Garter King of Arms 1505–34, carefully copied both of Richard's rolls for his own armorial records and recorded their ownership. Thomas was the son of John Writhe, Garter King of Arms 1478–1504. He pompously extended his name when he succeeded his father in the office.[39] John had been Garter when Richard III incorporated the Heralds and granted them Coldharbour on 2 March 1484. The loss of this house under Henry VII, who gave it to his mother, left the heralds without a home and apparently caused considerable disarray to the communal library that had already been instituted. There were bitter disputes over the ownership of the college's books: one complaint was that the two Writhes retained some of the books belonging to the whole office.[40] It is likely that Richard's two rolls were among the Writhes's booty and one at least may have been placed in the communal library by Richard's gift or command when he set up the college.

Richard's ownership of the rolls may have been an expression of gen-uine personal interest in heraldry, one of the trappings of chivalry and pride in family, but it was certainly an expression of the practical need for a member of the upper classes to be able to recognise the arms of all ranks and, above all, the need of the constable of England to do so. Richard was constable 1469–83, and in that office had the personal oversight of the heralds. He drew up ordinances encouraging the heralds to record both military and ceremonial events and the right of certain people to bear arms.[41] Richard proved his interest and concern for the heralds by creat-ing their college and by giving them a large house to live in and keep their records and library. He apparently added one magnificent roll of arms, a copy of what is now called 'St George's Roll', to the heralds' collection.

The original of 'St George's Roll' was made around 1285. It has been inferred that it contained 677 painted shields and measured about 93⁄4

---

38 *Ibid.*, p. xiii.

39 College of Arms, pp. 41–44, on the two Writhes/Wriothesleys. John Writhe apparently resigned, for no known reason, from office 5 January 1485, resuming office 22 August 1485.

40 *Ibid.*, pp. 41–44, and see Wagner, *Heralds and Heraldry*, pp. 94–5. See also ch. 7 above.

41 Wagner, *Aspilogia*, vol. 1, p. xvii, on the importance of Richard owning a general roll and his herald a 'great ordinary.' Wagner, *Heralds of England*, pp. 67–68, 75, 130.

inches × 8 feet 91⁄2 inches, the precise arrangement of the shields being uncertain.[42] The original does not survive but several copies or versions were made and some of these, dating from the sixteenth century and later do survive. One copy of the original, which may have been made in the fifteenth century, came into the ownership of Richard of Gloucester. His copy certainly had blazons dating from the fifteenth century added to each shield and these blazons alone were copied by Thomas Wriothesley. Wriothesley's copy is now College of Arms, MS M 14 bis, pp. 392–421 and 461, an old rebinding having carelessly split the text in two. Wriothesley's heading runs:

Ista arma sequencia habebantur in quodam veteri rotulo depicto quondam R ducis gloucester'

(These coats of arms were contained in an old painted roll that once belonged to R Duke of Gloucester)

The roll begins with the king of England followed by the king of Scotland, the earl of Warenne and then proceeds down the lower ranks. There are a few blanks, either due to blanks in Wriothesley's original or to its dilapidated state. It must have been a magnificent roll when originally made, however battered it may have become by the time Richard of Gloucester owned it.

The particular collection of arms now called 'Thomas Jenyns' Book' is thought to have been originally made around 1400 and based on an earlier collection of about the mid-fourteenth century with later additions. It comprised a large number of shields with blazons. One version (which may indeed have been the original) with 1,595 shields was owned by Queen Margaret of Anjou and still survives (now BL, MS Add. 40851). Another was owned by Thomas Jenyns, a gentleman of the household of Henry, Earl of Huntingdon, in the sixteenth century, who has given his name to the collection. Jenyns's version does not survive,[43] but several sixteenth-century and later copies of both Queen Margaret's and Jenyns's

---

42 The main description of this roll is in *Aspilogia*, vol. 1, pp. 19–21. See also Campbell, *Catalogue*, p. 155. Wagner says it was probably Wriothesley who copied the roll, but the new catalogue is more definite. See also ch. 4, above.

43 Wagner, *Aspilogia*, vol. 1, pp. 73–78, and pl. vi, for the main description, and Campbell, *Catalogue*, p. 155.

books do survive. All these versions begin with the arms and blazon of the kings of Spain and Almaigne (whose coats include lions) and then proceed down through the ranks, while grouping the coats by their devices: leopards follow the lions, then eagles, and so on. The whole has a markedly Yorkshire bias.[44] Richard of Gloucester also owned a version of this 'great ordinary',[45] which again does not survive, and Sir Thomas Wriothesley copied out the blazons, his copy being now College of Arms, MS M 14 bis, pp. 462–527. He headed it:

> En ung liure Ric' duc de Gloucester' en picture lequel liure son poursuyvant avoit en garde A° xx° E iiij[ti]

> (In a book with pictures of Richard, Duke of Gloucester, which book his pursuivant had in his keeping in the twentieth year of Edward IV).

The beauty of Richard's copy cannot now be compared to Queen Margaret's, but it was certainly a prestigious and useful manuscript for the duke of Gloucester as constable of England. He entrusted it to his own pursuivant: as an ordinary it was primarily a professional herald's working book. The pursuivant in question would have been Blanc Sanglier, a post held apparently by a son of John More, Norroy King of Arms (1478–85, 1485–91), who is reputed to have accompanied Richard III's body to burial in Leicester after the battle of Bosworth.[46]

Richard III's 'Family Books'

There are three illustrated manuscripts of particular family interest with which Richard can be associated, though not as owner. They are all well known: the Salisbury Roll, the Rous Roll and the Beauchamp Pageant. All three combine pride in family, descent and ancestral glory with an awareness of its 'advertising' value, an antiquarian interest and a love of heraldic display. Each reflects the interests of the maker as well as those of the patron and owner.

---

44 The next known owner of Queen Margaret's copy was Sir John Norton, of Norton Conyers, Yorks. (died 1489), Wagner, *Aspilogia*, vol. 1, p. 74.
45 Wagner's phrase, *ibid.*, p. xvii.
46 *College of Arms*, pp. 106, 238.

The Salisbury Roll, unlike the heraldic rolls described above, was of specific interest only to members of the Neville family. It was also more 'personal' in the sense that it uses human figures to display the coats of arms. The complete roll showed more than fifty knights and ladies dressed in armorial surcoats and robes, most of them in pairs and all of them earls of Salisbury, their countesses or their kin.[47] The roll was probably made on the occasion of the reburial of the father and uncle of Richard Neville, Earl of Warwick, at Bisham Priory, 14 February 1463, a ceremony so magnificent and memorable that the narrative was to become a manual on how to stage such events. A few months earlier Richard Neville had become earl of Salisbury and presumably even more interested in the history of his predecessors. Twenty years later a second version of this roll was made, a partial and crude copy with many differences in detail and only following the direct line of succession of the earls. Important additions were the figures of Richard III and his queen and there need be no doubt that it was made in their reign and during Anne Neville's lifetime. At the time Richard's son, Edward, held the title of earl of Salisbury and was the living symbol of the continuation of the line.[48]

Heraldry is still important, but more balanced by narrative, in another 'family book' that can be associated with Richard, the so-called Rous Roll. However deficient according to modern standards, it was the most 'scholarly' of the illustrated books discussed here.[49] Its maker, John Rous (c. 1411–91), chaplain of Guy's Cliff near Warwick, servant to the Beauchamp and Neville earls of Warwick, was an antiquarian in the class of William Worcester and John Hardyng, men who carefully collected, described and studied historical material, and combined scholarly competence and a varying critical sense with a cheerful, unwitting acceptance of the shortcomings of the sources available to them.

47 Cat. XX, below; Wagner, *Aspilogia*, vol. 1, pp. 103–04; vol. 2, p. 275; for a detailed study: Payne, 'The Salisbury Roll', pp. 187–98, and pls. The original roll is owned by the duke of Buccleugh, BL, Loan MS 90; the copy made temp. Richard III is partly in the same ms. (pp. 146–58), partly in a collection made by Sir Thomas Wriothesley, now BL, MS Add. 45133, ff. 52*–55v.

48 Created 15 Feb. 1478, see *Complete Peerage*, vol. 11, p. 399.

49 For the Rous Roll, Rous's life and the problem whether he was the artist as well as the author, see *Manual*, vol. 8, XXI [78]; Courthope, *Rous Roll*; Russell, 'Rous Roll', pp. 23–31, ill.; Wright, 'Rous Roll: The English Version', pp. 77–81, e.g. on the various hands that worked on the text; Gransden, 'Antiquarian studies', pp. 75–97, ill., esp. 84–87, pls. vi–viii. The mss of the two versions in Latin and English are London, College of Arms, MS Warwick Roll and BL, MS Add. 48976; several later copies were made of both, see Wagner, *Aspilogia*, vol. 1, pp. 116–20; vol. 2, p. 277.

Rous Roll is a history of the town and the earls of Warwick in the accessible and attractive format of a roll with full length pictures of individual figures each accompanied by a narrative text. The first part of the manuscript has legendary and historical characters of national importance associated with the locality of Warwick, from King Guthelinus, who founded the town 'in the time of Alexander the Great', to Richard III, who 'did gret cost off byldyng' in the castle. The second part is concerned with the earls themselves and leads from Aeneas, the forefather of all earls, to Sir Guy of Warwick, of romance fame, to the renowned Richard Beauchamp and Richard Neville, the Kingmaker, ending with Richard III, his wife and son. Every figure stands beneath his or her full coat of arms in colour, their heraldic beasts are at their feet, their descriptive text below. Rous made two versions, one in Latin, one in English. He was consistent and careful. He glorified the earls with as much interesting information as he could gather, including the elaborate heraldry, legendary and symbolic or historical and accurate. His depiction of the armour of his subjects – and to a lesser extent their dress – shows he was aware of historical change. Readers could enjoy such details as the piety of Henry Beauchamp, who used to say the full 'David psalter' every day when not prevented by 'gretter besines', the personal 'resons' (mottoes) of Henry and the later countesses, as well as such pictorial details – that go beyond Rous's text – as the lion resting its paws on Guy of Warwick's shield and looking gratefully up at its saviour.[50]

There is little doubt that the rolls were finished in time for them to have been shown to Richard III, Anne Neville, his queen, and their young son during their visit to Warwick in the summer of '83. They may have been well pleased with the description of themselves and with the visual presentation of the continuity of their family.[51] Young Edward is the last

---

50 Courthope, *Rous Roll*, nos. 54, 51–53, 56, 21; Guy saved the life of a lion about to be killed by a dragon and it followed him ever after.

51 The two versions and Rous's dismissal of Richard III as Anne Neville's 'unfortunate husband' and the other changes in the Latin one have been sufficiently discussed elsewhere; for the facts see the Courthope/Ross edition. The English version clearly shows the maker's intention of celebrating the reigning king, the queen, their heir and ancestors. It was completed after 8 September 1483, when young Edward was created Prince of Wales, a title he bears in the ms. There is no reason to assume that the Latin version did not originally contain exactly the same pictures and texts; the accepted theory is that this copy remained in Rous's possession and that he was thus able to adapt it to the new circumstances after August 1485, whereas the English copy which survives had already left his hands.

figure in the series, regally crowned and holding a sceptre, a (white) boar at his feet.

Patronage and flattery need not have been the only reasons for a manuscript's existence, however;[52] men like Rous and, for instance, William Worcester,[53] did much of their work in the service of a master, but they must have had their own motives for making a book, their own interests and preferences. In Rous's text there is mention of his wish 'to show folk the place', that is, Guy's Cliff hermitage, and it is arguable that he originally planned his roll for such a 'tourist' purpose, to bring him a little income from the offerings of pilgrims and other visitors. His Latin text would impress the more learned, others could read the English version. In this respect the Rous Roll can be compared to another Yorkist family production, the so-called Clare Roll, produced at Clare Priory, Suffolk, which supplied the interested visitor with information in Latin and English about the history of the priory and the patronage of the lords of Clare; it included the arms of the lords in full colour. Both the Clare Roll and the Rous Roll had the additional merit of flattering the maker's overlord.[54]

More magnificent even than the Rous Roll, but covering only a short period of history, is the Beauchamp Pageant, another illustrated manuscript that Richard may have known. It was perhaps made for his mother-in-law, Anne Beauchamp, Countess of Warwick in her own right, and possibly in order to entertain and educate her grandson, Richard's prince of Wales. The well-known series of fifty-three splendid, detailed drawings celebrate the life of Richard Beauchamp, Earl

---

52 See also the claims of the makers of the roll for Duke Philip of Burgundy, above. There is a danger of over-emphasising the ulterior motives of the makers of such mss (e.g. in Mason, 'Legends of the Beauchamps' ancestors', pp. 25–40). It was natural for authors to flatter their lord or the king – it would have been foolish not to do so – but Rous (and even less the probable maker of the Clare Roll, Osbern Bokenham, see below) was not entirely dependent on patronage for his living. A straightforward scholarly desire to inform people and organise one's knowledge on paper for safekeeping and in an accessible form should not be denied even to 15th-century writers. Rous's use of the past tense even in the sections about Richard III, Queen Anne and their son suggests that he was aware his work might be read by future generations and that he saw it in a slightly wider context than just getting a 'tip' from the royal visitors because they felt flattered. It is probable that some lords and patrons shared an interest in historical facts and liked to add another such book to their collection; it need not *always* have been essential to flatter them up to the hilt.

53 For Worcester see chs 4 and 5 above.

54 For the Clare Roll see ch. 2 above.

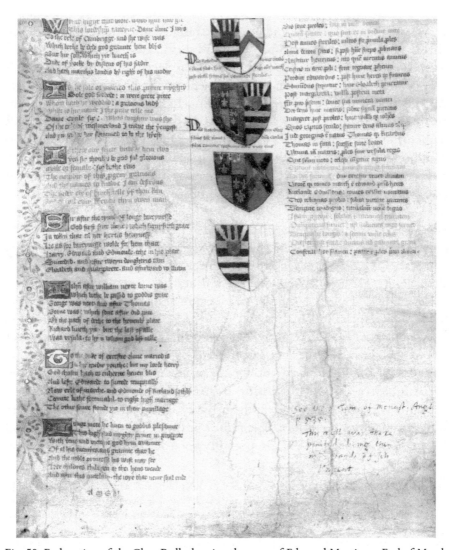

Fig. 50 End section of the Clare Roll, showing the arms of Edmund Mortimer, Earl of March (died 1425), Richard, Earl of Cambridge (died 1415), and Richard, Duke of York (died 1460). The last coat is that of Edward, Earl of March, the future Edward IV, the space for his wife's arms left blank. See also pl. III. London, College of Arms, MS 3/16. By permission of the Chapter of the College of Arms.

of Warwick (1381–1439), and are all extremely suitable to illustrate the chivalric virtues of martial prowess and service to king and country.[55] At the end of the manuscript are two small selective family trees, which may be presumed to contain the 'argument' of the book. The first shows Anne Beauchamp as daughter and eventual heir of Richard Beauchamp, as 'hole suster' of his only son, Henry, Duke of Warwick; the second depicts her again, this time with her husband, Richard Neville, her two daughters, three sons-in-law and three grandchildren. In what seems to be a conscious error, Anne, the younger daughter, is not only drawn in the position of the elder child, but also called the 'first' daughter in the text. She is flanked by her two husbands, Edward of Lancaster, Henry VI's son, and Richard III. Isabel and her husband George, Duke of Clarence, are on the right half of the page (heraldically the left) and Isabel is called the 'secunde doughter'. This lay-out gives 'Edward Plantagenet, son to kyng Richard' the status of principal heir to the earldom of Warwick. A scholar and local man like Rous would not have made such a mistake – in fact, in the Rous Roll he clearly distinguishes between Isabel and Anne as the elder and the younger, calling the latter 'on of the eyrys'[56] – but an unscrupulous or ignorant author, helped by an artist without historical knowledge or interest, could have organised this suggestive alteration. Anne Beauchamp herself, with a daughter who was queen and a grandson likely to be king, may have been only too happy to overlook this minor point of precedence: Isabel and Clarence were dead, their son possibly retarded, whereas Anne's regal

---

55 BL, MS Cotton Julius B iv; see *Manual*, vol. 8, XXI [80], and references given there. The facsimile editions are: Carysfort, *Pageants of Richard Beauchamp*, and Dillon and St John Hope, *Pageant of the Birth, Life and Death of Richard Beauchamp*; a new edition by Dr Alexandra Sinclair is being prepared.

56 In the Latin version of the Rous Roll, where Anne has been stripped of her regal robes, she is *secunda filia et una heredum*, see Courthope, *Rous Roll*, notes to no. 62. The position and regal attire of Anne and her husband in the Beauchamp Pageant also seem to argue strongly against this ms. having been made after 1485 to please the eyes of Henry VII for whatever purpose; compare Lowry, 'John Rous and the ... the Neville Circle', pp. 327–38, esp. 337–38; Lowry also seems to assume that most works by 15th-century authors or artists were produced in the service of 'calculated propaganda'. As to the sensational changes that Rous made to his roll and the stories he introduced into some of his other work after 1485 in order to blacken Richard III, we must remember that like all writers he tried to write what his readers would like. Visitors to Guy's Cliff would be pleasantly horrified by the childish stories about the trivial physical signs of Richard's evil character which Rous could tell and included in his *Historia* (see e.g. Hanham, *Richard III and his Early Historians*, pp. 118–24).

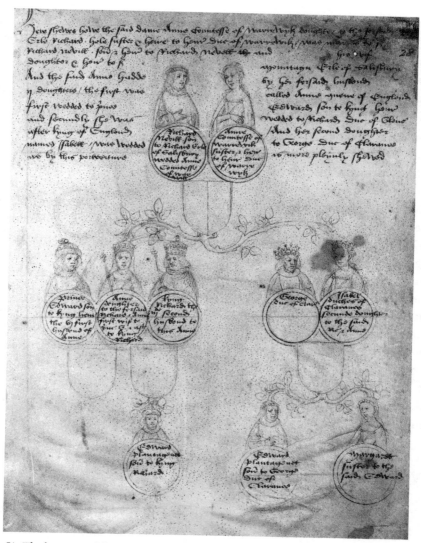

Fig. 51 The last page of the Beauchamp Pageant, showing Anne Beauchamp and her husband, Richard Neville, Earl of Warwick by right of his wife, and their daughters with their husbands. Anne the second daughter, who married first Edward, Prince of Wales, son of Henry VI, and second Richard, Duke of Gloucester, later Richard III, is shown on the left – the heraldic right – in the position of the elder; in the explanatory text she is called 'the first daughter'. Isabel, actually the elder, is shown in secondary position with her husband, George, Duke of Clarence. The children of these two marriages are, from left to right: Edward, Prince of Wales, Edward, later Earl of Warwick, and Margaret, later Countess of Salisbury. BL, MS Cotton Julius B iv. By permission of The British Library.

status put her more or less 'naturally' in a senior position. Such editing of family trees in favour of those in power had been common since they were first composed.

Anne Beauchamp was the heiress of several great and long-lived families; she was also largely dispossessed of her wealth from 1471 because of the political errors of her husband who had taken her title of Warwick. It is perhaps not surprising she was interested in her ancestry and in a grandson who was prince of Wales – she drank out of the cup of her ancestor, the Swan Knight, with the local antiquary John Rous; she built the magnificent chapel and tomb of her father and she may have commissioned the Beauchamp Pageant. Anne and her descendants are the *contemporary* focus of the line in another surviving roll made *c.* 1475 by Tewkesbury Abbey. This set out the many descendants of the legendary Oddo Dux and Doddo Dux, devout British lords, who lived long before the Conqueror. The coats of arms of all the intervening ancestors – the lords of Clare, the Despensers and others – which made up the remarkable collection of quarterings borne by Anne, are set out and explained in great detail. The Abbey claimed to have been founded by Oddo and Doddo and wished to advertise its very powerful, contemporary patrons and their long line of descent: the final two coats of arms, painted very large, are those of the two daughters of Anne Beauchamp impaling those of their husbands, the dukes of Clarence and Gloucester.[57]

'Virtue and Ancient Riches'

To ley the grownde of noblesse upon vertu joyned to possessions and Rychesses, thowe it be a mater disputabille and disputed … ; it is not of

---

57 Oxford, Bodleian Library, MS Lat. Misc. b. 2 (R), dorse. The obverse is a genealogy from Adam and Eve to the young Henry VI. The Tewkesbury 'descent' is crudely done, but elaborate; lesser connections are also noted as well as the main line down to Anne. The scribe appears to have had an excellent exemplar as far as Thomas le Despenser, but thereafter his layout deteriorates, although his attention to heraldry does not. This note corrects the present authors, 'RIII's books: Ancestry', p. 352 and n. 47.

eny scole dynyed [denied] but that Rychesse ys a propre instrumente of execucion of vertu ... [58]

This quotation is taken from the draft speech of Chancellor Russell for the opening of Edward V's parliament. The 'mater disputabille' referred to is the controversy about the nature of 'true nobility'. The fact that the chancellor could mention the subject in such a public context and expect to be understood indicates that the topic was generally discussed in Richard's time. Several books owned by Richard, his relatives and contemporaries touched on the controversy in various ways.

The question whether nobility (noblesse, gentilesse) was founded on inheritance and blood or on personal virtue and achievement had been mooted in classical times and rehearsed by several English authors in prose and verse. To Chaucer's Wife of Bath the idea that 'gentilesse ... is descended out of old richesse ... is nat worth a hen' and she refers to Seneca and Boethius who state 'that he is gentil that dooth gentil dedes'.[59] Boethius had actually been more specific, saying that nobility is worthless, based as it is on the borrowed fame of one's parents. The best one can do is live up to their reputation.[60] The tenet that nobility was based on inherited wealth was also familiar to John Gower:

The worldes constitucion
Hath set the name of gentilesse
Upon the fortune of richesse
Which of long time is fall in age.[61]

Like the Wife of Bath he does not accept this, for riches may fail and fortune change; nor is nobility based on lineage, for all men are born equally naked and all will return into the earth. Only he who eschews vice and sloth and follows virtue 'is a verrai gentil man'. Even when

---

58 From the draft speech of John Russell, the chancellor, for the opening of Edward V's parliament, printed in Nichols, *Grants*, pp. xl–xli. The speech continues: '... addyng there unto the defunicion that Aristotle maketh 4° Politicorum [*Politica*, 4, 8] *quod Ingenuitas est virtus et divitiae antiquae*, Noblesse is vertu and auncienne Richesse, ...'. See also Chrimes, *English Constitutional Ideas*, pp. 168–78.
59 *The Wife of Bath's Tale*, lines 1109–12, 1168–70.
60 Boethius, *De consolatione philosophiae*, book 3, prose 6.
61 John Gower, *Confessio Amantis*, in *Complete Works*, vol. 2, pp. 360–63, bk 4, lines 2200 ff.; *Confessio Amantis*, transl. Tiller, pp. 166–69.

virtue and wealth are combined in one person he must be vigilant and active:

> For nowther good ne gentilesse
> Mai helpen hem whiche ydel be.

An early fifteenth-century text that reviewed both sides of the argument was the *Controversia de vera nobilitate*, by the Italian Buonaccorso da Montemagno, which could have been known to Richard either in the popular French translation by Jean Mielot, or in the English one printed by Caxton in 1480.[62] In this debate the high-born Scipio states unreservedly that nobility consists in blood and riches, and the best part of nobility is the joy in the noble deeds of one's ancestors and the claim to have their privileges as of right. His opponent, the virtuous and learned commoner Flaminius, echoing Boethius, objects that Scipio has nothing to offer himself and that nobility is only proved by one's own merits, such as service to the state, virtuous living and study. To modern readers the two men seem to be talking at cross purposes, as Flaminius appears to be actually defending nobility of the soul, a concept apparently beyond his opponent's grasp. To the author and his Italian audience, brought up in the political climate of the city states and imbued with the ideal of civic humanism, combining service to the state with learning, it was perfectly clear which of the two contestants was right, even though this was not explicitly said. To Caxton, who printed and probably edited the English translation, and to Edward IV, to whom this edition was dedicated, the 'solution' may not have been quite so self-evident. They would have agreed with Scipio that only those descended from noble ancestors are themselves noble and that their ancient and famous deeds are of the utmost importance. Great riches, moreover, enable a man to exercise the typically noble virtue of liberality (largesse). William Worcester in his significantly entitled *Boke of Noblesse*, which exhorted Edward IV to invade France and regain his lost inheritance, used Scipio's eulogy of ancestral glory and status as his 'argument' to encourage the king to follow in his predecessors' footsteps.[63] He clearly expected the king to actively emulate his ancestors, a need which

---

62 On the *Controversia* see Vanderjagt, *Qui sa vertu anoblist*; the same, 'Three solutions'. On the English translation see Manual, vol. 3, VII; vol. 7, XX; and 'R III's books XII', pp. 157–58, 160–61, 163–65.

63 For William Worcester see chs 4 and 5 above.

the aristocratic Scipio failed to stress, except by saying complacently that the children of noble parents tend to perform noble deeds for the simple reason that fathers live on in their sons.

Personal virtue or inherited status and riches? Which of these make a man noble, especially in the eyes of the world? At the end of Richard of York's translation of a book of Claudian's *Consulship of Stilicho*, turned into a 'mirror' for princes and edited to fit York's position and political dilemma, an original dedicatory poem reiterates in the last line of each stanza *honor merces est virtutis*, 'worship is the reward of virtue'.[64] Is 'worship', or worldly honour, the equivalent of nobility? Would York have genuinely accepted such a maxim? It is more likely that Richard of York and his sons were realistic: they would not openly deny the importance of 'virtue', but to men whose nobility of blood was a fact of life, inherited status and 'ancient riches' were essential and enabled them to fulfil their ambitions.

> Just as the newly-rich often have worse habits than those who have always been wealthy, so men that have been recently raised up and come to power do not always live as well as others, because they are unused to such good fortune ...

Thus Giles of Rome in his *De regimine principum*, of which Richard of Gloucester owned a copy.[65] He was proving the advantages of hereditary monarchy and using arguments similar to those needed to support a belief in nobility of blood. Richard III would have agreed with him; his background suggests it and his interest in heraldry and family history, as proved by his ownership of the heraldic rolls and his links with various magnificent 'family books', leave few indications to the contrary. The existence of a different view among non-noble, didactic authors cannot have escaped him, however, nor would he have denied the moral duty of everyone to be virtuous. Aristotle's simple phrase – whatever

---

64 See ch. 2 above.
65 See ch. 5 above. Giles of Rome, *De regimine*, bk 3, pt 2, ch. 5, f. 273v.

the context he had used it in and whatever he had exactly meant by it[66] – with its convenient play on Richard's name (Richard/Richesse) gave the perfect solution:

nobility is virtue and ancient riches.

---

66 It is ironic that the simple but realistic definition of Aristotle – to him a mere side issue in his discussion of the ideal state – has echoed down the centuries, repeated by people to whom the existence of nobility of blood was the last thing they either could or wanted to ignore. See e.g. Lowes, 'Chaucer and Dante's *Convivio*', pp. 19–33, who apparently fails, however, to realise what was the origin of the phrase 'old richesse' / *antica ricchezza* shared by Chaucer and Dante (in spite of his note 7, p. 22, where Dante is quoted in *De monarchia*: *Est enim nobilitas virtus et divitiae antiquae juxta Philosophum in Politicis*). Dante and Chancellor Russell knew their Aristotle. On the blending of classical/humanist and 'medieval' concepts in contemporary Burgundian views of nobility see Keen, 'Some later medieval ideas', passim. Also his, 'Debate over nobility'.

SEVEN

History: Its Reading and Making

Richard III, like many men of his time and class, had more books in the category which can be called 'history' than any other, except for religious and liturgical books.[1] We know that he had access to at least one history/ romance and three substantial histories. As a boy he became familiar with tales from the Old Testament retold in verse, and the historical romance by John Lydgate describing the *Siege of Thebes*. As a young man he could refer to an anonymous chronicle, here called the 'Fitzhugh Chronicle', which covered English history from the conversion of the Anglo-Saxons to 1199, and he acquired one volume – covering the period 1270 to 1380 – of the *Grandes chroniques de France*, the standard history of France. As king he was delighted to acquire Guido delle Colonne's *Historia destructionis Troiae*, describing the fall of Troy from whose rulers the kings of England traced their descent, and Geoffrey of Monmouth's *Historia regum Britanniae*, which continued Guido's story with the foundation of Britain by Brutus, the reign of Arthur, and the defeat of the Britons by the Anglo-Saxons.

Richard's collection of history books thus covered much of the history of the known world, almost down to the years that people could still remember in his day. Some of these books contained a mixture of

---

1 The percentage depends on how the categories are made; many classical texts and early medieval and 15th-century literary works can also be seen as containing history, certainly in the eyes of contemporary readers. See for example: *Histoire des bibliothèques*, pp. 248–56; the list of Edward IV's books in 'Choosing a book'; the library of Philip of Cleves discussed in ch. 1, above; Kibre, 'Intellectual interests', pp. 257–97; Hirsch, *Printing*, pp. 30–31, 59 n. 47, 127–30, 133–34.

fact and fable, others were straightforward history by the standards of the time. Many of the fables were accepted as more or less true by Richard and his contemporaries, according to their motives, interests and learning, and some of these fictions remained acceptable in well-informed and educated circles until the seventeenth century and for far longer in the popular imagination.[2]

A simple and sensible, contemporary view of the value of history and the passage of time is to be found in the *Débat des hérauts d'armes* (1456), an imaginary debate between an English and a French herald each trying to prove that his country deserves the place nearest to the throne of 'Honour'.[3] Heralds were cast in this role because it was their duty to give honour where it was due, and to be able to do so they had to know the truth about the past and record the present faithfully themselves. As part of their argument about the superiority of their own countries the heralds of the *Débat* recalled the valiant deeds of their countrymen, and in order to do so effectively and systematically they divided time into three: *temps passé*, *temps moyen* and *temps présent*. They were not strictly consistent throughout their debate, but it is clear that for them the temps *passé* was a long period of time and included both legendary and historical figures, such as Constantine and Arthur, Clovis and Charlemagne, Roland and Oliver. In the *temps moyen*, further defined as 'within the memory of men', they placed such events as the battles of Creçy, Agincourt and Verneuil;[4] the *temps présent* was the period they themselves would record. They appear to take for granted that both *romans* and *chroniques* supplied evidence of the distant past, and that *romans* in particular served to keep fresh the memory of those long dead men of a more heroic age whose deeds should be emulated. For more recent events the French herald called to witness, with satisfaction, his opponent's '*own* chronicles' and the *Brut* in particular, which contained much evidence to the Englishman's disadvan-

---

2   For history, its study and its use in the middle ages see particularly: Guenée, *Histoire et culture historique*; and also e.g. Gransden, *Historical Writing in England II*, Epilogue; Fleischman, 'The representation of history and fiction'; Brandt, *The Shape of Medieval History*; Levine, *Humanism and History*, ch. 1, 'Caxton's histories: fact and fiction at the close of the middle ages'; D. Hay, 'History and historians', pp. 111–27.

3   Pannier, *Débat des hérauts d'armes*.

4   The time span of *temps moien, dites de memoire d'omme* agrees well with the conclusion reached by e.g. Guenée, that the (collective) memory of people, for instance of a family or a monastery, usually stretches back sixty or seventy years, with a limit of about a hundred, see his 'Temps de l'histoire', passim.

Fig. 52 The heralds of France (on the left) and of England (on the right) debate the merits of their respective countries; Prudence (in this case male) presides. Opening page of the *Débat des hérauts*, French, late fifteenth century. Paris, BN, MS fr. 5837, f. 1. By permission of the Bibliothèque Nationale.

tage but which had to be used for the sake of truth. For the *temps présent* they cited no written sources, but at the end of the debate the judge, Dame Prudence, demanded that both contestants put their arguments in writing. She announced that a little book would be made, called *Passe-temps*, which would be read with great profit by young noblemen and pursuivants; information would also be gathered from heralds in other Christian countries to help her reach her final judgment.

The *Débat* toucheed on many theoretical and practical aspects of history and historical writing. There was the undoubted didactic and 'exemplary' value of recorded history to later generations and its ability to entertain and occupy the mind, as well as prove a point or win a case. There was the need for professionalism, in this case that of the heralds, which included the essential and honest use of good sources, a knowledge of chronology and an ability to organise one's material. Lastly there was the duty of actually writing things up.

All these aspects of contemporary views on history are relevant to Richard III and his books. He owned the texts of the fabulous *Historia Troiae* and *Historia regum Britanniae* of the *temps passé*, and also examples of the chronicle type of history associated with the *temps moyen*, the 'Fitzhugh Chronicle' and the *Grandes chroniques*. The preoccupations of the heralds of the *Débat* offer a means of coming to terms with how Richard and his contemporaries rated works of history, what use they put them to, and how they organised the writing of the history of their own times. Richard's known close association with heralds suggests a lively interest in their duties and in what they might record in his lifetime. We also have to guide us the contemporary comments of Caxton – derivative or down to earth – as he invested in multiple copies of both the fabulous histories and the staid chronicles, compiled new annals of his own time, and assessed how all these works of history would sell.[5]

Temps Passé: 'Joyous and playsant hystoryes'

In his introductions to his publications William Caxton, the printer, had to find the right phrases to recommend his books to his readers. His need to advertise and his haste to produce yet another imprint meant that he usually avoided controversial statements and was content to copy much of the information of his original. His choice of source could be effective, and his skill in using it shows how thoroughly he agreed with it. This is the case with his long dissertation on the value of history copied from Diodorus Siculus, the Greek historian, and used in his preface to the *Polychronicon*; it was impeccably traditional and entirely acceptable to Caxton and his readers. Caxton's attitude to stories about the distant *temps passé* can be deduced from his comments, or lack of them, in the *Recuyell of the Hystoryes of Troye* and his *Jason*. The former work was the life and deeds of Hercules and described by Caxton as 'strange and mervayllous historyes', though he nowhere implied that he did not believe them. In *Jason* he offers no opinion at all, merely referring to the 'grettest fame' of the

---

5   All quotations in the sub-titles that follow are from Caxton's prologues and epilogues.

quest for the Golden Fleece and the order, which was named after it and which included Edward IV among its knights. In his prologues to both these works Caxton was adopting the tone of his author, the Burgundian Raoul le Fèvre, to whom Hercules and Jason were as sacred as they were to his patrons, the dukes of Burgundy, who venerated Hercules as the founder of their house and Jason as the patron of their order.[6]

Only in his edition of the *Morte Darthur*, did Caxton imply that he shared the doubts other people had about the existence of the great British hero of *temps passé*, Arthur. His purpose was to explain why he had taken so long to print anything about King Arthur and the Holy Grail. He told his critics that 'dyvers men holde oppynyon that there was no suche Arthur' because some chronicles make no mention of him, but that he himself had been persuaded by the following arguments: the tomb of Arthur was to be seen at Glastonbury and the story of its discovery was in the authoritative *Polychronicon*; Arthur was in Boccaccio's *De casibus virorum illustrium* and in Geoffrey of Monmouth's 'Brutysshe book'; relics of Arthur and his knights survived all over England (Arthur's seal was in Westminster Abbey, the Round Table could be seen at Winchester); and there were books about Arthur in every language.[7] Apart from conveniently providing a summary of everything known in favour of Arthur's existence which was available to a well-read and knowledgeable layman of his day, Caxton also tells us that certain of his contemporaries seriously doubted Arthur's existence.[8] Caxton does not say who these doubters were and how they presented their arguments, and it may be justifiable to assume it was Ralph Higden himself of whom Caxton was thinking in particular. Caxton had updated Higden's *Polychronicon* in Trevisa's translation and published it in July 1482; his edition is remarkable for not printing Trevisa'a defence of Arthur against Higden's attacks. Caxton the editor

---

6   Diodorus is used indirectly, and probably Caxton did not know the origin of the text; it takes up the first and greater part of the prologue to the *Polychronicon* (1482), Blake, *Caxton's Own Prose*, pp. 128–131, and see n. 56 below. For the prologues to the *Recueil* and *Jason*, *ibid.*, pp. 97–99 and 103–05.

7   Blake, *Caxton's Own Prose*, pp. 106–09.

8   Matheson, 'King Arthur and the medieval English chronicles', pp. 248–73, esp. 264, queries the truth of Caxton's statement that some people did not believe in Arthur's existence, and makes a connection with the *Polychronicon* edition of 1482 which we take much further here. Housman, 'Higden, Trevisa, Caxton and the beginning of Arthurian criticism', pp. 209–17, accepts Caxton's scepticism about Arthur as genuine and on the lines of Higden's, but he apparently failed to notice the absence of Trevisa's defence from Caxton's edition.

may have wanted to print unadulterated Higden and deliberately omitted Trevisa's addition out of respect for the great monk-historian who was being ticked off by a mere Cornish translator.[9] The result was that Caxton unleashed on his public a *Polychronicon* which dismissed the country's greatest hero as largely a work of fiction. No wonder men protested Arthur's existence to him between July 1482 and 31 July 1485, the date of the publication of the *Morte Darthur*. Can we even link Richard III's apparently enthusiastic acquisition of a rather untidy copy of Geoffrey of Monmouth's original Latin 'Brut', between 1483 and '85, to an interest in a lively historical debate precipitated by the printer? There was a need for those taking part in the debate to refer to a source so rigorously criticised by Higden! The controversy may equally have encouraged someone to bring Malory's pro-Arthurian text to Caxton or encouraged the printer himself to make a determined search for good Arthurian material.

Ultimately it is not possible to be certain whether Caxton believed in Brut and Arthur, or shared the sophisticated and learned doubts expressed by such as John Whethamsted, Abbot of St Albans (1420–40 and 1452–65),[10] about the Trojan foundation of Britain, or Higden's reservations about Arthur. Caxton left his reader free to believe or doubt the 'joyous and playsant histories' to be found in Sir Thomas Malory's *Morte Darthur*. The controversy was unlikely to hinder the sale of his book and the stories would certainly entertain because they contained all possible aspects of human interest:

noble chyvalrye, curtosye, humanyte, frendlynesse, hardynesse, love, frendship, cowardyse, murdre, hate, vertue and synne.[11]

---

9   Caxton clearly was using a text of Trevisa that included all his additions and he edited them in a variety of ways, see Babington and Lumby, *Polychronicon Ranulphi Higden*: e.g. vol. 2, p. 83 (an addition allowed by Caxton); vol. 2, p. 91 and n. 1 (the addition on Cornwall, Trevisa's home county, was summarised by Caxton who omits Trevisa's name); vol. 5, p. 337 and n. 15 (Arthur addition omitted).

10 Keeler, *Geoffrey of Monmouth*, pp. 80–85, briefly summarises Whethamsted's arguments, which are to be found in his *Granarium* (unpublished). And see 'R III's books VIII', pp. 221–22.

11 Blake, *Caxton's Own Prose*, p. 109, lines 111–13. For a recent commentary on the value of Malory's sober and factual approach to his material and his production of a text of more 'historical' weight, McCarthy, 'Malory and his sources', in Archibald and Edwards, *Companion*, pp. 86, 93–94. And see Meale, '"The hoole book"', *ibid.*, pp. 11–12, on Caxton's editorship.

We can be even less sure of Richard III's attitude to such 'joyous and play-sant hystoryes' of ancient Britain than we can be of Caxton's.[12] That he was interested – even deeply interested – is shown by his ownership of the recently rediscovered 'double' manuscript, now in St Petersburg, which was signed by him as king. These books have added dramatically to our knowledge of his library and his interests;[13] they contain two important and popular texts: Guido delle Colonne's *Historia destructionis Troiae* and, as already mentioned, Geoffrey of Monmouth's *Historia regum Britanniae*. Together they provided Richard III with the original sources, as they were accepted in his day, of the foundation of Britain and early British history and covered a fascinating section of the *temps passé*, whether he believed the details or not or was aware of any particular contemporary controversy over Arthur. His possessive signature at the beginning of each text seems to indicate his pleasure at acquiring the basic, authorita-tive information about the deeds of his ancestors and predecessors (figs 53, 54). The first volume covered the prelude and the full story of the Trojan War,[14] and it linked almost seamlessly to the material in the second volume, the founding of Britain by Brutus, the great-grandson of the Trojan prince Aeneas, and the subsequent history of the island to AD 688 as reported by Geoffrey of Monmouth.

Guido delle Colonne's version of the stories of Troy was written in 1278. The author may or may not have been the man of the same name mentioned by Dante as a member of the Sicilian school of poets which

---

12 Prologue to *King Arthur*, Blake, *Caxton's Own Prose*, p. 109. Doubts about early British history had been expressed since the first appearance of Geoffrey's *Historia regum Britanniae*, by such as William de Newburgh and Gerald of Wales, and remained a consistent, if largely ignored, undercurrent, see e.g. the much quoted statement of Jean Bodel (d. 1209–10) in his *La chanson des Saisnes*, pp. 2–3: 'There are only three "matters" [subjects] for any man of sense: those of France, of Britain and Rome the Great. The stories of Britain are idle and pleasant, those of Rome are wise and didactic, those of France are true, as we can see everyday'. For the fluctuating reception of British history and Arthur, esp. under the Yorkists and Tudors see 'R III's books VIII', p. 220, and 'R III's books VII and VIII', pp. 403–07.

13 The manuscripts' existence was noted by Bakhtin, 'Manuscripts', but the language his article was written in prevented the information from reaching western scholars generally. For details of the mss see the present authors' 'R III's books, VII and VIII' and Cat. VII, VIII below.

14 This text largely covers the same ground as Book III of Caxton's version of the *Recuyell*. Lefèvre had failed to make his own text describing the great siege, as he had planned, and as a consequence a translation of delle Colonne's work was often added to copies of his work as Book III; see Aeschbach, *Raoul Lefèvre*. Caxton used a similarly 'completed' manuscript.

was greatly influenced by French poetry, but he must have known the *Roman de Troie* composed by Benoît de Sainte-Maure in or about 1160.[15] It was Benoît who created the Troy story as it was known in the Middle Ages using the forged 'eye-witness' reports of Dares and Dictys; he added in Jason and the Golden Fleece and introduced the love story of Troilus and Cressida.[16] The lawyer delle Colonne, never mentioning his source, turned the French verse of Benoît's long romance into equally long (and turgid) Latin prose, lending it an air of authenticity and solemn reliability that deceived everyone. For centuries no one knew that delle Colonne had used the romance of Benoît as his source; the Latin text became an authoritative work of reference which was copied, translated, turned back into verse, and finally became one of the first books to be printed.[17]

Several vernacular versions of the stories of Troy were available to Richard and other English readers in the late fifteenth century: the '*Gest Hystoriale' of the Destruccion of Troy* of 1350–1400, the Laud *Troy Book* of about 1400, and John Lydgate's *Troy Book*, begun in 1412. Their authors clearly regarded the Troy story first and foremost as history of a distant and shadowy past, but they also liked it as literary entertainment; most important it supplied many examples of chivalric prowess and many moral lessons.[18] Both the city's ruins and Helen of Troy's vanished beauty were popular illustrations of the *ubi sunt* theme (... where are the snows of yesteryear?). The ten-year siege itself was a vivid example of the evils of a war started for an insignificant reason. Jason, Hector, Troilus and Achilles were paragons of martial conduct, Hector joining the ranks of the Nine Worthies, the patrons of chivalry, and Jason becoming the primeval questing knight and protector of the famous Burgundian order of chivalry, the Golden Fleece.

---

15 Meek, *Historia*, pp. xxviii–xxx; Griffin, *Guido de Columnis*, pp. xv–xvi; Benson, *Troy*, p. 4; 'R III's books VII', p. 195 n. 10.

16 On Benoît's sources: see Constans, *Le Roman de Troie par Benoît de Saint-Maure*; a brief modernised version is in Baumgartner, *Le Roman de Troie par Benoît de Saint-Maure*. The forged 'eye-witness' reports were written in the 1st and 5th or 6th centuries AD and ascribed to Dares and Dictys who were supposed to have fought on the Greek and Trojan sides respectively: trans. in Frazer, *Chronicles of Dictys of Crete and Dares the Phrygian*; Eisenhut, 'Spätantike Troja-Erzählungen', pp. 1–28; Griffin, 'Un-Homeric elements in the medieval story of Troy', pp. 32–52.

17 Edition: Griffin, *Guido de Columnis*; translation: Meek, *Historia*; and see Cat. VII below.

18 Benson, *Troy*, passim.

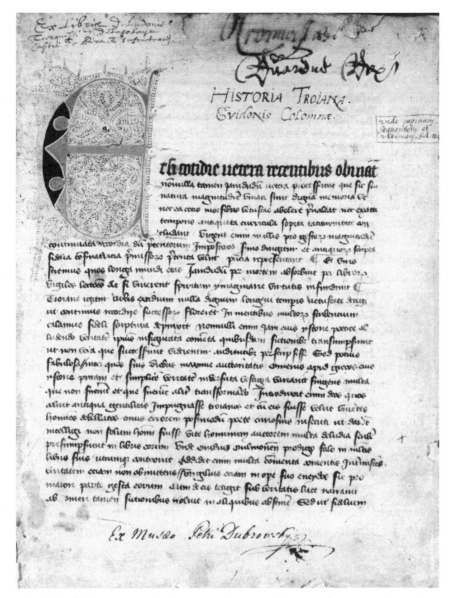

Fig. 53 The first page of Guido delle Colonna's *Historia destructionis Troiae*, showing the royal signature of Richard III, *Ricardus Rex*, and above it *O Cromwell 1656*. In the bottom margin is the *ex libris* of the Russian book collector Peter Dubrovsky. St Petersburg, Saltykov-Shchedrin State Public Library, MS Lat. F IV 74, f. 1. By permission of the State Public Library.

The authors of the middle English versions all admired delle Colonne's work, but they also made their own contributions. They had made some distinction between fact and fiction, preserving and separating the facts from delle Colonne's verbiage, and even clearing up some of his inconsistencies. William Caxton in his third book of the *Recuyell of the Hystoryes of Troye*, printed in 1473–74,[19] pruned Guido's moralising and decorative passages and left only the bare facts, intentionally or unintentionally turning the text into 'mere' history.

For Richard III delle Colonne's material held an interest similar to that felt by the dukes of Burgundy: it contained the accepted 'evidence' of his own high descent. The Trojan princes were thought to have dispersed after the fall of their city and were claimed as ancestors by many nations and dynasties of Europe. The Trojan Aeneas travelled to Italy, his descendant, Romulus, founded and named Rome, and his great-grandson, Brutus, did the same for Britain. Because of these claims the sympathy of most readers in Richard III's day was with the Trojans; the ancient Romans had regarded the Greeks as their adversaries and the West inherited their view, identifying the Turks with the Greeks.[20] The pope and other leaders of the West, such as Philip the Good of Burgundy and Richard III, still dreamed and talked of a real crusade against the traditional enemy.

Before Guido delle Colonne and even before Benoît the story of Troy had already been taken up by Geoffrey of Monmouth (died 1155). It was he who created the link between the classical Worthy, Hector, and the Christian Worthy, Arthur, and continued the line from the royal house of Troy into the dynasty of the kings of Britain. Geoffrey was born in England or Wales, probably of Breton parents, and by 1129 had become a member of the secular clergy at Oxford. It was there that he wrote his three most famous works. The first was the *Prophecies of Merlin*, probably

---

19 Benson, *Troy*, p. 165 n. 68. Sommer, *Recuyell of the Hystoryes of Troye*. Caxton's edition is mentioned in virtually every article or book on him as it was the first book printed in the English language (in Bruges). And see Finlayson, 'Guido de Columnis' *Historia destructionis Troiae*', pp. 141–62.

20 When Waleran de Wavrin, nephew of the Burgundian historian Jean de Wavrin who wrote the *Chronicles of England*, visited the Levant in 1443, he inquired about the exact site of Troy and especially the place where the Greek ships had beached. When told it was quite near and that he could not miss it, he expressed a fervent wish that the Turkish army would land in the very spot and that he could 'have at them' (*davoir a faire a eulz*); Wavrin, *Croniques*, vol. 5, pp. 38–9.

completed not long before 1135 and later incorporated in what he called his *Gesta Britonum* (*Deeds of the Britons*), the book Richard III owned; between 1148 and 1151 he finished a Latin verse romance, *Vita Merlini* (*Life of Merlin*).[21]

Geoffrey's success with the *Gesta Britonum* or *Historia regum Britanniae* was overwhelming and, in spite of occasional criticism, his account was both popular and authoritative until the eighteenth century.[22] His purpose had been to fill the gap in people's knowledge about the period between the arrival of Brutus in England – also to be briefly mentioned in delle Colonne's *Historia Troiae*[23] – and the flight from the island by Cadwalader, the last native king, after the Saxon invasion. Geoffrey used many known sources as well as a mysterious 'old book written in the British language', and he used them with great skill, creating a credible, orderly record set in a sound framework of the established chronology of the history of the rest of the known world. He chose Arthur, until then an obscure figure, as his principal hero, turning him into the conqueror of Scotland and thirty other kingdoms.

Geoffrey's creation was used in many ways.[24] The Norman poet Wace put it into verse and expanded it into the *Roman de Brut* as early as 1155; individual stories were fleshed out, for example by Chrétien de Troyes. As 'real' history the text became the basis of prose chronicles in Latin, French and English, commonly called the *Brut* after their first hero, Brutus; the author of the Fitzhugh chronicle, another of Richard III's history books, set out to write a continuation of Geoffrey; few chroniclers, in fact, failed

---

21 'R III's books VIII' and Cat. VIII below. The literature on Geoffrey of Monmouth is vast, see e.g. Griscom, *Historia regum Britanniae*; Hammer, *Geoffrey of Monmouth*; Lloyd, 'Geoffrey of Monmouth', pp. 460–68; Tatlock, *Legendary History of Britain*; Parry and Caldwell, 'Geoffrey of Monmouth', pp. 72–75; Gransden, *Historical Writing I*, pp. 201–09; of the comprehensive critical ed. the following vols have appeared, Wright, *The 'Historia regum Britanniae' of Geoffrey of Monmouth. I.*, and *II. The First Variant Version*; modern trans. with useful introd. by Thorpe, Geoffrey of Monmouth, *The History of the Kings of Britain*.

22 To date 215 mss have been identified. 'R III's books VIII', pp. 220–22 and 'VII and VIII', pp. 403–13.

23 Griffin, *Historia Troiae*, pp. 11–12, reports where the various Trojan princes went, Brutus settled in Britain, France was founded by Francus, etc. The *Historia Troiae* was written after Geoffrey's work, but readers would rarely have realised that.

24 See e.g. Loomis, *Arthurian Literature*, the articles on Wace, Layamon, Chrétien de Troyes, etc. Keeler, *Geoffrey of Monmouth*, passim.

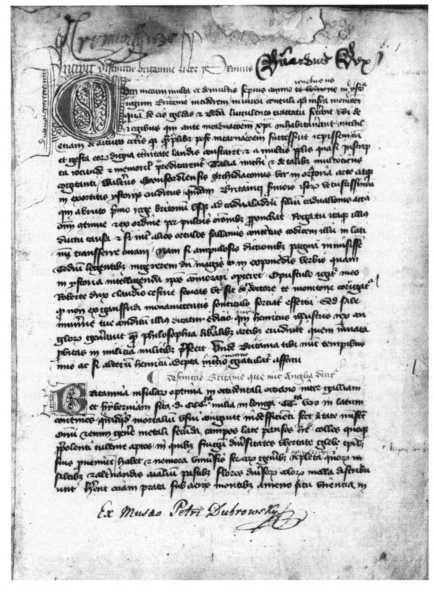

Fig. 54 The first page of Geoffrey of Monmouth's *Historia regum Britanniae*, showing the royal signature of Richard III, *Ricardus Rex*, and in the top margin on the left *O Cromwell 1656*. In the bottom margin is the *ex libris* of the Russian book collector Peter Dubrovsky. St Petersburg, Saltykov-Shchedrin State Public Library, MS Lat. F IV 76, f. 1. By permission of the State Public Library.

to use the *Historia regum* and by Richard III's day the *Brut*,[25] in many versions and with many continuations, was the standard national history of England and the only English work that bears any comparison to the French *Grandes chroniques* (see below). Usually Geoffrey's text was taken over wholesale into the histories of others, for example by the author of the Fitzhugh chronicle also owned by Richard (see below) and by John Hardyng (1463)[26] whom it inspired to make one of the better stanzas in his long work:

> But howe this ysle, enbrased with this sea,
> Unedified, was knowne first and founde,
> That Albion was named, of propertee
> Of dame Albione, that first therein had ground;
> And after long, how Brute therof was crowned,
> That of his owne name called it Brytayne,
> And buylded it, wher all before was playne.[27]

A very short version of the *Brut* came to be used as the narrative core of the schematic genealogical rolls showing the descent of English kings from Adam, via the kings of Troy and the kings of Britain. Many such rolls were produced in the reigns of Henry VI and Edward IV to prove the ruling prince's particular title to the crown.[28]

In Richard's copy of the *Historia regum Britanniae* there are a number of marginalia with a clear pro-British/English bias: it is noted that Rome was taken by the Britons to whom Rome paid tribute for some time, and how 'noble' the Britons were when they defeated Caesar. Elsewhere attention is drawn to the fact that Arthur 'first put into bondage' the Picts and the Scots. Though none of these notes can be attributed to Richard's hand it is likely that his interest would have focused on similar matters.

---

25 Brie, *The Brut or Chronicles of Britain*, for which his introd. has never been published in English, *Geschichte und Quellen*; Kingsford, *English Historical Literature*, ch. 5, pp. 113–39; Gransden, *Historical Writing II*, pp. 73–77, 220-27; at least 166 copies survive, Matheson, 'The middle English prose *Brut*. A location list', pp. 353–59; and his 'Historical prose', passim.

26 For Hardyng see also ch. 2 above.

27 Hardyng, *Chronicle*, last stanza of *Proheme*.

28 See ch. 8 below.

The first two items in Richard's collection of romances, now at Longleat,[29] supplemented the legendary history of Troy, telling the sequence of events that centred on the Greek city of Thebes, its siege and the aftermath. The first item in the manuscript was a copy of Lydgate's *Siege of Thebes*, probably regarded by fifteenth-century readers as an elaborate narrative of an essentially historical event, whatever the possibilities of the story as a 'mirror for princes' or didactic entertainment. Chronologically the *Siege* was followed by what is also the next item in the manuscript, Chaucer's *Knight's Tale*, of which the protagonists, Palamon and Arcite, had been taken prisoner during the capture of Thebes. These two romances filled in another section of the remote *temps passé* for Richard. A past where fact and fiction were inextricably interwoven and served to entertain readers and listeners, keep them from idleness and teach them virtue by example.

Temps Moyen: 'So precious and also profitable'

If the fables of the distant past, the legends and semi-history of the *Historia Troiae* and the *Historia regum*, could teach men what to do and what to avoid, how much more would true history move them:

> ... yf the terryble, feyned fables of the poetes have moche styred and moeved men to pyte and conservynge of justyce, how moche more is to be supposed that historye, assertryce of veryte and as moder of alle philosophye moevynge our maners to vertue, reformyth and reconcyleth ...[30]

Richard had two history books which can be termed genuine history, the Fitzhugh Chronicle and the *Grandes chroniques de France*. They were detailed narratives covering long periods of time and designed to be inclusive and informative. Of all Richard's books the Fitzhugh chronicle is now the least known;[31] it covers English history from the first prepara-

---

29 Longleat House MS 257, see Cat. II. See also chs 5 and 9.

30 Blake, *Caxton's Own Prose*, Polychronicon, p. 130, lines 72–76.

31 Cambridge, Corpus Christi College, MS 96. See 'R III's books VI' and Cat. VI below, for discussion of chronicler's sources and the provenance of ms. The only edition is that of Roger Twysden, *Historiae Anglicanae*, in 1652, cols 725–1284, with an indispensable introduction by John Selden.

tion for the conversion of the Anglo-Saxons in the sixth century to the coronation of King John in 1199.[32] The unknown author wrote his work between the 1350s and 1377 as a continuation and supplement to Geoffrey of Monmouth's *Historia regum Britanniae* which he says failed to describe the arrival of St Augustine.[33] He concentrated on the deeds of kings – as Geoffrey had done – and

> compiled the work for my own relaxation and for that of others who want to know of the deeds of kings. I did so not because I am clever or inspired but because I worked very hard, using everything I could find in books and chronicles.[34]

Like all such chronicles it is highly derivative and lifts large passages from the works of such writers as Bede or Ralph Higden. The author's choice of texts included several which were critical of the legends of King Arthur, notably Higden's strongly worded criticism, which would have enabled any of his readers to take an informed part in any Arthurian controversy. What may have intrigued other fifteenth-century readers of this chronicle in particular was its emphasis on the administrative and governmental history of England and inclusion of many legal texts and official documents of the twelfth century, such as Henry II's assizes, the text known as 'Glanvill' and the laws of the kings of England. The most unusual source used by this chronicler was the *Quadripartitus*, a legal compilation of the twelfth century, from which he had extracted the laws of each king in order to insert them in his own narrative at the end of each reign,[35] thereby giving each king additional authority. His bias towards official documents and the laws and deeds of kings, as well as his possible Northern bias, may have made his chronicle famous in Wensleydale in

---

32 The chronicle actually starts with a paraphrase of Bede's *Ecclesiastical History*, bk 1, ch. 3, but confuses dates, taking 588 as the year in which Augustine first attempted to go to England; this should be 596. The other ms. of the chronicle (BL, MS Cotton Tiberius C xiii) ends with the coronation of Richard I.

33 Twysden, cols 780, 784, 785, 787, 790, 814, 1152–54; he refers to Geoffrey's work as *liber de gestis Britonum* often adding *dictus le Brut*.

34 Twysden, col. 725. For a summary of the mistaken theories about monastic authorship, see Selden's introduction and 'R III's books VI', n. 35.

35 Liebermann, *Quadripartitus*, and his *Gesetze der Anglesachsen*. Plucknett, *Early English Legal Literature*, pp. 24–30. Robertson, *Laws of the Kings of England*, pp. ix–xi. Downer, *Leges Henrici Primi*, introd.

the fifteenth century; during its long career it has always attracted readers and scholars ranging from the fourth Lord Fitzhugh who had this
copy made, John Brompton, abbot of Jervaulx, John Bale, Peter Osborne
and Archbishop Parker to Felix Liebermann in the twentieth century, its
importance being sealed by the 1652 edition of John Selden, the jurist,
and Sir Roger Twysden. Twysden summed up the chronicle,

> an author wanted by many, seen by few, though not unworthy of being
> brought to light, if for no other reason than that the laws of the Saxons, in
> Latin, have been preserved in this work.[36]

Actual ownership of the Fitzhugh Chronicle by Richard of Gloucester
is not entirely certain. The copy was made for the fourth Lord Fitzhugh
of Wensleydale and Richmondshire (1425–52) whose arms appear in the
first initial. His son, Henry, succeeded him, and his name occurs on a
flyleaf at the end, just below Richard's; the names are written in a way
that suggests they were inscribed on the same occasion. Henry died on
8 June 1472 after a troubled career picking his way through the divided
allegiances of York and Lancaster; he married Alice, the sister of the
Kingmaker, and in 1471 led a small rebellion against Edward IV. He was in
favour again by the time that Richard of Gloucester was ready to replace
Warwick in Wensleydale and the North and marry Warwick's daughter, Anne Neville, Fitzhugh's niece. It is conceivable that the chronicle
was at Jervaulx Abbey soon after its making, acquired, according to an
inscription in the book, by John Brompton, abbot from 1436 until the
1460s and possibly much later; it was to remain at the Abbey until the
dissolution. Brompton may have 'procured' the book from a Fitzhugh,
or from Richard himself.[37] Richard's signature is a mature one; if he
did not sign the volume in the presence of Henry Fitzhugh before June
1472, he could have signed it as its owner or as a visitor to the library
of Jervaulx Abbey while lord of the North – the great tome was one to
be consulted in a library.[38] It seems likely that Richard's interest focused
on the same important characteristic of this chronicle that attracted all
its other known users: the laws of the English kings, a subject in which

36 Twysden, preface.
37 For Fitzhughs and Brompton, see *Complete Peerage*, vol. 5, pp. 421–30 passim; Pollard, 'The
    Richmondshire community', pp. 42–45; Emden, *Oxford*, p. 277; *CPR 1467–77*, p. 90.
38 See Cat. VI below for evidence of Leland consulting the book in Jervaulx Abbey.

Fig. 55 The first page of the Anonymous or Fitzhugh Chronicle; the initial contains the arms of William, fourth Lord Fitzhugh (died 1452). At the top of the page is John Bale's inscription erroneously ascribing the authorship of the chronicle to John Brompton, Abbot of Jervaulx. Cambridge, Corpus Christi College, MS 96, f. 1. By permission of The Master and Fellows of Corpus Christi College, Cambridge.

Richard is known to have taken an active and practical interest. In this chronicle the future king could see kings and their laws in an impressive, chronological sequence.

While duke of Gloucester, Richard acquired at least one volume – covering the period 1270 to 1380 – of another history of kings, the immensely successful *Grandes chroniques de France*.[39] This compilation started with the Trojan ancestors of the French monarchs and was largely the work of the monks of Saint-Denis, the royal necropolis, just outside Paris. The monks had a tradition of historiography glorifying the French kings that went back to the eighth century, but the inspiration for the vernacular *Grandes chroniques*, which gathered together and translated all previous works and continued them in French, may have come from St Louis IX (1226–70). The next king who took an active interest was Charles V (1364–80) who urgently required propaganda and royal panegyric to refurbish the French royal image, so badly tarnished by the defeats and imprisonment of his father in the Hundred Years War, and to defend the house of Valois against the claims of the Plantagenets to the French crown. The recension of the *Grandes chroniques* up to 1380 produced for Charles V under the overall guidance of his chancellor and friend, Pierre d'Orgemont, was to become the key manuscript in the later development of the chronicles; from this manuscript derived many fine and expensive copies made for the rich aristocrat and official, among them the one in which Richard of Gloucester placed his signature (fig. 134).[40] His volume was written in the last years of the fourteenth century and illuminated *c.* 1400–10.[41]

Richard's interest in the *Grandes chroniques* may have been purely practical. His volume covered the period of the worst reverses suffered by the French at the hands of the English, and also the withdrawal of the English from France at the end of Edward III's reign when all the English victories had come to nothing. Richard would have known that the great victories of Henry V had also come to nothing. Did he read the volume

---

39 BL, MS Royal 20 C vii. 'R III's books IX' and Cat. IX below. See esp.: Spiegel, *Chronicle Tradition*; and her 'Cult of Saint Denis', pp. 43–69. The editions are: Paris, *Grandes chroniques de France*; Viard, *Grandes chroniques de France*, which ends in 1350 and has to be used with Delachanel, *Chroniques des règnes de Jean II et de Charles V*.

40 See Delachanel, vol. 3, p. xiv ff; Spiegel, *Chronicle Tradition*, pp. 122–23; Delisle, 'Notes sur quelques manuscrits', pp. 211–12; his *Recherches sur la librairie de Charles V*; *La librairie de Charles V*; and see further refs. in Cat. IX below on Charles V's copy, BN, MS fr. 2813, and the illumination.

41 Dennison in 'R III's books IX', pp. 503–08.

Fig. 56 A page from Richard's finely illuminated copy of the *Grandes chroniques de France*, with his signature and a miniature illustrating the siege of Meaux and the death of the mayor of the town. French, written *c.* 1380–1400, illustrated *c.* 1400–10. BL, MS Royal 20 C vii, f. 134. By permission of The British Library.

in the hope of understanding what had gone wrong the first time, before he accompanied Edward IV on the third major invasion of France by the English in 1475? If he did, he would have been following the received wisdom expressed by Diodorus Siculus – and gratefully repeated by Caxton in his 'prohemye' to his edition of the *Polychronicon* – that history could advise the present.[42]

The *Grandes chroniques* were reasonably well known to the English in the fifteenth century although the circulation of the lavish manuscripts was necessarily limited to the rich in England as in France. Humphrey, Duke of Gloucester, had a copy, and sumptuous manuscripts originally made for French royal dukes passed to such men as Henry VII's last Garter King at Arms, while the City of London found it useful to acquire a less lavish copy.[43] Only when the *Grandes chroniques* were printed in three volumes by Pasquier Bonhomme at Paris on 16 January 1477 with a text ending in 1461 did the work become readily available to everyone.

It may have been apparent to readers like Richard of Gloucester – though it is much more clearly apparent to modern historians – that there was no precise counterpart of the *Grandes chroniques* in English historiography. The chronicles of the Abbey of St Albans almost had the scope and longevity of Saint-Denis but they were not an organised system of chronicles, they never received any official blessing and they certainly did not consistently hero-worship the kings of England. If any abbey had a special relationship with the king it was Westminster, but its few, semi-official chronicles never matched those of St Albans in scope, let alone those of Saint-Denis.[44] It was not until the London lawyer, Edward Hall, wrote his *The Union of the Noble and Illustrious Families of Lancaster and York* (1548) that an English history (from Henry IV) was attempted with the unifying theme of king-worship: Hall wrote in support of the well-ordered state and his hero-king was Henry VIII.[45]

---

42 Blake, *Caxton's Own Prose*, pp. 128–31. And see n. 48.
43 List of mss in England, 'R III's books IX', pp. 511–12 n. 37.
44 Farley, 'French historiography', ch. 5; Gransden, 'Propaganda in English medieval historiography', p. 375; and her 'Uses made of history by the medieval kings of England', passim.
45 Levy, *Tudor Historical Thought*, pp. 173–74.

The English counterpart of the *Grandes chroniques* was the *Brut* chronicle, mentioned earlier.[46] Both started with the mythical Trojan foundations of their respective kingdoms and then proceeded, by the means of many continuations by many compilers, to their own time, using kings' reigns as their basic structure. The *Brut* had a distinctive chivalric and patriotic tone, although it adopted no particularly royalist stance. The earliest *Brut* is the earliest extant work in Anglo-Norman prose; like the *Grandes chroniques* it was originally for a literate public of social standing that wanted a history of its own country in the vernacular and not in the more old-fashioned, less authoritative form of verse. It appeared at approximately the same time as the *Grandes chroniques*, and it was put into English during the period 1350 to 1380. The numerous, disorderly continuations, none of which had the advantages of the cosseted environment of Saint-Denis or the encouragement of kings, are a tribute to its popularity. The *Brut* probably reached far lower down the social scale and may have been read far more widely than the *Grandes chroniques*, at least until the latter were printed; it reached many through the medium of the London chronicles so often copied and continued by ordinary citizens, and it had the great advantage of being containable in one volume.

The *Grandes chroniques* and the *Brut* were the first national histories to be printed in their countries. In 1480 Caxton issued a version of the *Brut* as *The Chronicles of England*, with a continuation to 1461 compiled by himself,[47] only three years after the appearance of the French work in print also ending in 1461; he used the French chronicles for some events of the reign of John II probably from the printed edition. Caxton, like all Londoners, was part of the strong tradition of London chronicles which in the fifteenth century became entirely integrated with the *Brut* tradition. Instead of one abbey producing a history of the kings of France many citizens of London combined to produce a haphazard national chronicle with a bias towards the capital city. Caxton was undoubtedly emulating Bonhomme's *Grandes chroniques* of 1477 with his *Chronicles of England* in 1480 (see fig. 60); later Alderman Robert Fabian set out to

---

46 Caxton had no problem assuming that the *Brut* was the English equivalent. Hay, 'History and historians', p. 115, suggests Higden's *Polychronicon* as the nearest equivalent, but as the work of one man it is not an ideal comparison. The failure to consider the *Brut* as the equivalent seems to be partly a result of the lack of an adequate study, although that is now changing. See n. 25 above for sources behind this paragraph.

47 Matheson, 'Printer and the scribe', passim, and see below.

surpass the old *Brut*, the London chronicles and the *Grandes chroniques* in his *New Chronicles of England and France* (1516) making use of the London Guildhall's copy of the last for his work.[48]

For Richard III both the Fitzhugh chronicle and the *Grandes chroniques* were sources of facts and chronology, as were some other histories produced and circulating in his lifetime of which he would have been aware and which he may have used. John Capgrave's universal and almost wholly derivative chronicle, for example, was dedicated to Edward IV on completion in 1462–63.[49] Capgrave was an Augustinian friar, who appears to have had a passion for numbers and dates. In his dedication he explained how he would date each event from the creation of the world *and* from the birth of Christ (anno 5199 of the creation); he also made much of the year of Edward IV's accession, which he placed in 1460, and of the fact that Edward the *Fourth* 'entered by Goddis provision', while Henry the *Fourth* 'entered by intrusion'. His chronicle ended in 1417 and was intended more as a reference book than a narrative; he himself wrote 'we think that it myte be cleped rather *Abbreviacion*[50] *of Cronicles* than a book'. His entries were very brief, even Arthur being mentioned laconically:

> In these dayes was Arthure kyng of Bretayn, that with his manhod conqwered Flaunderes, Frauns, Norwey, and Denmark, and aftir he was gretely woundid he went into an ylde cleped Avallone, and there deyed. The olde Britones suppose that he is o-lyve.[51]

More interesting and of more practical use to Richard of Gloucester as lord of the North may have been the verse *Chronicle* of John Hardyng, the soldier/author who hated the Scots and fervently wished that their country would be occupied by the English: in his chronicle he included every historical fact and every document – some of them forged by himself

48 For London chronicles see esp. Kingsford, *London Chronicles*, pp. v–xlviii, and Gransden, *Historical Writing II*, ch. 8. For Fabian's works, *Great Chronicle*, pp. xv–lxxvi; Gransden, *Historical Writing II*, pp. 230–32, 245–48. Guildhall Library Muniment Room, MS 244, is the ms. which Fabian borrowed.

49 *Capgrave's Abbreviacion of Cronicles*; Gransden, *Historical Writing II*, pp. 389–90. And see *Manual*, vol. 8, XXI [36].

50 I.e. summary, abridgment.

51 *Capgrave's Abbreviacion of Cronicles*, p. 69; *thorn, u* and *v* modernised.

— that could prove English overlordship.[52] His book started with the founding of Britain and in its second and final version it ended in 1464, shortly before his death. Hardyng was of the opinion that Scotland could be subdued in three years and he offered careful advice about when a campaign should be started, which castles could be starved into surrender and which rivers were navigable. One of the surviving manuscripts, the one believed to have been Edward IV's presentation copy, had full colour maps of Scotland with rivers and castles drawn in. Richard of Gloucester was the commander who came closest to fulfilling Hardyng's desires, during his successful campaigns of 1482 and '83.[53]

Hardyng admitted that he would prefer the English king to invade Scotland rather than try and regain his inheritance in France, but a contemporary, the antiquarian William Worcester, was of the contrary opinion. Like Hardyng he did not care which king of England followed his advice, all he wanted was the reconquest of the lost territories in Normandy. He composed the *Boke of Noblesse*, which set out to persuade Edward IV and later Richard III to fulfil the obligations of their 'noblesse' and emulate the achievements of their ancestors, regaining what was theirs by right.[54] In the *Boke* itself Worcester used only a few examples from recent history and quoted mainly from philosophical and didactic texts to make his point. His antiquarian interests, however, made him well aware of the value of original sources, and he added a collection of historical documents to the literary text of the *Boke* illustrating the success of English military government in Normandy in the 1440s and, in the author's view, still of great practical use.[55] Worcester's son, who wrote an introduction to the *Boke of Noblesse* and the collection of documents when he re-dedicated them to Richard III, explained that the two texts combined the 'deciplyne' of literary authors and the 'experyence of men'.

Chronicles might start in the shadows of *temps passé* and resemble the fables and romances of poets, but they inevitably stretched down to the better-documented period that some men had experienced and could still remember. The value of these historical works which truthfully recorded facts and real events was greater than that of any other work of literature.

---

52 Ch. 2 above, for Richard of York's books; see also Riddy, 'John Hardyng's Chronicle', pp. 91–108.
53 Pollard, *North-Eastern England*, pp. 213–14.
54 See ch. 4 and Cat. XIIA below.
55 For his work in the context of other 'mirrors for princes', ch. 5 above.

Caxton in his borrowed prologue to the *Polychronicon* set out the dangers of mere 'eloquence' (that is literature): though eloquence has been used to teach men how to be virtuous, it has also been known to incite them to pleasure or to berate and punish rather than instruct, and it has even misrepresented the truth. In such cases the 'utylyte' of eloquence 'is mixt with harme', but

> historye, representynge the thynges lyke unto the wordes, enbraceth al utylyte and prouffite. It sheweth honeste and maketh vyces detestable. It enhaunceth noble men and depresseth wicked men and fooles. Also thynges that historye descryveth by experyence moche prouffyten unto a ryghtful lif ... historye is so precious and also prouffytable ...[56]

'A perpetuel conservatryce of thoos thynges that have be doone before this presente time': Attitudes to Recorded History in Richard III's Day

It was a commonplace of historians to claim in their prologues that they had started their work to preserve the *memory* of people and events; they wanted to 'put in memorye', to have 'in remembraunce', and to make people 'abyde in perpetuel memorye'.[57] Memory in medieval thought was of exceptional importance: one needed memory to have standards by which to make moral judgments and to distinguish between good and evil. Memory equalled learning and knowledge.[58]

Two allegorical figures, Prudence and *Fresche Memoire*, personifications of human faculties, were used, and can be used here, to illustrate the importance of knowledge of the past and the means by which it could be gained and preserved. Prudence, one of the four cardinal virtues, was sometimes depicted with three faces, young, middle-aged and old, looking into the past, the present and the future. In the *Débat des hérauts d'armes* Prudence did not have three heads, but she was also engaged, by means of the heralds, in looking back, in looking at her own time, and

---

56 Blake, *Caxton's Own Prose, Polychronicon*, p. 131, lines 101–16.
57 These quotes are all from Caxton's prologue to his *Siege of Jerusalem (Godfrey of Boulogne)*, Blake, *Caxton's Own Prose*, p. 137, but numberless examples could be given from English and Burgundian authors.
58 Carruthers, *Book of Memory*, pp. 1, 12–13, 71, 156, and passim.

looking forward. It was memory, as well as written history, the preserver of what had happened beyond the boundary of memory, that allowed observance of the past. Prophecy, closely related to history and almost as important, looked into the future.[59] In the work of the Burgundian chronicler and courtier Olivier de La Marche, it was *Fresche Memoire* (*Living Memory*) herself who graciously led the author, in his *persona* of the ageing *Chevalier délibéré* (composed in 1483), past the tombs of the famous dead of the distant past and allowed him to witness again the melancholy battles in which his lords, the Dukes Philip and Charles, and his beloved young lady, the Duchess Mary, had recently been defeated by *Weakness* and *Accident*.[60] With the aid of 'prudence' and 'memory' men might learn to live better and avoid disaster.

Memory and learning in their turn had to be aided by writing and books: another Burgundian courtier, the historian Georges Chastellain (died 1474), began his *Chroniques* by describing the ignorance, fear and amazement of the first human creatures who had to suffer the 'darkness of the world' because they had no written records and no way of gaining knowledge of what had happened before their time.[61] The wisdom of recording events was also stressed by Vegetius in his preface to Book 3 of his military manual *De re militari*, of which Richard owned an English translation. He praised the Athenians, who were 'wyse and cunnyng' because they had books made about wars and battles they had seen and heard of, and used them to teach the young – unlike the Spartans who concentrated on the waging of war and kept no records. It was generally assumed in Richard III's time that *all* written record could instruct; Caxton quoted the words of St Paul in several of his prologues: 'alle that is wryten is wryten unto our doctryne and for our lernynge'.[62]

The instruction received from history was seen in some ways as very practical. The future Richard III 'syttynge in his chambre or studye'

---

59 See ch. 8 below.

60 La March, *Chevalier délibéré*, ff. 27v–47v.

61 *sans lecture de nulle chose devant eux, sans aucune expérience précédente*, Chastellain, *Oeuvres*, vol. 1, p. 2. Compare the idea of Lorenzo Valla that mankind had only emerged from 'infancy' when history had been invented, Guenée, 'Temps de l'histoire', p. 25.

62 Romans 15:4. Blake, *Caxton's Own Prose, Game of Chess*, p. 87, lines 1–3; *History of Troy*, p. 101, lines 40–41; *Charles the Great*, p. 66, lines 1–2, and *Kyng Arthur*, p. 109, line 117. Caxton may have taken into account Higden's reminder that the Apostle had not said: 'All that is written is *true*', but 'All that is written is written for our instruction', Babington and Lumby, *Polychronicon*, vol. 1, p. 18. And see ch. 9 below.

Cp monstre fresche memoire a lacteur les sepultures des anciens trespassez. et par les escriptures voit ceulx qui ont este desconfiz par debile ou par accident. Et commence la tierce partie de ce liure.

Fig. 57   Fresh Memory (*Fresche Memoire*) showing the author (*lacteur*) the tombs of dead kings; among them is the monument of *le grant turc*; on the gate of the town is written 'success' (*bonne aventure*). Woodcut from Olivier de La Marche's *Chévalier délibéré*, printed at Gouda, *c.* 1486.

would have been able, according to the theory of the day, to 'understande the polytyke and noble acts of alle the worlde'.[63] The capacity of history to teach by example meant that a man did not need to experience person- ally the 'storms of adversyte' in order to acquire 'wysedom and polycye'.[64] This had been voiced by Diodorus Siculus as long ago as the first century AD and was still acceptable to Caxton and his contemporaries when he translated Diodorus to form an introduction to his edition of Higden's *Polychronicon*.[65] All the accumulated advice of past ages was made available in histories; the young could tap into the wisdom of those much older than themselves and the 'pryvate man' could become 'worthy to have the governaunce of empyres'.[66] Hardyng put it thus:

As out of olde feldes newe corne groweth eche yere,
Of olde bokes, by clerkes newe approved,
Olde knyghtes actes with mynstrelles tonge stere   [guide]
The newe corage of yonge knightes to be moved:
Wherefore, me thinketh, old thinges shuld be loved,
Sith olde bokes maketh young wittes wise,
Disposed well to vertuous exercyse.[67]

Political and practical examples were to be found in the past. When Chancellor Russell wrote his sermon for the opening of parliament in 1483 he quoted Livy, comparing the assembled house to the Roman senate and the speaker to the tribunes. Richard of Gloucester's protector- ship he linked to the consul Lepidus' 'tutele' and 'defense' of the young king of Egypt, who, according to Valerius Maximus, when he grew up did not know whether he had learned more from his father or his guardian.[68] Models were frequently to be found in the lives of great men,

---

63 Blake, *Caxton's Own Prose, Polychronicon*, p. 125, lines 23–25.
64 *Ibid.*, line 22.
65 Diodorus' introduction to his *Library of History*. Caxton probably knew a French version of Poggio Bracciolini's Latin translation, see Workman, 'Versions by Skelton, Caxton, and Berners', pp. 252–58.
66 Blake, *Caxton's Own Prose, Polychronicon*, p. 129, lines 40–46.
67 Hardyng, *Chronicle*, p. 32.
68 Nichols, *Grants*, pp. xxxix–lxiii, esp. xlv; Chrimes, *English Constitutional Ideas*, pp. 167–91, esp. 177. The quotations are from Livy, *Decades*, 1, 8 (the senate) and Valerius Maximus, *Facta*, 6, 1 (Lepidus).

especially those of rulers, whether historically accurate or idealised,[69] and in the lives of saints of which so many were written and re-written in Richard's time. In his introduction to the *Golden Legend* – the standard collection of saints' lives to be found in every library, however small – Caxton hoped that his readers would 'encrease in ... vertue and expelle vyce and synne' and 'by the ensaumple of the holy sayntes amende theyr lyvynge'.[70] To him the *Golden Legend* was the companion volume of the *Polychronicon*, both were history and both were 'precious and also prouffytable'.[71] Osbern Bokenham, who wrote many saints' lives at the request of acquaintances,[72] nowhere explicitly referred to the didactic value of his re-writing of old legends as it was probably understood. His compositions served as prayers or acts of homage to the saints and as a pleasure to his friends; his friends' motives are similarly unexplained, and in some cases it may simply have been that the story they wanted him to retell was unavailable.[73] St Katherine, of whom Pietro Carmeliano presented Richard III a *Vita*, was the embodiment of Christian scholarship and more learned than fifty heathen philosophers.[74]

There was also an expectation that history would entertain and comfort, occupying the mind and the imagination. Caxton used words such as 'joyfulle', 'joyous' and 'playsant' of his historical romances,[75] but not for his solid history books; he may have been concerned to have no hint of frivolity in his historical texts. Other writers were more explicit in their intentions. Hardyng wrote for the 'pleasaunce and consolation' of Duke Richard of York, who had 'delectacion' in chronicles.[76] John Kay, introducing his account of the recent siege of Rhodes by the Turks (1482), which ended so happily for the Christians, spoke of the 'joye and consolacyon' that his readers would experience.[77] Dame Prudence in the *Débat* predicted that their book of heraldic argument would make readers and

---

69 E.g. Plutarch's *Lives*, Curtius' *Alexander* or Xenophon's *Education of Cyrus*, all of which also served as 'mirrors of princes', see ch. 5 above.
70 Blake, *Caxton's Own Prose*, p. 90, lines 64–66.
71 *Ibid.*, *Polychronicon*, p. 131, lines 116 ff. And see ch. 2 above.
72 See ch. 2 above.
73 Referring to John Capgrave's version of the life of St Katherine, Bokenham says: '... that book is rare/ And straunge to gete ...', prologue to 'St Katherine', Bokenham, *Legendys*.
74 See also ch. 3.
75 Blake, *Caxton's Own Prose*, pp. 57, 109, 110.
76 Hardyng, *Chronicle*, p. 16.
77 Kaye/Caoursin, f. [1]. See also ch. 3 above.

listeners *joieusement passer temps*. The author of the *Comte d'Artois* (1453–67) – a romance/history – explained the need to occupy one's mind:

> Because idleness torments the human heart with various fantasies and with melancholy it is good and useful to listen to ancient stories (*anchiennes histoires*) being read pleasantly, and pass the time joyfully, fleeing the restlessness that is too great a burden to human nature.[78]

Raoul le Fèvre, the Burgundian whose *Istoire de Jason* Caxton translated, and who knew how important the story of Jason was to his master, Philip the Good, Duke of Burgundy, claimed in his introduction that the duke *toute sa vie a esté nourri en histoires pour son singulier passetemps* ('… all his time enclined … to here and see red the auncient histories … for his singuler passetemps').[79]

Historical facts also supported legal or political disputes. Authoritative chronicles and saints' lives as well as actual documents were raided for evidence to back up the pretensions of princes and nations in times of political need. Particularly well known is the instance of Edward I who ordered the archives of monasteries to be searched for proof of English overlordship in Scotland. The heralds of the *Débat* used the facts preserved by chronicles to prove that their own country was the most 'honourable' and valiant. Each enumerated great kings and great battles, but each also emphasised that his people was the most *christian* and had been converted before any other. In Richard III's time both France and England claimed to have been evangelised first: France by St Denis, England by Joseph of Arimathea. France also maintained the tradition that their kings had been unwavering in their loyalty to Rome, whereas John of England had been outlawed by the pope; England countered this with the story of St Helena, an English princess, who 'excavated' the true Cross and was the mother of Constantine the Great, the first Christian emperor.[80]

Descent and inheritance similarly needed the assistance of historians to be authoritatively proven. The French herald criticised his opponent

---

78 Seigneuret, *Roman du Comte d'Artois*, p. 1. And see ch. 9 below.
79 Quoted in Doutrepont, *Littérature*, p. 159. Caxton, *History of Jason*, p. 3.
80 Such matters were brought forward, for example, at the Council of Constance (1417), where it was important to prove that a country was a real 'nation' and worthy to vote, see e.g. Genet, 'English nationalism at the Council of Constance', pp. 60–78.

for naming Arthur as a great Englishman, when everybody knew he had been a Briton and that the present people of England were descended from the Saxons not the Britons. To claim the 'honour' due to somebody else in this way was shameless and the last thing of which a herald should be found guilty. For Richard III the histories of Troy and ancient Britain were particular confirmation of his ancestry; their facts could be worked into the family tree of the house of York and prove its right to the English crown beyond a shadow of doubt. While dedicating his chronicle to Richard III's father, Hardyng spent pages on explaining York's right to England, France, Spain, Portugal and many other countries in the east and west; he concluded:

> All these titles, the chronicles can recorde,
> If they be seen by good deliberacion,
> Many of theim to these full well accorde,
> As I have seen with greate delectacion,
> By clerkes wrytten for our informacion.
> As in olde feldes, cornes freshe and grene grewe,
> So of olde bookes commeth cunnyng newe.[81]

Similar arguments for writing were put forward by Olivier de La Marche (died 1504) when he introduced his *Mémoires* to the young Philip the Fair, Archduke of Austria and Duke of Burgundy. The first purpose of his work was to show the prince his high descent, the second to prove how and why he had inherited his many lands and lordships, and only the third was to remind him of the events that had happened in the author's lifetime.[82]

The many uses to which history could be put, the general awareness of the past, the authority and importance of historical example and precedent, all help to explain why most book owners, particularly men of noble birth had such a large proportion of history books in their collection.

---

81 Hardyng, *Chronicle*, p. 22.
82 La Marche, *Mémoires*, vol. 1, pp. 10–13.

Temps Présent: 'Grete thankynges … unto wryters of hystoryes':[83] The Writing of History in Richard III's Day

In the fifteenth century all sorts of people in England and Burgundy turned their hand to the writing of the history of their own time. Their work can be roughly divided into three categories, though many authors do not neatly fit into just one and most were not aware they were writing 'history'. At the most mundane level were the jottings of private individuals in their notebooks, commonplace books or letters, recording events of personal and local importance and occasionally including more important matters that came their way. At the next level were the professional scribes: secretaries, heralds and government officials, whose duty it was to compose and copy documents in order to record a particular transaction or event for future reference, and whose work in some cases turned out to be useful to historians. The serious chronicler and historian who made use of every kind of source, who actively searched for evidence and news and who attempted to make his facts into a coherent narrative, formed the most sophisticated category.

An example of the private jottings is the puny annals compiled year by year from 1483 to 1497 in the London household of Sir Thomas Frowyk and his widow Joan, probably at their town house, Ypres Inn; several persons added a sentence or so each year to what had originally been a simple, ready-made list of mayors and sheriffs of London probably bought at a scrivener's shop.[84] Another, more impressive, example of private historical writing which also survives in its original copy and allows a systematic analysis of the author's methods is a chronicle by an unknown Londoner of Caxton's day with interests similar to Caxton's own.[85] Here the compiler started out with a *Brut* chronicle that ended in 1419, inserted his own translations of sections of Higden's *Polychronicon*, and his own adaptation of episodes from literary works on legendary heroes and saints, such as Havelok and St Thomas Becket. He finished it in 1479, and then in 1482 made extensive alterations and insertions, using the newly printed *Polychronicon* in Trevisa's translation, updated by Caxton. The maker was

---

83 Blake, *Caxton's Own Prose*, 'Prohemye' to the *Polychronicon*, p. 128.

84 See the present authors' 'The making of a minor London chronicle'.

85 London, Lambeth Palace, MS 84; see Matheson, 'Printer and scribe', pp. 607–09, his 'The Arthurian stories of Lambeth Palace Library, MS 84', pp. 70–91, and his 'King Arthur and the medieval English chronicles', p. 255.

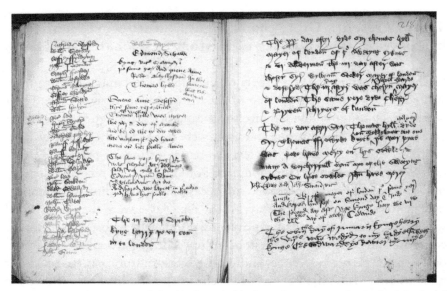

Fig. 58 Historical notes compiled in the household of Sir Thomas Frowyk. On the left a list of mayors of London, ending with Thomas 'Hylle', is followed by notes on the death of Queen Anne Neville, Richard III's defeat and death at 'Redmore feld' and Henry VII's entry into London. On the right the birth of Arthur, the battle of Stoke and the coronation of Elizabeth of York. BL, MS Harl. 541, ff. 217v and 218. By permission of The British Library.

greatly attracted by a good story, and if he read his work to his family for their entertainment they should have enjoyed it.

Other private compilers had other ambitions; some were more inchoate and less clear about their motives and their end product. They rarely got beyond making copies of official reports, political manifestos, broadsides and newsletters, as well as private documents. One such copyist was John Vale, the man-of-affairs or secretary of Sir Thomas Cook (Mayor of London 1462–63), who between *c.* 1478 and 1484 made an extensive collection of official accounts of events in the reigns of Henry V and Henry VI, broadsides produced by both Yorkists and Lancastrians in the 1450s, as well as diplomatic letters circulating in London between 1420 and 1480 and private documents relating to the affairs of the Cook family. Vale's exact intentions cannot be recovered but much of the material he copied was the same as that used by certain London chroniclers, such as

Alderman Robert Fabyan in his magisterial compilation known as the *Great Chronicle*.[86]

Private individuals who deliberately wrote narratives of events they had heard of or witnessed, for the benefit of their friends or business associates elsewhere, must have been more conscious that they were writing history than the mere collectors of interesting facts and documents. Their accounts varied greatly in quality and usually only survive if they were published widely and became (semi)-official; most of those surviving are not of English origin.[87] A German merchant in London wrote at length about the battle of Barnet (14 April 1471), its prelude and its aftermath, to his friends in Cologne, and his letter was filed in the records of the Hanseatic League;[88] Margaret of York, Duchess of Burgundy, wrote to her mother-in-law as soon as she had had certain news of Edward IV's victory at Barnet and the contents of her letter were of such immediate political importance that it was widely circulated.[89] Several people were so impressed by the magnificently staged wedding of Margaret of York and Charles the Bold in Bruges in 1468,[90] and by the latter's meeting with the emperor in Trier in 1473,[91] that they felt impelled to write up what they had seen. One such reporter wrote that he had made a *minute* (draft) during the event or he would never have remembered it all.[92] Guillaume de Caoursin's eye-witness account of the siege of Rhodes, the headquarters of the Knights of St John, by the Turks under Mehmet II, the conqueror of Constantinople, May to August 1480, became very famous. Caoursin's story was printed in Venice in the same year and was copied, printed and translated so often that it has been called a 'European bestseller'. John Kay, an otherwise unknown Englishman, dedicated a translation of it to Edward IV. In his preface he said that Edward's subjects reading about the defeat of the Turks would 'have joy and consolacyon and shal beter know

---

86 It should be emphasised that although Vale and Fabyan must have known each other in Cook's household, Fabyan did not use Vale's collection for his *Great Chronicle*; see the present authors, 'Provenance of the manuscript' in *John Vale's Book*.
87 Exceptions are the more of less narrative accounts surviving in letter collections such as those of the Pastons or Celys.
88 *Hanserecesse*, vol. 6, pp. 415–18.
89 See Visser-Fuchs, 'Edward IV's memoir', p. 204.
90 There are many versions and copies, see e.g. *Manual*, vol. 8, XXI [96].
91 There are many versions and copies, see e.g. *ibid.*, [97].
92 Haynin, *Mémoires*, vol. 2, pp. 18, 55.

by dayly myracles and goddes werkes the inestymable power and certentye of our crysten fayth'.[93]

The dramatic aftermath of the siege of Rhodes was also known in the West through a newsletter, in this case written by a Venetian merchant to his brother at home. It reported the death of the dreaded Mehmet II and his last wishes, as well as his magnificent funeral at Constantinople in which 20,000 people were said to have taken part. It ended with an account of the deadly struggle between the sultan's heirs, which wasted so much of the Turks' energy and resources that the Christian West had little to fear from them for several years. The letter became known as the *Testament of the Sultan*; Edward IV's son, Edward, Prince of Wales, owned a copy in French specially made for him in Flanders.[94]

The professional recorders of events – such as royal clerks and secretaries – were not necessarily aware that they were writing history, but they did know that their accounts would be used for a specific purpose. One official letter, a brief report in French produced in the signet office of Edward IV to inform Charles the Bold, his brother-in-law and ally against France, of the success of Edward's campaign in the spring of 1471 to recover his crown, became unusually popular. It had been composed merely for the duke's benefit, but he turned it into an instrument of propaganda to advertise the success of his alliance with England to his subjects. On the continent the text was used by many chroniclers, either in its entirety or worked into their own narrative (see pl. IX). In England it was also copied and used, after it had been translated into English: a longer version, composed by a different author, who did not acknowledge his source, became known as the *Arrivall of Edward IV*. Nicholas Harpisfeld, the signet clerk who wrote the original short text, produced it in the course of his normal duties but knew what was required; he wrote a factual report, but he also highlighted his king's virtues which had been so visibly endorsed by God's favour. The account must have been planned at the beginning of the campaign, with either the author or heralds attending Edward IV making notes of events as they happened, recording dates, places and distances for later use. The interest of the account for heralds is reflected in the fact that it survives in sixteenth-century heraldic miscellanies.[95]

---

93   Kaye/Caoursin, f. [15]. See above, and ch. 3.
94   Princeton University Library, MS Garrett 168; it bears his coat of arms between ostrich feathers and is also signed by two of his sisters.
95   Visser-Fuchs, 'Edward IV's memoir', passim.

Pl. I   First page of a book of hours of Richard's father, Richard, Duke of York (died 1460). The initial *O* of *Obsecro* contains his coat of arms. The book is small (6 x 9 cm). Durham, Ushaw College MS 43, f. 1. By permission of Ushaw College.

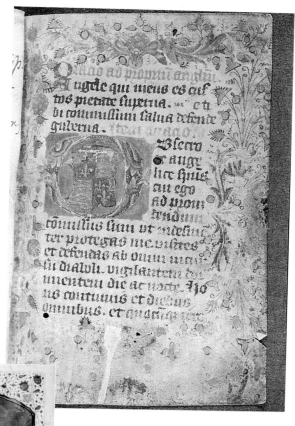

Pl. II   Presentation of a copy of the French translation of Boethius, *De consolatione philosophiae* to Margaret of York. Jena, University Library, MS EL F. 85, f. 13v. By permission of the University Library.

Pl. III   Top section of the Clare Roll, showing an Augustinian friar in conversation with a fashionably dressed visitor. The text contains their dialogue in which the history of Clare Priory and its patrons, the lords of Clare, is set out. The column on the left gives the English version, the column on the right the Latin one. The coats of arms of the lords run down the centre. English, 1456. London, College of Arms MS 3/16. By permission of the Chapter of the College of Arms.

Pl. IV   First page of a Burgundian treatise on nobility, the *Enseignement de la vraie noblesse*, showing the knight listening to the instructions of Lady Imagination. The manuscript was made for Richard Neville, Earl of Warwick, and has his coat of arms surrounded by the Garter in the lower margin and his emblem, the bear and ragged staff, in the right margin. Flemish, 1464. Geneva, Bibliothèque Publique et Universitaire MS fr. 166, f. 3. By permission of the Bibliothèque Publique et Universitaire.

Pl. V   The presentation miniature and the first page of the text of the Hours of the Guardian Angel presented to Queen Elizabeth Woodville by a devout lady. The scroll between the donor and the queen reads: 'with everlastyng ioy', a quotation from the hymn to the Guardian Angel which is part of the text. English, late 1470s to early 1480s. Liverpool, Liverpool Cathedral MS Radcliffe 6, ff. 5v–6. By permission of the Chancellor of Liverpool Cathedral.

Pl. VI   Two pages of the autograph copy of his *Life of St Katherine* which Pietro Carmeliano presented to Chancellor John Russell. On the left, p. 4, is the end of the text addressing Russell and the miniature of St Katherine with her sword and wheel; part of a prayer to the saint is written on the backdrop, and below the miniature is a prayer for the saint's intercession. On the right, p. 5, the title and the beginning of the poem. Cambridge, Gonville and Caius College, MS 196/102, pp. 4–5. By permission of the Master and Fellows of Gonville and Caius College, Cambridge.

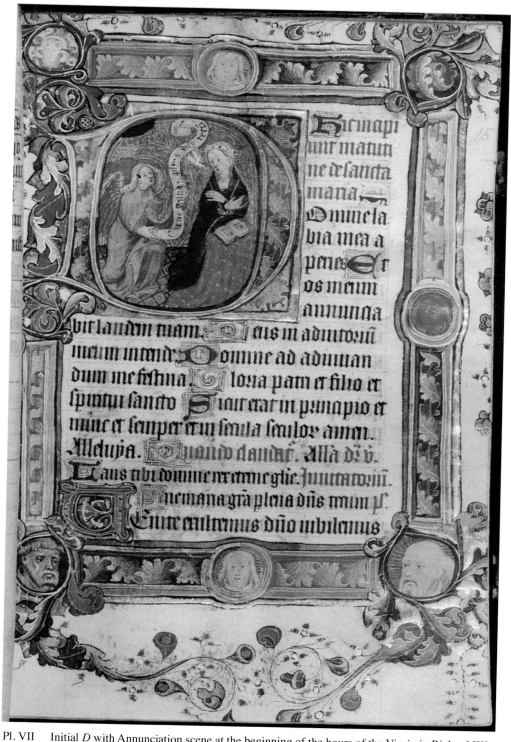

Pl. VII   Initial *D* with Annunciation scene at the beginning of the hours of the Virgin in Richard III's book of hours. The page has suffered severely at the hands of a sixteenth-century binder. London, *c.* 1420. London, Lambeth Palace Library MS 474, f. 15. By permission of Lambeth Palace Library.

Pl. VIIIa Equestrian portrait of Edward IV at the head of a genealogical roll showing his descent from Adam and Eve and his hereditary rights to the crowns of England, France, Leon and Castile. The arms of these countries appear on the trappings of his horse, the small scutcheon in the centre has the arms of Brutus, the legendary founder of Britain. On either side are quotations from the Bible indicating that Edward's accession was God's will.

Pl. VIIIb The final section of the same roll. Richard of York, by whom all hereditary claims were passed on to Edward IV, occurs in the rectangular space in the top centre. The roll is decorated with emblems and coats of arms, and scattered throughout is Edward's motto *comfort et liesse*, 'comfort and joy'. Philadelphia, Free Library MS Lewis E 201. By kind permission of the Free Library of Philadelphia.

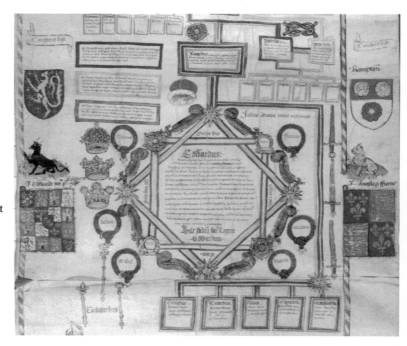

Pl. IX An example of contemporary rumour illustrated: Edward of Lancaster is killed by Edward IV's men after the battle of Tewkesbury, 4 May 1471, in a miniature from a copy of the so-called 'Short Version' of the *Arrivall of Edward IV*. The event is not described in the text, but the rumour was sufficiently wide-spread for it to be introduced by the artist on his own initiative. Flemish, early 1480s. Besançon, Bibliothèque Municipale MS 1168, f. 4v. By permission of the Bibliothèque Municipale.

Pl. X A chapter of the Order of the Golden Fleece presided over by Charles the Bold; miniature in a copy of the statutes of the order. The member knights are seated along the walls on either side; in the foreground the four officials of the order: Toison d'Or King of Arms (standing) and the Chancellor, the Clerk (*greffier*) and the Treasurer. The Clerk copied out the statutes of the order and recorded the deeds of the knights and the proceedings of the chapters. In 1473, towards the end of his life, Georges Chastellain was created a knight for his literary merits and became the official historian of the order. Flemish, 1468. The Hague, Royal Library MS 76 E 10, f. 5v. By permission of the Royal Library.

Pl. XI   A king of the 1480s, surrounded by his courtiers, receives a letter. From a French translation of William of Tyre's *History of the Crusades*, in a copy bearing the royal arms of England. Flemish, 1480s. BL MS Royal 15 E i, f. 185. By permission of The British Library.

Fig. 59 Secretaries at work recording events and writing letters 'in the field'. Miniature in Jean de Wavrin's *Chronicles of England*. Flemish, 1470s. Baltimore, Walters Art Gallery MS W 201, f. 147. By permission of the Walters Art Gallery.

The heralds of the imaginary *Débat* were performing some of the duties of their real-life counterparts. Heralds decided who were the victors in battle, they counted the dead and made lists of the slain in order of precedence. They supervised jousts and tournaments and arbitrated whenever a controversy arose between the participants. They organised and oversaw princely funerals and played an important part in other ceremonies, such as christenings, coronations and state visits. For their own information and that of their successors they kept records of all such occasions (see pl. X, fig. 62). A great number of accounts of such ceremonies that took place in Richard III's lifetime survive, although none of the authors are known:[96] the burial of some of his Neville relatives in 1463; the coronation of Elizabeth Woodville, 1465; the Anglo-Burgundian tournaments at Smithfield of 1467; the elaborate reburial of Richard, Duke of York, at Fotheringhay in 1476; the Garter ceremonies and the tournament and wedding ceremonies of Richard, Duke of York, and Anne Mowbray, 1477; the christening of Princess Bridget in 1480; the funeral of Edward IV, and the coronation of Richard III and his queen in 1483. Of all the Yorkist ceremonial events of which accounts survive, only the state visit of Louis of Gruuthuse in 1472, Edward's and Richard's host during their exile, was certainly written up by an officer of arms: Bluemantle Pursuivant. No English herald is known to have written a full-scale chronicle, like the Burgundian Jean le Fèvre, Toison d'Or king of arms (died 1468),[97] and it is difficult to name any author who was also an officer of arms. Thomas Whiting, Nucelles pursuivant and later Chester herald

---

96 No list of these ceremonial narratives is in print and many of them have no modern editions. For the subject generally see Keen, 'Chivalry, heralds and history', pp. 393–414; Green, *Poets and Princepleasers*, pp. 168–72; Lester, 'Literary activity of the medieval English heralds', pp. 222–29; the same, 'Fifteenth-century English heraldic narrative', pp. 201–12. Our list of Yorkist narratives is not exhaustive: for the Neville burial see e.g. Payne, 'The Salisbury Roll of Arms, *c.* 1463', pp. 187–98; coronation of Elizabeth Woodville: Smith, *Coronation*; Smithfield 1467: Anglo, 'Anglo-Burgundian feats of arms', pp. 271–83; Gruuthuse 1471: Madden, 'Narratives of the arrival of Louis de Bruges', pp. 265–86, and Kingsford, *English Historical Literature*, XV, Record of Bluemantle Pursuivant; reburial of York: present authors, *Reburial of Richard, Duke of York*; 1477 Garter: Stow, *Annales* (1615), p. 429; York and Mowbray: Black, *Illustrations of Ancient State and Chivalry*, pp. 25–40; the christening of Princess Bridget: Routh, 'Princess Bridget', pp. 13–14; funeral of Edward IV: Gairdner, *Letters and Papers*, vol. 1, pp. 3–10; coronation of Richard III: Sutton and Hammond, *Coronation*; see also *Manual*, vol. 8, passim.

97 Morand, *Chronique de Jean le Fèvre*; Le Fèvre's work is highly derivative, he copied extensively from Monstrelet, see Doutrepont, *Littérature*, pp. 436–37.

(died after 1496), has been suggested as the author of the accounts of the Smithfield tournament and York's reburial but these ascriptions cannot be substantiated.[98]

All such individual accounts and documents were potentially grist to the mill of the genuine chronicler or historian who set out to write a coherent survey of a longer period. In England there are a few examples to be found of Richard III's time. John Vale, the man-of-affairs of Sir Thomas Cook mentioned earlier, may be considered an example of the 'research' stage of composing a full-length history; he could have used the diverse and important material he collected himself or made it available to others. At least part of the well-known continuations of the *Crowland Chronicle* (1470–1486) seems to show how a collection of documents could be used and supplemented by the author's own knowledge. The continuations appear to contain excerpts and quotations from documents which the composer had to hand and which influenced his style and his choice of words: there are echoes of the signet letter concerning Edward IV's 'arrival' by Nicholas Harpisfeld,[99] phrases taken from a document concerning an embassy from Burgundy in 1472,[100] and a straightforward quotation – though apparently disguised as the author's personal knowledge – of the document recording the oath of the lords spiritual and temporal to young Edward, son of Richard III, taken in 'a certain room near the corridor which leads to the queen's quarters'.[101] The author worked such material into an existing local annals of the Abbey of Crowland and larded it with his personal knowledge, critical comments and quotations from the Bible.

The Burgundian chronicler of England Jean de Wavrin (died *c.* 1475) is an example of an industrious copier of existing texts who also made great efforts to obtain reliable information from witnesses of events. He

---

98 Lester, *Sir John Paston's 'Grete Boke'*, p. 109; present authors, *Reburial of Richard, Duke of York*, p. 12.

99 *Crowland Chronicle*, pp. 122–27. And compare the careers in Daly, 'Mixing business with leisure', pp. 99–115.

100 *Crowland Chronicle*, pp. 130–31; it is unlikely that the use of phrases such as *suam Serenitatem*, *Maiestatem suam* and *in prosperis and adversis* are examples of the author's irony; they are recurrent phrases in diplomatic documents.

101 *Ibid.*, pp. 170–71; documents recording oaths and solemn promises usually record in detail where the oath was taken or the promise made, and it is quite possible that the compiler had such an informative document to hand.

Fig. 60 An example of recent history illustrated: Edward IV, in bed, is betrayed by George Neville, Archbishop of York, and in the background the king is met and taken prisoner by the earl of Warwick and his army at the end of July 1469. From Jean de Wavrin's *Chronicles of England*, in a copy made for Louis de Gruuthuse and later owned by the kings of France. Flemish, 1480s. Paris, BN, MS fr. 85, f. 277. By permission of the Bibliothèque Nationale.

used the English accounts of the rebellion in Lincolnshire in 1469[102] and Edward's recovery of his crown in 1471,[103] but unfortunately he nowhere explains how he gained access to these documents. He does, however, report in detail how he set out for Calais in 1469 in an attempt to gather news from the earl of Warwick himself, 'wishing to know and have truthful material'. He was made very welcome, entertained lavishly for nine days, but was not given any information by the earl, being fobbed off with the promise that he could come back in two months' time. Wavrin consoled himself by reporting that he could see that the earl was obviously busy with 'great matters'. There is no evidence that he ever had another opportunity to gather such authoritative material for his chronicle.[104]

There is little doubt that Caxton was also a compiler of history. He never refers to himself as the maker of the continuation covering 1419–1461 which he added to a common version of the *Brut* to complete his *Chronicles of England*, published in 1480. He certainly implied, however, that he himself had compiled the *Liber ultimus*, covering 1357–1461, which incorporated much of the 1419–61 text of his *Chronicles* and which he used to complete his edition of Ralph Higden's *Polychronicon*, published in 1482. For his *Chronicles* Caxton had done a workmanlike job, probably using one or more texts of London chronicles that continued past 1419. He made a few personal additions and ended with a prayer for Edward IV; as the *Brut* was never claimed by any of its authors, neither did Caxton claim credit for his addition.[105]

In 1482 Caxton brought out the massive *Polychronicon*, a universal history by Ralph Higden, monk of Chester, translated into English by John Trevisa at the beginning of the fifteenth century. As the English of Trevisa was already dated, Caxton refurbished the entire text, and as it ended in the 1350s he decided to continue its original seven books with a *Liber ultimus* of his own, to bring it up to 1461. He naturally enough made use of his existing continuation of the *Chronicles of England* especially for the period 1419 to 1461; he actually tells his reader that he had looked at the *Fasciculus temporum* (1475), printed by John Veldener who had taught

---

102 Wavrin, *Croniques*, vol. 5, pp. 588–602; for the English text see Nichols, 'Chronicle of the Rebellion in Lincolnshire', pp. 3–28.
103 Visser-Fuchs, 'Edward IV's memoir', pp. 180–83.
104 Wavrin, *Croniques*, vol. 5, pp. 578–79.
105 Matheson, 'Printer and scribe', pp. 593–601.

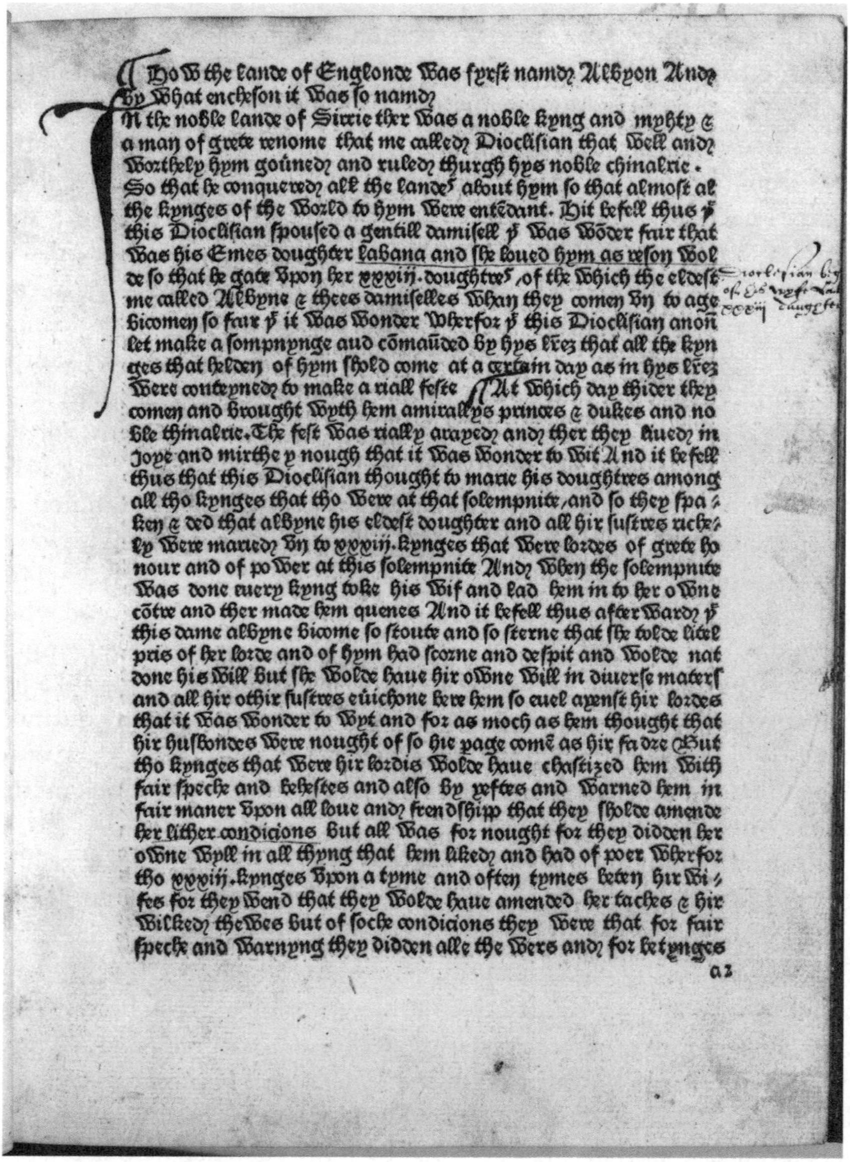
How the lande of Englonde was fyrst namd Albyon And by what encheson it was so namd
In the noble lande of Sirrie ther was a noble kyng and myghty & a man of grete renome that me called Dioclisian that well and worthely hym gouerned and ruled thurgh hys noble chiualrie. So that he conquered all the landes about hym so that almost al the kynges of the world to hym were entendant. Hit befell thus yt this Dioclisian spoused a gentill damisell yt was wonder fair that was his Emes doughter Labana and she loued hym as reson wolde so that he gate vpon her xxxiij. doughtres, of the which the eldest me called Albyne & thees damisellez whan they comen vn to age bicomen so fair yt it was wonder Wherfor yt this Dioclisian anon let make a sompnynge and comaunded by hys lres that all the kynges that helden of hym shold come at a certain day as in hys lres were conteyned to make a riall feste At which day thider they comen and brought wyth hem amirallys princes & dukes and noble chiualrie. The fest was rially arayed and ther they liued in Ioye and mirthe ynough that it was wonder to wit And it befell thus that this Dioclisian thought to marie his doughtres among all tho kynges that tho were at that solempnite, and so they spaken & ded that albyne his eldest doughter and all hir sustres richely were maried vn to xxxiij. kynges that were lordes of grete honour and of power at this solempnite And when the solempnite was done euery kyng toke his wif and lad hem in to her owne contre and ther made hem quenes And it befell thus afterward yt this dame albyne bicome so stoute and so sterne that she tolde litel pris of her lorde and of hym had scorne and despit and wolde nat done his will But she wolde haue hir owne will in diuerse maters and all hir othir sustres euichone bere hem so euel ayenst hir lordes that it was wonder to wyt and for as moch as hem thought that hir husbondes were nought of so hie parage come as hir fadre But tho kynges that were hir lordis wolde haue chastized hem with fair speche and behestes and also by yeftes and warned hem in fair maner vpon all loue and frendship that they sholde amende her lither condicions but all was for nought for they didden her owne wyll in all thyng that hem liked and had of poer Wherfor tho xxxiij. kynges vpon a tyme and often tymes betyn hir wiues for they wend that they wolde haue amended her taches & hir wikked thewes but of socke condicions they were that for fair speche and warnyng they didden alle the wers and for betynges
a2

Fig. 61 First page of Caxton's first edition of the *Chronicles of England* (10 June 1480); the second edition is dated 8 October 1482. Caxton concluded the text with a prayer for Edward IV. John Rylands University Library of Manchester, R26166, f. 8. Reproduced by courtesy of the Director and University Librarian, the John Rylands University Library of Manchester.

him printing,[106] and another, now unknown work *Aureus de universo* 'in whiche bookes I fynde ryght lytle mater'. He also used without acknowledgment the *Grandes chroniques* printed by Bonhomme in January 1477 and the *Chronique de la traison et mort de Richart Deux*.[107] It is interesting that Caxton added the complaint 'there can not be founden in these dayes but fewe that wryte in theyr regystres such thynges as dayly happen and falle ...'.[108] Despite all the activity of would-be chroniclers described above, little of their work fell into Caxton's hands when he needed it; the industry of twentieth-century scholars has apparently recovered more than he could obtain from his contemporaries.

Apart from Caxton few English chroniclers in Richard III's time explained *why* they wrote, or how they went about their work, or what standards they had set themselves. Jean de Wavrin started on his 'collection' of English chronicles because no continuous history of England existed, only smaller studies of separate kings and periods.[109] John Hardyng's and William Worcester's real reason for writing was their personal wish to prove the English rights to Scotland and France and to see these countries occupied. The purpose of John Carpenter in compiling the *Liber Albus* (1417), a collection of the customs of the city of London, had been to preserve in good order the customs of the city for posterity, because 'the fallibility of human memory and the shortness of life do not allow us to gain an accurate knowledge of everything that deserves remembrance' and also because all the knowledgeable men had died and the next generation had been left ignorant and perplexed.[110] Some authors, such as Hardyng and Wavrin, admitted that they felt old age approaching and they started to write with the double purpose of recording their experience and keeping both themselves and their readers from idleness.

The attitude of Richard III's contemporaries to the writing of history is summarised by the sensible remarks of an anonymous Burgundian who,

106 Corsten, 'Caxton in Cologne', pp. 1–18. Talk by Meg Ford on the *Fasciculus* at the conference of the Early Book Society, Dublin 1991.

107 Matheson, 'Printer and scribe', pp. 601–06.

108 Blake, *Caxton's Own Prose*, *Polychronicon*, p. 132. And compare the irritation of the scribe of a *Brut* (BL, MS Egerton 1435, f. 111), who lacked a 'trewe copy' of the 'Siege of Rouen', cited Scott, 'Limning and book-producing terms', p. 147.

109 Wavrin, *Croniques*, vol. 1, p. 2.

110 Riley, *Munimenta Gildhallae Londoniensis*, vol. 1, *Liber Albus*, pp. 3–4.

in the 1470s, decided to continue an earlier history into his own times and
pick up the history of France, England and Burgundy at the point where
it had been left by Enguerrand de Monstrelet:

> I have decided to make this chronicle to keep in perpetual memory the
> noble and great deeds of arms performed in the kingdoms of France,
> England, Italy, Flanders, Normandy, Germany and other parts of
> Christendom; to give comfort to my readers, and to set an example for
> all noble men to perform great and notable deeds of arms in imitation
> of those whom perpetual memory recommends to us even after their
> death, and to avoid idleness, the open door to all vices. I have sought
> information by long and thorough inquiry, not from one person but
> from several, and such as were present at the events, and seemed trust-
> worthy and truthful, and I have done this as far as I could without hate
> or favour, as one should in such matters. For as far as truth is concerned
> it is better *not* to report things than to report them falsely; it happens
> only too often that fear and love, hate or greed, deprive people of a true
> judgment. Furthermore I have informed myself very thoroughly and I
> did not have the accounts copied out fairly until a year had passed since
> the events happened in order to be more certain about them. And I beg
> those that read or hear them that they will forgive me if they should
> hear or read anything that does not please them, for it was my intention
> to tell the truth, following the reports of my informants. I begin my
> work with the year 1444, where Enguerrand de Monstrelet finished,
> and I end it with the year 1471.[111]

Richard III's Own Enthusiasms

It appears that Richard was surrounded by the history books of the past
and others in the making, but was he aware of these riches? His ownership or access to the books he signed offers only half an answer but it is
a positive indication of interest. No fifteenth-century king of England
commissioned works of history on the lines of the French royal patronage of the chronicles of Saint-Denis, and Richard is no exception. He
did, however, offer very important and practical assistance to the active

---

111 Wavrin, *Croniques*, vol. 1, pp. 607–08.

producers of some of the most useful works of history, those recorders of precedent, the heralds. The importance of his gift of a house, and with it the means to keep safely a joint library, to the incorporated heralds can hardly be overestimated. The loss of the house and the resulting disorder and quarrels over the library when Henry VII bestowed the house on his mother underlines the importance of both to the heralds' activities.[112] The rolls of arms that belonged to Richard ended up in this new library, probably put there by his ducal officers of arms during his reign.[113] He had supported the heralds while constable of England from 1469 to 1483, and his ordinances drawn up in the late 1470s emphasised their duties of recording deeds of valour and the ceremonies of knighthood and nobility. These were not new or original in concept but each generation needed reminders:

> Item nous voulons et chargeons que toutes manieres de solemnitees, actes solemnelz et faitz des nobles aussi bien touchant les faitz d'armes comme aultrement soient veritablement et indifferentement registrez, sans faveur, aucune parcialitee ou plaisir, …

> (Also we wish and command that all manner of solemn occasions, solemn acts and deeds of the nobility, those concerned with deeds of arms as well as others, be truthfully and indifferently recorded, without favour, without any partiality or sympathy …)[114]

As already mentioned, narratives of ceremonies and campaigns were made in the Yorkist period and lists of the people killed and taken prisoner were compiled after the battles.[115] Most of these texts were made by a professional with knowledge of what the king required to keep his subjects and allies informed of his successes. Even if many of the authors cannot be identified, some of them were heralds and English heralds can

---

112 Wagner, *Heralds of England*, pp. 130–31, 134–36; and his *Heralds and Heraldry*, pp. 95–96, which refers to the French heralds' acquisition of a regular library and meeting place in 1407. And see ch. 6 above.

113 See ch. 6 above.

114 On the ordinances see Wagner, *Heralds of England*, pp. 67–68; the text is printed in his *Heralds and Heraldry*, pp. 136–38, esp. 138. The ordinances were previously attributed to the Duke of Clarence, brother of Henry V, *Heralds and Heraldry*, pp. 59–63.

115 E.g. Worcester, *Itinerary*, pp. 203–05, 344–45; Visser-Fuchs, 'A Ricardian riddle', pp. 9–12.

Fig. 62 Jean LeFèvre, Toison d'Or King of Arms, at work writing up the life of the famous knight Jacques de Lalaing. He wears a tabard with the arms of the duke of Burgundy. Opening page of the *Livre des faits de Jacques de Lalaing*. Paris, BN, MS fr. 16830, f. 1. By permission of the Bibliothèque Nationale.

be credited with performing their tasks as competently as the heralds of other nations.[116] There is no sign, however, of any official chronicler for the Order of the Garter – although a narrative survives for the 1477 Garter ceremonies[117] – such as existed for the Golden Fleece (see pl. X). There was no Georges Chastellain for the English court and no *indiciaire* for the Garter survives to 'demonstrate' the deeds of its knights.[118]

The only accounts of ceremonial and political events for Richard's reign that survive are of his coronation,[119] his visit to York not long after,[120] and of the negotiations with Scotland at Nottingham in 1484, possibly the result of an official *aide mémoire*.[121] Richard may have been well aware that such records were being made, but presumably unknown to the king was the note-taking and copying of documents by one of his clerical councillors which were to form the basis of the account of his reign now embedded in the second continuation of the *Crowland Chronicle*. This author's activity was as much a private concern as the small burst of enthusiasm for a Neville queen that sparked off the notes that make up the Frowyk chronicle (see fig. 58), or the larger talent of the author of what is now called 'Gregory's Chronicle' (ends 1469).[122] Apart from the official encouragement given to the heralds, the writing of history in England was a private interest in the fifteenth century.

---

116 Compare Sicily Herald, *Le blason des couleurs*, and other works, *Parties inédits de l'oeuvre de Sicile héraut*; and Wagner, *Heralds of England*, p. 40 ff.

117 Preserved by Stow, *Annales* (1615), p. 429.

118 In 1473 Chastellain, the court historiographer of the duke of Burgundy, was officially made historian of the order of the Golden Fleece: *avecq tiltre de indiciaire, comme celuy qui demonstroit par escripture authentique les admirables gestes des chevaliers et confreres de l'ordre*, (with the title of *indiciaire*, as one who makes public in original writing the admirable deeds of the knights and the members of the order); for details see Naïs, '"Grands temps et long jours"', pp. 207–18; Doutrepont, *Littérature*, pp. 441–44, 470.

119 Sutton and Hammond, *Coronation*, pp. 195–99, 270–82.

120 York Minster Library, Bedern College Statute Book, p. 48 (which may only be a local and clerical record); printed Hammond, 'Richard III at York', pp. 3–4, and corrected Hammond and Sutton, *Road to Bosworth Field*, pp. 140–41.

121 Gairdner, *Letters and Papers*, vol. 1, pp. 63–67.

122 Gairdner, *Historical Collections*, pp. 57–239.

EIGHT

Prophecy and the House of York

At the end of Richard III's manuscript of the *Historia regum Britanniae* by Geoffrey of Monmouth the scribe added another short text which he called the *Prophecy of the Eagle*.[1] This text has long been known to scholars, but only recently studied in detail.[2] At first sight it has nothing to do with Richard III, but a closer look reveals that it is one of the many prophetic texts that Edward IV's supporters used in the campaign of political propaganda which had to justify his accession in 1461: the *Prophecy of the Eagle* predicts the return to power of a race and a dynasty that has long been put aside. The *Prophecy* can only be understood with the help of the last section of Geoffrey of Monmouth's *Historia*, to which the Eagle's words are, as it were, a *pièce justificative*. Richard's ownership of this particular prophecy is not unexpected, as such politically useful vaticinal texts were very popular, but it demands a discussion of the subject and the use of the genre by – and against – the Yorkist kings.

Prophecies, especially those of Merlin, were immensely popular from the twelfth to the late seventeenth century and they have always been in vogue at times of political crisis or heightened national sentiment. Even

---

1 See ch. 7 above, and Cat. VIII A and B below.
2 'R III's books VIII', pp. 290–304, 351–62. The first scholar to know and study the *Prophecy* was John Selden, who published his findings in his learned *Illustrations* to the *Poly-Olbion* of Michael Drayton (1612–22); for details see 'R III's books VII and VIII', p. 408 and nn.

in the twentieth century they are occasionally re-interpreted.[3] They were used to explain events, but could also influence them, for example by inciting or supporting rebellion. Men of all classes were intrigued by them and many prophecies had an international reputation, among them those of Merlin and the various texts ascribed to the classical Sibyl.[4] The English were often said to have a special predilection for prophecies: the Burgundian historian Philippe de Commines asserted they were never short of them.[5]

Prophecy claims to foretell what is bound to happen and by so doing gives a semblance of order to a series of events. The medieval love of prophecy, like that of typology (or foreshadowing), is closely associated with the frequently held belief that we learn from the past because history has a pattern and events repeat themselves. There were, for example, innumerable artificially created links between events in the Old and New Testaments and these were frequently depicted in medieval art. Isaac and David were thus foreshadowings or types of Christ; to what extent and in what way they were types depended on the interpretation of their actions in the light of Christ's later life and passion. In both typology and prophecy the significance of one event was enhanced by the other. A prophetic text or a typological precedent derived its value and interest from the event that it was supposed to have predicted or the figure it was thought to have foreshadowed, and any event became more momentous when it was thought to have been foreseen and planned by God or Nature.

Prophecies served to make the past, the present and the future one continuous cycle in the mind of the author and the reader. At a time when chroniclers and historians had, or chose to use, few other means to 'make sense' of a long narrative, it was a useful ordering device which emphasised God's plan for mankind. The historical plays of Shakespeare, *Richard II* to *Richard III*, abound with such foretellings. In *Richard III*, for exam-

---

3   One of the most recent interpretations of the Prophecies of Merlin is R.J. Stewart, *The Prophetic Vision of Merlin*, London 1986. On prophecies in the Middle Ages in England see: Webb, 'Translation', pp. 250–51; Taylor, *Political Prophecy*; Tatlock, *Legendary History*, ch. 17; Eckhardt, *Prophetia Merlini*; Southern, 'History as prophecy', pp. 159–80; Herrmann, 'Spätmittelalterliche englische Pseudoprophetien', pp. 87–116; Jansen, *Political Protest*; Lerner, *Powers of Prophecy*, 'Conclusions'; *Manual*, vol. 5, XIII, pp. 1516–36, 1714–25.

4   See Taylor, *Political Prophecy*, pp. 28–38; McGinn, '*Teste David cum Sibylla*'. The Sibyl's prophecies were popular because they were supposed to have predicted the coming of Christ.

5   Commines's memoirs in any edition, bk 4, ch. 10; see also Webb, 'Translation', p. 253; Taylor, *Political Prophecy*, pp. 84–86.

ple, Queen Margaret constantly appears throughout the play to remind the audience of her predictions and the inevitable consequences of past events. Her *persona* is largely the playwright's creation and so she could be presented as both prophet and interpreter. Any attempt to explain a prophecy could be as persuasive, disturbing and subversive as Margaret's interventions in the play.

An essential feature of all prophecies is their obscurity. This is achieved by ambiguous words and symbols, play on words and metaphor. Another common and effective device is to begin with a series of actual and thinly disguised historical facts and then go on to the 'real' prophecy, thereby implying that the latter is as revelatory and truly prophetic as the first part has already proved to be. As a result it is not surprising that some interpretations of prophetic texts start out full of confidence, but end more or less abruptly when they come up against the section which is entirely fictional and not yet made 'clear' by events.

For whatever purpose they were originally composed, the propaganda value of prophetic texts was obvious. They were used to impress people with the inevitability and consequent rightness of certain events, particularly political events of national importance. As a result it could be very dangerous to promulgate them and accusations of sedition and treason might follow. In 1402 and 1406, at a time when Henry IV was plagued with memories of Richard II, laws were passed in England against the use of 'false prophecies', threatening severe punishment. Early in Edward IV's reign a man was executed for proclaiming on the basis of prophetic texts that Henry VI was still king.[6] In Henry VIII's time many people suffered for criticising the government by the use of old prophecies.[7] Prophecies might lend respectability and confidence to the claims of both rebels and new dynasties, confirm the righteousness of military action, sanctify an important relic, or raise expectations about a specific event, such as the birth of a royal heir or a hoped-for crusade.

Explanations of prophetic texts survive in the shape of scholarly glosses, as quotations in historical works relating them to particular events, and in some instances prophecies themselves appear as political poems and songs that leave little doubt about the way in which

---

6   Bellamy, *Law of Treason*, p. 119.
7   Jansen, *Political Protest*, passim.

they should be interpreted.[8] When several interpretations of the same text survive they inevitably have similarities, particularly the sections that were originally composed after the event, but they also have endless variations, according to the preoccupations of each generation. Commentators are brief or prolix, and they have personal, regional or ethnic preferences. Most of them concentrate on the more dramatic, political happenings: battles and the deaths of kings.[9]

The *Prophecy of the Eagle*

To Geoffrey of Monmouth, the author of the *Historia regum Britanniae*,[10] must go most of the credit for popularising prophetic writing in England which had been comparatively unknown in this country before the twelfth century. Geoffrey's main prophet was Merlin, but he also created a prophetic eagle. Although in Geoffrey's writings there is no confusion between these two beings or their prophecies, there is later, so they must both be described. The Eagle only occurs briefly in the *Historia*, but Merlin is in all three of Geoffrey's works and is one of his most popular and enduring creations.

Geoffrey is now generally accepted as the author of the Latin verse romance *Vita Merlini*, his last work.[11] With the aid of Celtic traditions of a prophet, Myrdinn, he created the legend of Merlin, magician and seer, and used it throughout his work. The Merlin of the romance was a very different personality from the Merlin of the *Prophecies* and the *History of the Kings of Britain*, although to Geoffrey he was the same man grown old after Arthur's death. This disparity encouraged the creation of *two* Merlins by puzzled writers later in the twelfth century who thought they needed to clarify their puzzlement. The two prophets were separated as early as 1188

---

8 *Manual*, vol. 5, XIII, pp. 1516–36; Scattergood, *Politics and Poetry*, pp. 32, 118; Robbins, *Historical Poems*, pp. xliv–xlvi, 113–21, and notes; Taylor, *Political Prophecy*, passim.

9 See e.g. Eckhardt, *Prophetia Merlini*, pp. 13–15; Hammer, 'A commentary on the *Prophetia Merlini*', pp. 3–30; Curley, 'Fifteenth-century glosses on *The Prophecy of John of Bridlington*', pp. 321–29.

10 See also ch. 7 above.

11 It was written soon after 1148, dedicated to Robert de Chesney, Bishop of Lincoln (1148–67). The two main editions are Parry, *Vita Merlini*; Clarke, *Life of Merlin*. See also Ward, *Catalogue of Romances*, vol. 1, pp. 278–88; Faral, *Légende Arthurienne*, pp. 28–36, 341–85; Jarman, 'Welsh Myrdinn poems', pp. 20–30; Tatlock, *Legendary History*, pp. 171–77, 403–21.

Fig. 63 Merlin watches the red and white
dragons fighting at the foot of the tower that
Vortigern, King of Britain, is trying to build.
Woodcut from an unidentified printed edition
of Geoffrey of Monmouth's *History of the
Kings of Britain*. It was used without reference
to its origin in the Dutch *Divisie*-chronicle
(f. 17), printed in 1517, to illustrate the
founding of a legendary city.

when an interested person like Gerald of Wales was well informed about
their careers.[12] It is the Merlin of the *Vita* that the history of the *Prophecy of
the Eagle* is concerned with: he was a *silvester homo*, a 'man of the woods' of
North Britain, or Caledonia, a king of Demetia who went mad with grief
at the death of friends in battle and fled to the woods to live with animals.
Bouts of sanity alternated with madness for the rest of his life; he endured
suffering and various adventures, uttering a series of prophecies – many of
which refer to Geoffrey's own text and to the reign of Stephen, not surprisingly – until he retired permanently to live among the trees and prophesy
no more. The Merlin of the *Vita* not only inspired later romances but was
also, in part, the inspirer of the character Merlin Silvester or Celidonius to
whom the *Prophecy of the Eagle* was frequently attributed. This later creation
must not be confused with Merlin Ambrosius, the Merlin of Geoffrey's
Prophecies and his *History of the Kings of Britain*.

The *Prophecies of Merlin* was Geoffrey's earliest work, a series of statements and images couched in symbolic language, not necessarily linked
to each other and with no obvious argument or meaning, but purporting
to foretell the future if the reader can interpret the symbols and language
correctly. These were based on Welsh bardic sayings and prophecies, but

---

12 For Gerald of Wales, see below; *both* Merlins have received biographies in the *DNB*.

Geoffrey also took inspiration from the Bible and such sources as Lucan's *Pharsalia*, the epic describing the civil wars of Rome. He claimed that his prophecies were merely translations of an ancient book in Welsh. They were put together at some time between 1120, the year of the loss of the White Ship, in which Henry I's only legitimate son was drowned – an episode clearly 'foretold' in the *Prophecies* – and 1135.[13] Later Geoffrey included the *Prophecies* in his *History of the Kings of Britain*, where he attached them to the character of Ambrosius Merlin, the boy without a father and whose mother was the daughter of a king of Demetia. The boy prophesied to Vortigern, the British king who alternately fought against and cooperated with the Saxon invaders, and interpreted for him the battle of the Red and White Dragons.[14] The Red and White Dragons were to be one of the most successful of all motifs used in British vaticinal literature, and they also feature in the *Prophecy of the Eagle*. Geoffrey took the dragons and the boy, Ambrosius, from the ninth-century *Historia Brittonum* by Nennius, where the dragons represented the nations of the Britons (red) and the Saxons (white), as they were to do throughout their literary life. To Nennius' brief details Geoffrey added a life history for the boy-seer and his book of prophecies. Ambrosius Merlin went on to be of assistance to Aurelius Ambrosius, a general fighting the invaders of Britain, and it was he who enabled Uther Pendragon to disguise himself so that he could beget the future King Arthur – a king whom Merlin himself never met in the pages of the *Historia*. For Geoffrey, Merlin's later career was as the mad prophet-king of Demetia, and it was other, later, romance writers who created his role as Arthur's mentor and magician.[15]

In the text of the *Historia* there are two references to a prophetic eagle. In Book Two, while the walls of Shaftesbury were being built this eagle spoke. 'If I believed its sayings to be true I would not hesitate to hand them down to history with my other material', concludes Geoffrey, no doubt with his tongue well in his cheek.[16] At the end of his *Historia* he is not

---

13 See e.g. Wright, *Historia regum Britanniae I*, pp. v–xvi, for the date and composition of Geoffrey's works.

14 Geoffrey of Monmouth, *History of the Kings of Britain*, trans. Thorpe, pp. 167–87.

15 The *Prophecies* remained very popular throughout the middle ages and after, circulating by themselves or in the *Historia*. See e.g. Eckhardt, *Prophetia Merlini*, and her 'The first English translations', pp. 25–34; Hammer, 'Commentary'. Ambrosius Merlin is too well known to need discussion here. Merlin Silvester had a more modest career, see *Manual*, vol. 1, p. 46.

16 Geoffrey of Monmouth, *History of the Kings of Britain*, trans. Thorpe, p. 61.

so sceptical for he places the prophecies of the Eagle among the authorities consulted by King Alan of Brittany when he counselled Cadwalader about the Angelic Voice which had spoken to him. Cadwalader was to retire to Rome, leaving Britain to the conquering Saxons: one day the British race (the Red Dragon) would rule again in Britain.[17]

There is no precise precedent for Geoffrey's prophetic eagle. Some critics have suggested that the eagle of Sestos on the Hellespont, whose story is told by Pliny in his *Natural History*[18] was transmuted by Geoffrey into the eagle of Shaftesbury (*Seftonia*), but the classical story concerns a faithful pet eagle which immolated itself on the funeral pyre of the young girl who had trained it. More in keeping with the eagle of Shaftesbury are the folk-tales of animals and birds helping human beings, and of dead kings and gods speaking through the medium of animals. Also relevant is the comparable amplification by Geoffrey of another of Nennius' details, when he makes the sixty eagles of Loch Lomond announce marvels in his *Historia*.[19] Geoffrey littered his prophecies with animal symbols in a way that suggests he easily associated animals with prophecy. He was not unique in this usage, but he was undoubtedly the most significant and influential author who wrote in this way.

Although Geoffrey was sceptical of the Eagle's capabilities initially, it has been noticed that he was less so by the end of his *Historia*. Even less sceptical were his readers who rushed to put texts into the bird's beak. The text of the prophecy usually attributed to the Eagle was probably in circulation during the reign of Henry II and manuscripts began to proliferate in the thirteenth century. The Eagle of Shaftesbury soon became entangled with the Merlin of the Woods, Merlin Silvester or Celidonius (Caledonius, Caledonicus). Such authors as Wace, who did a French verse version of Geoffrey's *Historia* for a courtly audience, called *Le Roman de Brut* (1155), were partly responsible for turning the Eagle into a human being. Wace assumed, sensibly, that *aquila* was the name of a *bon devin* – it did not occur to him that *aquila* was merely Latin for an eagle.[20]

---

17   *Ibid.*, p. 257.
18   Pliny, *Naturalis Historia*, bk 10, 5.
19   Geoffrey of Monmouth, *History of the Kings of Britain*, trans. Thorpe, p. 219.
20   Wace, *Roman de Brut*, vol. 2, line 14814. Wace, too, in his time had to consider the risk of using prophecies that contained political material: he consciously omitted Merlin's long prophecies altogether, see Blacker 'Ne vuil sun livre translater', pp. 49–59.

Precisely when and how the group of texts now called the *Prophecy of the Eagle* became attached to the Eagle or Merlin Silvester is not clear. One section, here called the *Three Dragons*, may have been among the bardic texts found by Gerald of Wales about 1188. He asserts that such prophecies 'of Merlin' were commonly sung in Wales by bards but rarely written down. Henry II encouraged him to collect them and translate them into Latin. Gerald's collection of prophecies, which he intended to publish as the third book of his *Expugnatio Hibernica* (*The Conquest of Ireland*), does not survive, but separate vaticinal passages that may have been taken from Gerald's collection are quoted in the two surviving books. Some of these passages can also be found embedded in the *Prophecy of the Eagle*. Whether Gerald perhaps wrote his prophetic texts himself or is genuinely quoting, in this instance from a complete text of the *Prophecy of the Eagle*, is not certain. Translation would undoubtedly have altered details and he admits to knowing of Merlin Silvester whom he clearly distinguishes from Merlin Ambrosius.[21] What is certain is that the Giraldian sentences, those common to both Gerald and the Eagle, refer to twelfth-century events and can be presumed to have been composed before 1200; Merlin Silvester was already associated with several of them.

The long section of the *Prophecy* which was known, partly at least, to Gerald is here called the *Three Dragons* because its main feature is the use of Merlin's image of the Red and White Dragons, plus their counterpart and victor, the Dark Dragon.[22] To medieval interpreters this was the most promising and specific of all sections of the Eagle's prophecy: several detailed commentaries survive. The text is too long to be given here in full, but an impression will be gleaned from the beginning:

As the White Dragon expelled the Red Dragon so a Dark Dragon will throw out the White Dragon. The Dark Dragon, fierce and terrible, will come flying and burn up the whole island with the flaming fire of its mouth. From its loins will come forth a ram with a fine fleece who will strike with its horns in the east. A little king of

---

21 For more detail of Gerald's work see Gerald of Wales, *Conquest of Ireland*, pp. lxi–lxviii and index under Merlin; Gerald of Wales, *Journey through Wales*, pp. 66–67 and n. 22, 183 and n. 346, 192–93, 248, 280; see also 'R III's books: VIII, 2', p. 301 n. 35.

22 For details see the present authors, 'Dark Dragon', pp. 1–19.

venomous aspect will also come forth and under his gaze faith and religion will quake... .[23]

The other long section of the Eagle's prophecy is that called the *Prophecy of the White King*. Its origin is obscure, but it was probably composed as one piece and intended to refer to the troubled reign of Stephen. It clearly refers to a period of civil war, describing its abuses in ambiguous and disturbing images. Frequently copied but rarely interpreted from the twelfth to the seventeenth centuries, it has attracted little attention from historians of prophecy. No detailed commentary is extant, but one scribe accurately summed up its ominous contents by adding at its end: 'And then it will be the Day of Judgment. The end.' The prophecy begins:

> When the lion of justice is dead a white and noble king will rise up in Britain, first flying, then riding and then going down, and in this same going down he will be snared. Then he will be led through Britain and he will be pointed at with the finger and it will be said: where is the white and noble king?

One of its most ominous passages reads:

> Behold the greed and effusion of blood and how many churches become furnaces; what one sows another will reap and death of miserable life will prevail; the love of few men will remain entire and what is agreed in the evening will be violated in the morning.

It ends:

> Then the white and noble king will slide into death. Then the eagle's chick will build a nest on the highest point of all Britain and he will not be killed as a young man, nor will he live to old age. Then common goodness of heart will not suffer injury to him who goes to the peaceful kingdom.[24]

The third, shorter, section of the Eagle's prophecy is not always included but in Richard's text it is the opening passage. This *Vision of King Edward*

---

23 For a translation of the full text see, 'R III's books: VIII, 2', p. 353.
24 For a translation see *ibid.*, pp. 353-54

the Confessor, or the *Vision of the Green Tree* is the most ancient and best authenticated text among all this 'skimble-skamble stuff'.[25] The first, anonymous, life of the Confessor was composed before 1084–85 and all the early subsequent lives or accounts of Edward were indebted to its text: William of Malmesbury, Osbert of Clare, and the *Life* commissioned from Aelred of Rievaulx to celebrate the successful conclusion, in 1161, of the campaign to canonise the king. Edward's deathbed vision of the Green Tree is in all these lives. The Confessor's cult had begun probably during his lifetime among his Norman courtiers as a virgin, miracle-working king, but its main flowering was in the twelfth century when the Angevin kings were concerned to strengthen their claim to the English throne with reverence for Edward and marriages into the Anglo-Saxon royal line. Despite the twelfth-century enthusiasm and canonisation campaign, the earliest life of St Edward is thought to reflect genuine contemporary information.[26]

The *Vision* is short:

> A fruitful tree cut from its original trunk will be separated from its own root by a space of three acres. Without force of human hand and without any command it is returned to its trunk, that is to Kambrus and Kambria.[27] When it has restored itself to its trunk and regained its sap, it will flourish again and bear fruit: then a remedy can be hoped for to this trouble.

The earlier accounts of this deathbed vision – the doom of the felled tree unable to produce leaves or fruit until its parts are come together again without the help of a human agent – interpreted it pessimistically, in the context of the politics of their own day, the Norman Conquest or subsequent civil disturbances. In Aelred of Rievaulx's text of 1163, the only one to receive wide circulation, however, it was dramatically re-interpreted in a positive way: the felled tree was one again and Henry II was the heir to past divisions. To Aelred the tree was the English kingdom, which descended in direct succession from Alfred to Edward, was then divided from its 'trunk' in that it passed to another race, and after three kings – the three acres – Harold, William I and William II, was returned

---

25 Hotspur's description of prophecy, Shakespeare, *Henry IV*, part 1, act 3, scene 1, line 154.
26 See Barlow, *Vita Aedwardi Regis*, pp. xiii–xiv, xxii, xxv–xxvi, xxxvii, 112–16.
27 The words *scilicet ad kambrum et kambr[i]am* which occur in Richard's copy, are not part of the original text, but a gloss that was absorbed by the prophecy.

to the original race in the person of Henry I who married Matilda of the old royal house. The line flourished (the Empress Matilda) and bore fruit (Henry II).

The brief and delightfully simple text of the vision of the Green Tree was a perfect prophecy. It was capable of constant re-interpretation, once the knack was caught from Aelred, every time there was civil division followed by a period of reunion: Edward IV was as good an example of the working out of the prophecy as Henry II. It was also a text that must have been known to Geoffrey of Monmouth and one of the many influences on his prophetic style. Edward the Confessor's own inspirations include St Dunstan who prophesied the Norman Conquest, the green tree of Christ's parable and, in particular, the dream of King Nebuchadnezzar interpreted by Daniel. The last provides a clue as to why the vision of the Green Tree should sometimes be included in the Eagle miscellany. Not only did the dream contain the symbol of a green and fruitful tree cut down, but, like Merlin, Nebuchadnezzar went mad, was driven from his kingdom to live with animals and eat grass, and his hair 'was grown like eagle's feathers and his nails like birds' claws'.[28] It is hardly surprising that someone who knew the Book of Daniel linked the Confessor's vision of the Green Tree to Merlin Silvester, alias the Eagle.

The Commentary on the *Prophecy of the Eagle* in Richard III's manuscript was written by someone who had Geoffrey of Monmouth's *Historia regum Britanniae* to hand.[29] He copied words and complete sentences from the *Prophecies* of Merlin Ambrosius in Book Seven and from the events of the reign of Cadwalader in Book Twelve. His interpretation is unusual and pessimistic; he cannot have been aware of its connection with the Confessor and Aelred's *Life* was unknown to him. He relates the text only to Cadwalader and the Welsh and their defeat, and appears to think – as Gerald of Wales did – that there is little hope of the exiled Welsh ever returning since they have not reformed the sinful ways that were the original cause of their misery.[30]

---

28 Daniel 4; compare Luke 23: 31 and Ezekiel 31.

29 For more detail of other mss containing the *Prophecy of the Eagle* and other commentaries see 'R III's books: VIII, 2', esp. pp. 357–58 n. 1.

30 In Geoffrey's *Historia* the main sin of the Britons is their internal discord. Gerald names several others: inconstancy, cowardice, quarrelsomeness and homosexuality. The last they inherited from their Trojan ancestors, who, like them, lost their country because of it; see e.g. Thorpe translation, pp. 255–67.

The commentator displays a marked preoccupation with the racial symbolism of the Red (British), the White (Saxon) and Dark (Norman) Dragons and most of his interpretation is taken up by long lists of names not composed by him but borrowed from another source. The Red Dragon is illustrated by a list of names of British kings taken straight out of Geoffrey's *Historia*.[31] The Anglo-Saxon kings representing the White Dragon are not so easily allotted but they could have been taken from a lost chronicle, or inspired by a mnemonic list, of the type traditionally made of tribes, kings, heroes and elves by the Saxons' Germanic ancestors. The Dark Dragon was given the series of names known as the 'Companions of the Conqueror' which had a vigorous life from its creation in the time of Henry II until 1943, when it was finally shown to be spurious.[32]

Edward IV and Prophecy

As the first king of a 'new' dynasty Edward IV needed self-advertisement and his accession had to be justified and legitimised in every possible way. His use of straightforward genealogy has been discussed[33] and his claim of being descended from Edward III through the senior line is well known. Prophetic and other ancient and prestigious texts were also employed by Edward to great effect. These can be roughly divided according to the political purpose of the moment: insular authorities – usually Geoffrey of Monmouth – who had prophesied in the remote past that the disinherited Britons would come into their own again; continental prophets who had predicted in more general terms the coming of a golden age under a mysterious 'Last Emperor'; and finally religious texts that provided a theological background for the legal aspects of Edward's right to the crown.

The *Prophecy of the Eagle* belonged to the first category and its usefulness to the Yorkist kings depended on the information provided by Geoffrey of Monmouth in his *Historia* and on the popularity of his work. The Yorkist kings were conscious of their British/Welsh descent and they were in an

---

31 A comparison may be made to the list of kings in the convenient Time Chart in Thorpe's translation of the *Historia*, pp. 286–88. For more detailed information about the lists see, 'R III's books: VIII, 2', pp. 297–99, 355–56, and 'Dark Dragon', passim.

32 Douglas, 'Companions of the Conqueror', pp. 129–47.

33 Ch. 6 above.

excellent position to take complete political advantage of the fact that people knew Geoffrey and other *Brut* texts deriving from him so well. Edward IV's supporters could emphasise his impeccable Welsh lineage through Mortimer, Llewelyn the Great,[34] and Cadwalader back to Brut and the Trojans, and they could go one step further and cast the Lancastrians in the role of the usurping Saxons.[35] The many genealogies produced early in Edward IV's reign used, directly or indirectly, prophetic material to support their veracity.

The value of the Eagle's words was based on the role of Cadwalader, the last British king, and *his* importance again lay in the prophecy revealed to him by an angel, which promised that the defeated race, driven out of its native country for its sins, would eventually return and recover its land from the Saxons when the latter had become as sinful as the Britons had been when they were exiled. According to Geoffrey's *Historia* several authorities were consulted to explain and corroborate this prophecy: the prophecies of Merlin, the Sibyl and those of 'the Eagle which has proph-esied at Shaftesbury'; all these authorities, it is said, confirmed the Angel's message. For the Sibyl and Merlin various texts were known, but the words of the Eagle were not known and not given by Geoffrey. It was essential for those who looked for a justification of a 'return of race' to find words for the prophetic bird, and the *Prophecy of the Eagle* with its Galfridian dragons and ambiguous description of civil war under the *White King* – the period *before* the predicted return – met all their requirements. The *Three Dragons* could be used to great effect: Edward IV, like his father, was the 'Ryght eyre of Brute' and descended from the 'true heir of Cadwalader who was called the Red Dragon'. In some texts Edward himself *is* the Red Dragon, while Henry VI *is* the White Dragon and the Lancastrians the Saxons. The image of the mysterious tree which will flourish again could be vividly comple-mented by the White Rose of York triumphantly flowering: 'Oute of the stoke that long lay dede ... the floure to springe and rosse so white'.[36]

The actual words of the *Vision* of the Confessor were included sepa-rately in the unique pictorial propaganda roll, now BL, MS Harley 7353,

---

34 In 1230 Ralph de Mortimer had married Gwladys Ddu, daughter of Llewelyn, Prince of Wales; Edward's father was their heir. See also chs 2 and 6 above.

35 See Anglo, 'British History', pp. 17–48; Allan, 'Yorkist propaganda', pp. 171–92; the same, thesis, chs 7 and 8; the same, 'Royal propaganda', pp. 147–54; see also, 'R III's books: VII and VIII', pp. 403–05.

36 See the poem *Edward Dei Gratia* (*c.* 1461) on the accession of Edward IV, printed in Robbins, *Historical Poems*, pp. 221–22.

which celebrated the accession of Edward IV by depicting his descent, the victories that helped him to his crown and the prophets who predicted his coming.[37] The text about the felled tree was aptly written in near the top branches of the realistic, upward growing family tree which shows Richard II's branch being literally lopped off with a sword by Henry IV, both kings sitting in bowl-shaped flowers at the end of their sprig. Three generations on – the 'three acres' specified in the *Vision of the Green Tree* – Edward IV steps fully armed out of his own flower, ready to do battle with Henry VI, similarly armed and poised to fight.

Edward's supporters used many other prophecies in many versions and most of them elude attempts at classification. Only a few representative examples can be discussed here. The most compendious and apparently well organised is a series of short statements recently called the *Sayings of the Prophets*.[38] The inspiration behind most of these 'sayings' is to be found in continental prophecies concerned with the coming of the Last World Emperor, the prince who would defeat the forces of evil and take the world into an age of happiness. Because sources and authors were so numerous and the texts continually amended, misunderstood and rewritten it was not quite clear whether this age – called the Third Age or the Sabbath Age – would be short and precede the Day of Judgement, or follow it and last forever, whether it would be 'within' or 'beyond' history; there was also a general ambiguity and mingling of pessimistic and optimistic, spiritual and material elements. According to the influential theologian and prophet, Joachim of Fiore (*c.* 1135–1202), the age of bliss was to come before the Last Judgment and after the defeat of Antichrist, and although he himself did not accept a Last Emperor, many of his followers did and the roles of the tyrannous Antichrist and the saviour king were easily allotted on the various political stages of later ages, particularly in Germany.[39] In England some of the prophecies about the saviour king were used for a prince who would reconquer the Holy Land and

---

37 BL, MS Harl. 7353 is *c.* 5 feet 4 inches long and consists of a family tree at the bottom, large pictures of four major events in Edward's life on the right with their biblical precedent on the left, and at the top two scenes celebrating his accession: on the right Reason itself stopping the Wheel of Fortune with Edward sitting on top, on the left all the prophets that predicted Edward's coming gathering around Reason's throne; also ch. 6 above.

38 Jansen, *Political Protest*, pp. 110–24, 168, where no mss *temp*. Edward IV are mentioned, however, and the texts are considered just 'a crazy list of names'.

39 Reeves, *Influence of Prophecy*, pt 3, 'Antichrist and the Last World Emperor'; the same, 'Joachimist influences on the idea of a Last World Emperor', pp. 323–70, esp. 323–25.

Fig. 64 A roll recording the events leading up to Edward IV's accession and their biblical precedents. This is the last in the sequence of prophetic scenes and shows Reason (*Ratio*) presiding over a company of twelve saints and prophets who correctly predicted Edward's coming. It includes portents, such as the three suns that Edward saw at the battle of Mortimer's Cross, scrolls with biblical quotations and figures who perhaps represent the four Cardinal Virtues (see also fig. 66). BL, MS Harl. 7353. By permission of The British Library.

became connected with other texts which promised the coming of such a conqueror; this amalgamation of texts may have taken place in the reign of Edward I, as the name 'Edward' occurs several times. In Edward IV's time these texts were readapted to refer to his coming; in some versions the Holy Land is forgotten and only a 'king called Edward' is mentioned, whose accession, by implication, will bring joy and prosperity.

One of the clearest and 'best' copies of the *Sayings* survives in a large composite manuscript put together during Edward IV's reign.[40] This copy is not an authoritative one and has no claim to being more accurate than any other, but it is a good example and firmly datable to Edward's reign.[41] The heading of the prophetic section reads:

> These ben the names of seyntes and prophetys that prophesy of a kyng that shuld be callyd Edward.[42]

The prophesies are the following:

> *Seynt Thomas* of Caunterbury calleth hym the urgent kyng of bewte.
> *Rychard Scrope*, the hooly Bysshop of Yorke, calleth hym the trew blood of nativite.
> *Edmund Lacy*, the hooly Bysshop of Excestre, sayde that oon Edward shuld conquere for Harryes shuld reygne no mo.
> *Marlyn* calleth hym a bulle of iij fold nature, that ys of Englond, Fraunce and Spayne.
> *John* the heremyte calleth hym the brode fforthe, that ys he shalbe kyng of the broode sees.
> *Marlyn* Sylvester calleth hym a kyng of wreches, that ys there shuld be so many ryotous folk and so many theves within the xijth yere of his reygne that he shall have moche to do to correct them.
> *The monke* of Almayn calleth hym a lyon of the ayre the whyche shall take hys wynges and flee to Rome and there to be made Emperour.

---

40 Cambridge, Trinity College, MS R.3.21, f. 244r–v; James, *Catalogue of … Trinity College, Cambridge*, vol. 2, pp. 69–74; Boffey and Thompson, 'Anthologies', pp. 288, 308; *John Vale's Book*, pp. 110n., 112.

41 See also below.

42 E.g.: *qui inveniret sanctam crucem*, in Cambridge, Gonville and Caius College, MS 249/277, f. 228v (*c.* 1464); 'that shall wynne the holy cros', in Oxford, Bodleian Library, MS Lyell 35, f. 17v (*c.* 1478–91).

Alphen, the Patriark of Jerusalem, wroot in a booke and calleth hym
the westorn beste the whyche dyspirteth the blak bulle with the goldyn
hornes ffurst in the west he shalbegyn and he shall conquere a gret part
of the world and he shall make frewey in to the Holy Land.

Malyn, the abbot of Irelond, calleth hyn the syxth lyon the whyche
wyll be governyd by noman but by God alone and hymself.

Sybyll the prophete calleth hym the second lyon of the Gret Bretayne
that shall wynne the Holy Crosse.

Petyr of Belwelden in Almayn calleth hym the egyll the whyche shall
overcome vi kynges.

Mastyr Tullius of Varra calleth hym an unicorne whych shall never torne
hys face for any werre.

David the prophete calleth hym in the sawter booke filius honoris that
ys the son of worshyp.[43]

Banastre calleth hym a boore of cleene nature.

Seint Germayn[44]44 calleth hym a dragon whych shuld be crysenyd in hys font
and so shuld never noon but he alone and he shuld trede undyr hys feete the
kynge of pryde and he shulde have wyngys and flee to the Holy Land.

Robert, the scrybe of Brydlyngton, calleth hym the cok of the trew Brittes.[45]

Makamyte calleth hym the delyte [more usually: delightful rose] of
Crystyndome and he shall dystroy hym and all false pepyll by the power
of Almyghty God and also he shalbe callyd Edward[46] of Roone.[47]

Other, longer versions – and sometimes the 'original' text – of some of
these sayings can be identified. The impressive collection of pro-Edward
IV propaganda in BL, MS Cotton Vespasian E vii, for example, contains

---

43 This is the *filius hominis* (the son of man) of the Bible, which occurs in many prophecies; *filius
    honoris* (the son of 'worship' or 'honour') is the result of a scribal confusion; it shows how
    easily a prophecy could change 'meaning'.
44 In most copies the prophet is called the 'daughter of St Germain'.
45 *John* of Bridlington is associated with a Latin prophecy of which two English versions exist:
    The Cock in the North and *When Rome is removed into England*; see *Manual*, vol. 5, XIII [279],
    [281] and [285]; Haferkorn, *When Rome is Removed into England*.
46 'Makamyte' is presumably Mahomet; the Cotton collection (see below), no. 15, explains that
    ward (of 'Edward') means 'rose' in Arabic.
47 Capitals and punctuation modernised. Versions of the *Sayings* survive in the following mss:
    Cambridge, Gonville and Caius College, 249/277 (Latin, *c*. 1464); Oxford, Bodleian Library,
    Bodley 623 (*c*. 1465), Lyell 35 (*c*. 1478–91), Hatton 56 (15th c.); Cambridge, Trinity R.3.21
    (temp. Edward IV); BL Add. 24663 (16th c.), Lansdowne 762 (16th c.), Sloane 2578 (16th c.);
    Bodleian Library, Arch. Seld. B 8 (16th c.), Ashmole 1386 (16th c.).

an orderly list of fifty-six prophecies, neatly identified by their *incipit* and quoted in full under their numbers on the pages that follow.[48] Among them is, for example, number 44, the vision which Thomas Becket had had when in exile in France,[49] which contains a description of the king of England who would conquer the Holy Land.[50] It was known in the early fourteenth century and became of crucial importance to the kings of England because it concerned the miraculous oil entrusted to St Thomas by the Virgin for the anointing of future kings of England, who would be invincible, regain Normandy and Aquitaine, 'build many churches in the Holy Land and drive all pagans from Babylon'.[51] Richard Scrope, Archbishop of York, is well attested as a prophet of the house of York;[52] executed for rebellion against Henry IV in 1405 Scrope quickly became a martyr of the anti-Lancastrian cause and later a patron saint of the house of York. A full account of his death is section 32 of the Cotton manuscript, and he is one of the few prophets standing round the throne of Reason in the last picture of the Harley Roll who can be identified with certainty: he is dressed as a priest, holding a chalice with the host and *Ricardus* is written across him. 'Edmund Lacy, the holy bishop of Exeter'[53] is a corruption of St Edmund of Abingdon, Archbishop of Canterbury 1234–40, who opposed Henry III – another Henry who was succeeded by an Edward. In the Cotton manuscript, prophecy number 7, he is called St Edmund *de Pontiniaco* (Pontigny, France, where he was buried) and it is claimed that he was told by the Virgin that *E* would rule after *H*. This prophetic saying of St Edmund has not so far been found in another source.

The best researched text of the collection is the one here ascribed to 'Alphen, the patriarch of Jerusalem'.[54] This is the *Cedar of Lebanon* proph-

---

48   BL, MS Cotton Vesp. E vii, list on f. 81, texts on ff. 83v–133.

49   There are other prophecies of Thomas Becket, but these concern mainly a king who will devastate France, see Manual, vol. 5, XIII [293].

50   The words 'urgent king of beauty' cannot be traced in this text but 'urgent' may be a corruption of Latin *unctus*, 'anointed' which does occur in the 'vulgate' text of the Becket vision. Other English versions of this *Saying* have 'virgin king of beauty'.

51   Sandquist, 'The Holy Oil of St. Thomas of Canterbury', pp. 330–44, incl. a list of mss and printed editions of the prophecy. On the oil generally see *Coronation*, pp. 6–10 and references given there. On the use of the holy oil, the prophecy and similar ones by Edward II see Phillips, 'Edward II and the prophets'.

52   McKenna, 'Popular canonization'.

53   An Edmund Lacey was indeed bishop of Exeter 1420–55, see e.g. Emden, *Oxford*.

54   Lerner, *Powers of Prophecy*, passim.

ecy, traceable to Hungary in *c.* 1240, when a Cistercian monk claimed that
a supernatural message had been written on the wall while he was celebrating mass. The message concerned the frightening advance of the Mongol
hordes and ended on vague promises concerning the defeat of the Saracens.
The vision rapidly started out on a long career, travelling through Swabia,
Champagne and Italy to England.[55] Shortly after the fall of Tripoli to the
Saracens in 1289 the text was carefully rewritten, probably in Germany; of
the new version – number 18 of the Cotton collection – the *Sayings* only
preserve the 'western beast' and the free access of the faithful to the Holy
Land, but there is no doubt that it is a descendant of the same prophecy.

The fact that detailed research can reveal almost the whole 'life' of one of the
Sayings of the Prophets suggests that this could be done for most of them. Even
after cursory study some of the other prophets can also be tentatively 'identified', such as Merlin Silvester, and his 'king of wretches' who is presumably the
White King of the *Prophecy of the Eagle*, and 'John the hermit' who may well be
connected to the 'Friar John' whose *Vision* foresaw an age of disaster similar to
that described in the *White King*.[56] In the present context it need only be said
that this particular series of prophecies was very popular in Edward's time, and
survived in even more garbled versions to be used in the reign of Henry VIII –
another Henry succeeded by an Edward.[57] In Edward IV's time they were also
drawn together, for example, in a four-foot long, genealogical roll (BL, MS
Add. 18268 A) of which the sole purpose appears to have been to corroborate
the prophecies and explain some of the more simple 'code names' by which
Edward was known in these texts and other vaticinal literature: *taurus* (bull),
rosa (rose), *rubeus draco* (red dragon).[58] The roll traces *taurus* to Edward III, *rubeus
draco* to Cadwalader, the last British king, *rosa* to the Mortimer line. The final

---

55 In one of the English copies the Cedar got entangled with the Green Tree, BL, MS Arundel
    66, f. 291v, Lerner, *Powers of Prophecy*, p. 33 and n. 16.
56 Oliger, 'Ein pseudoprophetischer Text aus Spanien', pp. 13–28; Donckel, 'Visio seu prophetia
    fratris Johannis', pp. 361–79; Lerner, *Powers of Prophecy*, pp. 38–39, 100–101, 192-93; Reeves,
    Influence of Prophecy, p. 162. – Most of the other *Sayings* can be related to texts in the Cotton
    MS and Bodley 623.
57 Jansen, *Political Protest*, pp. 110–24, 168 and passim. For a similar set of prophecies predicting
    the coming of a French saviour-king: Chaume, 'Une prophetie'.
58 For a longer list of such names see e.g. MS Bodley 623, f. 71r–v, where Edward is *Sextus
    Hibernie, Angelus domini, Nuntius celi, Leopardus, Albus leo, Sol, Taurus, Alba rosa, Falco, Ternis,
    Brutus, Rubeus draco, Cadwalladrus, Animal occidentalis, Aquila, Filius hominis, Unicornus, Salus,
    Aper* and *Asinus*; Henry VI is *Talpa*(?), *Linx, Abrolle*(?), *Stella, Canis, Antilo/upus, Taurus, Albus
    Draco, Predator, Usurpator, Filius aquile,* and *Vulpes.*

text at the bottom of the roll explains everything: the Red Dragon will return and rule over 'all three porcions', England, Scotland and Wales, which will again bear the name of 'Britain'. The roll admits there are learned men who argue the contrary through the 'obstynacy of ther awyn wyll and so in derkness they walke and blynde the common pepul', but the truth about Edward's right has at last been revealed by the Holy Ghost through many holy men and women: the Virgin, the Angel, the Sibyl, 'the daughter of St Germain' and others, a list close to the one discussed earlier.[59]

To support Edward's right to the crown via the female line the text used was Moses' judgment concerning the daughters of Salphaad (Zelophehad, Numbers 27: 1–11). The daughters complained that they had not been given their father's inheritance and that his name and estate would pass out of his family. At God's command Moses decided that they would inherit and so would all daughters from that time on if their father had no son. The figure of Moses and a scroll with explanatory text was included in the life-like family tree of the Harley Roll, and in the collection of prophetic texts in Bodley MS 623 the judgment was included in two places.[60]

Another quotation of great importance to the House of York was the passage in St Bridget of Sweden's *Revelations* where Christ explains that it is vital for the well-being and survival of a kingdom that it is ruled by the rightful heir.[61] Not only did this text fit the Yorkist claim to the throne perfectly, St Bridget's status as saint and prophet in England lent it great prestige. Edward IV was a generous patron of the Bridgettine foundations in England in the tradition of the Lancastrian kings, but his patronage and that of his queen certainly owes something to St Bridget's convenient prophecy. The saint's prestige partly derived from another vision, which was of potential use to any king of England as it concerned the wars between France and England. It compared the two kings to 'fell beasts' and recorded the judgment of Christ on the two combatants. This judgment implied that one of the two kings 'had right', but did not specify which; as a consequence it could be used by either king to his own advantage and failed to contribute to a peaceful conclusion of the wars.[62]

---

59 BL, MS Add. 18268A.
60 F. 72 and at the very end of the ms.
61 Ellis, *Liber Celestis*, bk 4, ch. 3, p. 253; Johnston, 'English cult', pp. 75–93, esp. 87; Ellis, 'Flores ad fabricandam ... coronam', pp. 173–74.
62 Ellis, *Liber Celestis*, bk 4, chs 103–05; Johnston, 'English cult', p. 78.; Ellis, 'Flores ad fabricandam ... coronam', pp. 163–86, esp. 173.

The 'Yorkist' vision of St Bridget, concerning the rightful heir to the kingdom, is usually given an explanatory introduction:

> ... because the kingdom of England was taken from the elder brother, by election and by fear and violence, and given to the younger brother who was not the heir, it suffers this affliction and desolation, as is clearly set out in Book Four of the *Revelations* of St Bridget.[63]

In the fifteenth-century English translation Christ's words concerning the rightful heir end:

> And tharefore the kyngdome sall noght come to the first prosperite that it was inne, ne to that gode astate nawthir, to [until] the right ayre be sett up, that is of succession of the fadirs syde or elles of the modirs.[64]

This same text was the final and most important section of the ostentatious Philadelphia Roll described above.[65] At the end of the roll's intricate, colourful family tree (see pls VIII a and b, fig. 48), with its pictures of Adam and Eve, the Ark, and God Himself, tracing the royal houses of England, France and Spain, and illuminated with innumerable coats of arms, devices, symbols and mottoes, appears a simple, undecorated frame with the text of St Bridget, written in Latin; it provided the most visible part of the roll as it hung in the public view.

The prophecies of the Last Emperor who would overcome evil and bring happiness, and the revelation of St Bridget which recorded the words of Christ Himself, were the perfect legitimation for Edward's accession and explain his amazing motto, *comfort et liesse* 'comfort and joy', with its obvious messianic connotations. Both prophets and motto presented Edward IV as another Saviour.

Prophecy and Richard III

It is likely that Richard III's attitude to prophecy was the same as his brother's, though as the second king of his house his own direct need for

---

63   BL, MS Cotton Vesp. E vii, f. 116v (Latin); the same heading is used in the Philadelphia Roll (see below).
64   Thorn, yogh, *u* and *v* modernised. Ellis, *Liber Celestis*, bk 4, ch. 3, p. 253.
65   See also ch. 6 above.

it was less marked. In the manuscript containing the *Historia destructionis Troiae* and the *Historia regum Britanniae* he could find a complete early history of his race and his house from its remote and venerable Trojan beginnings, through the complicated generations of British kings and queens, who became Christians, who defeated and were defeated by the Romans and finally degenerated and had to leave their land to the Saxons – but not forever as the *Prophecy of the Eagle* testified. The Eagle's words were a *pièce justificative* for the other texts and a unifying supplement to the story as a whole, giving it an obvious propaganda value and putting it firmly in the cyclical tradition of history that allows no break and no change without an eventual return to the old situation. There is no reason to think that Richard regarded the stories of Troy and Britain as anything else than factual history, following God's plan towards an ordained end. It is true that doubts about the 'British history' and the origin of the English people were current[66] and that Richard probably knew them since he had ready access to scholars and their theories – one of them may have given him the manuscript that contains the *Prophecy of the Eagle* – but the Yorkist period did not experience any great controversy about the early history of the British islands. Between 1461 and 1485 genealogy and prophecy were, in fact, perfectly in tune with both the 'rights' and the wishes of the ruling house. They served the same purpose, and as both derived from the same sources – mainly Geoffrey of Monmouth – they inevitably and neatly agreed about the line of Brut and the return of the British Red Dragon.

Prophecies that can be linked to Richard III himself are all texts which were directed against him and his taking of the throne and they survive in copies written after his defeat at Bosworth in August 1485. The most famous is the so-called *Prophecy of G*, first used by the antiquarian John Rous in his *Historia regum Angliae*, written between 1489 and 1491:

And because there was a prophecy that after E, that is Edward IV, G would reign, on the strength of these obscure words George, Duke of Clarence, the middle brother between King Edward and King Richard,

---

66 See ch. 7 above.

because of this Duke George was killed. And the other G, that is
Gloucester, lived on until he had fulfilled the prophecy.[67]

Rous's text was probably the basis of the later assertions by Polydore Vergil,
the historian of Henry VII, and Thomas More. Vergil expressed doubts
about the prophecy as the cause of Clarence's downfall, but he repeated it:

> A report was eaven then spred emongest the common people, that the
> king was afeard, by reason of a soothsayers propecy, and so became incen-
> syd agaynst his broother George, which prophecy was, that after King
> Edward, showld raigne soome one the first letter of whose name should
> be G. And because the devels ar wont in that sort to envegle the mynds
> of them who concaeve pleasures in such illusions, which ther crafty con-
> ceytes and subtylties, menn sayd afterwardes that the same prophecy tooke
> effect, whan after Edward the duke of Gloucester usurpyd the kingdom.[68]

In the 'better' editions of Thomas More's *History of King Richard III* the
prophecy is not mentioned, but it does appear in the Hardyng-Hall-
Grafton editions of 1543–50; More himself could have got the story from
Rous or Vergil, or common report.[69] This version of his *History of King
Richard III* gives the prophecy a dramatic context and places it firmly
before the accession of Henry VII, but the drama is certainly More's
invention. The scene is Pontefract, the date presumably the historical one
of 25 June 1483, and the action the execution of Anthony Woodville,
Richard Grey, Thomas Vaughan and 'William Haute', arrested by
Richard of Gloucester two months earlier:

---

67 The first sentence is badly constructed, but the present translation follows the passage in BL,
    MS Cotton Vesp. A xii, illustrated in Hanham, *Richard III and His Early Historians*, opp. p. 121;
    and printed in Kelly, *Divine Providence*, p. 70 n. 23, from the edition by Thomas Hearne,
    Oxford 1716. See also Kelly, 'English kings and the fear of sorcery', p. 230 nn. 97–98. The
    Prophecy of G was used by Taylor, *Political Prophecy*, p. 85, to prove that Edward believed in
    prophecies; his sources were Shakespeare and the French royal servant and memorialist of the
    reign of Francis I, Martin du Bellay (died 1559) in his *Mémoires*, vol. 1, pp. 42–43, where it
    is said that Edward consulted the prophecies of Merlin 'a superstition existing since the days
    of King Arthur' and that they predicted that the king's brother whose name began with G
    would take the crown away from his children.
68 Vergil, *Three Books of Polydore Vergil's English History*, p. 167.
69 More, *History of King Richard III*, pp. xxiv and 58n., and the introduction on the editions.

... sir Thomas Vaughan goyng to his death sayd, A wo worthe them that toke the prophecie that G. should destroy kyng Edwardes children, meaning that by the duke of Clarence lorde George which for that suspicion is nowe dead, but nowe remayneth Richard G. duke of Gloucester, whiche now I see is he that shal and wyll accomplishe the prophecye and destroy kyng Edwardes chyldren and all their alyes and frendes, as it appeareth by us this day, ...

If this was a genuine prophecy the earliest possible date that could be given to it is the summer of 1483 after Richard of Gloucester's progress towards the throne had become evident. Only then could some wit have realised the ominous possibilities of the innocent coincidence of Gs, but there is little doubt that, in fact, the *Prophecy of G* was composed after the accession of Henry VII, and later cleverly ascribed, by More and others, to Vaughan as a bitter lament on his fate.[70]

Another text that claimed to be predicting the events of 1483 and after has been called the *Streets of London* prophecy.[71] It is a good example of the genre in the sense that it is totally confused and confusing, made up of parts of numberless, identifiable and unidentifiable texts and partial texts, of different ages, dating from perhaps the fourteenth to the sixteenth century, and offers tantalising glimpses of apparently factual events.[72]

The yere of our lorde m cccc lxxx iij
betuext the departyng of Aprell and not far from may
The bull shall departe and passe away
The same yere shalbe moche adoo
Walles shall be armys and to Albion goo
...
The Egill shall aryse and wyth hym com

---

70 The story occurs in Rous's 'blackest' description of Richard III. The fact that the 'William' Haute mentioned was actually called Richard and was *not* executed casts further doubts on the trustworthiness of the story. Some version of it was used by Edward Hall in 1548 (*Chronicles*, ed. H. Ellis, London 1908, p. 326); George Ferrers in 1559 ('How George Plantagenet ...', one of the verse tragedies in William Baldwin's *Mirror for Magistrates*, ed. L.B. Campbell, Cambridge 1938, p. 227); Shakespeare in 1593 (*Richard III*, act 1, scene 1); Thomas Heywood in *c.* 1594 (*King Edward IV*, *Part II*, London 1842, pp. 138–39).

71 *Manual*, vol. 5, XIII [276].

72 The only copy is BL, MS Lansdowne 762, ff. 63v–65, the only printed edition is in Scattergood, *Politics and Poetry*, pp. 386–90.

The bore shall mete hym in the way

...

The son shall slee the father the broder the broder
That the stretes of London shall ron all on blod

and so on for 134 lines. Again, there is little doubt that this 'prophecy'
was put together during the reign of Henry VII and attempted to gain the
reader's confidence by starting with a thinly veiled reference to the death
of Edward IV and, possibly, to the duke of Buckingham's rebellion.[73] The
whole prophecy is highly general and obscure, even in its mention of the
battle of Bosworth.

More vicious and openly hostile to Richard III is the so-called 'Prophetic
ode on the outcome of the battle of Bosworth', one of the texts in Welsh
that were made in Henry VII's time.[74] It leaves no doubt about its purpose
and its Welsh bias; most of it is exceptionally incoherent, for example:

> A servile boar wrought penance upon Edward's sons in his prison. If
> he slew without favour of the bench his two young nephews, I mar-
> velled in a measure of anger at God, that the earth did not swallow him.
> Success to whomsoever killed the dog slain in a ditch.

One of the main themes is Richard's killing of Henry VI and it stresses
Henry's saintliness. Richard himself seems to have inspired no other
prophets: after Bosworth he was too much a thing of the past to need a
'future', however fantastic.

'Wind of the head'[75] or the hand of God?[76]

It may be asked what Edward IV and Richard III and other literate people
of their time thought about the value of prophetic texts. The usefulness

---

73 Scattergood, *Politics and Poetry*, p. 211.
74 Printed in *Richard III*, p. 95.
75 Lull, *Ordre of Chyvalry*, trans. Caxton, p. 109, where divination is considered 'the wynde of
[the superstitious knight's] head'.
76 The view that prophecy was the work of God is discussed below; the involvement of
the hand of God in Edward IV's accession and the restoration of the House of York is
magnificently displayed in the Philadelphia Roll, see below.

of some of them for political propaganda cannot be doubted, but who owned or read these mysterious texts and complicated pictorial rolls? Such owners and users as can be traced came from various, but thoroughly literate, backgrounds.

Two examples of ordinary persons owning prophetic texts can be given. The earliest surviving manuscript to contain the *Sayings of the Prophets*[77] was compiled *c.* 1464 by John Harryson, a Yorkshireman who studied at Cambridge University and was vicar of Ashwell, Herts., till his death in 1473. In his book he briefly recorded the activities of several of his friends at Cambridge, works by Cicero, part of Higden's *Polychronicon*, notes about the antiquity of Cambridge University and many prophecies. All these entries appear to have been regarded as of more or less equal value and interest; they were all in Latin and only accessible to scholars.

The other example, the literary and prophetic collection in the manuscript now at Trinity College, Cambridge, is in English and had a London owner: Roger Thorney, mercer and merchant adventurer, who was a young man at the beginning of Edward's reign. In the 1490s he actively supported the printing press of Caxton's successor, Wynkyn de Worde; he was a book collector and generally involved with the trade and production of books. His Trinity collection consists of individual booklets, containing religious and historical lyrics, saints' lives, prayers and other devotional pieces, as well as a few political items. The booklets were probably acquired as ready-made, separate entities at a London bookshop, such as John Multon's;[78] where relevant the texts had been adapted to the change of kings. The Yorkist texts were not the most important sections, however: even the twenty-eight-leaf booklet that contains the *Sayings of the Prophets* is not exclusively political, though it does have another prophecy, verses on the kings of England and an anti-French poem. Thorney rated the prophecies as interesting as the encyclopaedic *Court of Sapience* or the 'Life of St Anthony'.

The organised and compendious Cotton collection of prophecies was probably compiled for the use of one of the first families in the land: the

77 Cambridge, Gonville and Caius College, MS 249/277.

78 Cambridge, Trinity College, MS R.3.21, f. 244r–v; James, *Catalogue of ... Trinity College, Cambridge*, vol. 2, pp. 69–74; Boffey and Thompson, 'Anthologies', pp. 288, 308; *John Vale's Book*, pp. 110n., 112.

Percys,[79] who from 1469 supported the House of York and apparently wished to record every available bit of Yorkist propaganda. The Percys appear to have taken particular interest in such matters, partly because of their close family connection with the Yorkists: they occur in the family tree explaining some of Edward's prophetic code names (described above),[80] where they are indicated by their own device, the moon (*luna*); they appear, with the moon, in the Philadelphia Roll; and they may have commissioned the only genealogical roll that included Richard III, his queen and his son, which is known to survive.[81]

Little is known about the ownership of the propaganda rolls, but many of them show the physical signs of having been actually hung up for display. Though the Philadelphia Roll is almost fourteen feet long the magnificent equestrian picture of Edward IV in full armorial trappings at the top could still have been visible if it had been displayed, for example, in a large hall or on a staircase.[82] The Harley Roll is much shorter and all its pictures would have been easily visible in any position. The fact that it records Henry III's foundation of the Dominican house at Gloucester may indicate that it was owned by the same house; only clerics would have understood all the biblical precedents and had sufficient Latin to read all the texts and quotations worked into the pictures.[83] Only people with sufficient learning would have been able to appreciate fully the intricacies and cleverness of all these pictures, symbols and texts, but there is little doubt that much of it filtered down in simplified but no less persuasive forms to all ranks of society. Prophecy was — and is — irresistible to everyone.

In his *Order of Chivalry* Ramon Lull had expressed disapproval of 'divination': a knight who believed in such things as 'the devynaylles and ... fleyng of byrdes doth ageynst god and hath gretter fayth and hope in the wynde of his hede and in the werkes that the byrdes done ... than in god'.[84] He scoffs at the knight who will not fight when he has seen a bareheaded woman in the morning, or believes that a bird flying on his right portends different events from one flying on his left. Lull's feelings on

---

79 BL, MS Cotton Vesp. E vii; Ward, *Catalogue of Romances*, vol. 1, pp. 320–24; Lerner, *Powers of Prophecy*, pp. 101–03 and nn., 179 and n., 224–25.
80 BL, MS Add. 18268A.
81 Oxford, Bodleian Library, Bodley Roll 5.
82 Philadelphia, Free Library, MS E 210.
83 BL, Harley Roll 7353.
84

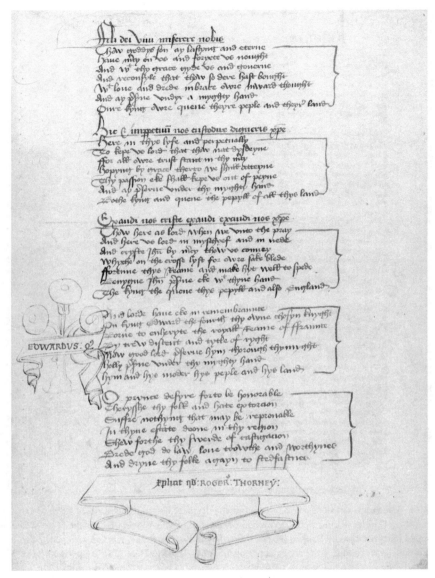

Fig. 65 Page from a composite manuscript containing Yorkist material collected by its owner. The page shown contains the last three stanzas of a mixed Latin and English prayer for protection against enemies to which two stanzas addressed to Edward IV were added. The scroll on the left has *Edwardus Quartus*; the one at the bottom of the page reads *Explicit quod Roger Thorney*, which probably refers to the author of the two additional stanzas who may also have been the owner of the book. Elsewhere in the manuscript is a text of Lydgate's *Verses on the Kings of England* at the end of which is a heading, *Edwardus Quartus*, but no text. Cambridge, Trinity College, MS R. 3. 21, f. 245v. By permission of The Master and Fellows of Trinity College, Cambridge.

Fig. 66 The culmination of a roll setting out the divinely inspired accession of Edward IV: this scene shows the new king sitting crowned on the top of the Wheel of Fortune. The Wheel is stopped in its rotation by Reason (*Ratio*), dressed as an English judge, who drives a spoke through it. Suitable texts reinforce the message (see also fig. 64). BL, MS Harl 7353. By permission of The British Library.

the subject were so strong that his disapproval fills several pages: a knight who credits such omens 'is not agreable to god ne mayteneth not thordre of chyvalrye'; he is 'a foole that useth no wytte ne reason' and ought to be defeated by his adversaries. It is clear that in Lull's time there were already people who were prepared to shake off such superstition and put their trust in reason and common sense, and any reader of Lull's text, including Richard III, could have appreciated Lull's emphasis on the contrast between 'reason' and 'divination'.

The flight of birds, however, is not the same as the word of God as embodied in the Bible and more specifically in the books of the prophets. To many Christians there was a clear link between faith and prophecy. Christ Himself explained the purpose of prophecy to St Bridget, emphasising that the prophets, apostles and 'holi doctours' had all spoken the truth concerning His coming. It was God's wish that His works should first be known through the word and then should follow in fact. 'All the misteris of mine incarnacion were told longe before to the prophetis', and the star that guided the Three Kings was proved right by the events. 'So mi wordes sall be told before, and eftirwarde, when the werkes come, than are thai more evidentli trowed'.[85]

A text that was well known during Richard's lifetime and used in the context of Yorkist propaganda is the statement of St Gregory the Great concerning faith and reason: 'faith has no merit where human reason supplies proof'. When quoted by members of the Frowyk family in their small commonplace book cum chronicle the words refer to the mystery of Christ's incarnation which man can only understand through faith: 'Theire feeith is lord; reson goth undre'.[86] In the large collection of Yorkist prophecies, now in the Bodleian Library, St Gregory's words are connected to the mysteries of vaticinal texts: they are written next to the lists of all the prophetic 'code names' that illustrate the iniquities of Henry VI and the virtues of Edward IV. St Gregory is paraphrased:

Sciendum nobis est quod divina operacio, si racio comprehenditur, non est mirabilis; nec fides habet meritum, ubi humana racio prebet experimentum.

---

85 Ellis, *Liber Celestis*, p. 57.
86 BL, MS Harl. 541, f. 207v; see the present authors, 'Making of a minor London chronicle'. For St Gregory's actual text see *Homilia in Ezechielem*, bk 2, homily 8, *PL*, vol. 76, col. 1034B,

(We should know that God's work, if it could be grasped by reason, would not be miraculous; and faith has no merit when human reason supplies proof).[87]

In their context the words imply that we should believe in prophecy even if we do not understand it rationally; there would be no divine miracles, including the fulfilment of prophecies, if we understood everything. In the most magnificent section of the Philadelphia Roll, the equestrian portrait of Edward IV at the top (see pl. VIIIa), his accession and his right to the thrones of England, France and Spain is clearly shown to have been God's doing: on either side of the king's image the right hand of God is depicted and from it floats a scroll saying: *Dextera Domini fecit virtutem* (The right hand of the Lord gave power).[88] By implication all the prophecies that predicted Edward's coming were correct.

In the detailed illustrations of the Harley Roll celebrating Edward's accession in pictures the argument was taken one step further: it was shown that Reason and prophecy could work *together*, towards the same goal.[89] In one picture Reason, dressed as a judge and watched by the three estates, stops the Wheel of Fortune with a long spoke at the very moment that Edward has safely reached the top position; this is a unique and effective scene, meant to leave no doubt in the mind of the onlooker that Edward was king by the will of Reason itself and that the changeable influence of Fortune had been brought to an end. In the parallel picture Reason sits enthroned (see fig. 65), presiding over a company of all those saints and holy prophets who had predicted Edward's coming; clearly God, through His chosen prophets, and Reason had worked together to make Edward of York king.

---

87 Oxford, Bodleian Library, MS Bodley 623, f. 71v.
88 Psalm 117: 16.
89 BL, MS Harl. 7353.

NINE

Passing the Time: Stories of Love and Example at the Yorkist Court

In the time of the Yorkist kings having 'time' that needed 'passing' was mainly a problem of the leisured classes.[1] Leisure allowed men and women to do something else than just working, eating and sleeping, but throughout the Middle Ages people were very aware of the danger of leisure becoming mere 'idleness'. The printer and translator William Caxton, whose views can be taken as representative of literate people of Richard's day, approvingly quoted conventional warnings against idleness, the 'moder of lies and stepdame of vertues' who 'overthroweth stronge men into synne, quenchyth vertues, nouryssheth pryde and makyth the waye redy to goo to helle'.[2]

In the thirteenth-century *Roman de la rose*, which was still widely read in the fifteenth century, it is the gracious and well-groomed, but distant Lady *Oiseuse*, personifying both 'leisure' and 'idleness', who opens the gate of the Garden of Love to the lover and enables him to have his adventures and find his beloved. Later in the story *Oiseuse* is both praised and blamed for letting the lover in: praised by the lover himself in his moments of success, but blamed by him in his misery as well as by the austere figure of Reason. Without *Oiseuse* neither the lover nor anyone else would be able to take an interest in love and

---

1   This chapter is a longer version of a talk given at the 1995 conference of the International Courtly Literature Society at Belfast.
2   Blake, *Caxton's Own Prose*, p. 89, prologue to the Golden Legend.

Fig. 67 A tapestry depicting a joust hangs behind this animated court scene of 1469. Dido kisses
Ascanius, the son of Aeneas, in the *Histoire de Troie*, a French version of Guido delle Colonna's
Historia destructionis Troiae. Flemish, 1469. Now Geneva, Collection Bodmer, MS 160, f. 225.

adventure, or have anything but an ordinary, every day life, which
rarely exercises the mind and the emotions, but her influence is not
necessarily positive.[3]

To 'pass the time', pleasantly or profitably, entertainment was needed,
and entertainment in the fifteenth century was essentially what it is
today, although resources were more limited. Courtly entertainment
ranged from hunting or dancing to the composition and playing of word
games and music and the telling and reading of stories. Stories of all kinds
were suitable to pass the time and it is stories that we are concerned with
here, particularly those that are usually classified as romances. Events and
adventures of almost any kind could be – and still can be – made into
a story: reassuring, intriguing, frightening, instructive or humorous.
Romances, too, in spite of all modern attempts to classify them, appear

3   Batany, 'Miniature, allégorie, idéologie', pp. 7–36.

to have ranged widely, from the serious and devout to the burlesque and purely amorous.[4]

The general and continuous popularity of romances is undeniable; they run from the earliest time to the present day. They are stories of adventure and love containing aspirations towards ideals of love itself, and of friendship, courage, constancy and generosity. They are normally set outside the present or outside the real world, but never completely lose touch with reality. Though their range knows few limits, they always focus on the hero's adventures and the love element is paramount. In a late fifteenth-century copy of the English *Sir Orfeo* (composed *c.* 1300), a version of the Greek myth of Orpheus, the ultimate minstrel and 'entertainer', the author lists the subjects of romances:

> Som of werre and som off wo,
> Som of myrthys and joy also;
> Som of trechery and som off gyle,
> Som of happys that felle som-whyle,
> And som be of rybawdry,
> And many ther ben off fary;
> Off all the venturrys men here or se
> Most off luffe, for-soth, thei be, ...[5]

Romances have gone out of fashion regularly and returned as regularly; they were re-written, re-shaped and re-interpreted, and after each flowering in a new shape their social standing slowly but surely declined.[6] Their popularity among men and women of the late fifteenth-century English court has been taken for granted on the evidence of the survival of a few copies owned by identifiable persons, the translation and printing of a

---

4 For definitions of romance see Stevens, *Medieval Romance*, esp. pp. 15–28; Pearsall, 'English romance', pp. 56–83, esp. 57–58; *Manual*, vol. 1, esp. Newstead, 'Romances: general', pp. 11–12; Barron, *English Medieval Romance*, introd. And see Keiser, 'Romances', pp. 271–73. And see Olson, *Literature as Recreation*, esp. chs 2, 3.

5 Thorn and ampersand modernised. The author is actually describing Breton *lais*, precursors of romances; the ms. is Oxford, Bodleian Library, MS Ashmole 61, f. 151 (for this ms. see also below), printed in Bliss, *Sir Orfeo*, p. 3.

6 Stevens, *Medieval Romance*, pp. 15–28.

supposedly large number of 'Burgundian' romances by Caxton[7] and the frequency with which such texts were printed in the early sixteenth century.[8] In general terms this picture of their popularity is acceptable, but we would suggest that as far as the reigns of the Yorkist kings are concerned there was a drop both in the status and the fashionableness of romances and that this was evident at their court. This is not to deny the appeal romances continued to have for some readers, particularly the increasing number of new readers of a lower social status, who were 'drawn to romance by its adventures rather than its ideals'.[9]

What is the evidence for the failure in popularity of romances in court circles *c.* 1465–85? Why were such texts going out of favour at this date, what did people of the time really think about them and why did they read them when they did? What influence can really be attributed to Burgundy and what part did Caxton play? These questions will be discussed using the evidence of the texts themselves and the testimony of their fifteenth-century users – copiers, translators and readers – as well as such evidence as is offered by the ownership of romances at the courts of the Yorkist kings and their contemporaries, the dukes of Burgundy.

Romances Owned by Richard III and His Nearest Contemporaries

Our starting points are the romances owned by Richard of Gloucester: a *Prose Tristan* and a one-volume collection of stories. All the stories in the volume save one are in verse and all are in English. Two are by Chaucer, *Palamon and Arcite* (the *Knight's Tale*) and *Griselda* (the *Clerk's Tale*), one by Lydgate, the *Siege of Thebes*, and lastly there is the one prose romance, *Ipomedon*. The volume is completed by thirteen exemplary and adventurous stories from the Old Testament retold in verse, such as *Joshua*, *Ruth*

---

7   On Caxton's supposedly large production see e.g. Pearsall, 'English romance', pp. 72, 75, and his 'torrent of Burgundian style chivalric prose romances poured from Caxton's pen and press'; like other commentators Pearsall includes *Godeffroy of Boloyne*, which is not a romance but William of Tyre's history of the first crusade.

8   On the printing of romances: Meale, 'Caxton, de Worde, and the publication of romance', pp. 283–98, who also denies the importance of Burgundian influence on Caxton and shows that it was de Worde who first printed a large number of romances in England.

9   Barron, *English Medieval Romance*, p. 8. And see Pearsall, 'English romance', pp. 64–67.

and *Job*.[10] The whole collection is impeccable in its taste and its moral viewpoint and eminently suitable for youthful reading.

Lydgate's *Siege of Thebes*[11] is difficult to classify; it contains historical, chivalric and courtly elements and has also been called a 'mirror for princes'. It is a story more of example than love, but the love element is not wholly lacking. For this long poem of 4,716 lines Lydgate possibly made use of the anonymous prose romance *Roman de Edipus*, a redaction of the verse *Roman de Thebes* (c. 1150), which was in its turn based on Statius' *Thebaid*. He was also inspired by Chaucer, his much admired master, and wrote the *Siege* as a supplement to *The Canterbury Tales*, introducing the poem with a description of himself joining the pilgrims at Canterbury and being persuaded by the host to tell the first tale for the journey home. This fictional background was accepted by the maker of Richard of Gloucester's collection who joined it to two of Chaucer's own tales.

Lydgate's version of the story of Thebes is very different from the classical original. In his prologue he tells the stories of the founding of the city and of Eddipus (Oedipus), concluding with Eddipus' self-mutilation on his discovery of his true parentage and that in his ignorance he had killed his father, Layus, King of Thebes, and married his mother, Iocasta. He dies after being pushed into a pit by his two sons, Ethiocles and Polymite. The second part of the poem concerns the quarrel between the sons over the control of Thebes; they are forced to agree to reign in alternate years. While Ethiocles is in power, Polymite leaves and by chance comes to the palace of King Adrastus of Arge on the same night that Tydeus, the banished son of the King of Calydoyne, seeks shelter there. They engage in a fight over whether Tydeus should be admitted to the palace. Adrastus stops the fight and the two young men become great friends, marry Adrastus' two daughters and share his kingdom between them. Ethiocles meanwhile is determined to keep Thebes for himself and when Tydeus tries to persuade him to keep the bargain with Polymite, plots to murder him. Tydeus manages to kill all but one of his fifty assailants and has his wounds skilfully cared for by the daughter of King Lycurgus of Thrace. Tydeus does not linger with the princess but returns home the next day.

10 *Exodus, Leviticus, Numbers, Deuteronomy, Joshua, Judges, Ruth,* 1–4 *Kings, Job, Tobit, Esther, Judith* and part of 2 *Maccabees*.
11 Lydgate's *Siege of Thebes*; Pearsall, *John Lydgate*, pp. 151–56; Renoir, *Poetry of John Lydgate*, pp. 117–25; Ayres, 'Medieval history, moral purpose'. For recent work on the *Siege of Thebes* see Edwards, 'Lydgate scholarship', esp. pp. 33–34; Allen, 'The Siege of Thebes', passim.

The third part of the poem concerns the war for the possession of Thebes. 'Bishop' Amphiorax strongly advises Adrastus not to go to war in support of Polymite and prophesies disaster for all. He is ignored and forced to accompany the invading army of the Greeks, which is soon in danger of dying of thirst. While reconnoitring Tydeus and Campaneus enter a garden and discover Isyphile, the exiled daughter of the King of Crete, nursing the heir of King Lycurgus. She is persuaded to leave the child and show them the way to water, but while she is gone her charge is killed by a snake. In despair she seeks out Tydeus and Adrastus, who intercede for her with Lycurgus and obtain her pardon. The siege of Thebes begins and, despite negotiations between Iocasta and Adrastus, bitter fighting and disasters take their toll. All except Adrastus and Campaneus are killed. Polymite and Ethiocles kill each other. Creon is elected king of Thebes and once in power refuses burial to the dead of the Greek army. Theseus, Duke of Athens, is passing, takes up the cause of Adrastus and the widows of the unburied dead, destroys Thebes and restores order. The ordinary people rebuild the city.

To Lydgate the importance of the work lay in his moral commentary and his concluding peroration for peace. To him and his readers the story was history, teaching moral lessons and patterns of behaviour. The didactic tone of the poem appealed to all fifteenth-century readers. Lydgate's purpose was to make a universally acceptable plea for peace instead of war, which is caused by greed and ambition and destroys everything.

In Richard of Gloucester's collection *Thebes* is followed by the tale of *Palamon and Arcite*, based by Chaucer on Boccaccio's poem *Il Teseida*.[12] The action of this story overlaps and follows on from *Thebes* for Palamon and Arcite are two kinsmen of the royal house of Thebes taken prisoner by Theseus of Athens during his capture of the city. They are incarcerated without hope of release. Emily, the sister of Theseus' Duchess Hippolyta, is seen by both the young men from their prison and both fall instantly in love with her. Their love turns their friendship into insane jealousy. Arcite is eventually set free through the intercession of a friend and returns to Thebes under threat of death if he ever comes to Athens again. He pines

12 The literature on Chaucer's *Knight's Tale* is vast. See e.g. Robinson, *Works of Geoffrey Chaucer*, pp. 4–5, 25–47 (text), 669–70; Pearsall, *Canterbury Tales*, pp. 2–4, 117–38; Neuse, 'The knight'; Brooks and Fowler, 'The meaning of Chaucer's Knight's Tale'; Hulbert, 'What was Chaucer's aim in the Knight's Tale?'

Fig. 68 A scene from Boccaccio's *Teseida*, on which Chaucer's *Knight's Tale* was based: the three protagonists pray in the temples of the gods before the great tournament at which Emilie's hand will be bestowed on the victor. On the left Arcite prays to Mars, the god of war, carrying spear and shield, in the centre Emilie begs the favour of Diana, goddess of chastity, seated on the moon sickle, and on the right Palamon worships Venus, goddess of love, here armed with bow and arrows. French, made for René of Anjou *c.* 1460. Vienna, Austrian National Library, MS 2617, f. 102. By permission of the Austrian National Library.

for the sight of Emily so much that he becomes unrecognisable and finally decides to risk everything and return to Athens. He enters her service and is raised to a position of honour near Theseus. On a May morning he rides into the woods, the very day that Palamon has escaped from his prison to this same wood. They meet and their jealous passion drives them to fight a private duel. Theseus finds out and stops it. He orders them to return to his court each with a 100 knights in fifty weeks, when a proper tournament will be held under his aegis. The victor will marry Emily. Elaborate preparations are made; Arcite prays to Mars for victory, as the god of war, but Palamon prays to Venus, the goddess of love. The tournament takes place; Palamon is captured by Arcite's knights and Arcite is declared the victor, but in his triumphant enthusiasm he is thrown by his horse and mortally injured. Dying he commends Palamon to Emily. A magnificent funeral is held and after an interval Theseus arranges the marriage of Palamon to Emily.

The story is undoubtedly a romance, a courtly and chivalric tale about exploits of arms and love, but there has been considerable debate as to Chaucer's precise intentions and meaning. It has been called a 'philosophical romance' about the ordering of the world, and also a 'loveless love-story' exposing the courtly problem: which of two equally worthy young men should win the lady? There is also great emphasis on the pageantry of the tournament and courtly life. Love is the ordering spirit of the action, but is seen, both by the story teller, Chaucer's Knight, and by Theseus, primarily as a useful motivator of youth to chivalry and deeds of arms – a sentiment also to be found in *Ipomedon*. Any reader, following the directives of the Knight, would be aware that the behaviour of the two lovers was not entirely to be admired, although sympathy for their predicament might be aroused.

The story of Patient Griselda (the *Clerk's Tale*), the next item in Richard of Gloucester's collection, has proved even more difficult to interpret.[13] As a straightforward story it may seem crude and pointless, but it was usually seen as an example of Christian patience in adversity. The story runs as follows: Walter, an Italian marquis, is persuaded unwillingly to marry. He makes the socially eccentric choice of the peasant girl, Griselda, after observing her loving and obedient character. He exacts from her a promise of complete obedience to all his commands without question or complaint. Griselda becomes the perfect wife and mother and the perfect marchioness dispensing justice and benevolence. Walter decides to test her. He takes their two children from her, pretending that they will be killed. She submits without complaint. Some years later he puts her from him, sending her back to her peasant home, and sets about finding a younger bride for himself. She goes home without complaint. He then insists she receive the new bride and praise her publicly. After a slight demur she obeys. Seeing her obedience and patience Walter finally relents and takes her back as his wife, the pretended bride turns out to be

---

13 The literature on this tale is considerable, see e.g. Robinson, *Works of Geoffrey Chaucer*, pp. 8–9, 101–14 (text), 709–10; Severs, *Literary Relationship of Chaucer's Clerk's Tale*; Griffiths, *Origin of the Griselda Story*; Sledd, 'The Clerk's Tale'; Pearsall, *Canterbury Tales*, pp. 265–77; Benson and Robinson, *Chaucer's Religious Tales*, passim and esp. Morse, 'Critical approaches', pp. 71–83, a useful summary of readers' reactions to the story since the 18th century.

the daughter taken from her years before, and her son is also restored to her. They all live happily ever after.

Medieval readers and commentators were divided over the merits of the story. Boccaccio, who used it in his *Decameron*, and Petrarch, in his *De obedientia ac fide uxoria mythologia* upon which Chaucer closely based his own text (along with the *Livre Griseldis*), were both careful to say that no wife owed such obedience to her husband. Many people must have been affected by the romantic elevation of a peasant girl to rank and riches and not too surprised that she should have to prove herself worthy. Chaucer made Walter more cruel and obstinate and Griselda more meek than had his sources, turning her into a saint and martyr. He may have been using the story as a contrast to the view expressed by the Wife of Bath, that everyone is much happier if the woman rules in a marriage, and to the Merchant's tale about an elderly husband cuckolded by his young wife. Chaucer repeated the moral conclusion of Petrarch, declaring that the story is an example for all men in their relationship with God, but then continued with comments from other characters in the *Tales* which undermined this conclusion and revealed a range of contemporary (male) reactions to the story.[14] Petrarch too had recorded diverse reactions to his story in a less dramatic setting. Philippe de Mézières, advisor to Charles VI of France, translated the story from Petrarch's Latin and made it popular in France; and when pleading for peace between England and France and recommending a French marriage for Richard II of England in 1395, he expressed the hope that Richard would be granted a wife like Griselda who, in his eyes, was perfect.[15] Christine de Pizan inserted a brief and delicate rendering of Griselda's story into her *Book of the City of Ladies* (1405): it is told by Rectitude as an example of the constancy, endurance and strength of women. In another place Griselda is hailed as a perfect example of how a child should humbly care for its parents.[16] In the same period the Goodman of Paris (1390s), the elderly bourgeois husband who copied out a French translation of the story for his young wife, admitted that he did not expect unquestioning obedience from her: he was not worthy, he was not noble or mad or stupid, nor so arrogant as to think

---

14 The 'envoy of Chaucer' to this story was in Richard's copy; for the problems of its placing and authorship, see e.g. Severs, 'Did Chaucer rearrange the Clerk's Envoy?', pp. 472–78.

15 Mézières, *Letter to King Richard II*, pp. xxix and n. 53, 42, 115. For Mézières's work and the story generally, Golenistcheff-Koutouzoff, *Histoire de Griseldis*, passim.

16 Pizan, *Book of the City of Ladies*, pp. 16, 170–76.

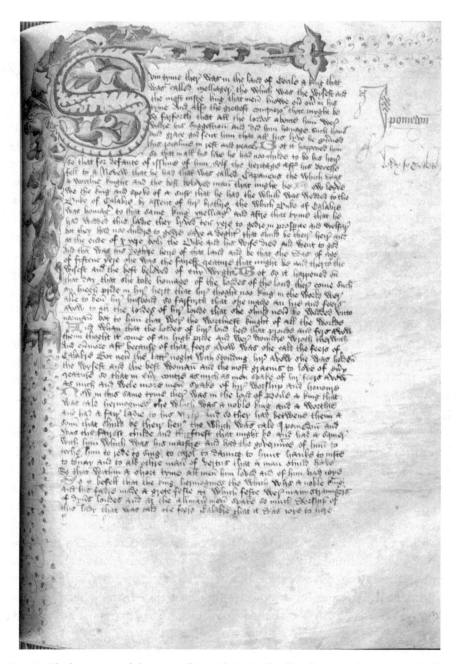

Fig. 69 The beginning of the story of *Ipomedon* in Richard's collection of romances; the first words read: *Svm tyme there was in the land of Cecile a king that was called melliagre.* Longleat, MS 257, f. 90. By permission of the Marquess of Bath.

he had a right to harm his wife in any way – but he *did* repeat the story![17] Suffering, humiliation and patience such as Griselda's were recurring elements in many romances and were the frequent lot of heroines; there can be no doubt about their general attraction for readers and, in this instance, their appeal to male fantasy.

The last story in the collection owned by Richard in his youth is the romance of *Ipomedon*, a short prose version of earlier Anglo-Norman and English texts.[18] It is the standard tale of a young man's quest for adventure, love and fame. Ipomedon is the son of the King of Poile; as a child he is taught 'to rede, to sing, to carol, to daunce, to hunt, to hauke, to iuste, to tournay and all othre maner of vertus that a man shuld have'. When he grows up he hears about La Fière, the Duchess of Calabria, who has vowed to marry 'the worthiest knight of all the worlde'. Ipomedon and his servant set out for the Lady's court and the youth becomes her squire and cupbearer without revealing his identity. He becomes popular with the ladies, but not with the men, because he prefers hunting to jousting. Proving himself in arms secretly he serves the Lady for three years. During a feast they finally fall in love, but the Lady, aware of his unmanly preference for hunting and his low estate, sends him away in order to forget him. He departs, determined to prove himself worthy of her love. Meanwhile the Lady's counsellors wish her to marry; she is determined to have only the man she loves and to delay matters proposes a three-day tournament, promising to marry the victor. Ipomedon takes part in the tournament in disguise while his friends think he is out hunting. He is victorious on each day, but in his own person he is despised and scorned. It take several more journeys, disguisings, adventures and battles with giants before Ipomedon and the Lady are finally united and married.

The disguises, the desire for 'fame', the unconsummated love, although anticipated and requited, with its constant separations and griefs, the hero's self-inflicted suffering of the scorn of his peers and the lady's suffering of grief and love (inflicted unnecessarily and with considerable thoughtlessness by the hero) had, and have, an immediate appeal and need no explanation. The adolescent in particular could identify with Ipomedon's aspirations to glory, the notion of hidden talents waiting

---

17 Power, *Goodman of Paris*, pp. 136–38; the story had become a 'mirror for married ladies' and the Goodman was not the only author to use it in this way.

18 Kölbing, '*Ipomedon' in drei englischen Bearbeitungen*; *Manual*, vol. 1, pp. 153–55, 309–11; 'R III's books II', pp. 327–32.

for the world's recognition, and the pangs of love for a distant object of desire. The motto *tant le desiree*, 'I have longed for it so much', together with his name, added to a page of the *Ipomedon* by Richard of Gloucester in neat handwriting may be dated to his adolescence and seems strikingly appropriate (see fig. 2).[19]

Richard owned one other undoubted romance, in a separate volume and in French, the first section of the *Prose Tristan*, a compilation, made shortly after 1200, which dominated the understanding of the love story of Tristan and Isolde in the later Middle Ages, and which is now known to English readers through the medium of the *Morte Darthur* by Sir Thomas Malory who used a version of the *Prose Tristan*. Richard's book covers the story of Tristan's ancestors, Sador and his wife, Chelinde, and their immediate descendants whose adventures seem to foreshadow those of Tristan, Tristan's birth, his troubled early life, his meeting with Isolde, the love potion, Isolde's marriage to King Mark, the discovery of the illicit lovers, the banishment of Isolde to live with lepers, and the lovers' escape to live in the forest. Whether Richard owned the rest of the story is not known. The *Prose Tristan* was a very long and influential compilation; so long that few manuscripts exist of it in its entirety, most being fragments like that owned by Richard of Gloucester. Its several authors drew what had been ancient, Celtic stories into the Arthurian cycle; Tristan became one of the greatest of the knights of the Round Table; he takes part in the quest for the Holy Grail and is a descendant of the brother of the first guardian of the Grail, Joseph of Arimathea (whom some in Richard's day held to be the evangelist of Britain); and he has every conceivable adventure. The uncontrollable passion of Tristan and Isolde was allotted a secondary place, redone in the 'courtly' style, and made into a tyranny endured by the lovers.[20]

What do his surviving books tell us of Richard's attitude to his romances? His one-volume collection is a moderately decorated, handsome vellum

---

19 It can also be found in an heraldic collection of contemporary mottoes and devices, of unknown provenance but made sometime during Richard's lifetime, BL, MS. Add. 40742, f. 5. For Richard's mottoes see below.

20 'R III's books X', gives a summary of all aspects of this work. There is an enormous amount of literature, e.g.: Löseth, *Roman en prose de Tristan*; Vinaver, *Études sur le Tristan en prose*; the same, 'Prose Tristan'; Newstead, 'Origin and growth of the Tristan legend', Whithead, 'Early Tristan poems', and Jackson, 'Gottfried von Strassburg', all in Loomis, *Arthurian Literature*; Curtis, *Roman de Tristan en Prose*; the same, *Tristan Studies*; Vinaver, *Roman de Tristan et Iseult*; esp. Baumgartner, *Tristan en prose*; esp. Ménard, *Roman de Tristan en prose*, edn in progress.

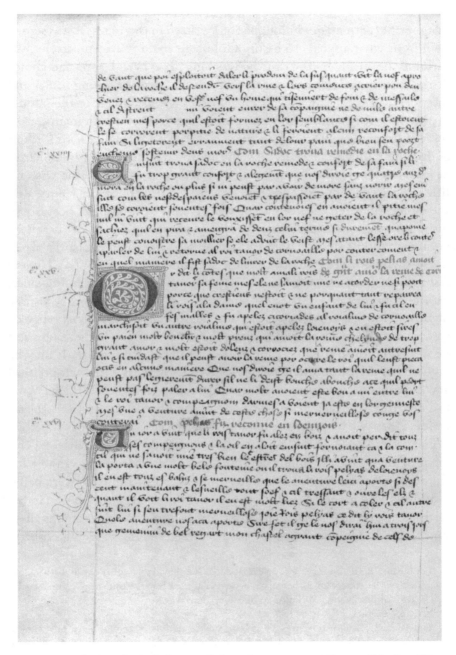

Fig. 70 A page from Richard of Gloucester's elegantly written copy of a part of the *Prose Tristan*. French, *c.* 1450. BL, MS Harl. 49, f. 5v. By permission of The British Library.

manuscript (with no gold illumination) written in the 1450s; it was signed
by him in what appears to be his adolescent hand with a motto he was
certainly not using by the time he was king. The overall tone and choice
of the texts in the volume suggest that it was aimed at a young reader and
intended to educate. Richard's *Prose Tristan* was also made in the middle
of the fifteenth century, another simple, handsome vellum manuscript,
with only some penwork to decorate it. It bears a formal *ex libris* for him
as duke of Gloucester written by an unknown hand. Beneath Richard's
ex libris his niece, Elizabeth, wrote a motto and her own name with no
title either as daughter of the king, Edward IV, or as queen of Henry VII;
she either inherited the volume or was given it by her uncle, possibly in
his reign when she had no title.[21] All the ownership details of these two
volumes contrast sharply with two other texts of which Richard's pleasure at owning is very obvious. These are Guido delle Colonna's *Historia
destructionis Troiae* and Geoffrey of Monmouth's *Historia regum Britanniae*,
the most authoritative versions of the history of Troy and the early history
of Britain known in Richard's day and the sources behind a vast range of
romances.[22] These he owned as king; they were companion volumes and
he signed both on the first page with his full royal signature. It may be
argued that these important and prestigious Latin texts with their political
and historical possibilities were more attractive to the adult Richard; he
had outgrown the tales of Palamon and Arcite, Ipomedon, and Tristan and
Isolde. He may have given the last away to his niece.

The pattern of Richard's ownership of romances accords with one element of their 'decline' in his day: such tales were becoming suitable for
children.[23] Romances that had once found an adult audience were being
moralised and given to children just as children are nowadays handed
Dickens: the prose *Ipomedon* and certain of Chaucer's tales were among these
suitable texts. This trend was to become stronger in the sixteenth century,

---

21 For the ms. 'R III's books X', pp. 26–27, and Cat. X below. For another of Elizabeth's books
    which can be connected to her uncle because she used his motto in it, see Visser-Fuchs,
    'Where did Elizabeth of York find consolation?', pp. 469–74.

22 See ch. 7 above.

23 E.g. Pearsall, 'English romance', pp. 64–67, on the decline of certain texts, but without
    reference to children. It has also been suggested that romances were adapted for children in
    another way: made cruder and simpler by the use of more direct speech, and more violent
    so as to hold the attention of boys in particular, to drive home the inevitable moral of virtue
    rewarded; see Shaner, 'Instruction and delight', pp. 5–15, using examples from the collection
    of short texts in Edinburgh, National Library of Scotland, Advocates MS 19.3.1.

but it had started much earlier. Richard read romances like any other aristocratic youth, for passing the time and learning the manners and customs of his class. His governors and tutors who gave them to him expected the texts to teach children in a palatable way. Authors, as well as booksellers like William Caxton and the Frenchman Vérard, emphasised in their prefaces the fact that romances had a teaching role and were particularly suitable for *young* men and women.[24] Adults were deemed to prefer the edification of history, mirrors for princes and other serious books of advice, though they, too, still read romances for their emotional or stirring qualities. Both young and old could gain a sense of pride in country and family from the traditional stories, or feel a desire to emulate the deeds or virtue of the hero or the heroine, and live and die as well and virtuously as they had done.

The fundamental change in the attitude to romances is suggested by the following comparison: in the early twelfth century chroniclers could still claim that before the battle of Hastings the fighting spirit of William the Conqueror's men had been fortified by a minstrel declaiming the *Song of Roland*,[25] and John Barbour tells us that Robert the Bruce passed the time for his troops during a tedious crossing of Loch Lomond by reading from the epic *Fierabras*.[26] It does not seem possible to transfer such an episode to either Edward IV on campaign or Richard III before Bosworth; times had changed.

Any general attempt to assess the popularity of romances among Richard's contemporaries from the evidence of surviving copies founders. Ninety-nine manuscripts of medieval romances in English have been identified, and of these sixty-six are of fifteenth-century manufacture.[27] Of the sixty-six volumes only twelve can be linked to definite localities or owners, and the only noble owner was Richard of Gloucester. Two of the remaining eleven volumes were apparently owned by the treasurer of his household, Sir William Hopton and his family.[28] An overall assessment

---

24 Caxton, *Blanchardyn and Eglantine*, p. 1; Pickford, 'Fiction and the reading public', pp. 430–36.
25 Douglas, 'The "Song of Roland" and the Norman conquest', pp. 99–116, esp. 99, 100.
26 Ramsay, *Chivalric Romances*, p. 20.
27 Guddat-Figge, *Catalogue*, passim; we are relying on her work without collation with more recent research on particular manuscripts. (Obviously all 99 mss had 15th-century owners, but this barely changes the total of known owners.) And see Doyle, 'English books in and out of court', for a study of all books known in English court circles.
28 *Ponthus*, Oxford, Bodleian Library, Digby 185: Mather, 'King Ponthus', pp. 1–150. *Generides*, Pierpont Morgan Library, MS M 876: Meale, 'The Morgan Library copy of *Generides*', pp. 89–104. Myers, *Household of Edward IV*, p. 288, Hopton was in office 4 July 1483 till his death, 7 Feb. 1484.

of the ownership of surviving romances in French in fifteenth-century
English courtly circles is not possible.[29]

If we turn to studying the ownership of romances, in French and
English, by Richard's immediate family, using all available evidence, the
figures hardly improve.[30] Edward IV himself is not known to have owned
any romance text by choice. Among other books that were part of the
royal library when he came to the throne in 1461 he inherited the composite volume of romances which John Talbot, Earl of Shrewsbury, gave to
Margaret of Anjou, Henry VI's queen, and which contained many favourites such as *Ogier le Danois*, *Les quatre fils Aymon*, *Ponthus et Sidoine*, *Gui de
Warewic* and *Le chevalier au cygne*, all in French.[31] Among the Flemish manuscripts that were executed in the right period and became part of the royal
library – though at an unknown date – and may therefore have belonged
to him, are Raoul Lefèvre's *Recueil des histoires de Troye*, in French, which
bears the royal arms in the marginal decoration,[32] and *Cleriadus et Meliadice*
and *Apollonius de Tyr* in another volume which has no signs of ownership.[33]
There is no direct evidence that Edward IV had any particular interest in
books – he never signed any, unlike his brother, Richard – and virtually
all the manuscripts that can be ascribed to his ownership, including the

---

29 E.g. Ward, *Catalogue of Romances* in the British Library does not systematically record all name
    inscriptions.
30 For a complete list of the books owned by them, 'Choosing a book', pp. 62–63, 84–86 and
    nn. 15–22, and ch. 2 above.
31 BL, MS Royal 15 E vi. Mandach, 'L'anthologie chevaleresque de Marguerite d'Anjou'. This
    much cited ms. (another case of the misleading evidence of mere survival) was, however, not
    the only means by which Edward could have known these popular stories!
32 BL, MS Royal 17 E ii, see e.g. Aeschbach, *Raoul Lefèvre*, p. 37. Caxton in his prologue to his
    Jason which he dedicated to the young prince of Wales wrote that he did not doubt that the
    king had the same book in French; he must have known from experience what the libraries
    of the rich contained.
33 BL, MS Royal 20 C ii. *Cleriadus et Meliadice* was probably composed in the early 1440s; it is
    a genuinely courtly romance, its action mainly set in England in a time when the kings of
    France and England *estoient tout ung et bons amis ensemble et les deux royaumes bien en paix*. Several
    mss made for Burgundian or French noble patrons in the 1460s or '70s survive, but their
    owners are mostly unknown. The British Library ms. is described by the editor of *Cleriadus*
    as a very bad copy, abbreviated by the scribe without any regard for coherence (though with
    attractive miniatures), which does not suggest royal ownership. Many of Edward's Flemish
    mss, however, are not as good as their counterparts made for Burgundian patrons. See Zink,
    Cleriadus et Meliadice. *Apollonius* is the ancient Greek story which Shakespeare used for his
    Pericles; the text of the British Library ms. differs from the other surviving copies of the
    period. See Zink, *Roman d'Apollonius de Tyr*.

Flemish ones, are historical, informative and didactic. Many of them were no doubt acquired for the education of the young prince of Wales, including a moralised French translation of Boccaccio's *Decameron*.[34]

The two eldest daughters of Edward may have acquired an illuminated fourteenth-century volume of Lancelot and the Holy Grail stories, and Queen Elizabeth Woodville herself probably owned a copy of Caxton's printed edition of the stories of Troy, which the printer had dedicated to the king.[35] Caxton also dedicated *Jason* to the prince of Wales. For Edward's brother, George of Clarence, and for his sisters no romances survive.[36] Neither of their parents can be associated with any romance.

Moving from the Yorkist royal family to their court the results are just as meagre. Queen Elizabeth Woodville's mother, Jacquetta of Luxemburg, owned a text of *Mélusine*; it was part of a collection of treatises on, and histories of, the crusades and the Holy Land and may have been considered history rather than romance. *Mélusine* was in fact an 'ancestral romance' of the families of Lusignan and Luxemburg, but was to become very popular in its printed editions with readers who were not interested in its historical features.[37] Elizabeth Woodville's father bought one lavishly illustrated fourteenth-century romance of *Alexander*;[38] her eldest brother, Anthony, despite his literary reputation, cannot be associated with any romance.[39] Taking a selection of courtiers: Sir William Hopton can be linked to two,[40] John, Duke of Norfolk, with three or four,[41] John

---

34 'Choosing a book', pp. 84–86.

35 BL, MS Royal 14 E iii; for the problems of the ownership of this volume, see the present authors' 'Queen Elizabeth Woodville', pp. 214–15. For the queen's copy of the *Recuyell*, *ibid.*, p. 230.

36 See above ch. 2.

37 BL, MS Cotton Otho D ii; see e.g. Stouff, *Essai sur Mélusine*, passim, esp. table 4; Willard, 'Duke of Berry's multiple copies of the *Fleur des Histoires d'Orient*', pp. 281–92.

38 Oxford, Bodleian Library, MS Bodley 246, see Guddat-Figge.

39 Anthony Woodville and John Tiptoft, Earl of Worcester, have been used as particular examples of the influence of the Burgundian courtly life style and as the most literary minded nobles of the period, but this certainly did not show itself in their owning any 'Burgundian' romance. Compare Kipling, *Triumph of Honor*, pp. 12–13.

40 Meale, 'The Morgan-Library copy of *Generides*', p. 102.

41 See the list of the books that he is assumed to have taken on the Scots campaign in 1484, Crawford, *Household Books of John Howard*, II, p. 277; it includes two texts of the histories of Troy (*La destruccion de Troye* and *La* [sic] *Recuel des histoires Troianes*), *Ponthus et la belle Sydoine* (*Pontius*), *Baudouin de Flandre* (*Sir Baudin, Comte de Flandres*), three texts from the cycle of Alain Chartier's *La belle dame sans mercy*, none of which can perhaps be considered romances, and *Paris et Vienne*.

Paston with five or six.[42] The evidence is so slender, erratic and miscellaneous that no firm conclusion as to the popularity of romances can be drawn from the evidence of the surviving copies, inventories, wills or any other chance reference.

Fifteenth-century Responses to Fiction

It has been reasonably said that romances were 'read to pieces' by their owners and therefore few survive.[43] It can also be suggested, perhaps even more plausibly, that they were as easily disposed of as a modern paperback novel; most of the surviving texts of English fifteenth-century romances have been found to be cheap, paper texts, some produced by amateur scribes for home use.[44] Clean, vellum, decorated copies were more likely to make the owner or inheritor of such manuscripts keep them, and all the surviving romances belonging to the Yorkist royal family fall into this category. Fiction was, and is, thrown out as old-fashioned, or as something felt to have been a waste of time to read. There is every reason to suppose that men and women at the end of the fifteenth century thought that fictional works were essentially frivolous and trivial when they bought, or made, their cheap, plain, paper copies. This opinion is expressed in the romances of the fifteenth century themselves, and it is also apparent from the usual contemporary meaning of 'passing the time' so frequently referred to in relation to reading romances.

The insidious idea that a pastime could be *merely* entertainment was creeping into use,[45] but it was still generally believed that time had to be passed or occupied *profitably*. The occupation of leisure was to be carefully planned and it was to result in learning and moral improvement. With this in mind romances, if they were not obviously exemplary or at least historical, were considered 'escapist fiction' and were therefore disposed

---

42 See Lester, 'The book of ... Sir John Paston', pp. 200–15; there are many gaps and illegible passages in this book list but it appears to include *Guy of Warwick* as well as *Guy and Colbrond*, *Richard coeur de lion*, Chaucer's *Troilus and Criseyde*, an unknown work, but probably a romance called 'Palatyse and Scitacus', and *Gawain and the Green Knight*.

43 Bennett, *English Books and Readers*, p. 149.

44 Guddat-Figge, *Catalogue*, pp. 20, 30–36. They were often copied into volumes containing a range of other works and thus seem to have been regarded as insufficiently important to stand by themselves, *ibid.*, pp. 25–29.

45 *OED*.

of. They are rarely mentioned in wills; writing your will encouraged a
serious frame of mind. Wills tend to mention liturgical, devotional or
professional books and give a different impression of book ownership
from the few surviving book lists, which usually contain at least some
romances.[46] Compare for example the will (1460) and the inventory of the
books (1474) of two ladies of similar background who may also have been
acquainted with each other, the one Burgundian, the other French. The
will contains nineteen book bequests, all religious and didactic except for
a copy of the prestigious *Roman de la rose* and a copy of *Lancelot du Lac*.[47]
The inventory lists about 163 books, among them twenty-one romances,
all well-known titles, such as *Tristan*, *Mélusine*, *Erec*, and *Paris et Vienne*.[48]

Romances in English excited criticism in England as soon as they
became popular. In *Sir Thopas* Chaucer parodied the long-winded,
unskilful romances that circulated in English in his day. His criticism
was of a literary and well-informed kind, but disapproval expressed in
clerical and educated circles was more concerned with moral than with
literary considerations. William of Nassington, a canon and a mystic,
scorned English romances in his *Speculum vitae* (*c.* 1380) as 'veyn spekyng';
his own writing, in contrast, was for the benefit of the soul.[49] This clerical critic disapproved of the *English* romances of his and Chaucer's day;
few had much literary merit, and what was worse, their very Englishness
made them available to a wide (and lower class) audience which might
be especially vulnerable to their corrupting influence. Nassington's criticism heralded Roger Ascham's fear of the potentially corrupting effect

---

46 See e.g. Moran, *Education and Learning*, passim, and Friedman, 'Books, owners and makers',
    pp. 111–27, who show that 15th-century wills in the north rarely mention romances and
    if they do they are usually historical stories such as those of Troy, 'classics' such as *The
    Canterbury Tales* or Boccaccio (whose work was considered eminently moral). And see Olson,
    Literature as Recreation, chs 1–4, passim.
47 The will of Marguerite de Boncourt, widow of Hugh de Lannoy, printed Lannoy, *Hugues de
    Lannoy*, pp. 281–95.
48 This inventory of her possessions was made after the death of Gabrielle de La Tour, Countess
    of Montpensier, in 1474: Boislisle, 'Inventaire des bijoux', pp. 269–309.
49 Thompson, '*Cursor mundi*, the 'Inglis tong', and 'romance', pp. 99–120, esp. 115–20; this essay
    contrasts the favourable reception of French and Anglo-Norman romances by the author
    of the *Cursor Mundi* 1300–25 to the hostility expressed by Nassington towards the *English*
    romances. For another comparable criticism of light reading, Thompson, 'Another look at
    the religious texts', p. 178. On Nassington, see also Owst, *Literature and Pulpit*, p. 13; and for
    the ambiguous relationship between secular stories and the sermon *exempla*, pp. 13–16, and
    ch. 4 'Fiction and instruction in the sermon "exempla"', esp. pp. 207–09.

of some romances. Ascham feared the religious and moral corruption of those unable to discriminate; it was not the wise man who was at risk, but the young who had no judgment. In his famous and oft-quoted denunciation of romances in his *Scholemaster*, written in the 1560s, he singled out the *Morte Darthur*: 'the whole pleasure of which booke standeth in two speciall poyntes, in open mans slaughter, and bold bawdrye'. He did not condemn romances as such, but feared them as papist books that would set a bad example, though not as bad as the 'merry' books that were translated out of Italian in his time.[50] This brand of criticism was not limited to England. Philippe de Mézières at the end of the fourteenth century had advised princes to avoid 'those books and romances which are full of nonsense and which entice the reader's mind to impossibilities, to folly, vanity and sin, like those telling of the deeds of Lancelot ...'. Erasmus adopted a similar tone in his *Instruction* of 1516: 'we see so many people these days who enjoy the stories of Arthur, Lancelot and others of that kind. These stories are not only about criminals, they are also coarse and sentimental'.[51] In Holland the presence of such criticism can also be concluded from the fact that certain romance texts were cleaned up and in due course became suitable for use by children. By the middle of the sixteenth century the *Chatelaine de Vergi* had been adapted for use by individual and less knowledgeable readers and its moral and religious lessons made simpler and more explicit; it was increasingly meant for the young and may even have been used in schools.[52] In the same period texts of *Amadis of Gaul*, *Floris and Blanchefleur* and *Fortunatus* are known to have been given as presents to quite small children, together with a new slate and a catechism.[53]

The increasing use of tidied-up romance texts for the education and entertainment of children seems to have been underestimated, but it was one of the factors contributing to the low value placed upon romances in late fifteenth-century England. The apparent 'fates' of Richard of Gloucester's romance volumes are cases in point. In the territories of the

---

50 Ascham, *Scholemaster*, pp. 57–80. If direct criticism of romances between the time of Nassington and Ascham in England is as limited as it seems, it may be that romances had been as well moralised as Ovid and the classical gods, see Owst, ch. 4.

51 Mézières, *Songe*, vol. 2, esp. p. 18. Erasmus, *Institutio*, pp. 179–80.

52 The *Chatelaine* dates from the 13th century. See Debaene, *Nederlandse Volksboeken*; Resoort, *Schoone historie*, passim; Gerritsen and van Melle, *Van Aiol tot Zwaanridder*, pp. 10–11.

53 Bredero, *Moortje*, lines 2637–45.

duke of Burgundy, however, and especially in the 1450s, it can be suggested, romances were enjoying an artificially induced 'Indian Summer', a phenomenon which complicates the historians' understanding of what was really happening to romances in this period. To this 'Indian Summer' we will return, but first let us ask why, if romances were considered frivolous and were criticised, *why* people read them, as they undoubtedly did? Why should anyone in fifteenth century England read a tale of adventure or love, usually set in an unreal world and in the distant past? More especially, what was the attraction such stories held for someone of the circle of Richard of Gloucester who had all the advantages of education, wealth and the culture of the time? The only way to answer this question is to look at the romances themselves and see what they can tell us in their prologues and epilogues. What reasons, and excuses, were given? The excuses especially should tell us about the general attitude to romances in the late middle ages.

Most late fourteenth- and early fifteenth-century romances in English tell us nothing. They may include a short prayer at beginning or end, but essentially they plunge into the story without ado and end as abruptly.[54] More cultivated story-tellers, those who retell the old stories as their own, like Chaucer and Gower, are more forthcoming. Gower tells us simply why he reads a love story: 'Min ere ... is fedd of redinge of romance of Ydoine and of Amadas', he says, choosing one of the most famous and virtuous of all love stories, 'that whilom weren in my cas'; his eyes fill with sympathetic tears and the story reminds him that sorrow cannot last forever and that hope always follows.[55] Gower reads love stories because he is in love and he finds solace in their example. We can all recognise this behaviour as universal, and if we do not, we can refer to the words written 200 years before Gower by the far greater poet, Gottfried of Strassburg (*fl.* 1210). In his long prologue to his tale of Tristan and Isolde he says that his work is 'a pastime, so that with my story people can bring

---

54 The texts included in the modern collections are all equally unforthcoming. See Rickert, *Early English Romances ... of Love*; the same, *Early English Romances ... of Friendship*; Fellows, *Of Love and Chivalry*; Mills, *Six Middle English Romances*; Mills and Andrew, *Ywain and Gawain*; the great Arthurian trilogy of *Grail*, *Lancelot* and *Morte* in French (Penguin edns), various dates.

55 *Confessio Amantis*, bk. 7, lines 876–89. *Amadas and Ydoine* rewrote and socialised the story of Tristan and Isolde, removing the adultery and unfaithfulness and ending with a marriage, Crane, *Insular Romance*, pp. 181–88.

Fig. 71 A gentleman reading a romance aloud to two others as *passe temps*. This drawing heads the prologue of the romance of the *Comte d'Artois* which stresses the benefits of such reading. Paris, BN, MS fr. 11610, f. 1. By permission of the Bibliothèque Nationale.

their keen sorrow half-way to alleviation ... For if we have something before us to occupy our thoughts it frees our unquiet soul and eases our heart of its cares'. The best occupation of a lover's leisure is a love story to distract any threatening 'langour' of spirit.[56] From Gottfried and from Gower we learn that love stories were read in the Middle Ages by lovers to ease their sufferings.

Gottfried introduces us to another main reason for reading romances: to pass the time in such a way that one does not fall into 'langour'. This applies not only to lovers but to anyone with time on his hands; essentially the classes who were educated and had adequate leisure. Similar reasons are given by the Burgundian author of the *Comte d'Artois*, about 1460, who wrote his story to guard against *diversez ymaginacions et merancolies* that trouble human beings; *lez plaisantez lectures dez anciennes histoires* passed the time and drove away the fantasies of idleness.[57] In England, John Metham of Norfolk expressed the same care more simply in 1457. His rhyming tale of *Amorys and Cleopas* would:

56 Gottfried von Strassburg, *Tristan, with the 'Tristan' of Thomas*, p. 42. And see Olson, *Literature as Recreation*, ch. 4, 'Literature as consolation'.
57 Seigneuret, *Comte d'Artois*, p. 1. Longer quotation in ch. 4 above.

To comfforte them that schuld fall in hevynes
For tyme on-ocupyid, qwan folk haue lytyl to do,
On haly-dayis to rede, me thynk yt best so.[58]

The bookseller and printer Caxton, who must have been very aware of what people considered acceptable and appropriate, used this theme twice to advocate the reading of romances. He used it most unaffectedly in the prologue to his first translation, the *Recuyell of the Histories of Troy*, which he had undertaken to 'eschewe slouth and ydleness'. He had chosen the stories of Troy because he took 'delyte' in them, because of their novelty, their 'fayr' French and because they were in prose and he could understand 'the sentence and substance of every mater'; and lastly they would pass the time for himself and others.[59] About ten years later he picked up the last idea more perfunctorily in the *Morte Darthur* (1485), 'for to passe the tyme thys book shal be plesaunte to rede in'.[60] Raoul Lefèvre, the original composer of the *Recuyell*, had had good reason to be more brashly confident – in his prologue to his *Jason* – that Philip the Good of Burgundy, the original dedicatee of both the *Recuyell* and *Jason*, loved to pass his time with such stories.[61] The whole of *The Canterbury Tales* and its reason for existence is based on the premise that stories are told to pass the time pleasurably. Again, the sentiment is readily recognisable 500 years later.

Stories, however, varied in quality, both in subject and presentation; inevitably subject drew forth most contemporary comment. Chaucer's Man of Law discriminates between stories of honest love and such tales of love as the story of the incest of Canace and her brother, which he commends Chaucer for not telling; he chooses the moral and improving tale of Constance's endurance. Similarly Chaucer's Clerk tells the story of Patient Griselda – which Richard of Gloucester knew in his youth – as an example of obedience to God's will,[62] the Nun's Priest's tale is told for its 'moralite',[63] and both the tales of the Canon's Yeoman and the Manciple have neat morals.[64] The Physician ends his tale urging his listeners to for-

---

58 Craig, *Works of John Metham, Amoryus and Cleopes*, p. 81, lines 2209–11.
59 Blake, *Caxton's Own Prose*, p. 97.
60 *Ibid.*, p. 109.
61 Caxton, *History of Jason*, p. 3; see also below.
62 Robinson, *Works of Chaucer*, p. 113, lines 1142–51.
63 *Ibid.*, p. 205, lines 3438–43.
64 *Ibid.*, p. 223, line 1473; p. 227, lines 359–62.

sake sin and gets exactly the right reaction from the Host who rails against the villain of the story.[65] When the Pardoner is about to tell his story the company insist that he

> ... telle us of no ribaudye!
> Telle us som moral thyng, that we may leere
> Som wit, and thanne wol we gladly heere.[66]

Bawdy and satire may be frequent in *The Canterbury Tales*, but the weight of the argument is that a good moral story is what is usually preferred. We are back already to our main contention that romances (or stories) are things of no account and disposable, unless they are bolstered by a good moral.

As a bookseller Caxton in particular had to address this issue, unlike Chaucer who could undercut his arguments as he chose with impunity. For Caxton all stories were meant to teach and improve the reader. He wrote seven prologues or epilogues to his eight romances and in all of these emphasised to varying degrees their value as examples for living. Three times he uses the words of St Paul, probably via *The Canterbury Tales*,[67] that all that is written is for our 'doctrine', a phrase that Caxton the publisher might have taken as his motto: he used it in the *Histories of Troy* (c. 1473), in the *Morte Darthur* (1485) and *Charles the Great* (1485). He knew, too, via *The Canterbury Tales* if not from sermons, that St Paul had reproved those who tell 'fables'.[68] The *Histories of Troy*, Caxton's first English translation, taught men the evil consequences of starting a war;[69] the prologue and epilogue of *Jason*, its sequel, make no specific reference to its moral value but its presentation to the prince of Wales implies that the life of the hero was an example to the prince.[70] In his next romance, the *Morte Darthur* (1485), Caxton was specific, perhaps because of the dubious morality of the love and adventures of such as Lancelot and

---

65   *Ibid.*, pp. 147–48.

66   *Ibid.*, p. 148, lines 323–36. For Chaucer's own attitude to storytelling and its social benefits, Olson, *Literature as Recreation*, pp. 145–46, 155–63.

67   *Ibid.*, the Nun's Priest's Tale, p. 205, lines 3441–42.

68   I Tim. 1: 4; 4: 7, and II Tim. 4: 7, all refer to *fabulae* of teachers that should not be listened to; prologue to the *Parson's Tale*, ed. Robinson, p. 228, lines 31–36.

69   Blake, *Caxton's Own Prose*, p. 101.

70   *Ibid.*, pp. 103–06.

Guinevere and Tristan and Isolde: 'Doo after the good and leve the evyl ... see and lerne the noble actes of chyvalrye ... al is wryton for our doctryne'.[71] In *Charles the Great* (1485) after the same safety-phrase of St Paul he reminds us that the deeds of 'olde peple ben for to gyve to us ensaumple to lyve in good and vertuous operations ...'.[72] He added nothing but the barest colophon to the well-known romance of *Paris and Vienne* (1485), but spent more time on the love and adventures of *Blanchardyn and Eglantine* (c. 1489) which were to encourage young men to act valiantly and thereby achieve 'grace' of their ladies, and to encourage young ladies to be constant to their male protectors; reading such virtuous stories would serve ladies as well as 'ouer moche' study of devotional books, ventured Caxton.[73] His last two romances, the *Four Sons of Aymon* (c. 1489) and *Eneydos* (c. 1490), were more routinely presented as sources of useful knowledge, example and, in the case of the last, straightforward ancient history and literature.[74] Those of Caxton's romances which had their own prologues and epilogues endorsed his opinion of their moral value, and in some cases furnished him with the cue for his additions.[75]

To cite the value of any fable, story (history or fiction) or romance as examples for good living was standard practice for nearly all writers in the late Middle Ages; they were inevitably conscious of the church's power of criticism. St Paul's stricture against the telling of 'fables' was a powerful threat, just as his assertion that everything written was for our doctrine was an ever useful protection. To conclude: stories could be read with enthusiasm, and criticism could be warded off fairly easily, but it was as well to preempt potential criticism whenever possible.

One way in which a reader could deal with the 'problems' of the frivolity of romance was to edit them and make them conform to social

---

71 *Ibid.*, p. 109, lines 100–19.

72 *Ibid.*, pp. 66–68.

73 Caxton's *Blanchardyn and Eglantyne*, pp. 1–2.

74 Blake, *Caxton's Own Prose*, pp. 33–34 (*Four Sons*); *ibid.*, pp. 78–81 (*Eneydos*). The version of the *Aeneid* that Caxton used has been said to be closer to Vergil's original than any other medieval version, Hall, 'Caxton's "Eneydos" and the redactions of Vergil', pp. 136–47, esp. 145–47.

75 The epilogue of the French text of Caxton's *Charles the Grete*, pp. 250–51, undoubtedly influenced the translator's choice of words; Caxton's *Blanchardyn and Eglantyne*, p. 11; Caxton's *Eneydos*, p. 10. The pseudo-chivalric romance, Caxton's *History of Reynard the Fox* also says much can be learnt from jokes, pp. 6, 111–12.

expectations.[76] Both professional and amateur redactors tried their hands at such editing and it was part of a continuous process, not unique to the fifteenth century. Editing and adapting had been going on in England since the thirteenth century, when the earlier romances were 'socialised' and made more accessible to an ever-widening public.[77] The popular story of *Ipomedon*, of which Richard of Gloucester possessed the only surviving copy of the prose version composed in the 1450s or early '60s – possibly even for Richard himself – had undergone a complete revision when translated from Anglo-Norman into English verse in the fourteenth century. That revision removed the original author's irony and sensuality and created an accessible and exemplary celebration of the perfect knight and his true love.[78] The prose version repeated this lesson in an abbreviated form to its fifteenth-century audience composed of, at least, the youthful duke of Gloucester.

A more subtle transformation of a twelfth-century romance is to be found in the mid-fifteenth-century English translation of *Partonope of Blois*. The competent, lively, 'courtly' translator frequently undermined the tale with an irony and detachment that owed much to the influence of Chaucer, and also added a didactic and moral dimension lacking in his original. His authorial interpolations distanced himself and his audience from the love and adventures of his protagonists. He emphasised the need to get on with the *story*,[79] and unlike his original (and Gower) he did not say he, too, was in love, but emphatically said he was not and did not want to be.[80] He also justified his entertainment by, again, quoting St Paul and saying that we can learn good from any written work. The most successful moral theme he introduced into the poem was that of good 'governance', of oneself and others,[81] thereby making it especially suitable for young ladies and gentlemen.

---

76 For rewriting of romances in the 15th century see Pearsall, 'English romance', pp. 64–83; he divides them into texts which descended to be popular entertainment (pp. 64–67), the adaptations influenced by Chaucer and Lydgate and adaptations in prose made for 'creamed off' audiences; he concludes that the changes were dictated by the needs of the *readers* who wanted comprehensive texts with no distractions (p. 74).

77 Crane, *Insular Romance*, passim, esp. pp. 210–11, 179–80.

78 *Ibid.*, pp. 158–74, 202–11.

79 Bödtker, *Partonope of Blois*, lines 928–35, 2343–51, 6170–74.

80 *Ibid.*, lines 2310–51.

81 Ihle, 'The English *Partonope of Blois* as *exemplum*', pp. 301–11, esp. 305–10; Windeatt, 'Chaucer and fifteenth-century romance', pp. 62–80; see also Meale, 'gode men …', pp. 222–24, for female owners of *Partonope*, which she calls a courtly work.

The translator of *Partonope* was working for an unnamed 'souereyne' (line 2335), presumably someone of standing, but such emendations of texts also went on lower down the social scale. The collection put together in the 1480s or soon after by someone called Rate, almost certainly of Leicester and a member of the town's Corpus Christi guild, illustrates how ordinary English people might edit romances and use them in their daily life. The manuscript contains five romances, *Sir Isumbras*, the *Earl of Toulouse*, *Libeaus desconnus*, *Sir Cleges* and *Sir Orfeo*, scattered through the volume among many other items in verse of an instructional, meditational or narrative kind, with a consistent bias towards devotion. The themes of the romances conform to this pattern with their emphasis on the survival of trials by the members of a family or by a marriage, fidelity, duty and sexual continence being among the virtues rewarded. Analysis of the texts has shown that the author actively edited them to make them suitable for an audience of family and friends. Rate has been proposed as a household chaplain, but he could equally have been a careful *pater familias* (or his wife) who entertained and morally improved his household and friends. The occupation of the idle minds of a household in the evening while the women sewed, or on a holiday, as John Metham advised, cannot have been uncommon in a prosperous household consisting of family, servants, apprentices and guests. What was probably unusual was the ability and concern of Rate to edit a collection of texts.[82]

The cleaning-up or moralising of romances in which adultery or sexual comments were prominent, and the pervasive and probably very effective criticism from clerics such as Nassington, combined with the poorer quality of many of the later English romances and their bland avoidance of complications and perhaps also the obligation which Chaucer's admirers such as the translator of *Partonope* felt to imitate the master's irony, all conspired against romances in England. In England, it can be suggested, there was not much future for the romance after Chaucer,[83] unless a maverick genius like Malory took them entirely seriously, ignoring both Chaucer and the oppressive moralities of the clerics. All these factors contributed to the change in status of romances by the time of the Yorkist kings – they were still popular and still read but they had become more disposable and mere pastimes.

---

82 Oxford, Bodleian Library, MS Ashmole 61; see Blanchfield, 'The romances in MS Ashmole 61'.
83 Compare Windeatt, 'Chaucer and fifteenth-century romance', p. 77.

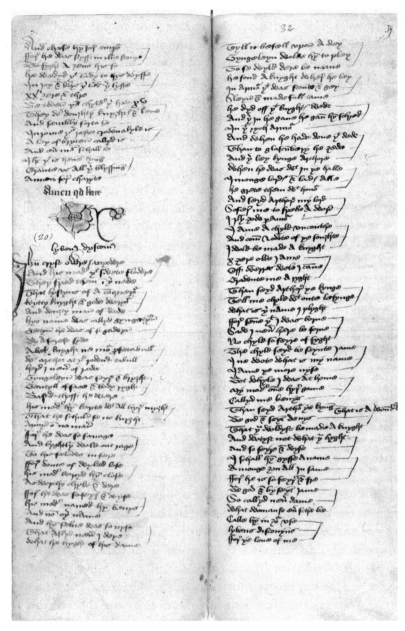

Fig. 72 The conclusion of the *Earl of Toulouse*, with *Amen quod Rate* and the beginning of *Libeaus Desconus* (The Fair Unknown). Rate, probably a guildsman of Leicester, compiled and rewrote a collection of improving romances and other texts for domestic reading, writing them into a tall, narrow 'account' book. Oxford, Bodleian Library, MS Ashmole 61, ff. 38v–39. By permission of the Bodleian Library.

The Duke of Burgundy's Love Affair with Romances

If we turn to the realms of the Duke of Burgundy again, something very different was apparently going on: romances were flourishing and being composed to a surprising degree. This appears to originate in the special interests of one man, Philip the Good, Duke of Burgundy (ruled 1419–67), older contemporary of Edward IV and Richard III. He is a rare example of a single man leaving a clear mark on the literary taste of his time and the people around him. After his death a decline in the popularity of romances set in among the upper classes of his domains, comparable to that found in England. His son, Duke Charles, had very different tastes from his father.

Duke Philip's romances were commissioned in magnificent manuscripts which have ensured their survival, whatever the merit of their contents; a survival which in its turn has allowed later commentators to assume that romances were generally flourishing in this period and that all nations, and especially England, were following Burgundy's lead. To Philip his romances rarely represented mere entertainment, each one had its own meaning. One example is *La belle Hélène de Constantinople*, the romance of a long-suffering heroine who wandered for many years from east to west. A modern literary historian has explained why the story attracted Duke Philip:

> It was for him a kind of *oeuvre nationale*, it took him on a tour of all his lands and neighbouring regions, which were so well known to him: Tournai, Douai, Courtrai, Ecluse, Bruges, Brussels. At the same time the south and the east, Rome and Jerusalem, were evoked for him, and this, too, did not displease him ...[84]

To others and to later generations *La belle Hélène* was merely a touching story; to the duke, for whom a special prose version was made, it was far more.[85]

Another example is the popular story of *Paris et Vienne*, of which a prose version was edited for Philip and which he probably liked for the same reasons as *La belle Hélène*, but also for the part played in it by the sons of the count of Flanders and the duke of Burgundy and for the addition made for him of the grand tournament attended by the dukes

---

84 Doutrepont, *Littérature*, p. 37.
85 Prose version by Jean Wauquelin; see Doutrepont, *Mises en prose*, pp. 242–46.

of Burgundy and Bourbon, the kings of England, France and Sicily.[86]
There is little doubt about the general success of *Paris et Vienne*; it figured
in many libraries, including the 'travelling' collection of John Howard,
Duke of Norfolk,[87] and it was frequently reprinted in French from *circa*
1480 to 1596, in English from 1485 (Caxton) to 1650, as well as in other
languages. On its own merit the story remained a 'good read' long after
the ancestral and chivalric fascination had faded.[88]

   The personal taste of Duke Philip impressed itself on that of his subjects in a way unknown in England. His interests were the result of his
needs, which were very similar to those of his French royal ancestors: to
legitimate his authority. For him romances were one important means of
personal propaganda; he had acquired many of his lands by foul means
rather than fair and was in permanent need of confirmation of his 'rights'.
From the 1440s until his death in 1467 any literary text which – however
indirectly – treated his overlordship as natural and celebrated his ancestors,
or his patron saints, or the history or unity of his lands was very welcome.[89]

   There are more telling examples than *La belle Hélène* and *Paris et Vienne*,
already cited. Philip directly inspired several new texts and reworkings of
older texts in which history, descent and inheritance played an important
part. One of the most remarkable and representative was the semi-historical
romance of *Girart de Rousillon*, hero of Burgundy and opponent of the king of
France. In the course of the story Girart, the 'good' rebel, is forced to exclaim:

   How can I make my peace with the King of France who has killed
   my father!?

The same words could have been spoken by Philip himself whose father,
John the Fearless, had been murdered at the command of the dauphin,
later Charles VII. The many similarities between Girart and Philip, not
only in their opposition to a king of France, but also in their deeply felt

---

86 Kaltenbacher, 'Paris et Vienne', gives the text unique to the 'Burgundian' version; Naber,
    'Manuscrits d'un bibliophile', p. 35, and the same, 'BR 9632/3: une version bourguignonne
    de … *Paris et Vienne*', pp. 19–27.
87 See above, n. 41.
88 Kaltenbacher, 'Paris et Vienne', pp. 338–688; Debaene, *Nederlandse Volksboeken*, pp. 133–40;
    Veyrin-Forrer, 'Caxton and France', p. 44; Caxton, *Paris and Vienne*.
89 See especially Lacaze, 'Le rôle des traditions', passim, but also Doutrepont, *Littérature*,
    pp. 22–69.

wish to be reconciled and loyal to the monarchy itself, gave this prose romance/version of the story composed for the duke profound meaning during his reign, which it never held again.[90]

The creation of his 'nation' was only one of Philip's preoccupations which affected his taste in romances. Like the other princes of the west he nurtured a never-fading dream of the reconquest of the Holy Land. Any romance, but also any treatise, that described the curious lands and people of the Orient or connected them to him, his ancestors or his vassals, fascinated him in a way that went beyond mere entertainment. In this context of political needs and crusading dreams should be mentioned the series of romance manuscripts produced in Lille between *c.* 1445 and the mid-1460s, all apparently closely connected with Jean de Wavrin, the ex-soldier and chronicler of England. Virtually all these texts were in prose, adaptations of older poems or new works cobbled together from existing narrative elements; all can be called 'historical novels' or 'ancestral romances' and many were part of Philip the Good's library at the time of his death. The texts themselves were not unique, but the manuscripts produced at Lille had unique additional features bound to please Duke Philip and the courtiers that followed his lead: their action was deliberately set in places known to their readers, they described the martial exploits of the ancestors of their aristocratic public and, in addition, all contained a crusading story or a description of the wonders of the Orient. Some of the texts behind the new stories are well known, such as *Apollonius de Tyre* or *Olivier de Castile*. Some of the new texts were given a very local background, like *Gilles de Chin* or the *Comte d'Artois*; many existing stories were made more local and contemporary by the addition of names, places and events of particular interest to Philip and his nobles. The majority of these manuscripts was illustrated by an artist whose numerous cartoon-like sketches give the books an extremely fashionable but also light-hearted air, suggesting that even in Duke Philip's circle not everybody took these texts absolutely seriously (see figs 38, 67, 71, 73).[91] Nothing like this 'centre of production' of romances ever existed in England; the only comparable phenomenon is the collections of stories gathered together in single manuscripts such as Rate's.

---

90 Doutrepont, *Littérature*, pp. 24–30; Thoss, *Epos des Burgunderreiches*, passim; compare other romances of the *cycle des barons révoltés*, such as *Raoul de Cambrai*, the 'Four Sons of Aymon' (*Les quatre fils Aymon*) and *Ogier le Danois*, which were also popular in 15th-century Burgundy.

91 See e.g. Winter, 'Manuscrits à peintures', pp. 233–56, esp. 251–56.

Fig. 73 A princess and a gentleman in conversation. From the romance of *Olivier de Castile*. Flemish, made for Jean de Wavrin, 1450s. Ghent, University Library, MS 470, f. 15v. By permission of the University Library, Ghent.

The tales of the Arthurian cycle, which Caxton recommended English knights to read to learn 'manhode, curtosye and gentylnesse',[92] were also extremely popular at the Burgundian court. Every aristocratic book collection, about which anything is known, contained several samples. Duke Philip took them as seriously as his other romances. On one occasion when the duke had ridden off in a fury and lost his way in the forest at night he was greeted the next morning by his friend and chamberlain, Philippe Pot, with the words:

> Good morning, monseigneur, what is this? Are you King Arthur now, or Sir Lancelot? Did you think there would be no Sir Tristrams wandering around who would be a match for you?[93]

---

92 Byles, *Ordre of Chyvalry*, p. 122.
93 Chastellain, *Oeuvres*, vol. 3, p. 279.

Chivalric romances certainly inspired the enacting and outward trappings of the jousts and *pas d'armes* held during Philip's reign.[94] The authors of Philip's preferred romances still put the knights of fiction and the historical heroes of their own lifetime on the same footing in their lists of examples for their readers to follow, just as John Metham and Caxton did in England.

It can be suggested that Duke Philip's particular – and it is tempting to say, naive – interests were not shared fully by his contemporaries, except to humour him, and certainly not by his successors. In their didactic writings, Gilbert de Lannoy (1386–1462) and Diego de Valera (1412–*c*. 1488) turned to the heroes of antiquity not of romances for their *exempla*; and Blaise de Monluc writing in the 1560s specifically advised prospective knights not to waste their time reading *Amadis of Gaul* and *Lancelot du Lac*.[95] Charles the Bold inherited his father's magnificent library and could have read all his father's 'novels', but there is no evidence that he did. In his youth, like Richard of Gloucester, Charles did indeed 'read, and had read to him, pleasant tales and the deeds of Lancelot and Gawain',[96] but as an adult he was fascinated by the heroes of antiquity, Alexander, Xenophon, and Caesar; he is known to have been indifferent to *histoires d'amours, farses joyeuses et plaisantes devises*[97] and he is not known to have added any such book to the ducal library. The most frivolous book in the surviving collection of Charles's third wife, Margaret of York, was Jean Mansel's universal history, the *Fleur des histoires*, a serious and voluminous work which included the stories of Griselda and Girart de Rousillon among its innumerable items, because the author regarded them as history.[98]

In spite of Duke Philip's preference the book collections of his own courtiers show a relatively low percentage of romances. The extensive library of Louis of Gruuthuse contained about twenty among more than two hundred (less than 10 per cent).[99] For Charles's half-brother, Anthony

---

94 For a brief survey with bibliography of such *pas* and their immediate inspiration see e.g. Lindner, 'L'influence du roman chevaleresque français sur le pas d'armes', pp. 67–78.

95 Vale, *War and Chivalry*, pp. 163–64, 164.

96 Doutrepont, *Littérature*, p. 182; La Marche, *Mémoires*, vol. 2, p. 217: *il s'appliquoit à lire et faire lire devant luy, du commancement, en joyeulx comptes et ès faictz de Lancelot et de Gavain, et retenoit ce qu'il avoit ouy mieulx qu'aultre de son eage*; compare *ibid.*, vol. 2, p. 334.

97 Doutrepont, *Littérature*, p. 177, 182; it is significant that Doutrepont's chapter on *Fabliaux et Nouvelles* does not even have to discuss Charles.

98 On Margaret see ch. 2 above.

99 Martens *et al.*, *Lodewijk van Gruuthuse*, pp. 198–99.

the Grand Bâtard, also a noted book collector, only one survives: *Gillion de Trazignies*, one of the ancestral romances produced at Lille under the aegis of Jean de Wavrin.[100] The inventory of Charles's younger contemporary and relative, Philip of Cleves, lists about ten texts out of 127 titles, that can be called romances (less than 8 per cent); among them a *Lancelot*, *Gillion de Trazignies*, *Buscalus*, the legend of the foundation of the town of Tournai, and the generally popular *Mélusine*.[101] Comparable numbers can be found in the libraries of the influential Croy family, but it is difficult to establish when each book was acquired by which member of the family.[102]

How did the attitude towards romances of the Burgundian dukes affect the romance reading of the English courtier-class at a time when most of them were still expected to read French with pleasure? Caxton has often been regarded as the main 'bridge' between Burgundian and English literary culture during his printing career, 1475–91, and it is the romances that have usually been singled out as examples of the 'courtly' works which Caxton is supposed to have personally wanted to publish because of his 'Burgundian' past.[103] In fact Caxton published very few romances: eight out of his seventy-two titles. His first two English translations were the *Histories of Troy* (the story of Hercules) and *Jason* in 1475 and 1477, both already printed by him in French, and had certainly been special favourites of Duke Philip because of their connection with his order of the Golden Fleece. Whether they were successful in England is a moot point; neither he nor anyone else in England reprinted them.[104] During the next nine to ten years Caxton printed no romances – he did print the satire of chivalric romance, *Reynard the Fox* in 1481 – and only in the middle of 1485 did he bring out his great discovery, the *Morte Darthur*, a wholly English

---

100 Boinet, 'Un bibliophile', pp. 255–69.

101 Finot, *Inventaire sommaire*, pp. 433–34; *Boeken van en rond Willem van Oranje*, pp. 26–27.

102 Bayot, *Martin le Franc*, pp. 52–55.

103 E.g. Lathrop, 'The first English printers and their patrons', pp. 71, 81–85, was especially concerned to answer the contemporary debate over whether Caxton followed or guided popular taste; Blake, 'William Caxton: his choice of texts', p. 307, and his later *Caxton and His World*; Kekewich, 'Edward IV, William Caxton and literary patronage', pp. 181–87; and Bornstein, 'William Caxton's chivalric romances and the Burgundian renaissance', pp. 1–10; Scanlon, 'Pre-Elizabethan prose romances in English', pp. 1–20; Keiser, 'Romances', pp. 274–75, 279–81; Barron, *English Medieval Romance*, pp. 56, 104.

104 It was Gerard Leeu, at Antwerp, who reprinted *Jason* in English in 1492, Pinkernell, *Histoire de Jason*, pp. 30, 17–31.

work.[105] The five other romances that followed 1485–90 all seem to have been produced because of their easy availability in printed editions made in France and hardly reflect any personal choice or preference.[106] He did not bother, or was unable, to find suitable texts in English.[107] Three of the romances printed in and after 1485 were suggested to him: *Charles the Great* (96 ff.) by his friend, William Daubeney; *Blanchardyn and Eglantine* (51 ff.) by Margaret Beaufort after she had bought a copy of the book from him; and the *Four Sons of Aymon* (278 ff.) by the earl of Oxford.[108] It is arguable that all three had bought a French printed copy in Caxton's shop. Caxton's own choice among the romances he printed, boils down to four texts. It can be suggested that the first two, the *Histories of Troy* and *Jason*, had little success and that this contributed to his failure to print any more romances for nearly a decade.[109] Caxton's other 'choices' were the short and universally popular *Paris and Vienne* (*c.* 1485; 36 ff.), one of his best translations, and the *Eneydos* (*c.* 1490; 86 ff.), also reasonably short and, as the story of the Trojan ancestors of the founder of Britain, fairly certain to appeal to an English readership. Both reached him as printed texts from France; they were not products of Burgundian influence. Caxton's greatest find and probably his only real success among his romances, and certainly the only one to become enduringly popular, was the *Morte Darthur*.[110]

---

105 Our conclusions here are based on our 'Choosing a book', pp. 69–71.

106 Until 1483 Caxton appears to have been ahead of French printers in the production of texts (but not of romances); his *Charles the Great, Paris and Vienne, Sons of Aymon* and *Eneydos*, were all based on editions printed earlier at Geneva and Lyons, see Veyrin-Forrer, 'Caxton and France', pp. 33–47, esp. 40–46.

107 *Guy of Warwick* may be an example of the lack of a suitable ms.: it was very popular and should have appealed to Caxton's so-called 'courtly/chivalric' tastes. Verse texts were presumably available but he never printed any verse romances. In fact it is unlikely he could get a copy of the French prose version (considered a better work than the poems) even if he knew of it. Three of the known mss belonged to the kings of England (BL, MS Royal 15 E vi given to Margaret of Anjou by Lord Talbot), to Jean d'Orleans? (BN, MS fr. 1476), and to the dukes of Burgundy (lost); the fourth is the unknown parent of the first printed edition of 1525. Conlon, *Rommant de Guy de Warwick et de Herolt d'Ardenne*, pp. 13–47. Crane, 'The vogue of *Guy of Warwick*', pp. 125–94.

108 Reprinted three times before 1550, Pollard and Redgrave (rev. ed. 1986), 1007–10. *Charles the Great* was never reprinted, *ibid.*, 5013.

109 *Histories of Troy* reprinted once before 1550, Pollard and Redgrave (rev. ed. 1986), 15375–82; *Jason* has only ever been reprinted once, *ibid.*, 15383–84. And see Hellinga, 'Caxton and the bibliophiles', p. 31.

110 Reprinted at regular intervals 1498 onwards, Pollard and Redgrave (rev. ed. 1986), 800–06.

There is therefore, in our opinion, little hard evidence that Caxton particularly wanted to print, or had any preference for, what are called the courtly romances of Burgundy. He also steered well clear of English verse romances, and no romance is known to have been reprinted by him.[111] Caxton's modest output of eight romances out of a total of seventy-two titles accords well with the overall profile of romances in the literature of his day: romances, tales and *facetiae* made up 3.81 per cent of early printed books in Europe; and in England only twenty-four 'vernacular secular romances, verse, and satires' were published out of a total of 413 titles to 1499, 5.8 per cent.[112] The evidence for specific Burgundian influence on Caxton's output is very slender.

While allowing for the unusual role played by the particular interests of Philip the Good and disposing of Caxton's role as a 'bridge' between England and Burgundy, there was an undoubted similarity between the interests of the English and continental aristocracy. The similarity did not result from an English dependence on Burgundian influence and it did not show itself necessarily in the same ways on both sides of the Channel. All noble families were fascinated by their ancestry and family history; in fifteenth-century England this showed itself more in the popularity of genealogical rolls[113] than in the survival of a few home-made ancestral or historical romances of which *Guy of Warwick* is the best example.[114] Written originally in Anglo-Norman verse in the first half of the thirteenth century to please Thomas, Earl of Warwick,[115] it was reworked and translated in verse and prose and remained popular with descendants of the original patron as well as with Englishmen generally. The reasons

---

111 Blake, 'Caxton's reprints', pp. 109, 117, notes that no chivalric text was reprinted by Caxton but asserts they were part of his printing policy which he may have made financial sacrifices to maintain. See also Keiser, 'Romances', pp. 279–81.

112 The European figures, compiled by Lenhart, are open to dispute, Hirsch, pp. 127–28; compare Pickford, 'Fiction and the reading public', pp. 430–31 and n. 1, 436–37. The figures for England alone are from White, ' Early print and purgatory', App. 1, esp. pp. ii–iii.

113 See ch. 6 above.

114 The term 'ancestral' romance has come under justified attack; perhaps 'historical' is a better word. See Crane, *Insular Romances*, ch. 1 (esp. pp. 16–18), p. 86, and Field, 'Romance as history, history as romance', pp. 163–74. In the cases of *Guy of Warwick* and the *Knight of the Swan*, the Beauchamps would certainly have taken an 'ancestral' interest, as did the house of Luxemburg in England and France in that of *Mélusine*, whatever the precise origins of the tales.

115 Legge, *Anglo-Norman Literature*, p. 162; *Manual*, 1, pp. 27–31; Crane, 'The vogue of *Guy of Warwick*', pp. 125–94.

for its continued success are obvious: Guy became a national hero, his deeds were accepted as historical and the story is impeccably exemplary, almost a saint's life.[116] In Richard's day the history of Guy was known and used: by John Hardyng in the final version of his chronicle dedicated to Edward IV; and by the antiquarian John Rous in his history of the earls of Warwick which ended with Richard III, his wife and son.

In England all Arthurian stories had the added advantage of being national and 'ancestral' history – though no king could claim *descent* from Arthur! Like Philip the Good Caxton thought of them as textbooks of knightly behaviour, providing as suitable examples to follow the deeds of historical figures such as Richard I, Sir John Chandos and the ancestors of Richard III's queen. The stories he recommended were 'Saynt Graal, of Lancelot, of Galaad, of Trystram, of Perse Forest, of Percyval, of Gawayn and many mo'.[117] These titles are all familiar except *Perceforest*, a text of Hainault origin which must have been known in England for Caxton to mention it without explanation. The only copy surviving in this country, however, is a late fifteenth-century Flemish manuscript that cannot have belonged to either Edward IV or Richard III. The story could have been popular in England since the days of Philippa of Hainault, when it was composed; it is set in England at a time when the island is in a state of decline; order is restored by Alexander the Great and chivalry is revived by his institution of the tournament. In the context of his *Order of Chivalry* and his enthusiastic plea for the holding of tournaments Caxton must have found this book highly recommendable; its actual popularity in his day and in England can only be guessed at.[118]

The crusades and the east were also of interest in England. Edward IV had Josephus' *Jewish Wars* in French, a translation of the *Siege of Rhodes*, a French

---

116 See above n. 107. Hibbard, *Medieval Romance*, pp. 127–39; Klausner, 'Didacticism and drama in *Guy of Warwick*', pp. 103–19.

117 Blake, *Caxton's Own Prose*, p. 126, Epilogue to the *Order of Chivalry*.

118 BL, MSS Royal 15 E v, 19 E iii and 19 E ii. The evidence contained in these mss is confusing; the claim that 15 E v is the *grosse* made by David Aubert for Philip the Good seems untenable in view of the very late, post-1485 date of the presentation miniature. It is likely that the volumes were completed over a number of years by various artists and they may have ended up in the possession of Henry VII. Copies of the text are known to have been owned by the dukes of Burgundy, Louis of Gruuthuse, and Jacques d'Armagnac. This vast epic of chivalric adventures was probably written 1337–44 for William I, Count of Hainault; it linked the Alexander cycle to that of Arthur. Sole printed eds 1528 and 1531; now being ed. Taylor, *Roman de Perceforest*. And see ch. 4 above.

Fig. 74 The romance of the *Three Kings' Sons*, which tells the story of the joint crusading adventures of the princes of France, England and Scotland. The miniature shows the presentation of the bride to the king of France by the emperor, followed by the wedding. Probably London, 1480s. BL, MS Harl. 236, f. 117v. By permission of The British Library.

and an English version of William of Tyre's history of the first crusade and Cardinal Bessarion's pleas to the princes of the west for a joint new crusade.[119] Richard III is known to have had a special crusading litany inserted in his personal book of hours.[120] It is therefore not surprising that an ancestral romance written for Philip the Good which described a fictional campaign against the infidel organised by the heirs of France, England and Scotland was found interesting enough to be translated in the 1470s or '80s, and an illuminated copy commissioned in London in the 1480s – the only fifteenth-century illuminated manuscript of a romance in English to sur-

---

119 'Choosing a book', pp. 84–86.
120 *Hours of Richard III*, pp. 62–66. And see chs 3 and 4 above.

vive. Both the French author and the English translator of the *Three Kings' Sons*,[121] are unknown. This text might be suggested as the best surviving example of direct Burgundian influence on the romance-reading of the Yorkist court, but it also illustrates the limitations of such influence: the manuscript is unique and the English version was never printed.[122]

Romances and Real Life

The idea that romances were particularly popular reading matter at the Yorkist court appears to have been based usually on two closely linked assumptions: that Caxton printed a great number of such texts *and* that he was very much influenced by the taste of the Burgundian court. Both can be rejected. Nor do the surviving manuscripts provide real evidence of the great popularity of romances. This is not to deny, however, that such stories were still well known or enjoyed. They were known because the process of socialising them, of making them *useful* in daily life, was being continued by such as Rate, and selected and revised texts were used to educate and to amuse. Despite all criticism they were still favourite source books for behaviour.[123] As Caxton wrote: 'There shalle ye see manhode, curtosye and gentylnesse'.[124]

Can we, by way of conclusion, find an example of the possible influence of romances on real life? It is well known how Duke Philip the 'Good' after the ruthless reduction of his cousin Jacqueline of Bavaria, and after robbing her of everything, sent her presents and treated her 'chivalrously'. The same duke lavishly received Margaret of Anjou after the defeat and flight of her husband, Henry VI, awarded her all the courtesy due to a queen, but would

---

121 Also called the *Chronique de Naples* and the *Histoire royale* in Burgundy.

122 Grinberg, '*Three Kings' Sons*: notes and critical commentary'; the same, '*Three Kings' Sons* and *Les Trois Fils de Rois*', pp. 521–29; Furnivall, *Three Kings' Sons*. The text was composed during the reign of Philip the Good and for him. Seven mss of the French text survive; known owners of these are Philip the Good, his sister Agnes de Bourgogne, Louise de Créquy, *née* de La Tour (her sister Gabriele also owned a copy according to her inventory, see above n. 48) and probably the Croy family. The French text was printed ten times between 1501 and 1579. It is suggestive that the ms. of the English translation also contains a short 'chronicle' proving the Yorkist claim to the crowns of England, France, Castile and Leon, composed between 1468 and 1483. On the illumination see Scott forthcoming.

123 Crane, *Insular Romance*, pp. 197–98.

124 Blake, *Caxton's Own Prose*, introduction to *Morte Darthur*, p. 126.

Fig. 75 Dancing during marriage celebrations. From Jean de Wavrin's *Chronicles of England*. Flemish, 1465–75. Vienna, Austrian National Library, MS 2534, f. 17. By permission of the Austrian National Library.

not discuss her affairs with her personally because *aux dames on ne doit parler que de joye* – to ladies one should only talk of joyful matters.[125] The cold reality of political expedience was hidden behind a façade as consciously constructed as any of Philip's specially composed romances.

But what of the Yorkist court? If a member of the Yorkist court were proposed for Gower's role of a man or woman reading a tale of love while in love and sympathising with the trials of other lovers, or acting out a part like a romance hero, or merely being aware that he or she was in a 'romantic' situation, who would it have to be? Edward IV is not a good example: he played the hot lover in the popular story of his wooing of his future queen, Elizabeth Woodville, but he also had too many mistresses to be cast for the part of the true 'romantic' lover. Richard of Gloucester would be a better candidate as his name can be linked to an episode that has many of the hallmarks of a genuine romance: the persistent wooer rescues a damsel in distress, defeats his jealous rival and marries the heiress. The story is given by one source only, the unknown Crowland chronicler, who may have been a prominent cleric at the Yorkist court.

> When the son of King Henry, to whom Lady Anne, the younger daughter of the Earl of Warwick was married, had been killed in the battle of Tewkesbury, Richard, Duke of Gloucester, wanted this same Anne as his wife. This wish did not suit the plans of his brother, the Duke of Clarence, who some time before had married the same Earl's elder daughter: he had the girl hidden away so that his brother would not know where she was, for he feared that the inheritance, which he wanted to come to himself alone by right of his wife, would be divided and he did not wish to share it with anyone. The cleverness of the Duke of Gloucester was even greater, however: he found the girl dressed as a kitchen-maid in the city of London and had her brought to the sanctuary of St Martin's.[126]

As with all medieval stories of love, true or fictional, all is not quite as simple as it sounds, not for the male lover and certainly not for the woman. Anne Neville, the lady in this case, was the potential co-heiress of her mother, the last of the Beauchamps, Anne, Countess of Warwick. The countess was still alive and both her position and that of her daughter was entirely overcast by

---

125 Chastellain, *Oeuvres*, vol. 4, pp. 284–94.
126 *Crowland Chronicle*, p. 132, the translation is our own.

the treason of her dead husband, Richard Neville, the 'Kingmaker', whose own estates were forfeit to Edward IV, the king he had betrayed, brother to Richard of Gloucester. The villain of the piece was George, Duke of Clarence, brother of Edward and Richard and husband of Anne's sister, Isabel. Like his father-in-law George had betrayed Edward IV and his behaviour had been in sharp contrast to the loyalty of Richard. In this situation Anne was an object of desire, of love in theory, whose possession would yield power and wealth, exactly like a heroine of romance. The historian knows that it was not the lovers' courage and virtue but merely the political power of the king and the good relationship between him and Richard of Gloucester that allowed the hero to gain the heroine and the heroine to realise her potential. Her only alternative to marrying the king's brother was poverty and seclusion with her equally powerless mother whose estates were desired by the York brothers. In the event the mother was treated as though she was dead and her lands divided between her two sons-in-law.

The politics of this real life case can be compared to two romances we know Richard of Gloucester owned. In *Ipomedon* the heroine is wealthy and an object of desire not only for herself but also for her estates, the hero has to prove himself worthy of her and he also has to rescue her from an evil rival. She plays an essentially passive role, like Anne Neville, but at least the reader knows she is loved and loves. The story of Palamon and Arcite has other similarities: there is a jealous rival and 'brother' who is defeated and the lady, Emily, is a totally passive object awarded to the victor by the 'king', in this case Duke Theseus.

A thin veneer of love and marriage was undoubtedly contrived to soften the contours of many a real-life battle between rivals and many a ruthless search for wealth and status, mimicking romances in a practical way, just as surely as courtly entertainment and tournaments went out of their way to imitate them at a more fantastic level. Real-life protagonists such as Anne Neville, Richard of Gloucester and Duke Philip could have compared their experiences to those of Ipomedon and his lady. The validity and relevance of these examples may be questioned but they do suggest that the events and conventions of romances played a part in real life: directly for known admirers of the genre like Duke Philip and more indirectly for such as Richard of Gloucester, both of whom may have remembered the stories from their childhood.[127]

---

127 Compare Stevens's conclusion on the all-pervasive nature of romance, *Medieval Romance*, pp. 227–37.

TEN

The Reign of Richard III and the Trade in Manuscript and Printed Books, with Special Reference to the Proviso of 1484

... we secured the acquaintance of stationers and booksellers, not only within our own country, but of those spread over the realms of France, Germany, and Italy, money flying forth in abundance to anticipate their demands; nor were they hindered by any distance or by the fury of the seas, or by the lack of means for their expenses, from sending or bringing to us the books that we required.[1]

By the late 1470s any persistent scholar, 'any person with initiative, patience and the necessary cash' could obtain any existing book.[2] The diverse collections in manuscript and print that survive for scholars and diplomats like Shirwood and Russell, acquired all over England and Europe, are examples of such successful persistence.[3] Richard III's only parliament reaffirmed and passed several acts to restrain the activities of aliens in England as artisans and merchants, but made a very specific exception of all aliens trading in books or working in any aspect of the

---

1   Richard de Bury, *Philobiblon*, p. 62.
2   Hirsch, *Printing*, p. 147.
3   Allen, 'Bishop Shirwood', passim; Kuil, 'John Russell', passim.

book trade within the country.[4] Precisely who secured this exemption is not known. No one so far has been tempted to study its background, despite the fact that it had a considerable effect on the development of printing and the native book trade in England for fifty years. No one has asked seriously what the anti-alien legislation of this parliament was actually setting out to do, nor who reacted swiftly enough to put in this very specifically directed proviso. At some moment during the last week of January 1484 someone realised the possible effect that the full range of the anti-alien bills before parliament could have on the work and trade of aliens in the book trade and reacted strongly on this specific issue close to his heart: What about my books?

Who were the men on Richard's council who could have reacted like this and who took steps to protect the book trade and the untrammelled circulation of learning? Who else in the book trade and outside it lobbied their MPs and the council on this issue? Was Richard III personally involved? The proviso is unexpected and remarkable and merits discussion for its own sake. In the context of 'Richard III's books' the special treatment accorded to books and their makers by him and his principal counsellors is in line with everything else we have learned about him and again suggests at the very least a *positive*

---

4   1 Richard III, caps. 9, 10 (= 22 Edward IV, cap. 3), 12: *Statutes of the Realm*, vol. 2, pp. 489–96; *Statutes at Large*, vol. 2, *1 Edward IV – Elizabeth*, London 1770. It is important to remember that the proviso applied to all these acts although it formed part of cap. 9. Pollard, 'The company of stationers', p. 16, does not comment on who might have instigated the proviso; Hellinga, 'Importation', pp. 208–9, assumes mistakenly that the act excluded 'foreign merchants from the right to carry out trade of any kind', whereas it only concerned the retail trade. She continues: '[the proviso] is thought to have been influenced by educated people who did not wish to lose the benefits brought by alien book dealers'; Steinberg, *Five Hundred Years*, p. 108, who adds 'this enlightened view was very likely due to the personal interest of the King and the men of his court and council'; Christianson, *Directory*, pp. 42–43, quotes the proviso and continues, 'The proviso ... would appear to have run counter to the business interests of London stationers. Throughout their history, however, London book craftsmen had regularly been affected by overseas competition, both from less expensive imported manuscripts ... and from aliens working in England, often on expensive commissions ... the novel challenge ... came from ... the proviso's main intent, the development of commerce in printed books, both by imports and through domestic production'. Armstrong, 'English purchases', p. 276, emphasises Russell's support, repeated by Christianson, 'Rise of London's book trade', p. 8, who also suggests the importer of books, Peter Actors; Ross, *Richard III*, does not mention the proviso at all; Kendall, *Richard III*, p. 285, ends: 'To Richard and his councillors belongs the honour of having devised the first piece of legislation for the protection and fostering of the art of printing and the dissemination of learning by books.'

attitude to literateness and learning. The proviso was, after all, enacted during *his* reign, by *his* only parliament.

Anti-Alien Legislation and the Parliament of 1484

The parliament that finally assembled on 23 January 1484 had been long in people's minds. The political adjustments that had accompanied the replacement of Edward V with Richard III and the subsequent rebellions of the autumn of 1483 had led to three parliaments being summoned, two of which were cancelled.[5] The act against aliens which includes the famous proviso relating to books may therefore have had a long gestation; it certainly had precedents.

Anti-alien feeling was never far below the surface and the citizens of London, who can be credited with the promotion of this act,[6] had a long history of anti-alien riots. They had been at their worst in the 1450s against the Italians, but there were also sporadic outbursts against the 'Doche', a word used to describe anyone from the Low Countries, Germany and Northern Europe, such as the foiled attack on them in Southwark in 1468 or the burning of their brewhouses there in 1470–71. The craft and merchant guilds or companies of London were all jealous of alien activity in London: the Mercers were notorious for their hatred of the Italians who dominated the supply of silks and the luxury mercery small goods, which might always include books; the Drapers eyed with suspicion any Italian or Low Country merchant who meddled in the English cloth industry; and all leading merchants who were Merchant Adventurers or Merchants of the Calais Staple resented any alien profiting from the export of English cloth and wool respectively. Lower down the scale at the artisan level, trades like the skinners, leathersellers, pewterers, goldsmiths or brewers disliked the many skilled aliens who had set up workshops in or near London. Generally, the London companies exercised a jealous tolerance towards alien craftsmen which varied with economic conditions

---

5 The first parliament had been summoned on 13 May for 25 June; 16–17 June postponed; the second was summoned *c.* 25 September for 6 November, and cancelled 2 November; the third, which met, was summoned on 9 December for 23 January. *Coronation*, pp. 17, 22, 191 n. 2; Wedgwood, *History of Parliament: Register*, pp. 465, 473, 475.

6 See Roskell, *House of Commons 1386–1421*, vol. 1, pp. 78–79, for the petitions from 'individuals' that became acts applying to the whole country.

— they admitted them to their ranks and they often turned a blind eye to illicit retailing by the non-free — but there are signs that this tolerance was lessening in the late fifteenth century and it is possible that the anti-alien legislation of 1484 was the first sign of this change. Some aliens acquired royal letters of denisation and then bought their way into membership of the appropriate company and became free of the city with six citizens acting as their sureties; others who could not afford to go through this process or who lacked the right contacts might work as subcontractors or piece-workers for native freemen. Others lived in places like Southwark and endured sporadic attacks from citizens; even the alien who was a paid-up member of a city company was spied on for his incorrigible habit of employing his fellow countrymen as servants and apprentices despite guild regulations forbidding him to do so.[7] This particular grievance over servants and the complaints that aliens spent their profits abroad, drained bullion out of the country and stole the jobs of Englishmen were standard usage in the middle ages and little different from those in use today.

In 1483–84 the several companies of London — merchant and artisan — seem to have been able to combine over the presentation of their separate grievances against aliens, or they presented several bills which were run together by the legislators. There are also signs that in 1483 there was a considerable body of opinion in the city that the numbers of alien artisans, in particular, should be controlled: the court of aldermen had been the recipients of several complaints and fears from artisan companies from the 1470s,[8] and the alien subsidy collected on 16 June 1483 had provided the civic authorities with ample evidence of the large numbers of aliens in London and its environs. Some citizens were extremely busy on parliamentary business in January 1484: the Pewterers paid out for labouring the restraint of tin, and another 7s 4d for 'the sute at Westmynster', and later on 30 January recorded 'And God save kyng Rechard', presumably in satisfaction at the work of the parliament;[9] the Leathersellers paid 10d

7   Thomas, *Plea and Memoranda Rolls 1364–81*, pp. xlvii–xlviii. Flenley, 'London and foreign merchants', pp. 289–91, largely corrected by Bolton, 'City and the crown, 1456–61', pp. 11–24. Thrupp, 'Aliens in and around London', pp. 251-72 (a confusion is caused by Thrupp's referring to the subsidy of 1483 as '1484'). Sutton, 'Richard III, the city of London and Southwark', pp. 289–91. Bolton, 'The alien subsidy of 1483', forthcoming. The new rates of the alien tax set in 1482 and assessed with great assiduity in 1483 may be an indication of growing anti-alien feeling.

8   Sharpe, *Letter Book L*, pp. xx–xxii.

9   Pewterers' Wardens' Accounts, f. 82v. Welch, *Pewterers' Company*, pp. 56–57.

for a 'supplecacyon at the parleament tyme', another 13s 4d for a 'sewte to the parleament with othir craftes', and 8d for 'a powche for a burges of the parleament' who was presumably to present their point of view.[10]

There was nothing new about this activity; the artisan companies of London were as practised as their richer fellow citizens at lobbying parliaments.[11] They had, for example, acted in concert over alien competition during the parliament of 1461: the rare survival of a fragment of a Lords' Journal and the accounts of the London artisan companies of Cutlers and Pewterers combine to show that the 'handicraftmen' and women secured two acts prohibiting the import of a wide range of small manufactured goods. In 1461 the rallying call had been that English men and women were put out of work,[12] and it was to be re-employed in 1484. Richard III's parliament was to re-enact the two anti-alien acts of Edward IV's first parliament: the prohibition of the import of a wide variety of small goods, mostly made of metal and leather but including such things as painted images, and the mercery goods made by silkwomen (caps. 12 and 10).[13] Part of the 'new' act of 1484 was also a re-affirmation of an act of 1478 which had tried to force aliens to spend their profits on English goods and not take bullion out of the country.[14] Perhaps a new king coming to the throne in the hazardous manner of an Edward IV or a Richard III was particularly vulnerable to the chauvinist arguments of Londoners: in 1461 the king himself had put in the bill of the merchants,[15] and it is not impossible that Richard III made a comparable gesture of friendship to

---

10 London, Leathersellers' Company, Liber Curtes, p. 49.

11 Barron, 'London and parliament', pp. 343–67, for all aspects of this subject, much of which applies to the parliament of 1484 in general terms.

12 Dunham, *Fane Fragment*, pp. 65–71, esp. n. 8. Barron, 'London and parliament', pp. 360–61. Barron adds details about the preoccupations of the merchants of London with controlling the Hanse and collecting debts owed to them, matters which did not secure the new king's approval as they had financial implications for himself. And see Bolton, 'City and the crown', esp. pp. 18–21.

13 These were re-enactments of 3 Edward IV, cap. 3, 4. See Dunham, *Fane Fragment*, p. 67, for the finishing off of legislation begun in 1461 in the parliament of 1463. The act protecting silkwomen had been first passed in 1456 and was regularly renewed: 3 Edward IV, cap. 4; 22 Edward IV, cap. 3; 1 Richard III, cap. 10, and later. Neither ms. nor printed books were mentioned. And see Cobb, *Overseas Trade*, p. xxxvii.

14 17 Edward IV cap. 1 was designed to last for seven years; it was later reaffirmed in 3 Henry VII, cap. 8, to last for ever. Munro, *Wool, Cloth and Gold*, p. 179 n. 86.

15 Dunham, *Fane Fragment*, pp. 19, 65. But see n. 12, above, for Barron's correction and expansion of Dunham.

the city. It was as easy for Richard III as it had been for Edward IV in 1461 to endorse acts like these which pleased his subjects and did not affect royal finances directly. For that reason especially, the proviso over books stands out: suddenly someone, perhaps the king himself, was concerned about what was going on.

There is every sign that Londoners found in Richard III a king very willing to listen to them: he needed money. He had had to pay for a coronation, a progress, and an expensive autumn of rebellion and he had not yet had a chance to ask for the usual parliamentary grant of customs revenue.[16] London had been almost as helpful to Richard during his accession as it had been to Edward IV; and it had been alarmed but firm, under the command of the duke of Norfolk and its mayors, Edmund Shaa and Robert Billesden, in the face of the rebellion in Kent and the southern counties.[17] On 6 January Richard invited the leading citizens to his Epiphany feast in the White Hall and gave them a gold and jewelled cup, worth 100 marks, for use on civic occasions, and offered to bestow on them the borough of Southwark as part of the city's liberties, with £10,000 to build walls and ditches around it. What else was discussed on this propitious occasion? Anti-alien legislation or the suppression of the hated benevolences, the forced loans that had recently caused trouble between leading Londoners and Edward IV in January 1483. Future loans may have not been high on the agenda because it seems the king had already negotiated the money he needed with leading Londoners, mostly on pledges of jewels and plate, and he had sold outright other plate worth over £500. What he needed most was a smooth passage in parliament for a life-grant of the customs revenues of the realm, and, of course, an unopposed acceptance of his title to the crown.[18]

By 10 January Richard was at Canterbury, continuing the post-coronation progress of the previous year which had been interrupted by rebellion, while boroughs and counties began to hold parliamentary elections throughout the country.[19] The London men chosen on the

---

16 Horrox, 'Financial memoranda of the reign of Edward V', pp. 197–244, for the financial situation of his protectorship and early reign.

17 The change-over was 28 October. The fact that Billesden was the only one of Richard's mayors not to receive a knighthood may indicate that he had little to do with London's defence.

18 Sutton, 'Richard III, the city of London and Southwark', pp. 289, 292–93.

19 For this progress see e.g. Sutton and Hairsine, 'Richard III at Canterbury', pp. 343–48. Leicester held elections very promptly, Bateson, *Records of the Borough of Leicester*, vol. 2, no. ccxix.

13th[20] were Sir William Haryot, a draper and past mayor famous for his trade with Italy, several of his sons living in Milan;[21] John Fenkyll, another draper and relative of Haryot; Thomas Fitzwilliam, a member of a well-to-do Northern family and the city's recorder (its chief lawyer and spokesman), who had been elected 19 June 1483 with an eye on the Northern connections of the anticipated new king, Richard of Gloucester; and fourthly John Pickering, mercer and governor of the Merchant Adventurers in the Low Countries (1471–98), from whom Richard III had just purchased nearly £1300 worth of goods.[22] Any or all of these men may have energetically supported all or part of the measures that became chapter nine of Richard's statutes; they may also have been cynically aware that that part of the act which affected the Italians was unlikely ever to be implemented. As three sophisticated merchants and one lawyer they may have understood how foolish were the chauvinist fears of the less well-informed petitioners to parliament.[23]

Richard III returned from the south counties, via Sandwich and Dover, to Westminster to open parliament on 23 January. Wearing crimson velvet furred with ermine[24] and seated on his throne in the Painted Chamber, he listened to the opening sermon of Chancellor Russell, which was based on a quotation from the Bible: '… in a single human body there are many limbs and organs, all with different functions'.[25] The chancellor related this text to the 'politike body' of England and its members, whose duty it was to give each other mutual support.[26] By the time Russell was addressing parliament the wheels of the machinery that turned bills into statutes

---

20 For all these men see Sutton, 'Richard III, the city of London and Southwark', pp. 293–94; other references follow.

21 For Richard III's letters to the duke of Milan concerning Haryot's sons, 10 Feb. 1484, *Harl. 433*, vol. 3, pp. 53–57; Richard paid Edward IV's debts to Haryot and he had assisted Richard over his coronation costs, PRO, E 404/78/3, no. 39. Haryot's trade with Italy would not necessarily have ensured his opposition to anti-Italian legislation: compare William Cantelowe who was deeply involved in both the trade and the anti-Italian riots of 1455, Bolton, 'City and the crown', pp. 12–15, 17; Holmes, 'Anglo-Florentine trade in 1451', pp. 371–86.

22 For Fitzwilliam, *Coronation*, p. 23. Pickering had supplied Richard with arras in 1475, etc., Horrox and Sutton, 'Expenses of Richard Duke of Gloucester, 1475–77', pp. 267–68.

23 There is no evidence in the city's journals of how the aldermen and common council wanted the city's official views presented to parliament or what these were.

24 See Sutton and Hairsine, 'Richard III at Canterbury', for his progress. The robe is described in his great wardrobe accounts, *Coronation*, pp. 82, 175.

25 Rom. 12: 4.

26 *RP*, vol. 6, p. 237; and see below.

had already begun to move. Whoever instigated the bill against aliens, it had to be drawn up in its proper form by lawyers or expert scriveners, after enquiries had been made about its legal possibilities and prospects.[27] At the end of the chancellor's speech it would be announced when petitions were to be presented – usually within a few days – to the 'receivers of petitions', whose names would be read out.[28] Private bills were either handed in personally, or via an individual member of parliament, or, as was becoming more frequent, by the commons as a body. The chancellor and even the king sometimes deigned to present a bill themselves. In 1461 the predecessor of the 1484 bill 'conteyning the hurts and remedies of marchaudises made by the marchaunts of London was put in by the kings owne hande'.[29] If Richard III was indeed as willing as his brother had been to lend support to his London merchants he may have done the same, before or after the proviso was added.

The receivers did little more than receive, but they could reject a petition when it was not suitable in form or content. One of the receivers in 1484 was Dr Thomas Hutton, clerk of parliament and diplomat in Richard III's service.[30] It is not known whether he or any of his colleagues had any links with the book trade or the printing press or had a particular love of books. At the next stage the 'triers of petitions', prelates, noblemen and justices, could again refuse a petition, or pass it on to the king and council. It had become usual that even private bills were presented by the commons as a body and were handed directly to the clerk of the parliament.[31] This was the quickest and most successful method for individuals and groups of private

---

27 Dunham, *Fane Fragment*, p. 65; Myers, 'Parliamentary petitions', pp. 386–88.
28 Myers, 'Parliamentary petitions', pp. 389, 393–94.
29 Dunham, *Fane Fragment*, pp. 19, 65.
30 Emden, *Cambridge*, pp. 323–24; Pollard, 'Fifteenth-century clerks of parliament', p. 156. The other receivers of English petitions were Thomas Barowe, William Bolton and Richard Skipton, masters in Chancery, Wedgwood, *History of Parliament: Biographies*, p. 486.
31 Myers, 'Parliament 1422–1509', p. 168. The triers of English petitions of 1484 included Thomas Bourchier, Archbishop of Canterbury, Thomas Kemp, Bishop of London, Robert Stillington, Bishop of Bath and Wells, James Goldwell, Bishop of Norwich, John Howard, Duke of Norfolk, Edmund Grey, Earl of Kent, Francis, Viscount Lovell, and the lawyers William Husee and Richard Neele. Any of these men could have realised the implications of the act for the book trade at this early stage.

persons, particularly when the clerk was encouraged by gifts to speed the bill on its way.[32]

The speaker chosen by the commons and formally presented to the king on 26 January was William Catesby, already Richard's councillor and trusted servant.[33] His was an important office: in an earlier draft of his opening speech Chancellor Russell had compared the speaker to the powerful tribunes of the people in Rome: 'yn the lower house … alle ys directed by the speker *quasi per tribunum*'.[34] From the middle of the fifteenth century the speaker was usually very much the king's man, but at the same time he was by duty bound to represent the commons and their wishes. The least he could do for a petition was to have it read at an advantageous moment.[35] Catesby's usefulness to the city may be reflected in the gift of a livery gown, as a royal councillor, on 15 December 1484.[36]

A bill would be read out several times to the lords as well as to the commons; in the process it could be amended, merged with others, or its scope could be changed, and discussion would take place.[37] It must have been at this stage, while it was being considered whether the petition against aliens and particularly the Italians was 'reasonable' and 'behofull' and 'not prejudicial to the crown', that one of the listeners – lord, bishop or the king himself? – pointed out that a proviso *had* to be made. Provisos often originated with the government and the king, usually because they affected the king personally, especially his finances or his property or those of members of his family.[38] Less material motives may have played a part this time.

---

32 Myers, 'Parliamentary petitions', pp. 398–402.

33 Roskell, *The Commons and Their Speaker*, pp. 294–7, 351–2; the same, 'William Catesby, counsellor to Richard III', passim; Williams, 'The hastily drawn up will of William Catesby', passim.

34 Nichols, *Grants*, pp. lviii–lxiii and liii–lvi.

35 Myers, 'Parliament 1422–1509', pp. 173–74; 181–82; Roskell, *The Commons and Their Speaker*, pp. 278–97.

36 CLRO, London Journal 9, f. 10(42). Catesby's cultural interests are not well documented. He owned the 'Bedford Hours and Psalter', BL, MS Add. 42131, a magnificent volume which he seems to have acquired as an executor of its previous owner, Anthony, Earl Rivers.

37 Dunham, *Fane Fragment*, pp. 70–73; Myers, 'Parliament 1422–1509', p. 174.

38 Mainly exemptions from acts of resumption; *ibid.*, pp. 175–76.

The Anti-Alien Act of 1484

The act in restraint of aliens set out first the well-tried grievances of the commons of England on this subject as presented in the original bill, and second the remedies authorised by king and parliament. Italian merchants were the main target: they kept their goods in store until they fetched high prices; they tampered with their goods; they sold by retail and not merely wholesale; they took the profits out of the country as bullion and did not buy English goods with them; they plotted deceits and carried out secret business deals with other aliens in the numerous houses they owned or leased throughout the country; they hosted other aliens; and they bought up English wool and woollen cloth which they resold in England, while part of the wool they gave to clothmakers to be made into cloth 'at their pleasure'. Turning to alien artisans the act asserted that they took the 'easy occupations' and employed only people from their own country, putting Englishmen out of work; they imported vast quantities of wares which they sold by retail, and they spent their profits abroad.[39]

The act insisted that all Italian merchants who had not acquired royal letters of denisation should from henceforth sell their imported goods wholesale only, and buy English goods with the proceeds within a set period after their arrival in the country; unsold goods were to be taken away again; none of them were to traffic in English wool or woollen cloths within the realm or commission cloth to be made. Forfeits and fines were imposed. The misconceptions over how the Italians conducted their trade which lay behind these chauvinist rulings and the fact that there was no possibility of the latter being enforced hardly concern us here. The timing of the act was part of the cut and thrust of commercial rivalries at a time when English merchants were taking an ever increasing role in the Italian trade, shipping wool to the Mediterranean in English ships and using Pisa as the staple port for English wool.[40] The Italians of London – a tight community of about fifty – ensured that the clauses in this act which affected them were soon a matter of discussion between the citizens of London and Richard III's council and were repealed in

39 1 Richard III, cap. 9, *Statutes of the Realm*, vol. 2, pp. 489–93; *Statutes at Large*, vol. 2, pp. 60–62.
40 Mallett, 'Anglo-Florentine commercial relations', pp. 250–65, esp. 257.

the next parliament.[41] The particular clauses that tried to ensure that all bullion or profit was spent on English goods did not get repealed and was reaffirmed in 1488; these applied to *all* aliens and were standard copy for anti-alien legislation with a long series of precedents, the most recent being a statute of 1478.[42]

Alien *artisans* had less power than wealthy Italian merchants to protect themselves against the section of the act that concerned them. No person not born within the realm was in future to work as an artisan in England, unless they were in the employment of a native; no alien who had not bought letters of denisation could make or commission cloth; those already working in England would only be able sell their wares wholesale; and no alien artificer would be able to take apprentices or servants unless they were his own children or native born. To encourage prosecution half of the fine paid by those caught was to go to the civic authority concerned. Essentially this legislation was directed against new artisans who might come to the country, and the main vexation for those already in the country was that they could now be prosecuted for their alien apprentices and servants with a statute and not just guild regulations as encouragement. The recent returns of the alien tax levied in June 1483 had provided plenty of ammunition for the civic authorities on this point: a wealthy 'Doche' goldsmith and court supplier like Marcellus Maures had a household of sixteen aliens, and the printer John Lettou and his partner William Ravenswalde employed four aliens.[43] Some prosecutions are known to have started on this issue, but they depended largely on local enthusiasm.[44]

---

41 On 10 January 1485 two aldermen and four common councilmen were assigned by the court of aldermen to consult the king's council about this act *concernen' mercator Italie* and its execution, CLRO, Journal 9, f. 63. 1 Henry VII, cap. 10 (*Statutes of the Realm*, vol. 2, pp. 507–08; *Statutes at Large*, vol. 2, pp. 66–67). De Roover, *Gresham on Foreign Exchange*, pp. 38–49, esp. 42.

42 3 Henry VII, cap. 8 (*Statutes of the Realm*, vol. 2, pp. 517–18; *Statutes at Large*, vol. 2, pp. 70–71). Munro, *Wool, Cloth and Gold*, p. 178 and n. 86; see also De Roover (preceding note).

43 PRO, E 179/242/25, mm. 8d (Lettou), 9d (Maures). *Coronation*, p. 371.

44 Veale, *English Fur Trade*, p. 153, gives examples of prosecution in the 1490s. And see PRO, C 1/83/44, 105/32.

In all Richard III's parliament was of keen interest to Londoners. The mere abolition of benevolences was sufficient in itself to call forth the Pewterers' exuberant goodwill: 'God save King Richard!'[45]

The Proviso and the Book Trade of London in 1484

As mentioned above the 1484 parliament saw the reissue of two existing anti-alien acts and a new act.[46] The proviso regarding the book artisans and dealers applied to all these acts and all legislation in this parliament, although it was appended to the 'new' act, chapter nine.

> Provided alwey that this Acte or any parcel therof, or any other Acte made or to be made in this present parliament, in no wise extende or be prejudiciall any lette hurte or impediment to any Artificer or merchaunt straungier of what Nacion or Contrey he be or shalbe of, for bryngyng into this Realme, or sellyng by retaill or otherwise, of any manner bokes wrytten or imprynted, or for the inhabitynge within the said Realme for the same intent, or to any writer lympner bynder or imprynter[47] of suche bokes, as he hath or shall have to sell by wey of merchaundise, or

---

45 There were *three* acts of this parliament aimed at the alien: the one under discussion here; the extension by ten years of the act of the 1483 parliament which prohibited the import of silkwomen's goods (silk laces, ribbons, etc., cap. 10); and the act that prohibited the import of small wares in general (cap. 12) which was essentially a reissue of that drafted for Edward IV's first parliament in 1461 and made law in 1463 (3 Edward IV cap. 4), certainly of interest to any artisan manufacturing small metal and leather goods in England. It included 'peynted glasses, paynted Papers, peynted forcers [caskets], paynted images, paynted Clothes, any beten gold or neten silver wrought in papers for Payntours ...'. It is not certain that any of these items were directly relevant to the book trade, but it is obvious that the proviso was not concerned to safeguard the importation of works of *art*, only of books as vehicles of learning.

46 Caps 9, 10 and 11.

47 Some printed translations e.g. the *Statutes at Large* have: 'scivener allumynour *reader* or printer' (our italics).

for their abode in the same Reame for the exercisyng of the said occupacions, this Acte or any parte therof notwithstondyng.[48]

The proviso is concerned with the making, importation and selling, both
wholesale and retail, of any kind of book, but does not go into detail. It
has to be remembered here that the act against aliens itself did not prohibit
the wholesale trade in books. There is a slight emphasis on written books:
they and their makers are mentioned first. This is probably due to the still
prevailing unfamiliarity with printing rather than to the greater importance of manuscript books in the context of the proviso. The phrases used
do not point to a 'professional' having chosen the words. Parchmeners as
well as stationers were omitted. 'Scrivener' was probably used in a non-
technical sense and merely means 'scribe'. Binders and printers, though
they were mentioned last, were proved by later events to be the craftsmen
most affected by the proviso.

There were foreign scribes in England, especially from the Low
Countries, who worked for long or short periods in England and would
have welcomed the proviso. Many of these worked in the university
milieu, copying mainly Latin scholarly texts, for themselves or wealthier
patrons and scholars. There were also foreign bookbinders.[49] Some of these
scribes and binders no doubt worked for native stationers. One can assume
that there were illuminators, too, in similar situations, working for a single
book collector, or in professional workshops, collaborating so closely with
English artists that it cannot be established which painter was actually
foreign or merely trained in foreign countries or inspired by continental
trends. Very few of their names are known and they belonged to a section

---

48 The French text reads: 'Purveu toutz foitz que cest acte ou ascune part dicell, ne ascune
autre acte fait ou affaire en le dit parlement, en null maner extende ou soit prejudiciall ascun
destourbance damage ou empediment au ascun artificer ou marchaunt estraunge, de quell
nacion ou paiis it soit ou sera, de ou pur amesnance en cest Roialme ou vendicion par retaille
ou autrement dascuns maners livres escriptez ou enpressez, ou pur lenhabitacion deinz le dit
Roialme pur mesme lentent, ou au ascun escrivener alluminour liour ou enpressour autrement
dit imprintour de tielx livres, quelx il ad ou avera a vendre par voie de marchandice, ou pur
leur demeure en mesme le Roialme pur lexcercicion de les ditz occupacions; cest acte ou
ascune part dicell nient contristeant'. *Statutes of the Realm*, 1816, vol. 2, p. 493. Both texts are
here given in full because at times they have been badly rendered by commentators.
49 Mynors, 'Werken', p. 97; *Duke Humphrey's Library* mentions several. No alien scribe,
illuminator or bookbinder is described as such in the 1483 poll tax for London, but John
Richardson, described as a stationer, has been identified as a bookbinder, Christianson, 'Rise
of London's book trade', p. 9. Scott, *Mirroure*, pp. 43, 52, 55, 58.

La tresfamde et tref
biouenxeufe loenge et
magnificonte de noftre
fauuenr Jhefucaft et defa tref
douce et treftjlorieufe mere gui
font canfe et mouuement de

Fig. 76 A copyist at work. The manuscript belonged to the chronicler Jean de Wavrin, whose arms appear in the initial *A*. Flemish, 1450s. Ghent, University Library, MS 470, f. 1. By permission of the University Library.

of the craft that was to die out.[50] They would not have been numerous or influential enough to lobby for or support the proviso, but some of the members of the council may have been their employers or patrons.

There were several, much more prominent, groups of people in the book trade who might have objected to the proviso and supported the alien act: the native stationers, who were concerned to keep all aspects of book production in their own control, and the printers already established in England, who were mainly aliens themselves and who were being forced out of business by the flood of books from abroad. The stationers of London were not only handicraftmen. They were the dealers of the book trade – not great entrepreneurs like the merchant adventurers, Caxton or Wylcocks, but lesser men who supplied the required text from an exemplar, having it copied, decorated and bound, in-house or out as necessary. The mistery which was to become the Stationers'

---

50 Scott, 'A mid-fifteenth-century illuminator's shop', pp. 173, 194; *Hours of Richard III*, pp. 8–9. We do not even know whether, for instance, any of the famous illuminated Flemish mss of Edward IV were finished or altered in England, but there may have been someone in London who had the talent to paint the Tower of London in the well-known copy of the poems of Charles of Orleans, BL, MS Royal 16 F ii, f. 73. Scott, *Caxton Master*, represented the 'Caxton Master' as a Low Countries artist working in England.

Company[51] had been founded in 1403 when the textwriters and limners combined. Without the approval of this company it is unlikely any alien stationer or printer could have been admitted to the freedom of London or operate very successfully,[52] but it is equally true that they would not necessarily have opposed him. There is little sign of organised opposition to the actual trade of printing, for example, before the famous assault on Richard Pynson in 1500, but the friction between alien and native over selling books could be intense and the pressure of the stationers to control all printing and destroy the aliens' privileges granted by the proviso of 1484 and assimilate them into the company *increased* in the sixteenth century and was finally successful in 1534.[53]

By 1484 printing was an established part of the London book trade. Its benefits were well understood by royal officials, the clergy, as well as by such professions as the law, as it meant cheaper and readily available textbooks, advertisements, broadsheets, proclamations, religious souvenirs and indulgences. Members of parliament and lawyers were particularly aware of the advantages of having multiple copies of parliament's own statutes swiftly available: sessional printing was first tried out in 1484.[54] Unlike manuscript production, printing was largely dominated by aliens. Those who were interested could find out precisely how many aliens in London were in the trade from the lists of those paying the poll tax levied on aliens on 16 June 1483 at Guildhall. The surviving lists show that someone carefully inserted 'bokprynter' above the names of John Lettou, John Hawkes, Henry Frankenberg and Bernard van Stando, his partner. One of the assessors of the tax was the mercer, William Pratte, Caxton's friend of fifty years standing, so Caxton was well informed of his competitors if he did not know them personally already. All these men were householders and may have protected themselves by becoming denizens and free of the city, so they stood in no personal danger from the legislation except over its encouragement of prosecution for the employment and apprenticeship of aliens. John Lettou, along with William Ravenswalde – presumably to be identified as William de Machlinia – had four workers in 1483, Frankenberg had five, Caxton in Westminster is known to

---

51 Pollard, 'Company of stationers', esp. pp. 9–13, 45.
52 *Ibid.*, p. 19.
53 Pollard, 'Company of stationers', pp. 17–18, 20, shows conflict; countered by Christianson, *Directory*, pp. 43–44.
54 See below.

have had Wynkyn de Worde working for him and probably still had an entirely alien workforce for his press at this date.[55]

Caxton may have been concerned at the potential effect of the legislation, but only in relation to his workforce; otherwise, as a native, a merchant adventurer and mercer of considerable standing, and as an inhabitant of Westminster sanctuary he had no personal fear of repercussions; he also specialised in English books, for which there was no competition as yet from the continent.[56] If the increased supervision of the activities of alien merchants selling books concerned him, he would surely have been able to circumvent it and even profit from it.[57] The one known English entrepreneur of the printed book in the 1480s, besides William Caxton, was William Wylcocks, a draper and common councilman of London, a royal supplier and controller of the subsidies in the port of London and, like Caxton, a merchant adventurer.[58] He paid for the first two known productions of the printer, John Lettou, in 1480–81, the Latin texts of Antonius Andreas's commentary on Aristotle's *Metaphysics*, edited by Thomas Penketh (a man well known to Richard III) and Thomas Waleys's commentary on the psalms.[59] Wylcocks probably encouraged Lettou to set up business in the city and may have acted as one of the citizen sureties required to vouch for an alien being admitted to the freedom of the city – he himself was married to an alien.[60] A merchant adventurer background was the most likely to encourage a man to promote the printed book, not only because of the nature of 'venturing', but also because he could himself import the large quantities of paper

55 PRO, E 179/242/25, mm. 8d, 9d, 10, other trades were also inserted between the lines (e.g. m. 8d), but 'bokprynter' is always inserted. See also Sutton, 'Caxton was a mercer', pp. 134–38. The Westminster returns on the alien tax of 1483 do not include a workforce identifiable as Caxton's.

56 Gerard Leeu of Gouda was to print English texts in Antwerp in the early 1490s, his own *Paris and Vienne* in 1492 and Caxton's *Chronicles of England* in 1493; see *Cinquième Centenaire de l'Imprimerie*, items 136, 138.

57 On Caxton's importation see e.g. Kerling, 'Caxton and the trade in printed books'.

58 Biography, *Coronation*, pp. 414–15, and see Sutton, 'Caxton was a mercer', pp. 134–35.

59 Duff, *Fifteenth-Century Books*, nos. 26 (Aristotle) and 396 (Waleys). Rhodes, *Incunabula*, pp. 17, 33, nos. 80 and 1721. Arber, *Revelations to the Monk of Evesham*, pp. 3–4 (Arber miscalls him Thomas Wylcocks). For Penketh see also below.

60 Plomer, *Wynkyn de Worde*, p. 57. Pollard 'Company of stationers', pp. 18–22, on the importance of the freedom without which Lettou would have found it very difficult to operate successfully. For Wylcock's other printing ventures, Duff, 'Early chancery proceedings', pp. 410, 416–17.

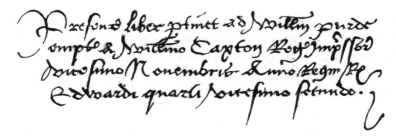

Fig. 77 *Ex libris* in a copy of Caxton's edition of Ralph Higden's *Polycronicon* (after July 1482): *Presens liber pertinet ad Willelmum Purde emptus a Willelmo Caxton regis impressore vicesimo Novembris Anno Regni Regis Edwardi quarti vicesimo secundo* (this book belongs to William Purde; [it was] bought from William Caxton the king's printer on 20 November in the twenty-second year of the reign of King Edward IV [1482]). Private collection.

required – the single most expensive investment of any printing venture – and avoid another middleman. Little else is known about Wylcocks and nothing indicates whether he knew Penketh personally, although it goes without saying he would have known of such a famous preacher. Nor is there much to be found about the two other known English entrepreneurs in this field, Roger Thorney and John Tate. Both were at the height of their careers too late to be significant in relation to the 1484 proviso, but both were merchant adventurers like Wylcocks and Caxton and both were mercers like Caxton. Thorney provided at least one copy text to Wynkyn de Worde and promoted two reissues of Caxton's *De proprietatibus rerum* and *Polychronicon* in 1495, and John Tate set up the first paper mill in England in the 1490s no doubt with an eye on the needs of printers. Wynkyn de Worde in his poem praising Caxton in *De proprietatibus rerum* had no hesitation in linking their names and activities with those of his former master – Wylcocks and Lettou are ignored.[61] Thorney and Tate may not have been involved in the events of 1484 but they are a rare indication of how the book trade was viewed by the more cultivated of English entrepreneurs. Alien and Englishman worked together for profit when opportunity existed, but this could be a temporary alliance.

Which printers were well known to royal officials and in particular those of parliament and council in 1484? It was either William de Machlinia, the partner and successor of John Lettou who probably died late in 1483 or early

---

61 Blake, *England's First Publisher*, pl. 63, gives most of the poem. For Thorney see Bone, 'Extant manuscripts', pp. 284–306, esp. 296 (some of the poem quoted, but not the lines on Tate); Hellinga, *Caxton in Focus*, p. 49 (includes the lines on Tate). On Tate himself see Hunter, *Papermaking*, pp. 115–16 (lines quoted); Hills, *John Tate*, passim.

1484, or possibly Caxton, who printed the statutes of the 1484 parliament (in law French).[62] Caxton certainly printed those of 1485–90 (in English) by which date it is usually supposed Machlinia's business had failed.[63]

It is worth considering the idea that Caxton was the king's printer by the end of Edward IV's reign. The straightforward evidence is slight as it derives solely from an inscription in a copy of Caxton's *Polychronicon* made by its purchaser, William Purde, who wrote that he bought it from Caxton, *regis impressor*,[64] William Purde was a mercer like Caxton and may have been well informed and interested. The posts of the king's ser-jeants, ranging from his tailor to pavilioner and goldsmith, were all long established; these officers took 12d a day and seasonal liveries and were usually citizens of London.[65] By 1482 the 'king's printer' may have been

---

62 There is still not sufficient evidence to prove beyond doubt who printed these statutes, see Duff, *A Century*, pp. 24, 97; Elton, 'Sessional printing of statutes', pp. 68, 72–75; Pantzer, 'Printing the English statutes, 1484–1640', pp. 69–114. Elton opts for Caxton and points out how quickly the advantages of printing the statutes were realised; from the first the texts were sacrosanct and carefully produced (p. 70). He does not refer to the problem of whether Caxton could have been the first king's printer, and also, surprisingly, accords Caxton the *initiative* for the printing (pp. 75–76). It seems more likely the initiative was official and done with more than the mere 'aid of the clerks of the parliament who controlled the records on which the prints depended'. Pantzer assumes that Machlinia printed the statutes because printing in law French was his speciality (p. 71), but goes on to say that 'special sorts were not actually necessary to print law French'. Another argument put forward by Pantzer in Pollard and Redgrave, no. 9347, p. 420, is the fact that at least three of the surviving fragments of Richard's statutes come from bindings of de Machlinia's *Nova Statuta*; it may be added, however, that binding waste is usually found in the binder's shop, not in the printer's.

63 There seems to be no hard evidence that Machlinia's business really failed, or that it continued to be run by Pynson, Plomer, *Wynkyn de Worde*, pp. 110–12. As there was such a tied market for the year books and law French works in which he is assumed to have specialised, it seems reasonable to assume his business escaped the fate of printers who unwisely competed in the Latin market and that he survived.

64 Blake, *Caxton's World*, pp. 75–76, citing Blades, *Life and Typography of William Caxton*, vol. 2, p. 128: *Presens liber pertinet ad Willelmum Purde emptus a Willelmo Caxton regis impressor vicesimo Novembris anno Regis Edwardi quarti vicesimo secundo* [20 Nov. 1482]; see fig. 77.
It is known that from 1503 William Faques (Fawkes) and others bore the same title officially; this may mean that even in 1482 the words denoted an office and were more than merely descriptive. It was in editions of the *statutes* that Richard Pynson and William Fawkes *claimed* to be 'king's printer'; no patent of their privileges survives. Fawkes's claim only survives in this manner; Pynson was granted an annuity on 20 June 1512, *Letters and Papers Foreign and Domestic, Henry VIII*, vol. 1, pt 1, 1509–13, p. 364; Winger, 'Regulations', p. 164. Pollard and Redgrave, nos. 9356–57.

65 Admitted to Mercers 1467, Mercers' Company, London, List of Members from 1347. For other king's craftsmen, *Coronation*, pp. 61–65.

one of them. As said above the conveniences of printing were already acknowledged by the 1480s: proclamations were prime candidates for official printing and from 1484 the printing of the statutes is likely to have been sessional.[66] The surviving print of the so-called *Promise of Matrimony* from 1482, publishing to Edward IV's subjects his grievances over the king of France's breaking of the treaty of Picquigny and the betrothal of the dauphin to Edward's eldest daughter, is clear evidence of government awareness of the value of printing for propaganda.[67] Again it is not certain who printed this item; Caxton was in Westminster and may have been the obvious choice. If he was printing such items as the *Promise of Matrimony* he could have referred to himself as king's printer. It is arguable that it was in 1482–85 that Caxton took his editorial duties as a publisher most seriously and began to make improvements to the layout and internal organisation of his books; it was the period when his press was at its busiest.[68] Whether he was indeed the king's printer by patent or only in his own and others' opinion, it remains debatable whether he would have used his undoubted expertise in diplomacy and his acquaintance with such men as Chancellor Russell – whose speech to Charles the Bold of Burgundy on the occasion of the duke's receiving the Garter he had once printed – to argue the cause of the alien book artisan and dealer.

What printers, apart from those in London and Westminster, had the ability to organise any protest against the 1484 legislation? The answer seems to be none. A printer was operating in Oxford from 1478 and, although the first books issued bear no publisher's name, they were probably the work of Theodoric Rood of Cologne, who produced a number of books there 1481–86. The first books were Latin texts aimed at the university and clerical market, but after 1481 more works by English authors were printed in an attempt to put on the market other books than those already being published abroad at lower prices. By 1485 at least Rood had a partnership with Thomas Hunt, an Oxford bookseller, and

---

66 Elton, 'Sessional printing', p. 75; the statutes were not consistently printed sessionally from then on; their printing was also a natural development in their publication which had formerly been done extensively in manuscript.

67 One copy survives, formerly BL, MS Royal 17 D xv, now IB 55451 (Pollard and Redgrave, no. 9176: *W. de Machlinia*, 1483, '... possibly printed in connection with the opening of parliament on 20 January 1483'). Duff, *Fifteenth-Century Books*, no. 351, dates it to 'after March 1486'. Picot and Stein, *Recueil de pièces*, p. 303, date it to 1483–85. See also *John Vale's Book*, pp. 253–55.

68 Blake, *England's First Publisher*, pp. 119, 127.

together in that year they produced the *Epistolae* of Phalaris in Latin by Francesco Griffolini with a verse prologue by Pietro Carmeliano.[69] Rood and Hunt did object to the importation of printed books as is clear from the verse at the end of this edition. It boasts that the Venetians had needed a Frenchman, Nicholas Jenson, to teach them the art of printing, but that native genius had taught England. The text continues:

Celatos Veneti nobis transmittere libros
Cedite: nos aliis vendimus, o Veneti.[70]

(Stop sending us your printed books,
Venetians, *we* now sell them to others.)

Rood and his English patrons and partners inserted no such advertisement in their other surviving imprints. His last book, printed in the next year, was an English book of sermons, the *Festial* by Mirk, and later the same year, it seems, the flood of books from abroad discouraged his investors and stopped his press.[71] At no time in the 1480s can Rood be seen as a successful entrepreneur capable of lobbying parliament, although possibly Thomas Hunt could have tried on his behalf. Only James Goldwell, Bishop of Norwich, briefly patron of the Oxford press,[72] could have presented the aliens' case, but his personal inclination may have favoured a good supply of books from abroad. Small printers, already established in England in the 1480s and desirous of printing Latin texts really needed legislation that would stop the flood of imports, something that the alien act of 1484 could not hope to stop – even without the proviso – because it did not prohibit the wholesale trade.[73] The same flood destroyed the only other provincial English printing press of the 1480s, that at St Albans. Like

---

69 Bodleian Library, 4° C 40 jur.; Duff, *Fifteenth-Century Books*, no. 348; De La Mare, *Humphrey*, no. 121; Weiss, *Humanism*, p. 172. And see above ch. 5.

70 The text goes on to say 'the art of printing Latin that was yours, is now here, and though Vergil wrote that the British live at the far end of the world [*Eclogues*, 1, 67], the Latin language pleases them well'.

71 Blake, 'The spread of printing in English', pp. 57-61.

72 For Goldwell see below.

73 The success of Caxton and Günther Zainer is attributable to their concentration on vernacular books and their own translations and their avoidance of competition with Italian production of Latin texts, Hirsch, *Printing*, p. 53. And see Armstrong, 'English purchases', pp. 286–89.

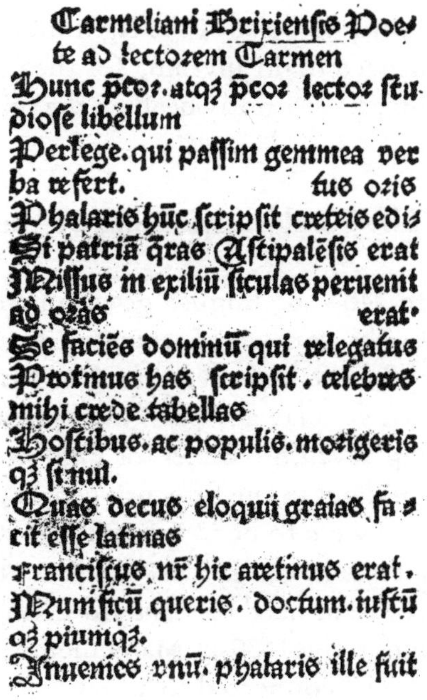

Carmeliani Brixiensis Poe
te ad lectorem Carmen

Hunc preor.atqz preor lector stu
diose libellum

Perlege.qui passim gemmea ver
ba refert.   tuo ocis

Phalaris huc scripsit ceteis edi
Si patria quas Astipalesis erat
Missus in exiliu siculas peruenit
ad oras   erat·

Se facies dominu qui relegatus
Protinus has scripsit. celebres
mihi crede tabellas

Hostibus.ac populis.morigeris
qz simul.

Quas decus eloquii graias fa
cit esse latinas

Franciscus. nr hic aretinus erat.
Mumificu queris. doctum. iustu
qz piumqz.

Inuenies vnu. phalaris ille fuit

Fig. 78 Pietro Carmeliano's recommendation of the *Letters of Phalaris* to the reader, in the edition of the *Letters* printed by Theodoric Rood and Thomas Hunt, Oxford. The poem differs slightly from the original version in Carmeliano's surviving autograph manuscript copy (see fig. 43). John Rylands University Library of Manchester printed book 15835. Reproduced by courtesy of the Director and University Librarian, the John Rylands University Library of Manchester.

Rood at Oxford it began to print English texts, probably in 1485, and like Rood it apparently failed in 1486.[74] The dates of the disappearance of these presses begs the question whether the proviso actually caused the growing influx of imported books, or whether it merely happened to be enacted at the moment the continental printers started to flood the English market in earnest.

It is just possible that the alien printers in the city and elsewhere, along with such major alien importers of books and dealers as John of Westphalia and Peter Actors of Savoy (the latter imported over 480 books into London between 16 May and 30 June 1483),[75] might have combined to lobby someone they knew on the king's council: a Goldwell or a Russell. But their ability, degree of influence, and above all, their oppor-

---

74 Blake, 'The spread of printing in English', pp. 61–63. It is not known who operated this press or whether the workforce included aliens; it was in operation by 1479, printing Latin works, one pirated from Caxton; it may have had the support of the Abbey.

75 Public Record Office, Petty Custom Account, E 122/ 73/41, mm. 1, 2v, 3.

tunity to do so at the right moment are unknown.[76] They may not have
needed to do anything for the personal sympathies of several councillors
may have already been on the side of the alien book trader and artisan.

The Real Supporters of the Proviso

In 1484 the English government had no reason to check the influx of
books from the continent. The fear of religious unorthodoxy, which was
to be the main reason in the future for restrictions and censorship, did
not yet play any part. Continental printers had not thought of producing Wycliffite Bibles for English readers, none of the texts imported into
England in the fifteenth century contained controversial theology, and
few were to be in English.[77] It was the professional men and scholars at
all levels, clergymen, lawyers, doctors and schoolmasters, who were in
constant need of standard Latin texts and benefited from foreign printing in the 1480s.[78] Many members of the clergy on Richard III's council
can be connected to a surviving book collection or a bequest of books,
both manuscript and printed. Some were authors or editors of texts, and
some had their work printed in Italy and/or in England. Most of them
were well aware of the need of the universities and other institutions for
cheap text books. Whether these men can be called humanists or not is
irrelevant to assessing their interest in the printing press.[79] All members
of the council, both lay and religious, who were most likely to have wor-

---

76 Painter, *Caxton*, pp. 139–40, imagines a fraternal consortium of all available printers, with
    Bishop Waynflete as their spokesman, converging on Richard III while he stayed at Magdalen
    College, Oxford, in July 1483. For the quarrelling capacity of printers and entrepreneurs, see
    Duff, 'Early chancery proceedings', pp. 410, 416. Christianson, 'Rise of London's book trade',
    p. 8, adds at least fifteen names of alien importers of books, and gives Peter Actors, Henry
    VII's stationer from 1486, the pre-eminent position of influence.
77 Hirsch, *Printing*, p. 93; for Gerard Leeu, see n. 56, above. There had, of course, been
    regulations against Wycliffite translations since the beginning of the century.
78 E.g. Armstrong, 'English purchases', p. 268.
79 E.g. Richard Fitzjames (died 1522), chaplain to Edward IV and Henry VII, bishop of London
    from 1506, can hardly be called a humanist (Emden, *Oxford*, vol. 2, pp. 691–92); he left to
    Merton College only mss, nearly all religious treatises and Bible studies, and Erasmus, who
    disliked Scotus and his followers, despised him as a 'superstitious and unmovable follower
    of Duns Scotus', but he was also the man who bought Johan Veldener's *Fasciculus temporum*
    (printed Louvain 1475) in Oxford as early as 1479 (BL, IB 49104; Armstrong, 'English
    purchases', p. 273).

ried about *any* curtailment of their supply of books, and all the bishops who might have gained access to the king and who were attending parliament, whether they were leading lights of the council or not, deserve consideration.[80]

John Shirwood, bishop-elect of Durham, was a classical scholar as well as a churchman and diplomat. His knowledge of Greek, apart from Latin, was remarkable and officially appreciated by Richard III, who emphasised it in his letter to the pope recommending Shirwood for the cardinalate. Shirwood's surviving library is impressive: seven manuscripts and no less than thirty printed books, virtually all classical texts produced in Italy. All but one of his Greek texts are lost but he inevitably needed foreign scribes to make these, whether in Italy or England. In 1482, in Rome, he had one work printed: the *Arithmomachia* (the Battle of Numbers), a complicated game that required great skill in arithmetic and geometry (as well as good Latin to read the rules!).[81]

James Goldwell, Bishop of Norwich, was a noted book collector from the 1440s to his death, bequeathing most of his collection to All Souls College, Oxford, where he had been a fellow. About fifteen manuscripts and thirty printed books are known to have been his, legal books, classical texts, philosophical and religious treatises; some of these were purchased while he was abroad on diplomatic missions and during his long stays in Italy as king's proctor (1467–73), and from the earliest date he bought printed works, including at least eleven produced in Rome. He is the first Englishman known to have owned an incunable.[82] The size of his collection and his careful bestowal of it in ways that furthered the cause of learning, means he must be regarded as a important voice on the subject of books in Richard's council. It has also been suggested that Goldwell actively promoted the setting-up of the first printing press in the university town of Oxford, and in

80 Lander, 'Yorkist council and administration, 1461–85' and 'Council, administration and councillors, 1401–85', in his *Crown and Nobility*, pp. 171–219, 309–20. The composition of Richard's council awaits detailed study.
81 Emden, *Oxford*, vol. 3, pp. 1692–93; Allen, 'Bishop Shirwood'; Weiss, *Humanism*, pp. 149–53. It is not certain that Shirwood was still in England at the time of the opening of parliament; in late February he was in Rome.
82 Emden, *Oxford*, pp. 783–86; he also gave books to Gonville and Caius, to the Carnary College, Norwich, and to Eastwell church, Kent; Armstrong, 'English purchases', p. 268: when in Hamburg in 1465 Goldwell bought a copy of Durandus, *Rationale divinorum officinorum*, printed in 1459, now Oxford, All Souls College Library L. R. 5. i. 1–3.

1478 backed the first book printed there, Rufinus' *Expositio Symboli*. He was probably the owner of the printer's copy manuscript, which he had bought from the Florentine bookseller, Vespasiano da Bisticci, while in Italy.[83] That this manuscript served as the printer's exemplar is certain, and that the whole enterprise involved Goldwell closely is proved by the decoration of a copy of the printed edition produced in exactly the same manner as the original manuscript with the addition of Goldwell's coat of arms.[84] It is possible that it was Goldwell who first encouraged a printer – probably Theodoric Rood – to set up his press in Oxford and supply the needs of students and dons.[85] Such an enterprise would have been an obvious object of encouragement to a man who had been profiting from printing for over a decade. He must be seen as an early enthusiast, backing one edition in the pursuit of his bibliophile and scholarly interests, but it is unlikely he was the initiator of the Oxford press as he did not continue to support it.[86]

One of the genuinely learned men among Richard III's councillors was John Gunthorpe, diplomat, humanist and friend of John Free, whose scholarship was acknowledged even by the Italians.[87] In 1484 Gunthorpe was dean of Wells and keeper of the privy seal; he had been on Edward IV's council and his long service to the Yorkist kings on many diplomatic missions may have made his voice a strong one. To a man in his position his love of books and his scholarly activities were merely a recreation from his political and ecclesiastical duties, but there is no doubt that his learning was also appreciated and used: it was Gunthorpe who was chosen to give the flattering public address in Latin to the duke of Burgundy on the occasion of the duke's wedding to Margaret of York, Edward IV's sister, in June 1468. This intellectual 'performance' had as much diplomatic value, showing the king's 'wor-

83 BL, MS Sloane 1579.

84 Cambridge, University Library Pr. Bk. 4159.

85 De la Mare and Hellinga, 'The first book printed in Oxford', pp. 184–244. And see De La Mare, 'The first Oxford book', p. 346.

86 Blake, 'Spread of printing in English', pp. 57–61, expands on the De La Mare and Hellinga material and sees Goldwell as the real initiator of the press, bringing a printer to England, and then losing interest after a year. There is no evidence to support this.

87 Gunthorpe and Free were both described as *homines doctissimi*, Schirmer, *Frühhumanismus*, p. 134. On Gunthorpe: Emden, *Oxford*, vol. 2, p. 837, *Cambridge*, pp. 275–77; *DNB*, vol. 23, pp. 351–52; Weiss, *Humanism*, pp. 122–27; Pollard, 'Fifteenth-century clerks of parliament', pp. 152–25; Mitchell, *John Free*, pp. 134–39.

ship' to the world, as the sartorial splendour of the bride's retinue, and in its own way it parallelled the magnificent chivalric display of the jousts laid on by the Burgundian court. Gunthorpe 'lived' with books. In the late 1450s and early 1460s he had been a student in Italy, just in time to attend the lectures of the famous grammarian Guarino da Verona, who had attracted so many English students. During that period Gunthorpe copied texts himself in a neat hand, writing his lecture notes in the margin.[88] He was to collect books for the rest of his life and often inscribed them with the place, date and price of acquisition. A twelfth-century manuscript of a late classical text was bought in London in 1465 for 5s 4d;[89] a manuscript of a Latin translation of the *Odyssey* written abroad, was found by him at Westminster on 12 May 1475 and purchased for 13s 4d.[90] Earlier in the same year he had acquired a commentary on Valerius Maximus printed in Strassburg *c.* 1471.[91] Though John Gunthorpe had many opportunities in the course of his diplomatic career to find books in other countries, these three purchases make it clear that he also depended on what was available in England. He was interested in many kinds of texts, from Bede's historical works[92] to Petrarch's,[93] from classical poetry[94] to Frulovisi's comedies[95] and whether the text he coveted was manuscript or printed, plain or illuminated,[96] was apparently of no importance to him.

The central figure in any council meeting was the chancellor, and the interest in books of John Russell, Bishop of Lincoln, Richard III's chancellor, cannot be doubted. His opening speech to king and parliament on

---

88 BL, MS Harl. 2485, Seneca *Tragedies*.

89 Cambridge, Trinity College, MS 824, Macrobius and Chalcidius.

90 Cambridge, University Library, MS Mm.3.4, translated by Leonzio Pilato (died 1365), a friend of Petrarch and Boccaccio.

91 Oxford, Bodleian Library, MS L Auct.N.4.4.; 7 February 1475, probably bought in England; Armstrong 'English purchases', p. 271 n. 4.

92 Cambridge, Emmanuel College, MS 3, Bede, *Historia Anglorum* and Gerald of Wales, *Topographia Hiberniae*.

93 Oxford, Brasenose College, MS UB/S.1.89, Petrarch, *Rerum memorandum libri*, printed, bought 16 July 1495.

94 San Marino, Huntington Library, MS EL 34 B 6, Persius and Juvenal.

95 Cambridge, St John's College, MS 60.

96 He owned several illuminated mss: Emmanuel MS 3, Sidney Sussex MS 46.

23 January was redolent with learning.[97] Unfortunately only a few of the
quotations Russell used in his sermon – both in the speech he drafted for
the parliament of Edward V that was never held and in the one he actually
gave – can be traced to texts of which he is known to have owned a copy.
He had Boccaccio's *De casibus virorum illustrium*[98] and the earlier books of
Pliny the Younger's *Historia naturalis*[99] in manuscript to inspire him and it
has to be assumed he had many other books at his disposal from which he
could cull his examples of political acumen and virtue. His known collection was varied like Gunthorpe's and, like his, was acquired over the years
in England and the Low Countries. Russell's diplomatic missions had taken
him to Bruges, Utrecht and Brittany, but probably never to Italy. He is
notable for buying the oldest surviving printed book that reached England
and a manuscript on the same day, both works of Cicero.[100] A short speech
of his addressed to Charles, Duke of Burgundy, on the occasion of the latter's investiture with the Order of the Garter, January 1470, was printed

---

97 Nichols, *Grants*, pp. xxxix–lxviii. These speeches have been linked to one of Russell's books
    by Lowry but his argument needs modification: Russell's reference – in the speech that he
    did not actually give – to Romulus making Rome an *azylum* and thereby attracting so many
    people that he had to select rulers and created the senate of one hundred noble and wise men,
    is not from Plutarch's *Romulus*, but from Livy, bk 1, ch. 8, and therefore there is no 'perfect ...
    coincidence', as noted by Lowry, of Russell buying Jenson's edition of Plutarch of 1478 with
    the 'manuscript notes indicating that Russell used it' (*pace* Lowry, 'The arrival', p. 456, and
    his 'Diplomacy', p. 133 and n. 35). On the evidence of the speech it is likely Russell owned
    more of Cicero's work than survives among his books: part of the cosmography of Pius II,
    Pomponius *De usucapionibus*, the popular preachers' manual *Pupilla oculi* of Thomas of Burgh,
    and Valerius Maximus. The quotations from Aristotle and Sallust were too common to prove
    that he owned a text, but it is likely that he did.
98 Oxford, New College, MS 263, acquired 1482.
99 Oxford, New College, MS 274, bought in London, 3 March 1471, given to New College in
    1482.
100 Cicero *De officiis* and *Paradoxa* in one volume, printed by Fust and Schoeffer, Mainz 1466, now
    Cambridge, University Library Inc. 28; and a ms. produced in Venice in 1467, of Cicero's
    Epistolae ad familiares, now London, Lambeth Palace Library, MS 765.

by Caxton, probably in 1475.[101] A man of Russell's interests and position in government may well have been the prime instigator of the proviso.

Thomas Rotherham, Archbishop of York, whose position at the time of parliament after his fall from favour in 1483 is not clear, *could* have been a major influence in favour of the proviso. It is known that he gave to Jesus College, his recent foundation at Rotherham, many printed books imported from Germany, and that the new library at Cambridge similarly acquired, by his gift, a great number of printed books, many produced at Venice in the 1470s.[102]

There were several secular, non-professional councillors who might have objected to any curtailment of their acquisition of beautiful manuscripts. There is no evidence of any particular interest in printed books among the noble or gently born members, but it is likely that most of them owned several illuminated texts. The books owned by John Howard, Duke of Norfolk, included standard texts in French, such as the histories of Troy and the *Game of Chess* and he seems to have liked his books enough to take a selection with him on the expedition to

---

101 *Propositio ad Carolum ducem Burgundie*, Duff, *Fifteenth-Century Books*, no. 367. When and why the speech was printed is not known but it was presumably at a time when many copies were needed to advertise the alliance between England and Burgundy, either immediately after the speech was delivered or for a diplomatic mission preparing the invasion of France in 1475. Only two copies survive but there must have been many more. Like the *Promise of Matrimony* (see above) the *Propositio* can only have been printed *because* many copies were needed, probably for propaganda purposes, but they were relevant only to the situation of the moment and quickly lost their value and disappeared. Whatever the paper and typographical evidence, about which there is still no unanimity, it is most likely that Russell's speech was printed in Bruges not too long after the event. Doyle, 'Ebesham', p. 309, n. 4, refers to Sheppard, 'Mansion', and the possibility that Caxton's type 2 was already used by him in Bruges.

102 Dobson, 'Archbishop Thomas Rotherham'. pp. 73, 82; Oates, *Cambridge University Library*, pp. 37–60; Emden, *Cambridge*, pp. 489–91, *Oxford*, vol. 3, pp. 1593–96. About some of the other clerical members of the council only a little is known, but they may have played a part. John Alcock, Bishop of Worcester: tutor to Edward V when prince of Wales, wrote religious tracts and sermons and was later to have them printed by Wynkyn de Worde and Richard Pynson, see Emden, *Cambridge*, pp. 5–6; Duff, *Fifteenth-Century Books*, nos. 11–20. Thomas Langton, Bishop of St Davids: three of his mss are extant, BL, MSS Royal 11 E iv (Latin), 10 E iii (Latin), 17 E viii (French); the first was copied at Langton's expense by a foreign scribe in 1472, Emden, *Oxford*, pp. 1101–02. William Waynflete, Bishop of Winchester: in his eighties by 1484; he was no great supporter of the 'new learning', but had been an active educationalist all his life and is said to have supported the printing press, particularly for the production of indulgences; he had given most of his books to Magdalen College, Oxford, in 1483, and it is not known with certainty whether there were any printed books among them, Davis, *William Waynflete*, pp. 90–98.

Scotland in the early 1480s.[103] The families of Blount, FitzAlan, Percy and Scrope – of which several members were on Richard's council – are all known to have been book owners. Among the gentry there were Robert Brackenbury, to whom Pietro Carmeliano presented a Latin verse life of St Katherine,[104] Sir John Donne,[105] and Thomas Thwaites,[106] who commissioned and owned Flemish manuscripts. Some of these men spent part of their life at Calais or travelled there frequently and were in a position to know and acquire whatever was available on the continent. Any ban on the commercial import of manuscripts or books probably did not affect them personally; they either had their manuscripts made and illuminated locally in England or brought their acquisitions into the country.

Among the people who were not members of the council but who may have had a personal influence on the king and were certainly aware of the advantages of the printing press, was the Austin friar Thomas Penketh, prior provincial of the order in England. Since his death he has been maligned by Thomas More, John Bale,[107] John Pits and by modern scholars[108] for preaching officially in favour of Richard III's title to the throne at St Mary's Hospital without Bishopsgate at Easter 1484.[109] More's rhetorical slander of Penketh that he was 'of more learning than virtue, of more fame than learning' is ingenious calumny for there can be no doubt about the friar's learning. Contemporaries described him as so well versed in the teaching of Duns Scotus – a notoriously 'difficult' philosopher

---

103 Crawford, *Household Books of John Howard*, introd. p. xix; II, p. 277.

104 See ch. 3 above.

105 Backhouse, 'Sir John Donne's Flemish manuscripts', pp. 48–53, ills.

106 Backhouse, 'Founders', p. 30. 'Choosing a book', p. 82.

107 For Penketh, Emden, *Oxford*, vol. 3, p. 1457, *Cambridge*, p. 448; Roth, *English Austin Friars*, vol. 1, pp. 122–25, vol. 2, passim. Perhaps More's attitude to Penketh can be linked to Erasmus' contempt of followers of Duns Scotus, even though Scotus was generally popular with English scholars, see e.g. Smith, *Erasmus*, pp. 21–23. John Bale's reasons were apparently also personal, Roth, p. 124.

108 Sylvester, *Complete Works of St Thomas More*, vol. 2, Richard III, p. 234 n. 58/23: Sylvester refers to Bale and Pits and adds, 'there is some *irony* in the fact that he [Penketh] wrote an *Ars sermonicandi*' (our italics). Penketh was famous as a preacher and drew large crowds, Rosser, *Medieval Westminster*, p. 277.

109 The 'Spital Sermons' at Easter were a civic event; all the leading London citizens attended and the mayor and aldermen nominated the preacher, CLRO, 'Historical Notes on the Spital Sermons', compiled by P.E. Jones, Research Papers 1.19.

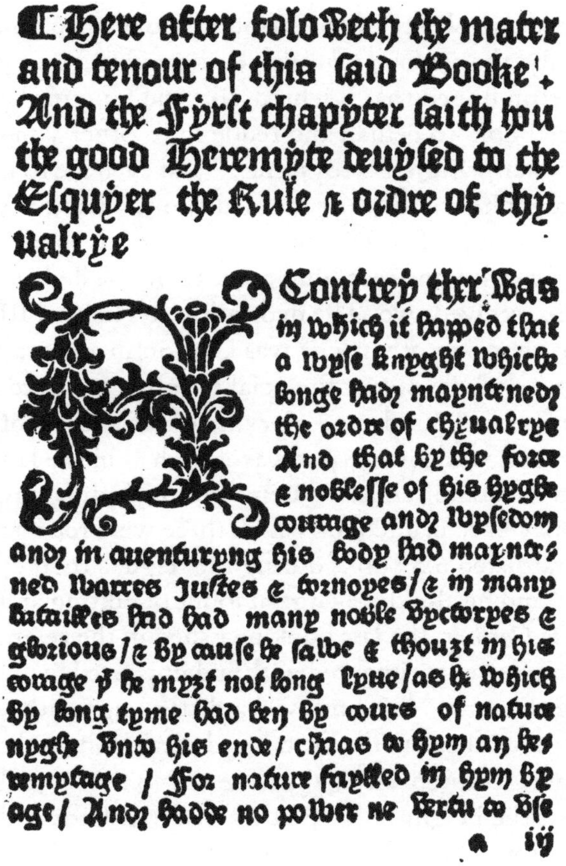

Here after foloweth the mater and tenour of this said Booke'. And the Fyrst chappter saith hou the good Heremyte deuysed to the Esquyer the Rule & ordre of chyualrye

Contrey ther was in which it happed that a wyse knyght which longe had maynteyned the ordre of chyualrye And that by the force & noblesse of his hyghe courage and wysedom and in auenturyng his body had maynteyned warres Iustes & tornoyes/ & in many batailles had had many noble vyctoryes & glorious/ & by cause he sawe & thouzt in his corage y̆ he myzt not long lyue/as he which by long tyme had ben by cours of nature nygh vnto his ende/ chaas to hym an hermytage/ For nature faylled in hym by age/ And had no power ne vertu to use

a ij

Fig. 79 Large floriated *A* at the beginning of Caxton's edition of the *Order of Chivalry* by Ramon Lull, printed in 1484 and presented to Richard III. John Rylands University Library of Manchester, 12105, f. 2. Reproduced by courtesy of the Director and University Librarian, the John Rylands University Library of Manchester.

— that if Duns's work had been lost Penketh could have rewritten it.[110] Penketh's interest in having his editions of Scotus's work published and becoming widely available cannot be doubted.

What did the king himself do? It is not known that Richard III took any particular action to advance printing, but he undoubtedly had a positive attitude to books and it can be suggested that he shared his councillors' concern to prevent any physical restraint on learning in the country. As we have said elsewhere little can be concluded about Richard's patronage

---

110 Roth, *English Austin Friars*, p. 123, and references given there. John Leland confirmed this, quoted by Roth, p. 564; Roth's own comments p. 123 n. 222. For Penketh's editions of Duns Scotus, printed in Padua (1474) and Venice (1477) and later reprinted in various places see e.g. *Short-Title Catalogue of Books Printed in Italy*, pp. 27, 229. Bishop Goldwell of Norwich owned several of these books.

of books. Taking the particular object of the printed book, only one can be linked to him directly, the *Order of Chivalry*, dedicated to him by Caxton early in 1484. Caxton hoped that Richard, like the king in the book, would command the book 'to be had and redde unto other yong lordes, knyghtes and gentylmen within this royaume',[111] and even see to it 'that every noble man ... might have a copye of the sayd book'.[112] Caxton's thoughts ran optimistically on his profits. The *Order* was one of the books he dedicated to named persons, no one receiving more than one dedication except Edward IV who received two. The dedication to Richard III is thus no more significant than any other, nor was Caxton in any way dependent on his or anyone else's favour or financial support. Richard, however, does benefit from a certain reflected glory from the success of Caxton's press during his reign, when its output was as high as in the last years of Edward IV's reign: a total of eighteen items (not including any parliamentary statutes he may have printed) of which three were reissues of earlier books. Caxton translated 6.5 books during the reign, a total of approximately 714 folios,[113] and he also did a large amount of editing and adapting for Malory's *Morte Darthur*, the last book he issued in the reign. As referred to above, Caxton also experimented with and improved many aspects of his books during the early 1480s and Richard III's reign: titles, explicits, tables of contents and foliation. He introduced paragraph marks and printed initial letters and acquired a new typeface in 1483–85.[114] All this indicated that he was at the height of his powers as a translator and printer, and that his business was doing well. No direct patronage from Richard III is ascertainable but there was nothing in the political climate

---

111 Epilogue to the *Order*, Blake, *Caxton's Own Prose*, p. 127. See also ch. 4 above.

112 *Ibid.*, p. 14.

113 He began the translation of the *Golden Legend* under Edward IV and printed it in 1484; the translation of *Charles the Great* was finished 18 June 1485 and printed under Henry VII. We have used the chronological list of his books in Blake, *England's First Publisher*, pp. 192–96, but have allotted the printing of the *Four Sermons* to Edward IV's reign and the *Sex Epistolae* to Richard III's, as well as the *Royal Book*, as its translation was definitely finished during Richard's reign. The *Golden Legend*'s massive number of folios has been divided between Edward and Richard, as translation started under the former and was finished and printed under the latter. *Charles the Great* has been counted as translation of Richard's reign and a publication of Henry's, the *Knight of the Tower* as a translation of Edward's reign and a publication of Richard's. The full *foliation* figures of De Ricci have been used with no allowance for blanks. Caxton's failure to date all his works means that it is impossible to do a precise year-by-year analysis; nor do we know anything about his print-runs.

114 Blake, *England's First Publisher*, pp. 153 ff., 110–19, quotation p. 119, 127–30. And see his, 'Caxton prepares ... *Morte Darthur*', pp. 272–85.

to discourage him; Caxton was a businessman who operated successfully without political affiliations.[115]

Just as we do not know precisely how Richard III responded to Caxton and his books, so we do not know precisely how either the king or the first English printer responded to the proviso of 1484. It can be assumed that Caxton's reactions would have been governed by profit and those of the king by his interest in learning and the promotion of the universities, which supplied useful men, both secular and religious, for clerical posts and high positions in government – precisely the kind of men whom he met around his council table. We come full circle to the proviso itself: the council and the king determined to agree that the proviso should be made and thereby proved to posterity their interest in books and learning.

115 See 'R III's Books VI', pp. 116–18. Caxton's overall output fell in Henry VII's reign.

ELEVEN

Richard III and His Books

Our research into the books of Richard III has been conducted out of an interest in the reading material which was available during the later fifteenth century, but also in the hope that the books might tell us something about the owner. The same wish to resurrect the owner motivates most manuscript and incunable researchers. Both statistics and personal details help to identify contemporary interests. There are several caveats to be discussed before any conclusions are hazarded about Richard III's books. First, did Richard really own all the books discussed here and did he read them? In most cases there is no doubt about Richard's ownership: the presence and the phrasing of the inscriptions or the inclusion of his arms leave no room for argument. It is possible, however, that he never owned, in the full sense of the word, the Fitzhugh or Anonymous Chronicle, which he could have seen at Jervaulx Abbey and signed merely to please the monks who were happy to welcome such noble visitors as the Duke of Gloucester and the Lord Fitzhugh. The *Booke of Gostlye Grace* by Mechtild of Hackeborn may have belonged to his wife. Though a duke of Gloucester is mentioned in the Latin *ex libris* in the *De regimine principum* there is no initial or Christian name. The manuscript's date of manufacture precludes ownership by Thomas of Gloucester, but it might conceivably have been Humphrey's. Richard's signature in the New Testament is also unusual in lacking initial or first name, but as neither signature or motto tie in with those of the other two dukes of Gloucester Richard remains the most likely owner. Three of Richard's books were dedications: Caxton's *Order*, Worcester's *Boke* and Carmeliano's *Life of St Katherine*. These must be regarded as only partly reflecting Richard's personal interests, as the authors wished to bring their work to the attention of the king of England, whoever he was, though they did hope to please Richard and gain rewards. No copy of Caxton's *Order of Chivalry* owned by Richard III survives, though it can be presumed that the printer formally presented one to the king, either printed, or perhaps more likely, in manuscript, as it was his *translation* which was the important gift to the king;[1] he expected, no doubt, to sell more copies of the printed edition if it had a royal dedicatee. Whatever William Worcester's own aim was when he compiled his treatise on the reconquest of France, his son certainly hoped to profit from 'doing up' the book and presenting it to the new king; it is likely Richard did indeed own the surviving copy. Pietro Carmeliano had already dedicated books to Edward IV and the prince of Wales, and copies of his *Life of St Katherine* were also addressed to Chancellor Russell and Robert Brackenbury, constable of the Tower. In the preface to the latter the author calls on Brackenbury to bear witness to the excellence of the king, to whom he had 'consecrated' the work, 'a prince who honours both learning and learned men'. Brackenbury and Russell's copies, written by the poet's own hand, survive unlike Richard's copy, but there is no reason to suppose it was not presented to the king in due form.[2]

One important way in which princes such as Richard heard of 'new' texts was by presentation, usually a simple process of self-advertisement by an author like Carmeliano who, in the hope of reward, created a new version of a life of a saint for Richard III, but which could be part of a more complex series of events. In one case where the details are known, both the making of the text and its acquisition by the prince were the result of devotion to a particular saint, and the presentation scene itself was subtly 'staged'. In 1459 Hubert le Prevost of Lille journeyed round various religious houses to collect as much material as he could find about his patron saint, St Hubert. He then had this written up into a Latin *vita*. Later he commissioned the scribe, Colard Mansion (a future printer and associate of Caxton) to translate it into French and make two manuscript copies. In 1462 or '63 le Prevost read from his book in the presence of Philip the Good who – as Prevost probably knew – had a

---

1 For our argument that Caxton presented a manuscript copy of his *Dicts* to Edward IV, see 'R III's books: mistaken attributions', pp. 303–07, and Cat. XXI below.
2 See above, ch. 3.

particular devotion to St Hubert. Philip was so pleased with it that he
had his scribe, David Aubert, make a copy worthy of the ducal library.
It was illuminated by Loyset Liédet, Aubert improved the text, and the
work was finished in a few months.[3] The *Vie de S. Hubert* was only one
of many volumes, chronicles, histories and romances, known to have
been presented to Philip the Good of Burgundy; no English king of the
fifteenth century received so many. Edward IV can be credited with thirteen, possibly fourteen presentation volumes, and Richard III with three,
or five if we add the double volume of the *Historia Troiae* and *Historia
regum Britanniae* which may well have been a gift. Of these only one was
a new text specially composed for the king, that by Carmeliano. In most
cases of presentation there was nothing unusual or unexpected for the
prince who was used to receiving gifts, but he might be especially pleased
if the gift was successfully linked to his personal interests, as was the life
of St Hubert to the taste of Philip the Good and the *Life of St Katherine*
to Richard III – and Richard could have a gracious way with gifts.[4]
The average presentation was of more importance to the donor than to
the recipient as the following 'timeless' account preserved in a letter to
Cardinal Bessarion from his printer, Fichet, on 22 March 1472, proves.
Bessarion had composed a book of *Letters and Prayers concerning the Defence
against the Turks* which was intended to convince the kings and princes of
Europe that a crusade could no longer be put off. Fichet personally pre-
sented a copy to Louis XI and reported to the author:

> The king accepted your book with pleasure and read part of the brief
> preface that I added to the beginning of your work. He turned the pages
> and studied the illustrations in the margin. Next he read almost all your
> notes ... they were, after all, marked with gold and various colours ...
> He then turned to the beginning of the book and several times read the
> verses below the presentation miniature. Finally the secretary who was
> present accepted the book for safe keeping.[5]

This was as much as an author could expect from a busy king.

---

3   De Rooy, *Vie de Saint Hubert*, pp. lxxxiii–iv.
4   For Edward's presentation volumes, 'Choosing a book', pp. 84–86. For Richard and 'gifts',
    see ch. 5.
5   Claudin, *Histoire de l'imprimerie*, vol. 1, p. 52 n. 2.

Fig. 80 Standard presentation scene, 1482, in one of the large manuscripts probably acquired by Edward IV but bearing the royal arms only. From the French translation of Bartholomaeus Anglicus' *On the Properties of Things*. Flemish, text finished 25 May 1482. BL, MS Royal 15 E ii, f. 7. By permission of The British Library.

In the final analysis it has to be acknowledged that book owners do not necessarily read all, or any, of their books and it is possible that Richard did not read his most difficult and long texts from cover to cover. The enormous Fitzhugh Chronicle was the kind of book to be dipped into or used to look up a particular episode of English history, and Richard of Gloucester and Henry Fitzhugh may have been doing just that on one brief occasion. The inaccurate texts of the *Historia Troiae*, *Historia regum Britanniae* and the *Prophecy of the Eagle* would have discouraged all but the most determined of readers – some of the marginalia *may* be Richard's however. If his collection of romances and Bible stories, his *Grandes chroniques* or the *De regimine principum* were youthful possessions he may still have had time to read them carefully or have had them read to him. Ultimately we can only be certain he knew his book of hours well.

The dangers of speculating about any library, such as Richard's, which lacks a surviving, complete, regularly updated and reliable inventory, are great. We have suggested how and when Richard acquired his books, but we are very conscious that we do not know precise details of time, place or circumstance for the acquisition of any of his books, although we do know he received at least eight texts (seven books) when king (the *Historia Troiae*, the *Historia regum Britanniae* with the *Prophecy of the Eagle* and its *Commentary*, the Vegetius, the *Vita Sanctae Katherinae*, the *Boke of Noblesse* and its accompanying Collection, and his book of hours). There is no reliable statistical method of computing the size of a medieval library from the surviving books,[6] especially when it is composed of secular material liable to be over-used, vulnerable to wilful destruction as well as changes in fashion.[7] Only an inventory can give information about the breadth of interest of the collector, but even the most complete of inventories may reveal only that the owner wanted his collection to be complete and fashionable, containing what everyone else expected a library to contain. Studies of long inventories produced in Italy, France and England have revealed the uniformity of the contents of Latin libraries, the increasing use of vernacular translations of the classics by the princes of those countries, and that all libraries had similar proportions of Latin, vernacular,

---

6   Ker, *Medieval Libraries*, pp. xi–xv.
7   Harris, 'Patrons, buyers and owners', pp. 163–99, esp. 165–66.

scriptural, and other texts.[8] Large libraries, whether of institutions or princes, inevitably repeated each other then, as they do now.

Faced with a large inventory of a prince certain conclusions can be drawn, but above all warnings taken: the 1424 inventory of Charles V's library contains 1,239 manuscripts, of which only 198 were French literary works, the rest being Latin and mostly religious and service books (113 Bibles, 5 'liturgies', 43 breviaries and hymnals, 51 missals and gospel books, 57 books of hours, etc.). These did not represent the king's choice but his needs as a Christian prince, the needs of his household, his priests and his private chapel. Charles V's personal interest may have been indicated by the more unusual 80 books on astronomy and 136 on astrology and the occult, but the library also had 171 historical texts and 39 encyclopaedias.[9] As a *collector* Charles may have been far more interested in acquiring books for their own sake, as prestigious objects, rather than for reading on any particular subject; he could have bought job-lots of other collectors' libraries. The sad conclusion is that if Richard III ever owned such a large collection a full inventory would tell us little about his real interests.

One needs more than an inventory, one needs the books themselves, and other clues, like Charles V's use of royal propaganda and historiography, which informed much of his bibliophilia, or the statement of his counsellor, Philippe de Mézières, that Charles read the Bible through each year.[10] Annotations, signatures and personal mottoes help to prove that the owner's appreciation of his books went beyond mere possessiveness. A few of these clues survive to be used and pieced together for Richard III, notably his habit of putting his name in his books, a practice not apparently shared by others of his family, and his occasional use of a motto for additional identification. A motto not only could act as an ownership mark on a book but contrariwise it derived its life from books and skill with words.[11] Before we turn to the more complicated issue of whether Richard's books help us to understand his choice of mottoes, can his books offer further information about his use of a white boar as his cognizance?

---

8 Kibre, 'Intellectual interests', pp. 257–97. And see ch. 1 above for our comparisons taken from the collections of Savoy and Philip of Cleves.
9 Pickford, 'Fiction and the reading public', pp. 425–26, n. 1.
10 Mézières, *Songe*, p. 20.
11 There is little written on the use of devices and mottoes in the 15th century, see e.g. Beaune, 'Costume et pouvoir', pp. 125–46; Piponnier, *Costume et vie sociale*, pp. 231–61.

As the supporters of his arms a pair of white boars only identify one book as his, Vegetius' *De re militari*. The boar was a popular heraldic charge, used long before heraldry became standardised. The *sanglier* was the most dangerous and difficult animal to hunt, a *beste noire* (like the wolf and the bear) whose killer was greatly honoured. In contrast to the stag (one of the *bestes rouges*) which came to symbolise the Christian virtues – a flying stag was particularly associated with the kings of France – the boar stood for the sinner,[12] but at the same time the boar's very ferocity and power caused it to develop from a symbol of evil to an emblem of him who defeated it. In most stories the boar of evil is black and it is likely Richard very consciously chose a white boar to exorcise in advance all the vices of the animal and leave it only its virtues. The image of the boar fighting for its rights, as the king of England should do in France, used by William Worcester in the *Boke of Noblesse* has already been mentioned;[13] in the *Knight's Tale* Palamon and Arcite fight furiously like wild boars, foaming with mad anger;[14] and more appropriately in Lydgate's *Siege of Thebes* the ever courteous, wise and brave Tydeus bears a boar on his shield, his 'gypon [was] wroght of the bristles of a wylde boar' and the same beast was

> ... wroght and bete upon [his] banner,
> Displaied broode whan [he] shulde fight.[15]

If Richard read his *History of the Kings of Britain* – and 'everybody' did know at least the internationally popular *Prophecies of Merlin* included in it – he must have rejoiced at the mention of the 'fierce Boar, which will try the sharpness of its tusks in the forests of Gaul; for it will lop down all the larger oak-trees, taking care, however, to protect the smaller ones. The Arabs shall dread the Boar and so shall the Africans ...'.[16]

---

12 Thiebaux, 'The mouth of the boar', pp. 281–99.
13 See ch. 3.
14 Chaucer, *Knight's Tale*, lines 1658, 1699.
15 Lydgate, *Siege of Thebes*, lines 1546–49.
16 Thorpe, trans., Geoffrey of Monmouth, *History*, p. 176. It is unlikely that Richard ever knew the German tradition that Tristan's device was the boar, a black one in the poem by Gottfried von Strassburg. Other arms attributed to him were a lion on a red ground (or blue in French sources); and in the *Prose Tristan* two gold crowns on a red ground. See Gottfried von Strassburg, *Tristan ... with the surviving fragments of the Tristan of Thomas*, p. 130 and app. 3, and esp. Pastoureau, 'Armoiries de Tristan', pp. 9–32.

Tant le desieree is one of the earliest of the three mottoes associated with Richard III (see fig. 2). It is known from two sources: in this spelling it accompanies Richard's boar with a note, 'my lorde of gloscester', and another variant *illa treztant desyre* in a small collection of drawings of heraldic beasts and mottoes made 1461–70;[17] it also occurs in Richard's own hand above his signature on a page of the prose *Ipomedon*.[18] The date of this insertion is not certain but the neat hand and the general tenor of the texts contained in this manuscript incline us to place it before 1470. The purpose of this motto is speculative: it may have been a motto adopted in tournaments and courtly entertainments by the young Richard, such fancies being essential to these activities. The most likely translation is: 'I have longed for it so much', the past tense presenting a slight problem in so far as the thing desired seems to have been attained and a chivalrous ideal must be continually desired.

Another motto to be associated with Richard as duke is that in his New Testament: *a vous me ly* occurs above his title alone (see fig. 6).[19] The motto *a vostre plaisir* engraved round a metal plaque with a central motif of a linked *RA* discovered at Middleham Castle[20] may also be Richard's, but as the predecessors of Richard of Gloucester and Anne Neville at Middleham Castle were Richard Neville and Anne Beauchamp and before them, Richard Neville and Alice Montague, this is not certain. Both *a vous me ly* and *a vostre plaisir* have a clear personal connotation: the first is the

---

17 The collection of heraldic drawings has been in the British Library since 1923 as BL, MS Add. 40742; they were found in a mutilated condition in 1779 by the antiquarian John Fenne, who salvaged them, cut them out and pasted them on to new sheets of paper, carefully recording his actions. He correctly dated the collection to 1450–70 (ff. 1v, 21v–22); it might be more precise to date it to 1461–71 because the devices include those of Richard, created duke of Gloucester in 1461, and Richard Neville, Earl of Warwick, died 1471. There are two boars both with coronets round their necks in the collection: one jolly-looking beast has no note of ownership (f. 13); the other is a fierce animal with the motto beneath the animal, and Richard's title above, in contemporary script (f. 5), below the title a line records a variant of the motto (ill. in Ross, *Richard III*, fig. 18a). The variant is scarcely legible but a reading *illa treztant desyre* 'il l'a trestant desiré', 'he has longed for it so much', fits with the re/ er abbreviation over the fifth and sixth letters and the number of letters available; the third person singular *il* might then be coupled to the 'my lorde' of the line above. This also allows a sensible translation in the past tense of the visible variant: *tant le desirai* is possible since in many cases the pronunciation of *ai* and *e* was identical in Old French and Anglo-Norman and the spelling interchangeable, see Pope, *From Latin to Modern French*, paras 529–32 and 1284.

18 Longleat, MS 257, f. 98v.

19 New York Public Library, MS De Ricci 67, f. 1.

20 *A vos plaisir* has been extended. Illustrated, *Richard III*, item 47.

stronger expression and the latter is the equivalent of the current idiom 'at your service'. *Dame, a trestot vostre plaisir*, says Jason to Medea in *Le Roman de Troie*.[21] Many courtiers, knights and ladies, changed their *devise*, *raison* or 'word', or had several, for use in love, in courtly games, in war or in tournaments, as apparently Richard of Gloucester had.[22] The boy-hero of Christine de Pizan's *Book of the Duke of True Lovers* chose 'a device and a motto in which was the name of my lady in such a form that none could recognise it'; he also chose rich liveries according to his device.[23] The *Assembly of Ladies*, an English poem written for a courtly milieu in the 1470s is set in the maze and arbour of Pleasaunt Regard, where the lady of the highest estate is Lady Loyalty, and is packed with mottoes which are clearly expected to appeal to its audience.[24] Attractive 'coupled' mottoes of man and wife that seem to give an insight into their relationship were those of John, Duke of Bedford's *a vous entier* (I am wholly yours) and that of his first wife, Anne of Burgundy, *j'en suis contente* (it pleases me well), or the ambitious *je l'ay emprins* (I have undertaken it) of Charles the Bold and the cautious *bien en aviengne* (may it turn out well) of Margaret of York that completes it. Unfortunately we do not know Anne Neville's 'word' or whether it could be joined to her husband's, nor is it known when and for how long Richard used these mottoes – *a vous me ly, tant le desiere(e)* and *illa treztant desyre* – or whether they can be associated with his private and family life in contrast to the official *loyaulte me lie*.

Loyaulte me lie, 'loyalty binds me' seems to have emerged later as a motto for Richard as all its occurrences are datable to 1483–85 (see also figs 10, 13). It first appears, bracketed with his signature on a scrap of paper also bearing the regal signature of Edward V and that of Henry, Duke of Buckingham, with his motto, certainly datable to between May and early June 1483.[25] The most important surviving public use of this motto

---

21 Constans, *Roman de Troie*, line 1443. It is the kind of saying that could be inscribed on any love token. *Vostre plaisir* was also the motto of the contemporary Lannoy family.

22 E.g. Charles the Bold had a separate motto for tournaments: *ainsi je frappe* (this is how I strike), see e.g. De Smedt, *Chevaliers de l'Ordre de la Toison d'Or*, no. 34. For his other motto see below.

23 Pizan, *Book of the Duke of True Lovers*, pp. 17, 22.

24 Pearsall, *The Floure and the Leafe and The Assembly of Ladies*, pp. 105–26.

25 BL, MS Cotton Vesp. F xiii, f. 123 (a scrapbook). A few weeks later a reference to this motto seems implied in a letter from George Brown to John Paston: 'Loyalte Ayme. Hyt schal newyr cum howte for me'. Brown was hostile to Richard as king and later took part in the rebellion of 1483 and was executed; the letter seems to sum up his hostility. *Paston Letters*, ed. Davis, vol. 2, p. 443.

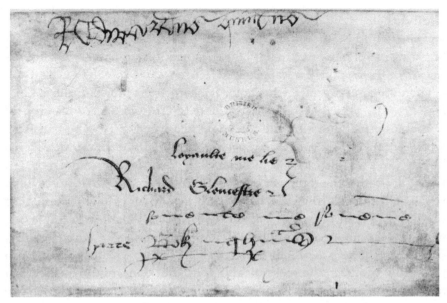

Fig. 81 The signatures of Edward V, Richard of Gloucester and Henry, Duke of Buckingham. Richard has added his motto *Loyaulte me lie* and Buckingham his *Souvente me souvene*. Written at some date in April 1483. BL, MS Cotton Vesp. F xiii, f. 123. By permission of The British Library.

is the charter of incorporation granted the Wax Chandlers' Company of London on 16 February 1484 where it is written on a scroll behind the crowned arms of the king painted in the initial *R* of the text.[26] Numberless mottoes witnessed to their owners' loyalty, faith and love for an overlord or beloved lady and loyalty occurred in almost as many mottoes as love; this knightly virtue was ideal for public use in a motto despite the more realistic attitude to the virtue adopted by knightly families on a day-to-day basis.[27] 'Loyalty' and 'loyal' were commonly used 'good' words and they were readily used in connection with and by members of the York

26 The Wax Chandlers' Company hold their charter; a facsimile may be consulted at the Guildhall Library, London.

27 See numerous variants in, e.g. Chassant and Tausin, *Dictionnaire de Devises*. The minor Margetson family had the identical motto, *ibid.*, *Supplement*, p. 207. Mary Hungerford, heiress of Hungerford, Botreaux and Moleyns, who married Edward, the second lord Hastings, also took the same motto, and in her case it is unlikely she did not know it had been Richard III's, Bodleian Library, Digby MS 233, f. 228. Two prominent Northern families had the word in their own motto: the Parrs of Kendall used *amour avec loyaulte* and Lord Dacre (d. 1525), one of Richard's henchmen as a boy, used *forte en loiaute*.

family: the epitaph of Richard, Duke of York, said he *bien ama loyaulte sans envye*; and Margaret of York when presenting a manuscript life of St Colette to the Poor Clares at Ghent signed it, *votre loyale fylle margarete dangleterre pryez pour elle et pour son salut* (see fig. 23).[28]

There are some aspects to the motto Richard used as an adult and as king, *loyaulte me lie*, which need to be considered in the context of his view of himself as prince and king and the books he owned and can be associated with, especially *De regimine principum*.[29] Various authors have interpreted 'loyalty' to mean 'justice', or rather 'doing what the law commands'. To Dante discussing the four ages of man in his *Convivio* (1308) loyalty, *lealtà*, is one of the principal virtues of an adult man in his prime; it consists of obeying and carrying out the dictates of the law.[30] Dante's example of a man who was above all 'loyal' was Aeneas, the founder of Rome. In classical times Aeneas was usually given the epithet *pius*, which does not mean primarily 'pious' in the sense of 'religious', but denotes the quality that makes a man behave as he should in relation to others, treating everyone according to his status and merit and obeying God's law and man's.[31]

In the *Bréviaire des nobles* ('book of prayers for noblemen') of Alain Chartier (*c.* 1390–1430) are listed twelve virtues which a noble should possess to do his 'job' properly. Edward IV owned a copy of this popular text in his collection of didactic works which also contained Ramon Lull's *Order of Chivalry*, Jean de Courcy's *Chemin de vaillance*, and two other works with similar messages.[32] The *Bréviaire* consists of a series of prayers that *Dame Noblesse* expects her followers to say every day to purge the evils of the world. The first prayer is to *Foy* (troth, fidelity), the second is to *Loyaulté* and defines 'loyalty' as the virtue which makes noblemen deserve the high honour they receive, by fulfilling their obligations to inferiors and superiors, defending their dependants and not exploiting

---

28 The epitaph is printed in present authors, *Reburial of Richard, Duke of York*, pp. 28–29. Ghent, Monasterium Bethlehem, *Vita Sanctae Coletae*, f. 163r, see Corstanje *et al.*, *Vita Sanctae Coletae (1381–1447)*, pp. 196–97.

29 Esp. the discussion of justice and the law, see ch. 5 above.

30 See e.g. Wicksteed, *Convivio of Dante Alighieri*, pp. 363–64.

31 *Pius* can be translated in many ways, including pious, conscientious, kind, loyal and patriotic. Chastellain in his biography of the Burgundian hero, Jacques de Lalaing, described him as *pieux comme Enée*, but his exact meaning or range of meanings is not clear, see *Les Faits de Messire Jacques de Lalaing*, in Chastellain, *Oeuvres*, vol. 8, p. 252.

32 BL, MS Royal 14 E ii; the text also survives in MSS Royal 15 E vi (1445), 17 E iv and 19 A iii (both late 15th century).

them, supporting their king and not abandoning his cause: *Servir leur roy et leurs subgez deffendre* is the refrain of this prayer.[33]

Loyalty was not only a virtue of the nobility. A popular proverb in the fourteenth and fifteenth century, which appears in many forms and variations, vividly describes what happens to society when *loyaulté* is not active:

> Parlons bas, car Loyaulté dort.
> Las! en quoy est elle endormie?
> Par son dormir fait on maint tort, ...

> (Speak softly for Loyalty is asleep.
> Alas! why did she fall asleep?
> Because she sleeps much wrong is done, ...)[34]

And elsewhere, in a collection of illustrated proverbs:

> On ne voit maintenant
> Ame qui soit d'accort
> D'estre la main tenant
> A vivre en bon accort.
> Plusieurs font du droit tort;
> Le plus puissant l'emporte:
> Dame Loyauté dort
> Et Verité est morte.

(These days you do not see a soul willing to help another to live in harmony; many turn right to wrong and the stronger comes out on top: Loyalty sleeps and Truth is dead).[35]

In this last version the words are accompanied by a drawing of one lady asleep in a chair, her head resting on her hand, and another lady lying dead at her feet. In most versions of the proverb Loyalty is mentioned together

---

33 See Laidlaw, *Poetical Works of Alain Chartier*, pp. 393–409, esp. 396–97.

34 Morawski, *Les Diz et Proverbes des Sages*, vol. 2, pp. 138–40.

35 Frank and Miner, *Proverbes en rimes*, pp. 65, 91.

with Truth, Reason and/or Justice, who all suffer while she dozes and are either fled away, asleep or dead themselves, leaving society in disarray.

It has been argued successfully that in Langland's *Piers Plowman* 'lewte' has several shades of meaning, but appears particularly to refer to 'justice' in the sense of 'living righteously'.[36] This 'loyalty' can be described as being directed not just to one person or cause – which is sometimes misguided – but to the community as a whole. It is to be identified as Aristotle's 'form of justice' which only exists in relation to others. 'Justice in this sense then, is not part of virtue but virtue entire'.[37] This concept was taken up by St Thomas Aquinas and later by Giles of Rome. Giles's *justitia legalis*, 'which is, as it were, every virtue in one', may be regarded as the equivalent of the 'lewte' of Langland. 'Lewte' and 'loyalty' both found their origin in Latin *legalitas*, which in its turn derives from *lex*, 'law'.

It is unlikely Richard was consciously aware of all these possibilities and literary trends, but he expressed an interest in the law, he did use the word 'loyalty' in his adult motto, and he is likely to have known at least Alain Chartier's definition of loyalty as fulfilling one's obligations as a nobleman to all classes of people; probably some version of the well-known proverb, and certainly Giles of Rome's *justitia legalis*, were familiar to him – as was *Piers Plowman* (see below). The connotations that people gave – and give – to personal mottoes and devices are numberless and impossible to gauge with certainty; one idea leads to another on an entirely irrational basis. This being so there may also have been a link between Richard's *loyaulte me lie* and his brother's *comfort et liesse* (comfort and joy): *lié* and *lie* are also derived from *liesse* meaning 'joyful', 'happy'. Richard's sense of justice and his position that allowed him to dispense it may indeed have given him pleasure. *Loyaulte me lie* could therefore have an alternative translation: 'justice rejoices me'. Such double meanings were the essence of good mottoes. We can conclude that Richard used his mottoes both effectively and consciously – perhaps he really enjoyed these more trivial trappings of a courtly knight – and the many meanings of *loyaulte* outlined above suggest that his last motto was the choice of a man who read books.

A unique clue about Richard and his books and his attitude to them is to be found in the fact that he was able to quote from them. As we have

---

36 Kean, 'Love, law, and *lewte* in *Piers Plowman*', pp. 241–61; see also Sutton, 'Curious searcher', p. 62 and n. 31.

37 Aristotle, *Ethica Nicomachea*, 5, 1, 1129b–1130a; quoted by Kean, 'Love, law, and *lewte* in *Piers Plowman*', p. 256.

seen, a document of great personal interest to the king quoted from and improved upon an image from the *Mirror of the World* (see fig. 47).[38] Even more interesting is the king's personal quotation from William Langland's *Piers Plowman*, a poem already referred to above. He called Nottingham Castle his 'Castle of Care',[39] a phrase from the prologue of Passus One of *Piers Plowman*, where the Castle of Care, ruled by Wrong, is contrasted to the Tower of Truth.[40] If Richard was quoting directly from the poem he was saying that at Nottingham he had experienced despair and betrayal: he had learnt there of the death of his son and later awaited news of Henry Tudor's invasion. *Piers Plowman* is one of the most moving works of medieval English literature:[41] if it were among Richard's books it would considerably raise the literary quality of his collection in modern eyes. A multiple dream poem, it consists of several visions, with intervening waking periods, witnessed and participated in by the author in his search for truth. Its subject is the state of human society, perverted by the power of money and greed; it asks how the human condition can be bettered and how men can lead more Christian lives under a king ruled in his turn by Conscience and Reason.

The number of manuscripts surviving supports the possibility that Richard III could have read the poem and known it well enough to quote from it, and so does both the variety of the recorded owners in the fifteenth century and the kind of reader the poem demanded. Richard would have had no trouble locating a copy if he had wanted one; he could easily have been given one. Copies are known to have been owned by a canon of York Minster in 1396, by clergy of Arncliffe in Craven and Grimston in Yorkshire in the first half of the fifteenth century, by Sir Thomas Charlton in 1465 (a

---

38 See ch. 5.

39 No other example of the phrase, 'the Castle of Care', has been found. Sutton, 'Richard III's "Castle of Care"', pp. 303–06. *Hours of Richard III*, pp. 83, 112.

40 Compare Charles d'Orléans's use of the Castle of No Care, *château Nonchaloir* (only once actually called a castle, also referred to as a manor), to where the bereaved Lover retires from Love's Court. There he is to live out his life as an anchorite occupied with dispassionate social activities and be cured of his lovesickness. The porter of No Care is significantly called 'Tyme-Apast' or Pastime. See esp. Arn, *Fortunes Stabilnes*, pp. 3–10,, 14, 28, 54, 241–48 (text). It has been claimed that Orléans developed his No Care from a theme of Alain Chartier (Fox, *Lyric Poetry of Charles d'Orléans*, pp. 63–64) and Machaut (Wilkins, *One Hundred Ballades*, p. 141). We are grateful to Julia Boffey for this comparison.

41 Skeat, *Vision of William concerning Piers the Plowman in Three Parallel Texts*; Kane, *Piers Plowman: the A Version*; Kane and Donaldson, *Piers Plowman: the B Version*; Pearsall, *Piers Plowman by William Langland, an Edition of the C-text*. All versions include the image of the castle of care.

Fig. 82 A king and courtiers in 'a bookshop', *c.* 1480–85. The first illustration of a French translation of Caesar's *Commentaries*. Flemish. Oxford, Bodleian Library, MS Douce 208, f. iv. By permission of the Bodleian Library.

distant cousin of Richard's queen), and Sir Adrian Fortescue in 1532, the last writing out a copy himself.[42] Readers from the fourteenth to the sixteenth centuries came from all classes: members of parliament, lawyers, clerics, as well as dissidents and Lollards. The poem attracted an attentive and literary-minded reader who was interested in the condition of mankind under God, in government, education and the spiritual betterment of the human race.[43] It was not an easy work to understand as a whole, though it was full of enter-taining characters and had sections of lively narrative and 'adventure'. It demanded intellectual involvement; it was 'designed to cast off the slothful reader'.[44] Looking at the contents of Richard's other books it is fairly evident that he could have been an industrious and committed reader.

If we cannot add any great new dimension to Richard III's personal-ity from our study of his books, it is nevertheless certain we know more than we did about both him and them. We know more of him and his books than of any other English medieval king for the simple reason that he *signed* so many of them. The number of his surviving books *is* con-siderable, their nature *is* revealing, and they are not the non-committal, arbitrary remnants of an official royal collection, but individually marked, personal belongings. It is justifiable to read their message with care; con-clusions, in the past, have been based on far less.

There is enough material to provide an adequate basis for a study and also to convince that even if more survived it would not change the tenor of the final picture, though it might change its proportions. Admittedly there are subjects on which Richard appears to have owned no books; he had, for example, no works of theology, no medical, agricultural or alchemical texts. It is more relevant, however, that we know he *wished* to own most of the manuscripts that survive and took pleasure in mark-ing each as his own. Particularly revealing is his book of hours with his chosen additions: his birthday in the calendar, the collect of St Ninian, the crusading litany and the long, cathartic prayer for comfort. Equally

---

42 Middleton, 'Audience and public', pp. 108–09, 147–48 nn. 6–8. Charlton and Anne Neville were both descendants of Adam Fraunceys, mayor of London 1352–54, present authors, 'The making of a minor London chronicle', p. 90, corrected p. 199.

43 Middleton, 'Audience and public', pp. 101, 103–04, 108, 147–48 nn. 6–8. See also Burrow, 'Audience', passim.

44 Pearsall, *Piers Plowman*, p. 16. Middleton, 'Audience and public', passim, and especially pp. 109–23. She discusses the other works the poem is found with in the surviving mss to establish its appeal and its perceived *genre*, and finds it alongside romances and histories as well as works on piety.

interesting, and perhaps even more unusual, is the Latin compendium of the early history of his race and his country, which he acquired late but was pleased to claim as his own with his royal signature; it is one of the few books to have marginal comments throughout and even if none of them can be proved to be Richard's own, some of them were already there to focus his attention. This volume, in combination with the French and English chronicles he had, allowed him to survey the whole of world history from the siege of Troy to almost his own day. It is Richard's interest in history and chronicle information, so evident even in his relatively small collection – though not unusual at the time – that impresses most; religion, in the shape of his very personal book of hours and his Bible texts, follows; and thirdly, partly overlapping with these two other categories, he owned a substantial amount of narrative entertainment.

All the facts seem to point to Richard, both as duke and king, having a 'positive' attitude to books, being conscious of their existence and their value, and capable of protecting them by the 1484 proviso. He did not collect books as objects but used them for what they could give him and others in the way of instruction, consolation and entertainment:

> Books delight us ... they comfort us ... no serious judgments are propounded without their help.... . In books we climb mountains ...[45]

Above all books gave advice and remained to give advice long after formal education had ceased. A prince, more than any other, relied on advice – mostly from human counsellors, both secular and clerical. Proper education for his subjects, so they might become loyal servants and counsellors, was a prince's everyday concern: his household took boys for a military and courtly education; he patronised places of religious instruction for his clergy, both for the good of his own soul and the state. Books were needed by all men and for all these processes of learning, and books remained to advise the pupil once the teacher had been outgrown. It is arguable that of all those who needed continual advice and impartial counsel princes had the greatest need of books, described by Richard de Bury as those most secret, unsleeping and uncritical of counsellors:

> no one can rightly rule a commonwealth without books.[46]

---

45 Richard de Bury, *The Love of Books*, p. 94.
46 *Ibid.*, pp. 89 (and 11–12).

Catalogue of Richard III's Books and Books Associated with Him

The following handlist is based closely on the sequence of articles on the individual books which appeared in *The Ricardian* 1986–96 and fuller references and more bibliographical details are to be found there. Here more detailed information is only given where no library catalogue entry exists or where the information is particularly relevant to Richard's ownership or use of the book.

A. Richard III's Books

I. MECHTILD OF HACKEBORN, THE *BOOKE OF GOSTLYE GRACE*

A fourteenth-century translation of the *Liber Spiritualis Gratiae* of the German mystic and teacher Mechtild of Hackeborn, who was a nun at the Cistercian convent at Helfta, Saxony, in the thirteenth century. The English version became very influential and fragments and redactions can be found in other devotional treatises.

The Manuscript. BL, Egerton MS 2006. The text begins: *Capitula prime partis. Here begynneth the ferst chapitere* … (f. 1), and ends: *Explicit liber Sancte Matildis virginis Et Monache* (f. 212). Written in one mid-fifteenth-century hand, probably in the north or north-east Midlands. Vellum; *c.* 250 × 170 mm., written space *c.* 185 × 110 mm., 212 folios (one pasted-down flyleaf at the beginning and one at the end). Text in one column, 32–36 lines to a page. Modern foliation. A seven-line blue and red initial *H* at the beginning of the table of chapters; initial letters in this table are alternately red and blue. There are blue capitals with red pen flourishes at the beginning of each chapter of the text; rubrics are in red ink. There are some scribbles and marginal marks.

Binding. Original untooled rough leather binding over chamfered boards; fragments of three straps remain on the front and of a central boss on the back.

Illumination. None.

Ownership and Use. On the pasted-down front flyleaf are the fifteenth-century signatures *Anne warrewyk* and *R Gloucestr'* and, in a later hand, *lying legend alias Romance* *de Sancte Matilde*. On the last pasted down flyleaf *R Gloucestr'* is repeated and another *R* probably in his hand; this page also has some names, pen-trials and Latin tags, the most interesting of which is *Equore cum gelido zepherus fert maximis kymbris*, an example of a standard pen-trial containing virtually all the letters of the alphabet (compare Bischoff, 'Elementarunterricht', p. 15).

Other Manuscripts. Oxford, Bodleian Library, MS Bodley 220; see Halligan, *Booke*, pp. 1–3.
Catalogue. BL, *Catalogue of Additions to the Manuscripts, 1861–1875*, pp. 945–46.
Edition. Halligan, *Booke*, used the ms. for collation with her base text, MS Bodley 220.
Other Main References. 'R III's books I'; *Manual*, vol. 9, XXIII [65].

II. COLLECTION OF ROMANCES AND OLD TESTAMENT STORIES
A. COLLECTION OF ROMANCES: JOHN LYDGATE, *SIEGE OF THEBES*, GEOFFREY CHAUCER, THE *KNIGHT'S TALE* AND THE *CLERK'S TALE*, PROSE *IPOMEDON* (*IPOMEDON* C)

The collection starts with Lydgate's *Siege of Thebes*, ff. 1–48v; the text begins with the prologue: *Whan that Phebus passed was the Ram / Mid of Aprill and into the bole cam*, and ends abruptly in the third book: *Oute of citees and royall tounes / Comen all the ladies and women of estate / Ful hevy chered and disconsolate / In this assemble afforn as i you told*. Ff. 49–52 are lost and *c.* 300 lines of the poem are therefore missing at the end.

The second item is Chaucer's *Arcite and Palomon*, ff. 53–77; it begins: *Whilom as olde stories tellen us / There was a duke that hight theseus*, and ends: *Explicit Arcite and Palomon*. F. 68 is missing in the middle, otherwise the text is complete. Chaucer's *Grisild* follows, ff. 77v–89v; it begins: *There is at the west side of Italie / Down at the rote of Vesuvius the old*, and ends with *lenvoie Chaucer* (*Grisild is dead and eke hir pacience ...*) and *Explicit Grisild full of Pacience*. Ff. 81–82 and 87–88 are missing. The final romance text is the prose *Ipomedon*, ff. 90–105v, it begins: *Sum tyme there was in the land of Cecile a king ...* , and ends at the bottom of the page in the middle of a sentence: ... *And Ipomedon said, the quene of Poill*. F. 101, and f. 106 which had the end of the story, are lost.

B. COLLECTION OF OLD TESTAMENT STORIES: A MIDDLE ENGLISH VERSE PARAPHRASE OF THE OLD TESTAMENT

The text includes Exodus, Numbers, Deuteronomy, Joshua, Judges, Ruth 1–4, 1–4 Kings, Job, Tobit, Esther, Judith and parts of 2 Maccabees (6: 10 and 18–31; 7: 1–41; 9: 4–29, called *De matre cum septem pueris*), filling ff. 119–212. Ff. 111–18 (which originally included Genesis), 145–48, 151, 154–55, 188 and part of 211 are lost. The text begins abruptly in Exodus: *Thre monethes theym hym hyd and lenger they durst noght abyde / Bot in a case hym did and layd hym by the see syde*, and ends: *Pray we to god forthy with the modre and hire sonnes seven / That we may be werthy to wonne with theim in heven. Explicit*.

The Manuscript. Longleat House, Library of the Marquess of Bath, MS 257 (formerly MS 25). The ms. as a whole was written in the third quarter of the fifteenth century in two different but very similar hands. Modern commentators are not unanimous about the provenance of the text or the scribes; the language of the romances is a mixture of southern and northern elements; the Old Testament appears to be markedly northern. Vellum; *c.* 300 × 210 mm., written space *c.* 200 × 110 mm., originally 212 folios, of which 187 remain. Both prose and verse pages are written in one column, most have 46 lines. Modern foliation, which allows for the lost leaves. The ms. consists of two clearly separate parts, the first containing the romances, the second the Bible stories. Between the two parts there were a number of blank leaves, four of which survive, ff. 107–110 (see below **Ownership and Use**). In the romances, subdivisions of

the text are marked by alternate blue and red capitals; on many pages the initial of the first line is decorated with penwork. In the Bible text each stanza of six lines starts with a blue or red capital.
Binding. Late nineteenth-century.
Illumination. F. 1 has a full vinet of green, blue, pink and orange foliage and an 11-line capital *W* in pink and blue, on a yellow ground suggesting gold. The decoration of this page is now the most elaborate of the book and f. 1 may have been the front page from the first; the first page of the Bible section is missing. In the romance section the decoration of f. 1 continues in the same style. Some capitals have shields of arms, 'hanging' on a buckled strap; all the arms have been completely erased. In the Bible section the illumination is again similar; all Bible books except Deuteronomy are introduced by large initials, about half of them with shields of arms, one of them erased, the others never filled in.
Ownership and Use. On f. 98v, about half-way through the *Ipomedon* and about half-way through the ms., in the bottom margin is written: *tant le desieree / R Gloucestre* in Richard's own hand. F. 107 has pen-trials, f. 107v some verse by Francis Thynne, beginning: *That kinge that first gave life to the in/Cres theye happie dayes, Oh kinge.* F. 108r–v has more pen-trials and scribbles. F. 109r–v has two sets of household rules, one on each side, the first headed: *the order how a jentylman hysher schall scerwe hys gret master in doying the sarwyse for the afternon,* and the second: *howe and in wat maner a jentyllman howsschar schalle sarwe hys greet master or mestres ther lewery for alle nyt*; both are written in a late fifteenth or early sixteenth-century hand. On the opposite page, f. 110, a sixteenth-century hand copied out the second set of rules. On f. 110v Francis Thynne wrote some anti-women verse, most of them later obliterated; at the top of the page two lines in his hand appear to read: *Heye that in yeuthe nowarteue wylleues, in age all honore shall heyme refeues* followed by a date *1597*, indicating that he had the use of the ms. at that time. On f. 212v two fifteenth-century hands wrote out some facts about weights and measures used in England and *a medicine for the axes* (ague).
On some pages of the Bible text the hand of the scribe (or one very close to it) added marginal notes, drawing attention to events in the text. A later owner, who may also have added the chapter numbers according to the Vulgate, made comments on the errors of the translator.
Richard of Gloucester's ownership need not be doubted and in view of the date of the ms. he may have been the first owner. Indications of later ownership are the poetic efforts of Francis Thynne, antiquarian and Lancaster Herald, who died childless in 1608. An earlier candidate is his father, William Thynne, collateral ancestor of the Marquess of Bath and the first editor of Chaucer (d. 1546). He was Clerk of the Kitchen and Master of the Household to Henry VIII and in a position to acquire a royal manuscript; he could also have been the copyist of the rules for the conduct of the usher. For more detail see the sources listed under **Other Main References.**
Other Manuscripts. Many mss survive for the Lydgate and the Chaucer texts; the Ipomedon text is unique. Of the Old Testament stories Oxford, Bodleian Library, MS Selden Supra 52 provides the only other – more complete – copy.
Catalogue. None.
Edition. There are many editions of the Chaucer texts. Lydgate's *Siege* was edited by Erdmann and Ekwall. The *Ipomedon* was edited by Kölbing. The Old Testament paraphrase was edited by Kalén and Ohlander.
Other Main References. 'R III's books II'; *Manual*, vol. 1, I [102]; Meale, 'Middle English romance of *Ipomedon*'; Guddat-Figge, *Catalogue*, no. 63; Manly and Rickert, pp. 339–42 (Ll¹).

III. THE ENGLISH NEW TESTAMENT (Wycliffe translation)
All the books of the New Testament, with introductions to individual sections, but not the General Prologue or the glosses, in an early – but not very early – version of the Wycliffite

translation and is preceded by a simple calendar with the Bible readings for various feast-days inserted.

The Manuscript. New York, Public Library, MS De Ricci 67. The Bible text begins: *Mathewe of jewerie born* ... (p. 1); and ends: ... *the grace of oure lord ihesu crist with you all Amen* (p. 276). The ms. was perhaps written *c.* 1390, probably in the East Midlands; the Bible readings for the various feast days were inserted in the calendar by a different but almost contemporary hand. Vellum, size of book *c.* 289 × 185 mm., page size *c.* 275 × 175 mm.; written space *c.* 205 × 135 mm. 6 and 276 pages. There are also 8, originally 12, paper flyleaves at the beginning, and 12 at the end; the first of the flyleaves was originally, and the last still is, pasted to the cover. Text in two columns, 43–47 lines to a page. No original foliation; the six pages of the calendar are unnumbered, the New Testament text has a pagination added *c.* 1700, 1–276. Three-line blue initial capitals with red flourishing begin all chapters. There are corrections by the original scribe or a near-contemporary hand in the margin.

Binding. Probably original; flexible, 'old English sheepskin' according to De Ricci, with an incised rule around the edges of front and back. A paper label with 67 written on it is stuck on the spine. The remains of two metal and leather clasps survive.

Illumination. There is no other decoration than the flourished chapter initials.

Ownership and Use. There are many inscriptions, underlinings, marginal notes and other signs of ownership and use. The most important signs of ownership are: f. ii verso (flyleaf), in black ink, nineteenth-century hand, in upper right corner, *Thomas Banister Inner Temple*; on the first page of the calendar, in the lower margin, *A vo⁹ me ly Gloucestre* (*A vous me lie*). On p. 276 fifteenth-century and early sixteenth-century pen-trials and copies of bills mention the names John Glyd?, John Merten?, John Thomas of Westfyrle? and Richard Mygmore?. A large, late hand added the numbers of pages, chapters and verse.

Thomas Banister (*c.* 1793–*c.* 1875), soldier and lawyer in the Inner Temple, owned the ms. when Forshall and Madden used it for their edition of the Wycliffite Bible. When the book was sold by Sotheby, Wilkinson and Hodge on 8 June 1875 – to Quaritch for £331 – it was claimed that Banister could 'trace its existence in the family for at least four generations' and with the book were sold letters from various authorities claiming it had been owned by Thomas, Duke of Gloucester (d. 1397), Humphrey, Duke of Gloucester (d. 1447), or Richard of Gloucester, and early members of the Banister family were named as possible recipients of the gift of the book from one or other of these dukes. In the absence of other evidence the script of the signature on the first page of the calendar and the similarity of the motto to Richard's other mottoes make him the most likely writer of the inscription. The ms. was given to the New York Public Library by J.J. Astor in 1884.

Other Manuscripts. Many mss of this translation of the New Testament and its later version survive, see Forshall and Madden, and Fristedt.

Catalogue. De Ricci and Wilson, *Census*, no. 67, p. 1325.

Edition. Forshall and Madden used this ms. for collation with others.

Other Main References. Forshall and Madden, vol. 1, p. lxiii, item 162, manuscript *S*; Fristedt, *Wycliffe Bible*, manuscript *S*; 'R III's books III'; sale catalogue of Sotheby, Wilkinson and Hodge, 8–9 June 1875, lot 333, pp. 30–31.

IV. FLAVIUS VEGETIUS RENATUS, *DE RE MILITARI* (Walton translation)

A work of practical instruction in the art of war written by a minister of finance at the Roman Imperial court towards the end of the fourth century AD when the first barbarian invasions threatened the Empire. Divided into four (sometimes five) books covering exercise and physical training, the ideal composition of an army and its officers, the general rules governing the practice, strategies and tactics of war, and lastly fortifications and war at sea. Widely disseminated, translated, copied and reworked throughout the Middle Ages and later. The text owned by Richard III is a copy of an English translation made for Thomas, Lord Berkeley, in 1408, probably by John Walton.

The Manuscript. London, BL, MS Royal 18 A xii. The text begins: *Here begynneth a short tretise* …; and ends with the colophon of the translator: … *This boke was translate in to English in the vigill of All Hallowes the yere of oure lord god ml cccc and viijth yere etc.* The ms. was written in 1483–84 in London (see **Illumination**, below), in an unremarkable English hand. Vellum; *c.* 240 × 155 mm.; 123 ff. (three modern paper free flyleaves, two vellum ones and one additional modern paper leaf at the beginning; three ruled but blank vellum flyleaves and three modern paper free ones at the end). On the second vellum flyleaf at the beginning is written *Vigesius* in a fifteenth-century hand. Text in one column, 25 lines to a page. Modern foliation. Important words such as headings, names of certain persons, regions and military ranks (some left in Latin) are in red; paragraph marks throughout are in red, blue or gold, with red or blue penwork. Each chapter begins with an initial letter of gold on a coloured ground – dark rose and blue, over-painted with white sprays of pinnate leaves – with ornamental pen-sprays extending into the margin and terminating in curls dotted with green, seed-heads or other shapes filled with gold.

Binding. Red leather stamped with the arms and monogram of George II, dated 1757.

Illumination. No miniatures. Each of the four books opens with a full 'vinet', that is a decorated 6, 7, 8-line initial letter on gold with a decorated border of formal and naturalistic foliage and flowers enclosing all sides of the text. Book One (f. 1) has an *H* enclosing the arms of England supported by the silver (now oxidised) boars of Richard III beneath an imperial crown; in the centre of the lower border, a gold griffin on a green mound for the earldom of Salisbury held by Richard's son and derived from the family of Queen Anne Neville; naturalistic flowers in the borders are pink roses and columbines. Book Two (f. 26) begins with an *I* composed of entwined acanthus leaves; with naturalistic pink marshmallows and yellow acorns in bright green cups in the borders. Book Three (f. 49) has an *H* enclosing the arms of Queen Anne Neville; the naturalistic flowers in the border are thistles, daisies and violets. Book Four (f. 98) has an *H* filled with formalised foliage; the naturalistic plants in the border are periwinkles, thistles, strawberries, pinks, acorns and a single mauve crocus. For the illuminated chapter initials and paragraph marks see **The Manuscript**, above. The quality of the illumination is not outstanding but it is a pleasant and decorative book; it can be directly linked to other work produced in London, such as the Wax Chandlers' Charter granted 16 February 1484, also decorated with the same repertoire of formal and naturalistic flowers.

Ownership and Use. The sole owner, commissioner or recipient is indicated by the arms of Richard III, his queen and the griffin of his son. It must be presumed that the volume has remained in the Royal Collection since Richard's day. No signs of use or annotations.

Other Manuscripts. Eleven of this translation, listed by Lester, *Earliest English Translation*, pp. 17–23.

Catalogue. Warner and Gilson (not in the old catalogues of the old Royal and Kings' Collection).

Edition. Made from Bodleian Library, Douce MS 291, Lester, *Earliest English Translation*.

Other Main References. 'R III's Books IV'; Lester, *Earliest English Translation*; *Richard III*, no. 131.

V. AEGIDIUS ROMANUS (GILES OF ROME), *DE REGIMINE PRINCIPUM*

A book of moral and practical guidance for princes and others, composed for the future Philip IV of France in 1277–79 by Aegidius Romanus, Augustinian friar and one of the most influential teachers of the University of Paris (d. 1316). Three books, of which One treats of the virtues essential for a prince; Two, the management of the household and family, and of education; Three, the state and its government in peace and war.

The Manuscript. London, Lambeth Palace Library, MS Arc. L 40.2/L 26 (formerly London, Sion College, MS Arc. L 40.2/L 26). The text begins (f. 1): *Ex regia ac sanctissima prosapia* ...; and ends (f. 96): ... *benedictus in secula seculorum*. All the contents of the ms. were written towards the end of the second quarter of the fifteenth century and in one professional hand, in heavily abbreviated Latin; some corrections to text were added by same hand in margin (ff. 37v, 38v). Vellum; *c.* 400 × 280 mm., 2 and 101 and 1 ff. (one missing). F. 1 is badly stained and rubbed. Text in two columns. A 12-line initial *A* of blue decorated with white opens the text on f. 1; chapters are opened with 4-line initials in blue with fine red penwork, occasionally enlivened by a hooded head, a dragon or a yawning bear or dog, etc. Paragraph marks are in red or blue. Each new letter of the alphabetical index is given 3-lines and each item has a paragraph mark in red and blue alternately. There is an alphabetical index to contents at the end (ff. 96-100), and a scribal tag (f. 100):

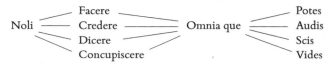

Binding. Seventeenth-century.

Illumination. Only the first folio, which is badly rubbed, has a vinet or full border of foliage; this incorporates two coats of arms, a small, originally gold, eagle with half-spread wings and perched on a pedestal, decorated with two small red crosses, and another, now unidentifiable, bird. Coats of arms decorate the opening initials of each of the divisions of the book, with tendrils of foliage extending along the margin: the prologue, the three books divided into four, three and three parts respectively, and the list of contents. The books have 6- or 7-line initials and their parts have 5-line initials. F. 1 has two coats as part of the original scheme: (1) in the initial letter, Edward the Confessor impaling France modern and England quarterly, with a crest of a lion passant or on a cap of maintenance, to represent Richard II; (2) in right-hand border, England, a label three points azure, each point charged with three fleur-de-lis or (?), with a crest as in (1), to represent the house of Lancaster. In its bottom margin three ill-executed coats have been added to f. 1: (i) sable three escallops argent (?) for Strickland, or Jervaulx Abbey; (ii) sable a chevron argent (?); (iii) per chevron argent and azure, three escallops countercoloured (?). None of these arms have been identified, nor do they seem to be family connections of Francis Babington. F. 6v: or, an eagle displayed argent, to represent St John of Beverley. F. 22: azure, a cross fleury between four lions rampant, all argent, for the Monastery of St Cuthbert, Durham. F. 27v: or, nine mascles gules, 3, 3, 2, 1, probably for St William Fitzherbert, Archbishop of York (d. 1154). F. 32: argent, a cross gules, for St George. F, 42: France modern and England quarterly, a label of three points argent, each point charged with three (roundels gules ?), in pretence a shield of Mortimer, probably for Richard, Duke of York. F. 51v: quarterly, 1 and 4, or, a lion rampant azure, and 2 and 3, gules three luces argent, impaling gules, a saltire argent, that is Percy impaling Neville. Probably to represent Henry Percy, 1st Earl of Northumberland who married Eleanor, daughter of Ralph

Neville, Earl of Westmorland in 1414. F. 60v: argent, a cross gules, in the dexter chief quarter a sword erect also gules, for London. F. 68: argent on a cross gules, five lions passant guardant or, for York. F. 84: quarterly 1 and 4, or, an eagle displayed argent; 2 and 3, argent, three bars wavy azure, on a chief also azure a beaver or with its head turned biting its fur, to represent Beverley (the tinctures are in error). F. 84v: azure, three crowns or, for St Edmund; possibly an error for azure, three crowns in pale or, for Hull. The painter placed the last coat of arms, intended for the index, by mistake, in the 4-line space reserved for the simpler initial of the second chapter of the third part. Later a 5-line *S* was added to begin the index in the same style but with only a little foliage for decoration. Throughout the colours are very bright: vivid crimson, dark orange, blue and green.

Ownership and Use. The heraldry of the book, with its strong northern bias, suggests that Henry Percy, 1st Earl of Northumberland (d. 1455), was its commissioner, as his is the only non-royal personal coat in the sequence. This is reinforced by the close Percy associations with Durham, Beverley, York, and the possible Hull coat. The royal arms may be explained by a desire to commemorate the year 1416, when he received a new grant of the earldom of Northumberland from Henry V. The identification of the arms on f. 42, as those of Richard, Duke of York, may be justified by York's marriage to Cecily, sister of Northumberland's wife, Eleanor, which had taken place by 1424. In the top right-hand corner of f. 1, a now illegible inscription read: *Egidius de Regimine Liber illustrissimus Principis Ducis Gloucestr'* ('the most illustrious book of the Prince, the Duke of Gloucester'). This has generally been accepted as most likely to refer to Richard of Gloucester. How the volume passed to his ownership is not known. The next known owner is Francis Babington, the book collector (d. 1569), who wrote his name and the date of 1550 on f. 1. It was presented to Sion College by Walter Travers, the Puritan divine, chaplain of Lord Burghley and tutor to Robert Cecil, 1635–36.

Other Manuscripts. Hundreds of mss and many recensions and abridgements, but no convenient list in print.

Catalogue. Ker, *Medieval Manuscripts in British Libraries*, vol. 1, pp. 282–83.

Edition. No modern edition of Latin text. Frequently printed, e.g. Rome 1556, reprinted Frankfurt 1968.

Other Main References. 'R III's books V'; *Richard III*, no. 157.

VI. THE FITZHUGH or ANONYMOUS CHRONICLE, also called BROMPTON'S CHRONICLE

A Latin chronicle from the first preparations for the conversion of the Anglo-Saxons to the coronation of King John in 1199. The author is unknown; probably a layman with an administrative background; possibly with a northern bias; he wrote between the 1350s and 1377 (and no original copy survives). He states that he compiled the work for his own entertainment and to record the deeds of kings, as did Geoffrey of Monmouth, whom he aimed to continue and whom he criticised for not including the conversion of the Anglo-Saxons. He used a vast number of sources but it is difficult to know which he used direct and which he derived from such writers as Higden (his most recent source): Bede, Gerald of Wales, William of Malmesbury, Ralph Diceto, William of Newburgh, Benedict of Peterborough, Roger of Hoveden. He cited many documents in full and included, unusually, the texts of 'Glanvill', Henry II's Assizes, and the laws of the kings of England taken from the unusual *Quadripartitus*, a legal text book of 1114. Latin.

The Manuscript. Cambridge, Corpus Christi College, MS 96. The text begins: *Postquam contigit Britones modo Waleorum Guallone* ... (f. 1), and ends: ... *et temeraria presumpcione accepit*

(f. 237v). The ms. was written in the early fifteenth century, *c.* 1425, presumably in the North. Vellum; *c.* 365 × 240 mm., 239 folios (2 unfoliated flyleaves at beginning, 2 at end (ff. 239 and 240) the last one being pasted to cover). Text in one column, 48 lines to a page. There is no original foliation as the top right corner of all the pages is missing with no damage to the text. The only decorated initial is that opening the chronicle, a 5-line *A* with unremarkable *fleuronné* work. All other 2- and 3-line initials are plain with no flourishes in red or blue. Paragraph marks and brackets are in red or blue and line-endings are in red. Larger line-fillers are in red or blue. The original scribe added a lot of attention marks and dates in the margins. Some later writers have done the same and given sources of passages. Much of the text is underlined.

Binding. Rebound 1954. In excellent condition, apart from the missing top right corner.

Illumination. The opening 6-line initial *P* of the author's prologue (f. 1) is decorated and contains the arms of William, 4th Lord Fitzhugh (1425–52) in bright colours with a little gold, against a background of olive green, and the entire text is surrounded by a simple, neat border of foliage tendrils in green, red and blue, of no particular artistic merit. The seal of William II of Sicily is illustrated in yellow, blue and red (f. 164), the drawing done as if the seal is tagged to the preceding text of the charter.

Ownership and Use. William, 4th Lord Fitzhugh, 1425–52, whose arms are in the opening initial, probably commissioned the volume. The signature of his son, Henry, 5th Lord Fitzhugh, 1452–72, appears on the last flyleaf as *Henry ffytzhugh* (f. 240, stuck to the cover). Immediately above this signature is that of *Richard Gloucestr'*. The book was procured at some date for the Abbey of Jervaulx by its abbot, John Brompton (1436–60s or later?) according to the text, *Liber monasterii Jorevall[is] ex procuracione domini Johannis Bromton abbatis eiusdem loci. Si quis hunc librum alienaverit delebitur de libro vite* (f. 237v). This assertion that Brompton actively acquired the book for his abbey and the unknown length of his abbacy makes the extent of the interest in the volume of both Henry Fitzhugh and Richard of Gloucester difficult to assess. The chronicle was seen at Jervaulx by the antiquarian, John Leland, 1534–43 (compare *De Rebus Britannicis Collectanea*, vol. 4, p. 44, to Twysden, cols. 800–990); and almost certainly passed to the Royal Library of Henry VIII at the dissolution of the abbey.

The 'mr Osborne' (f. 1) shows that Peter Osborne, 1521–92, the lawyer who became keeper of Edward VI's privy purse, 1551–52, and remembrancer to the lord treasurer of the exchequer in 1553, acquired it from the Royal Library or possibly from the estate of John Leland, via Sir John Cheke, the uncle of his wife. John Bale, the antiquarian and book collector (d. 1563), consulted the book and wrote *Chronicon Johannis Bromton Abbatis Jorevallensis Cisterciensis instituti* (f. 1), thus starting the notion that Brompton wrote the chronicle, an idea he also promulgated in his *Index Britanniae Scriptorum*; the book was still owned by Osborne in 1548 when the *Index* was published. Archbishop Parker exchanged with Osborne a copy of Higden's *Polychronicon* for this chronicle, probably after 1560: *[H]ec Chronica comparata est a Mro Petro Osburne pro Chronica Ranulphi Cestrensis sive polichronicon in magno volumine* (verso of flyleaf, opposite f. 1). No sign of Parker's red chalk has been found in the book, but his secretary, John Joscelyn, added a list of the chronicle's sources on the same page. The volume formed part of Archbishop Parker's bequest to Corpus Christi College, Cambridge, in 1575. Many users, besides the original scribe, made notes in the margins and gave sources of passages. For details of the unattributed scribbles, cipher, and tags on the last two flyleaves, probably all dating from the period of monastic ownership, see 'R III's books VI', p. 110; James, *Corpus Christi College*.

Other Manuscripts. BL, MS Cotton Tiberius C xiii is the only other surviving copy of this chronicle; fifteenth-century, but later than Corpus Christi College 96; the two mss are in no way related. Vellum. Undecorated and with no ownership marks before those of Sir Robert Cotton (f. 3); he acquired it in 1604 (f. 265v).

Catalogue. James, *Corpus Christi College.*

Edition. Twysden, *Historiae Anglicanae Scriptores*, cols. 725–1284, with an introduction by John Selden.

Other Main References. The Selden introduction is still invaluable. 'RIII's books VI'; Liebermann, *Gesetze*, pp. xix–xx, and his *Quadripartitus*, pp. 65, 70 ff.; Keeler, *Geoffrey of Monmouth*, pp. 20–23; Robertson, *Laws*, pp. ix–xi.

VII. GUIDO DELLE COLONNE, *HISTORIA DESTRUCTIONIS TROIAE*

The *Historia destructionis Troiae* by Guido delle Colonne (fl. *c.* 1259–80) is a Latin prose reworking of Benoît de Sainte-Maure's French *Roman de Troie*. According to its colophon the text was composed in 1278. It covers the legends of Jason and the Golden Fleece, the building of the first Troy and its destruction by Hercules, and the Trojan War itself. The latter is based on the 'eye-witness' accounts of Dictys the Cretan, who fought on the Greek side, and Dares the Phrygian, who helped to defend Troy. These accounts were only exposed as first and fifth- or sixth-century forgeries in the early eighteenth century. The book introduced, for example, the love story of Troilus and Briseis (Troilus and Cressida) into western European literature.

The Manuscript. St Petersburg, Saltykov-Shchedrin State Public Library, MS Lat. F IV 74. The text begins (f. 1; capitals and punctuation modernised): *Et si cotidie vetera recentibus obviant* [sic] *nonnulla tamen jamdudum vetera processerunt* [sic] *que sic sui natura magnitudine vivaci sunt digna memoria ut nec ea cecis morsibus vetustas abolere prevaleat ...,* and ends (f. 114v): *Et specialiter ille summus poetarum Virgilius quem nichil statuit,* [sic; last word underlined by a commentator] *latuit ne eius veritas incognita remaneret ad presentis operis perfectionem efficaciter laboravi. Explicit liber de casu Troie. deo gracias.* The ms. was written in the first half of the fifteenth century in an English hand, showing French influence. Paper; c. 290 × 210 mm., 117 ff. (i, 116, incl. two folios 26, f. 116 and f. 116 bis). Text in one column, 30 to 35 lines to a page. A 10-line opening initial *E*, decorated with penwork, on f. 1; two-line chapter initials and paragraph marks in blue and red throughout. Eighteenth-century pagination only. Catchwords on every sixteenth page. On the first folio a seventeenth-century hand has added a title: *Historia Troiana Guidonis Columna.* Secundo folio: *peregit.* Watermarks: common, used all over the continent from the late fourteenth to the mid-fifteenth century, but pointing to an Italian origin; both this ms. and the next one, Cat. VIII, *Historia regum Britanniae*, have a bow and arrows similar to Piccard, *Wasserzeichen. Werkzeug und Waffen*, nos. 1071–1771, see the description of Cat. VIII, below.

Binding. Eighteenth-century; both this ms. and its companion, the *Historia regum Britanniae*, Cat. VIII, are covered with the green velvet in which Dubrovsky had his most valuable books bound.

Illumination. None.

Ownership and Use. There are many and various marks of ownership: on f. iv, on a note stuck to the pasted down flyleaf: *1.C.1.G.10 1774 14 Fevr. L'an mil s[e]pt Cent soixante-quator[ze] Fevrier, Madame la Princesse de Rohan a donne, pour la Bibliotheque de M. le prince de Soubise, Ce manuscrit intitule historia Trojana Guidonis Columnae, lequel a ete presente par M. Marchand son homme d'affaires de sa part.* On the flyleaf itself is written: *Guido de Columna, Natione Siculus* [last two words cancelled and altered to: *ordinis fratrum predicatorum*] *Patria Romanus archiepiscopus* [last two words inserted] *Messanensis, restauravit ac scholiis ornavit tam Dyctis Cretensi,* [sic] *quam Daretem Phrygium in historiis* *de Bello troyano, ut habet Bosconius Buriensis in suo cathalogo, et scripsit plenissime quidquid in tota historia universaliter ac particulariter fuerit gestum, editique Chronicon magnum lib. 36 De Bello troiana Lib. 1. De Regibus ac rebus Anglorum et alia* [last two words inserted] *plura tradit.* [last word cancelled] *Hic Guido de Columnae claruit anno Dom. 1287. P. Dubrovsky.*

On f. 1, in the top right corner, Richard III's signature: *Ricardus Rex*, and above it Oliver Cromwell's: *O Cromwell 1656*; in the top left corner: *Ex libris domini Ludovici Turquesti domini Lasolaye castri de Piru usufructuarii*; at the foot of the page: *Ex musaeo Petri Dubrovsky*.

On f. 114v, the last page of the text: *James R* (James I) and *Carolus R* (Charles I) and *Ex musaeo Petri Dubrovsky*; on f. 115v: *Louis Turquest Sire de Lasolaye advocat au parlement de Bretaigne residant au chateau de Perier pres Guigamp Evesché de Treguier* and *Roland Riwallon Richard Sire du pontglaz Lez guingamp en Bretaigne*; there are various notes in Russian concerning the number of pages of the ms.

There are many marginalia throughout, mostly in fifteenth- and sixteenth-century hands which cannot be attributed to any known owner of the ms. This ms. and that of the *Historia regum Britanniae*, Cat. VIII, were not produced as one book, but they were probably produced at the same time and always remained together. From *c.* 1650 they were mistakenly regarded as one text, probably bound together and referred to in the singular.

It is not known who owned this ms. and its companion before they were signed by Richard III. It presumably remained in the Royal Library to be signed by James I and Charles I and found there by Cromwell in 1656 (for these owners' interest in the texts see 'RIII's books VII and VIII', passim). Both the *Historia Troiae* and the *Historia regum* may have been taken to the continent by the Protector's son, Richard, and presented to his Breton hosts, the next owners being probably Roland Richard (f. 115v, d. 1662), Louis Turquest (f. 1, d. 1676), and the latter's nephew of the same name (f. 115v). In 1774 the Princess of Rohan presented them to the Prince of Soubise (d. 1787). Sold for *six livres* in May 1789 to Peter Dubrovsky, the Russian book collector whose activities saved many mss. from the ravages of the French revolution, they passed into the Imperial Public Library in 1805.

Other Manuscripts. The full number of surviving mss has not yet been established; Griffin's edition was based on eight mss.

Catalogue. None.

Edition. The text is essentially the same as the one printed in Griffin.

Other Main References. Bakhtin, 'Manuscripts'; Golubeva, 'The Saltykov-Shchedrin Library'; 'RIII's books VII and VIII'. Translation : Meek, *Historia*.

VIII A. GEOFFREY OF MONMOUTH, *HISTORIA REGUM BRITANNIAE*

A copy of the so-called 'vulgate' text of the famous compendium of British history by Geoffrey of Monmouth (d. 1155); it covers the flight of the great-grandson of Aeneas, Brutus, from Italy; his discovery, conquest and naming of Britain; the history of the island before, during and after the Roman occupation; its defence against the Saxon invaders; Arthur and all his victories at home and abroad and the final abandonment of the island by the Britons under Cadwalader, to whom an angel prophesied the eventual return of his people. Geoffrey included in the text his long prophecies of Merlin and he created the figures of Arthur and, for example, Lear and Cymbeline.

The Manuscript. St Petersburg, Saltykov-Shchedrin State Public Library, MS Lat. F IV 76. The text begins (f. 1): *Cum mecum multa et de multis sepius animo revolvens in ystoria regum Britanie inciderem ...* (the scribe wrote *te volvens* but was corrected), and ends (f. 79v): *... reges vero Saxonum Willelmo Malbusberiensi* [sic] *Henrico Contendonensi* [sic] *quos de regibus*

Britonum tacere iubeo cum non habeant librum illum Britannici sermonis, quem Walterus Oxenefordensis archidiaconus ex Britannia advexit quem de [ise] hestoria istorum veraciter editum in honore principum hoc modo in latinum sermonem transferre curavi. The text has the single dedication to Robert of Gloucester. Paper; *c.* 290 × 210 mm., 83 folios (83, i), text in one column, 30–35 lines to a page. Apart from the watermark with the bow and arrows mentioned above, Cat. VII, this ms. also has a three-topped hill in a circle similar to Briquet, nos 11847–50 and 11868–81. Five-line intial *C* decorated with penwork on f. 1. Many chapters have descriptive headings in red, and all have two-line intials in red or blue. Paragraph marks in red. Secundo folio: *partes.* For further details see the description of the previous ms., Cat. VII.

On the first folio a seventeenth-century hand has added a title: *Incipit distinctio britannie liber primus,* presumably because this part of the double manuscript was regarded as a section of Guido delle Colonne's work. The manuscript has many scribal and textual errors, many of them corrected by an early hand, perhaps the scribe's own.

Binding. See previous ms., Cat. VII.

Illumination. None.

Ownership and Use. F. 1, top right corner, the signature of Richard III: *Ricardus Rex,* top left: *O Cromwell 1656,* at the foot of the page: *Ex musaeo Petri Dubrowsky.* F. 83v, at the end of the text: *James R* (James I), *Carolus R* (Charles I) and *Ex musaeo Petri Dubrowsky.* Compare the description of the *Historia Troiae,* Cat. VII, above.

Marginalia in this ms. are few and often illegible, partly because the pages have been cropped; many show an English bias.

Other Manuscripts. So far *c.* 215 other mss have been identified, see e.g Crick, *HRB III,* but the process continues.

Catalogue. None.

Edition. The edition by Hammer remains important, but as part of a plan to provide a comprehensive critical edition of all versions the following have been published: Wright, *HRB I* and *HRB II.*

Other Main References. 'RIII's books VIII'; Crick, *HRB III,* no. 78, and the same, *HRB IV,* no. 78.

VIII B. THE *PROPHECY OF THE EAGLE,* AND ITS COMMENTARY

The *Prophecy of the Eagle* is a composite text made up of various prophecies also known from other sources. As a whole it dates from *c.* 1259, but its parts are older: the *Vision of Edward the Confessor,* the *Here Prophecy,* the *Three Dragons,* and the *Prophecy of the White King.* The *Three Dragons* was so called by the present authors because it contains the images of Merlin's White Dragon (of the Saxons) and Red Dragon (of the Britons) with the Dark Dragon (of the Normans) added to it in a way not found anywhere else. The commentator partially explained the text and, more remarkably, illustrated the three races by long lists of names: a list of British kings, clearly taken from Geoffrey of Monmouth; a list of the Norman 'Companions of the Conqueror', also known as the 'Battle Abbey Roll' and here appearing in its earliest known version; and a unique list of the Saxon kinsmen of King Harold. In the present ms. the *Prophecy of the Eagle* is an additional text to the *Historia regum Britanniae* and closely related to it. It occurs on ff. 79v–80v of St Petersburg, Saltykov-Shchedrin State Public Library, MS Lat. F IV 76 (Cat. VIII A), its Commentary on ff. 80v–83v. The text is headed: *Hic incipit prophetia aquile,* and begins: *Arbor fertilis a primo trunco decisa …,* and ends: *Tunc generalis* [sic] *probitas non patietur illi erogare iniuriam qui pacifico regno accidit.* The Commentary begins: *Arbor fertilis, sanguis Bruti interpretatur …,* and ends with the scribe's: *Explicit. Deo gracias.*

The text has a few marginal notes, mere repetitions of names of people and places mentioned in the text.

Other Manuscripts. 'R III's books VIII', pp. 357–58, n. 1.

Edition. Latin text from another ms.: Parry, *Brut y Brenhinedd*, pp. 225–26. Translation: 'R III's books VIII', pp. 352–57.

Other Main References. 'R III's Books VIII'; present authors, 'Dark Dragon'; Crick, *HRB III*, no. 78; the same, *HRB IV*, pp. 35, 65–66.

IX. *GRANDES CHRONIQUES DE FRANCE*

One volume of the chronicle of the kings of France from their Trojan ancestors to 1461 compiled by the monks of the Abbey of St Denis, covering the period 1270 to 1380, that is from the accession of Philip III to the unsuccessful siege of Nantes by the English. It is generally identical to that of the other copies made *c.* 1380–1400 from the recension made for Charles V; there is the usual abridged version of the visit of the Emperor to Charles V.

The Manuscript. BL, MS Royal 20 C vii. The text is headed by the rubric (f. 1): *Cy commence lystoire du roy philippe filz au roy saint loys*, begins: *Nous avons du bon roy saint loys ...* and ends (f. 216v): *Et sen alerent aucuns et emmenerent grant foison de biens*. Made in Paris; written 1380–1400 and illuminated *c.* 1400–10. Vellum; *c.* 290 × 400 mm., written space *c.* 177 × 256 mm., 216 ff. (two modern paper free flyleaves and two vellum ones at the beginning; one ruled but blank vellum flyleaf and two modern paper ones at the end). Text in 2 columns, 42 lines to a page. Part 1 ends on f. 106v with the colophon, *Cy fenissent les croniques du roy philippe de valoys. Et apres sensuit le couronnement du roy jehan filz du roy phelippe. C.B.* The identity of C.B. is unknown. One folio, blank on both sides, follows and part 2 begins on f. 107. Illuminated three-line initial letters introduce chapters after rubrics; they are foliated on a gold background with sprays of leaves in the margin. Line fillers are blue, wine-red and gold. Paragraph marks are blue or red with red or blue flourishes. A few two-line letters in red or blue with blue or red flourishes introduce sub-sections within chapters at the end of the text. One-line illuminated letters introduce the articles on f. 49r–v.

Binding. Eighteenth-century.

Illumination. Paris, the atelier of the Virgil Master, *c.* 1400–10. 250 large and small miniatures with 57 blank spaces unpainted. An unusual sequence of 9 pictures for the text of the visit of the Emperor to Charles V which otherwise only occurs in Charles V's own copy of the *Grandes chroniques* (BN, MS fr. 2813) and in a copy probably made for Charles VII (BN, MS fr. 6465); Richard's volume may therefore have been started for a royal patron, possibly the duke of Anjou. The illumination was unfinished when the book was originally bound and it is marred by a sequence of very poor work at its beginning, a combination not uncommon in books produced by this atelier. Five closely related illuminators are identifiable including the Virgil Master, and a sixth. Detailed analysis by L. Dennison, 'R III's books IX'.

Ownership and Use. The heraldic knowledge displayed by the illuminators suggests that the original commission was for someone affiliated to the dukes of Anjou. Sole owner indicated is *Richard Gloucestre* whose signature occurs in a space on f. 134. There is no evidence that this was a companion volume to that owned by Humphrey of Gloucester as has been suggested (BL, MS Royal 16 G vi, made *c.* 1350). The book may have come to England by one of many routes. Presumably it has remained in the Royal Library since Richard III's time.

Other Manuscripts. List of copies of the *Chroniques* in England, 'R III's books IX', pp. 511–12 n. 37.

Catalogue. Warner and Gilson, and Delisle, 'Notes', p. 212.

Edition. Paris and Viard; the Viard edition only goes up to 1350 and has to be used with Delachanel.
Other Main References. 'R III's books IX'; Spiegel, *Chronicle Tradition*; Meiss, *Limbourgs*; Avril *et al.*, *Grandes chroniques*; Hedeman, 'Valois legitimacy', pp. 171–81; Fowler, *Plantagenet and Valois*, has many of the miniatures.

X. PROSE TRISTAN

A compendium of the Tristan stories made by several unknown authors in the thirteenth century. It fully integrated their Celtic setting with that of Arthur's court and made Tristan a knight of the Round Table, comparable to Lancelot. It is the largest of all medieval romance compendia and became the sole source of the Tristan and Isolde story until the nineteenth century rediscovered its lost originals. Richard of Gloucester's copy contains less then a tenth of the whole: the story of Tristan's ancestors, his birth, his meeting with Isolde, the love potion, Isolde's marriage to Mark and the lovers' escape to the forest.
The Manuscript. BL, MS Harley 49. The text now begins (f. 1): ... *Sadoc vient cel part et regardoit* ... and ends (f. 148): ... *et toutvoies s'en est eschapee par sa proesce. Quant li prodom* ... in mid sentence. French, written in the middle of the fifteenth century. Vellum; *c.* 276 × 192 mm., written space *c.* 202 × 130 mm., 156 ff. (including one original flyleaf at the beginning and one at the end; there are also modern unnumbered paper flyleaves). Text in one column, 43 to 44 lines to a page. The modern foliation runs 1*, 1–155. The text is divided into sections A–G; at the head of each recto page the appropriate capital is repeated in red. The small chapters have headings in red ink, blue two-line initials and are numbered in Roman numerals in the margin. There is an index of chapter headings at the end.
Binding. Nineteenth-century.
Illumination. None.
Ownership and Use. On the original end-flyleaf is a formal *ex libris*: *Iste liber constat Ricardo duci Gloucestre*. At the foot of the page is a motto and the autograph signature of Elizabeth of York, queen of Henry VII: *sans re[mo]vyr / elyzabeth*. On f. 148v is written: *George Tubervyle / A Turbervyle a monster is that loveth not his friend / or stoops to foes, or doeth forget good turns and so I end*. On f. 154v: *Judith Turbervil*. George Turberville (*c.* 1544–after 1588), the poet, was the grandson of John Turberville, who was associated with the Mortons and served Henry VII; Judith may have been his daughter. The ms. passed to Sir Simonds D'Ewes, to Robert Harley and so to the BL in 1773.
Other Manuscripts. There are too many mss to be listed here.
Catalogue. *A Catalogue of Harleian Manuscripts in the British Museum*; Ward, *Catalogue of Romances*.
Edition. A complete edition is in progress under the general editorship of P. Ménard.
Other Main References. 'R III's books X'; Löseth, *Roman*; Vinaver, *Études*; the same, 'Prose Tristan'; Curtis, *Roman*; the same, *Tristan Studies*; Baumgartner, *Tristan en prose*; Wright, *Fontes Harleiani*; *Richard III*, no. 161.

XI. RAMON LULL, *ORDER OF CHIVALRY*, translated and printed by William Caxton

A treatise of instruction for young men in the virtues of knighthood, written as a dialogue between a squire and a retired knight of long experience. Their meeting is described in the first book, and books two to eight are the treatise, explaining the mythological origins of knighthood and the correct training of knights; the duties of the Christian knight; the examination of candidates and their character; the ceremonies of creation; the symbolic significance of a knight's arms; the customs and virtues he must observe; the honours due to the order of knighthood. The text was written by Ramon Lull, born in Majorca *c.* 1235, a knight and learned author who became a missionary to the Saracens in North Africa, where he was killed in 1315. Caxton's epilogue picks up the author's device of a young squire being given a treatise which he is to take to a king's court for dissemination among prospective knights. Caxton has a squire give the treatise to him for publication and the printer begs Richard III to have his translation given to all knights of the realm. Caxton was also inspired by Lull's enthusiasm to write one of his finest pieces of prose.

Richard III's copy of Caxton's edition does not survive. The five extant copies show that it was a quarto book (130 × 80 mm.), had 52 leaves, the first and the last being blank, and 26 lines to a page. It was printed in Caxton's type 3*, with some of his type 4. The large decorative *A* that opens the text was otherwise only used in Caxton's *Aesop*, printed 26 March 1484, and suggests the *Order* was close in date to the *Aesop*.

Illumination. None.
Catalogue. De Ricci, *Census*, no. 81; Duff, *Fifteenth-Century English Books*, no. 58.
Edition. Byles.
Other Main References. 'R III's books XI'; Minervini, *Ordre*.

XII A. WILLIAM WORCESTER, THE *BOKE OF NOBLESSE*

Composed by Worcester probably not long after 1451, perhaps to please his master, the veteran of the French wars, Sir John Fastolf, the *Boke* was meant to persuade first Henry VI, then Edward IV, and later Richard III, to emulate the deeds of their ancestors and reconquer the English territories in France for the sake of the 'common good' – thus living up to the *noblesse* of the title. Worcester used many authorities, among them Christine de Pizan and Cicero. The *Boke* provided the theoretical and philosophical background for Worcester's argument, while the Collection of Documents (Cat. XII B, below) supplied the documentary evidence.

The Manuscript. BL, MS Royal 18 B xxii. The text begins with the heading (f. 1): *The boke of noblesse compiled to the mest hygh and myghty prince kyng Edward the ivth for the avauncing and preferring the comun publique of the royaumes of England and of Fraunce*, and ends (f. 42): *Here endyth thys epistle undre correccion the xv day of June the ueere of crist m^l iiii^c lxxv. and of the noble regne of kyng Edward iiii^the the xv^ne*. Written in a mid- to late fifteenth-century cursive hand, probably not long after 1461. Paper; very simply and consistently executed; *c.* 283 × 205 mm., written page *c.* 175 × 125 mm., 45 ff. (three modern paper flyleaves and three parchment ones at the beginning; two original ruled but unused paper flyleaves, two parchment ones and three modern paper ones at the end; the first and the last paper flyleaves are stuck down; the parchment leaves may be the remains of an earlier cover). Text in one column, 30 lines to a page. Modern foliation. Decoration consists of a four-line initial *H* with green penwork at the beginning of the actual text and two-line red initials and blue and red paragraph marks throughout. Chapter headings are underlined.

Binding. Eighteenth-century, but some of the thick parchment 'flyleaves' may originally have formed the cover of the book.

Illumination. None.

Ownership and Use. The *Edward* of the heading on f. 1 was underlined and *herry* was added in the margin by way of correction; *ivth* was altered to another, illegible, number (*vj* or *vij*); both alterations were crossed out again and *iiij* restored. Some phrases in the text leave no doubt that the present version was meant for Edward IV, but had been altered from a text meant for Henry VI. Richard III's ownership depends on the evidence found in the dedication of the Collection of Documents, Cat. XII B, below. The ms. has contemporary marginalia, corrections and long additions mostly in Worcester's own hand. There are numerous scribbles containing the names of later owners.

Other Manuscripts. No other copy survives and it is likely no other copy ever existed.

Catalogue. Warner and Gilson.

Edition. J.G. Nichols.

Other Main References. 'R III's books XII'; McFarlane, 'Worcester'.

XII B. WILLIAM WORCESTER, COLLECTION OF DOCUMENTS ON THE WAR IN NORMANDY

These (copies of) documents include lists of Frenchmen who served under the duke of Bedford, regent of France, with some summary biographies, lists of estimated revenues from English possessions in France, of various wages, receipts and expenses, of numbers of soldiers in various garrisons, of the value of lands; ordinances, military inventories, Sir John Fastolf's report and advice on the management of France and similar 'advertysements and instruccion' made by him and others when Richard, Duke of York, and Edmund, Duke of Somerset, were governors. The dedicatory introduction begins: *Most hyghe myghtye and excelente Cristen prince Edwarde by the dyvyne prudence of God the thred kyng of Englande and of Fraunce* ... The first three letters of *Edwarde* are written on an erasure, *thred* is underlined in different ink and *fourth* added in the margin in the same ink as the underlining. The introduction was written by Worcester's son, as he himself says, and the way the relatives of the king are described proves that it was originally meant for Edward IV and altered for Richard III – *your most nobill brodyr and predecessoure*. The items in the Collection of Documents are listed in detail and the *Boke* is also described, though not very accurately; the text was meant to introduce both books together. The Documents, according to Worcester's son, contain the 'experiense of men' and complement the 'deciplyne' of the literary authorities used in the *Boke*.

The Manuscript. London, Lambeth Palace Library, MS 506. Smaller than the *Boke* (Cat. XII A, above) – *c.* 250 × 150 mm., written space *c.* 180 × 90 mm. – and neatly written, the Collection is a jumble of notes and copies. Vellum, i and 75 ff. The first gathering contains the introduction and a list of contents, probably in the hand of Sir Robert Cotton, but is otherwise blank. This gathering was clearly added; the rest of the ms. is in a fifteenth-century hand with some additions by Worcester himself.

Binding. Probably seventeenth-century.

Illumination. None.

Ownership and Use. See the description of the ms. above.

Other Manuscripts. M.R. James refers to a sixteenth-century transcript in the library of the Society of Antiquaries. BL, MS Cotton Nero C x, ff. 91v–92v, has some extracts said to be in the hand of Edward VI.

Catalogue. James, *Lambeth Palace*.

Edition. Stevenson, *Wars of the English in France*, vol. 2, pt 2.

Other Main References. 'R III's books XII'; McFarlane, 'Worcester'; *Richard III*, no. 168.

XIII. ROLLS OF ARMS

A. St George's Roll

The original of this roll of arms, now lost, was made *c.* 1285. It probably contained 677 shields, both painted and blazoned, and measured 9¾ inches × 8 feet 9½ inches. Several copies or versions, some dating from the sixteenth century and later, do survive. Richard's version is also lost, but the evidence of his ownership is found in the copy of the blazons made by Thomas Wriothesley (College of Arms, MS M 14, pp. 392–421 and 461) which is headed: *Ista arma sequencia habebantur in quodam veteri rotulo depicto quondam R ducis gloucester'*. See Wagner, *Aspilogia*, vol. 1, pp. 20–21; Campbell, *Catalogue*, p. 155; 'R III's books: ancestry and "true nobility"', pp. 347–49.

B. 'THOMAS JENYNS' BOOK'

An ordinary (a roll which groups coats together by devices such as the lion), of which the original was made *c.* 1400. It was based on an earlier collection of *c.* 1350 and comprised a large number of shields with blazons. One version, with 1,595 shields, was owned by Queen Margaret of Anjou (BL, MS Add. 40851), another by Thomas Jenyns in the sixteenth century, which does not survive. Richard of Gloucester's version is also lost, but Thomas Wriothesley copied out the blazons (now College of Arms, MS M 14 bis, pp. 462–527) and headed them: *En unq liure Ric' duc de Gloucester' en picture lequel liure son poursuyvant avoit en garde A° xx° E iiijᵗⁱ*. See Wagner, *Aspilogia*, vol. 1, pp. 73–78, and pl. vi; Campbell, *Catalogue*, p. 155; 'R III's books: ancestry and "true nobility"', p. 49.

XIV. PIETRO CARMELIANO, *BEATAE KATERINAE EGYPTIAE CHRISTI SPONSAE VITA*

The ms. that Carmeliano presented to Richard III does not survive, but there is little doubt that it resembled closely the two copies dedicated to Chancellor John Russell (Cambridge, Gonville and Caius College, MS 196/102) and Sir Robert Brackenbury (Oxford, Bodleian Library, MS Laud Misc. 501). It would have been written in the author's own attractive humanist hand on vellum; it would have been small (*c.* 200 × 130 mm., paper size *c.* 195 × 125 mm., written space *c.* 140 × 95 mm.) and thin (18 ff.); a bifolium was probably inserted at the beginning with the laudatory dedication, praising the king's patronage of learning, his justice and his good government in peace and war. The ms. is likely to have had a half-page miniature of St Katherine on the last page of the dedication and some marginal decoration on the opposite page which bore the beginning of the text itself. See Orbán for the edition of the text, and also 'R III's books XIV' and Carlson, *English Humanist Books*, pp. 42–48.

XV. BOOK OF HOURS

The standard Hours of the Blessed Virgin Mary, with the Hours of the Cross and the Hours of the Compassion of the Virgin added in, but also many additional devotions.

The Manuscript. London, Lambeth Palace Library, MS 474. Written in 'a tall narrow English hand', according to M.R. James, *c.* 1420. Vellum; *c.* 193 × 140 mm. (originally at least 236 × 173 mm.), written space *c.* 117 × 83 mm., 184 ff. (several leaves missing, two unruled flyleaves at the end). Modern foliation in pencil. Text in one column, 18 lines to a page. At the beginning are a collect to St Ninian, added for Richard III (f. 1), and memorials to Sts Christopher and George (f. 2r–v), followed by a calendar (ff. 3–8v) and instructions for the seasonal variations for the Hours of the Virgin (ff.9–14). The Hours (ff. 15–54) are followed by the Penitential and Gradual Psalms with the Litany (ff. 54v–71v), the Office of the Dead (ff. 72–90), the Commendation of Souls (ff. 90v–100v), the Psalms of the Passion (ff. 101–12), the Psalter of St Jerome (ff. 112–22v), the Verses of St Bernard (ff. 122v–23v), prayers to God and Christ (ff. 124–45), the Fifteen Oes (ff. 145v–51v), long prayers to the Virgin (ff. 152–62), more devotions to the Virgin and miscellaneous prayers to saints and for various purposes (ff. 162v–80), and devotions added for Richard III, including the so-called 'Prayer of Richard III' and his crusading litany (ff. 181–84v). There are one-line initials in gold or blue decorated with blue and red flourishes; strokes of ochre mark certain lesser capitals in the text. Rubrics and paragraph marks in red. Line fillers are blue and gold.

Binding. Mid-sixteenth-century, with some gold tooling; recently rebacked. The binding was executed in the workshop of the King Edward and Queen Mary Binder, which was active in the 1540s and 1550s doing work for Henry VIII, Edward VI and Mary, as well as lesser customers.

Illumination. Produced in London *c.* 1420. Simple but rich illumination – few openings lack decoration. Three historiated initials mark the beginning of the Hours of the Virgin (f. 15, Annunciation), the Penitential Psalms (f. 35, this would have been a Last Judgment but has been cut out), and the Vigil of the Dead (f. 72, three clerics singing *placebo* and *dirige*). Full vinets accompany these initials. Nine-, eight-, seven-, five- and four-line initials introduce the key items in the book; most prayers rate a three-line initial. All initials are illuminated and decorated with elaborate foliage which extends into the margin. Richard III's additional prayers are introduced by initials in the style of London in the 1480s. The calendar has little decoration. The finest page has the full vinet opening the Hours of the Virgin with an Annunciation depicted in the manner common to London manuscripts of this date, but with two unusual features: the Virgin crosses her hands on her breast and wears a jewelled coronal. The elaborate border includes first-class three-dimensional foliage and patterns, 'portrait' heads of angels and Sts Peter and Paul, all in monochrome; the three-dimensional patterns in monochrome also occur elsewhere in the book.

Ownership and Use. The book was probably made for a cleric *c.* 1420, but no signs of such ownership remain except the unusually large number of additional devotions. Richard III added in his birth-date to the calendar (f. 7v, October 2): *hac die natus erat Ricardus Rex Anglie iijus apud ffodringay anno domini mccc[clij].* The collect of St Ninian was added for him, as was the long prayer on ff. 181–83v, which had *me famulum tuum Regem Ricardum* worked into the text twice, now partly obliterated. The remaining pages of the crusading litany on ff. 148–84v, in the same script and on the same paper as the other additions, show that this was also put in for the king. On one of the end flyleaves was the inscription: *In the honor of god and Sainte Edmonde / Pray for Margarete Richmonde*, noted by M.R. James but now lost. It can be presumed that the book was with Richard III at Bosworth and passed via the Stanleys to Margaret Beaufort, Countess of Richmond, mother of Henry VII. She gave the book to an unknown person. There are some sixteenth-century inscriptions by unidentifiable hands in the calendar, and various erasures and mutilations throughout.

Catalogue. James, *Lambeth Palace.*

Edition. A detailed description and calendar, including the full texts of the collect of St Ninian, the 'Prayer of Richard III' and his crusading litany can be found in *Hours of Richard III.*

Other Main References. Sutton and Visser-Fuchs, 'Richard III and St Julian'.

B. BOOKS ASSOCIATED WITH RICHARD III

XVI. *EPISTOLAE* OF THE PSEUDO-PHALARIS, edited by Pietro Carmeliano

The Latin translation (early 1440s) by Francisco Aretino of Griffolini of a collection of letters in Greek ascribed to the Sicilian tyrant Phalaris (sixth century BC) but written by an unknown third- or fourth-century author. It is preceded by the editor's verse recommending the book and the translator's introduction recommending its reputed author, Phalaris.

The Manuscript. Dublin, Trinity College, MS 429. The author's recommendatory poem begins (f. 3v): *Hunc precor atque precor, lector studiose, libellum perlege* ...; the translator's introduction begins (f. 4): *Vellem Malatesta novelle Princeps* ..., and ends with the author's colophon. Written by the editor, 1482–84. The ms. was probably one of several identical ones that Carmeliano produced at the time. Parchment; *c.* 208 × 138 mm., written space *c.* 125 × 75 mm., 63 ff., 20 to 21 lines to a page. The 63 folios include two original flyleaves at the beginning and two at the end. After the flyleaves at the beginning a single leaf was bound in; this contains the editor's recommendation of the book to the reader, a half-page space for a miniature (filled in with a drawing of two crossed branches and some foliage) and the coat of arms of the recipient in the lower margin. The ms. also has some classical Latin quotations, and on f. 63 a verse translation of the Latin oath of homage taken by temporal peers at the coronation of the kings of England, with one line from the oath taken by the spiritual peers inserted.

Binding. Eighteenth-century.

Illumination. Ff. 3v and 4 have borders of leaves and flowers in blue, green and red, and some gold. The editor's recommendation has a 6-line initial *H*; the text starts with a 2-line initial *V*; both are gold on a crimson background. A red or blue two-line initial opens each letter.

Ownership and Use. The coat of arms on f. 3v is that of the Lee family, of London and Kent (azure, on a fess cotised or, three leopards' faces gules), and the most likely owner of the ms. was John Lee (*c.* 1430–95), doctor of canon law and master of Maidstone College. The inclusion of the Latin version of the oaths taken at the coronation suggests a royal dedication of the ms. to either Edward V or Richard III. The ms. predates the more complete, printed edition of the same letters by Carmeliano in August 1485.

Other Manuscripts. Though Carmeliano very probably produced other copies none are known to survive. The printed edition of 1485, at Oxford by Thomas Hunt and Theoderic Rood, is essentially the same: Carmeliano's recommendatory verse was slightly altered and four more letters were included.

Catalogue. Colker, *Trinity College*.

Edition. There is no modern edition of this Latin translation of these letters.

Other Main References. 'R III's books XIV'; Modigliani, 'Nuovo manoscritto'.

XVII. WILLIAM LANGLAND, *THE VISION OF PIERS PLOWMAN*

The basis for the assumption that Richard III knew *Piers Plowman* is the tradition that he called the castle of Nottingham his 'castle of care', a phrase which occurs in passus 1 of all versions of the poem. The local tradition which ascribes the phrase to Richard III can be traced back to the early eighteenth century, the first reference being in George Charles Deering, *Nottinghamia vetus et nova* ..., Nottingham 1751 (p. 171). See especially 'R III's books: mistaken attributions', p. 384; Sutton, 'Richard III's "Castle of Care"'.

There are many surviving mss of this poem, but none can be ascribed to Richard's ownership.

XVIII. THE ROUS ROLL

A history of the earls of Warwick and the town of Warwick with illustrations of each earl and other eminent personages associated with the town and the castle, compiled by John Rous, chantry priest of Guy's Cliff, Warwick. The roll includes illustrations and texts for the last countess, Anne Beauchamp, her daughter, Anne, wife of Richard III, Richard himself as king, and their son as prince of Wales, and was clearly composed to celebrate this connection, presumably at the time of

Richard's and Anne's visit to Warwick after their coronation, summer 1483, and certainly before the prince died in April 1484. Rous's first version survives in English and is laudatory of Richard; his second, written after Bosworth, is in Latin and is highly hostile to the king.

BL, MS Add. 48976 (English) has no signs of Richard's signature or ownership. The facsimile edition by William Courthope, 1859, was reissued in 1980 with a new introduction by Charles Ross.

For College of Arms MS Warwick or Rous Roll (Latin) see Wagner, *Aspilogia*, 1, pp. 116–20, and *Aspilogia*, 2, p. 277. See also 'R III's books: ancestry and "true nobility"', pp. 350–51.

XIX. THE BEAUCHAMP PAGEANT

A life of Richard Beauchamp, Earl of Warwick, with 53 'pageants' or scenes from his life. The author of the text was possibly John Rous; the artist of the delightful and very fine pen and ink illustrations is not known. It concludes with two pages of pedigree running from Richard Beauchamp through the last countess, Anne, his daughter, her daughters, Isabel and Anne, and their husbands. Anne and Richard III and their son, the prince of Wales, take the senior place on the last page. The pedigree dates the making of the book firmly to Richard's reign and before the death of his son in April 1484; it seems most likely that it was commissioned by Anne Beauchamp for her grandson before he died.

BL, MS Cotton Julius E iv; no signs of Richard's signature or ownership. Facsimile edition, Dillon and St John Hope, 1914; new edition planned by A. Sinclair. See also Scott, *Caxton Master*; 'R III's books: ancestry and "true nobility"', pp. 351–52.

XX. THE SALISBURY ROLL

A pictorial pedigree of the earls of Salisbury, probably composed about the time of the burial of Richard Neville, Earl of Salisbury in 1463 at Bisham Priory founded by the first earl. The roll ends with Richard Neville and his two sons, Richard, Earl of Warwick in right of his wife, and of Salisbury, and Thomas, also buried at Bisham in 1463. The roll consists of 50 full-length figures of the earls and their spouses with full heraldic trappings.

A copy was made of this roll in the reign of Richard III – his son, the Prince of Wales, had been Earl of Salisbury since 1478 when the lands and title of Richard Neville the Kingmaker were divided between the husbands of his two daughters. The roll ends with Richard III and his queen in heraldic mantles. This is a much coarser work than the original of which the commissioning has been attributed to John Writhe, Garter, possibly intended for the king, and the queen – as daughter of the Kingmaker – and their son.

BL, Loan MS 90 and Additional 45133 (the original, which is fragmentary; vellum); no signs of Richard's signature or ownership.

BL, MS Add. 45122 (the copy; paper); no signs of Richard's signature or ownership.

Payne, 'Salisbury roll'; Wagner, *Aspilogia*, 1, pp. 103–04, *Aspilogia*, 2, p. 275; 'R III's books: ancestry and "true nobility"', p. 350.

C. BOOKS WRONGLY ATTRIBUTED TO RICHARD III'S OWNERSHIP

XXI. GUILLAUME DE TIGNONVILLE, *THE DICTS AND SAYINGS OF THE PHILOSOPHERS*, translated by Anthony Woodville, Earl Rivers, manuscript copy of the printed edition of William Caxton

The *Dits moraulx* is a collection of moral stories and maxims, often arbitrarily ascribed to ancient philosophers. It was put together by Guillaume de Tignonville, provost of Paris and counsellor of Charles VI of France (d. 1414). An English translation by Anthony Woodville, Lord Rivers, brother of Queen Elizabeth, was printed by William Caxton in 1477 and 1478. A manuscript copy was made from Caxton's edition, now London, Lambeth Palace Library, MS 265. It was written, according to its colophon, in December 1477 *Apud sanctum Jacobum / in campis per haywarde* ('at St James-in-the-Fields, by Hayward'). One leaf was inserted at the beginning; its verso side has the miniature of the presentation scene (see below) and a dedicatory poem stating that the text was translated by Rivers and that the ms. is presented to 'youre noble grace', i.e. Edward IV; it is not said *who* is presenting the book to the king. Rivers's title was obliterated or never filled in; at the end of the book Rivers's title was again erased twice. The manuscript text hardly differs from Caxton's editions, the only essential difference being the scribe's announcement that Caxton 'emprinted many bokes after the tonour and forme of this boke ...'. There is no evidence that this manuscript was actually presented by Rivers; it is most likely to be a more 'presentable' copy commissioned by Caxton and the printer's advertisement of his publication.

On the inserted leaf at the beginning is the only miniature of the manuscript: the presentation of the translation – not necessarily the presentation of the present ms. – showing, on the left, Rivers, kneeling on his right knee, wearing armour and a surcoat with his intricate coat of arms; he is handing the book to the king. In the foreground, on the earl's right and half behind him, is another kneeling man, presumably the original author, his hands half-raised and empty; he is tonsured and wears a black gown. On the right is the king, crowned and seated, flanked by his queen and, in the foreground, the little prince of Wales, for whom the translation was made. On the king's right, in the background, stand six courtiers, one of them royally dressed like the king and the prince, but wearing no crown or coronet – presumably the latter was meant to represent Richard of Gloucester, George of Clarence being already in prison at the time.

Richard's ownership of the ms. was a hypothesis of M.R. James based on the illegible signature on the last flyleaf. Examination of the signature under ultra-violet light has not confirmed this hypothesis. For details of the controversy surrounding the text, the ms. and the miniature, see 'R III's books: mistaken attributions', pp. 303–07.

XXII. THE ELLESMERE CHAUCER

The finest surviving manuscript of Chaucer's *Canterbury Tales*, each tale illustrated by a 'portrait' of the story-teller. The book is also remarkable for the number of its annotations and inscriptions made by owners and readers, the longest of which is a poem *per Rotheley* which is in praise of the de Vere family. The penultimate stanza is addressed to the 'royal boar' – the badge of the de Veres was a blue boar and they claimed royal descent. In 1926 E.F. Piper suggested that the royal boar addressed was Richard III and that the poem was to recommend the exiled de Vere earl of Oxford to the king; also that the manuscript had belonged to the de Veres and to Richard. In fact there is no ownership recorded in the book before that of the Drury family of Essex around 1500; Sir Robert Drury (d. 1536) was an executor of the 13th earl of Oxford in 1513 and probably had the poem added to the book. There is no evidence to make either Richard III or any de Vere an owner of the Ellesmere Chaucer.

San Marino, CA, Huntington Library, MS EL 26 C 9, Dutschke, *Guide*, pp. 41–50; 'R III's books: mistaken attributions', pp. 307–10; Piper, 'Royal boar', pp. 331–35; *Manual*, vol. 5, XIII [215]; Hanna and Edwards, 'Rotheley'.

XXIII. A BOOK OF HOURS

On 21 June 1994 a small book of hours was sold at Sotheby's, lot 103. According to the sale catalogue it is of the use of Sarum, in Latin, on vellum, has 197 leaves and has been illuminated probably in Bruges *c*. 1450–75. Size 105 × 73 mm, fourteen large illuminated initials with full borders and seventeen historiated initials with three-quarter illuminated borders. Among the saints depicted in the initials are both Sts John, the martyrdom of Becket, St George, St Anne, St Mary Magdalene, St Katherine, St Barbara and St Margaret. On f. 74v, in the lower margin and upside down there are two inscriptions: *Rychard B / Rychard Brg* in a late fifteenth- or early sixteenth-century hand. On f. 101 it reads: *Whoo so euer on me dothe looke: I am Iaspar lodges booke*. Cuttings from a nineteenth-century bookseller's catalogue, now stuck into the ms., describe it erroneously as: 'A most interesting volume containing the undoubted autograph of Richard III … pronounced by an expert to be unquestionably genuine' and '… autograph being found in this volume reminds us of the scene in Shakespeare's Play where Richard enters between two Bishops, "a book of prayer in his hand, true ornaments to know a holy man"'. Below these cuttings is the bookplate of 'Alfred Cock of the Middle Temple'. The text of this book of hours is standard and has no features of interest.

Bibliography

Manuscripts

The manuscripts owned by or associated with Richard III are not listed here but in the Catalogue, above.

Cambridge, Corpus Christi College 98, pedigree of Richard, Duke of York.
——, Gonville and Caius College 196/102, life of St Katherine.
——, Trinity College R.3.21, literary and political collection.
Durham, Ushaw College 43, hours of Richard, Duke of York.
Liverpool, Liverpool Cathedral Radcliffe 6, Hours of the Guardian Angel.
London, British Library, Add. 11814, translation of *De consulatu Stiliconis*.
——, Add. 18268A, genealogical roll.
——, Add. 46354, 16th-c. copy of pedigree of Richard, Duke of York.
——, Cotton Vesp. E vii, collection of prophecies.
——, Harl. 541, miscellaneous texts.
——, Harl. 7353, propaganda roll of Edward IV.
——, Royal 14 E ii, miscellaneous texts.
——, Royal 14 E iii, Arthurian romances.
——, College of Arms, 3/16, Clare Roll, pedigree of the lords of Clare.
New Haven, Yale University Library, Beinecke 323, *Brut* chronicle.
Oxford, Bodleian Library, Bodley 623, collection of prophecies.
——, Bodley Rolls 5, genealogical roll.
——, Lat. Misc. b. 2 (R), genealogical roll.
Philadelphia, Philadelphia Free Library, E 201, pedigree of Edward IV.
The Hague, Royal Library, 75 A 2/2, genealogical roll.
——, 78 B 24, genealogical roll.

Printed Works

With a few exceptions all titles used have been included. For medieval writers usually known by their surname see under their surnames for editions of their works; the texts of lesser known or early medieval writers will be found under their christian names; anonymous works will be found under the names of their editors.

Aegidius de Colonna (Aegidius Romanus), *see* Giles of Rome.

Allan, A., 'Yorkist propaganda: pedigree, prophecy and the "British history" in the reign of Edward IV', in Ross, ed., *Patronage, Pedigree and Power*.

——, 'Political propaganda employed by the House of York in England in the mid-fifteenth century, *c.* 1450–71', PhD thesis, Swansea 1981.

——, 'Royal propaganda and the proclamations of Edward IV', *BIHR*, 59 (1986).

Allen, P.S., 'Bishop Shirwood of Durham and his library', *EHR*, 25 (1910).

Allen, R.S., '*The Siege of Thebes*: Lydgate's Canterbury Tale', in J. Boffey and J. Cowen, eds, *Chaucer and Fifteenth-Century Poetry*, King's College London Medieval Studies 5, London 1991.

Allmand, C.T., 'France-Angleterre à la fin de la Guerre de Cent Ans: le "Boke of Noblesse" de William Worcester', in *La France anglaise*. 111e *Congrès national des sociétés savantes*, Poitiers 1986.

——, 'Changing views of the soldier in late medieval France', in Contamine *et al.*, eds, *Guerre et Société*.

Altamura, A., ed., *Riccardo da Bury, Philobiblon*, Naples 1954.

Anderson, A., *Studia Vegetiania*, Uppsala 1938.

Anderson, M., *St Ninian, Light of the Celtic North*, London 1964.

Anglo, S., 'The British History in early Tudor propaganda', *BJRL*, 44 (1961).

——, 'Anglo-Burgundian feats of arms: Smithfield, June 1467', *Guildhall Miscellany*, 2 (1965).

Arber, E., ed., *The Revelations to the Monk of Evesham ... edited ... by William de Machlinia about 1482*, London n.d.

Archibald, E., and A.S.G. Edwards, *A Companion to Malory*, Cambridge 1996.

d'Ardenne, S.R.T.O., and E.J. Dobson, eds, *Seinte Katerine*, EETS SS 7 (1981).

Armstrong, C.A.J., 'The piety of Cecily Nevill, Duchess of York: a study in late medieval culture', in the same, *England, France and Burgundy in the Fifteenth Century*, London 1983.

Armstrong, E., 'English purchases of printed books', *EHR*, 94 (1979).

Arn, M.-J., ed., *Fortunes Stabilness. Charles of Orleans' English Book of Love. A Critical Edition*, Binghamton, New York, 1994.

Ascham, Roger, *The Scholemaster*, ed. E. Arber, Birmingham 1870.

Ashby, George, *George Ashby's Poems*, ed. M. Bateson, EETS ES 76 (1899).

Ashmole, E., *The Institutions, Laws and Ceremonies of the Noble Order of the Garter*, London 1672.

Aston, M., 'Lollardy and Literacy', in the same, *Lollards and Reformers. Images and Literacy in Late Medieval Religion*, London 1984.

Avril, F., M.-T. Gousset and B. Guenée, *Les Grandes Chroniques de France. Reproduction intégrale en fac-similé des miniatures de Fouquet. Manuscrit français 6465 de la Bibliothèque nationale de Paris*, [Paris] 1987.

Ayres, R.A., 'Medieval history, moral purpose and the structure of Lydgate's *Siege of Thebes*', *Publications of the Modern Language Association of America*, 73 (1958).

Babington, C., and J.R. Lumby, eds, *Polychronicon Randulphi Higden monachi Cestrensis (from the creation to 1352); together with the English translations of John Trevisa and of an unknown writer of the fifteenth century*, 9 vols, Rolls Series, London 1865–86.

Backhouse, J., 'Founders of the Royal Library: Edward IV and Henry VII as collectors of illuminated manuscripts', in Williams, ed., *England in the Fifteenth Century*.

——, 'Sir John Donne's Flemish manuscripts', in Monks and Owen, eds, *Medieval Codicology*.

Bagge, S., *The Political Thought of the King's Mirror*, Odense 1987.

Baillie-Grohman, W.A. and F., *The Master of Game, by Edward Duke of York: The Oldest English Book on Hunting*, London 1909.

Bakhtin, V.S., 'Manuscripts from the collection of Oliver Cromwell', *Kniga o Knige*, 2 (1929), pp. 207–19.

Barlow, F., ed. and trans., *Vita Aedwardi Regis. The Life of King Edward who rests at Westminster*, London 1962.

Barnie, J., *War in Medieval Society*, London 1974.

Barratt, A., ed., *The Seven Psalms. A Commentary on the Penitential Psalms translated from French into English by Dame Eleanor Hull*, EETS OS 307 (1995).

Barron, C.M., 'London and parliament in the Lancastrian period', *Parliamentary History*, 9 (1990).

—— and A.F. Sutton, eds, *Medieval London Widows, 1300–1500*, London 1994.

Barron, W.R.J., *English Medieval Romance*, London 1987.

Batany, J., 'Miniature, allégorie, idéologie: "Oiseuse" et la mystique monacale récupérée par la "classe de loisir"', in J. Dufournet, ed., *Études sur le Roman de la Rose de Guillaume de Lorris*, Geneva 1984.

Bateson, M., ed., *Records of the Borough of Leicester, 1103–1603*, 3 vols, Cambridge 1899–1905.

Baumgartner, E., *Le Tristan en prose. Essai d'interpretation d'un roman médiéval*, Geneva 1975.

Bayot, A., *Martin le Franc, l'Estrif de Fortune et de Vertu*, Brussels 1928.

Beaune, C., *Naissance de la nation France*, Paris 1985.

——, 'Costume et pouvoir en France à la fin du moyen âge: les devises royales vers 1400', *Revue des sciences humaines*, 55 (1981).

Bellamy, J.G., *The Law of Treason in England in the Later Middle Ages*, Cambridge 1970.

Bellay, Martin du, *Mémoires de Martin et Guillaume du Bellay*, ed. V.-L. Bourrilly and F. Vindry, 4 vols, Paris 1908–19.

Bennett, H.S., *English Books and Readers, Being a History of the Booktrade, 1475–1557*, Cambridge 1952.

Benoît de Sainte-Maure, *Le Roman de Troie par Benoît de Sainte-Maure*, ed. L. Constans, 6 vols, Paris 1904–12.

——, *Le Roman de Troie de Benoît de Sainte-Maure*, ed. E. Baumgartner, Collection 10/18, 1987.

Benson, C.D., *The History of Troy in Middle English Literature*, Woodbridge 1980.

——, and E. Robertson, *Chaucer's Religious Tales*, Cambridge 1990.

Benson, L.D., and J. Leyerle, eds, *Chivalric Literature: Essays on Relations between Literature and Life in the Later Middle Ages*, Kalamazoo 1980.

Berges, W., *Die Fürstenspiegel des hohen und späten Mittelalters*, Monumenta Germaniae Historica, Schriften 2, Leipzig 1938.

Bernier, A., ed. and trans., *Journal des Etats généraux de France tenus à Tours en 1484*, Paris 1835.

Bischoff, B., 'Elementarunterricht und *probationes pennae* in der ersten Hälfte des Mittelalters', in L.W. Jones., ed., *Classical and Medieval Studies in Honor of E.K. Rand*, New York 1938.

Black, A., '*Jehan de Saintré* and *Le Livre des Faits de Jacques de Lalaing*: a common source?', *Notes and Queries*, 232 (1987).

Black, W.H., *Illustrations of Ancient State and Chivalry from Manuscripts preserved in the Ashmolean Museum*, Roxburghe Club, London 1840.

Blacker, J., '"Ne vuil sun livre translater": Wace's omission of Merlin's prophecies from the *Roman de Brut*', in I. Short, ed., *Anglo-Norman Anniversary Essays*, Anglo-Norman Text Society, Occasional Publications Series 2, London 1993.

Blades, W., *The Life and Typography of William Caxton*, 2 vols, London/Strasbourg 1861–63.

Blake, N.F., *Caxton and His World*, London 1969.

——, *Caxton's Own Prose*, London 1973.

——, *Caxton. England's First Publisher*, London 1976.

——, *William Caxton and English Literary Culture*, London 1991.

——, 'William Caxton: his choice of texts', *Anglia*, 83 (1965).

——, 'The "Noble Lady" in Caxton's "The Book of the Knight of the Tower"', *Notes and Queries*, 210 (1965).

——, 'Caxton's language', in the same, *William Caxton and English Literary Culture*.

——, 'Revelations of St Matilda', *Notes and Queries*, 218 (1973).

——, 'William Caxton: the man and his work', in the same, *William Caxton and English Literary Culture*.

——, 'Caxton prepares his edition of the *Morte Darthur*', in the same, *William Caxton and English Literary Culture*.

——, 'Caxton's reprints', in the same, *William Caxton and English Literary Culture*.

——, 'The spread of printing in England during the fifteenth century', in the same, *William Caxton and English Literary Culture*.

Blanchfield, L.S., 'The romances in MS Ashmole 61: an idiosyncratic scribe', in Mills *et al.*, eds, *Romance in Medieval England*.

——, 'Rate revisited: the compilation of the narrative works in MS Ashmole 61', in J. Fellows *et al.*, eds, *Romance Reading on the Book. Essays on Medieval Narrative presented to Maldwyn Mills*, Cardiff 1996.

Bliss, A.J., ed., *Sir Orfeo*, Oxford 1954.

Bloch, M., *The Royal Touch. Sacred Monarchy and Scrofula in England and France*, trans. J.E. Anderson, London/Montreal 1973.

Blockmans, W., 'The devotion of a lonely duchess', in Kren, ed., *Margaret of York*.

Bodel, Jean, *La Chanson des Saisnes*, ed. A. Brasseur, Geneva 1989.

Bödtker, A.T., ed., *The Middle English Versions of Partonope of Blois*, EETS ES 109 (1912, for 1911).

Boeken van en rond Willem van Oranje, catalogue of an exhibition at the Royal Library, The Hague, 1984.

Boffey, J., and Thompson, J.J., 'Anthologies and miscellanies: production and choice of texts', in Griffiths and Pearsall, eds, *Book Production and Publishing*.

Boinet, A., 'Un bibliophile du xve siècle: le Grand Bâtard de Bourgogne', *Bibliothèque de l'École des Chartes*, 67 (1906).

Boislisle, A. de, 'Inventaire des bijoux, vêtements, manuscrits et objets précieux appartenant à la comtesse de Montpensier, 1474', *Annuaire-Bulletin de la Société de l'Histoire de France*, 17 (1880).

Bokenham, Osbern, *Legendys of Hooly Wummen*, ed. M.S. Serjeantson, EETS OS 206 (1938, for 1936).

Bolton, J.L., 'The city and the crown, 1456–61', *The London Journal*, 12 (1986).

——, *Alien subsidy of 1483*, forthcoming.

Bone, G., 'Extant manuscripts printed from by W. de Worde with notes on the owner, Roger Thorney', *The Library*, 4th series, 12 (1932).

Born, L.K., 'The perfect prince: a study in the thirteenth- and fourteenth-century ideals', *Speculum*, 3 (1928).

——, 'Erasmus on political ethics: the *Institutio Principis Christiani*', *Political Science Quarterly*, 43 (1928).

Bornstein, D., 'Military manuals in fifteenth-century England', *Medieval Studies*, 37 (1975).

——, 'William Caxton's chivalric romances and the Burgundian renaissance in England', *English Studies*, 57 (1976).

Bossuat, R., 'Jean Mielot, traducteur de Cicéron', *Bibliothèque de l'École des Chartes*, 99 (1938).

Bradley, R., 'Background of the title *Speculum* in medieval literature', *Speculum*, 29 (1954).

Brandenberg, T., *et al.*, *Heilige Anna, Grote Moeder. De cultus van de Heilige Moeder Anna en haar familie in de Nederlanden en aangrenzende streken*, catalogue of an exhibition held at the Museum voor Religieuze Kunst, Uden, 1992.

Brandt, W., *The Shape of Medieval History*, New York 1973.

Braswell, L., 'Utilitarian and scientific prose', in *Middle English Prose*.

Brie, F.W.D., *Geschichte und Quellen der mittelenglischen Prosachronik 'The Brute of England' oder 'The Chronicles of England'*, Marburg 1905.

——, ed., *The Brut or the Chronicles of England*, EETS OS 131, 136 (1906, 1908).

Briquet, C.M., *Les Filigranes*, 4 vols, Leipzig 1923.

Britnell, R., 'Richard, Duke of Gloucester, and the death of Thomas Fauconberg', *The Ricardian*, 10 (1994–96).

Bromberg, OP, R.L.J., *Het Boek der Bijzondere Genade van Mechtild van Hackeborn*, Zwolle 1965.

Brooks, D., and A. Fowler, 'The meaning of Chaucer's *Knight's Tale*', *Medium Aevum*, 39 (1970).

Bruce, J., ed., *Historie of the Arrivall of Edward IV in England*, CS, Old Series, 1838.

Burrow, J.A., 'The audience of Piers Plowman, *Anglia*, 75 (1957).

Butler, A., H. Thurston, and D. Attwater, *The Lives of the Saints*, 12 vols, London 1937–38.

Byles, A.T.P., *see* Lull, Ramon.

——, 'William Caxton as a man of letters', *The Library*, 4th series, 15 (1934).

Bynum, C.W., *Jesus as Mother. Studies in the Spirituality of the High Middle Ages*, Berkeley 1982.

Calendar of the Letter Books of the City of London, L, ed. R.R. Sharpe, London 1912.

Calendar of Patent Rolls: Edward IV, Henry VI 1467–77, London 1900; *Edward IV, Edward V, Richard III 1476–85*, London 1901.

Calendar of Plea and Memoranda Rolls ... of the City of London ..., 1364–81, ed. A.H. Thomas, Cambridge 1929.

Campbell, L., with F. Steer and R. Yorke, *A Catalogue of Manuscripts in the College of Arms. Collections*, vol. 1, London 1988.

Capgrave, John, *John Capgrave Abbreviacion of Chronicles*, EETS OS 285 (1983).

Carey, H.M., 'Devout literate laypeople and the pursuit of the mixed life in later medieval England', *Journal of Religious History*, 14 (1987).

Carlson, D.R., *English Humanist Books. Writers and Patrons, Manuscript and Print, 1475–1525*, Toronto 1993.

Carlyle, R.W. and A.J., *A History of Medieval Political Thought in the West*, 6 vols, Edinburgh/London 1903–36.

Carruthers, M., *The Book of Memory*, Cambridge 1990.

Carysfort, William, Earl of, ed., *The Pageants of Richard Beauchamp, Earl of Warwick*, Roxburghe Club 1908.

Catto, J., *et al.*, eds, *Wyclif and his Followers: An Exhibition to Mark the 600th Anniversary of the Death of John Wyclif*, Oxford 1984.

Caxton, William, *Caxton's Blanchardyn and Eglantine, c. 1489*, ed. L. Kellner, EETS ES 58 (1890, repr. 1962).

——, *Game and Playe of the Chesse, see* Cessolis, James de.

——, *Caxton's Eneydos, 1490*, ed. W.T. Calley and F.J. Furnivall, EETS ES 57 (1890).

——, *The History of Jason, see* le Fèvre, Raoul.

——, *The History of Reynard the Fox*, ed. N.F. Blake, EETS OS 263 (1970).

——, *The Lyf of the Noble and Crysten Prynce Charles the Grete*, ed. S.J.H. Herrtage, EETS ES 57 (1890).

——, *Caxton's Mirrour of the World*, ed. O.H. Prior, EETS ES 110 (1913, repr. 1966).

——, *Ordre of Chyvalry, see* Lull, Ramon.

——, *Paris and Vienne, translated from the French and printed by William Caxton*, ed. M. Leach, EETS OS 234 (1957, for 1951).

——, *Polychronicon, see* Babington and Lumby, eds.

——, *The Recuyell of the Historyes of Troye, see* Sommer, H.O.

Cessolis, James de, *The Game of Chess. Translated and Printed by William Caxton c. 1483*, introd. N.F. Blake, facsimile, London 1976.

Chalon, R., ed., *La Chronique du Bon Chevalier Messire Gilles de Chin*, Mons 1837.

Chartier, Alain, *see* Laidlaw, J.C.

Chassant, A, and H. Tausin, eds, *Dictionnaire des devises*, Paris 1878–95, repr. Geneva 1978.

Chastellain, George, *Oeuvres*, ed. Kervyn de Lettenhove, 8 vols, Brussels 1863–66.

Chaucer, Geoffrey, *see* Robinson, F.N.

Chaume, M., 'Une prophétie relative à Charles VI', *Revue du Moyen Age Latin*, 3 (1947).

Childress, D.T., 'Between romance and legend: "Secular hagiography" in Middle English literature', *Philological Quarterly*, 57 (1978).

Childs, H.E., 'A Study of the unique Middle English translation of the *De regimine principum* of Aegidius Romanus', PhD thesis, Washington 1932.

Chrimes, S.B., *English Constitutional Ideas in the Fifteenth Century*, Cambridge 1936.

Christianson, C. P., *A Directory of London Stationers and Book Artisans 1300–1500*, The Bibliographical Society of America, New York 1990.

——, 'The rise of London's book trade', typescript.

Le cinquième centenaire de l'imprimerie dans les Anciens Pays-Bas, Brussels 1973.

Clarke, B., *Life of Merlin*, Cardiff 1973.

Claudin, A., *Histoire de l'imprimerie en France au xve et au xvie siècle*, vol. 1, Paris 1900.

Clough, C.H., ed., *Profession, Vocation and Culture in Later Medieval England. Essays dedicated to the memory of A.R. Myers*, Liverpool 1982.

Cobb, H.S., ed., *The Overseas Trade of London. Exchequer Customs Accounts 1480–1*, London Record Society 27 (1990).

Cockshaw, P., *et al.*, *Charles le Téméraire*, catalogue of the exhibition at the Bibliothèque Royale, Brussels 1977.

The College of Arms ... with a Complete List of the Officers of Arms, H. Stanford London, London Survey Committee, 1963.

Colonna, Aegidius de, *see* Giles of Rome.

Commines, Philippe de, *Memoirs*, ed. and trans. M. Jones, Harmondsworth 1972.

——, *Mémoires de Philippe de Commynes*, ed. E. Dupont, 3 vols, Paris 1840–47.

Complete Peerage of England, Scotland, Ireland and the United Kingdom, ed. G.E. C[okayne]; new edn by V. Gibbs, H.A. Doubleday *et al.*, 13 vols, 1910–59, repr. Gloucester 1982.

Conlon, D.J., ed., *Le Rommant de Guy de Warwick et de Herolt d'Ardenne*, Chapel Hill 1971.

Contamine, P., 'L'art de guerre selon Philippe de Clèves, seigneur de Ravenstein (1456–1528): innovation ou tradition?', *Bijdragen en Mededelingen betreffende de Geschiedenis der Nederlanden*, 95 (1980).

——, C. Giry-Deloison and M.H. Keen, eds, *Guerre et société en France, en Angleterre et en Bourgogne, XIVe–XVe siècle*, Lille 1991.

Corstanje, C. van, *et al.*, eds, *Vita Sanctae Coletae (1381–1447)*, Tielt/Leiden 1982.

Corsten, S., 'Caxton in Cologne', *Journal of the Printing Historical Society*, no. 11 (1976–77).

Courthope, W., ed., *The Rous Roll*, 1859, repr. with an introduction by C. Ross, Gloucester 1980.

Craig, H., ed., *The Works of John Metham including The Romance of Amoryns and Cleopes*, EETS OS 132 (1916).

Crane, R.S., 'The vogue of *Guy of Warwick* from the close of the Middle Ages to the romantic revival', *Publications of the Modern Language Association of America*, 30 (1915).

Crane, S., *Insular Romance. Politics, Faith and Culture in Anglo-Norman and Middle English Literature*, Berkeley 1986.

Crawford, A., 'Victims of attainder: the Howard and de Vere women in the late fifteenth century', *Reading Medieval Studies*, 15 (1989).

——, introd., *The Household Books of John Howard, Duke of Norfolk, 1462–1471, 1481–1483*, Stroud 1992.

Crick, J.C., *The Historia Regum Britanniae. III. A Summary Catalogue of Manuscripts*, Cambridge 1989.

——, *The Historia Regum Britanniae. IV. Dissemination and Reception in the Later Middle Ages*, Cambridge 1991.

Crotch, W.B., *The Prologues and Epilogues of William Caxton*, EETS OS 176 (1928).

The Crowland Chronicle Continuations: 1459–1486, ed. N. Pronay and J. Cox, London 1986.

Curley, M.J., 'Fifteenth-century glosses on *The Prophecy of John of Bridlington*: a text, its meaning and its purpose', *Mediaeval Studies*, 46 (1984).

Curtis, R.L., *Le Roman de Tristan en prose*, 3 vols, Munich 1963, Leiden 1976, Woodbridge 1985, reprinted as *Arthurian Literature*, 12, 13 and 14, Woodbridge 1988–89.

——, *Tristan Studies*, Munich 1969.

Daly, K., 'Mixing business with leisure: some french royal notaries and secretaries and their histories of France c. 1459–1509', in C.T. Allmand, ed., *Power, Culture and Religion in France c. 1350–c. 1550*, Woodbridge 1989.

Davies, C.S.L., 'Richard III, Brittany and Henry Tudor', *Nottingham Medieval Studies*, 37 (1993).

——, 'The alleged "sack of Bristol": international ramifications of Breton privateering, 1484–85', *Historical Research*, 67 (1994).

Davies, R.G., 'The episcopate', in Clough, ed., *Profession*.

Davis, N. 'The epistolary usages of William Worcester', in D.A. Pearsall and R.A. Waldron, eds, *Medieval Literature and Civilisation. Studies in Memory of G.N. Garmondsway*, London 1969.

Deanesly, M., *The Lollard Bible and other Medieval Biblical Translations*, Cambridge 1920.

Debaene, L., *De Nederlandse Volksboeken. Ontstaan en Geschiedenis van de Nederlandse Prozaromans tussen 1475 en 1540*, Antwerpen 1951.

De Jonghe, B., *Belgium Dominicanum*, Brussels 1719.

Delachanel, R., ed., *Chroniques des règnes de Jean II et de Charles V*, 4 vols, Paris 1810–20.

De La Mare, A., *Catalogue of the Collection of Medieval Manuscripts bequeathed to the Bodleian Library, Oxford, by James P.R. Lyell*, Oxford 1971.

——, and L. Hellinga, 'The first book printed in Oxford: the *Expositio Symboli* of Rufinus', *Cambridge Bibliographical Society Transactions*, 1982.

Delisle, L., 'Notes sur quelques manuscrits du Musée Britannique', *Mémoires de la Société de l'Histoire de Paris et de l'Isle de France*, 4 (1877).

——, *Recherches sur la librairie de Charles V*, 2 vols, Paris 1907.

Dennison, L., *see* Sutton, A.F. and L. Visser-Fuchs.

De Ricci, S., *A Census of Caxtons*, Bibliographical Society Illustrated Monographs 15, Oxford 1909.

——, and W.T. Wilson, *Census of Medieval and Renaissance Manuscripts in the United States and Canada*, New York 1935–37.

De Roover, R., *Gresham on Foreign Exchange*, Cambridge, Mass., 1949.

De Rooy, F., ed., *La vie de Saint Hubert dite d'Hubert le Prevost*, Zwolle 1958.

De Schryver, A., 'The Louthe Master and the Marmion case', in Kren, ed., *Margaret of York*.

De Smedt, R., ed., *Les Chevaliers de l'Ordre de la Toison d'or au xve siècle*, Frankfurt am Main 1994.

Dictionnaire des lettres françaises. Le Moyen Age, ed. R. Bossuat *et al.*, 1964.

Dillon, Viscount, and W.H. St John Hope, eds, *Pageant of the Birth, Life and Death of Richard Beauchamp Earl of Warwick K.G. 1389–1439*, London 1914.

DiMarco, V., and L. Perelman, eds, *The Middle English Letter of Alexander to Aristotle*, Amsterdam 1978.

Dobson, R. B., *Durham Priory, 1400–1450*, Cambridge 1973.

——, 'Richard III and the church of York', in Griffiths and Sherborne, eds, *Kings and Nobles*.

——, 'The educational patronage of Archbishop Thomas Rotherham', *Northern History*, 31 (1995).

Donckel, E., 'Visio seu prophetia fratris Johannis', *Römische Quartalschrift*, 40 (1932).

Douglas, D.C., 'Companions of the Conqueror', *History*, 28 (1943).

——, 'The "Song of Roland" and the Norman conquest of England', *French Studies*, 14 (1960).

Doutrepont, G., *La littérature française à la cour des Ducs de Bourgogne*, Paris 1909, repr. Geneva 1970.

——, *Les Mises en prose des Epopées et des Romans chevaleresques du xive et xve siècle*, Brussels 1939.

Downer, L.J., ed., *Leges Henrici Primi*, Oxford 1972.

Doyle, A.I., 'The work of a late fifteenth-century English scribe, William Ebesham', *BJRL*, 39 (1956–57).

——, 'More light on John Shirley', *Medium Aevum*, 30 (1961).

——, 'English books in and out of court', in Scattergood and Sherborne, eds, *English Court Culture*.

Dubuc, B.D., '"Le Chemin de Vaillance": mise en point sur la date de composition et la vie de l'auteur', in Monks and Owen, eds, *Medieval Codicology*.

Duff, E.G., *Fifteenth-Century English Books. A Bibliography of Books and Documents printed in England and of Books for the English Market printed abroad*, Bibliographical Society Illustrated Monographs 18, Oxford 1917.

——, *A Century of the English Book Trade*, London 1948.

——, 'Early chancery proceedings', *The Library*, 2nd series, 8 (1907).

Duke Humphrey's Library and the Divinity School, 1488–1988. An Exhibition at the Bodleian Library, June–August 1988, Oxford 1988.

Dunham, W.H., *The Fane Fragment of the 1461 Lords' Journal*, New Haven 1935.

Dutschke, C.W., ed., *Guide to Medieval and Renaissance Manuscripts in the Huntington Library*, 2 vols, San Marino, Cal., 1990.

Dyboski, R., and Z.M. Arend, *Knyghthode and Bataile*, EETS OS 201 (1936 for 1935).

Eckhardt, C.E., *The Prophetia Merlini of Geoffrey of Monmouth. A Fifteenth-Century Commentary*, Speculum Anniversary Monographs 8, Cambridge, Mass., 1982.

——, 'The first English translations of the *Prophetia Merlini*', *The Library*, 6th series, 4 (1982).

Edmunds, S., 'The medieval library of Savoy', *Scriptorium*, 24 (1970); 25 (1971); 26 (1972).

Edwards, A.S.G., 'The transmission and audience of Osbern Bokenham's *Legendys of Hooly Wummen*', in Minnis, ed., *Late Medieval Religious Texts*.

——, ed., *Middle English Prose. A Critical Guide to Major Authors and Sources*, New Brunswick, New Jersey, 1984.

——, 'The manuscripts and texts of the second version of John Hardyng's *Chronicle*', in Williams, ed., *England in the Fifteenth Century*.

——, 'Lydgate scholarship. Progress and prospects', *Fifteenth-Century Studies. Recent Essays*, ed. R.F. Yaeger, Hamden, Conn., 1984.

——, 'ISTC, the literary historian and the editor', in L. Hellinga and J. Goldfinch., eds, *Bibliography and the Study of Fifteenth-Century Civilisation*, British Library Occasional Papers 5, London 1987.

Eisenhut, W., 'Spätantike Troja-Erzählungen mit einem Ausblick auf die mittelalterliche Troja-Literatur', *Mittellateinisches Jahrbuch*, 18 (1983).

Ellis, H., 'Copy of an historical document ... dated 1475' [*The Promise of Matrimony*], *Archaeologia*, 32 (1847).

Ellis, R., ed., *The Liber Celestis of St Bridget of Sweden*, vol. 1, Text, EETS OS 291 (1987).

——, '"Flores ad fabricandam ... coronam": an investigation into the uses of the revelations of St Bridget of Sweden in fifteenth-century England', *Medium Aevum*, 51 (1982).

Elton, G.R., 'The sessional printing of statutes, 1484–1547', in E.W. Ives, R.J. Knecht and J.J. Scarisbrick, eds, *Wealth and Power in Tudor England. Essays presented to S.J. Bindoff*, London 1978.

Emden, A.B., *A Biographical Register of the University of Cambridge to A.D. 1500*, Cambridge 1963.

——, *A Biographical Register of the University of Oxford to A.D. 1500*, 3 vols, Oxford 1957–59.

Erasmus, Desiderius, *Institutio principis christiani*, ed. O. Herding, in *Erasmi Opera Omnia*, vol. IV, 1, Amsterdam 1974.

D'Evelyn, Ch., ed., *Peter Idley's Instructions to His Son*, Modern Language Association of America, Monograph Series 6, Boston/London 1935.

Fahrenbach, W.J., 'Vernacular translations of classical literature in late-medieval Britain', PhD thesis, Toronto 1975.

Faral, E., *La Légende Arthurienne, Études et Documents*, vol. 2, 'Geoffrey of Monmouth', Bibliothèque de l'École des Hautes Études, vol. 256, Paris 1929.

Farley, S.M., 'French historiography in the later middle ages with special reference to the *Grandes chroniques de France*', PhD thesis, Edinburgh 1969.

Fellows, J., ed., *Of Love and Chivalry. An Anthology of Middle English Romances*, London 1993.

Ferguson, A.B., *The Indian Summer of English Chivalry*, Durham, North Carolina, 1960.

Field, R., 'Romance as history, history as romance', in Mills *et al.*, eds, *Romance in Medieval England*.

Finlayson, J., 'Guido de Columnis' *Historia Destructionis Troiae*, The *"Gest Hystorial"* of the *Destruction of Troy*, and Lydgate's *Troy Book*: translation and the design of history', *Anglia*, 13 (1995).

Finoli, A.M., ed., *Jean d'Avesnes*, Milan 1979.

Finnegan, OP, M.J., *The Women of Helfta. Scholars and Mystics*, Athens, Georgia, 1991.

Finot, M.J., ed., *Inventaire sommaire des Archives Départementales antérieures à 1790*, vol. 8, *Archives Civiles. Série B, Chambres des Comptes de Lille, nos. 3390–3665*, Lille 1895.

Fleischman, S., 'On the representation of history and fiction in the middle ages', *History*, 22 (1983).

Fleming, P.W. 'The Hautes and their "circle": culture and the English gentry', in Williams, ed., *England in the Fifteenth Century*.

Flenley, R., 'London and foreign merchants in the reign of Henry VI', *EHR*, vol. 25 (1910).

Flügel, E., 'Eine mittelenglische Claudian-Uebersetzung (1445)', *Anglia*, 28 (1905).

Forshall, J., and F. Madden, *The Holy Bible, containing the Old and New Testaments, with the Apocryphal Books, in the earliest English Versions made from the Latin Vulgate by John Wycliffe and his Followers*, 4 vols, London 1850.

Fortescue, Sir John, *De laudibus legum Anglie*, ed. S.B. Chrimes, Cambridge 1942.

——, *'The Governance of England' by Sir John Fortescue*, ed. C. Plummer, Oxford 1885.

Fossier, R., 'Chroniques universelles en forme de rouleau à la fin du Moyen-Age', *Bulletin de la Société nationale des antiquaires de France*, 1980–81.

Fouw, A. de, *Philips van Kleef*, Groningen 1937.

Fowler, K.A., *The Age of Plantagenet and Valois*, London 1967.

Fox, J., *The Lyric Poetry of Charles d'Orléans*, Oxford 1969.

Frank, G, and D. Miner, eds, *Proverbes en rimes. Text and Illustrations of the Fifteenth Century from a French Manuscript in the Walters Art Gallery, Baltimore*, Baltimore 1937.

Frazer Jr., R.M., *The Trojan War. The Chronicles of Dictys of Crete and Dares the Phrygian*, London/Bloomington 1966.

Friedman, J.B., 'Books, owners and makers in fifteenth-century Yorkshire: the evidence from some wills and extant manuscripts', in A.J. Minnis, ed., *Latin and Vernacular. Studies in Late-Medieval Texts and Manuscripts*, Cambridge 1989.

Fristedt, S., *The Wycliffe Bible*, pts 1, 2 and 3, Stockholm Studies in English 4, 21 and 28, Stockholm 1953, 1969 and 1973.

Furnivall, F.J., ed., *The Three Kings' Sons*, EETS ES 67 (1805).

Gagnebin, B., 'L'enluminure de Charlemagne à François Ier', *Genava*, 24 (1976).

Gairdner, J., ed., *Letters and Papers, Richard III and Henry VII*, 2 vols, Rolls Series, London 1861–63.

Gallet-Guerne, D., *Vasque de Lucene et la Cyropédie à la cour de Bourgogne (1470). Le traité de Xenophon mis en français d'après la version latine de Pogge*, Geneva 1974.

Genet, J.-P., 'Les idées sociales de Sir John Fortescue' in *Économies et sociétés au moyen age. Mélanges offerts à Edouard Perroy*, Publications de la Sorbonne, série 'Études' 5, Paris 1973.

——, ed., *Four English Political Tracts of the Later Middle Ages*, CS, 4th series, 18, London 1977.

——, 'Political theory and local communities in later medieval France and England', in J.R.L. Highfield and R. Jeffs, eds, *The Crown and Local Communities in England and France in the Fifteenth Century*, Gloucester 1981.

——, 'English nationalism at the Council of Constance', *Nottingham Medieval Studies*, 28 (1984).

Geoffrey of Monmouth, *Geoffrey of Monmouth, Historia Regum Britanniae: a Variant Version*, ed. J. Hammer, Medieval Academy of America, Cambridge, Mass., 1931.

——, *The Historia Regum Britanniae of Geoffrey of Monmouth with Contributions to the Study of its Place in Early British History*, ed. A. Griscom, London 1929.

——, *The 'Historia Regum Britanniae' of Geoffrey of Monmouth I. Bern, Burgerbibliothek, MS 568*, ed. N. Wright, Cambridge 1985.

——, *The 'Historia Regum Britanniae' of Geoffrey of Monmouth. II. The First Variant Version: A Critical Edition*, ed. N. Wright, Cambridge 1988.

——, *The History of the Kings of Britain*, trans. L. Thorpe, Harmondsworth 1966.

——, *see also* Clarke, B.; Crick, J.; Eckhardt, C.E.; Lloyd, J.E.; Keeler, L.; Parry, J.J.

Gerald of Wales, *The Conquest of Ireland by Giraldus Cambrensis*, ed. A.B. Scott and F.X. Martin, Dublin 1978.

——, *The Journey through Wales and the Description of Wales*, trans. L. Thorpe, Harmondsworth 1978.

Gerritsen, W.P., and A.G. van Melle, eds, *Van Aiol tot Zwaanridder. Personages uit de middeleeuwse verhaalkunst en hun voortleven in literatuur, theater en beeldende kunst*, Nijmegen 1993.

Geschichte der Wissenschaften in Deutschland, repr. London / New York / Hildesheim 1965.

Gilbert, A.H., *Machiavelli's 'Prince' and Its Forerunners. The 'Prince' as a Typical Book 'de Regimine Principum'*, New York 1938.

Giles of Rome (Aegidius Romanus, Aegidius de Colonna), *De Regimine Principum Libri III*, Rome 1556, repr. in facsimile Frankfurt 1968.

——, *Li Livres du Gouvernement des Rois. A XIIIth Century French Version of Egidio Colonna's Treatise De Regimine Principum*, ed. S.P. Molenaer, New York 1899.

Gillingham, J., ed., *Richard III: A Medieval Kingship*, London 1993.

Golenistcheff-Koutouzoff, E., *L'Histoire de Griseldis en France au xive et au xve siècles*, Geneva 1933.

Goodman, A., and D.A.L. Morgan, 'The Yorkist claim to the throne of Castile', *Journal of Medieval History*, 11 (1985).

Gossuin de Metz, *L'Image du monde de maître Gossouin, redaction en prose, texte du ms. Bibl. nat. fr. 574*, ed. O.H. Prior, Lausanne/Paris 1913.

Gottfried of Strasburg, *Tristan ... with the surviving fragments of the Tristan of Thomas*, trans. A. Hatto, Harmondsworth 1960.

Gower, John, *The Complete Works*, ed. G.C. Macaulay, 4 vols, Oxford 1899–1902.

——, *Confessio Amantis*, trans. T. Tiller, Harmondsworth 1963.

Gransden, A., *Historical Writing in England I, c. 550 to c. 1307*, London 1974.

——, *Historical Writing in England II, c. 1307 to the Early Sixteenth Century*, London 1982.

——, 'Propaganda in English medieval historiography', *Journal of Medieval History*, 1 (1975).

——, 'Antiquarian studies in fifteenth-century England', *Antiquaries Journal*, 60 (1980).

——, 'The uses made of history by the medieval kings of England', in *Culture et l'idéologie dans la genèse de l'état moderne*, Collection de l'École Française de Rome, 82 (1985).

Grant, A., 'Foreign affairs under Richard III', in Gillingham, ed., *Richard III: A Medieval Kingship*.

——, 'Richard III and Scotland', in Pollard, ed., *The North of England in the Age of Richard III*.

The Great Chronicle, ed. A.H. Thomas and I.D. Thornley, London 1938.

Green, R. F., *Poets and Princepleasers. Literature and the English Court in the Late Middle Ages*, Toronto 1980.

Griffin, N.E., 'Un-Homeric elements in the medieval story of Troy', *Journal of English and Germanic Philology*, 7 (1903).

Griffith, D.D., *The Origin of the Griselda Story*, University of Washington Publications in Language and Literature 8, Seattle 1931.

Griffiths, J., and D. Pearsall, eds, *Book Production and Publishing in Britain, 1375–1475*, Cambridge 1989.

Griffiths, R.A., and J. Sherborne, eds, *Kings and Nobles in the Later Middle Ages*, Gloucester 1986.

Grinberg, H., 'The *Three Kings' Sons*: notes and critical commentary', PhD thesis, New York 1968.

——, '*The Three Kings' Sons* and *Les Trois Fils de Rois*. Manuscript and textual filiation in an Anglo-Burgundian romance', *Romance Philology*, 27 (1975).

Guddat-Figge, G., *Catalogue of Manuscripts containing Middle English Romances*, Munich 1976.

Guenée, B., *States and Rulers in later Medieval Europe*, trans. J. Vale, Oxford 1985.

——, *Histoire et culture historique dans l'Occident médiéval*, Paris 1980.

——, 'Temps de l'histoire et temps de la mémoire au moyen âge', in the same, *Politique et histoire au moyen âge*, Paris 1981.

Guido delle Colonne, *Guido de Columnis, Historia Destructionis Troiae*, ed. N.E. Griffin, Cambridge, Mass., 1936.

——, *Guido delle Colonne 'Historia Destructionis Troiae'*, trans. M.E. Meek, Bloomington 1974.

Hachez, F., 'Un manuscrit de l'Enseignement de la vraie noblesse, provenant de la bibliothèque de Charles de Croy, comte de Chimay', *Annales du Cercle archéologique de Mons*, 23 (1892).

Haferkorn, R., *When Rome is Removed into England. Eine politische Prophezeiung des 14. Jahrhunderts*, Leipzig 1932.

Hales, J.W., and F.J. Furnivall, eds, *Bishop Percy's Folio Manuscript*, 4 vols, London 1867–68.

Hall, L.B., 'Caxton's "Eneydos" and the redactions of Vergil', *Medieval Studies*, 22 (1960).

Halligan, T.A., ed., *The Booke of Gostlye Grace of Mechtild of Hackeborn*, Toronto 1979.

Hammer, J., 'A commentary on the *Prophetia Merlini* …', *Speculum*, 10 (1935)

Hammond, P.W., *The Battles of Barnet and Tewkesbury*, Gloucester 1990.

——, 'Richard III at York', *The Ricardian*, no. 41 (June 1973).

——, 'Richard III's books: III. English New Testament', *The Ricardian*, 7 (1985–87), pp. 479–85.

——, ed., *Richard III: Loyalty, Lordship and Law*, London 1986.

——, and A.F. Sutton, *Richard III. The Road to Bosworth Field*, London 1985.

Hanham, A., *Richard III and His Early Historians 1483–1535*, Oxford 1975.

——, ed., *The Cely Letters*, EETS OS 273 (1975).

——, *The Celys and Their World*, Cambridge 1985.

Hanna III, R., and A.S.G. Edwards, 'Rotheley, the De Vere circle and the Ellesmere Chaucer', *Huntington Library Quarterly*, 58 (1996).

Hanserecesse von 1431–1476, ed. G. von der Ropp, 7 vols, Leipzig 1876–92.

Hardyng, John, *Chronicle*, ed. H. Ellis, London 1812.

Harris, K., 'Patrons, buyers and owners: the evidence for ownership and the rôle of book owners in book production and book trade', in Griffiths and Pearsall, eds, *Book Production and Publishing*.

Harriss, G.L. ed., *Henry V: The Practice of Kingship*, Oxford 1985.

Hay, D., 'History and historians in France and England during the fifteenth century', *BIHR*, 35 (1962).

Haynin, Jean de, *Mémoires*, ed. D.D. Brouwers, 2 vols, Liège 1905–06.

Hedeman, A.D., 'Valois legitimacy: editorial changes in Charles V's *Grandes Chroniques de France*', *Studies in Art History*, 16 (1985).

Hellinga, L., 'Caxton and the bibliophiles', *Actes du XIe Congrès International de Bibliophile*, ed. P. Culot, [Brussels] 1979–81.

——, *Caxton in Focus*, London 1982.

——, 'Importation of books printed on the continent into England and Scotland before c. 1520', in Hindman, ed., *Printing the Written Word*.

——, 'The codex in the fifteenth century: manuscript and print', in N. Barker, ed., *A Potencie of Life. Books in Society. The Clark Lectures, 1986–1987*, London 1993.

Helmholz, R.H., 'The sons of Edward IV: a canonical assessment of the claim that they were illegitimate', in Hammond, ed., *Richard III: Loyalty, Lordship and Law*.

Hemnant, M., ed., *Select Cases in the Exchequer Chamber before all the Justices of England*, vol. 2, *1461–1509*, Selden Society, 1948

The Heralds Exhibition Catalogue 1934, catalogue of the *Heralds' Commemmorative Exhibition 1484–1934, held at the College of Arms*, London 1970.

Herrmann, E., 'Spätmittelalterliche englische Pseudoprophetien', *Archiv für Kulturgeschichte*, 57 (1975).

Hewson, M.A., *Giles of Rome and the Medieval Theory of Conception*, London 1975.

Hibbard, L.A. (Loomis née Hibbard), *Medieval Romance in England*, New York 1963.

Hicks, M., 'Descent, partition and extinction: the Warwick inheritance', *BIHR*, 52 (1979).

——, 'The last days of Elizabeth, Countess of Oxford', *EHR*, 13 (1988).

——, 'The cartulary of Richard III as duke of Gloucester in British Library Manuscript Cotton Julius B XII', in the same, *Richard III and His Rivals: Magnates and Their Motives in the Wars of the Roses*, London 1991, ch. 14.

Hills, R., *John Tate, England's First Papermaker*, talk at Stationers' Hall, 24 Feb. 1993, printed.

Hilpert, H.-E., 'Geistliche Bildung und Laienbildung: Zur Ueberlieferung der Schulschrift *Compendium historiae in genealogia Christi* (Compendium veteris testamenti) des Petrus von Poitiers († 1205) in England', *Journal of Medieval History*, 11 (1985).

Hindman, S.L., 'Fifteenth-century Dutch bible illustration and the *Historia Scholastica*', *Journal of the Warburg and Courtauld Institutes*, 37 (1974).

——, ed., *Printing the Written Word. The Social History of the Book, circa 1450–1520*, Ithaca / London 1991.

Hinkle, W.M., *The Fleurs de Lis of the Kings of France 1285–1488*, Carbondale/Edwardsville 1991.

Hirsch, R., *Printing, Selling and Reading 1450–1550*, Wiesbaden 1967.

Histoire des bibliothèques françaises. Vol. 1. *Les bibliothèques médiévales. Du VIe siècle à 1530*, introd. by A. Vernet, 1989.

Hoccleve, Thomas, *Selections from Hoccleve*, ed. M.C. Seymour, Oxford 1981.

Horrox, R.E., 'Financial memoranda of the reign of Edward V. Longleat Miscellaneous Manuscript Book II', *Camden Miscellany*, 29 (1987).

——, and P.W Hammond, eds, *British Library Harleian Manuscript 433*, 4 vols, Gloucester 1979–83.

——, and A.F. Sutton, 'Some expenses of Richard, Duke of Gloucester, 1475–77', *The Ricardian*, 6 (1982–84).

Horstmann, C., ed., *Sammlung Altenglischer Legenden*, Heilbronn 1878.

——, *The Life of St. Katherine of Alexandria*, EETS OS 100 (1893).

Housman, J.E., 'Higden, Trevisa, Caxton and the beginning of Arthurian criticism', *Review of English Studies*, 23–24 (1947–48).

Howard, J.J., ed., *The Visitation of Suffolke*, vol. 1, Lowestoft/London 1866.

Hudson, A., *The Premature Reformation. Wycliffite Texts and Lollard Scholarship*, Oxford 1988.

Hughes, J., *Pastors and Visionaries*, Woodbridge 1988.

Hulbert, J.R., 'What was Chaucer's aim in the *Knight's Tale*?', *Studies in Philology*, 26 (1929).

Hunter, D., *Papermaking*, New York 1978.

Hutchison, A.M., 'Devotional reading in the monastery and in the late medieval household', in M.G. Sargent, ed., *De cella in seculum: Religious and Secular Life and Devotion in Late Medieval England*, Cambridge 1989.

Ihle, S., 'The English *Partonope of Blois* as *exemplum*', in K. Busby and E. Kooper, eds, *Courtly Literature, Culture and Context*, 5th Congress of the International Courtly Literature Society, Amsterdam/Philadelphia 1990.

Ipomedon, *see* Kölbing, E.

Ives, E.W., 'The common lawyers', in Clough, ed., *Profession*.

Jackson, W.T.H., 'Gottfried von Strassburg', in Loomis, ed., *Arthurian Literature*.

Jähns, M., *Geschichte der Kriegswissenschaften, in Geschichte der Kriegswissenschaften in Deutschland*, vol. 21, repr. London / New York / Hildesheim 1965.

James, M.R., *A Descriptive Catalogue of the Manuscripts in the Library of Trinity College, Cambridge*, 4 vols, Cambridge 1900–04.

——, *A Descriptive Catalogue of the Manuscripts in the Library of Corpus Christi College, Cambridge*, 2 vols, Cambridge 1909–12.

——, *A Descriptive Catalogue of the Manuscripts in the Library of Lambeth Palace: The Medieval Manuscripts*, Cambridge 1932.

Jameson, A.B., *Sacred and Legendary Art*, 2 vols, London 1891, 1890.

——, *Legends of the Madonna*, London 1909.

Jansen, S.L., *Political Protest and Prophecy under Henry VIII*, Woodbridge 1991.

Jarman, A.O.H., 'The Welsh Myrdinn poems', in Loomis, ed., *Arthurian Literature*.

Jeremy, M., 'The English prose translation of the *Legenda aurea*', *Modern Language Notes*, 59 (1944).

John Vale's Book, *see* Kekewich, M.L., *et al.*, eds.

Johnson, P.A., *Duke Richard of York, 1411–1460*, Oxford 1988.

Johnston, F.R., 'The English cult of St Bridget of Sweden', *Analecta Bollandiana*, 103 (1985).

Joliffe, P.S.A., *A Checklist of Middle English Prose Writings of Spiritual Guidance*, Toronto 1974.

Jones, R.H., *The Royal Policy of Richard II. Absolutism in the Later Middle Ages*, Oxford 1968.

Kalén, H., ed., *A Middle English Paraphrase of the Old Testament*, Göteborgs Högskolas Arsskrift 28, 5 (1923).

Kaltenbacher, R., 'Der altfranzösische Roman *Paris et Vienne*', *Romanische Forschungen*, 15 (1904).

Kane, G., ed., *Piers Plowman: the A Version ...*, London 1960.

——, and E.T. Donaldson, *Piers Plowman: the B Version*, London 1975.

Kaye, John / Guillaume Caoursin, *The Siege of Rhodes (1482)*, ed. D. Gray, facsimile, New York 1975.

Kean, P.M., 'Love, law, and lewte in *Piers Plowman*', *Review of English Studies*, 15 (1964).

Keeler, L., *Geoffrey of Monmouth and the Later Latin Chroniclers 1300–1500*, Berkeley/Los Angeles 1940.

Keen, M. H., 'Treason trials under the law of arms', *Transactions of the Royal Historical Society*, 5th series, 12 (1962).

——, 'Brotherhood in arms', *History*, 47 (1962).

——, 'Chivalry, heralds and history', in R.H.C. Davis et al., eds, *The Writing of History in the Middle Ages. Essays presented to R.W. Southern*, Oxford 1981.

——, *Chivalry*, New Haven/London 1984.

——, 'Some late medieval ideas about nobility' in the same, *Nobles, Knights and Men-at-arms in the Middle Ages*, London 1996.

——, 'The debate about nobility: Dante, Nicholas Upton and Bartolus', in the same, *Nobles, Knights and Men-at-arms*.

——, 'English military experience and the court of chivalry: the case of Grey v. Hastings', in Contamine et al., eds, *Guerre et société*.

——, Introduction, in Contamine et al., eds, *Guerre et société*.

Keiser, G.R., 'The romances', in *Middle English Prose*.

Kekewich, M.L., 'Edward IV, William Caxton and literary patronage in Yorkist England', *Modern Language Review*, 66 (1971).

——, C. Richmond, A.F. Sutton, L. Visser-Fuchs, J.L. Watts, eds, *The Politics of Fifteenth-Century England: John Vale's Book*, Stroud 1995.

Kelly, H.A., *Divine Providence in the England of Shakespeare's Histories*, Cambridge, Mass., 1970.

——, 'English kings and the fear of sorcery', *Medieval Studies*, 39 (1977).

Kendall, P.M., *Richard III*, London 1972.

Kendrick, T.D., *British Antiquity*, London 1949.

Ker, N.R., *Medieval Manuscripts in British Libraries*, 4 vols, Oxford 1969–92.

——, *Medieval Libraries of Great Britain. A List of Surviving Books*, second edn, London 1964.

Kibre, P., 'The intellectual interests reflected in libraries of the fourteenth and fifteenth centuries', *Journal of the History of Ideas*, 7 (1946).

Kingsford, C.L., *English Historical Literature in the Fifteenth Century*, Oxford 1913.

——, *The London Chronicles*, Oxford 1905.

——, 'The first version of Hardyng's chronicle' (with extracts), *EHR*, 27 (1912).

Kipling, G., *The Triumph of Honour*, Leiden 1977.

Kirchner, J., ed., *Scriptura gothica libraria*, Munich / Vienna 1966.

Klausner, D.N., 'Didacticism and drama in *Guy of Warwick*', *Medievalia et Humanistica*, n.s. 6 (1975).

Kölbing, E., '*Ipomedon* in drei englische Bearbeitungen', Breslau 1889.

Kren, T., ed., *Margaret of York, Simon Marmion and The Visions of Tondal. Papers Delivered at a Symposium Organized by the Department of Manuscripts of the J. Paul Getty Museum in collaboration with the Huntington Library and Art Collections, June 21–24, 1990*, Malibu 1992.

Kuil, R., 'John Russell en het vroege Engelse humanisme', in *Excursiones Medievales, opstellen aangeboden aan Prof. A.G. Jongkees door zijn leerlingen ...*, preface by H. Schulte Nordholt, Groningen 1979.

Kupelwieser, L., *Die Kämpfe Ungarns mit den Osmanen*, Vienna/Leipzig 1895.

Lacaze, Y., 'Le rôle des traditions dans la genèse d'un sentiment national au xve siècle. La Bourgogne de Philippe le Bon', *Bibliothèque de l'École des Chartes*, 129 (1971).

Laidlaw, J.C., ed., *The Poetical Works of Alain Chartier*, Cambridge 1974.

La Marche, Olivier de, *Mémoires*, ed. H. Beaune and J. d'Arbaumont, 4 vols, Paris 1883–88.

——, *Chevalier Délibéré*, in A.V., ed., *Collection de Poésies, Romans, Chroniques, etc... .*, Paris 1842.

Lander, J.R., *Crown and Nobility 1450–1509*, London 1976.

——, *Government and Community, England 1450–1509*, London 1980.

Lang, C., ed., *Flavi Vegeti Renati Epitoma Rei Militaris*, repr. Stuttgart 1967.

Langland, William, *see* Kane, G.; Pearsall, D.; Skeat, W.W.

Lannoy, Comte B. de, *Hugues de Lannoy, le bon seigneur de Santes*, Brussels 1957.

——, and G. Dansaert, *Jean de Lannoy, le bâtisseur, 1410–1493*, Paris / Brussels 1937.

Lannoy, Gilbert de, *Oeuvres de Ghillebert de Lannoy*, ed. C. Potvin, Louvain 1878.

Larson, L.M., ed. and trans., *The King's Mirror*, New York 1917.

La Sale, Antoine de, *Petit Jehan de Saintré*, ed. J. Misrahi and C.A. Knudson, Geneva 1987.

Lathrop, H.B., 'The first English printers and their patrons', *The Library*, 4th series, 3 (1922–23).

Leeuwen, G.C. van, *Denkbeelden van een Vliesridder. De Instruction d'un jeune Prince van Guillebert de Lannoy*, Amsterdam 1975.

Le Fèvre, Raoul, *Raoul Le Fèvre, The History of Jason*, trans. William Caxton, ed. J. Munro, EETS ES 111 (1913, for 1912).

——, *see also* Pinkernell, G.

——, *Raoul Lefèvre – Le Recoeil des Histoires de Troyes*, ed. M. Aeschbach, Bern 1987.

——, *The Recuyell of the Hystoryes of Troye*, *see* Sommer, H.O.

Legg, L.G. Wickham, *English Coronation Records*, Westminster 1901.

Legge, M.D., *Anglo-Norman Literature and its Background*, Oxford 1963.

Leland, John, *De Rebus Britannicis Collectanea*, ed. Thomas Hearne, 6 vols, London 1774.

Lemaire, C., *et al.*, *Isabella van Portugal*, catalogue of an exhibition at the Royal Library, Brussels, 1991.

Lerner, R.E., *The Powers of Prophecy. The Cedar of Lebanon Vision from the Mongol Onslaught to the Dawn of the Enlightenment*, Berkeley/Los Angeles 1983.

Lester, G.A., *Sir John Paston's 'Grete Boke'. A Descriptive Catalogue with Introduction of British Library MS Lansdowne 285*, Woodbridge 1984.

——, *The Earliest English Translation of Vegetius' De Re Militari*, Middle English Texts 21, Heidelberg 1988.

——, 'The books of a fifteenth-century English gentleman, Sir John Paston', *Neuphilologische Mitteilungen*, 88 (1987).

——, 'The literary activity of the medieval English heralds', *English Studies*, 3 (1990).

——, 'Fifteenth-century English heraldic narrative', *Yearbook of English Studies*, 22 (1992).

Levine, J.M., *Humanism and History. Origins of Modern English Historiography*, Ithaca/London 1987.

Levy, F.J., *Tudor Historical Thought*, San Marino 1967.

Lewis, P.S., 'Two pieces of fifteenth-century political propaganda: b) the English kill their kings', *Journal of the Warburg and Courtauld Institutes*, 27 (1964).

——, 'War propaganda and historiography in fifteenth-century France and England', *Transactions of the Royal Historical Society*, 15 (1965).

——, 'France in the fifteenth century: society and sovereignty', in the same, *Essays in Later Medieval French History*, London 1985.

——, 'Jean Juvenal des Ursins and the common literary attitude towards tyranny in fifteenth-century France', in the same, *Essays*.

La Librairie de Charles V, catalogue of an exhibition at the Bibliothèque Nationale, 1968.

Liebermann, F., *Quadripartitus ...*, Halle an der Saale 1892.

——, *Die Gesetze der Angelsachsen*, 3 vols, Halle an der Saale 1903–16.

Lindner, A., 'L'influence du roman chevaleresque français sur le pas d'armes', *Publications du Centre Européen d'Études Bourguignonnes (XIVe–XVIe s.)*, 31 (1991).

Lloyd, J.E., 'Geoffrey of Monmouth', *EHR*, 57 (1942).

Löseth, E., *Le 'Roman en prose de Tristan', le 'Roman de Palamède' et la Compilation de Rusticien de Pise. Analyse critique d'après tous les manuscrits de Paris*, Bibliothèque de l'École des Hautes Études, 82, Paris 1891, repr. New York 1970.

Loomis, R.S., ed., *Arthurian Literature. A Collaborative History*, Oxford 1959.

Louis, C., ed., *The Commonplace Book of Robert Reynes of Acle. An Edition of Tanner MS 407*, New York/London 1980.

——, 'A Yorkist genealogical chronicle in Middle English verse', *Anglia*, 109 (1991).

Lovat, R., 'The library of John Blacman and contemporary Carthusian spirituality', *Journal of Ecclesiastical History*, 43 (1992).

Lowes, J.L., 'Chaucer and Dante's *Convivio*', *Modern Philology*, 13 (1915–16).

Lowry, M., 'Caxton, St Winifred and the Lady Margaret Beaufort', *The Library*, 6th series, 5 (1983).

——, 'Diplomacy and the spread of printing', in L. Hellinga and J. Goldfinch, eds, *Bibliography and the Study of Fifteenth-Century Civilisation*, London 1987.

——, 'John Rous and the revival of the Neville Circle', *Viator*, 19 (1988).

——, 'The arrival and use of continental printed books in Yorkist England', in P. Aquilon *et al.*, eds, *Le Livre dans l'Europe de la Renaissance*, Paris 1988.

Lull, Ramon, *The Book of the Ordre of Chyvalry* translated and printed by William Caxton, ed. A.T.P. Byles, EETS OS 168 (1926, repr. 1971).

——, *see also* Minervini, V.

Lydgate, John, *Lydgate's Troy Book*, ed. H. Bergen, vol. 1, EETS ES 97 (1906).

——, *Lydgate's Siege of Thebes*, ed. A. Erdmann and E. Ekwall, 2 vols, EETS ES 108 (1911) Text; 125 (1930, for 1920) Introduction.

McCarthy, T., 'Malory and his sources', in Archibald and Edwards, *A Companion to Malory*.

MacCracken, H.N., 'Vegetius in English', in *Anniversary Papers by Colleagues and Pupils of G.L. Kittredge. Presented on the Completion of his Twenty-Fifth Year of Teaching in Harvard University, June 1913*, Boston/London 1913.

Macdougall, N., *James III. A Political Study*, Edinburgh 1982.

——, 'Richard III and James III: contemporary monarchs, parallel mythologies', in Hammond, ed., *Richard III: Loyalty, Lordship and Law*.

McFarlane, K.B., 'William Worcester: a preliminary survey', in the same, *England in the Fifteenth Century. Collected Essays*, London 1981.

MacGibbon, D., *Elizabeth Woodville*, London 1938.

McGinn, B., '*Teste David cum Sibylla*: the significance of the Sibylline tradition in the Middle Ages', in J. Kirstner and S.F. Wemple, eds, *Women in the Medieval World*, Oxford 1985.

McKenna, J.W., 'Popular canonization as political propaganda: the cult of Archbishop Scrope', *Speculum*, 65 (1970).

Madden, F., 'Narratives of the arrival of Louis de Bruges …', *Archaeologia*, 26 (1836).

Maerlant, Jacob van, *Het Leven van St Franciscus*, ed. J. Tideman, Leiden 1874.

Mallett, M.E., 'Anglo-Florentine commercial relations, 1465–91', *Economic History Review*, 15 (1962–63).

Mandach, A. de, 'L'anthologie chevaleresque de Marguerite d'Anjou (BM Royal 15 E vi) et les officines Saint-Augustin de Cantorbury, Jean Wauquelin de Mons et David Aubert de Hesdin', *Actes des VIe Congrès International de Société Rencesvals pour l'étude des épopées romanes*, Aix-en-Provence 1974.

Manly, J.M., and E. Rickert, *The Text of the Canterbury Tales, studied on the basis of all the known manuscripts*, vol. 1, *Description of the Manuscripts*, Chicago 1940.

A Manual of the Writings in Middle English, 1050–1500, gen. eds J. Burke Severs / A.E. Hartung, 9 vols, New Haven, Conn., 1967–93.

Manzaloui, M.A., ed., *Secreta Secretorum. Nine English Versions*, EETS OS 276 (1977).

Marks, R., 'The glazing of Fotheringhay church and college', *Journal of the British Archaeological Association*, 131 (1978).

——, and A. Payne, *British Heraldry*, catalogue of an exhibition at the British Museum 1978, London 1978.

Martens, M.P.J., *et al.*, *Lodewijk van Gruuthuse, Mecenas en Europees Diplomaat, ca. 1427–1492*, catalogue of an exhibition at the Gruuthuse Museum, Bruges 1992.

Mason, E., 'Legends of the Beauchamps' ancestors: the use of baronial propaganda in medieval England', *Journal of Medieval History*, 10 (1984).

Mather, F.J., 'King Ponthus and the fair Sidone', *Publications of the Modern Language Society of America*, 12 (1897).

Matheson, L.M., 'Historical Prose', in *Middle English Prose*.

——, 'The Middle English prose *Brut*: a location list of the manuscripts and early printed editions', *Analytical and Enumerative Bibliography*, 3 (1979)

——, 'Printer and scribe: Caxton, the *Polychronicon*, and the *Brut*', *Speculum*, 60 (1985).

——, 'The Arthurian stories of Lambeth Palace Library MS 84', *Arthurian Literature*, 5 (1985).

——, 'King Arthur and the medieval English chronicles', in V.M. Lagorio and M.L. Day, eds, *King Arthur through the Middle Ages*, New York 1990.

Mathew, G., 'Ideals of knighthood in late fourteenth-century England', in R.W. Hunt *et al.*, eds, *Studies in Medieval History presented to F.M. Powicke*, Oxford 1948.

Meale, C., ed., *Readings in Medieval Romance*, Cambridge 1994.

——, 'Patrons, buyers, and owners: book production and social status', in Griffiths and Pearsall, eds, *Book Production and Publishing*.

——, 'The Middle English romance of *Ipomedon*: a late medieval "mirror" for princes and merchants', *Reading Medieval Studies*, 10 (1984).

——, 'Manuscripts, readers and patrons in fifteenth-century England: Sir Thomas Malory and Arthurian romance', *Arthurian Literature*, 4 (1985).

——, 'The Morgan Library copy of *Generides*', in Mills *et al.*, eds, *Romance in Medieval England*.

——, 'Caxton, de Worde, and the publication of romance in late medieval England', *The Library*, 6th series, 14 (1992).

——, '"gode men / Wiues maydens and alle men": romance and its audiences', in the same, ed., *Readings in Medieval English Romance*.

——, '"The hoole book": editing and the creation of meaning in Malory's text' in Archibald and Edwards, *A Companion to Malory*.

Meijer, A. de, 'John Capgrave, O.E.S.A.', *Augustiniana*, 5 (1955).

Meiss, M., *The Limbourgs and their Contemporaries*, 2 vols, London 1974.

Ménard, P., *et al.*, *Le Roman de Tristan en prose*, Geneva 1987– [in progress].

Metcalf, W.C., *A Book of Knights*, London 1885.

Mézières, Philippe de, *Le Songe du Vieil Pelerin*, ed. G.W. Coopland, 2 vols, Cambridge 1969.

——, *Philippe de Mézières, Letter to King Richard II*, ed. G.W. Coopland, Liverpool 1975.

Middleton, A., 'The audience and public of *Piers Plowman*', in D. Lawton, ed., *Middle English Alliterative Poetry and its Literary Background*, Woodbridge 1982.

Mielot, Jean, *Vie de Ste Catherine d'Alexandrie*, ed. M. Sepet, Paris 1881.

Migne, J.P., *Patrologiae cursus completus. Series Latina*, 221 vols, Paris 1844–64.

Mills, M., ed., *Six Middle English Romances*, London/Melbourne 1973.

——, and M. Andrew, *Ywain and Gawain*, London 1992.

——, J. Fellows, and C. Meale, eds, *Romance in Medieval England*, Cambridge 1991.

Milner, N.P., trans., *Vegetius: Epitome of Military Science*, Liverpool 1993.

Minervini, V., *Ramon Lull, Livre de l'Ordre de Chevalerie*, Bari 1972.

Minnis, A.J., ed., *Late Medieval Religious Texts and their Transmission. Essays in honour of A.I. Doyle*, York Manuscripts Conferences Proceedings Series 3, Cambridge 1994.

Mitchell, R.J., *John Free. From Bristol to Rome in the Fifteenth Century*, London 1955.

Modigliani, Anna, 'Un nuovo manoscritto di Pietro Carmeliano: le "Epistolae" delle pseudo-Falaride nella Trinity College Library di Dublino', *Humanistica Lovaniensia*, 33 (1984).

Molinet, Jean, *Chronique*, ed. G. Doutrepont and O. Jodogne, 3 vols, Brussels 1935–37.

——, *Les faictz et dictz de Jean Molinet*, ed. N. Dupire, 3 vols, Paris 1937–39.

Monks, P.R., and D.D.R. Owen, eds, *Medieval Codicology, Iconography, Literature, and Translation. Studies for Keith Val Sinclair*, Leiden 1994.

Monmouth, Geoffrey of, *see* Geoffrey of Monmouth.

Mooney, L.R., 'Lydgate's "Kings of England" and another verse chronicle of the kings', *Viator*, 20 (1989).

Moore, S., 'Patrons of letters in Norfolk and Suffolk, *c.* 1450', *Publications of the Modern Language Association*, 27 (1912), 28 (1913).

Moran, J.H., *Education and Learning in the City of York*, Borthwick Papers 55, York 1979.

Morand, F., ed., *Chronique de Jean le Fèvre*, 2 vols, Paris 1876–81.

Morawski, J., *Les diz et proverbes des sages*, Bibliothèque de la faculté des lettres, 2nd series, vol. 2, Paris 1924.

More, Thomas, *The Complete Works of St. Thomas More*, vol. 2, *The History of King Richard III*, ed. R. Sylvester, New Haven/London 1963.

Moreton, C.E., 'The "library" of a late-fifteenth-century lawyer', *The Library*, 6th series, 13 (1991).

Morey, J.H., 'Peter Comestor, biblical paraphrase and the medieval popular bible', *Speculum*, 68 (1993).

Morgan, N., 'Texts of devotion and religious instruction associated with Margaret of York', in Kren, ed., *Margaret of York*.

——, *Early Gothic Manuscripts (I) 1190–1250 (A Survey of Manuscripts Illuminated in the British Isles*, gen. ed. J.J.G. Alexander), Oxford/London 1982.

——, *Early Gothic Manuscripts (II) 1250–1285*, Oxford/London 1988.

Morse, C., 'Critical approaches to the *Clerk's Tale*', in Benson and Robertson, *Chaucer's Religious Tales*.

Munro, J.H.A., *Wool, Cloth and Gold. The Struggle for Bullion in Anglo-Burgundian Trade, 1340–1478*, Toronto 1972.

Myers, A.R., 'Parliamentary petitions in the fifteenth century', *EHR*, 52 (1937).

——, 'Parliament 1422–1509', in R.G. Davies and J.H. Denton, eds, *The English Parliament in the Middle Ages*, Manchester 1981.

——, ed., *The Household of Edward IV. The Black Book and the Ordinance of 1478*, Manchester 1959.

——, 'The household of Queen Elizabeth Woodville, 1466–7', in the same, *Crown, Household and Parliament in Fifteenth Century England*, London 1985.

Mynors, R.A.B., 'A fifteenth-century scribe: T. Werken', *Transactions of the Cambridge Bibliographical Society*, 1, no. 2 (1950).

Naber, A., 'Les manuscrits d'un bibliophile bourguignon du xve siècle, Jean de Wavrin', *Revue du Nord*, 72 (1990).

——, 'BR 9632/3: une version bourguignonne de … *Paris et Vienne*', *Rencontres médiévales en Bourgogne (XIVe–XVe siècles)*, 1 (1991).

Naïs, H., '"Grands temps et long jours sont, monsieur l'indiciaire"', *Travaux de linguistique et de littérature publiés pour le Centre de philologie et de littérature romanes de l'Université de Strasbourg*, 11 (1973).

Nemitz, R., and D. Thierse, *St. Barbara. Weg einer Heiligen durch die Zeit*, Essen 1995.

Neuse, R., 'The Knight: the First Mover in Chaucer's Human Comedy', in J.A. Burrow, *Chaucer: A Critical Anthology*, Harmondsworth 1980.

Nevanlinna, S., and I. Taavitsainen, eds, *St Katherine of Alexandria*, Cambridge 1993.

Newstead, H., 'Romances: General', in *Manual*, vol. 1.

——, 'The origin and growth of the Tristan legend', in Loomis, ed., *Arthurian Literature*.

Nichols, J.G., ed., *Grants etc. from the Crown during the Reign of Edward the Fifth*, CS, Old Series, 1854.

——, ed., 'Chronicle of the Rebellion in Lincolnshire, 1470', *Camden Miscellany*, 1, London 1847.

——, *see also* Worcester, William.

——, and J. Bruce, eds, *Wills from Doctors' Commons*, CS, Old Series, 1863.

Nicolas, N.H., *Privy Purse Expenses of Elizabeth of York: Wardrobe Accounts of Edward the Fourth*, London 1830.

Oates, J.C.T., *Cambridge University Library: A History from the Beginnings to the Copyright Act of Queen Anne*, Cambridge 1986.

Ohlander, U., ed., *A Middle English Paraphrase of the Old Testament*, Gothenburg Studies in English, 5, 11, 16, 24, Göteborg 1955, 1960–61, 1963, 1972.

Oliger, L., 'Ein pseudoprophetischer Text aus Spanien', in *Kirchengeschichtliche Studien P. Michael Bihl*, Colmar 1941.

Olson, G., *Literature as Recreation in the Later Middle Ages*, Ithaca / London 1982.

Orbán, A.P., ed., *Vitae Sanctae Katharinae*, 2 vols, Corpus Christianorum Continuatio Medievalis, vols 119 and 119a, Turnhout 1992.

Orme, N., *From Childhood to Chivalry*, London / New York 1984.

[Owen, H., and J.B. Blakeway], *A History of Shrewsbury*, 2 vols, London 1825.

Owst, G.R., *Literature and Pulpit in Medieval England*, Cambridge 1938.

Painter, G.D., *William Caxton*, London 1976.

Pannier, L., ed., *Le débat des hérauts d'armes*, Paris 1877.

Pantzer, K.F., 'Printing the English statutes, 1484–1640: some historical implications', in K.E. Carpenter, ed., *Books and Society in History,* New York/London 1983.

Paris, P. ed., *Grandes chroniques de France*, 6 vols, Paris 1836–38.

Parry, J.J., *The Vita Merlini*, Illinois University Studies in Language and Literature, vol. 10, no. 3 (1925).

——, *Brut y Brenhinedd*, Cambridge, Mass., 1937.

——, and R.A. Caldwell, 'Geoffrey of Monmouth', in Loomis, ed., *Arthurian Literature*.

Paston Letters, ed J. Gairdner, 6 vols, London 1904.

Paston Letters and Papers of the Fifteenth Century, ed. N. Davis, 2 vols, Oxford 1976.

Pastoureau, M., 'Les armoiries de Tristan dans la littérature et l'iconographie médiévales', *Gwechall. Bulletin de la Société finistèrienne d'histoire et d'archéologie*, 1 (1978).

Patch, H.R., *The Tradition of Boethius. A Study of His Importance in Medieval Culture*, New York / Oxford 1935.

Payne, A., 'The Salisbury roll of arms, *c.* 1463', in Williams, ed., *England in the Fifteenth Century*.

Pearsall, D., ed., *The Floure and the Leafe and the Assembly of Ladies*, London 1962.

——, *John Lydgate*, London 1970.

——, 'The English romance in the fifteenth century', *Essays and Studies*, n.s., 29 (1976).

——, ed., *Piers Plowman by William Langland, an Edition of the C-Text*, Berkeley/Los Angeles 1982.

——, *The Canterbury Tales*, London 1985.

——, 'Lydgate and literary patronage at the Lancastrian courts', International Courtly Literature Society, 8th Triennial Congress, Belfast, Trans. 1995 [forthcoming].

Peck, R.A., ed., *Heroic Women from the Old Testament in Middle English Verse*, Kalamazoo 1991.

Petre, J., ed., *Richard III, Crown and People*, Gloucester 1985.

Phillios, J.R.S., 'Edward II and the prophets', in W.M. Ormrod, ed., *England in the Fourteenth Century. Proceedings of the 1985 Harlaxton Symposium*, Woodbridge 1986.

Piaget, A., '*Le Chemin de Vaillance* de Jean de Courcy', *Romania*, 27 (1898).

Piccard, G., ed., *Wasserzeichen. Werkzeug und Waffen*, Stuttgart 1980.

Pickford, C.E., 'Fiction and the reading public in the fifteenth century', *BJRL*, 45 (1963).

Picot, E., and H. Stein, *Recueil de pièces historiques imprimées sous le règne de Louis XI*, Paris 1923.

Pinkernell, G., ed., *L'Histoire de Jason*, Frankfurt 1971.

Piper, E.F., 'The royal boar and the Ellesmere Chaucer', *Philological Quarterly*, 5 (1926).

Piponnier, F., *Costume et vie sociale: la cour d'Anjou aux xive et xve siècles*, Paris 1970.

Pizan, Christine de, *The Book of the City of Ladies*, trans. E.J. Richards, New York 1982.
——, *The Book of the Duke of True Lovers*, trans. A. Kemp-Welch, London 1908.
——, *The Book of the Faytes of Armes and Chevalrye*, trans. William Caxton, ed. A.T.P. Byles, EETS OS 189 (1932, repr. 1971).
Platnauer, M., ed., *Claudian*, Loeb edn, 2 vols, London / New York 1922.
Plomer, J.H., *Wynkyn de Worde and His Contemporaries*, London 1925.
Plucknett, T.F.T., *Early English Legal Literature*, Cambridge 1958.
Pollard, A.F., 'Fifteenth-century clerks of parliament', *BIHR*, 15 (1938).
Pollard, A.J., *Richard III and the Princes in the Tower*, Stroud 1991.
——, *North-Eastern England during the Wars of the Roses. Lay Society, War and Politics 1450–1500*, Oxford 1990.
——, ed., *The North of England in the Age of Richard III*, Stroud 1996.
——, 'The Richmondshire community of gentry during the Wars of the Roses', in Ross, ed., *Patronage, Pedigree and Power*.
——, 'St Cuthbert and the hog', in Griffiths and Sherborne, eds, *Kings and Nobles*.
Pollard, A.W., and G.R. Redgrave, *A Short Title Catalogue of Books printed in England ... 1475–1640*, rev. edn, London 1986.
Pollard, G., 'The company of stationers before 1557', *The Library*, 4th series, 18 (1937).
Power, E., ed., *The Goodman of Paris*, London 1928.
Raine, James, 'The statutes ordained by Richard, Duke of Gloucester, for the College of Middleham. Dated July 4, 18 Edw. IV, (1478)', *Archaeological Journal*, 14 (1857).
Ramsay, L.C., *Chivalric Romances. Popular Literature in Medieval England*, Bloomington, Indiana, 1983.
Reeves, M., *The Influence of Prophecy in the Later Middle Ages. A Study in Joachimism*, Oxford 1969.
——, 'Joachimist influences on the idea of a Last World Emperor', *Traditio*, 17 (1961).
Reiss, E., 'Romance', in T.J. Hefferman, ed., *The Popular Literature of Medieval England*, Tennessee Studies in Literature 8, Knoxville 1985.
Renoir, A., *The Poetry of John Lydgate*, London 1967.
Resoort, R.J., *Een schoone historie vander borchgravinne van Vergi. Onderzoek naar de intentie en gebruikssfeer ven een zestiende-eeuwse prozaroman*, Hilversum 1988.
Reynaert, J., 'Het middelnederlandse gebedenboek van de Brigitinessen van Dendermonde', *Jaarboek van de Koninklijke Souvereine Hoofdkamer van Retorica 'De Fonteine' te Gent*, tweede reeks, no. 24 (1980–81).
Reynolds, L.D., ed., *Texts and Transmission. A Survey of the Latin Classics*, Oxford 1986.
Rhodes, D.E., *A Catalogue of Incunabula in All the Libraries of Oxford University Outside the Bodleian*, Oxford 1982.
Richard of Bury, *The Love of Books, the Philobiblon*, trans. E.C. Thomas, London 1903.
Richmond, C., *John Hopton*, Cambridge 1981.
——, '1485 and all that', in Hammond, ed., *Richard III: Loyalty, Lordship and Law*.
Rickert, E., trans., *Early English Romance in Verse ... Romances of Love*, London 1908, repr. New York 1966.
——, trans., *Early English Romances in Verse ... Romances of Friendship*, London 1908, repr. New York 1967.
Rickert, M., 'The so-called Beaufort Hours and Psalter', *Burlington Magazine*, 104 (1962).
Riddy, F., 'John Hardyng's Chronicle and the Wars of the Roses', *Arthurian Literature*, 12 (1993).
Riley, H.T., ed., *Munimenta Gildhallae Londoniensis*, 3 vols, Rolls Series, London 1859–60.
Robbins, R.H., *Secular Lyrics of the XIVth and XVth Centuries*, Oxford 1955.
——, *Historical Poems of the XIVth and XVth Centuries*, New York 1959.
Robertson, A.J., ed., *The Laws of the Kings of England from Edmund to Henry I*, Cambridge 1925.
Robinson, F.N., *The Works of Geoffrey Chaucer*, second edn, Oxford 1957.
Rogers, N.J., 'Books of Hours produced in the Low Countries for the English market in the fifteenth century', 2 vols, M. Litt. thesis, Cambridge 1982.

——, ed., *England in the Fifteenth Century. Proceedings of the 1992 Harlaxton Symposium*, Stamford 1994.

Romanus, Aegidius, *see* Giles of Rome.

Rosenthal, J., 'Richard, Duke of York: a fifteenth-century layman and the church', *Catholic History Review*, 50 (1964–65).

Roskell, J.S., *The House of Commons 1386–1421, The History of Parliament*, vol.1, Stroud 1993.

——, *The Commons and their Speakers in English Parliaments, 1376–1523*, Manchester 1965.

——, 'William Catesby, counsellor to Richard III', *BJRL*, 42 (1959).

Ross, C. D., *Edward IV*, London 1974.

——, *Richard III*, London 1981.

——, 'Some "servants and lovers" of Richard in his youth', *The Ricardian*, 4: 5 (Dec. 1976).

——, 'Rumour, Propaganda and Popular Opinion during the Wars of the Roses', in R.A. Griffiths, ed., *Patronage, the Crown and the Provinces*, Gloucester 1981.

——, ed., *Patronage, Pedigree and Power in Later Medieval England*, Gloucester 1979.

Rosser, G., *Medieval Westminster, 1200–1540*, Oxford 1989.

Roth, F., *The English Austin Friars, 1249–1538*, vol. 1: History, New York 1966; vol. 2: Sources, New York 1961.

Rotuli Parliamentorum, ed. J. Strachey *et al.*, 6 vols, London 1767–77.

Routh, P.E., 'Princess Bridget', *The Ricardian*, 3: 49 (June 1975).

Rowe, B.J.H., 'A contemporary account of the Hundred Years' War from 1415 to 1429', *EHR*, 41 (1926).

——, 'King Henry VI's claim to France in picture and poem', *The Library*, 4th series, 13 (1932–3).

Russell, A.G.B., 'The Rous Roll', *Burlington Magazine*, 30 (1917).

Ryan, G., and H. Ripperger, ed. and trans., *The Golden Legend*, New York 1987.

Saenger, P., 'Colard Mansion and the evolution of the printed book', *The Library Quarterly*, 45 (1975).

Salvat, M., 'Barthélemi l'Anglais, traités du soleil et de la lune, traduits par Jean Corbechon (1372)', in *Le soleil, la lune, et les étoiles au Moyen Age, Sénéfiance*, no. 13, Aix-en-Provence 1983.

Sandler, L.F., *Gothic Manuscripts 1285–1385 (A Survey of Manuscripts Illuminated in the British Isles*, gen. ed. J.J.G. Alexander), 2 vols, Oxford / London 1986.

Sandquist, T.A., 'The Holy Oil of St. Thomas of Canterbury', in T.A. Sandquist and M.R. Powicke, eds, *Essays in Medieval History Presented to Bertie Wilkinson*, Toronto 1969.

Sargent, M.G., 'Minor devotional writings', in *Middle English Prose*.

Scanlon, P.A., 'Pre-Elizabethan prose romances in English', *Cahiers elisabéthains*, 12 (1977).

Scattergood, V.J., *Politics and Poetry in the Fifteenth Century*, London 1971.

——, and J.W. Sherborne, eds, *English Court Culture in the Later Middle Ages*, London 1983.

Schirmer, W.F., *Der englische Frühhumanismus, ein Beitrag zur englischen Literatur-geschichte des 15. Jahrhunderts*, Leipzig / London 1931.

——, *John Lydgate. A Study in the Culture of the XVth Century*, trans. A.E. Keep, Westport, Conn., 1961.

Scholz, R., *Die Publizistik zur Zeit Philipps des Schönen und Bonifaz VIII. Ein Beitrag zur Geschichte der Politischen Anschauungen des Mittelalters*, Stuttgart 1903.

Schullian, D.M., 'A revised list of manuscripts of Valerius Maximus', in *Miscellanea Augusto Campana, Medioevo e Umanesimo*, 45, Padua 1981.

Schulz, H.C., 'Thomas Hoccleve, scribe', *Speculum*, 12 (1937).

Science, M., ed., *Boethius: De Consolatione Philosophiae translated by John Walton*, EETS OS 170 (1927 for 1925).

Scofield, C.L., *The Life and Reign of Edward the Fourth*, 2 vols, London 1923.

Scott, K.L., *The Caxton Master and His Patrons*, Cambridge Bibliographical Society Monographs 8, Cambridge 1976.

——, *The Mirroure of the Worlde. MS Bodley 283 (England c. 1470–80). The Physical Composition, Decoration and Illustration*, Roxburghe Club 1980.

———, 'A mid-fifteenth-century English illuminating shop and its customers', *Journal of the Warburg and Courtauld Institutes*, 31 (1968).

———, 'A late fifteenth-century group of *Nova Statuta* manuscripts', in A.C. De La Mare and B.C. Barker-Benfield, eds, *Manuscripts at Oxford. R.W. Hunt Memorial Exhibition*, Bodleian Library, Oxford 1980.

———, *Later Gothic Manuscripts: 1390–1490*, in 2 vols (vol. 6 of *A Survey of Manuscripts Illuminated in the British Isles*, gen. ed. J.J.G. Alexander), London 1997.

———, 'Limning and book-producing terms and signs *in situ* in late-medieval English manuscripts: a first listing', in R. Beadle and A.J. Piper, eds, *New Science Out of Old Books. Studies in Manuscripts and Early Printed Books in Honour of A.I. Doyle*, Aldershot 1995.

Searle, W.G., *History of Queens' College Cambridge*, Cambridge Antiquarian Society Octavo Publication 9, 2 vols, 1867–71.

Seigneuret, J.-C., ed., *Le Roman du Comte d'Artois*, Geneva 1966.

Severs, J.B., *The Literary Relationship of Chaucer's Clerk's Tale*, Yale 1942.

———, 'Did Chaucer rearrange the Clerk's Envoy?', *Modern Language Notes*, 69 (1954).

Shailor, B.A., *Catalogue of the Medieval and Renaissance Manuscripts in the Beinecke Rare Books and Manuscript Library, Yale University*, 2 vols, New York 1984–87.

Shaner, M.E., 'Instruction and delight: medieval romances as children's literature', *Poetics Today*, 13 (1992).

Sheppard, L.A., 'A new light on Caxton and Colard Mansion', *Signature*, n.s. 15 (1952).

Short Title Catalogue of Books Printed in Italy and Italian Books Printed in Other Countries from 1465–1600, now in the British Library, London 1986.

Shrader, C.R., 'A handlist of extant manuscripts containing *De re militari* of Flavius Vegetius Renatus', *Scriptorium* 33 (1979).

Sicily Herald, *Le blason des couleurs*, ed. H. Cocheris, Paris 1860.

———, *Parties inédits de l'oeuvre de Sicile héraut*, ed. P. Roland, Mons 1867.

Simons, W., *et al.*, *Het Pand*, Tielt 1991.

Singer, B., *Die Fürstenspiegel in Deutschland im Zeitalter des Humanismus und der Reformation*, Munich 1981.

Skeat, W.W., *The Vision of William concerning Piers the Plowman in Three Parallel Texts ...*, 2 vols, Oxford 1886.

Sledd, J., 'The *Clerk's Tale*: the monsters and the critics', *Modern Philology*, 51 (1953).

Smith, G., *The Coronation of Elizabeth Wydeville*, London 1935.

Smith, P., *Erasmus, A Study of His Life, Ideals, and Place in History*, New York 1962.

Sommé, M., 'Le testament d'Isabelle de Portugal et la Dévotion Moderne', in *Publications du Centre Européen d'Études Bourguignonnes (XIVe–XVIe s.)*, 29 (1989).

Sommer, H.O., ed., *The Recuyell of the Hystoryes of Troye*, London 1894.

Southern, R.W., 'Aspects of the European tradition of historical writing, 3. History as prophecy', *Transactions of the Royal Historical Society*, 5th series, 22 (1972).

Spiegel, G., *The Chronicle Tradition of Saint-Denis: A Survey*, Brookline, Mass., and Leiden 1978.

———, 'The cult of Saint Denis and Capetian kingship', *Journal of Medieval History*, 1 (1975).

Springer, M., 'Vegetius im Mittelalter', *Philologus*, 123 (1979).

Squibb, J.D., *The High Court of Chivalry*, Oxford 1959.

Statutes of the Realm, ed. A. Luders *at al.*, 11 vols, Record Commission 1810–28.

The Statutes at Large, vol. 2, *1 Edward IV – Elizabeth*, London 1770.

Steele, R., ed., *Three Prose Versions of the Secreta Secretorum*, EETS ES 74 (1878).

———, ed., *Lydgate and Burgh's Secrees of Old Philosoffres*, EETS ES 66 (1894).

Steinberg, S.H., *Five Hundred Years of Printing*, Harmondsworth 1977.

Stevens, J.E., *Medieval Romance*, London 1973.

Stevenson, J., *Letters and Papers Illustrative of the Wars of the English in France during the Reign of Henry VI*, Rolls Series, 2 vols in 3 pts, London 1861–64.

Stouff, L., *Essai sur Mélusine, roman du xive siècle par Jean d'Arras*, Dijon / Paris 1930.

Stow, John, *Annales or General Chronicle of England*, London 1615.

Stratford, J., 'The royal library in England before the reign of Edward IV', in Rogers, ed., *England in the Fifteenth Century*.

Strubel, A., 'Écrire la chasse: le prologue du *Livre de chasse* de Gaston Fébus', *Le Moyen Age*, 95 (1989).

Sutton, A.F., 'Richard III, the City of London and Southwark', in Petre, ed., *Richard III, Crown and People*.

——, ' " A curious searcher for our weal public": Richard III, piety, chivalry and the concept of the "good prince"', in Hammond, ed., *Richard III: Loyalty, Lordship and Law*.

——, 'The court and its culture in the reign of Richard III', in Gillingham, ed., *Richard III. A Medieval Kingship*, ch. 5.

——, 'Richard III's "Castle of Care"', in Petre, ed., *Richard III, Crown and People*.

——, 'Richard III's "tytylle & right": a new discovery', in Petre, ed., *Richard III, Crown and People*.

——, 'Caxton was a mercer: his social milieu and friends', in Rogers, ed., *England in the Fifteenth Century*.

——, 'Alice Claver, silkwoman (d. 1489)', in Barron and Sutton, eds, *Medieval London Widows*.

——, 'Lady Joan Bradbury', in Barron and Sutton, eds, *Medieval London Widows*.

——, and R.C. Hairsine, 'Richard III at Canterbury', in Petre, ed., *Richard III, Crown and People*.

——, and P.W. Hammond, eds, *The Coronation of Richard III. The Extant Documents*, Gloucester and New York 1983.

——, and L. Visser-Fuchs, 'Choosing a book in late fifteenth-century England and Burgundy', in C. Barron and N. Saul, eds, *England and the Low Countries in the Late Middle Ages*, Stroud 1995.

——, *The Hours of Richard III*, Stroud 1990, repr. 1996.

——, 'Richard III's books: I. *The Booke of Gostlye Grace* of Mechtild of Hackeborn', *The Ricardian*, 7 (1985–87), pp. 287–92.

——, 'Richard III's books: II. A collection of romances and Old Testament stories: 1. *Ipomedon*', *The Ricardian*, 7 (1985–87), pp. 327–32.

——, 'Richard III's books: II. A collection of romances and Old Testament stories: 2. Old Testament Stories [and] 3. *The Siege of Thebes* by John Lydgate', *The Ricardian*, 7 (1985–87), pp. 371–85.

——, 'Richard III's books: II. A collection of romances and Old Testament stories: 4. *Palamon and Arcite* and *Griselda* by Geoffrey Chaucer [and] 5. The Collection and Its Purpose', *The Ricardian*, 7 (1985–87), pp. 421–36.

——, 'Richard III's books: IV. Vegetius' *De re militari*', *The Ricardian*, 7 (1985–87), pp. 541–52.

——, 'Richard III's books: V. Aegidius Romanus' *De regimine principum*', *The Ricardian*, 8 (1988–90), pp. 61–73.

——, 'Richard III's books: VI. The Anonymous or Fitzhugh chronicle', *The Ricardian*, 8 (1988–90), pp. 104–19.

——, 'Richard III's books: VII. Guido delle Colonne's *Historia destructionis Troiae* and VIII. Geoffrey of Monmouth's *Historia regum Britanniae*, with *The Prophecy of the Eagle* and Commentary', *The Ricardian*, 8 (1988–90), pp. 136–48.

——, 'Richard III's books: VII. Guido delle Colonne's *Historia destructionis Troiae*', *The Ricardian*, 8 (1988–90), pp. 190–96.

——, 'Richard III's books: VIII. Geoffrey of Monmouth's *Historia regum Britanniae* with *The Prophecy of the Eagle* and Commentary. 1. The *Historia regum Britanniae*', *The Ricardian*, 8 (1988–90), pp. 217–22.

——, 'Richard III's books: VIII. Geoffrey of Monmouth's *Historia regum Britanniae* with *The Prophecy of the Eagle* and Commentary. 2. The Prophecy and Commentary', *The Ricardian*, 8 (1988–90), pp. 290–304.

——, 'Richard III's books: VIII. Geoffrey of Monmouth's *Historia regum Britanniae* with *The Prophecy of the Eagle* and Commentary. 2. The Prophecy and Commentary (continued)', *The Ricardian*, 8 (1988–90), pp. 351–62.

——, 'Richard III's books: VII and VIII. Guido delle Colonne's *Historia destructionis Troiae* and Geoffrey of Monmouth's *Historia regum Britanniae*, with *The Prophecy of the Eagle* and Commentary. The interest of these books for Richard III and later owners', *The Ricardian*, 8 (1988–90), pp. 403–13.

——, with Lynda Dennison, 'Richard III's books: IX. The *Grandes chroniques de France*', *The Ricardian*, 8 (1988–90), pp. 494–514.

——, 'Richard III's books: X. The *Prose Tristan*', *The Ricardian*, 9 (1991–93), pp. 23–37.

——, 'Richard III's books: XI. Ramon Lull's *Order of Chivalry*, translated by William Caxton', *The Ricardian*, 9 (1991–93), pp. 110–29.

——, 'Richard III's books: XII. William Worcester's *Boke of Noblesse* and his Collection of documents on the war in Normandy', *The Ricardian*, 9 (1991–93), pp. 154–65.

——, 'Richard III's books: XIII. Chivalric ideals and reality', *The Ricardian*, 9 (1991–93), pp. 190–205.

——, 'Richard III's books: XIV. Pietro Carmeliano's early publications: his *Spring*, the *Letters of Phalaris*, and his *Life of St Katherine* dedicated to Richard III', *The Ricardian*, 10 (1994–96), pp. 346–86.

——, 'Richard III's books: mistaken attributions: *The Dictes of the Philosophers*, translated by Anthony Woodville; the *Ellesmere Chaucer*', *The Ricardian*, 9 (1991–93), pp. 303–10.

——, 'Richard III's books: ancestry and "true nobility"', *The Ricardian*, 9 (1991–93), pp. 343–58.

——, 'Richard III's books observed', *The Ricardian*, 9 (1991–93), pp. 374–88.

——, '"Richard liveth yet": an old myth', *The Ricardian*, 9 (1991–93), pp. 266–69.

——, 'Richard III and St Julian: a new myth', *The Ricardian*, 8 (1988–90), pp. 265–70.

——, 'Richard of Gloucester and *la grosse bombarde*', *The Ricardian*, 10 (1996), pp. 461–65.

——, '*Loyaulte me lie*: another user of this motto', *The Ricardian*, 8 (1988–90), pp. 120–21.

——, 'The making of a minor London chronicle in the household of Sir Thomas Frowyk (died 1485)', *The Ricardian*, 10 (1994–96), pp. 86–103, 198–99.

——, 'The cult of angels in fifteenth-century England: a book of hours of the Guardian Angel of Queen Elizabeth Woodville', in *Women and the Book*, ed. J. Taylor and L. Smith, London 1997.

——, '"A most benevolent queen": Queen Elizabeth Woodville's reputation, her piety and her books', *The Ricardian*, 10 (1994–96), pp. 214–45.

——, 'The device of Queen Elizabeth Woodville: a gillyflower or pink', *The Ricardian*, 11 (1997–99), pp. 17–24.

——, 'The Dark Dragon of the Normans: a creation of Geoffrey of Monmouth, Stephen of Rouen, and Merlin Silvester', *Quondam et Futurus. A Journal of Arthurian Interpretations*, 2 (1992).

——, with P.W. Hammond, *The Reburial of Richard, Duke of York, 21–30 July 1476*, London 1996.

Tatlock, J.S.P., *The Legendary History of Britain. Geoffrey of Monmouth's 'Historia Regum Britanniae' and Its Early Vernacular Versions*, Berkeley / Los Angeles 1950.

Taylor, J.M.H., *et al.*, eds, *Le Roman de Perceforest*, pts 1, 3 and 4, Geneva 1979–93.

Taylor, R., *The Political Prophecy in England*, New York 1911.

Temple, Sir W., *Sir William Temple's Essays On Ancient and Modern Learning and On Poetry*, ed. J. Springarn, Oxford 1909.

Testamenta Eboracensia; wills registered at York, 6 vols, ed. J. Raine and J.W. Clay, Surtees Society 1836–1902.

Thiebaux, M., 'The mouth of the boar as a symbol in medieval literature', *Romance Philology*, 22 (1969).

Thompson, J.J., 'Another look at the religious texts in Lincoln, Cathedral Library, MS 91', in Minnis, ed., *Late Medieval Religious Texts*.

——, 'The *Cursor Mundi*, the "Inglis tong", and "Romance"', in Meale, ed., *Readings*.

Thomson, J.A.F., *The Later Lollards 1414–1520*, Oxford 1965.

——, 'Orthodox religion and the origins of Lollardy', *History*, 74 (1989).

Thoss, D., *Das Epos des Burgunderreiches*, Graz 1989.

Thrupp, S.L., 'Aliens in and around London in the fifteenth century', *Studies in London History Presented to P.E. Jones*, ed. A.E.W. Hollaender and W. Kellaway, London 1969.

Tilander, G., ed., *Gaston Phébus. Livre de Chasse*, Cynegetica 18, Stockholm 1971.

Trapp, J.B., 'Verses by John Lydgate at Long Melford', *Review of English Studies*, n.s., 6 (1955).

Tudor-Craig, P., *Richard III*, catalogue of an exhibition at the National Portrait Gallery 1973, London 1973, 1977.

Twysden, Roger, introd. John Selden, *Historiae Anglicanae Scriptores X e vetustis manuscriptis nunc primum in luce editi*, London 1652.

Tyerman, C., *England and the Crusades 1095–1588*, Chicago and London 1988.

Tymms, S., ed., *Wills and Inventories ... of Bury St. Edmund's*, Camden Society, Old Series, 1850.

Urwin, K. ed., *Le Lyon Coronné (1467)*, Geneva 1958.

Vale, M.G.A., *Piety, Charity and Literacy among the Yorkshire Gentry*, Borthwick Papers 59, York 1976.

——, *War and Chivalry. Warfare and Aristocratic Culture in England, France and Burgundy at the End of the Middle Ages*, London 1981.

——, 'Warfare and the life of the French and Burgundian nobility in the late Middle Ages', *Adelige Sachkultur des Spätmittelalters. Internationaler Kongress Krems an der Donau 22 bis 25 September 1980*, Wien 1982.

Valerius Maximus, *Facta et dicta memorabilia*, ed. C. Kempf, Leipzig 1888.

Vanderjagt, A.J., *Qui sa vertu anoblist. The Concepts of noblesse and chose publique in Burgundian Political Thought*, Groningen 1980.

——, 'Three solutions to Buonaccorso's *Disputatio de nobilitate*', in *Non nova sed nove. Mélanges de civilisation médiévale dediés à Willem Noomen*, Groningen 1984.

Vaughan, R., *Philip the Good*, London 1970.

Veale, E., *The English Fur Trade in the Middle Ages*, Oxford 1966.

Vergil, Polydore, *Three Books of Polydore Vergil's English History*, ed. H. Ellis, CS, Old Series, 1844.

Veyrin-Forrer, J., 'Caxton and France', *Journal of the Printing Historical Society*, no. 11 (1976–77).

Viard, J., ed., *Les grandes chroniques de France*, 10 vols, Paris 1920–53.

Vinaver, E., *Études sur le 'Tristan en prose', les sources, les manuscrits, bibliographie critique*, Paris 1925.

——, 'The Prose Tristan', in Loomis, ed., *Arthurian Literature*.

——, *Le 'Roman de Tristan et Iseult' dans l'oeuvre de Thomas Malory*, Paris 1975.

Visser-Fuchs, L., 'Richard in Holland, 1461 and 1470–71', *The Ricardian*, 6 (1982–84), pp. 182–89, 220–28.

——, 'The Splendour of the Sun', *The Ricardian*, 7 (1985–87).

——, 'A Ricardian riddle: the casualty list of the battle of Barnet', *The Ricardian*, 8 (1988–90).

——, 'Edward IV's "memoir on paper" to Charles, Duke of Burgundy: the so-called "Short Version of the Arrivall"', *Nottingham Medieval Studies*, 36 (1992).

——, 'Where did Elizabeth of York find consolation?', *The Ricardian*, 9 (1991-93)

Vos, D. de, *Hans Memling. The Complete Works*, Antwerp / Ghent 1994.

Wace, *Le Roman de Brut de Wace*, ed. I. Arnold, 2 vols, Paris 1938–40.

Wagner, A.R., *Aspilogia, being Materials of Heraldry*, vol. 1, *A Catalogue of English Medieval Rolls of Arms*, Harleian Society, 100 (1950); vol. 2 Harleian Society, 113 and 114 (for 1961 and 1962).

——, *The Heralds of England*, London 1967.

——, *Heralds and Heraldry in the Middle Ages*, second edn, Oxford 1957.

Walsh, R.J., 'Charles the Bold and the crusade: politics and propaganda', *Journal of Medieval History*, 3 (1977).

Ward, H.L.D., *Catalogue of Romances in the Department of Manuscripts in the British Museum*, 3 vols, London 1883.

Warner, G.F., and J.P. Gilson, *Catalogue of the Western Manuscripts in the Old Royal and King's Collection in the British Museum*, 4 vols, London 1921.

Watts, J.L., '*De Consulatu Stiliconis*: texts and politics in the reign of Henry VI', *Journal of Medieval History*, 16 (1990).

Wavrin, Jean de, *Recueil des Chroniques et Anchiennes Istories de la Grant Bretaigne ...*, ed. W. Hardy, 6 vols, Rolls Series, London 1864–91.

Webb, J., 'Translation of a French metrical history of the deposition of Richard II ...', Appendix IV, *Archaeologia*, 20 (1824).

Wedgwood, J., *History of Parliament: Register 1439–1509*, London 1938.

——, *History of Parliament 1439–1509: Register 1439–1509*, London 1936.

Weiss, R., *Humanism in England during the Fifteenth Century*, Oxford 1967.

Welch, C., *The History of the Worshipful Company of Pewterers of the City of London*, London 1909.

White, R.L., 'Early print and purgatory: the shaping of an Henrician ideology', PhD thesis, Australian National University, Canberra 1994.

Whithead, F., 'The early Tristan poems', in Loomis, ed., *Arthurian Literature*.

Wicksteed, P.H., ed., *The Convivio of Dante Alighieri*, Temple Classics, London 1903.

Wieck, R.S., *The Book of Hours in Medieval Art and Life*, London 1988.

Wilkins, N., *One Hundred Ballades, Rondeaux and Virelais from the Late Middle Ages*, Cambridge 1969.

Willard, C.C., *Christine de Pizan. Her Life and Works*, New York 1984.

——, 'Isabel of Portugal, patroness of humanism?', in *Miscellanea di studi e richerche sul quattrocento francese*, ed. F. Simone, Turin 1967.

——, 'The Duke of Berry's multiple copies of the *Fleur des Histoires d'Orient*', in *From Linguistics to Literature. Romance Studies offered to F.M. Rogers*, ed. B.H. Bichakjan, Amsterdam 1981.

Williams, D., ed., *England in the Fifteenth Century, Proceedings of the 1986 Harlaxton Symposium*, Woodbridge 1987.

——, 'The hastily drawn-up will of William Catesby, esquire, 25 August 1485', *Leicestershire Archaeological and Historical Society Transactions*, 51 (1975–76).

Williams, E., 'Hunting the deer: some uses of a motif-complex in Middle English romance and saint's life', in Mills *et al.*, eds, *Romance in Medieval England*.

Windeatt, B., 'Chaucer and fifteenth-century romance: *Partonope of Blois*', in *Chaucer Traditions. Studies in Honour of Derek Brewer*, ed. R. Morse and B. Windeatt, Cambridge 1990.

Winger, H.W., 'Regulations relating to the book trade in London, from 1357 to 1586', *The Library Quarterly*, 26 (1956).

Winter, P.M. de, 'Manuscrits à peintures produits pour le mécénat lillois sous les règnes de Jean sans Peur et Philippe le Bon', *Actes du 101e congrès national des sociétés savantes, Lille 1976. Archéologie et histoire d'art. Archéologie militaire. Les pays du Nord*, Paris 1978.

Wiseman, J.A., 'L'Epitoma rei militaris de Vegèce et sa fortune au moyen âge', *Le Moyen Age*, 85 (1979).

Wolpers, T., *Die Englische Heiligenlegende des Mittelalters*, Buchreihe der Anglia 10, Tübingen 1964.

Worcester, William, *William Worcestre, Itineraries, Edited from the Unique Manuscript Corpus Christi College, Cambridge, 210*, ed. J.H. Harvey, Oxford 1969.

——, *The Boke of Noblesse*, ed. J.G. Nichols, Roxburghe Club 1860.

Workman, S.K., 'Versions by Skelton, Caxton, and Berners of a prologue by Diodorus Siculus', *Modern Language Notes*, 56 (1941).

Wright, C.E., 'The Rous Roll: The English Version', *British Museum Quarterly*, 20 (1955–56).

——, *English Vernacular Hands from the Twelfth to the Fifteenth Centuries*, Oxford 1960.

——, *Fontes Harleiani. A Study of the Sources of the Harleian Collection of Manuscripts in the Department of Manuscripts in the British Museum*, London 1972.

Wright, T., *Political Poems and Songs relating to English History*, 2 vols, Rolls Series, London 1859–61.

——, ed., *Feudal Manuals of English History. A Series of Popular Sketches of Our National History ... from the Thirteenth Century to the Fifteenth ...*, London 1872.

Zink, G., ed., *Cleriadus et Meliadice*, Geneva 1984.

Zink, M., *Le Roman d'Apollonius de Tyr. Roman en prose du xve siècle*, Geneva 1982.

Ziolkowski, J., 'The nature of prophecy in Geoffrey of Monmouth's *Vita Merlini*', in *Poetry and Prophecy. The Beginnings of a Literary Tradition*, ed. J.L. Kugel, Ithaca / London 1990.

Index